KV-144-199

Contents

Preface ix

Contributors xi

Part One
TRENDS AND ISSUES

Introduction 1

Defining a Field: A Case Study of the Development of the
1994 Definition of Instructional Technology 2
   Rita C. Richey, Barbara Seels

Current Literature in Educational Media and Technology 18
   Donald P. Ely

Part Two
THE PROFESSION

Introduction 24

—New Curriculum Developments—

Preparing Instructional Technologists for the 21st Century 26
   James A. Pershing, Ph.D.

Association for Educational Communications and Technology
1993 Presidential Address 41
   Addie Kinsinger

—Research and Development—

The Learning Technology Center at Vanderbilt University 44
   Cognition and Technology Group at Vanderbilt (CTGV)

Educational Technology at TERC 49
   Robert F. Tinker, Susan L. Schoenberg, Heidi H. Nyland

—Criticism—

Beware the Computer Technocrats: Hardware Won't Educate Our Kids 64
   Michael Schrage

An Incomplete Caution: "Beware the Computer Technocrats" 66
   Randall G. Nichols

Analysis of Computers in Education as a Cultural Field 70
   Andrew R. J. Yeaman, Ph.D.

Part Three
CURRENT DEVELOPMENTS

Introduction 73

Improving Student Performance Through Learning Technologies 74

Promoting Success in Educational Partnerships Involving Technology 82
   Linda M. Baker

Networking in 1993 106
   John Clement, Janice Abrahams

The Eisenhower National Clearinghouse for Mathematics and
Science Education: Working Toward Education Goal 4 120
   Len Simutis

The National Center to Improve Practice: Promoting the Use
of Technology in Special Education 126
   Judith Zorfass, Arlene Remz, Patricia Corley

Changing Directions in Higher Education Media and Technology
Programs: An Interview with Robert M. Diamond 132
   Donald P. Ely

The Federal Role in Educational Technology 142
   Malcolm V. Phelps

Alternative Assessment and Technology 151
   Dorothy Bennett, Jan Hawkins

School-University Partnerships and Educational Technology 155
   Bernard J. Dodge

Telecommunications and Distance Education 159
   Alexander Romiszowski

EDUCATIONAL MEDIA AND TECHNOLOGY YEARBOOK

EDUCATIONAL
MEDIA AND
TECHNOLOGY
YEARBOOK

Donald P. Ely, Barbara B. Minor, Editors

1994   VOLUME 20

Published in Cooperation with the
ERIC® Clearinghouse on Information & Technology
and the
Association for Educational Communications
and Technology

1994
Libraries Unlimited, Inc. • Englewood, Colorado

LIBRARIES UNLIMITED, INC.
P.O. Box 6633
Englewood, CO 80155-6633
1-800-237-6124

Library of Congress Cataloging-in-Publication Data

Suggested Cataloging:

Educational media and technology yearbook,
    1994 volume 20 / Donald P. Ely and Barbara B. Minor, editors.—
Englewood, Colo.: Libraries Unlimited, 1994.
    xii, 409 p. 17x25 cm.
    Includes bibliographical references and index.
    ISBN 1-56308-267-5
    ISSN 8755-2094
    Published in cooperation with the ERIC Clearinghouse on Information
& Technology and the Association for Educational Communications and
Technology.
    1. Educational technology—yearbooks. 2. Instructional materials
centers—yearbooks. I. ERIC Clearinghouse on Information & Technology.
II. Association for Educational Communications and Technology.
III. Ely, Donald P. IV. Barbara B. Minor
LB 1028.3.E372   1994   370.778

Television Violence and Behavior: A Research Summary 164
   Marilyn E. Smith

Part Four
LEADERSHIP PROFILES

Introduction 169

Carolyn Guss 170
   Beverly Teach, William J. Cuttill

Mendel Sherman 174
   Dennis Pett

Part Five
THE YEAR IN REVIEW

Introduction 178

ADCIS: Association for the Development of Computer-Based
Instructional Systems 179

AECT: Association for Educational Communications and Technology 181

AMTEC: Association for Media and Technology in Education in Canada/
L'Association des Media et de la Technologie en Education au Canada 184

ISTE: International Society for Technology in Education 186

IVLA: International Visual Literacy Association 188

NSPI: National Society for Performance and Instruction 190

SALT: Society for Applied Learning Technology 192

Part Six
ORGANIZATIONS AND ASSOCIATIONS
IN NORTH AMERICA

Introduction 194

United States 195
   Classified List 195
   Alphabetical List 203

Canada 254

Part Seven
GRADUATE PROGRAMS

Doctoral Programs in Instructional Technology 257

Master's Degree and Six-Year Programs in Instructional Technology 273

Graduate Programs in Educational Computing 303

Scholarships, Fellowships, and Awards 317

Part Eight
MEDIAGRAPHY
Print and Nonprint Resources
Nancy R. Preston

Introduction 332

Mediagraphy 334
    Artificial Intelligence and Robotics 334
    CD-ROM 335
    Computer-Assisted Instruction 336
    Databases and Online Searching 344
    Distance Education 345
    Educational Research 348
    Educational Technology 350
    Electronic Publishing 354
    Information Science and Technology 355
    Instructional Design and Training 359
    Libraries and Media Centers 364
    Media Technologies 372
    Simulation and Virtual Reality 379
    Telecommunications and Networking 381

Index 387

Preface

In the United States we seem to have a preoccupation with anniversary dates, whether of political events or natural disasters. This thought comes to mind as the 20th edition of the *Educational Media and Technology Yearbook* goes to press. In 1973, the editor of the first edition, James W. Brown, noted that the date coincided with the 50th anniversary of the founding of the Association for Educational Communications and Technology (first known as the Division of Visual Instruction of the National Education Association). He noted in his preface that "the *Educational Media Yearbook 1973* [is] bringing together the historical, statistical, and factual data needed to gain a perspective of the field."

Brown went on to say that "a publication of this type will provide information to help media professionals 'see themselves' in a changing, expanding field, and to become better informed about the purposes, activities and accomplishments of the many organizations with activities relative to the utilization of media." The same statement could be made 20 years later, as the editors put together this volume. The tradition of the *Yearbook* is to chronicle the development of a relatively new profession. It is interesting to note that the first edition included an article, "Defining the Field of Educational Technology," by Donald P. Ely! In the current volume, the article by Seels and Richey describes in detail the development of the most recent (1994) definition of the field of *instructional* technology. The definition of the field has evolved over the years and this publication has been the chronicle of its development.

Although the content of the *Yearbook* has changed, its purpose has not. The first edition was divided into eight sections: (1) Educational Media Developments; (2) Manpower (what a difference 20 years can make!) and the Media Professions; (3) Research and Development Activities; (4) Sales and Business Outlook; (5) International Educational Media Developments; (6) Educational Media-Related Organizations; (7) Directory of Foundations and Federal Granting Agencies; and (8) Multimedia Resources Directory. The same categories are not used in the current volume, but certainly most of the concepts are still intact—perhaps with new terms and new applications, but certainly still helping "media professionals 'see themselves' in a changing, expanding field." Today we see trends, professional development, research, current developments, and a directory now called "mediagraphy." A section on criticism and one on leadership profiles have been added to the resource directories of organizations, associations, and graduate programs. It is still a rich menu.

The *Yearbook* will continue to be the chronicle of the field. With the rapid growth of technology, one can't help but wonder what the 25th and 50th editions might bring forth.

Donald P. Ely

Contributors to the
Educational Media and Technology Yearbook 1994

Janice Abrahams
President, J3 M3
14 Vandeventer
Princeton, NJ 08540

Gordon Ambach, Executive Director
Council of Chief State School Officers
One Massachusetts Avenue NW, Suite 700
Washington, DC 20001

Linda M. Baker, Research Assistant
College of Education
Miller Hall DQ-12
University of Washington
Seattle, WA 98195

Dorothy Bennett, Senior Researcher
Center for Children and Technology
Education Development Center, Inc.
96 Morton Street
New York, NY 10014

John Bransford, Centennial Professor and
    Co-Director
Learning Technology Center
Vanderbilt University
Nashville, TN 37203

John Clement, Program Officer
Research, Evaluation, and Dissemination
    Division
Education and Human Resources Directorate
National Science Foundation
1800 G Street NW
Washington, DC 20550

Patricia Corley, Associate Project Director
National Center to Improve Practice
Education Development Center
55 Chapel Street
Newton, MA 02160

William Cuttill, Facilities Coordinator
Office of Integrated Technologies
Indiana University-Purdue University
Indianapolis, IN 46202

Bernard J. Dodge, Associate Professor
Educational Technology Department
San Diego State University
San Diego, CA 92182-0311

Jan Hawkins, Director
Center for Children and Technology
Education Development Center, Inc.
96 Morton Street
New York, NY 10014

Addie Kinsinger, Director
ASSET/KAET Channel 8
Arizona State University
Box 871405
Tempe, AZ 85287-1405

Randall G. Nichols, Professor
Department of Curriculum and Instruction
College of Education
608 Teachers College Building
University of Cincinnati
Cincinnati, OH 45221-0002

Heidi H. Nyland, Researcher
Technology Education Research Centers
    (TERC)
2067 Massachusetts Avenue
Cambridge, MA 02140

James A. Pershing, Associate Professor
Department of Instructional Technology
W. W. Wright Education Building
Indiana University
Bloomington, IN 47405-1006

Dennis Pett, Professor Emeritus
Indiana University
RR2—Box 120
Brattleboro, VT 05301

Malcolm V. Phelps, Chief
Technology and Evaluation Branch
Education Division
National Aeronautics and Space
    Administration
Washington, DC 20546

Nancy R. Preston, Consultant
ERIC Clearinghouse on Information
    & Technology
4-194 Center for Science and Technology
Syracuse University
Syracuse, NY 13244-4100

Arlene Remz, Associate Project Director
National Center to Improve Practice
Education Development Center
55 Chapel Street
Newton, MA 02160

Rita C. Richey, Professor and Program
    Coordinator
Instructional Technology
Wayne State University
Detroit, MI 48202

Alexander Romiszowski, Professor
Area of Instructional Design, Develop-
    ment, and Evaluation
School of Education
Syracuse University
Syracuse, NY 13244-2340

Susan L. Schoenberg, Software Engineer
TERC
2067 Massachusetts Avenue
Cambridge, MA 02140

Michael Schrage, Columnist
Los Angeles Times Syndicate
Times-Mirror Square
Los Angeles, CA 90053

Barbara Seels, Associate Professor
Instructional Design and Technology
4A16 Forbes Quadrangle
University of Pittsburgh
Pittsburgh, PA 15260

Len Simutis, Director
Eisenhower National Clearinghouse for
    Mathematics and Science Education
The Ohio State University
1929 Kenny Road
Columbus, OH 43210-1079

Marilyn E. Smith, Database Coordinator
ERIC Clearinghouse on Information &
    Technology
4-194 Center for Science and Technology
Syracuse University
Syracuse, NY 13244-4100

Beverly Teach, Director
Media Resources
Instructional Support Services
Indiana University
Bloomington, IN 47405-5901

Robert F. Tinker, Chief Science Officer
TERC
2067 Massachusetts Avenue
Cambridge, MA 02140

Andrew R. J. Yeaman
Yeaman & Associates, Consultants
7152 West Eighty-fourth Way #708
Arvada, CO 80003

Judith Zorfass, Principal Investigator
National Center to Improve Practice
Education Development Center
55 Chapel Street
Newton, MA 02160

Part One
Trends and Issues

Introduction

Past editions of *EMTY* have highlighted studies about trends and issues in the field of educational media and technology. Several editions featured *trends* and issues; last year a study of the *future* was included. This edition reports on *issues* surrounding the definition of the field and the *trends* surrounding the development of the definition that have been central to AECT for more than 30 years. The most recent definition was published this year by AECT. The driving forces behind the new definition were Barbara Seels and Rita Richey. Their chapter documents the multiyear process that yielded the new monograph, *Instructional Technology: The Definition and Domains of the Field.* The change of title from the 1977 definition of *educational* technology to the current *instructional* technology is discussed in this chapter along with other issues that arose during this difficult undertaking. Never before has the process of defining a field been described in such detail. It will serve as a milestone for others who certainly will be involved in the creation of future definitions.

As new publications become available, trends emerge from an analysis of the literature. Professionals usually report their current activities through books, journal articles, and conference papers (that often find their way into ERIC). Publications are the documentation of a field's growth. They report the research; they describe the development of new products and procedures; they help others to understand innovations and, in some cases, provide specific instructions about using new approaches in a variety of settings. This chapter looks at the current literature, classifies it, and provides sources of information. It is, in a sense, an organized inventory that helps us to see, in one place, what media and technology professionals are doing at this time.

Defining a Field
A Case Study of the Development of the 1994 Definition of Instructional Technology

Rita C. Richey
Professor, Instructional Technology, Wayne State University

Barbara Seels
Associate Professor, Instructional Design and Technology
University of Pittsburgh

BACKGROUND

In 1994 the Association for Educational Communications and Technology (AECT) published Seels and Richey's *Instructional Technology: The Definition and Domains of the Field.*[1] This book is a capstone of five years of collective work dedicated to developing a new definition of the field that was not only examined and endorsed by the Association, but by a broad base of the professionals in the field, including both scholars and practitioners. The new definition is:

> Instructional Technology is the theory and practice of design, development, utilization, management, and evaluation of processes and resources for learning.

This definition describes the field in terms of five domains, which are shown in the diagram in Figure 1. This new definition is the fourth officially endorsed definition of the field, and now replaces the 1977 definition.[2]

We have been asked to document the process followed in the construction of this new definition for the *Educational Media and Technology Yearbook* to preserve a record of the field's development for future researchers. To do this, we will:

- present a chronology of the development and the key factors that influenced the process; and

- describe the issues confronted.

CHRONOLOGY OF THE PROCESS

Emerging Discourse on the Definition of the Field

General Discussion in the Profession. In 1983 Ely suggested that "the ferment over the definition of the field of educational technology seems to have subsided" (p. 2). This was 20 years after AECT had published the first definition and terminology monograph, and six years after it had published the third definitional monograph. He thought that because there was then little emotional debate on the topic, it was a propitious time to raise related issues as yet unresolved.

Figure 1. The domains in instructional technology.

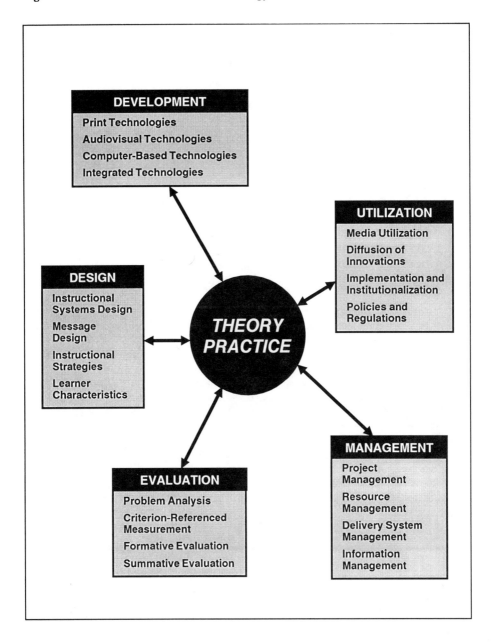

The lull was short-lived, however, and in the late 1980s there was a growing uneasiness with the current definition. The 1977 statement was unwieldy, and the monograph explaining that definition was difficult to use in academic settings. In essence, the definition was being challenged in terms of the very points Ely cited in 1983—clarity and utility.

In addition, many were raising questions in relation to Ely's third criterion for definitional stability—currency. The issues in this regard grew to a great extent out of the rapid growth of the field, growth that encompassed:

- the capabilities and applications of technology, especially with respect to the computer;

- the organizational contexts in which practice occurs, especially in relation to private and public sector training; and

- theoretical expansion.

The computer had become an integral part of the lives of virtually everyone, as well as every profession and discipline. Technology was no longer the province of only educational technologists. Technologists were everywhere, and the field at times found itself cut off from those doing related work. External communication concerns were being raised. These phenomena were coupled with the fact that our impact was growing in the training arena even as, in many instances, it was declining in teacher education and K-12 educational settings. To many, the 1977 definition seemed to be out of step with these trends.

Finally, in the late 1980s, a variety of new theoretical paradigms were being introduced and debated throughout the field. Not only had the old behavioral orientation been replaced with a cognitive viewpoint, but even newer ideas were being advanced. Constructivism, situated cognition, and postmodernism enjoyed increasing support. Was the old definition compatible with these new ideas? Many were not sure.

Urging Formal Consideration. By 1987, a proposal had been sent to the AECT's Committee on Definition and Terminology (D&T) asking that the committee assume responsibility for revising the definition.[3] After reviewing the 1977 definition monograph, the committee seriously considered undertaking this task, but eventually decided that there were insufficient resources and redirected its energies toward a glossary of terminology in the field.

Nevertheless, the pressure for a revised theoretical framework for the field continued. Questions were raised about the validity of the old definitions, the instructional systems design basis, the relationship of the domains to each other, and the relationship of instructional design to Instructional Technology. As the area of instructional design grew, many saw it as being separate but equal to, rather than a subset of, Instructional Technology.

It was difficult to communicate and defend the identity and the uniqueness of the field on the basis of the old definitions. In addition, the field had some inherent problems that could be resolved only by a reexamination of its values and theoretical framework, including the components of the definition and the domains. For example, the terms "Instructional Technology" and "Educational Technology" were being used as process, as product, as software, as field, and as specialty. The field could neither lead nor reflect until these issues were resolved. Generally, practitioners were unconcerned and remained convinced that their work was defined adequately by what they did and that a description in a book would not change the field. Nonetheless, a few academicians urged that attention be directed toward revising the definition.

Professors in Instructional Design and Technology (PIDT) Debates

The issues surrounding a definition of the field arose at a series of meetings of Professors in Instructional Design and Technology (PIDT). This setting provided an opportunity for groups to analyze the issue first in a rather free-form manner, and later in a much more organized fashion. The topic was addressed over a four-year period in this forum.

1989 and 1990 Meetings. The issue came to the forefront first at the annual meeting of PIDT in May 1989. There were continuing debates and discussions on the utility of the current definition and the need for a new definition.[4] Two events at the meeting led to further action related to revising the definition of the field. The first was a conversation between Bob Holloway, of Northern Arizona University and president-elect of AECT, and Barbara Seels about the need for a revised definition. As a result of this conversation, Holloway later asked Seels to chair the AECT Definition and Terminology Committee.

The second event was the decision by Mike Molenda from Indiana University and Barbara Seels to begin the process of redefinition themselves by forming a PIDT working group to prepare a report for the next year's meeting. Based on her demonstrated interest, Rita Richey from Wayne State University was asked to join the group. Molenda named it the Working Group on Typology and Geography of the Field, and members were solicited at a PIDT general session. Barbara Seels agreed to coordinate the effort. It was hoped that the group would serve as a catalyst for thought and action.

Members tentatively agreed to share a one-page or less definition of the field and a page or less on domains in the field.[5] In October, these statements on definition and domains were shared with the group as a whole. Members were asked to react to the set of statements keeping these questions in mind:

- What is the integrating paradigm for our field?

- What has changed since the last definition?

- Where do we want to go in the future?

- Is the relationship among domains and functions shown in the last definition still appropriate?

Members felt it was too difficult to react to the statements as a whole. Instead of preparing a report, the group agreed to request that small group meetings on the topic be scheduled for the 1990 PIDT conference. At the 1990 PIDT conference, the discussion continued primarily among Barbara Seels, Rita Richey, Mike Molenda, and Denis Hlynka. They centered around the type of definition that should be drafted and what it should include.

1991 Meeting. At the 1991 PIDT conference, there was continued interest in the redefinition effort. Many joined the debates and proposed their versions of a definition or critiqued other definitions and domains put forth.[6] The general sessions and theme groups at the 1991 conference were devoted to topics such as postmodernism and situated learning. One outcome for the Working Group on Typology and Geography of the Field was the recommendation that any publication on definition include alternative perspectives to reflect the postmodern emphasis on multiple paradigms.

Near the end of the conference, Barbara Seels and Rita Richey drafted a definition and representation of proposed domains.[7] This draft was circulated at a general session with the 1977 definition and domains, and participants were asked to react by commenting on both. The comments were grouped, and the proposed definition and domains were revised before the end of the conference. There was general agreement that the 1977 definition was no longer adequate. Reactions to the proposed definition, however, ranged from "Excellent, a good start" to "Not good! This definition is too much like ISD." It was clear there was no general consensus yet on what the new definition should be.

1992 and 1993 Meetings. Open meetings on the topic continued at the 1992 and 1993 PIDT conferences. Another survey on the proposed definition was conducted at the 1992 conference, and participant suggestions were incorporated wherever possible. In 1993, the proposed definition and a draft of the related book were available for review and comment. Small group discussions also continued.

The continuing interest at PIDT conferences was due to the academicians' perceptions of the need for a definition that would provide a basis for a research agenda, improve communications, and substantiate the field's unique identity and value. The involvement and debates at PIDT were crucial to the success of the redefinition effort.

The AECT Committee on Definition and Terminology

Devising a Definition Strategy. Concurrent with the debates at PIDT, the AECT Definition and Terminology Committee moved in the same direction. Barbara Seels now chaired the committee.[8] At the AECT meeting in Anaheim, the committee agreed to undertake a revision of the 1977 definition monograph and developed the following strategy:

- Those committee members present at other conferences would use the opportunity to meet on the definition problem, starting with the 1990 NSPI (National Society for Performance and Instruction) conference, and continuing with PIDT and other AECT conferences.

- This would be a three-year project, with the first year devoted to obtaining committee consensus on the definition, the second year devoted to drafting the document, and the third year dedicated to refining the document.

- A survey would be published in *TechTrends* and hearings would be held each year at the AECT conference to obtain widespread input.

- Members of the committee interested in the project would be reappointed for the duration of the project. New committee appointments would reflect needed expertise in the domain areas.

- The chair could appoint a steering committee if necessary.

- Input would be solicited from AECT divisions and affiliates.

- Rita Richey would coordinate the definition effort with the revision of the NCATE (National Council for the Accreditation of Teacher Education) Standards.

Implementing the Strategy. In March 1990, after the convention, Barbara Seels submitted a three-year budget plan to cover expenses associated with the project. She and Rita Richey met with Stan Zenor, the executive director of AECT, at AECT headquarters in June 1990 to discuss the project strategy and needed resources. The AECT Board of Directors' allocation of funds for the project was based on the rationale that the budget should not exceed projected revenue from sales of the anticipated publication.

The *TechTrends* survey was printed in the second issue of 1990. Out of the approximately 4,500 AECT members, 20 responded that the definition of the field was very important or important to them. There was general agreement that the 1977 definition was dated in many ways, was difficult to use, and that a revised definition could serve many purposes.

Attendance at hearings held at AECT's 1991 and 1992 conventions was negligible due to scheduling conflicts and a lack of interest.[9] The poor attendance at hearings led to a different strategy in 1993. Instead, a symposium on the knowledge base of the field, as reflected in the proposed definition, was held in New Orleans.[10] More than 75 people attended the symposium and offered comments from the audience. The symposium was co-sponsored by the AECT Committee on Definition and Terminology and the NCATE Guidelines Task Force.

In the fall of 1990, each division of AECT was asked to appoint a representative who would be invited to the D&T meetings at conventions and placed on the D&T mailing list. Several divisions did so. Members of the D&T committee were periodically updated by mail and asked to react to changes and issues. The next step was the writing meetings.

Writing Meetings in Pittsburgh

1991 Meeting. Barbara Seels appointed a steering committee of Ellen Wagner, Rita Richey, and herself. This group met July 19-21, 1991, at the University of Pittsburgh. Their work was based on the definition and domain documents that had emerged from the last D&T committee meeting, together with input from the PIDT debates and survey and the *Tech Trends* survey. An outline for the book was developed and critical visuals were drafted at this 1991 writing meeting.

The outline was circulated to the full D&T committee prior to the 1992 AECT convention in Washington, DC, then reviewed and modified at that convention. The committee recommended inviting contributors to write short papers on their areas of expertise that could be incorporated into the book. These were requested, and contributors were asked to supply them before the next writing meeting, which was to be held during the summer of 1992.

1992 Meeting. Ellen Wagner resigned from the D&T committee to chair another AECT committee. Therefore, the next writing meeting was broadened beyond the original steering committee. Rita Richey, Barbara Seels, Fatemeh Olia, and Denis Hlynka participated in this second meeting from July 30-August 2, 1992. They were joined at times by Lou Berry of the University of Pittsburgh, Susan Heide from the University of Wisconsin-Superior, and Barbara Good, a professional editor from the Allegheny General Hospital in Pittsburgh. There were several outcomes of this meeting;[11] nevertheless, it was clear that large gaps remained in the proposed book.

After the writing meeting, Barbara Seels reviewed the progress made so far and concluded that the task was too large to be completed satisfactorily using the strategy of infrequent meetings of a group of three to six persons.[12] As a consequence, Seels decided a new strategy was warranted if the document was to be completed. She decided to author the book if Rita Richey would agree to co-author. The book would incorporate the contributions made to sections whenever possible, and would reflect the consensus of the Committee on D&T. Rita Richey agreed.

Writing Meetings in Detroit

1992 Meetings. A series of meetings were held in Detroit to write the definition book in 1992 and 1993. In the two 1992 meetings (November 19-22 and December 3-6), the authors reorganized the manuscript to establish a more cohesive flow. In the process, a new concluding chapter was conceptualized.[13] Some contributions for "Chapter 2—The Domains of the Field" were especially helpful.[14] The first draft of the book was produced at these November and December meetings. After further work, this draft was mailed to D&T committee members and section contributors on December 29, 1992.

1993 Meetings. The authors held three additional writing meetings in Detroit in 1993. At the first two, the manuscript was fine-tuned and rewritten. In addition, at the April 22-26 meeting, the D&T committee recommendations were incorporated into the manuscript. At the August 24-26 meeting, the recommendations of the AECT Board were incorporated. The final manuscript was submitted for publication September 30, 1993. Another writing meeting was held in Detroit October 27-31. This meeting was devoted to completing the index and working on dissemination strategies.

Review and Endorsement

In anticipation of review by the AECT Board of Directors, Don Ely and Barbara Seels met with Stan Zenor in June 1993 at the AECT headquarters. At this time, a schedule and standard for the review and production of the book were formulated. The schedule called for a revised manuscript by July 1, 1993, with immediate mailing to each of the Board members. The Board met and discussed the manuscript at the August meeting at the AECT Leadership Conference.[15] After this discussion, the Board voted to endorse the book and the statement of definition and domains of the field.

SUMMARY

The process of reaching consensus on the definition and domains of the field was open and participatory. The process included:

- surveys and discussion groups;
- open hearings;
- continuous peer review;
- a symposium;
- coordination with other AECT committees and divisions;
- contributions from individuals;
- review meetings; and
- writing meetings.

A chronology of the process is shown in Figure 2.

Figure 2. A chronology of the process of defining the field.

Date	PIDT Meetings	AECT Activities	Writing Meetings

1989	•Debates
	•Formation of
	  Working Group
	  on the Typology
	  and Geography
	  of the Field		

1990	•Working groups
	  meet and
	  develop draft
	•Survey
		•Meeting at AECT
		  headquarters
		•Budget
		  established
		•Strategy
		  developed
		•*Tech Trends* survey	

1991	•Theme group
	  meetings
	•Survey
	•Alternative
	  perspectives
	  recommendation
		•Survey at hearing
		•D&T reaches
		  consensus
			•Outline book
			•Modify domain
			  visual

1992	•Open meetings
	•Survey
		•Two hearings held
		•Outline revised by
		  D&T Committee
			•Revise overall
			  strategy
			•Write first draft
			  of book
			  manuscript

1993	•Open meeting
	•Copy of
	  manuscript
	  available for
	  review
		•Symposium
		•Meeting at AECT
		  headquarters
		•New NCATE
		  Standards
		  proposed
		•Manuscript
		  reviewed by
		  Gustafson,
		  Braden, and Ely
		•AECT Board
		  endorses definition
			•Manuscript
			  refined and edited
			•Indexing
			•Developed
			  dissemination
			  strategy using
			  articles

1994	•Book discussed	•Book published	•Articles published

The resulting document presented a definition and domains broad enough to encompass AECT's membership, but specific enough to clarify identity. Because the resolution of issues was completed carefully over time, the definitional effort reflects the best judgment of those who care a great deal about it.

DEFINITIONAL ISSUES CONFRONTED

A variety of issues were confronted throughout the five-year development period. The resolution of the problems posed by these issues typically involved examining the topic from a variety of perspectives before synthesizing a solution. This process typically included considering the issue from:

- a historical perspective by listening to those involved in the development of earlier definitions;
- alternative theoretical paradigms, including those not in the mainstream of current thought;
- an international perspective; and
- the orientation of those in a range of jobs in the field.

Although some "executive decisions" were made during the writing process, these never involved key philosophical or fundamental issues.

THE CHARACTERISTICS OF AN ACCEPTABLE DEFINITION OF THE FIELD

Most involved in the definition process had their own views of what an acceptable definition would look like. In retrospect, it is clear that key criteria were used to evaluate the definitions that were proposed. Some of these criteria were specifically articulated and supported; others evolved through examination of the issues. It was concluded that the final definition had to *demonstrate the uniqueness of the field,* but in addition it had to possess a number of other characteristics. The endorsed definition should also be:

- brief, simple, and easily understood;
- useful as a way of communicating with those in the field as well as those outside of the field;
- explained with a visual, as well as a textual dimension, if possible; and
- embraced by persons in the field with a range of experience, interests, job responsibilities, and national affiliations.[16]

By and large, these criteria were not controversial in nature, even though debates on a specific definition were often intense.

THE CONCEPTUAL NATURE OF THE DEFINITION

There have been many intellectual debates related to the definition over the past five years. Here we describe five of the most important issues that emerged.

The Focus of the Definition. The 1977 definition described the field as a process that can be used to solve problems in "all aspects of human learning." In contrast, the 1994 definition describes the field not as a process, but as theory and practice. This is a fundamental change that reflects the maturation of the field and a newer orientation toward the field as an area of study, *in addition to* being an area of practice. There was a difference of opinion on this point. Some felt that the field should emphasize its practical orientation; others felt that it should encompass both theory and practice and be considered both an area of study and a profession. The current definition is more consistent with the 1963 definition, which described the field as a branch of educational theory and practice (Ely 1963).

Outcome Orientation. A second, but related, issue centered on whether the efforts of our field should be directed toward processes and resources for instruction, or processes and resources for learning. The issue has two parts. The first is the semantic redundancy that occurs when Instructional Technology is directed toward instruction. The second, and more significant aspect, concerns the rightful emphasis on a learning outcome rather than the intermediate step of instruction. This conclusion was arrived at through mutual problem solving rather than debate.

The Role of the Systems Paradigm. Instructional systems design and use of the systems approach in general is the most commonly held paradigm in the field. The domains of the field in the 1994 definition reflect the stages in the systems model, and the previous definitions of the field have at the minimum implied the use of such a model. However, an early version of the 1994 definition also explicitly referred to "systematic design, development, utilization, and management." The discussions surrounding deletion of the term *systematic* reflect the current examination in the field of alternative approaches to design, and to the emphasis in some quarters on systemic, rather than systematic, design (Beckwith 1988; Richey 1992). The deletion was also reflective of an attempt to present a more philosophically neutral definition.

The Influence of Philosophy and Values. The participants in the discussions and debates that shaped the 1994 definition were very cognizant of the influential role played by individual and collective philosophies and values on Instructional Technology theory and practice. These areas were considered to be important foundations of the field. The question was precisely how to portray this role in the definition and domain statement and visuals. Early drafts of the domain taxonomies showed philosophy, research, and theory as common foundations of each domain. After further discussion, history and technology were also added to the taxonomy visual to emphasize their comprehensive impact on the domains.

These discussions were concurrent with the debate on whether practice should serve as the primary focus of the field. The resolution of these issues forced us to recognize that if the definition were to be brief and simple enough to promote widespread communication, many of the complexities would have to be explained in the book-length exploration of the topic rather than the basic definition statement. Ultimately, "Chapter 3—The Sources of Influence on Instructional Technology" was used to address the topics surrounding historical influences, research and theory, values, and technology. At the same time, it was decided that the definition and the matching domain visual should explicitly refer only to theory and practice. The underlying assumption was that theory encompasses research, values, and philosophy, whereas practice encompasses technology and history.

Alternative Perspectives. The last of the key issues addressed during development of the 1994 definition was the role and emphasis to be placed upon alternative perspectives of the field. These viewpoints included those emerging ideas which, though not yet dominant, are still important parts of the culture of the field. These perspectives are of increasing importance with the exploration of performance technology, postmodernism, feminist interpretations, and constructivist views becoming more common in the literature (Duffy and Jonassen 1992; Hlynka and Belland 1991; Stolovitch and Keeps 1992). The question was the amount of emphasis to place upon these views in the explanation of the field. Should there be a separate chapter devoted to alternative perspectives, or should this content be incorporated in another chapter? Finally, this content was also incorporated into Chapter 3 and presented as an influence on the field.

THE SCOPE AND NATURE OF THE DOMAINS

The notion of domains was introduced in the monograph on the 1977 definition. However, in 1977 domains were equated to functions of the field and varied substantially from the five domains of the 1994 definition. Nonetheless, elements of each of the domains can be found in the 1977 monograph. In spite of the fact that there was precedent for the domains, they still posed conceptual problems. In summary, the domain issues related to their scope, the best way to communicate them to the typical professional, their components, and the extent to which they were inclusive of the entire field.

Scope and Visualization of the Domains. Four domains—Design, Development, Management, and Evaluation—were identified early in the definition process. The domain of utilization emerged midway through the definition construction process.[17] The addition of this fifth domain resolved many theoretical inconsistencies that were being recognized in the domain structure.

However, even with the addition of the fifth domain, there was an uneasiness with the visual format of the domain taxonomy. It was a matrix, and seemed too linear. This format seemed to suggest a procedural relationship among the domains—a natural conclusion given the similarities between the domains and the major phases of most instructional systems models. The problem was solved with the design of a wheel-like visual showing the domains connected to a foundational hub labeled "theory and practice." This new visual captured the major elements of the definition statement and emphasized the nonlinear relationships among the domains themselves.[18]

The Components and Inclusiveness of the Domains. From the very beginning, there was no attempt to completely explicate the domain taxonomies beyond a very general breakdown at the first level. Even so, these subcategories demanded a great deal of analysis. Was there a logical consistency among the subcategories in each domain? Did the subcategories adequately cover the domain as an area of study? Did the subcategories adequately cover the domain as an area of practice? In other words (as we kept asking each other), can every professional in the field find a "home" in the domain taxonomies?

Not surprisingly, the least problematic domain to explicate was Design, the domain with the strongest theoretical foundation. "Instructional Systems Design" is viewed as a part of the domain rather than the comprehensive title of the domain. The remaining subcategories encompass the bulk of the current design-related research and practice.

The most difficult problems were encountered in the Development Domain and the overlaps between the Management and Utilization Domains. Development is the domain most in flux because of the rapid changes in technology. There were repeated attempts to construct the development taxonomy, and the final configuration was not arrived at until the third year of work. This domain is portrayed here in terms of the range of products developed, all seen as types of technologies. The problem was constructing a category system that was comprehensive *and* discriminating, especially in relation to nonprint, nonintegrated technologies such as television.[19]

The Management and Utilization Domains were also continuing problems. These domains probably are the least developed in the field, in terms of both theory and practice. This is especially evident in the list of glossaries at the end of the definition book, which show a scarcity of terminology literature in these two domains. There were particularly problematic issues related to distinguishing Management and Utilization, including:

- the correct placement of "Diffusion of Innovations";

- the conceptualization of "Implementation and Institutionalization"; and

- the role of "Information Management" in this field.

The Evaluation Domain issues centered on a recurring problem of identifying only those parts of the domain that were the primary province of Instructional Technology, rather than topics "belonging" to other fields. Consequently, the measurement subcategory was specifically labeled "Criterion-Referenced Measurement." This is our *primary* concern, even though Instructional Technologists clearly use other types of measurement.

These domain taxonomies are a starting point in summarizing the field in terms of the areas of study and practice. One would expect that these would be more fluid than the definition itself. These are the categories that will change as the field matures and technology advances.

TERMINOLOGY AND GLOSSARY

An important part of the new definition book is the glossary of terms. This is especially critical to a field that has a history of proliferating new terms. Issues focused not only on selecting definitions that were clear and brief, but on eliminating multiple definitions for one term, and multiple terms for the same definition.

Representative points of concern were:

- the many meanings of "design" in the literature;

- defining terms currently in a state of flux, such as "micro-design" and "macro-design"; and

- defining new and emerging terms, such as "confirmation evaluation."

The Distinction Between a Discipline and a Field

After all key issues had been resolved, two terminology decisions remained. The first focused on how "Instructional Technology" itself was labeled. Specifically, the question centered on whether it was a field or a discipline. The judgment related to whether the profession has progressed to the point at which the bulk of its theoretical growth is within its own parameters, deals with its own issues, and is advanced by its own scholars. Few disagreed that there had been considerable progress in this respect since the 1977 definition. Although most agreed that the Design Domain was more mature than the other domains, there was not a consensus that Instructional Technology as a whole had progressed to a point that would warrant it being called a discipline.

This issue was not entirely unrelated to one's preference for portraying the field as an area of study or as an area of practice. Those with a more applied emphasis tended to prefer describing Instructional Technology as a field. Those with a more theoretical emphasis tended to prefer describing Instructional Technology as a discipline.

The Name

Finally, there were debates on whether the field should be known as "Educational Technology" or "Instructional Technology." Historically, both terms have been used, and nearly 30 years ago Finn noted that many had used the terms interchangeably for some time even then (Finn 1965). This seems to be the case still. Nevertheless, the term "Instructional Technology" was selected primarily because it:

- is more commonly used today in the United States;

- encompasses many practice settings; and

- describes more precisely the function of technology in education.

CONCLUSION

It should be apparent that the process of constructing a definition for a field is not only an intellectual exercise, but also a matter of orchestrating complex joint decision making. It is not an isolated task, but rather an ongoing exercise requiring a re-examination of the state of one's field in relation to recent advancements in the profession and society at large. It is especially important that there be not only a continuing examination of the definition and its implications, but also of the domains. The domain taxonomies need additional refinement to maintain their relevancy in a world of rapidly changing technology. Ultimately, the definition and domains of the field should parallel the field's evolution.

Of equal importance is the need for dissemination and discussion of the definition, as the original impetus for the project was to aid communication both within the field and with those in other professions. The definition can affect the field in a variety of ways. It can contribute to the culture of the field through its use in the training of new professionals and by stimulating discussion. It also has historical significance, to the extent that the definition and its fuller explanation document the maturation of the field and identify influential professionals and ideas. Finally, if the definition is successful, it will serve as an impetus to further research and development, which, in the end, advances the field of Instructional Technology.

NOTES

1. This book describes the field of Instructional Technology today through a comprehensive explanation of the definition. Its components are: "Chapter 1—The 1994 Definition of the Field" (including the definition's underlying assumptions, components, and evolutionary nature); "Chapter 2—The Domains of the Field" (including their role and description); "Chapter 3—The Sources of Influence on Instructional Technology" (including the field's historical development, research and theory, values and alternative perspectives); "Chapter 4—The Practice of Instructional Technology" (including the elements that shape practice, ethics, and role of practice in the field's evolution); "Chapter 5—Implications of the Definition of Instructional Technology" (including the definition's role in growth, communication, and agenda-building); "Glossary of Terms"; "List of Glossaries in the Field, Associations and Journals, and the AECT Code of Ethics"; "References" (comprehensive list).

2. A shortened version of the 1977 definition is: Educational technology is a complex, integrated process involving people, procedures, ideas, devices, and organization, for analyzing problems and devising, implementing, evaluating, and managing solutions to those problems, involved in all aspects of human learning.

3. The proposal was submitted in a letter from Barbara Seels, of the University of Pittsburgh and a member of the D&T Committee, to Tony Arabia, outgoing chair of the committee, dated February 19, 1987. The letter suggested that the committee collaborate on this project with the newly formed organization of Professors in Instructional Design and Technology (PIDT).

4. These conversations were precipitated by a meeting held by Paul Welliver, of Pennsylvania State University, to gather input on the mission of AECT, at the request of AECT president Elaine Didier.

5. Don Ely from Syracuse University, Denis Hlynka from the University of Manitoba, Mike Molenda, Rita Richey, Barbara Seels, and Ron McBeath from San Jose State University participated in this working group.

6. Among those expressing their views strongly were John Keller of Florida State University, Bob Heinich from Indiana University, Dave Merrill from Utah State University, and Alan Januszewski from the State University of New York at Potsdam.

7. The draft was based on a concept developed by Rita Richey and Ellen Wagner from the University of Northern Colorado at the 1990 annual meeting of the National Society for Performance and Instruction (NSPI) in Toronto.

8. Seels agreed to assume the D&T chair's position only after obtaining assurances that key people, such as Don Ely, Rita Richey, and Mike Molenda, would be willing to serve on the committee.

9. Two hearings were requested for the 1991 convention. One was scheduled opposite Don Ely's forum, which appealed to the same audience. The other was scheduled Sunday morning. The next year the hearing was scheduled opposite a forum on instructional design offered by Barbara Seels and Rita Richey. Don Ely assumed chair of that hearing.

10. The symposium included papers on each of the proposed domains. The Design Domain was presented by Rita Richey, the Evaluation Domain by Barbara Seels, the Utilization Domain by Mike Molenda, the Management Domain by Ed Caffarella from the University of Northern Colorado, and the Development Domain by Mike Simonson from Iowa State University. Other members of the D&T Committee also contributed to the papers (for

example, Kent Wood and Nick Eastmond from Utah State University, who sent a section for the Evaluation Domain paper).

11.   Considerable progress was made on "Chapter 1—The Definition of the Field" by Barbara Seels. Of special note was the useful contribution to this chapter made by Alan Januszewski on the history of the definitions. In addition, Rita Richey progressed with "Chapter 3—The Sources of Influence on Instructional Technology" and the reference list. An outline for "Chapter 4—The Practice of Instructional Technology" was developed by Fatemeh Olia and Barbara Seels. Progress was also made in conceptualizing other areas.

12.   To validate this perception, Barbara Seels asked AECT Board member Roberts Braden from the California State University at Chico, who was in Pittsburgh during September for the 1992 conference of the International Visual Literacy Association, to review the document developed so far. He concurred with her assessment that the remaining work was extensive and probably more suited to individual rather than group efforts.

13.   Barbara Seels wanted the last chapter to speak to the metaphor of "community." It was decided to draw on Rita Richey's original statement of definition for the PIDT Working Group on Typology and Geography of the Field as a starting point for the new concluding chapter.

14.   Lou Berry's description of the Development Domain, Kent Wood and Nick Eastmond's description of the Evaluation Domain, and Mike Molenda's description of the Utilization Domain were especially useful. Much of their material was incorporated, although some conceptual and editorial changes had to be made based on peer reviewer comments.

15.   Extensive review of the manuscript was done before the Board meeting by Kent Gustafson from the University of Georgia and president-elect of AECT, and Roberts Braden. Board members were reminded that the proposed NCATE standards were also based on the revised definition.

16.   The importance of an international perspective was emphasized by Denis Hlynka from Canada, and Don Ely, who has had extensive international experience in the field.

17.   The Utilization Domain was added primarily because of the conceptualization and urging of Michael Molenda.

18.   A breakthrough on this issue came at the first writing meeting in Pittsburgh when Rita Richey devised the new graphic presentation.

19.   Using the development taxonomy shown in Figure 1, one can see that traditional television would fall under audiovisual technologies. However, if the television were part of an advanced telecommunications delivery system, it would then be classified as an integrated technology.

REFERENCES

Association for Educational Communications and Technology. (1977). *The definition of educational technology*. Washington, DC: Author.

Beckwith, D. (1988). The future of educational technology. *Canadian Journal of Educational Communications 17*(1), 3-20.

Caffarella, E. P., Earle, R. S., Hanclosky, W., and Richey, R. C. (1994). *Guidelines for the accreditation of programs in educational communication and information technologies* (3d ed.). Washington, DC: Association for Educational Communications and Technology.

Duffy, T. M., and Jonassen, D. H., eds. (1992). *Constructivism and the technology of instruction: A conversation.* Hillsdale, NJ: Lawrence Erlbaum.

Ely, D. P., ed. (1963). The changing role of the audiovisual process in education: A definition and a glossary of related terms. TCP Monograph No. 1. *AV Communication Review 11*(1), Supplement No. 6.

Ely, D. P. (1983). The definition of educational technology: An emerging stability. *Educational Considerations 10*(2), 2-4.

Finn, J. (1965). Instructional technology. *Audiovisual Instruction 10*(3), 192-94.

Hlynka, D., and Belland, J., eds. (1991). *Paradigms regained: The uses of illuminative, semiotic and post-modern criticism as modes of inquiry in educational technology.* Englewood Cliffs, NJ: Educational Technology Publications.

Richey, R. C. (1992). *Designing instruction for the adult learner: Systemic training theory and practice.* London: Kogan Page.

Richey, R. C. (1993). *The knowledge base of instructional technology: A critical examination.* A symposium presented at the 1993 Conference of the Association for Educational Communications and Technology in New Orleans, LA. Papers included: Richey, R. C. The knowledge base of the design domain; Simonson, M. The knowledge base of the development domain; Caffarella, E. The knowledge base of the management domain; Molenda, M. The knowledge base of the utilization domain; and Seels, B. The knowledge base of the evaluation domain.

Seels, B. A., and Richey, R. C. (1994). *Instructional technology: The definition and domains of the field.* Washington, DC: Association for Educational Communications and Technology.

Stolovitch, H. D., and Keeps, E. J., eds. (1992). *Handbook of human performance technology: A comprehensive guide for analyzing and solving performance problems in organizations.* San Francisco: Jossey-Bass.

TechTrends survey definition of the field. (1990). *TechTrends 35*(2), 51.

Current Literature in
Educational Media and Technology

Donald P. Ely
Professor, Instructional Design, Development and Evaluation
Associate Director, ERIC Clearinghouse on Information and Technology
Syracuse University

Current developments in the literature of educational technology are not easy to find. No one journal systematically lists all or most new publications. Conferences in the field do not feature displays of written works. Unless a person is on many mailing lists to receive announcements of new publications, it is unlikely that information about recent publications will be known.

The list of publishers is extensive. Almost every publisher in the general field of education has several titles about some aspect of educational media and technology. Five publishers in the United States print most of the books in the field;[1] two are professional organizations and three are commercial houses. With the catalogs of these three sources, most of the 1992-94 titles can be found. There are, of course, publishers in other parts of the English-speaking world that add significantly to the annual output of educational technology literature, for example, The National Council for Educational Technology in the United Kingdom, and Kogan Page, which has North American representation through Oryx Press and Nichols Publishing. The international publications are not included in this chapter.

The difficulty of awareness is compounded by the multiple perceptions of "the field." No single definition is sufficiently comprehensive to cover all aspects included in these multiple perceptions. With emerging digital technologies and the rapid expansion of telecommunications, the scope of the field is enlarged. The existing areas of instructional technology—instructional design, instructional science—begin to blend with the new delivery systems and create an expanded literature.

The ERIC system, through the ERIC Clearinghouse on Information and Technology, attempts to keep pace with the growing body of literature. Currently the Clearinghouse indexes 38 journals related to educational technology in the *Current Index to Journals in Education*.[2] Approximately 400 new educational technology documents are entered into the system with abstracts and are available in full text on microfiche. These documents are in the public domain and usually do not reach potential users through conventional channels, unless the user sees items listed in the columns of the half-dozen journals[3] that carry selected lists of current ERIC documents or conducts an ERIC search.

Yet professional educational technologists must keep up with new developments. The literature of the field is one way of assessing current trends and new developments. The purpose of this article is to help individuals who are seeking information about new literature in the field. The sources used are the exhibits at the annual meeting of the American Educational Research Association, the advertising literature that floods the desk of the professor of education, and information that has been sent to the ERIC Clearinghouse on Information and Technology. There is no attempt to review the literature in any comprehensive manner. Categories have been established to group items of like content, although there is often overlap. Complete citations for publisher source, date of publication, and number of pages are listed in the Mediagraphy of this *Yearbook*. The list is limited to publications that carry a 1992, 1993, or 1994 copyright date. All are available from commercial publishers. Prices are not included because they frequently change and often postage and shipping charges are added.

If this information is useful to you, the editor would like to know if it should be continued in future editions of *EMTY*. There are bound to be some omissions. Please contact the editor if you know of other items that should be added. They will be included in the next edition.

CONCEPTUAL ORGANIZATION

Five categories have been established to report the current published literature. Where there is overlap, an attempt has been made to determine the dominant category.

1.	The Field of Educational Technology	Definitions, conceptual background, theory, dissemination, organizations, policy
2.	Design Functions	Resources, tools, models, procedures, techniques, evaluation
3.	Delivery Options	Hard and soft technologies, telecommunications, media
4.	Applications and Settings	Implementation, context, case studies, use
5.	Emerging Issues	Legislation, cost-effectiveness, research findings, trends, futures.

THE FIELD OF EDUCATIONAL TECHNOLOGY

Carey, D., Carey, R., Willis, D. A., and Willis, J. (1993). *Technology and teacher education annual 1993.* Needham Heights, MA: Allyn & Bacon.

Eckel, K. (1993). *Instruction language: Foundations of a strict science of instruction.* Englewood Cliffs, NJ: Educational Technology Publications.

Hawkins, J. (1993). *Technology and the organization of schools.* New York: Center for Technology and Education.

Honey, M., and Henriquez, A. (1993). *Telecommunications and K-12 education: Findings from a national survey.* New York: Center for Technology and Education.

International Board of Standards for Training, Performance and Instruction. (1993). *Instructional competencies: The standards.* Batavia, IL: International Board of Professional Standards.

Johnson, J., ed. (1993). *Graduate curricula in educational communications and technology: A descriptive directory*, 4th ed. Washington, DC: Association for Educational Communications and Technology.

Kearsley, G., and Lynch, W. (1994). *Educational technology leadership perspectives.* Englewood Cliffs, NJ: Educational Technology Publications.

Moore, D. M., and Dwyer, F. M. (1993). *Visual literacy: A spectrum of visual learning.* Englewood, Cliffs, NJ: Educational Technology Publications.

Muffoletto, R., and Knupfer, N. N. (1993). *Computers in education: Social, political, and historical perspectives.* Cresskill, NJ: Hampton Press.

Thompson, A., Simonson, M., and Hargrave, C. (1993). *Educational technology: A review of the research.* Washington, DC: Association for Educational Communications and Technology.

DESIGN FUNCTIONS

Balestri, D., Ehrmann, S., and Ferguson, D. L., eds. (1992). *Learning to design, designing to learn.* Bristol, PA: Kogan Page.

Dempsey, J. V., and Sales, G., eds. (1993). *Interactive instruction and feedback.* Englewood Cliffs, NJ: Educational Technology Publications.

Duffy, T. M., and Jonassen, D. H. (1992). *Constructivism and the technology of instruction: A conversation.* Hillsdale, NJ: Lawrence Erlbaum.

Duffy, T. M., Lowyck, J., and Jonassen, D. H., eds. (1993). *Designing environments for constructive learning.* New York: Springer-Verlag.

Duffy, T. M., Palmer, J. E., and Mehlenbacher, B. (1992). *On line help: Design and evaluation.* Norwood, NJ: Ablex Publishing.

Eggleston, J. (1992). *Teaching design and technology.* Bristol, PA: Taylor & Francis, Open University Press.

Farr, M., and Psotka, J. (1992). *Intelligent instruction by computer.* Bristol, PA: Taylor & Francis.

Fleming, M., and Levie, W. H., eds. (1993). *Instructional message design: Principles from the behavioral and cognitive sciences*, 2d ed. Englewood Cliffs, NJ: Educational Technology Publications.

Kaufman, R., Rojas, A. M., and Mayer, H. (1993). *Needs assessment: A user's guide.* Englewood Cliffs, NJ: Educational Technology Publications.

Leshin, C. B., Pollock, J., and Riegeluth, C. M. (1992). *Instructional design strategies and tactics.* Englewood Cliffs, NJ: Educational Technology Publications.

Merrill, M. D., Tennyson, R., and Posey, L. O. (1992). *Teaching concepts: An instructional design guide.* Englewood Cliffs, NJ: Educational Technology Publications.

Myers, D., and Lamb, A. (1992). *Hypercard authoring tools for presentations, tutorials and information exploration.* Orange, CA: Career Publishing.

Piskurich, G. M. (1993). *Self-directed learning.* San Francisco, CA: Jossey-Bass.

Richey, R. (1992). *Designing instruction for the adult learner: Theory and practice for employee training.* Bristol, PA: Taylor & Francis.

Schuler, D., and Namioka, A., eds. (1993). *Participatory design, principles and practices.* Hillsdale, NJ: Lawrence Erlbaum.

Schwier, R. A., and Misnachuk, E. R. (1993). *Interactive multimedia instruction.* Englewood Cliffs, NJ: Educational Technology Publications.

Smith, P. L., and Ragan, T. J. (1993). *Instructional design.* New York: Macmillan.

Spector, J. M., Polson, M. G., and Muraida, D. J., eds. (1993.) *Automating instructional design: Concepts and issues.* Englewood Cliffs, NJ: Educational Technology Publications.

Tessmer, M., and Harris, D. (1992). *Analyzing the instructional setting: Environmental analysis.* Bristol, PA: Kogan Page.

Wileman, R. (1993). *Visual communication.* Englewood Cliffs, NJ: Educational Technology Publications.

Williamson, J., and Henderson-Lancett, eds. (1993). *Interactive multimedia: Practice and promise.* Bristol, PA: Taylor & Francis.

Yoder, S. (1992). *HyperTalk for educators: An introduction to programming.* Washington, DC: Association for Educational Communications and Technology.

DELIVERY OPTIONS

Bailey, G. D., ed. (1993). *Computer-based integrated systems.* Englewood Cliffs, NJ: Educational Technology Publications.

Best, A., and Mathis, J., eds. (1993). *The 1992-93 Educational Software Preview Guide.* Eugene, OR: International Society for Technology in Education.

Gayeski, D. M., ed. (1993). *Multimedia for learning: Development, application, evaluation.* Englewood Cliffs, NJ: Educational Technology Publications.

Hakes, B. T., Sachs, S. G., Box, C., and Cochenour, J. (1993). *Compressed video: Operations and applications.* Washington, DC: Association for Educational Communications and Technology.

Pettersson, R. (1993). *Visual information,* 2d ed. Englewood Cliffs, NJ: Educational Technology Publications.

Piazza, D. (1992). *Macintosh step by step.* Eugene, OR: International Society for Technology in Education.

APPLICATIONS AND SETTINGS

Beynon, J., and Mackay, H., eds. (1992). *Computers into classrooms: More questions than answers.* Bristol, PA: Taylor and Francis.

Duning, B., VanKekerix, J. J., and Zaborowski, L. M. (1993). *Reaching learners through telecommunications.* San Francisco: Jossey-Bass.

Hawkridge, D. (1992). *Learning difficulties and computers.* Philadelphia, PA: Jessica Kingsley.

Lochte, R. H. (1993). *Interactive television and instruction: A guide to technology, technique, facilities, design and classroom management.* Englewood Cliffs, NJ: Educational Technology Publications.

Male, M. (1993). *Technology for inclusion: Meeting the special needs of all students,* 2d ed. Needham, MA: Allyn & Bacon.

Scaife, J., and Wellington, J. (1992). *Information technology in science and technology education*. Bristol, PA: Taylor & Francis, Open University Press.

Stolovitch, H. D., and Keeps, E. J., eds. (1992). *Handbook of human performance technology*. San Francisco: Jossey-Bass.

Willis, B. (1993). *Distance education: A practical guide*. Englewood Cliffs, NJ: Educational Technology Publications.

EMERGING ISSUES

Braden, R., and Beauchamp, D., eds. (1992). *Imagery and the arts*. Washington, DC: Association for Educational Communications and Technology.

Collins, A. (1993). *Design issues for learning environments*. New York: Center for Technology and Education.

Dukelow, R. (1992). *Library copyright guide*. Washington, DC: Association for Educational Communications and Technology.

Fawson, E. C., ed. (1992). *Focus on reform: State initiatives in educational technology*. Washington, DC: Association for Educational Communications and Technology.

Johnson, S. (1993). *Appraising audiovisual media: A guide for attorneys, trust officers, insurance professionals, and archivists in appraising films, video, photographs, recordings and other audiovisual assets*. Washington, DC: Association for Educational Communications and Technology.

Simonson, M., ed. (1993). *Research proceedings: 1993 AECT National Convention*. Washington, DC: Association for Educational Communications and Technology. ERIC no. ED 362 144; individual papers, ED 362 145-215.

Vlcek, C. (1992). *Adoptable copyright policy: Copyright policy and manuals designed for adoption by schools, colleges and universities*. Washington, DC: Association for Educational Communications and Technology.

NOTES

1. Major publishers of educational media and technology publications:

   Association for Educational Communications and Technology (AECT)
   Educational Technology Publications
   International Society for Technology in Education (ISTE)
   Lawrence Erlbaum Associates, Inc.
   Libraries Unlimited

2. Educational media and technology journals indexed in the *Current Index to Journals in Education* by ERIC (Educational Resources Information Center):

American Journal of Distance Education	*Computers in the Schools*
British Journal of Educational Technology	*Computing Teacher*
Collegiate Microcomputer	*Distance Education*
Computers & Education	*Educational & Training Technology*
Computers in Human Behavior	*International*

Educational Media International
Educational Technology
Educational Technology Research and
   Development
Educom Review
Electronic Learning
Human-Computer Interaction
Instructional Science
International Journal of Instructional
   Media
Journal of Artificial Intelligence in
   Education
Journal of Broadcasting and Electronic
   Media
Journal of Computer Assisted Learning
Journal of Computer-Based Instruction
Journal of Distance Education
Journal of Educational Computing
   Research

Journal of Educational Multimedia and
   Hypermedia
Journal of Educational Technology
   Systems
Journal of Educational Television
Journal of Instruction Delivery Systems
Journal of Research on Computing
   in Education
Journal of Visual Literacy
Knowledge: Creation, Diffusion,
   Utilization
Media and Methods
Open Learning
Performance and Instruction
Performance Improvement Quarterly
Simulation & Gaming
Simulation/Games for Learning
Technos
TechTrends
T.H.E. Journal

3. Educational media and technology journals that publish columns listing selected ERIC documents:

Educational & Training Technology International
Educational Technology
Educational Technology Research and Development
Journal of Computer-Based Instruction
Performance Improvement Quarterly
TechTrends

Part Two
The Profession

Introduction

There are three sections to this part: (1) new curriculum developments and the state of the Association for Educational Communications and Technology—our professional association; (2) research and development; and (3) criticism.

In recent years, each edition of *EMTY* has profiled new academic programs that are on the "cutting edge." In one case, it was a master's program in educational technology offered at a distance. In another, it was a new graduate program based in the cognitive sciences. One other was an innovative doctoral program that blended traditional and contemporary approaches to educational technology. One or two new programs seem to appear every year, while others are phased out.

This year we highlight one of the pioneer universities in the field. Indiana University has served as the model for more graduate programs in the field of media and technology than any other program anywhere in the world. It was one of the earliest graduate programs and has graduated more people with advanced degrees in the field than any other program in North America. So why focus on an established program?

The news is that Indiana University has gone through a rigorous three-year process to completely revamp its curriculum. Not only have content, sequence, and credit hours of courses been changed, but the approach to delivering the curriculum is completely new. The complete story is told in this edition of the *Yearbook* by Jim Pershing, who led the faculty team in the curriculum development effort. It is thus consistent with the articles in previous editions that reported only "new" programs. The Indiana University Instructional Systems Technology program is one of the premier new programs in the United States.

The other article in this section is a report to the profession by Addie Kinsinger, the Immediate Past President of the Association for Educational Communications and Technology. This is the report she gave to the members attending the AECT National Convention in New Orleans, Louisiana, in February 1994. It is an overview of the state of the Association as well as a status report about the field.

Much of the research in media and technology is fragmented. Doctoral students and faculty at many universities pursue their own research interests and report their findings from time to time. Most of this research is idiosyncratic; that is, the inquiries often seem to be isolated from other research. Some of it is related to other studies, some of it is not. There is not a lot of programmatic research in educational media and technology these days, even though programmatic research helped to call attention to this emerging field and provided a base for its further development. The Yale University Film Studies and the Pennsylvania State University studies of film and later, television, launched a series of research projects that were connected. They built on one another and provided rich results for their sponsors and professionals in the emerging field.

The two articles in the section on research and development provide contemporary examples of programmatic research as they describe the studies at Vanderbilt University and TERC. Vanderbilt's Cognition and Technology Group has begun a series of studies in which the principles of cognitive science are applied to software development and delivered through computers and telecommunications. The systematic studies of the TERC group are also highlighted. Both of these programs are deeply involved in the application of technology to teaching and learning, but it is not the technology itself that is important; it is the design of the learning materials that make the results of these research programs useful beyond the walls of each organization. Both are worthy of note here and further exploration is recommended.

The section on criticism is new. The critics of media and technology have always been visible, but they often go unchallenged. A syndicated column by Peter Schrage is an example of responsible criticism. Media and technology professionals may not like what he says, but his points are well taken.

We have reprinted his column (with permission) and have asked two individuals, both of whom are actively concerned about the areas of philosophy and theory in the field, to respond. Their comments on the Schrage column are thoughtful and penetrating. Andrew Yeaman analyzes the article from a "theories of resistance" perspective. Randall Nichols reconstructs the argument and gives it more depth, sometimes agreeing with and sometimes rejecting the premises of the original article.

If you were asked to respond to Schrage, what would you say?

—NEW CURRICULUM DEVELOPMENTS—

Preparing Instructional Technologists
for the 21st Century

James A. Pershing, Ph.D.
Department of Instructional Technology, School of Education
Indiana University

The Instructional Systems Technology Department (IST) at Indiana University recently completed the laborious task of revising its curriculum.[1] This complex project is faced periodically by most departments, and we offer this article on our curriculum revision for the insight of those facing similar problems as well as for those interested in the development of IST at Indiana University. The impetus for change is discussed, followed by a description of the stages in the process of revision, a brief synopsis of two relevant field studies, a description of major new features in the curriculum, and a brief discussion of the effect of revision on the faculty.

Indiana's IST program has been in place since 1940 and is one of the oldest and largest academic instructional technology programs in the United States. It has enjoyed a worldwide reputation and its graduates are easily placed. Currently it offers a master's degree and two doctoral degrees, the Ed.D. and the Ph.D.

The School of Education has echoed the boom and bust cycle of economics for the country as a whole in the 1970s through 1990. The curriculum in IST was most recently revised in 1970 during a period of expansion. The program had experienced a period of overall growth; budgets and enrollments had increased, staffing was stable, and there was a significant influx of research, development, and service money. The program was able to support a proliferation of specialty courses and tracks; 58 courses were "on the books."

Unfortunately, the School of Education as a whole has confronted dwindling resources since then and all of the departments, including IST, have been affected.[2] The gains made earlier were reversed: there was a net loss of faculty and staff positions and declining financial support for graduate assistants,[3] a gloomy situation that has stabilized only recently.

The IST faculty decided to approach the problem of curriculum revision in 1990 as a challenge and to do more than simply cut a few courses. The decision was made to thoroughly rethink the curriculum. The faculty agreed to conduct a needs assessment for the program and create a curriculum that would reflect society's changing ideas of education and prepare our students for new roles in the next century.

RATIONALE

The challenge to the Indiana University program was to recognize and incorporate information resulting from changes in three areas: changes in the instructional technology field (IT); external, societal pressures; and changes in the I.U. School of Education.

Changes in the Field

General systems theory was the dominant paradigm when IST last changed its curriculum in 1970.[4] It is still a major paradigm. Reiser and Salisbury, for example, state that "the systems approach definition and others like it . . . have become the standard view of many professionals who claim instructional technology as their field of endeavor" (1991, p. 228). Although this article is quite recent, the authors found it necessary to address those practitioners who are still "equating instructional technology with media" (1991, p. 228). The field of instructional technology is, of course, historically rooted in audiovisual education; early developments focused on the instructional uses of film, radio, and television, and emphasized hardware utilization and the production of instructional programs. Production has remained a part of the curriculum, but the approach to it has changed. The IST program in 1970 focused on hardware but had shifted attention to "technological *processes* [applied] to the design, management, and improvement of instruction" (Indiana University 1970, p. 1121, emphasis added). Since then, "audiovisual education" degree programs have been radically transformed into programs that prepare instructional systems designers. The focus has shifted to instructional theory, systematic design, formative evaluation, and issues of transfer and business impact. The general systems approach itself has undergone refinement and is now applied to corporate as well as school and university settings. In addition, new paradigms are gaining ground (Ertmer and Newby 1993; Duffy and Jonassen 1992). Constructivism and cognitive instructional theory hold increasing interest for the field and may prove to be of value for our students in gaining "a comprehensive understanding of the way people learn" (ASTD Handbook 1993, Sec. 32.3).

In addition, the arrival of the information era has had a resounding impact on the field. Computers seem to have engaged the imagination and entered the consciousness of educators and the public much more than that of earlier "media." The most visible change has been the burgeoning variety of computer and telecommunications devices that can be utilized in teaching and learning processes.[5] Instructional technology practitioners must keep abreast of developments in these areas.

Societal Changes

American society has begun debating the role and nature of education in this country, and there is a movement afoot to make meaningful changes in schooling. The very foundations and paradigms of schooling are being questioned and reevaluated (see Molenda 1992; Reigeluth 1987). Technology is being touted as one way to enhance teaching and learning at all levels and in all settings. Instructional technologists will play a key role in these debates and in reshaping traditional schooling. The redesign of instruction and the development of new means for its delivery are in the domain of instructional systems design. These emerging societal demands must be addressed in IT programs and courses.

Increasingly, the concept of education as an early, single event in an individual's life is giving way to a concept of education as an ongoing and lifelong process. Most institutions now prepare instructional developers not only for education but also for such nontraditional educational settings as corporate education centers, health care institutions, government and military training facilities, libraries, textbook publishing companies, and producers of computer software.[6] U.S. corporations alone now spend more money per year on education and training for their employees than do all institutions of higher education combined, and the systematic design of instruction is an important part of human resources development.

Demand for instructional technologists has accelerated for the past 10 years and shows no signs of abating.

Changes in the I.U. School of Education

The School of Education, in common with programs across the country, has been affected by reduced budgets, decreasing numbers of faculty, and smaller student enrollment. The School has downsized. Despite replacement of some faculty, attrition has resulted in a net loss of 9 IST faculty in the past 10 years. Fewer faculty are available for teaching, and the breadth of faculty expertise has been significantly reduced. In addition, the new faculty members who have arrived have brought with them skills and knowledge not always fully utilized by the existing program.[7]

The IST Department teaches a heterogeneous student body. Increasing numbers of students work part-time while pursuing their degrees and some are medium- to long-distance commuters.[8] Demand for evening and weekend classes has resulted. International students comprise a substantial portion of the student body, about 35 percent.[9] In common with their fellow U.S. students, these students aspire to nontraditional careers. In the past, approximately 75 percent of IST students expected to find careers in traditional audiovisual education programs in schools and universities. Now, approximately 75 percent seek careers as instructional systems designers in business, industry, and government. Those students interested in the public school and university domains focus more on technology's role in school restructuring and its integration into the school curriculum than on traditional audiovisual concerns.

An additional resource for the faculty has been I.U.'s new School of Education building and the Center for Excellence in Education. One emphasis has been on the incorporation of the latest in technical capabilities. Distance education studios have been built for the Bloomington and Indianapolis campuses, and interactive multimedia courses delivered for inservice teachers in Indianapolis. The Bloomington building is equipped with teaching, photographic, computer, and science laboratories, a 14-station multimedia lab, and television studios. An auditorium featuring interactive multimedia and a touch-screen podium has been added. These new facilities provided an opportunity for the IST program to fully integrate technology into its curriculum.

CURRICULUM REVISION OVERVIEW

Curriculum revision has been a three-year effort for all of the IST faculty. An associate chair position was added on a temporary basis to provide leadership during the revision process. Release time and support during the summer months ensured that continuity and momentum were not lost. A steering committee was appointed. One of the two faculty meetings per month was devoted to reporting, discussion, planning, and decision making. In addition, department faculty participated in five one-day retreats on the topics of department direction and curriculum revision. Some faculty members accomplished major tasks; their efforts were integrated into their service loads and evaluated in the annual performance reviews. Assistance in data collection and analysis, logistics, and clerical tasks was given by half-time graduate students.

STRATEGIC PLANNING AND DIRECTION

The goal for the 1989-90 academic year was to complete a plan for revising the curriculum for the IST Department. The first step for the IST faculty was to gather relevant information. A literature review was undertaken of trends and issues pertinent to the field of instructional systems technology, particularly in relation to university programs. Faculty also reviewed several sets of data concerning the history and future of the IST program: 10 years of data showing trends in enrollments, faculty and staff resources, course offerings, and budgets; an account of facilities, equipment, furnishings, and supplies currently used by the program; and responses to a 1987 follow-up study of program graduates. Supplemental information was gleaned from relevant reports and planning documents generated by the School of Education and the Center for Excellence in Education. Finally, the faculty conducted a self-inventory to determine collective and individual faculty expertise, expectations, and needs.

After much discussion, the faculty agreed upon the following specifics for planning the curriculum over the following two years:

- Any changes would be consistent with the IST program's history of leadership and scholarship and maintain the department's high status in the field of instructional systems technology.[10]

- The faculty would cut the 58 course offerings by one-third. Breadth would be sacrificed for depth and quality.

- The program emphasis favoring production and hardware utilization over instructional analysis and design would be reversed.

- The size of the faculty must be stabilized at a minimum of eight full-time faculty. Additional support staff were required to assist the one full-time department secretary.

- Student enrollment for the master's degree might be increased. The number of doctoral student admissions will be decreased to ensure that the faculty can provide adequate time for mentoring and dissertation guidance.

RESEARCH AND LITERATURE REVIEW

One of the most important tasks for the IST Department's revision was the identification of skills and competencies required by instructional systems technology practitioners[11] and the evaluation of the curriculum in light of those competencies. Practitioners in both academic and industry settings have been concerned about the skills and competencies required now and in the future. McLagan and Bedrick (1983) summarized the results of the massive American Society for Training and Development study by describing roles performed and the products created. These studies were of particular interest to us. In addition, several studies have attempted to link competencies to education and curriculum. Pinto and Walker (1978), Kennedy (1982), and Trimby (1982) conducted research in this area. Trimby's goal was to assist academic institutions in preparing students for industry settings. She surveyed training team members and supervisors to ascertain entry-level competencies for instructional development specialists and established 70 competencies. Interestingly, interpersonal skills were the highest ranked competency, and communication skills also received high rankings. Cameron (1988) surveyed industrial trainers in Tennessee, who ranged widely in education and position, and asked them to identify tasks for which it was important to have additional training. Palmer (1987) also conducted a study to identify competencies; in this case, the goal was specifically to provide data useful for curriculum development. The five competencies ranked as extremely useful were oral and written communication skills, group facilitation skills, platform presentation skills, and needs assessment techniques. Production skills received low rankings. Spitzer's survey (1988) of National Society for Performance and Instruction professionals was conducted specifically to guide curriculum decisions for Boise State's developing program. Needs assessment, performance analysis, and task analysis were the highest rated competencies.

Information from two studies intimately connected with I.U. proved particularly useful in planning curriculum changes. The first was a small, informal effort initiated by the faculty and restricted to Indiana University graduates. Surveys of IST graduates revealed both strengths and weaknesses in our program. The second study was formal and included instructional technology graduates from numerous programs. Synopses of the two studies follow.

Survey of I.U. Graduates

During the spring and summer of 1987, the IST Department contacted by letter approximately 50 IST program graduates. Thirty-eight graduates responded. These were master's, specialist's, or doctoral graduates who had been working in the field from one to five years. The letter stated that information was sought for the purpose of making major changes in the departmental curriculum. Three open-ended questions were asked:

1. Indicate the strengths and weaknesses of the IST program in preparing you for a career as an instructional technologist.

2. Cite areas that need to be expanded or added to the IST curriculum.

3. Cite areas that need to be de-emphasized or deleted from the IST curriculum.

We were very pleased that all of the respondents were supportive of the IST program in general. There were numerous reports that the positive reputation of Indiana University and the IST Department were keys in these graduates' securing employment.

Communication skills were foremost in the minds of the respondents. An emphasis on writing, particularly skills necessary for the preparation of proposals and reports, was regarded as very important. Developing the necessary skills to work effectively with multidisciplinary teams was also mentioned.

There was unanimity in reporting that the field of Instructional Technology is in flux. New and emerging technologies, particularly those that are computer-related, are significantly affecting the field. Respondents requested more "hands-on" experiences with these technologies.

Respondents also stated that the IST program should place less emphasis on administering instructional programs and more on project management and evaluation. Respondents felt they lacked the knowledge and the tools to justify and measure the impacts of training and development programs in economic terms. Some recommended the addition of business or labor studies minors for the doctorate.

Production skills were seldom used by our graduates, particularly skills involving traditional technologies such as graphic art, sound, and still and motion pictures. Practitioners valued their familiarity with these processes but indicated that, in the workplace, technicians are usually called upon to carry them out.

Finally, nearly all of the respondents suggested integrating more experiential learning into the IST program. Many rated their most valuable program experiences at Indiana University as the simulated assignments, practica, and internships.

Corporate Instructional Designers:
A Curriculum Needs Assessment Survey

During the summer and fall of 1990, the IST Department of Indiana University and Arthur Andersen, Inc., one of the world's largest employers of instructional technologists, collaborated on a national needs assessment study. The purpose was to identify competencies needed in corporate training and development now and in the next five years. Another purpose was to assess the adequacy of training: respondents were asked to compare the skills needed on the job with those taught by their programs. The population for the study was instructional technologists employed in U.S. corporations, government, and military. Instructional technologists employed in school settings were not included. The 204 respondents were alumni of 14 instructional technology programs.

Information from this study had great import for the I.U. faculty working on the curriculum revision. An open-ended question of particular interest was "Describe what curriculum changes universities should make to accommodate new developments." Of the 180 individuals who responded to this question, 17 were identified as Indiana University graduates. Graduates from 13 other programs were among the respondents, greatly increasing confidence in the wide applicability of the results. A content analysis of the responses indicates agreement among the graduates from the various university programs. (The responses are also in agreement with those received three years earlier in the IST Department follow-up study.) A full description of the corporate instructional designers study will be published elsewhere, but several findings particularly affected the IST faculty's work on the curriculum. The practitioners requested:

- More exposure to and experience with the *new and emerging technologies* impacting the field.

- Better preparation in understanding the "bottom line" of training and development in the private sector—a focus on *economic* and *business* principles. These skills were declared *critical* to job performance and appear to be a real void in IT programs.

- More emphasis on *communications skills*, including writing, speaking, and practice in writing proposals and reports.

- Special emphasis on the social skills necessary for consulting, negotiating, and working as a team member. Practitioners seldom work in isolation.

- An increase in the number of real-life or *hands-on experiences* in the program through group projects, case studies, simulation assignments, and practica.

- Active involvement by students in the teaching and learning processes—let the faculty assume the roles of supervisor, coach, and consultant.

ANALYSIS AND DESIGN

Based on analysis of the preceding materials, faculty enumerated goals for the curriculum revision during the early part of the 1990-91 academic year and then developed specifications for the master's and doctoral degrees. Many of the goals were derived from the literature review and the results of the surveys. The faculty agreed upon the following points as goals for program revision:

- Require computer skills as a prerequisite and make technology utilization an integral part of the curriculum. Eliminate the separation of the various media formats. Establish a series of courses of increasing complexity integrating production and development.

  —Reflect the needs and expectations expressed by those practicing in the field. Specifically:

  —Emphasize experiential and hands-on learning in all courses. Make more extensive use of case methods, simulations, and project-based teaching methodologies.

  —Establish a sequence of courses which culminate in a "portfolio presentation" to demonstrate the student's mastery of program knowledge.

  —Increase group learning in classes, providing students with a chance to develop consulting and teamwork skills.

- Increase oversight of each student's progress by increasing the steps requiring an advisor's approval and by mentoring.

- Increase prescription in the program. Establish a set of required core courses and criteria for the selection of electives.

- Set the number of program focus areas at four. Develop one required and three to seven elective courses for each focus area:

  —Foundations

  —Instructional Analysis, Design, and Development

  —Instructional Development and Production

  —Implementation and Management

- Establish a set core of courses that teach essential concepts, providing students with a coherent overview of the field.

During the 1990-91 academic year, the IST faculty worked on the design phase of the curriculum revision, writing specifications for the IST master's and doctoral programs that would change these programs substantially. At the end of the year, the following operational criteria were accepted by a unanimous vote by the faculty. These criteria are now the operating criteria for the IST program.

1. Establish a 12-hour core of required courses. The core course sequence is the heart of the new program. The first six-credit block is offered in the first semester, the second six hours in the second semester. The content of the courses is integrated; instructional design process, instructional theory, and learning theory are merged. The core competencies reflect

competencies currently in demand in the marketplace: evaluation, implementation, project management, group processes, and communication skills. Extensive use of technology is included in all aspects of the core. Students survey and learn about multiple technologies by example and use. A description of the core as it was envisioned and developed follows:

- R511—Instructional Technology Foundations I (semester 1)—2 credits
  IT: Field and Profession
  Basic Media Selection and Appraisal

- R521—Instructional Design and Development I (semester 1)—1 credit
  ISD: A Process Approach

- R522—Instructional Design and Development II (semester 1)—3 credits
  Instructional Strategies
  Task Analysis and Objective Writing
  Content Analysis and Sequencing

- R541—Instructional Development and Production Process I (semester 2)—3 credits
  Basic Production Skills
  Multimedia Production and Process
  Lab Practice, Presentation Software, and Authoring

- R561—Evaluation and Change in the Instructional Development Process (semester 2)—3 credits
  ID Evaluation
  Adoption and Use of Instructional Products

The core courses focus on analysis, design, and development, de-emphasizing media in the first semester, followed by elaboration on media selection, design, and production in the second semester. Formative and summative evaluation, implementation, and project management are added in the second semester. During the third and fourth semesters, students deepen their knowledge of each area.

Practical skills are developed in graduated steps. For instance, in R522 students design a 30-minute workshop on a simple procedural task. They then prepare a course outline for teaching a complex task or domain, demonstrating knowledge of selection, sequencing, and overall strategy. Next they design a complete course that includes remember-level and application-level learning.

2. The widespread agreement on the necessity of computer skills makes mastery of these skills essential. Computer literacy is now a prerequisite for the program. Students entering the IST graduate program with very little or no computing experience are required to take R501, Instructional Computing Basics (1-3 credits). The course consists of three units, each equivalent to one credit: computer awareness and literacy, basic applications, and educational computing basics. Students requiring training in one or more of the sections would undertake highly structured study in a lab setting, for one to three credits.

3. Basic communications skills, specifically writing and presenting, are emphasized in the new program. A student who is deficient in these skills, or who is judged deficient by a faculty member, receives instruction directly related to the problem. The student might receive instruction from mentors or tutors, or work at the campus Learning Resource Center.

4. Recruitment efforts are being stepped up to increase graduate student enrollments at the master's level. The goal is to increase class size by 50 percent in 5 years. Qualifications for entrance to the doctoral programs are being raised.

DEVELOPMENT AND IMPLEMENTATION

The most difficult and time-consuming phase was development and implementation. During the 1991-92 academic year, faculty could report the following accomplishments:

- A fully revised IST master's program was developed and prepared for testing during the first semester of the 1992-93 academic year.

- Detailed course outlines for all basic, core, and new elective courses were completed.

- Transition plans were developed to deal with the needs of all current master's students, guaranteeing that they are not penalized or burdened as revised programs are implemented.

- Specifications for all new departmental promotional and student advisement materials were developed. Drafts of these materials were produced during the summer months of 1992.

To facilitate a smooth transition to the new curriculum, information concerning the IST program revisions was widely disseminated to prospective students, alumni, and academic and professional colleagues in the summer of 1992 and throughout the 1992-93 academic year.

FEATURES OF THE NEW CURRICULUM

The following is a brief overview of the requirements for each IST degree: M.S., Ed.D., and Ph.D. After that is a description of major features of the revised curriculum, some parts of which are common to all three degrees.

Redefinition of the Degrees

Faculty decided that the three degrees should be more sharply delineated than they had been in the past. Differences between the two doctoral degrees, the Ed.D. and the Ph.D., were particularly indistinct. Studies by Andersen (1983), Dill and Morrison (1985), and Carpenter (1987) demonstrated that the philosophical assumptions underlying the two degrees are seldom reflected in university requirements and curriculum. Growth in the field and increasing numbers of professionals in nonacademic settings, however, called for a clear delineation of the two.

Master of Science. The Master of Science degree program is designed for individuals seeking to be practitioners in the field of instructional technology. Graduates typically assume design and/or development roles in public or private agencies and organizations.

The program is a 40-credit-hour (minimum) graduate program for individuals who have completed a bachelor's degree from an accredited institution. The required set of courses consists of 16 credits (4 core courses, colloquia, and an instructional product or master's thesis). Most students will complete an instructional project as their final experience, but, if there is a compelling reason, a student will be allowed to write a traditional master's thesis under the guidance of a faculty advisor. (The core course system was explained earlier and the project requirement is explained later.) Outside electives (12 hours) are chosen with a faculty member responsible for overseeing the student's path to his or her career goal and may be taken in adult education, business, curriculum and instruction, telecommunications, or other departments.

Prerequisites	0 to 3 hrs.
Core Courses	12 hrs.
Colloquia	1 hr.
Industrial Project	3 hrs.
Courses Inside IST	12 hrs.
Courses Outside IST	12 hrs.
	40 hrs. to 43 hrs. total

Doctor of Education, Ed.D. The Doctor of Education degree program is designed for individuals seeking to be practitioners in the field of instructional technology. The program prepares students to bridge the gap between research and practice. The student learns to apply the findings of basic and applied research and to build and test processes, products, and services intended for use in education and training settings. Ed.D. graduates typically assume management and leadership roles in public or private organizations. Sixty post-master's credit hours are required; nine must be credit hours in inquiry. Ed.D. students must meet the portfolio examination requirement and fulfill the dissertation requirement, which may be project-based.

Doctor of Philosophy in Education, Ph.D. The Ph.D. program is designed to train researchers in the field of instructional technology rather than practitioners. The IST program prepares students to conduct basic and applied research. Ph.D. program graduates typically teach in universities or work as researchers in research and development centers involved in instructional technology. The program is a 90-credit-hour post-bachelor's degree graduate program that culminates in a research-based dissertation. Twenty-seven hours of credit must be in inquiry. The Ph.D. student must also fulfill a publication requirement, the portfolio examination requirement, and participate in a research colloquium.

Major Curriculum Elements

Basic Computer Skills. Elementary computer skills are no longer developed as an integral part of the curriculum—they are a prerequisite. Those students lacking essential computer skills and knowledge in one or more areas will be required to take R501 for 1, 2, or 3 credits, as described earlier.

Colloquia. Weekly meeting attendance is required of master's and doctoral students. Presentations by faculty, advanced students, visiting scholars, and guest practitioners are intended to expose students to trends and issues in the field. The colloquia allow for the development of student-centered professional activities and a strong student support group.

Core Courses. The system of core courses was described in an earlier section. These courses are requirements common to the master's, Ed.D., and Ph.D. degrees, enhancing articulation between the levels of the program.

Instructional Project Development Course. This course is required of students in all three degree programs, ensuring that all students receive practical experience in instructional product development under the guidance of a faculty member. The project is one of the main features of the portfolio. The project must address a real-world instructional problem and contain evidence of the student's successful application of at least three of the five components of the instructional systems development process: analysis, design and development, production, evaluation, and implementation and management.

Portfolio Examination Requirement. The portfolio requirement is perhaps one of the department's most innovative features. It is required of all master's students who choose not to write a thesis, and of all Ph.D. and Ed.D. students. It is intended to demonstrate the student's facility in the types of projects and tasks that will be required in a career position. The portfolio is expected to be a valuable aid in displaying the student's talent and experience to prospective employers or clients. In addition, the portfolio examination is an opportunity for the faculty to conduct an early evaluation of the potential success of students in the doctoral programs and to provide them with good career counseling.

Each portfolio includes two sets of data: a set including a project or projects and a set of information related to the student's career goals. Students in the master's program will develop a project during the last semester of residency. Ed.D. and Ph.D. students must submit the portfolio after completion of a specific number of credit hours. Each student chooses a portfolio mentor from the IST faculty, who assists the student in finding real clients and coaches the student through the project. The product developed in course R681, Instructional Project Development, is featured, but additional projects undertaken in other courses on research or development, or via practica and internships, may be included.

Master's-level students must provide four items to fulfill the second part of the portfolio examination: a completed program of studies form, a statement of career goals, a resume, and a list of professional references. An advisory committee, including the student's mentor, examines each portfolio and meets with the student to provide career counseling.

For doctoral students, the second set of information is composed of five items. A statement of the student's career goals and a list of competency areas the student believes are important for attaining those goals are two. The student must also document his or her attainments within each competency area. Identification of competencies yet to be acquired and a plan for achieving them must be included. (The latter includes the doctoral program plan.) Lastly, identification of the topical area in which the dissertation is to be conducted and the professor who has agreed to serve as director of the dissertation must be added. The dissertation director and an advisory committee meet to examine and discuss the portfolio and then provide counseling to the student and recommendations to the IST Department Chair.

Ph.D. Publication/Paper Requirement. Prior to acceptance of the dissertation proposal, each student must publish an article in a reputable journal or present a paper at an acceptable conference. The student must receive approval from the faculty prior to undertaking this effort.

Minors and Outside Electives. The competencies named by former IST students indicated that the program must utilize the outside minor requirement more efficiently than in the past. Practitioners' concerns about their lack of knowledge of business procedures and economic principles suggested that minors could be initiated in labor studies, business, or similar fields, depending on the career goal of the student. All courses taken outside IST are now reviewed by the student's advisor and chosen in accordance with the student's career goals and objectives.

EFFECTS ON THE FACULTY

The curriculum revision has had the secondary but important effect of unifying the IST faculty. The development effort alone, long and arduous as it was, contributed to building a spirit of camaraderie. Too often faculty members had little detailed knowledge of the curriculum apart from their own courses. The faculty is now more fully committed and better informed than it would otherwise have been, and the benefits to both students and faculty members are expected to far outweigh the time cost.

In addition, the core has been restructured in a way that requires changes in our teaching methods. The faculty decided to teach the core courses in teams of three or four people and to rotate the assignments so that everyone becomes fully immersed in the core curriculum. The faculty are modelling behavior for the students through team teaching. The team meets weekly to plan activities and is present during instruction. Structured activities and specific assignments are shared among the faculty members. Activities include small and large group lectures and discussions, projects, and guided self-study. Team teaching the core portion of the new curriculum provides an ongoing shared experience for all IST faculty and contributes to the spirit of collegiality. The faculty have found the approach refreshing.

CONCLUSION

As we begin the 21st century, we must all adapt innovatively to new technologies and changing societal demands, finding ways to accomplish our goals with fewer and smaller resources. Instructional Technology departments must lead the way in preparing instructional technologists for the public school system, the service industry, business, and government, both here and abroad. To do so, they must continue to revise their curricula in the light of recent research on learning and meet the needs of practitioners.

NOTES

1. IST is one of six departments in the School of Education at Indiana University's main campus in Bloomington, Indiana. The others are Counseling and Educational Psychology, Curriculum and Instruction, Educational Leadership and Policy Studies, Language Education, and Teacher Education.

2. In 1970, the IST faculty numbered 20, but all had split appointments with the campus audiovisual center, resulting in an actual 10.4 full-time equivalent (FTE). Currently, the IST faculty is nine, with only three split appointments (none with the audiovisual center), totalling 7.55 FTE. IST has fared relatively well within the School of Education, whose entire faculty peaked at 203 in 1970 and has dropped to 100 at present. Fortunately, the School expects to add 10 to 15 new positions over the next five years.

3. During the 1970s, the IST Department and the Audio-Visual Center combined provided most IST students with graduate assistantships. During that period, the number peaked at 80. Since then, the number of available positions has fallen to 30. Fortunately, numerous other School of Education and University departments and programs have compensated by employing IST graduate students as instructional developers, consultants, media technicians, and so on.

4. The curriculum revision in 1970 was driven by a total systems approach to instructional systems development. It was assumed that instructional technologists would work on development teams consisting of specialists in systems design, development, diffusion and adoption, message design, and evaluation. Thus, five curriculum emphasis areas were established: (1) instructional design and development; (2) product evaluation and curricular integration; (3) systems design and management of learning resources; (4) diffusion and adoption; and (5) message design and research.

5. Note Clark and Sugrue's critiques of the myriad studies on instructional media (1988) and Ely and Plomp's interesting evaluation of the role of educational technology (1988).

6. The stream of instructional technologists into business and industry has been well reported. For example, one study comparing 1982 and 1986 data showed that approximately half of the master's and doctoral graduates did not obtain employment in educational settings (Logan 1988, p. 163-64).

7. Of the 20 faculty members in IST in 1970, only 2 were still teaching in 1990.

8. Approximately 25 percent of students in 1990, compared to 10 percent in 1970. No doubt the decrease in the number of available assistantships is a relevant factor.

9. The percentage of foreign students in IST at I.U. is fairly stable; it has ranged between 30 and 40 since 1950.

10. Moore and Braden's (1988) study of prestige in the field of instructional technology found that I.U. was the only institution named first, second, or third most prestigious by more than 50 percent of the respondents.

11. The most useful prior research on ID competencies was conducted by the International Board of Standards for Training, Performance, and Instruction in 1986. Mary Kennedy (1982) and Patrick Pinto and James Walker (1978) also conducted research in this area, but their findings were no longer current in 1990.

REFERENCES AND ADDITIONAL READING

American Society for Training and Development. (1993). *The ASTD handbook of instructional technology.* New York: McGraw-Hill.

Andersen, Dale G. (1983). Differentiation of the Ed.D. and Ph.D. in education. *Journal of Teacher Education 34*, 5-58.

Anglin, Gary J., ed. (1991). *Instructional technology: Past, present, and future.* Englewood, CO: Libraries Unlimited.

Branch, Robert C., Moore, David M., and Sherman, Thomas M. (1988, October). Evaluating potential instructional technology and design professionals for academic and business settings: Criteria for decision-making. *Educational Technology 28*(10), 34-37.

Cameron, Walter A. (1988). *Training competencies of human resource development specialists in Tennessee.* Knoxville, TN: Tennessee University Department of Technological and Adult Education. ERIC no. ED 303 674.

Carpenter, D. Stanley. (1987). On-going dialogue: Degrees of difference? *Review of Higher Education 10*, 281-86.

Clark, Richard E., and Sugrue, Brenda M. (1988). Research on instructional media, 1978-1988. In *Educational Media and Technology Yearbook 14,* ed. D. P. Ely (Englewood, CO: Libraries Unlimited), 19-37.

Dill, David D., and Morrison, James L. (1985). Ed.D. and Ph.D. research training in the field of higher education: A survey and a proposal. *Review of Higher Education 8,* 169-86.

Duffy, Thomas M., and Jonassen, David H., eds. (1992). *Constructivism and the technology of instruction: A conversation.* Hillsdale, NJ: Lawrence Erlbaum.

Ely, Donald P., and Plomp, Tjeerd. (1988). The promises of educational technology: A reassessment. In *Educational Media and Technology Yearbook 14,* ed. D. P. Ely (Englewood, CO: Libraries Unlimited), 5-18.

Ertmer, Peggy A., and Newby, Timothy J. (1993). Behaviorism, cognitivism, constructivism: Comparing critical features from a design perspective. *Performance Improvement Quarterly 6,* 50-72.

Indiana University Audio-Visual Center. (1970). *1970 catalog: Educational motion pictures.* Bloomington, IN: I.U. Office for Academic Affairs.

International Board of Standards for Training, Performance, and Instruction. (1986). *Instructional design competencies: The standards.* Author.

Kennedy, Mary. (1982). *Guidelines for graduate educational technology programs with an emphasis in training in the business and industry milieu.* Unpublished doctoral dissertation, Indiana University.

Logan, Edwin. (1988). Highlights of the status and trends of instructional technology/media related programs at the doctoral and master's level. In *Educational Media and Technology Yearbook 14,* ed. D. P. Ely (Englewood, CO: Libraries Unlimited), 153-64.

McLagan, Patricia A., and Bedrick, David. (1983, June). Models for excellence: The results of the ASTD Training and Development Competency Study. *Training and Development Journal 37,* 10-20.

Molenda, Michael. (1992). Technology and school restructuring: Some clarifying propositions. In *Educational Media and Technology Yearbook 18,* ed. D. P. Ely and B. B. Minor (Englewood, CO: Libraries Unlimited), 77-90.

Moore, David M., and Braden, Roberts A. (1988, March). Prestige and influence in the field of instructional technology. *Performance and Instruction 27*(3), 19-22.

Palmer, Teresa M. (1987, October). *Needed training competencies and university offerings: Designing a good match.* Paper presented at the annual meeting of the American Association for Adult and Continuing Education, Washington DC. ERIC no. ED 287 059.

Pinto, Patrick, and Walker, James. (1978). *A study of professional training and development roles and competencies.* Madison, WI: American Society for Training and Development.

Reigeluth, Charles M. (1987). The search for meaningful reform: A third wave educational system. *Journal of Instructional Development 10,* 3-26.

Reiser, Robert A., and Salisbury, David F. (1991). Instructional technology and public education in the United States: The next decade. In *Instructional technology: Past, present, and future,* ed. G. J. Anglin (Englewood, CO: Libraries Unlimited).

Spitzer, Dean R. (1988, August). Instructional/performance technology competencies. *Performance and Instruction 27*(7), 11-13.

Trimby, Madeline J. (1982, May). *Entry level competencies for instructional developers.* Paper presented at the annual meeting of the Association for Educational Communications and Technology, Dallas, TX. ERIC no. ED 222 174.

Wallington, Clint. (1984). Industry and instructional development. In *Instructional development: The state of the art,* ed. Ronald K. Bass and Charles R. Dills. (Dubuque, IA: Kendall/Hunt). ERIC no. ED 298 927.

Association for Educational Communications and Technology 1993 Presidential Address

Addie Kinsinger
President AECT—1993/94

The other day the newspaper section called *Perspectives* had a headline that caught my eye: "Key to the Future? or Lock on the Past?"

It was an article by Mike Elliott, Washington Chief of the *Economist*. He started out by saying that each new year is anticipated for the promise of *change*, but that if this year or any other year is to be a watershed year, we (all of us) will have to do more than simply talk *change*. He went on to say, "A mere switching of the control of the executive branch has far less significance in America than it would have in most other countries. The essentials of American life remain unchanged." This statement is applicable to AECT as well. The essentials of your lives will remain pretty much unchanged . . . even though there is a new AECT president.

The desire to push through novel personally held ideas forms little part of being president of AECT. A change of presidents does not mean the association will be turned upside down or will do so of its own accord. Reality overrules those philosophical soul mates, "What you hope to do" and "What you are able to do."

Equally germane to the future of AECT is that we not allow ourselves to think of the Board of Directors in the simplistic terms of "doers" or "them" as in them and us, or as the only decision makers.

Indeed, this president believes strongly in change, viewing it as a challenge and with my usual enthusiasm. I also believe in a certain continuity of ideas and ideals that have shaped this professional organization. They should not be tampered with, but polished vigorously and made to shine as our guiding principles. A central question is whether we will be willing to embrace new ideas and a more focused vision which may come from the intellectual wellsprings of the VISION 2000 Task Force. Or will we reject the recommendations because they mean change—because they mean messing around with our comfort zones? We've done long-range planning before. We bring hope to the table. We don't commit. The essentials of our AECT lives remain unchanged.

Of all this commentary on concerns of commitment to change, one of the most pervasive centers on your view of the association, its business, and the Board's relations with you, the membership, and vice versa. Elected officers of divisions and affiliates, committee chairpersons, regional coordinators, committee and task force persons have already committed to leadership roles and responsibilities. Many members are already involved in offering ideas to bring about change and direct visionary thinking of what issues and/or problems need solutions.

At the Summer Leadership Development Conference over 50 people signed on for a "Great Ideas Task Force." Much discussion was generated about the issues the association and the profession are facing as well as what are some of the solutions. Everything from the need for professional impact; legislative advocacy; membership services; creativity and flexibility in addressing learner needs; unequaled professional development courses and activities; modeling the use of technology; an 800 number; networking; multigenerational leadership emerging from every aspect of the membership; electronic communication for all governance and members; be *the* voice in standardization of cutting-edge technology; a resource for the exchange of ideas; to an association that "touches me daily." I know that one well.

I would expand that list. I would place before you that the *learner* is the significant recipient of our efforts, and the manner in which we use communications and technology as the interface for advancing that learner is the most significant reason for our collective professional presence.

In order to provide the association the image, vitality, and foundation as *the* organization for professionals in educational communication and technology, it is my belief that the direction, focus, and targeted goals for AECT governance, staff, and membership will need to:

- Acquire and efficiently utilize human and financial resources to the best possible advantage in building a new convention/exposition (InCITE).

- Direct and empower leadership development activities as a continuing and concentrated focus involving broad opportunities for participation, nurturing, and mentoring.

- Extend, promote, and advocate equitable access to information, ideas, technological advantages, and exemplary teaching for all learners.

- Vigorously pursue and increase contributions of human energy, mind power, time, and expertise of AECT members for writing, speaking, teaching, networking, researching, and producing for the advancement of our professional field.

- Strengthen the infrastructure of AECT with responsible workplans, business and fiscal accountability for proportional improvement in performance and productivity.

- Strive for representation of persons from diverse multicultural backgrounds in all aspects of the association.

Each new president inherits an association financial situation where room for maneuvering is strictly limited. Aspirations for doing something new are quickly sobered. Productive changes usually require a second look for whatever financing needs are necessary for implementation. As the association presses forward in new ventures, services, and images, there will have to be tough decisions made. . . . Choices, I remind you, do not have to be negative. Merger or consortium possibilities certainly have the potential to expand the ventures, services, and image, provided the membership and leaders negotiate, with caution and expertise, an agreement that will curry favor and encompass a sense of security for all parties concerned.

Every issue does not need lengthy debate at the expense of common sense; if we can't afford it, we can't do it.

You, the membership, constituents if you will, who are demanding change, will have to ultimately determine how sound the solutions are and at what pace they should be implemented.

I don't want to be known as the president who was high on enthusiasm but brought very little change. The hope I have is that the AECT I know today will see some interesting change at the policy level, and for the membership—a planning guide for continuing changes—some revolutionary, some evolutionary, for the next few years which may be examined, evaluated, and adjusted as necessary.

In the grand sweep of things, I may not alter AECT's course at all. Change is not easy. I ask then, "Are comfort and change natural enemies? Will we focus on the learner?"

—RESEARCH AND DEVELOPMENT—

The Learning Technology Center at Vanderbilt University

Cognition and Technology
Group at Vanderbilt (CTGV)*

The Learning Technology Center (LTC) at Vanderbilt University is an unusually collaborative, multidisciplinary group of approximately 70 researchers, designers, and educators who are internationally known for their work on technology in education. Members of the LTC are currently working on a variety of projects in the areas of mathematics, science, social studies, and literacy. All LTC projects are research-based and all products undergo extensive evaluation before being implemented.

The personnel profile of the Learning Technology Center reflects a heterogeneous group of individuals in terms of their disciplinary backgrounds and relationship to the university. Faculty members who participate in the LTC have their university appointments in a variety of departments, including Computer Science, Psychology, Teaching and Learning, Special Education, Mathematics, Chemistry, Organizational Administration, and Public Policy. Other research staff are appointed to the LTC and supported on grants and contracts. The research staff includes postdoctoral research scientists, research analysts, and design specialists in video, multimedia, and computer applications. The administrative structure of LTC includes a director of administration, an administrative assistant, and various secretarial/clerical personnel. There is also a technical support person responsible for our video editing suite. The LTC also has a number of collaborative relationships with Nashville-based experts in video scripting, production, and design.

Members of Vanderbilt's LTC publish individually as well as collaboratively under the name "The Cognition and Technology Group at Vanderbilt (CTGV)." Since 1990, the CTGV has authored over 25 articles.

REPRESENTATIVE PROJECTS

All LTC projects share the idea of anchoring (situating) instruction in meaningful environments that invite thinking and inquiry. Videodisc, CD-ROM, and simulation technologies make it possible to create integrated media environments that are rich in content and easy to explore. Telecommunications technologies make it possible to connect diverse sites in order to create learning communities. A major goal of the learning environments developed by the LTC is to encourage generative rather than passive learning, and to encourage collaboration. Some representative projects are described here.

---

*This article was authored by John Bransford, Centennial Professor and Co-Director of the Learning Technology Center.

The Jasper Woodbury Problem-Solving Series

The Jasper series consists of 12 videodisc-based adventures that focus on mathematical problem finding and problem solving while also providing links for cross-curricular explorations relevant to science, social studies, literature, and other subjects. The adventures are designed for students in grades 5 and up. Each videodisc contains a short (approximately 17-minute) video adventure that ends in a complex challenge; students work collaboratively in small groups to re-explore the video (usually over a period of 3 to 5 class periods) to find the data needed to solve the challenge. They then present their solutions to their fellow classmates and discuss strengths and weaknesses of each set of solutions. Students then work on extension challenges that help them engage in "what if" thinking by revisiting the original adventures from new points of view (e.g., what if the ultralight used to rescue the eagle faced a 4-mph headwind rather than flying on a calm day?).

Jasper's "Adventure Maker" software provides additional opportunities to extend students' learning by encouraging them to create their own problems that they can present to others. The computer software lets students create new adventures, keeps track of their answers to problems, and then provides a simulation of the consequences of the answers that they have proposed.

The Jasper series is funded by the National Science Foundation and the James S. McDonnell Foundation. It has been shown to significantly improve complex problem solving as well as attitudes toward mathematics and other types of challenges. The series has won awards for its video production (from the New York Film Festival) and its instructional design (from the Association for Educational Communications and Technology). It also received Optical Data's 1993 "Product of the Year" award.

Scientists in Action

The Scientists in Action series is a research-based series funded by the National Science Foundation. A major goal of the series is to engage students in inquiry characteristic of real scientists. Especially important is its emphasis on scientific activities in everyday settings, as opposed to in isolated laboratories, and in settings that depict collaboration rather than isolated work.

The Scientists in Action series builds upon and extends the anchored instruction principles used in the Jasper series. At present, four video-based adventures, plus accompanying software, are being developed. The series will eventually be on CD-ROM.

Your Explorer Series (YES)

The Your Explorer Series is an extensively researched, multimedia literacy program for grades K-3 that is designed to help students develop important attitudes, concepts, and skills necessary for reading to learn and for lifelong learning. YES is based on the principles of the Jasper Woodbury Problem-Solving Series and takes students to new levels. Developed from the perspective of "no floor, no ceiling," YES is especially useful for children who are at risk for school failure, yet the series is equally challenging for all learners. YES supplements existing curricula in reading, science, and math.

At each grade level, YES is organized around compelling and original video-based "anchor" adventures that culminate in motivating challenges for students to solve. Students use specially designed software as they work in small groups to solve the challenges and, in the process, develop important skills in comprehension, communication, and decoding. As they work through the series, students move systematically from a reliance on oral and visual presentations to the ability to decode and understand text. Products created by the students (e.g., books and multimedia presentations) are taken home and shared.

Adult Literacy Program

The Adult Literacy Program utilizes integrated media technology to help adults learn to read in a relevant contextual environment. The Program provides instruction in word recognition, decoding, and comprehension of text passages centered on topics relevant to the learners (for example, work-related subjects or broader contemporary topics). These topics are presented by CD-ROM in QuickTime format. Unique features of the program include:

- A personalized tutor that provides the learner with digitized human-voice instruction and feedback.

- Voice recognition software that assists the learner in word recognition, decoding, and fluency.

- Focused instruction keying off the 400 most frequently used words in the English language, with which a learner can read between 50 and 60 percent of the text later encountered.

- A set of decoding and semantic tools that permits the learner to hear a word spoken, get a definition of the word, see and hear the word used in context, hear individual phoneme or morpheme sounds, and record the learner's pronunciation of the word to compare it with the tutor's.

- A set of researched-based instructional principles in fluency training which includes:

  (a) assessment prior to instruction,

  (b) small instruction sets,

  (c) systematic presentation of new material,

  (d) guided practice, and

  (e) independent practice.

- QuickTime video reinforcement of key word definitions.

- Over 10,000-word digitized human-voice-recorded dictionary.

- Programmed tracking of each learner, which includes the ability to adjust the instructions to fit the learner's assessed level.

One module of the Adult Literacy Program merges with the Young Explorers Series by providing opportunities for adults to learn to read the materials in the YES series to their children. A prototype of the Adult Literacy Program was a winning entry among some 800 contestants in a competition at the Smithsonian Institute that was conducted by Johns Hopkins University.

The SMART Assessment Project

SMART stands for Special Multimedia Arenas for Refining Thinking. Its goal is to explore ways to increase achievement by removing teachers and students from the isolation of individual classrooms and engaging them in opportunities for frequent formative assessments that provide feedback about their progress and suggest "just-in-time tools" for improving their abilities to learn and understand. SMART assessments have utilized teleconferencing and telecommunications technologies and are designed for eventual use with distance learning technologies that permit online interactivity. SMART programs are currently being piloted in conjunction with the Jasper Woodbury Problem-Solving Series and have been shown to have even more beneficial effects on attitudes and achievement than programs that utilize Jasper without the SMART component. Designed as a model for any problem- or project-based curriculum, SMART assessments will soon be tested in other areas such as science.

Preservice Education Programs

In addition to the preceding programs for K-12 are a number of innovative technology-based programs for use with preservice students studying to be teachers. Programs in mathematics, science, literacy, and special education are four of the major areas in which technology is currently being studied and used. The Learning Technology Center also oversees the Peabody computer lab, which is used by all students at Peabody.

REPRESENTATIVE PUBLICATIONS

Representative publications of the CTGV include the following:

1. Bransford, J. D., Sharp, D. M., Vye, N. J., Goldman, S. R., Hasselbring, T. S., Goin, L., O'Banion, K., Livernois, J., Saul, E., and The Cognition and Technology Group at Vanderbilt. (in press). MOST environments for accelerating literacy development. In *International perspectives on the psychological foundations of technology-based learning environments,* eds. S. Vosniadou, E. DeCorte, R. Glaser, and H. Mandl (New York: Springer Verlag).

2. Cognition and Technology Group at Vanderbilt. (in press). From visual word problems to learning communities: Changing conceptions of cognitive research. In *Classroom lessons: Integrating cognitive theory and classroom practice*, ed. K. McGilly. (Cambridge, MA: MIT Press/Bradford Books).

3. Cognition and Technology Group at Vanderbilt. (in press). Using multimedia environments to develop literacy. In *Technology and educational reform: The reality behind the promise*, ed. B. Means (San Francisco: Jossey-Bass).

4. Goldman, S. R., Petrosino, A., Sherwood, R. D., Garrison, S., Hickey, D., Bransford, J. D., and Pellegrino, J. W. (in press). Multimedia environments for enhancing science instruction. In *International perspectives on the psychological foundations of technology-based learning environments,* eds. S. Vosniadou, E. De Corte, R. Glaser, and H. Mandl (New York: Springer Verlag). (A seven-page summary version of this paper is in press in *Psychological and educational foundations of*

technology-based learning environments, eds. S. Vosniadou, E. DeCorte, R. Glaser, and H. Mandl [New York: Springer Verlag].)

5. Moore, J. L., Lin, X., Schwartz, D. L., Petrosino, A., Hickey, D. T., Campbell, J. O., Hmelo, C., and The Cognition and Technology Group at Vanderbilt. (in press). The relationship between situated cognition and anchored instruction: A response to Tripp. In *Perspectives on situated learning,* ed. H. McLellan (Englewood Cliffs, NJ: Educational Technology Publications).

6. Zech, L., Vye, N. J., Bransford, J. D., Swink, J., Mayfield-Stewart, C., Goldman, S. R., and The Cognition and Technology Group at Vanderbilt. (in press). Bringing the world of geometry into the classroom: The adventures of Jasper Woodbury. *Mathematics Teaching in the Middle School Journal (MTMS).*

7. Cognition and Technology Group at Vanderbilt. (1993, March). Anchored instruction and situated cognition revisited. *Educational Technology 33*(3), 52-70.

8. Cognition and Technology Group at Vanderbilt. (1993). The Jasper experiment: Using video to furnish real-world problem-solving contexts. *Arithmetic Teacher: Mathematics Education through the Middle Grades 4,* 474-78.

9. Cognition and Technology Group at Vanderbilt. (1993). The Jasper series: Theoretical foundations and data on problem solving and transfer. In *The challenges in mathematics and science education: Psychology's response,* eds. L. A. Penner, G. M. Batsche, H. M. Knoff, and D. L. Nelson (Washington, DC: American Psychological Association), 113-52.

10. Cognition and Technology Group at Vanderbilt. (1993). Integrated media: Toward a theoretical framework for utilizing their potential. *Journal of Special Education Technology 12,* 71-85.

11. Cognition and Technology Group at Vanderbilt. (1992). The Jasper experiment: An exploration of issues in learning and instructional design. *Educational Technology Research and Development 40*(1), 65-80. Winner of the 1993 Outstanding Journal Article Award, presented by the Division for Instructional Development (DID) of the Association for Educational Communications and Technology (AECT).

12. Cognition and Technology Group at Vanderbilt. (1992). The Jasper series as an example of anchored instruction: Theory, program description and assessment data. *Educational Psychologist 27,* 291-315.

13. Sharp, D. L., Bransford, J. D., Vye, N., Goldman, S. R., Kinzer, C., and Soraci, Jr., S. (1992). Literacy in an age of integrated-media. In *Elementary school literacy: Critical issues,* eds. M. J. Dreher and W. H. Slater (Norwood, MA: Christopher-Gordon Publishers), 183-210.

14. Cognition and Technology Group at Vanderbilt. (1990). Anchored instruction and its relationship to situated cognition. *Educational Researcher 19*(6), 2-10.

Educational Technology at TERC

Robert F. Tinker
Susan L. Schoenberg
Heidi H. Nyland
TERC*

The Global Laboratory class at the Pease Middle School in San Antonio, Texas, had a problem. As a result of the class enrolling in Global Lab's research strand on indoor air quality, the students discovered that the quality of air in their classroom was poor. With the teacher's help, the students organized themselves into an "Air Force," delegating tasks to each member for investigation.

In the 1992-93 school year, TERC's Global Laboratory Project had 100 participating schools in 18 countries. Each class chose a study site where they would make detailed scientific observations of the local environment. In the case of the Pease Middle School, the selection was simple. Because the students of this inner city school were prohibited from leaving school grounds, the class chose its own classroom. Led by teacher Linda Maston, a three-year veteran of the TERC Global Lab Project, the students examined the environmental conditions in their classroom with qualitative activities followed by a battery of measurements. The students became concerned with the air quality in their room and decided to conduct in-depth research.

TERC supported the Global Lab students with the TERC air pump, a variety of other air-testing tubes, and instructional materials. After a series of tests, the students found consistently high levels of carbon dioxide in the air. They determined that over the course of the day, CO_2 levels exceeded the recommended limit of 1,000 parts per million set by the American Society of Heating, Refrigerating and Air Conditioning Engineers.

Equipped with their Global Lab tools, the students conducted a school-wide survey and found that CO_2 in some classrooms was as high as 2,100 ppm. The CO_2 measurements were presented to the school board, which contacted four environmental control officers to investigate. The officers showed up with the same (but more expensive) equipment that the students had used and got exactly the same readings. The students' actions had demanded responsibility and gotten results; the ventilation system was repaired. Not only had the students conducted real scientific research, but their findings made a difference in the lives of others in their community.

These students had been stimulated not by academic problems presented in textbooks, but by real-world problems that clearly affected their lives. For the educational process to be most effective, students must want to learn. They are motivated to do so when they appreciate the relevance of the curriculum. What could be more relevant than examining the air you breathe?

---

* TERC (formerly Technology Education Research Centers) is a nonprofit education research and development organization committed to improving science and mathematics learning and teaching. Founded in 1965, it is located in Cambridge, Massachusetts. Illustrations courtesy of TERC.

This Global Lab experience is extraordinary, but by no means unique. It illustrates many goals that lie within TERC's mission of improving science and mathematics learning and teaching. Our goal at TERC is to advance all aspects of education, including fundamental research, technology, curriculum, and professional development. We strive for projects that will have the maximum impact on education. The funding for our projects comes primarily from grants, which we often combine to allow work to continue over an extended period of time. For example, our work on microcomputer-based laboratories, Kids Network, and the Global Laboratory Project, described in this article, have evolved over the past decades. In addition, by working with publishers and businesses, such as EduQuest and the National Geographic Society, we are able to build upon the grant-supported work. We disseminate our work through publications, workshops, and other methods, both providing materials and serving as a catalyst to others for innovation and change in science and mathematics education.

By relying on a multifaceted strategy, TERC projects introduce teachers and students to real-world, hands-on investigations, technologies, communications, and collaboration—all of which support student-based research, teacher enhancement, cognitive research, data collection and analysis, and curriculum development. This article presents examples, illustrations, and stories about many of TERC's technology-based projects and the motivation behind them.

LEARNING AS DOING

The model of learning in much of science and math education today is to drill students in facts and operations in the hope that this will lead to an understanding of the underlying concepts. The goal is to stock students' intellectual storehouse with facts, formulas, and definitions against some day in the future when they will need to draw from their supply. The problem with this model of science and math education is that, for many students, it has proven ineffective, and has led to a dead end that finds students turned off, poorly prepared, or even dropping out. The alternative is to create a learning environment that encourages students to construct and communicate their knowledge and understandings.

Learning science and math, like the processes of science and math themselves, must be active. Learning requires attention, active participation, communication, inquiry, and thought. At TERC, our approach is to focus on the *doing* of mathematics and science, on encouraging students and teachers to explore new areas, to formulate new questions, and to search for answers in ways that mirror as closely as possible the experience of practicing mathematicians and scientists (Figure 1). This approach supports in-depth, interdisciplinary, collaborative study, puts the student in charge of his or her own learning, and leads to learning that is relevant and interesting.

The story from Global Lab illustrates much of what TERC aims to accomplish. Students and teachers investigate a real-world problem that affects their lives directly, using their science skills to collect and analyze data and to attempt to improve the outcome. They use low-cost, high-tech instrumentation in their investigations, and they work collaboratively in the classroom and as part of a larger community through telecomputing.

Much of the work at TERC explores aspects of this style of learning. For example, we emphasize microcomputer-based labs because they expand the range of investigations students can undertake; we use electronic networking because it supports collaborative student projects; we are working with at-risk and gifted students to understand the range of applicability of our approach; and we have developed a strand of applied mathematics for the K-6

Figure 1. Students and their teacher investigate chaotic motion with a water wheel.

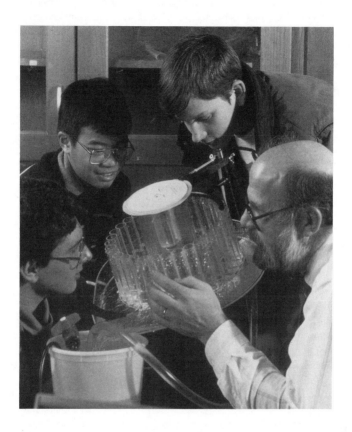

mathematics curriculum in order to convey a more realistic view of mathematics. The results are often spectacular—student motivation, learning, and interest in mathematics and science soar, sometimes exceeding teacher expectations. Many teachers find this approach so exciting that it rekindles their interest in teaching; teachers sometimes use project participation as the centerpiece of a profound, integrated, interdisciplinary learning experience that encompasses science, mathematics, geography, communication, and social studies.

Technology gives students a wide range of tools they can apply to their investigations and new collaborators with whom to communicate and learn. The technologies that TERC has developed and applied offer new opportunities for collaboration and communication; simplify acquiring and displaying data; provide mechanisms to control experiments; increase the sophistication of theory building, modeling, and data analysis; provide new outlets for creative expression; and grant access to vast databases of information. In the best implementations, technology enters the culture of the school and becomes woven into learning in many more ways than its original promoters could possibly have anticipated.

SOFTWARE TOOLS THAT ENABLE

Microcomputers and computer-based telecommunications offer flexible tools for communication, data acquisition, instrumentation, computation, analysis, and visualization. These tools support students in doing science, in undertaking interesting investigations, and in building durable science concepts. Communication about their work and about the process of learning itself with peers, teachers, and collaborators is an indispensable part of students' learning.

In the sections that follow, we present examples of the use of software tools to empower students, including communications software, microcomputer-based labs, data analysis software, and video analysis.

Microcomputer-Based Labs

Microcomputer-based labs (MBL)—the use of microcomputers for student-directed data acquisition, display, and analysis—give students unprecedented power to explore, measure, and learn from their environment. Using MBL, students have a flexible instrument that can measure force, light, pressure, temperature, pH, heart rate, speed, acceleration, response time, brain waves, muscle signals, and many other phenomena in the world about us. These measurements can be performed by powerful, general-purpose software that speeds analysis and provides real-time feedback. MBL can make meaningful science instruction possible earlier and at a much more profound level than educators have typically believed possible.

In collaboration with EduQuest (an IBM company), TERC has developed the Nature of Science software and curriculum. The software uses IBM's Personal Science Laboratory (PSL) hardware and the PSL temperature, motion, and light probes, and runs on IBM PC compatibles. Designed for grades 3 to 6, the curriculum enables students to explore natural phenomena in their everyday surroundings through direct experiences and to develop their own investigations of these phenomena. The curriculum includes units on light, motion, solar energy, and the human body. The PSL software helps students understand such complex concepts as temperature, light, and motion by the collection of real-time data and the simultaneous display of these data as graphs (see Figure 2).

Probe data are displayed as they are captured in a variety of graphic representations that may be selected by students and teachers. These representations include one-dimensional bar graphs, two-dimensional bar graphs, and line graphs. Several new types of graphs have been invented to aid young users in exploring graphical data presentations, thus providing more concrete expressions for children learning to read graphs.

Students view the graphs while running experiments and may attach "flags" to specific events represented by the graph, either during or after the experiment. They may record notes for each of these flags with the word-processing capabilities of the ScienceWriter, a built-in note-taker. The software spans the wide developmental needs of elementary school children by providing different levels that control the complexity and number of features available. The software supports these levels and the pedagogical needs of teachers by providing structured individual lessons or activities that are part of the PSL curriculum units or are created by the teacher or the students themselves. Running the PSL software on a local area network (LAN), students can interact with other students and with teachers. Students can share their data and observations through an online bulletin board.

Figure 2. The Nature of Science software. In this curriculum unit, students investigate light. The experiment shown explores how well sunglasses block a light source.

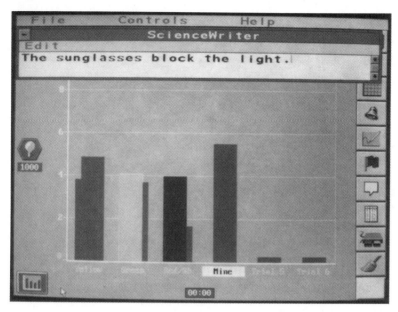

For older students, TERC has developed PSL Explorer software, which allows students to manipulate variables, to analyze data that can be presented in both graphical and tabular modes, and to see immediate results from their experimental procedures. The software uses IBM's Personal Science Laboratory (PSL) hardware and the PSL temperature, motion, light, and pH probes, as well as the Digital Multimeter (DMM) module to measure voltage, current, and power, and the Digital Input/Output (DIO) module with the rotary motion probe or photo event probe. Using these probes, students can study such areas as motion, temperature, angular rotary motion, and pulse analysis. The software allows students to create and save their own experiment setups; to display graphs of their data in real time as the data are being collected; and to store, display, and analyze their data once they have been collected. The software has built-in analysis features for manipulating the data, including the ability to perform logarithmic operations, compute power operations, calculate sines and cosines, and differentiate and integrate. The graphing functions include the ability to mark a graph and to perform and display a least-squares fit on the data.

MBL has been used in many different school settings for a variety of educational goals. This past year TERC introduced MBL into the science curriculum in Zimbabwe as a way to augment the use of microcomputers and enhance computer literacy in schools there. TERC has also adapted a Human Physiology curriculum, enhanced by MBL, to allow students with learning disabilities to carry out meaningful science activities both in a technology-equipped resource room and in the regular classroom. As part of the emphasis on the literacy component of each activity, the curriculum invites students to communicate orally and in writing about their findings, using the word processor and telecommunications.

TERC researchers are using MBL to help explore students' understandings of the mathematics of change and variation. The focus is on how high school students who have not taken calculus courses learn about differentiation and integration of notions when problems are posed in the context of physical changes that students can control, predict, and measure (Figure 3).

Figure 3. Students using MBL (microcomputer-based labs) to explore the mathematics of change and variation.

Many of the students in this study work with a computer-based motion detector. The motion detector enables the user to produce graphs of a moving object in real time on the computer screen. Students use toy cars moving along a straight path and flowing water to generate graphs. Most of the problems involve the translation between a given graph of position vs. time and its corresponding graph of velocity vs. time, or vice versa. The research explores students' learning of ways of symbolizing kinesthetic actions and the roles that MBL tools can play in their learning. The research findings are used to inform curriculum and software development.

Networked Learning

Scientists and other researchers increasingly rely on telecommunications and electronic databases to collect and distribute masses of data and to share analyses. Many of the projects at TERC involve individuals and groups who form a community to work collaboratively on a common problem or agenda. Community members include students, teachers, scientists, volunteers, and facilitators from all over the world. Scientists play a key role in developing curricula and evaluating student data; in return, these data are often useful to the scientific community. For teachers, telecommunications decreases isolation and helps to build support networks with other educators. For students, networking with each other and with local community officials and scientists helps them begin to see themselves as active participants in the process of real science.

To support such collaborative inquiry, TERC is developing easy-to-use, flexible network and tool software that enables users of different computer systems to share data, graphics, and text. The software, currently called Alice Network Software, is complemented by compelling curricula that support large-scale data sharing. With the simple tools of computer, modem, and telephone lines, scientists, teachers, and students from around the world collaborate on project-based investigations. The goals of the Alice Network Software are to provide a core set of tools that are easily available to beginning users, to allow the use of a variety of existing products in a seamless fashion, and to provide a growth path as users get more sophisticated.

The Alice Network Software includes a simple word processor, data table, graphing and mapping utilities, electronic mail, and telecommunications functions (Figure 4). Because participants use the same tools, they are able to work collaboratively and develop a sense of community. For example, a student in Hawaii can use the Alice mapping tool to see the locations of other classes on her project. Transmission of data and photographs from these colleagues helps her visualize the differences in their study sites and local environments. By using the common data templates, members of an inquiry team help to ensure discipline and reliability in the collective database. All of the sites can submit their data to a common database. Data consolidation on the network server provides mail-mediated submission and retrieval of community data and other data resources on an Alice server. Standard file formats allow interchange with other Macintosh or IBM-compatible tools and Internet-hosted data. Alice can transport mail and files as standard RFC822 Internet mail messages. Anyone who can originate and receive RFC822 mail may participate in the community; anyone who is Internet mail-connected or mail-gatewayed may participate. Participants who do not use Alice software can thus exchange mail and files with Alice users. Currently, the software is in its prototype phase and is being used by a variety of test sites to support real-world investigations.

Figure 4. The opening screen of the Alice Network software. The software includes a word processor, a data table, a map utility, and telecommunications capabilities.

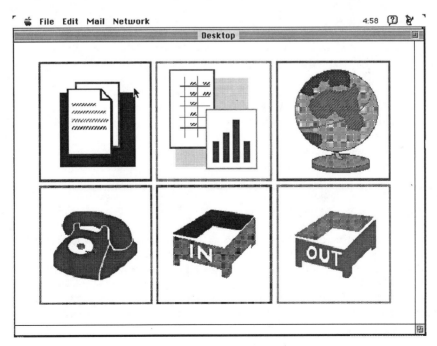

One such investigation is the Global Lab Project discussed earlier. The core philosophy of Global Lab is to teach investigative skills, methodologies, and scientific ethics to students as a foundation for undertaking advanced research projects. These goals are achieved by closely directing student research at the beginning of the year and offering open-ended research opportunities in the second half of the year.

In the first semester, the curriculum guides the students through a series of skill-building procedures called Environmental Snapshots. At the same time, on prearranged days Global Lab schools make synchronized environmental measurements of their study sites, using low-cost, high-tech tools. For this project, TERC has also developed specialized, yet inexpensive, instruments, such as the Total Column Ozonometer, which uses surface measurements to provide vital information about the ozone layer in the upper atmosphere. Students collect their data into templates, and these data form a project-wide database. These directed research procedures prepare students with invaluable skills of data collection and collaboration techniques. In the second semester, students choose one of nine topics for additional investigation. They are supported by the TERC staff with instrumentation, online scientists, and joint methodologies, but the students develop and implement their own research strategies.

Also using the Alice Network Software is National Geographic Kids Network/Middle Grades, whose four curriculum units—Soil, Sound, Water, and Human Body—are currently being field-tested in approximately 35 sites throughout the United States. For more than 6 years, students in more than 22 countries have used the published NGS Kids Network/Elementary curriculum to collaborate on a wide variety of experiments, including acid rain, nutrition, weather variation, solar energy availability, nitrates in drinking water, school trash, and pet choices.

The units regularly generate excitement and earnest participation among student-scientists. The youngsters sense that what they do matters, that this is not just another exercise. The act of sending off the data is taken seriously because they understand that someone—other classes and the unit scientist—will look at their work and that this work will contribute to a pattern that they will all have the opportunity to discuss and analyze. This curriculum unit has awakened genuine excitement for many classes: students with learning disabilities shine; teachers report that many students exhibit talents that had been dormant.

TERC uses telecommunications to help students with learning disabilities develop their literacy skills in a science context. In the Literacy in a Science Context (LISC) Project, students collaborate to collect, make sense of, and report on real-time data about the functioning of their own bodies. Teachers and students use a network to communicate with other participants about their findings.

Telecommunications can also provide a medium for supporting teachers in their professional growth. The LabNet Project at TERC uses telecommunications for building a supportive community of practice among science teachers trying to make inquiry, project-based science happen in their classrooms. The LabNetwork currently provides a meeting place for more than 400 teachers to support one another in experimenting with new teaching strategies, reflect on their teaching experiences, solve problems, share resources, and build collegial connections with their peers. The network was designed for and with teachers, and its evolution is linked to teacher contributions. Teacher-moderators help to initiate, contribute, moderate, and sustain dialogues, and help to link reflections on the network with action in the classroom.

The evidence from the last three years of LabNet supports the value of project-enhanced science learning. New standards for science education are increasingly asking teachers to make a dramatic shift away from encyclopedic coverage of science topics and toward a more learner-centered approach that emphasizes student inquiry and investigation. The experience of the first three years of LabNet is documented in the book, *LabNet: Toward a Community of Practice,* published in 1993 by Lawrence Erlbaum Associates.

TERC is working as a partner in the Eisenhower Regional Alliance for Mathematics and Science Education Reform in the Northeast and Islands to develop The Hub, a collection of information and services allowing educators to take advantage of the power of the Internet. Hub services range from custom information searches and electronic conversations (fast-paced, participatory sharing of ideas) to publishing and distributing very thin-market materials that might otherwise never be shared: lab manuals, material for physically challenged students, student research findings, ideas for uses of software applications, schematics, textbook reviews, and policy papers.

More and more, organizations are discovering that the Internet is an important means of obtaining and disseminating valuable information. Like many new tools, while it provides a great deal of power, it also comes with a number of attendant problems: locating information in an information space literally hundreds of times bigger than any library, discerning the quality of material once it is found, and dealing with all the technical issues associated with running a complicated computer system. Overcoming these problems can be an overwhelming task, and certainly daunting to educators who typically have very little time or money to spare. The Hub is part of the solution to these problems; it is the educator's librarian for the Internet. Using The Hub, one can retrieve and contribute materials without spending hours trying to find the appropriate location, or worrying about the intricacies of maintaining an Internet server.

Consider, for example, a teacher preparing a weather unit as part of an Earth Sciences curriculum. Although considerable extremely timely and useful weather information is available throughout the Internet, it is so difficult for a teacher untrained in the vagaries of Internet searching to find that it might as well not be there: it's useless! The Hub will empower this teacher much as a librarian empowers her or him to use the resources in the local library.

The Hub maintains several focus areas of interest to educators and, on request, can create others. The teacher in the preceding example could contact Hub staff and speak to people who will identify a group of resources especially tailored to his or her needs. Among these services, in addition to the obvious information searches, might be putting a class in touch with an expert who can help answer a difficult problem, or helping students and teachers find others with whom to collaborate on a given project or electronic publication facilities.

Telecommunications plays an important role in many of TERC's efforts to foster collaborative learning. Although a project-oriented instructional strategy does not require telecommunications, this technology can support project-based learning in many ways, fostering interesting projects that are easy to implement and feasible in a broad range of classrooms. In support of students' projects, telecommunications can connect student collaborators worldwide. This enables them to gather and distribute data in a timely manner among many sites. Students also have access to databases of information, research in support of projects, and scientists and others to assist them with their projects.

Data Modeling and Analysis

Much of the work of scientists and mathematicians, and hence of science and mathematics education, involves data modeling and analysis. One of the great challenges of science and mathematics education is to find ways that enhance students' abilities to build theories about the phenomena they are exploring. To make sense of a set of data, students must find ways of organizing and representing it. In the past, tools such as software applications were based on the idea that the developer puts a model into the software, then the students learn about the model by varying one or more parameters. A more valuable computer application comes from engaging the students directly in constructing models and exploring the consequences of different models.

A great deal of the work at TERC involves tools for collecting data that describe real-world phenomena and for analyzing what those data have to teach about the world. For example, the Alice Network Software, which is used in several TERC telecommunications projects, as described earlier, contains a data table with statistics functions that enables students to look at the data in a variety of graphs and a word processor for writing about the experiment. Similarly, both the Nature of Science PSL software (elementary school level) and the Explorer PSL software (high school level) contain many features designed to help students represent their data in a variety of ways and analyze its implications.

TERC has also developed some other tools to help students learn about organizing and representing information and about data analysis and statistics. Tabletop and Tabletop Junior are two software programs that allow direct manipulation of data by the student. The Tabletop was developed for students aged 9 and older, including adults, and the Tabletop Junior is appropriate for students aged approximately 5 to 11.

In Tabletop, data are represented by animated, movable icons that are graphed on a variety of graphs, such as Venn diagrams, histograms, and scatter plots. These icons have an almost three-dimensional presence on the screen, and they "animate" to new positions of a new graph rather than jumping from one arrangement to another without continuity (see Figure 5). This approach has proven effective in helping students to understand basic manipulations and representations of data. The user can query any icon to see the textual data associated with that icon. Students can work with predefined databases or create their own. Many of the uses of Tabletop involve project activities in which students collect their own data, enter them on the computer, analyze the data, and present their conclusions.

Figure 5. The Tabletop software. Here, a student examines the weight distribution for male and female cats in a database containing 20 cats.

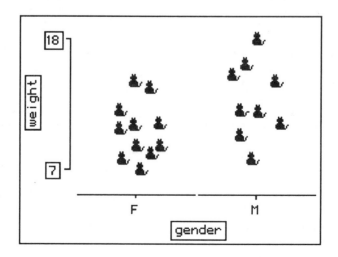

Like Tabletop, Tabletop Junior allows direct manipulation of data. In this playful, appealing environment, students create objects that simply stand for themselves, rather than representing information about the outside world. However, these icons have underlying structures similar to the real-world data students will eventually learn to collect and analyze. Included in the software are several icon construction "kits," such as *Animals, Party Hats,* and *Stick Figures* (Figure 6). Different kinds of kits support different kinds of thinking and activities.

Figure 6. In this Tabletop Junior example, objects have been arranged in a Venn diagram according to two features, and a new object is being created.

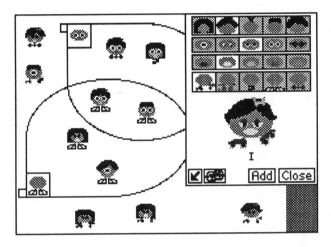

Another tool that TERC is exploring as an exciting and powerful vehicle for student scientific investigation is video. In the Video for Exploring the World project (VIEW), TERC is developing software called CamMotion™ to support the use of video as a laboratory instrument. Video provides students with an expanded world of phenomena to analyze because it can stop time and make events repeatable. By making measurements on single frames of video they have made themselves, students can explore in detail events that take place quickly, such as balls bouncing, or paper airplanes being thrown. They can also examine patterns of motion in jump rope, juggling, or gymnastics.

CamMotion™ provides a palette of on-screen measurement tools, immediate graphical feedback, and the ability to manipulate variables to support these mathematical and scientific investigations. Students can measure distances by clicking on each of two points and using a calibrated ruler provided by the software. Using a set of synchronization tools, students can set up a correspondence between a graphical representation or symbolic expression and the video images. Students are able to go back and forth between a mathematical representation and the original image.

In addition, the VIEW project is developing investigations that use mathematics tools to illuminate science concepts. Using this approach, it is expected that students can master concepts of change over time, and the fundamental concepts of calculus, at a much younger age than is currently thought. The important characteristics of video as a medium include its ubiquitousness and accessibility, its permanence, its ability to distort time, and its manipulability.

Teacher Enhancement and Curriculum Development

Many of the teachers with whom TERC works are in the midst of change. They feel trapped in a delivery system of education in which tests and textbooks shape the curriculum. The curricula developed at TERC guide students and teachers to explore and use the skills they acquire to pursue investigations. All TERC curricula are rigorously grounded in scientific and mathematical content, based on research, and undergo extensive field testing.

With teacher enhancement, TERC gives teachers opportunities to interact with each other, to collaborate with scientists and researchers, and to engage in serious mathematics and science themselves. At the same time, researchers benefit from the teachers who offer their daily experience and expertise of how students learn and who help keep curriculum development grounded in the realities of the classroom.

The central goal of TERC's Hands-On Elementary Science project (HOES) is to develop workshops to help elementary school teachers (grades 4-6) adopt a constructivist approach to teaching science with enhanced technology. The project's teacher-as-learner approach to professional development is based on the premise that if teachers are to provide alternative ways of learning to their students, they must experience these ways of learning themselves. Additionally, if professional developers are to support teachers in implementing alternative models, they must also have the opportunity to experience these alternatives.

In the workshops, trainers (teachers and other educators) first engage in prototype activities that serve as technology-enhanced science inquiry projects. They pose their own questions, plan and carry out investigations, negotiate understandings with other learners, and reflect on the results of their investigations. They learn how to design this type of activity, plan project work for their students, and consider ways of weaving this type of learning into their existing curriculum.

The TERC project Video Case Studies on Scientific Sense-Making illustrates ways in which teachers and students construct understanding of scientific concepts and practices. The video case studies are being developed along with a handbook that can be used for teacher development workshops, mini-courses, or long-term sustained development programs.

The case studies are based on research into practices that help teachers build scientific understanding and sense-making communities in their classrooms. The cases are framed in three themes: teacher as learner, teacher as practitioner, and teacher as researcher. This framework is intended to highlight three critical perspectives:

1. the need for teachers to become involved with scientific content and make sense of their activity both conceptually and epistemologically;

2. the need for teachers to experiment with new teaching practices derived from their activity as learners; and

3. the need for teachers to make sense of their students' understandings and how they construct those understandings in classroom practice.

The fundamental idea is that teachers must become sense-makers in order to understand their students' learning and thinking.

Technology for Science is a TERC curriculum development project that is creating and testing a series of design-oriented science problems called *Science Challenges* for general-level, secondary physics, and physical science students. These *Science Challenges* are being devised so that they create authentic situations for students to explore and learn about concepts such as motion and energy in the context of project-based learning. The challenges will fit into a series of units that will cover a number of overarching themes in physics and will eventually make up an entire year of instruction. Specific units being developed include: heat—"Emergency Solar Shelter System"; waves—"Transmission of Energy and Information"; and component and composite motions—"Mechanical Animation Theater." Still in the planning stages are units on force, magnetism, electricity, and optics.

A Science Challenge Source Book for students and a Teacher Resource Book will accompany the curricula. The source book will contain activities for the students. Teachers are encouraged to customize these materials to fit their classroom needs and employ a wide range of pedagogical strategies, which are described in the Teacher Resource Book.

The technology used in this project is widely available in schools already. It is deliberately "low tech," while still engaging students in the phenomena of physics. They will be able to gather data with a variety of measuring tools, for example, bulb and digital thermometers, MBL probes, and thermally sensitive liquid crystal thermometers. Templates for paraboloid and other concave shapes, small electronic motors, and batteries are among the common core of materials used throughout the curriculum.

Informal Learning Environments

Schools are only one place in which learning takes place. TERC is actively pursuing ways of fostering education in a variety of other, perhaps more informal settings. Playgrounds, for example, are part of most children's lives and present many opportunities for kinesthetic discovery of varied physical phenomena. Playgrounds are available, free, popular, and heavily used. They appeal to a heterogeneous population of all abilities and economic circumstances. By incorporating equipment that encourages exploration of scientific concepts, playgrounds can be important places to learn science.

New Directions for Science Playgrounds is a TERC project involved in researching and creating a new type of playground equipment that facilitates the learning of elementary notions of physics. The project goal is to extend the experience of kinesthetic learning that is already inherent in playground activities. TERC is designing new equipment that provides opportunities for children to explore their own movements and get immediate, symbolic feedback in the form of numerical or computer-driven graphical displays. This equipment allows children to test questions about time, rate, the fundamentals of motion—distance, velocity, and acceleration—momentum, and force. Sample design ideas include a large digital stop clock, strategically placed on the playground where it can spawn many games about time; a track of flashing lights that allows children to control the speed and sequence of the lights and, watching a visual display, to calculate their own speed as they run beside the lights; a jump counter that displays the number, time, and speed that children can jump; a mini-merry-go-round that tells children how fast they are spinning; and a jungle gym that shows the forces children exert as they climb, stand, hang, or jump. Children can control variables and see the effect of these variables on their own movements.

Museums are another example of informal places where much learning can take place. Smog Watch is a program involving youngsters and their families at 11 museums and nature/science centers nationwide in a study of ground-level ozone, a key component of smog and a pressing health risk. Participants learn about the sources and effects of ozone as well as behavioral changes appropriate for dealing with smog. Families participate in a variety of hands-on activities, including measuring their daily exposure to ozone with passive dosimeter badges, mapping sources of air pollution in their community, and making personal action plans to reduce air pollution in their communities and to reduce their own exposure to ozone.

CONCLUSIONS

The most important product of the past two decades of work on educational technology has been the emergence of a vision of what technology has to offer science and mathematics education. Earlier thinking focused on technology as supporting the more rote and mechanical aspects of learning. The new vision focuses on using technology to support excellence in learning. In this vision, students tackle much harder problems, work on larger-scale and more meaningful projects, have a greater and more reflective responsibility for their own learning, and are able to work in a variety of styles that reflect differences in gender, ethnicity, or simply individual personality.

The project-oriented, hands-on approach to education is not new, but the advent of inexpensive microcomputers and telecommunications adds new dimensions to the concept, allowing it to be a more powerful learning strategy while simplifying its implementation. All the TERC initiatives and projects share certain fundamental premises:

- People actively construct mental models and develop theories about the world.

- Hands-on activities are the foundation for effective learning.

- Students need to investigate meaningful problems and use real data about themselves and the world.

- Mathematics and science curricula must emphasize depth rather than exposure.

- Technology provides tools that enable learners to investigate their own questions.

- Collaboration and communication are critical skills and must be part of the context in which students learn math and science.

- Teachers are the primary agents for adopting and implementing educational change.

- Education must recognize the diversity of learners and build on their individual strengths.

TERC's activities in the fields of technology development, networks and telecommunications, teacher enhancement, curriculum development, data modeling and analysis, and cognitive research all serve its primary mission: to design, develop, and effectively implement educational strategies in which students acquire key mathematical and scientific skills through the process of questioning, investigating, and discovering.

For more information about TERC activities, contact TERC Communications, 2067 Massachusetts Ave., Cambridge, MA 02140, or by electronic mail at communications@TERC.edu.

FURTHER READING

Bagnall, L. (in press). *Tabletop and Tabletop Jr.: Two tools for hands-on exploration for kids.* 1994 Sig Chi Proceedings of the Association for Computing Machinery.

Berenfeld, B. (Fall, 1993). A moment of glory in San Antonio, a Global Lab story. *Hands On! 16*(2), 19-21.

Crismond, D., Falk, J., Hart, R., Noble, T., Pfister, M., and Touger, J. (1993). *Technology for science case study: Learning through science challenges.* Cambridge, MA.: TERC.

IBM Corporation, TERC. (1992). *Personal Science Laboratory, Explorer Version 1.0 Extended users guide.* Boca Raton, FL: IBM Corporation.

Nemirovsky, R. (1992). *On ways of symbolizing: The case study of Laura and the velocity sign.* TERC Paper presented at the NATO Advanced Workshop Microcomputer Based Laboratories-Educational Research Standards, Amsterdam. Cambridge, MA: TERC.

Nemirovsky, R. (Spring, 1993). Rethinking calculus education. *Hands On! 16*(1), 14-17.

Rosebery, A., Warren, B., Puttick, G. M., and Conant, F. R. (Fall, 1992). Sense-making practices in science: Case study of an ESL teacher. *Hands On! 15*(2), 4-5, 19.

Rubin, A. (1993). Video laboratories: Tools for scientific investigation. *Technology in Education, Communications of the Association for Computing Machines 36*(5), 64-65.

Ruopp, R., Gal, S., Drayton, B., and Pfister, M. (1993). *LabNet: Toward a community of practice.* Hillsdale, NJ: Lawrence Erlbaum Associates.

Spitzer, W., and Foster, J. (Fall, 1991). Tools of the trade. *Hands On!, 14*(2), 4-6, 10.

TERC. (1991). *25th year report.* Cambridge, MA: Author.

TERC. (1993). *Collaborative inquiry in networked communities: The Alice testbed phase I, year I, annual report.* Cambridge, MA: Author.

TERC. (1993). *Hands-On Elementary Science Project final report.* Cambridge, MA: Author.

TERC. (1993). *The Regional Alliance for Mathematics and Science Education Reform. First annual conference on networking and communications: Conference report.* Cambridge, MA: Author.

TERC, IBM Corporation. (1992). *PSL/EL software functional specification.* Cambridge, MA: TERC.

Tinker, R. F. (1992). *Science for kids: The promise of technology.* Washington, DC: American Association for the Advancement of Science.

Tinker, R. F., and Kapisovsky, P. M., eds. (1992). *Prospects for educational telecomputing: Selected readings.* Cambridge, MA: TERC.

Tinker, R. F., and Papert, S. (1988). *Tools for science education.* Association for the Education of Teachers in Science Yearbook Series. Columbus, OH: Ohio State University.

Weir, S. (1993). *Literacy in a science context.* Unpublished document. Cambridge, MA: TERC.

—CRITICISM—
Beware the Computer Technocrats
Hardware Won't Educate Our Kids*

Michael Schrage
Columnist, Los Angeles Times

While parents and taxpayers look upon our public schools and despair, the nation's software entrepreneurs and investment bankers can scarcely wipe the drool off their double chins. "Educational multimedia will be the investment opportunity of the '90s," asserted investment banker Paul Stephens of Robertson, Stephens & Co., the San Francisco-based investment house, at a recent educational technology conference. "Computer technology will help make students and teachers more productive."

It is that oh-so-rare investment opportunity to do well by doing good. Everyone from Chris Whittle's Edison Project to the prestigious National Academy of Science now champions technological innovation as essential to profitably transforming the U.S. public school system. Just give the little kiddies their computers and watch those test scores skyrocket.

"School is where all the really neat stuff in computers is going to happen," says John T. Kernan, chairman of Jostens Learning Corp., one of the largest educational technology vendors. "There are 46 million students in [kindergarten] through 12th grade in America; average per pupil expenditure is $5,000 per year. . . . The schools have plenty of money."

Taxpayers and parents beware. Rather than improving schools, the computers-in-education technocrats are likelier to become the welfare queens of the Information Age.

California, Texas, and Florida are actually funding computer curriculum development with taxpayer dollars rather than relying on private investment. In about 20 states, educators are exploring how to make computer technologies required, just like textbooks.

Consequently, this aspiring multibillion-dollar "market" for educational computing is growing less as a function of dire need and demonstrable performance than of pie-in-the-sky promises and public subsidies.

This is all going on despite one plain fact: Computers are irrelevant to the quality of education.

Consider the International Assessment of Educational Progress survey released last year; in science proficiency, American 13-year-olds placed behind those of Canada, England, France, Hungary, Israel, Italy, South Korea, Scotland, Slovenia, the former U.S.S.R., Spain, Switzerland, and Taiwan. Math proficiency was even worse.

Other cross-country evaluations consistently rank American students beneath their Asian and Western European counterparts.

Not one of the countries with higher performing students relies on computer technology in any way, shape, or form. Somehow, the students in Italy, Taiwan, and so forth manage to do well without being connected to a multimedia Intel chip or wired to an Apple-generated mathematics simulation.

*This article appeared in the *Washington Post*, May 7, 1993. Copyright © 1993, Los Angeles Times. Reprinted with permission.

In other words, in an increasingly global marketplace, technological endowment has nothing to do with the quality of public education. Only in the United States do we seek technological solutions to problems that are manifestly not technological.

Of course, organizations such as the Software Publishers Association issue reports like "The Effectiveness of Technology in Schools," which purport to demonstrate how vital computers can be to improving educational performance.

But if you really look at these studies, what you find isn't that new technology has made a fundamental difference—it's all the new attention being paid to the students that has made the difference.

Should anyone be surprised that students perform better when more people who care pay more attention to them?

Even when computers can help, merely installing them isn't enough.

"School systems think that buying computers will solve their educational problems, when it's actually a much bigger process" observes Connie Connors of Connors Communications, a marketing firm specializing in educational technology. "They simply don't understand the level of human resources required to make the process work."

For example, Connors points out that most of the school systems that bought scads of personal computers in the 1980s paid top dollar for machines that would soon plummet in price.

She says the schools didn't even have the internal resources available to effectively use the machines they bought.

Any school board that would import computer technology without insisting on explicit guarantees for improved student performance richly deserves to be impeached, voted out of office, or sued for malpractice.

But the real waste here is the pathetic hope that American hardware and software will have any significant role in improving school quality. It's a sad commentary indeed that our belief in the potential of our technology exceeds our faith in the potential of our children.

That respected educators such as former Yale University president Benno Schmidt and leading public officials such as Vice President Gore invest their reputations in supporting educational technologies shows just how warped our education policy dialogue has become.

Issues such as school choice, mainstreaming, bilingual education, class size, community participation, day care, and so forth each matter more to the future of American education than any piece of software hacked out by some profit-seeking company.

If we really cared about a successful public school system—which we clearly do not—we would forbid computers in the schools and force educators, parents, taxpayers, and teachers to face reality. We can't profitably computerize our problems away.

An Incomplete Caution
"Beware the Computer Technocrats"

Randall G. Nichols
University of Cincinnati

If we listen closely toward a place beyond the incessant whir of the fans cooling millions of computers, those of us who care about educational technology may hear the sound of Michael Schrage's (1993) voice as it echoes ever so faintly around the hallways of school houses. It is so faint that in the wide world almost nothing like he is saying about educational technology in "Beware the Computer Technocrats: Hardware Won't Educate Our Kids" gets spoken. It really is rare to have someone go against the grain of commonly accepted characteristics of educational technology, though occasionally it is done. For example, Taylor and Johnsen (1986) called the frenzy over spending for educational computing the "gold rush mentality."

It is good to hear Schrage, in as public and widespread a forum as the *Washington Post*, point out the economic ramifications of unresisted spending for educational technology. He says, for instance, "Taxpayers and parents beware. Rather than improving schools, the computers-in-education technocrats are likelier to become the welfare queens of the Information Age," especially since more and more schools and state and local governments (not the computer-selling companies) are paying for technologies that do not make appreciable differences in kids' learning. After showing that America is educationally behind countries with far fewer technological resources, Schrage is mostly right to claim loudly that "technological endowment has nothing to do with the quality of education."

Schrage is mostly right, but not completely. His echoes don't tell the whole story when he claims that "computers are irrelevant to the quality of education." They are close to irrelevant if we consider the common quantitative measures of education (national test scores and the like), but when we are immersed in computer worlds, the quality of our educational lives is changed profoundly, even if we are unaware of the effects. Computers are not irrelevant.

With computers, as with all technologies, we learn technological ways, even if we are less than fully conscious of these ways. That is to say, we almost imperceptibly learn to live efficiently. We accept systematic and systemic approaches to everyday basic human activities. We learn to expect that life will be predictable. We learn to accept that most technologies equate with positive social progress. We learn that we are in control of the earth and our own destiny; existence is bequeathed to us to do with as we please. We learn that problems of technology are to be solved with even more technology. We learn that the tacit, aesthetic, mythical, and creative aspects of humans are second-rate in matters such as learning, knowing, and teaching.

Perhaps the most profound change associated with computers and other educational technologies is that oral language and, so, all human meaning change as the technologies of writing, printing, computers, and other electric communications mutate meaning's poetic, historic, communal, moral, and educative senses. For example, among the many differences between oral and written (technological) cultures, Ong (1982) points out that "writing fosters abstractions that disengage knowledge from the arena where human beings struggle with one another. It separates the knower from the known. By keeping knowledge embedded in the human lifeworld, orality situates knowledge within a context of struggle" (p. 43). A bit further on, he also suggests that "the other side of agonistic name-calling . . . is the fulsome expression of praise which is found everywhere in connection with orality" (p. 45). So technologies can disengage us, to some extent, from the closest and fullest possibilities for relating with one another, whether the possibilities are by virtue of struggle or praise.

But there are other questionable technological effects that Schrage does not describe. One effect related to computers and other technologies is that they widen the educational chasm between those who have technology and use it for their advantage and those who do not. Sutton's (1991) summary of a decade of research findings concludes that in countries where computers were used throughout the 1980s:

> The uses maintained and exaggerated existing inequalities in education input, processes of computer learning, and output. Poor, female and minority students had less access to computers at school. . . . Poor and minority students were more likely to use computers for drill and practice than were middle-class and White students, and females outnumbered males in word processing but were under-represented in programming. Teachers, while concerned about equity, held attitudes which hindered access: They believed that better behaved students deserved computer time and that the primary benefit of computers for low-achieving students was mastery of basic skills. . . . Thus, children who were minority, poor, female, or low achieving were likely to be further behind after the introduction of computers in schools. . . . These inequities were found in the U.S.A., Great Britain, Australia, Canada, and New Zealand (p. 494).

These conditions might be changing, but I haven't found evidence of widespread change.

Schrage commits another omission when he does not tell us of the other social problems (education is a social entity) related to educational technologies. The social difficulties related to general technologies are pretty well known, if not well dispersed and/or believed. Langdon Winner (1993) notes that "technology reweaves the fabric of society," and in large measure we have a "technological somnambulism" about these changes. We are somewhat unable to do anything about technology except to see it and use it in economic and positive terms. Winner says:

> Take the building of the national highway system after World War II. The system was inspired by a wish to improve commerce, foster social mobility, and bolster national defense. In actual usage, its grid of arteries and ring roads permanently changed the American social landscape. Among other consequences, the inter-state highways amplified a growing split between urban centers and outlying communities, a serious and troublesome split characterized by today's suburbia as compared with the inner cities. As it built physical boundaries between neighborhoods, the highway system modified not only the nation's economy, but our personal relations as well (p. B1).

Winner acknowledges some of the wondrous accomplishments we have in terms of water, sewage, transportation, electricity, and so on. But he concludes also that:

> These have been accomplished at a serious cost—the weakening of American democracy. Decisions about infrastructure have been bureaucratized, professionalized, "technicized," and removed from the decision-making competence of ordinary citizens and local political bodies. When these conditions double back on us—for example, in the "energy crisis" of the 1970's or in today's predicaments about waster disposal and water supply—the very remoteness of large technological systems looms as an intractable political problem (p. B2).

There is every reason to believe that, like technology in general, educational technology fosters social turbulence. It does so by perpetuating the same beliefs and assumptions noted earlier for general technology. And the consequences can be the same. Representative George Brown (1993), Chair of the Committee on Science, Space, and Technology of the U.S. House of Representatives, points out that "the government plans to link the nation's grade schools to a national computer network over the next several years; meanwhile urban libraries can't afford to stay open or buy new books" (p. B1), so inner-city readers may be harmed by the great leap forward to the network.

There is a fourth profound effect that Schrage's argument does not address. Look to the deepest beliefs modern Western culture uses to buttress technological proliferation. I take *culture* partly to be what people do and how we act at levels that are usually taken for granted. In many cases the beliefs of educational technologists (be they instructional designers, students, teachers, parents, or professors) are at this below-active-consciousness level. Bowers (1993) examines our culture in terms of several historically received assumptions, including individualism and a deep rationalism. Both assumptions embody notions of the authority of reason and a consciousness that is separate from the body. He concludes that these beliefs are encouraging the decline of the ecology and are related to American schooling:

> Since current approaches to framing the ecological crisis are conditioning us to accept the rationalist approach to problem solving, they help to insure that the human dimensions of the crisis are never really understood at the deepest levels. The argument [Bower's] is not against being rational; rather the main issue is an overly narrow view of the well-spring of human thought and behavior. . . . Our main concern here is with the middle class culture which exerts such a dominant influence in American society, and with how the belief system of this group, which underlies so many environmentally disruptive practices, is perpetuated in the public schools and universities (p. 15).

So Schrage misses good bets when he does not warn us about educational technology and its difficult relationships to human communication, educationally disadvantaged learners, social upheaval, and ecological peril. But then most of the people within the field of educational technology are not inclined to listen for ideas beyond the computer whirr because much of our lives is devoted to believing in the potentials of technology for individualizing instruction, improving learning outcomes, energizing what may otherwise be boring learning experiences, and so on.

The faint echo referred to in the opening paragraph of this piece is the echo of warning or caution about too great a belief in and application of educational technology. That echo is most interesting when it comes from a few disenchanted advocates who are voicing concern about the closet full of old computer models, the teachers who no longer buy into a pervasive techno-vision, and the students for whom little technology appears to matter educationally.

REFERENCES

Bowers, C. A. (1993). *Education, cultural myths, and the ecological crisis.* Albany, NY: State University of New York Press.

Brown, G. (1993, June 30). Technology's dark side. *Chronicle of Higher Education,* B1-B2.

Ong, W. (1982). *Orality and literacy. The technologizing of the word.* New York: Methuen.

Schrage, M. (1993, May 7). Beware the computer technocrats: Hardware won't educate our kids. *Washington Post.*

Sutton, R. E. (1991). Equity and computers in the schools: A decade of research. *Review of Educational Research 61,* 475-503.

Taylor, W. D., and Johnsen, J. B. (1986). Resisting technological momentum. In *Technology and education (85th yearbook of the National Society for the Study of Education),* ed. J. A. Culbertson and L. L. Cunningham (Chicago: University of Chicago Press).

Winner, L. (1993, August 4). How technology reweaves the fabric of society. *Chronicle of Higher Education,* B1-B3.

Analysis of Computers in Education as a Cultural Field

Andrew R. J. Yeaman, Ph.D.
Yeaman & Associates, Consultants
Arvada, Colorado

For most of this century educational communications and technology research concentrated on the efficiency of learning stimuli, instructional techniques, and matching these with student characteristics. Those who study the technological delivery of educational messages tend to ignore daily realities. The abstract discussion of educational computers in a yearbook is likely to overlook the meaning of *using* computers in education. However, in anthropology, rituals and everyday events symbolize cultural meaning. Interpretation can connect these meanings to factual observations (Geertz 1973). This response to Schrage is founded on three beliefs:

- It is possible to decode the symbol systems of group beliefs.

- It is possible to determine the pressures causing group beliefs.

- It is possible to match symbol systems and pressures.

These beliefs are applied here in the context of computers in education. In contrast to naive assumptions that machines are superior to teachers and students, it seems it may be right for people to resist computers. Giroux gives insights into schooling in *Theory and Resistance in Education* that can be adapted to provide an explanation (1983, p. 46):

1. Computers in education cannot be analyzed apart from the socioeconomic context in which they are situated.

2. Computers in education are politically involved in the construction and control of discourse, meaning, and subjectivities.

3. The common-sense values and beliefs that guide and structure use of computers in education are not a priori universals, but rather social constructions based on specific normative and political assumptions.

A recent analysis of sociocultural aspects of computers in education from a poststructural, literary position resulted in several observations:

- Computers are sold to schools, as to any other customer, by corporations whose central concern is to produce profits.

- Computers in schools increase public knowledge about how to use computers and that increase facilitates sales and the rate of adoption.

- Computers are vehicles for social stratification.

- Computers are not easy to use and are difficult to learn to use well.

- Computers do not always work well.

- Computers are not always useful.

- Computers can be a hindrance to getting things done.

- Computer-to-student ratios are a false measure of the quality of education. (Yeaman 1993)

The critical problem is not overcoming teacher and student resistance to computers but the need to teach resistance. In this sense, *resistance* is redefined (Giroux 1983):

Theories of resistance provide a study of the way in which class and culture combine to offer outlines for a cultural politics. Central to such a politics is a semiotic reading of the style, rituals, language, and systems of meaning that constitute the cultural field of the oppressed. (p. 101)

Exploitation by computers may not be intentional but it is effective:

Whatever has been gained by introducing computers into the classroom, a great deal has already been lost, all of it unnecessarily, and not just because of a further crowding of the curriculum. The machine's lust for uniformity is leaving its mark in many ways as our society and culture reproduce themselves and conform to the contours of this newly constructed educational mold. (Dublin 1991, p. 169)

Given these social limitations, schools prepare the workers of tomorrow for using computers and for learning from computerized instruction on the job. The computerizing of work is enabled mostly through computer education in schools and colleges; on-the-job training; and self-instruction through media such as books, magazine articles, audio recordings, CAI, television broadcasts, and videos. In human factors engineering, this is called fitting the people to the machine. It is the last resort for overcoming inadequate design. Here the cognitive science viewpoint and the ergonomic viewpoint converge in that *things* need fixing, not people.

Therefore, workers, managers, and teachers are right to resist the problems of computerizing society. The situation is comparable to resistance to literacy (Giroux, 1983, p. 231). Passivity and indignation are just responses. They can become a powerful foundation for reflection, action, and making influential decisions.

Consider the following quotation, modified from Thrift's paper on the culture of clocks and watches and the timekeeping economics of the industrial revolution (1984, p. 62). Imagine a historian writing this passage one day in the future:

Somewhere between 1980 and 2030 a point would be reached where computers existed among all classes. It is hardly a coincidence that this diffusion should occur at the exact moment when the developments of the information revolution would demand a greater computerization of labor.

REFERENCES

Dublin, M. (1991). *Futurehype: The tyranny of prophecy*. New York: Dutton.

Geertz, C. (1973). *The interpretation of cultures*. New York: Basic Books.

Giroux, H. A. (1983). *Theory and resistance in education: A pedagogy for the opposition*. New York: Gergin & Garvey.

Thrift, N. (1984). Owners' time and own time: The making of a capitalist consciousness, 1300-1880. *Lund Studies in Geography 48*, 56-84.

Yeaman, A. R. J. (1993). The mythical anxieties of computerization: A Barthesian analysis of a technological myth. In *Computers in education: Social, political, and historical perspectives*, ed. R. Muffoletto and N. N. Knupfer (Cresskill, NJ: Hampton Press), 105-28.

Part Three
Current Developments

Introduction

This section has consistently been one of the focal points of *EMTY*. It offers a potpourri of new programs, informed perceptions, and responsible promotions. As usual, there is no theme or set of categories to unify the various articles. There are two articles on new media-oriented clearinghouses that are national in scope. There is one article on educational technology in federal agencies. A status report on networking in education focuses on a "hot topic," as does the piece on partnerships involving technology. For the schools, there is the policy paper about learning technologies prepared by the Council of Chief State School Officers. For higher education, there is an interview with one of the pioneers of instructional development in postsecondary education. And to round out the mix, there are four ERIC Digests, which discuss Telecommunications and Distance Education, School-University Partnerships, Alternative Assessment and Technology, and Television Violence and Behavior. Taken together, there is a sense of much activity in the world of media and technology in education. Pick and choose those articles that are close to your interests.

Improving Student Performance
Through Learning Technologies*

Policy Statement 1991
Council of Chief State School Officers (CCSSO)

The Council of Chief State School Officers (CCSSO) is a nationwide non-profit organization of the 57 public officials who head departments of public education in the 50 states, 5 U.S. extra-state jurisdictions, the District of Columbia, and the Department of Defense Dependents Schools. It has functioned as an independent national council since 1927 and has maintained a Washington office since 1948. CCSSO seeks its members' consensus on major education issues and expresses their views to civic and professional organizations, to federal agencies, to Congress, and to the public. Through its structure of committees and task forces, the Council responds to a broad range of concerns about education and provides leadership on major education issues.

Because the Council represents each state's chief education administrator, it has access to the educational and governmental establishment in each state and to the national influence that accompanies this unique position. CCSSO forms coalitions with many other education organizations and is able to provide leadership for a variety of policy concerns that affect elementary and secondary education. Thus, CCSSO members are able to act cooperatively on matters vital to the education of America's young people.

Council of Chief State School Officers
Werner Rogers (Georgia), President
Bill Honig (California), President-Elect
Gordon M. Ambach, Executive Director

IMPROVING STUDENT PERFORMANCE THROUGH LEARNING TECHNOLOGIES

Potential

Learning technologies have an enormous capacity to support and advance restructuring of teaching and learning. Our nation must use technology's potential to improve elementary and secondary education and to provide all learners with the knowledge, skills, and experience they need to be responsible and caring family members, productive workers, and informed global citizens.

Learning technologies encompass a wide range of equipment and applications that directly or indirectly affect student performance. Learning technologies range from ordinary telephones, which connect parents with teachers, to complex networks of satellites, cable, and fiber optics, which deliver interactive, multimedia learning opportunities. Technologies are tools. Their power as learning instruments is not inherent; their effectiveness is derived from the teachers and students who use them. This effectiveness is measured by whether they improve student performance and help students reach full potential.

Technologies offer information in a variety of formats—text, video, and audio—allowing students to use the medium most effective for their learning. General or standard transmission of information through the technologies enables teachers to focus their energies on coaching students with their individual growth. Teachers can give special attention to certain individuals without neglecting the progress of others who are successfully guiding their own learning. Technologies enable students working individually or in small groups to take advantage of vast sources of information and work with complex connections among varied disciplines. Technologies stimulate students as active learners who control the pace and direction of content, questions, and responses.

Learning technologies can provide students and teachers equitable access to learning no matter what the geographic location or fixed resources of the school. Telecommunications provide students and teachers with the information resources of distant libraries, museums, and universities. Telecommunications offer courses, degree programs, and career development. Learning technologies expand the opportunities of teachers, students, and parents to connect learning activities in school with those in homes, community centers, and other institutions. They provide access to colleagues and specialists around the world and connect student work to the problems and real work of other students and adults.

Learning technologies are the tools for productive, high-performance workers in the 21st century. In the "Information Age," the workforce must be prepared to manage substantial amounts of information, analyze complicated situations for decision making, and react rapidly in a well-informed manner. Equitable availability of learning technologies is essential to prepare all students to be adults with access to productive employment and community and political power. To keep up with the tools of the future workplace and the technologies of the home, all students must have access to them and master their use.

Technologies are productive tools for teachers and administrators to automate record-keeping, student information, and data for accountability. They help provide convenient and timely access to essential information on student outcomes, thereby helping teachers tailor instructional programs to meet specific student needs.

State Action

Most states, districts, and schools have successfully used some technologies to develop effective, exciting, and innovative learning environments. To stimulate systemic change and move beyond isolated model programs toward widespread integration of technology into learning, we must commit our efforts to these activities: planning at the state and local levels; funding; ensuring equitable access to technology; human resource training and support; expanding telecommunications networks; developing technology-based assessment tools; and establishing national leadership for learning technologies. To realize the potential for learning technologies, states must take action, both individually and together, as stated in the following "Recommendations for Implementation."

States are at different stages in the development and use of learning technologies. Some have made bold moves or are ready to make a quantum leap in their actions. Many have completed steps such as those recommended here. Where bold actions have been taken, they are applauded as examples for other states to emulate. The comprehensive order of this paper is in no way intended to slow progress of any state to back-track or adjust its previous actions to the systemic approach suggested here. Quite to the contrary, the intention is to encourage the leaders who have accomplished certain steps to maintain their leadership toward complete implementation.

The recommendations that follow provide guidance for a comprehensive approach to incorporating technologies into the center of teaching and learning. These are generic proposals intended for all states but not detailed to apply to any specific state. Each state must develop its own application, informed by this comprehensive design and cognizant that each of the components must be included in some form to ensure a complete and effective state strategy.

RECOMMENDATIONS FOR IMPLEMENTATION

Develop a State Plan for the Use of Technology in Education

States should establish a clear, long-term, strategic plan for learning technologies. The plan should provide a vision of technology's role in education services, propose effective uses of funds, ensure equitable access to technology, and maximize connections among technologies.

Provide a State Vision of Technology's Role in Education. States must communicate a clear and persuasive vision of technology's role in education to ensure that all key persons—the governor, legislators, state education agency staff, higher education authorities, school board members, administrators, teachers, parents, and students—work toward a common goal for technology use.

Include Certain Key Components in State and Local Plans. State and local plans for implementing the use of learning technologies should include an identification of needs; clearly defined goals and objectives; an evaluation of each selected technology's capabilities and cost-effectiveness; a description of the governance structure and systems operation; a delineation of current and future funding sources; a strategy for teacher, administrative, and support staff training; strategy and schedule for implementing the plan; procedures for assisting local education agencies in the development of local technology plans; an evaluation plan; and a mechanism for modifying the plan itself. Planning is an ongoing process. Plans should be continually re-evaluated based on program outcomes, analysis of program effectiveness, new research, and technology development.

Outline the Responsibilities at the State, District, and Building Levels to Ensure That the Technology Plan Is Successfully Developed and Implemented. Each state should determine the planning process that best fits its needs; there is no single planning process for all states. With a trend towards site-based decision making, districts and schools are increasingly responsible for planning and implementing technology programs to meet their specific needs. At the same time, the economies of scale derived from aggregate purchases and the use of telecommunications networks for large-scale delivery drive planning to higher levels within and among states.

Although specific responsibilities vary by state, educators from different levels of each state's education system should participate in planning to achieve full integration of technology into education and to ensure clarity of responsibility and action at each level. Technology plans at each level should be developed by teams that include financial and policy decision makers; teacher and administrator representatives; postsecondary and higher education representatives; technical experts; individuals with experience in curriculum development, instructional management, and assessment; and other major stakeholders in education.

Ensure That Plans for Other Programs Within State Education Agencies Incorporate the Use of Appropriate Technology. State education agency plans for the state and federal programs should incorporate the use of appropriate technology to ensure that technology is effectively integrated into each state education service and across the services.

Ensure That the States, Districts, and Schools Have Sufficient Funding to Initiate and Sustain Ongoing Use of Technology as Articulated in the State Plan

Develop a Bold New Plan to Provide Steady Funding for Learning Technologies. Technology is an integral part of education; consequently, the federal, state, and local governments are responsible for providing funds to initiate and sustain the use of educational technology. Funding should cover all costs associated with the technology and the necessary support for continuing effective use, such as training, maintenance, and upgrades. Avenues to decrease the cost of technology by aggregating purchases across the nation, state, or regions should be developed to the full extent. To supplement federal, state, and local funds, alternative funding options, such as business-state partnerships and foundation grants, should also be pursued.

Initiate State Development of Learning Technologies. States are in a unique position to stimulate and initiate the development of learning technology products. States should use this opportunity to undertake cost-effective projects in technology that support the state's curriculum frameworks and education goals.

Include Expenditures for Technology as Part of Capital Outlay. Investments in educational technology should be considered capital expenditures, which may be depreciated over the life of the product.

Ensure That Students and School Personnel Have Equitable Access to Technologies for Their Learning, Teaching, and Management Needs

Equitable access must be addressed at the national, state, district, and building levels. Access to current technologies and fully interactive information networks that transfer voice, video, and data must be provided.

Federal and State Policies Should Ensure Access to Learning Technologies. Many current federal and state policies were developed prior to the introduction of new technology into education. Such policies may now limit access to technology; therefore, it is imperative to review them for currency and equitable access. The following issues are especially important for policy review and update:

Cost of access: To ensure that students and school personnel have affordable access to technology and information networks, it is necessary for technology providers to establish rates and other policies specifically for educational purposes. What is affordable for education may not be what is affordable for profit-making corporations. For example, state public utility commissions and the Federal Communications Commission should establish special telephone rates for education. The rates must be low enough to enable students and school personnel to take advantage of the voice, video, and data services transmitted over the telecommunications systems. The rates must also be sufficient to ensure continued investment in development of future applications for the education market. In addition, telecommunications costs should be equitable regardless of the factor of geographic location.

Information access: Intellectual property and copyright laws must be revised to increase student and school personnel access to information and provide them the flexibility to use the information for instructional purposes. These laws must also ensure that the owners and originators receive adequate recognition and financial reward. In addition, these laws and other policies should encourage development of electronically accessible information sources.

School facilities design: School facility design requirements, whether for new schools or for building rehabilitation, must support the use of learning technologies. Electrical outlets and voice, video, and data lines are critical components of the modern school. School facilities must also support new instructional strategies that use technology (including individual or small-group learning, and varied workstations).

Use of federal and state funds: Federal and state policies should authorize purchase of learning technologies with funds currently earmarked for textbooks, instructional materials, and learning resources.

Provide Access to Learning Technologies Both in and Outside the School Building, Just as Access to Textbooks Is Provided Both in and Outside School. To compensate for unequal technology resources in the home and among schools, extra effort must be made by states, districts, and schools to provide all students access to learning technologies both in and outside school buildings. Schools should establish programs to loan equipment to students and school personnel for home use. Schools, libraries, and other information sources should make their resources accessible during extended or nonschool hours.

Ensure That Educators Have the Staff Support, Training, Time, Authority, Incentive, and Resources Necessary to Use Technology Effectively

Encourage Local Districts and Schools to Develop "Technology Teams." To effectively integrate technology into the classroom, teachers need to work closely with strong support teams that include principals, library media specialists, technicians, and other support staff. Technology teams should include individuals with decision-making authority and expertise in technology, curriculum design, instructional design, and student assessment. Technology teams should provide teachers with technical support to keep equipment operating; inform them about emerging technologies and programs; suggest ways to renew the curriculum through technology; and assist in assessing the outcomes of the learning technologies.

Provide Professional Development Activities to Facilitate Full Integration of Technology into Education. States must provide rigorous, continuous training to ensure that all educators develop the skills necessary to use technology in their work. Ongoing professional development activities should be offered cooperatively by states, local districts, and vendors to provide training along with technology purchases and upgrades.

As learning technologies become more powerful and complex, teachers must increase their capacities to use technology. Teachers must learn how to operate available equipment and applications; evaluate the potential of instructional applications; integrate the technology into the curriculum; use technology for administrative and assessment purposes; and develop a willingness to experiment with technology. They must receive training to develop the group management, decision-making, and coaching skills necessary to help students use technology effectively.

State and local education agency staff must be provided training that helps them understand technology's potential as an instructional, administrative, and assessment tool. They must also be encouraged to experiment with technology-based programs.

State education agency staff must join with higher education authorities to ensure that licensure requirements encourage professionals to use technology effectively in the learning environment.

Provide the Time, Authority, Incentives, and Resources Necessary to Use Learning Technologies. The integration of learning technologies at the center of teaching and learning requires substantial changes from the practice of the traditional classroom. Many of the changes pertain to the role of teachers—their use of time, incentives, relationships between colleagues, and the resources available to them. Examples of necessary changes follow.

Educators must have convenient access to a wide range of technologies in their schools, classrooms, and homes. These include the technologies of the contemporary workplace of other professionals as well as specialized learning technologies. The more opportunity educators have to become comfortable with and competent with technology, the more likely they are to use it in teaching.

Many elements of the school day must be reviewed. Use of learning technologies may require substantially different class schedules, class lengths, and class sizes. Such changes cannot be made in isolation, but must be part of decisions that authorize different arrangements for cooperation and logistics.

Evaluation criteria and processes for teachers must ensure that they are fairly judged in the effective use of technology and are encouraged to use it. Current criteria and processes may effectively penalize teachers who use technology. For example, if the criterion is to require a teacher to deliver instruction, the teacher who coaches the students to use technology for "delivery" may be penalized.

Encourage the Development and Expansion of Telecommunications Networks

State, interstate, national, and international telecommunications networks are critical for providing students and educators equitable access to resources outside the school and establishing connections between the school and the home, the community, and other outside resources.

Plan, Fund, and Build Telecommunications Networks. Governors and state legislators, the President, and Congress are encouraged to provide support for the coordination and expansion of current telecommunications networks and to develop new statewide, interstate, national, and international telecommunications networks to serve education.

Advocate National Standards to Increase Connections Among and Use of Voice, Data, and Wide-Band Video Networks. Telecomputing networks should operate as national, nonproprietary standard telephone networks do. A telephone user can communicate with another user regardless of which telephone companies provide the service. A routing system is needed to communicate across telecomputing networks. National standards and policies for telecommunications are needed to ensure that the networks serve education.

To Expand Distance Learning and Ensure That It Meets Acceptable Standards, Multistate Cooperative Agreements Are Necessary for Teacher Qualifications and Course Specifications. Varying state requirements for certification and course approval currently require teachers of distance learning to meet multiple state certification and course approval requirements. In some cases, teachers are required to take physical exams and demonstrate knowledge of the state's history and government, even though they are not teaching those subjects. Multistate agreements are needed to promote high standards for teachers in a manner that facilitates the expansion of distance learning.

Multistate agreements on standards for courses offered by distance learning are also needed to ensure effective expansion of learning opportunities.

Support the Use of Technology in Student Assessment to Measure and Report Accumulated Complex Accomplishments and New Student Outcomes

Learning technologies are valuable tools for strengthening the teaching and learning of critical thinking and problem-solving skills and for measuring these capacities. Technology-based assessments help educators monitor student performance by allowing for: clear statement of multiple student outcomes; measurement of complex indicators of student learning; collection of data; management of information in such forms as portfolios; and the analysis, processing, and timely reporting of testing.

The effective development of technology for student assessment should be encouraged through collaboration among the states, along with key stakeholders at national and local levels.

Develop National Leadership for Learning Technologies

The Federal Government Should Establish Leadership in Learning Technologies. The federal government should institute processes to develop a coordinated vision for the effective use of technology in education. This vision should be based on the Office of Technology Assessment's reports, *Power On!* and *Linking for Learning.* Federal leadership is essential to the nation's efforts in research and development; to provide direction in the development of the national telecommunications infrastructure; and to ensure that all federal education programs incorporate the use of technologies, as summarized here.

The Federal Government Should Provide Increased Investment in Research and Development of Learning Technologies. To realize the full potential of learning technologies, systematic research must be conducted on how students learn, the capabilities of current and emerging technologies, and the effect of technologies on student outcomes and the learning environment.

A national research agenda related to technology in education must be developed collaboratively by federal, state, and local education agencies with the federal government playing the primary role in providing increased and consistent funding for research and development of learning technologies and instructional strategies.

The Federal Government Should Take Leadership in the Rapid Establishment of an Infrastructure to Support Learning Technologies. The use of learning technologies across the nation requires the federal government's leadership in establishing an infrastructure that includes fiber-optic cable and other carriers to transmit all signals throughout the nation.

This infrastructure must have the capacity to handle all signals, including telephone calls, data transmission, fax, graphics, animation, compressed television, full-motion television, and high-definition television.

The Federal Government Should Ensure the Transfer of Technologies from Federal Agencies to State and Local Education Agencies. The Department of Education should lead an effort to identify and disseminate learning technologies developed and used by the Departments of Defense, Energy, Commerce, and other federal agencies. The federal investment in learning technologies in such agencies is far more extensive than in the Department of Education. State and local educational systems need access to these technologies through a coordinated dissemination program.

CCSSO and Other National Education Organizations Should Increase Advocacy for Education's Technology Needs at the National Level. Federal policies and actions on learning technologies are critical to the availability of such technology at the state and local levels. CCSSO and other national education organizations must increase their efforts of advocacy to ensure that federal telecommunications and technology decisions support improvement of teaching and learning. Strong appeals need to be made to the President, Congress, the federal courts, the Federal Communications Commission, and the Departments of Education, Commerce, and Agriculture. Specifically, CCSSO should continue to take positions on learning technologies authorizations, appropriations, and legislation that affect the national information infrastructure and education's access, as it has on the recent legislation and court ruling concerning the Bell Operating Companies' right to manufacture telecommunications equipment and provide information services. As Congress debates future actions concerning such issues as cable interconnectivity, spectrum allocation debates, and intellectual property rights, CCSSO should represent educational concerns.

CONCLUSION

The potential for technological advances in support of teaching and learning seems limitless. Each new generation of computers, each advance in multimedia applications, and each gain in telecommunications delivery opens more opportunities. Information Age realities seem close to the reach of some students, but the gap between current opportunity and actual use of technology in most schools is enormous.

We hope this paper captures a vision of the opportunities that learning technologies might provide for all. This vision will keep changing as invention follows new paths for technological creation. The vision will help us only if the states and our nation take the steps recommended here to bring the next generation's tools to the hands and minds of our students. The Council of Chief State School Officers is committed to bringing the vision and recommendations here to reality for all American students.

Promoting Success in Educational Partnerships Involving Technology

Linda M. Baker

College of Education, University of Washington
Seattle, Washington

BACKGROUND

Schools have always received some degree of community support, such as parental assistance, volunteer efforts, donations of money and equipment, and provision of needed expertise. Nevertheless, fueled by reports such as *A Nation at Risk*, calls for school reform by almost every major political candidate, and ceaseless media accounts of apparent educational failure, there is a growing public perception that American schools are in a crisis professional educators cannot fix by themselves. One positive result of this perception is more organized and substantial involvement in schools by influential community institutions, which band together in *educational partnerships* to provide resources and services to schools.

Such educational partnerships are increasing dramatically. There are thousands of them, big and small, and more all the time; the National Alliance of Business (NAB) estimated 140,000 in 1985. As might be expected with a growing phenomenon, these partnerships are as diverse in their purposes as they are in their membership. Small collaborations, such as those between a single local school and a neighborhood business, are usually focused on providing a particular service for a specific school group, such as business mentors for science students or tutors for at-risk kids, or they may provide in-kind assistance, such as free printing of school materials. They may also donate items to the school. Larger partnerships, involving bigger businesses or corporations and/or universities and groups of schools, usually have more ambitious and far-ranging goals, including effecting comprehensive school reform.

For many reasons, the goals of these larger educational partnerships often include the purchase of educational technology—both hardware and software—and promotion of its integration into the daily life of schools. Educational technology is new and exciting, has a high public profile, and is often cited in popular and professional literature as a catalyst for major changes in teaching and learning. At the same time, however, technology is expensive and adopting it can be complex, so the purchase and effective use of educational technology may tax the means and experience of individual schools or school districts. It is likely, then, that professionals in businesses, universities, and schools interested in educational technology will find themselves reaching out to and working with other community groups to make possible together what might not be possible alone.

For those contemplating such collaborations and those currently involved in one, it would be helpful to know the experiences of others. A description of what has worked in educational technology partnerships from the point of view of those who have been involved in such relationships should be beneficial.

Yet, unfortunately, although quite a bit has been written about educational partnerships in general, not very much of it has been specific to technology. This is true whether one examines the business, educational, or technology management literature.

The older business literature tends to focus on the perception that schools are doing an inadequate job of preparing the future work force as a rationale for business initiating involvement in education through partnerships. More recent analyses are often clear-eyed reassessments of the efficacy of partnership arrangements, frequently citing corporate frustration with slow or superficial change and a lack of accountability for resources used (Chion-Kennedy 1989; Edelstein 1989; Mann 1987a and 1987b; Rist 1990). Both the early and the recent analyses sometimes refer in passing to a lack of technical sophistication among today's students, but they generally do not single out technology or technology partnerships for special notice.

Educational analysts largely divide into two camps, those who consider partnerships as one more form of school change initiative and those who consider them as policy-making bodies. Like business observers, school change writers do not distinguish technology partnerships from other collaborations. Instead, these writers point to the difficulty of effecting comprehensive and lasting change regardless of the innovation (Fullan and Steigelbauer 1991; Lieberman and Miller 1990; Sarason 1982, 1991; Senge 1990a; Sirotnik 1991). An exception here is the work of Larry Cuban (1986), who focuses on the failure of teachers to adopt educational technology in significant ways. However, Cuban does not speak to partnerships.

Educational policy analyses frequently emphasize that no matter who does it, educational policy making is largely political, as the process of determining "who gets what, when and how" is essentially a process of exercising power and influence no matter what the reasons or who the involved parties (Campbell and Mazzoni 1976; Easton 1965; Lasswell 1936; Pawley 1992). This literature is just beginning to speak to partnerships as policy-making bodies and so does not consider technology partnerships separately.

Last, the technology management literature has a substantial group of analyses concerned with both technology and partnerships. But these studies are largely focused on evaluating university/corporate research and development collaborations and their success in developing and promoting commercially viable and competitive technologies (Fassin 1991; McBrierty and O'Neill 1991; Phillips 1991). The findings of these studies might relate to educational partnerships, at least where universities are involved with schools, but that connection has not yet been drawn directly.

To summarize, although it would be beneficial for professionals in business, universities, and schools who might work together to know what factors help lead to success in educational partnerships involving technology, not much research has yet been done that is specifically helpful.

RESEARCH QUESTIONS

The major research question for this study, then, is: What are the common features of successful technology partnerships?

Related research questions are:

- How is *success* defined and measured?
- Which features are identified as successful most often?
- Which features are identified as problematic most often?

- Does the nature of the group involved (i.e., business, school, university) make a difference in which features are identified as successful or problematic?

- What suggestions for success are made by partnership participants?

The wording of these questions indicates an emphasis on identifying factors that contribute to the success of technology partnerships from the point of view of those currently involved in one. The intent of these questions is therefore descriptive and pragmatic rather than conceptual or theoretical. It is hoped that answers to these questions will be of practical help to professional people contemplating or involved in partnerships. It is only just now that many partnerships are of sufficient duration that their participants can assess their progress and draw conclusions to share with others, so answers to these questions should be timely and helpful.

METHOD

Preliminary analysis was done on a pool of professional literature derived from a comprehensive review of education, business, and technology management literature, and a test sample of Department of Education (DOE) partnership grant reports (e.g., Danzberger 1990). Using a rough content analysis, those sections of pool documents that referred to helpful or problematic features of partnerships or that offered advice for improvement were examined closely for commonalities.

In this preliminary analysis, the following features were identified most often as contributing to success:

- Shared vision

- Clearly defined goals

- Equal relations among partners

- Local decision making

- Sufficient resources

- Involvement of top-level administrators

- Personal and professional rewards for collaboration

- Careful choice of project coordinators

- Sufficient time.

This analysis also suggested that most problems arose as a consequence of disparate organizations with different standards, operating procedures, and goals ("culture") trying to work together to distribute much-needed resources (e.g., Sirotnik 1991).

However, these preliminary results had some limitations. First, materials specific to technology partnerships were limited. Second, the reports and articles that were available were universally positive in tone and far more likely to identify successful features than problematic ones, probably reflecting a natural tendency to play up successes when reporting publicly on a project. Yet it could be as helpful for others to know what did not work as what did. Third, the documents examined often did not distinguish the disparate views of particular participants. Instead, they were consensual, making it impossible to determine if, for example, the business partner disagreed with the school partner on what was successful and why. Last, because there were not many summary articles and reports readily available that covered more than a few cases, and because few were the result of systematic, formal research into partnerships, the preliminary analysis was based on a relatively small amount of data. For these reasons, a second method was used to elicit more complete information.

Additional data were collected nationally by a 45-minute, semistructured telephone interview with 23 representatives of 15 educational partnerships. Each had at least two years' experience with a partnership, collaboration, or consortium of some complexity, involving at least two parties and administration of a large federal grant specifically focused on educational technology (DOE-FIRST [Fund for the Improvement and Reform of Schools and Teaching] grants, with an average award of $117,214 per year for two or three years). For most of the respondents, the school year 1992-93 marked the final year of a three-year grant that began in 1989-90. For some, the grant ended in 1991 or the summer of 1992, so each had completed or was completing the project. Many had written or contributed to one or more assessment reports as part of their grant reporting requirements, and so had experience evaluating the success of their projects.

All 23 respondents were somehow involved with managing the federal grant and/or the partnership related to it, being the ones empowered by their institutions to make decisions and allocate resources for shared partnership activities. Five persons were school district representatives of some kind, five represented corporations, eleven were from universities, and two were from state or regional education departments or centers.

Results of the preliminary analysis were used along with the research questions to guide design of the interview questionnaire, which solicited comments on how each partnership organized collaborative work, how the representative felt about being part of a partnership, how the partnership evaluated success, and what features aided or impeded success. Respondents were also asked to state their advice to people beginning partnerships.

Statements in response to the questionnaire were examined for similarities and then grouped into categories to make dominant patterns apparent. These patterns are discussed in the results section, which also includes some individual statements that were not widely replicated but appear to be interesting or insightful.

In a final step, those features identified by technology partnership participants as helpful or problematic were compared with features identified in the preliminary analysis to see if technology partnerships differ in any consistent way from other kinds of partnerships. Any such differences could suggest avenues for further research.

RESULTS

There is little question that professionals from all three groups—universities, businesses, and schools or school organizations—generally enjoyed being part of a partnership. Many respondents described their participation as "stimulating," "challenging," and even "fun," presenting a definite "change" from their usual activities and affording them "opportunities" for both personal and professional growth. Most also felt greatly rewarded by their contact with a new set of "colleagues," whom they often described as "friends" as well as "innovative," "creative," and "exciting" peers.

About a third of the respondents saw the partnership as a means to expand their range of personal "connections" and "professional opportunities." A third also appreciated their chance to be involved in a "real" project and watch the educational process unfold from an "insider's view" rather than from a distance as an outside professional observer or lay citizen.

Almost half found pride and gratification that they had been part of something that "made a difference," elicited "good feedback," or had an "impact" on education. (Categories are not mutually exclusive. Respondents could give two or more answers to a single question and so be counted in more than one category.)

Respondents also liked being part of a partnership for the unique benefits they felt collaboration brought, including much-needed "money and other resources," the "synergy" afforded by sharing "information," "ideas," and "purposes," and the "new perspectives" brought to educational problems and circumstances when multiple people from disparate backgrounds interact.

In addition, more than half the respondents signaled their intent to continue the partnership in some way after the initial three-year grant period ended and federal monies disappeared. Some of these were writing other grants for support, whereas others planned to absorb ongoing costs among involved institutions. Of the 11 respondents who said "no" or "maybe" to continuing their partnerships, none said they would never participate in another partnership, and most were actively soliciting new partners for new purposes. The general consensus on participating in partnerships appears to be, as two respondents put it, "Go for it!"

MEASURING SUCCESS

However, that participants generally enjoyed being part of a partnership does not mean their partnerships were successful. *How did partners define and measure success?* This question is particularly important in light of the preliminary analysis, which suggested that differences in institutional cultures—which affect the kinds of results that are valued, typical reward structures, and standard operating procedures—and differing institutional agendas for participating in partnerships can cause serious disagreements about what constitutes success and how to recognize when it is reached.

In this group, only two respondents were not sure if their project had been successful overall, one citing that she was too "close to it to tell objectively," and the other that he regretted "they could only go so far since it was important not to go too fast." The 21 others described their projects variously in laudatory terms such as "a model others can use," "110 percent effective," or "it reinforced our initial beliefs."

Fifteen of the respondents stated that their projects used specific concrete products to gauge success, including improvement in student test scores, production of curriculum units and lesson plans, development of multimedia prototypes or educational software, and measurements of technology usage, such as hours spent in computer labs, or cost of online connect time. The others used accomplishment of specific grant goals, such as attainment of "objectives" and "outcomes," or adherence to "benchmarks" and "timelines." Or they used qualitative measures of student and/or teacher attitudes and behavior, such as "comments," "feedback," and "evaluations" as measures of accomplishment. Many had a mix of ways to gauge their success, including formal evaluation by paid, outside evaluators (often university staff).

Even though the majority of respondents felt their projects were successful overall, they nonetheless expressed reservations about how evaluation was done. Six persons said they either did not agree with the methods used to gauge the success of their projects or were not sure of their effectiveness, and many of the 17 others agreed overall with the methods used but had some specific concerns. These concerns were divided about equally between those who wished more traditionally rigorous, quantitative assessments of progress, and those who thought qualitative measures more appropriate. Comments indicating a desire for more rigor included "need more evaluation at the school level—it was hard to document what the teachers were doing," "there was no control group," "I'd prefer more concrete benchmarks," and "there were little pre- and posttest differences." Those arguing for more qualitative measures stated, "it's hard to measure long-term goals," "I'd prefer to judge investment in people, not scores," "traditional evaluation took too much time for the results gained," "I'd add qualitative measures of attitudes or the energizing effect of collaboration," and "usual methods are merely 'add-ons' at end of the project, but no one will give you grant money for formative evaluation."

The concerns expressed about the effectiveness of evaluation in this group suggest that measuring success is one of the more problematic aspects of a partnership. Although on the one hand partners are convinced they have been largely successful, on the other hand they are not satisfied with how that is proved. Their measures of success often appear to be at odds with their perceptions of success. This may be because participants feel torn between their generally positive inside experience of collaboration and the need to justify its fruits to influential outsiders, such as grant officers, tenure committees, or school district administrators. Or it could be that differing cultural expectations of partnership institutions do mean differing perceptions of measuring success. Or it could be something else altogether. This study did not sufficiently address *why* these differences occur, but only points out that they do, just as the preliminary analysis suggested they might. But this result suggests that evaluation is a feature that those contemplating a partnership should consider for frank discussion and negotiation among partners at the beginning of their association.

What Features of the Partnership Were Identified as Problematic Most Often?

Answers to this research question came from three sources: the responses to questions about what partnership features impeded success, what partners did not like about being in a partnership, and the things that partners disagreed about.

Failures of Planning and Implementation. Failures of planning were mentioned most often as impeding success, including picking project "school districts too far apart geographically," having a "too-fast production schedule," or a "contract too binding," "contradictions in project goals," "too much money spent on hardware with none for training," and "not designing technology centrally enough into the project."

It is relatively easy to recognize failures of planning after the fact when what has not worked becomes apparent. It is much harder to anticipate problems as you are beginning a project, especially when technology partnerships are a relatively new phenomenon, local conditions vary dramatically, and there are few established guideposts to follow. As one respondent said, "This is an experiment, and we are learning as we go along." Another respondent suggests that one conclusion to be drawn from these experiences is to devote as much time as possible to planning, trying to anticipate problems, for "the more you plan, the easier it is to implement."

Planning problems were followed in importance by implementation problems, such as excessive "changes in personnel" and introducing the project on too grand a scale with "the 'big pitch' which scared school participants."

Some of these barriers to success cannot be anticipated or well controlled either, particularly excessive turnover in personnel, which was also mentioned prominently among things respondents did not like about being part of a partnership. When people change, it takes time to "know the new ones," or "bring them up to speed"; when key people go, they sometimes "take the commitment of their institutions and their resources with them." Yet, although participants can discourage each other from leaving partnerships, they cannot prevent each other from going, particularly because participation in the partnership is seldom anyone's main job, and most need to meet the demands of their primary jobs first. Personal and institutional agendas change with time, and preservation of the original membership in the partnership is rarely more important to participants than these other agendas.

Stress. In discussing what they did not like, many of the respondents also decried the stress associated with belonging to a partnership—stress mostly linked to the amount of time and emotional energy that collaboration requires. Many partnership participants felt their institutions did not provide them with sufficient personal support for their positions, mentioning that they needed more "clerical help," more "staff" or "assistants," and most importantly, "time," particularly release time from their regular institutional duties. In a few cases, participation in a partnership was even added on top of someone's other job duties with no extra support at all: "I inherited it when someone else left."

One corporate officer and one university professor both felt they deserved a "promotion" for the work they had put in, but clearly did not expect that their institutions would reward them that way for their participation. It appears that partnerships are still viewed as peripheral commitments by many organizations, and their success relies quite a bit on the willingness of involved parties to go beyond what is provided, out of personal commitment.

Logistical Problems. On a more basic level, respondents also frequently mentioned persistent logistical problems that arose from the complexity of group-managing a large project. These ranged from major decisions, such as deciding who would "manage the money" or be "responsible to outside auditors," to minor but consistently annoying hassles over details such as "conflicting school and corporate calendars," "different business office procedures and techniques," and "free parking at the university." One university grant coordinator pointed out that her university was not used to producing anything but written materials, and so its procedures could not easily support her work with outside multimedia producers who required large amounts of cash and rapid production and payment schedules to do their work.

Respondents found that resolving these logistical challenges took a surprising amount of time, yet, if left untended, could erupt into bad feelings. One school district technology coordinator laughingly referred to trying to park his car at the university without getting a ticket he had to personally pay as a "constant thorn in his side." Although this was a minor irritation, it was a constant reminder to him that he was not on his "turf."

These differences in routine institutional procedures were surface manifestations of more profound institutional differences that often caused considerable conflict. These differences surfaced in respondent answers about disagreement among partners. Only 4 of the 23 respondents reported no conflict of note, one explaining that disagreements varied by the persons involved, with "no major consistent" pattern, and another adding that their small working group made "agreement more possible than it would be among a large number of people." All of the others reported some major disagreements.

In fact, the representatives of one project contacted declined to participate altogether because their collaborative work had proved so difficult the first several years that, in the interest of remaining together in this better final year, they didn't wish to "drag it all up again" by being interviewed. In addition, one multimedia production company was considering revising corporate policy to do educational media development entirely in-house rather than through partnerships with outside educational organizations because the "investment in time, money and energy" involved in collaborations was considered too taxing for the return.

Disagreements Between Partners. The kind of disagreements most of the other respondents denoted varied by the organizations involved, as different concerns surfaced among partnership representatives than between representatives and teachers or representatives and technology vendors. Among partnership representatives, three areas of disagreement were mentioned most often: allocation of resources, partnership roles, and pedagogy.

Representatives often had to choose among many competing uses for the money, technology, and services their partnership had to provide schools. Hard choices therefore had to be made on who and what would be funded, what hardware and software would be chosen, and what direction staff time and energies would take. As one project director said, "We can think of 40 things to use the money for and can only do 3 or 4, so deciding what you're *not* going to do with resources is important. . . . It was hard for us to say no."

Dissension also arose about what role each partner was to take in the project. Often it was not clear what each organization was expected to provide or each representative to do, and so representatives felt others were not doing their jobs or, as one project coordinator said, "holding up their part of the bargain." This led to resentment. In addition, as projects evolved, there was often a reevaluation of partnership roles, with some partners becoming more active than others in different stages of the project. Agreeing on who should take an active role at any given time also caused dissension.

Last, partners did not always agree on pedagogy. This was most evident in discussions on the proposed content of educational materials, such as curricular units, lesson plans, computer programs purchased or developed for use in classrooms, and prototype educational CD-ROMs or videos. The director of research and development for a national professional association setting standards for the teaching of science pointed to this problem in his particular project. "There is a wide range of philosophical differences on how to teach science . . . the clash of ideas sometimes led to belittling and ridiculing of opposite positions."

In addition to these primary disagreements, as mentioned earlier, partners also disagreed to a lesser extent about the methods used to assess the accomplishment of project goals, with some wanting more "concrete benchmarks" than others, and about the project implementation process, particularly how to speed it up.

Disagreements Between Partners and Teachers. Two major kinds of disagreements arose between partnership representatives and teachers. The problem mentioned most often was competing ideas over the amount and content of training offered. Teachers often preferred elementary training in how to operate a computer and use basic application software, whereas partnership representatives were emphasizing classes in integration of the computer into classroom activities and development of original educational materials. One school district technology coordinator described this as, "We were determined to integrate technology and the teachers were determined not to."

The other primary disagreement was over methods for assessment and evaluation. Project managers were often required by their grants to regularly evaluate progress and sometimes had concerns about teacher performance, so they were interested in timely and telling evaluations. Teachers, in contrast, found some evaluation procedures intrusive or overly time-consuming and tedious.

To summarize, all but four of the partnership participants questioned were able to describe disagreements among partners. The nature of the disagreements varied by who was interacting, but there was dissension across a broad range of people and activities, including the most fundamental work of the partnerships, such as allocating money, assigning roles, choosing among educational alternatives, providing goods and services, training staff, and evaluating progress. This pattern suggests that these partnerships do not escape the conflict which the preliminary analysis suggested can characterize collaborations among disparate institutions.

Conflict Resolution. Because disagreements can present major obstacles to success, it is also helpful to know how partners tried to resolve conflict and whether the methods they chose were successful. It is interesting to note, then, that regardless of their position or the kind of conflict they were discussing, respondents overwhelmingly described their primary method of resolving conflict as building "consensus" by "talking it out."

Consensus. Each described a process of dispute resolution that began with asking for alternatives, describing the advantages and disadvantages of each suggestion from each partner's point of view, and then choosing one alternative through "negotiation" and "compromise." Many mentioned that they thought this process of group decision making through discussion and negotiation represented the essence of collaboration. One corporate education representative characterized it as "looking for a compromise. Seeing how we can change so that everybody enjoys a winner . . . a good partnership will give everybody something to win about." Others described it as reaching a "common understanding" or "tandem decision-making."

Most recognized, however, some limits to this method of resolving conflicts. First, it can take a long time; as one project director noted, "Collaborative work has its own time-line. It is much slower than when telling them [others] what to do. That isn't bad . . . it's just a different pace which takes adapting to."

In addition, many responses pointed to a set of attitudes that must be present for this kind of conflict resolution to work. People must trust each other, know each other's working styles, and be willing to critically examine and change their own opinions and, occasionally, behavior. The same person continued, "You must be willing to work as much on the relationship between people as on tasks. That was a personal learning for me as a project director. You must be open to change and be a co-learner." Another project coordinator felt that facilitating group process was the most challenging part of her project, indicating that most adults, even teachers, have no formal training in collaboration and do not automatically know how to solve problems and make decisions together. The needed attitudes and actions were therefore learned—sometimes painfully—in the process of working together.

Role of the Project Coordinator/Manager. Many of the responses outlined a critical role in the dispute resolution process for the project director or coordinator, those partnership managers who are responsible for the day-to-day operation of the project. One said she would only hire project coordinators like theirs who had "experience running complex projects and getting people to work together." Another said a crucial part of her role as project coordinator was to do the "summing up" at the end of meetings which helped people choose among alternatives.

In addition, if people were not able to reach consensus, which many said happened occasionally, the project coordinator or director often made a final determination, sometimes by "delaying a decision until a better time arose," or "dropping one idea and substituting another," or even by "taking the project and running with it," that is, making the decision he or she thought best for the project. When this last happened, the coordinator or director usually justified the decision to the others by reference to the original purposes of the project as represented in project documents or by citing grant demands made by the government funding agency. Respondents clearly linked group decision making to the idea of a partnership, and felt it "heavy-handed" when either they, or someone else in the partnership, made decisions unilaterally. As one said, "It takes longer to make decisions together but telling people what to do doesn't work, so it works out better this way in the long run."

In 3 of the 23 cases, this process of consensus did not work at all. Two of these cases involved school districts and hardware or software companies, and one concerned a school district and a group of teachers. In the first cases, the school district partners found the vendors to be uninterested in true collaboration. They claimed corporations either disappeared after the sale of hardware, providing little further support, or overly limited school district participation in joint activities with tightly worded partnership agreements. In one partnership between a school district and a multimedia development company, a contract outlining the duties and obligations of each partner was considered too restrictive by the school district representative, who felt left out of decision making about the educational content of the product. Yet the same contract was considered routine by the corporate representative, who was used to the highly competitive software industry in which protection of corporate creative processes is paramount in any collaborative work.

This misunderstanding points to a clear difference of organizational culture, as reflected in the documents and standard operating procedures that embody organizational values. The corporate representative explained school district concerns as resulting from a scheduling problem. "It was not anyone's fault. It was just circumstances. There are differences in the way schools and corporations carry out their work day. We're in a production mode whether schools are in summer break or not, so if kids and teachers aren't around, I make do with other kids, other classes."

She added that the consensual process of solving conflicts such as this was different for her as a corporate partner. "Production and creative decisions are made by huge numbers of people bantering about ideas in a software company. It takes time, and feelings get hurt. I was relieved to work in a situation [in the schools] where people liked my ideas." She detailed a process in which she presented the partnership with production company ideas about the educational content of the medium being produced, followed by some discussion in which there was minimal objection on minor issues ("no red flags") after which she tried to "follow the consensus" in the subsequent production. She did not feel she had to "fight for [her] ideas" as she would have had to in a corporate environment.

However, the school district representative on the same project felt the district had only minimal impact on the educational content of the product. She cited contract provisions that would financially penalize the school district for making any changes that slowed down the production schedule. She felt these legal provisions inhibited her group from persisting in its pedagogical concerns. The corporate representative apparently did not realize that her school district counterpart felt so strongly, as she thought there were no major disagreements on content.

False Consensus. This points to a danger focused on by another of the respondents—the problem of acceding to a false consensus. The desires to get along amicably, make deadlines, and meet the goals of the project and demands of the funding agency can cause people to agree to what they think everyone else wants even if they or their organization feels that what is being proposed is a bad idea—a kind of "group think." The director of research and development responsible for one project referred to this as the "Abilene paradox," after the work of management analyst Jerry B. Harvey (1988), saying "a lot of decisions are based on people agreeing because they think it is what the group wants, but no one wants it really." To avoid this false consensus, this director preferred open and pointed disagreement to acquiescence in the interest of collegiality or expedience.

"Exiting." The unresolved conflict between teachers and the school district referred to earlier was over the content of training and demonstrates the success of the "exit" strategy in influencing group processes. School district partnership representatives, sensitive to the outlines of the grant funding the partnership, wanted teachers to integrate technology into the classroom, bypassing or hurrying through the process of learning the basics of computing and common application programs like word processing. But teachers did not want integration classes and chose not to attend them, no matter how many were offered by the district, at what times, and for what pay. They "exited": a powerful ploy used by those not in power to frustrate the aims of those above them with whom they do not agree. This conflict was never resolved to the district's satisfaction, and this part of their project went unrealized as a result.

"Exiting" was also used as a strategy by partnership representatives in many of the other projects, even where consensus did work to resolve most issues. At least five respondents mentioned partners who had withdrawn, usually the corporate partners, individual school districts, or individual schools. Four others mentioned changes in personnel, moving partnership representatives around until they found a "stable working group" that could "deliver on what they promised." Indeed, as mentioned earlier, high turnover in personnel was cited in three cases as a major obstacle to accomplishment of project goals, as new people had to be "brought up to speed" before the partnership could proceed.

Four partnership representatives also mentioned threatening to exit, that is, stating their intent to withdraw partnership resources from school districts, schools, or teachers who were not fulfilling their obligations. These threats were often first carefully stated in writing, with follow-up telephone calls or site visits by project directors or coordinators. Usually such threats were effective. When partners or participants withdrew, it was of their own accord; few were "dropped" by the others.

In summary, most partnerships resolve conflicts by identifying and weighing alternatives and talking things through to a consensus. This is a time-consuming process of negotiation and compromise which partners recognize as requiring special skills in group process and a willingness by partners to learn new things, be open, trust each other, and change positions.

In addition, project coordinators or directors, as the day-to-day managers of most technology partnerships, frequently have a special role to play in conflict resolution as the ones who make partners confront each other and the issues, who summarize positions so decisions can be made, and who take over decision making when an impasse is reached. They are often the facilitators of conflict resolution and the guardians of group process. It is seen as part of their job by the others involved.

Also, when consensus fails to resolve disputes, the exit strategy is often used by partnership representatives, who either withdraw or threaten to withdraw their organizational resources from the partnership. Exiting can be represented formally, by threats to retract manifested in documents, phone calls, or visits, or informally, by nonparticipation in meetings or activities. Partners can leave or they can fade away; they are seldom booted out.

Last, beware of false consensus. The desire to please each other and forge ahead can lead people to agree to what they do not really like or think practicable, which can create problems when differing organizational cultures and standard operating procedures undermine underexamined goals.

What Features Are Identified as Successful Most Often?
What Advice Do Participants Have for Others Beginning Partnerships?

Answers to these research questions came from responses to three questions on the questionnaire:

- What features of the partnership led to success?

- What would you change if you could begin again?

- What advice do you have for those beginning partnerships?

Answers to the first and third questions overlapped significantly, so they are discussed together.

When respondents were asked what they would change about their partnerships if they could start over, 8 out of 23, almost a third, said nothing. Half of these did not identify any major problems in the course of their partnerships, and the other half did not feel the problems they experienced were debilitating enough to warrant making any changes. Overall, these representatives were fairly satisfied with the way things went.

Choose People and Sites Carefully. The other two-thirds would change their partnerships in a variety of ways, most frequently by including either different people or a wider range of people. Eleven references were made to being "choosier" in selecting the other members of the partnership. These comments were usually made by representatives of the initiating partner, the organization that first solicited other partners and drafted the grant proposal. Respondents who felt the push to find sites and encourage participation sometimes brought people and organizations together without due consideration for their true willingness or ability to actively participate. Several representatives mentioned the importance of being able to pick the persons they worked with, whether that was someone in a partner organization with whom they "already had a working relationship," someone who could demonstrate his or her ability to "deliver what [had been] promised," or someone who chose to be included rather than being assigned by administrative staff.

Respondents would also be more selective in picking project sites, choosing fewer districts or schools, sites geographically closer to the project administration point, or those that represented "ideal conditions." Two mentioned having some kind of competitive process for inclusion in the project. One project director who had worked with a large number of schools and districts over the three years of her project said, "I would be choosier . . . look for optimal conditions rather than anyone who wanted to work, and put conditions on schools to be selected. Have them put in writing what they will do to support us."

Eight references were made to including a wider range of people, usually to ensure critical support from interested "stakeholders," particularly principals. As the persons primarily responsible for decision making and allocation of resources in school buildings, principals are crucial to the success of any K-12 educational change effort, technology projects included. One project director said about administrative support for her teacher training project, "There should be some really. For the most part, they didn't support. There wasn't an administrator at the schools who knew and who cared. It made it hard for teachers to request individual support." One school district technology director who had helped choose sites for a project by mailing a survey to the schools added, "Now I'd go to individual schools and interview principals and technology teachers. . . . I'd do more personal interfacing with principals. It was more important than I realized."

Do You Have Any Advice for Those Starting Partnerships Now That Will Help Them Be Successful?

Some answers to this question corroborated the emphasis on including all important stakeholders. Three references were made to soliciting comments from impacted groups during the grant-writing and planning stages to secure their ideas and interest early, and others mentioned including everyone at all levels in every phase of the project (planning, implementation, evaluation) and securing organizational, rather than merely personal, buy-in. This last suggestion reflects the experience of projects where a critical person or persons exited during the project, taking their organizational commitment with them. Representatives who had experienced this problem suggested getting an institutional commitment in writing before the project begins. Others mentioned "keeping the original personnel if possible."

Have Clear Roles and Expectations. When giving advice to those starting partnerships, respondents overwhelmingly pointed to the necessity of outlining clear, specific roles and responsibilities for each partner, which are stated *in writing* and agreed to *before* the project begins. Suggestions for inclusion in these kinds of written agreements were a "few clear, simple and direct statements of project goals," a "formal team structure," "defined outcomes," and a timeline for the accomplishment of project "benchmarks." The purposes of such written agreements were stated variously as to "make expectations clear," "assign responsibilities," allow for consideration of each partner's "real constraints," get to "know each other's strengths," and make sure the team is "moving in the same direction, not on individual agendas." One corporate education manager described it as setting up a "win/win situation" from the beginning, and advised renegotiating the agreement every year to adapt it to current conditions, making it a "living document."

Cultivate Collaborative Skills. Another large group of advice responses centered on cultivating the personal characteristics that collaboration requires. Partnership representatives suggested involving or developing persons who are flexible, open, creative, willing to "share ideas," and capable of working on a basis of trust and respect. They should also be daring, "willing to push the limits of what is possible." In addition, four references were made to the need to be dedicated and hard-working, that is, individuals for whom this is not just a job but a passion. The primary reason for the latter suggestion is because of the huge amount of time collaborative partnership work requires, often far beyond what participants feel they are paid for or what their institutions anticipated when assigning them.

Pay Attention to Group Process. The last major group of suggestions for those starting partnerships had to do with group process and dynamics. Here the most frequent suggestion was to meet often and communicate regularly so that people feel included and know what is going on. Several representatives also mentioned picking a good project coordinator or director, someone who could provide a strong "anchor" for the project. Still others advised openly recognizing outside constraints on the group, such as limits on time, staff, and resources; "systemic influences" such as school district politics; and the impact of cultural differences between organizing institutions. One school district technology coordinator said, "You must understand and accept the culture differences. If you don't, then there will be continual problems. For example, university people must get something publishable out of an experience but teachers couldn't care less about that. The need to publish has implications for how you spend time . . . this must be understood and acknowledged."

To summarize, the primary advice of this seasoned group of partnership representatives was to be specific and clear about the goals of the partnership and to clearly define in writing, before the project begins, what each partner will be expected to do to advance those goals. They also strongly recommended promotion of the personal values and characteristics that make collaboration easier—qualities of flexibility, openness, trust, and respect for others mixed with creativity, daring, and dedication. Last, respondents thought it wise to pay attention to group process by meeting regularly, talking about things, relying on the guidance of a strong project coordinator or director, and acknowledging systemic limits on what can be accomplished.

Are There Differences Between Partners in What Features Are Seen as Successful or Problematic?

Answering this question for the group of respondents as a whole proved difficult, largely because corporations were underrepresented among those interviewed (5 of 23 respondents). When more than one person was interviewed from a project (8 of 23 cases), the responses were compared to each other to look for differences. Many of those differences have been discussed in earlier analysis. However, more definitive conclusions would be possible with a larger corporate sample.

It is interesting to note, however, why businesses are not more represented. Business partners were the hardest to find to interview, in many cases because their personal or institutional commitment was relatively short-term and they were no longer active, working members of the partnership. In the special case of technology vendors as partners, corporate involvement often ceased or was sharply curtailed after the original purchase or donation of hardware or software. Businesses that had long-term, ongoing commitments to a partnership were rare, even though, as one corporate education manager avowed, "it's the only way to be truly effective . . . roll up your sleeves and get involved in every aspect."

THE UNIQUE CHARACTERISTICS OF TECHNOLOGY PARTNERSHIPS

The final step in this study was aimed at examining whether technology partnerships differ in any consistent way from other kinds of educational partnerships. This exploration was done by comparing the categories of response given by technology partnership participants to the categories of response given by educational partnership participants generally. In order to make this comparison possible, a subset of the preliminary analysis document pool was drawn. This subset was composed of six major partnership syntheses done between 1986 and 1991 (see Appendix A). Content analysis was used on those sections of the syntheses that described successful or problematic features of partnerships or made suggestions for improvement. The features cited were then sorted into one of five categories: *leadership* (who should lead and desired leadership qualities); *governance* (who should be included and how the organization should be organized and structured); *support* (resources and support services required); *process* (group interaction and project implementation); and *purpose* (vision or mission). Those features mentioned most often in this subset covering all kinds of educational partnerships were then compared to those features mentioned most often by technology partnership participants (see Figure 1, page 96).

Figure 1. Analysis of Partnership Syntheses.

Leadership
- top-level
- brokering/linking abilities
- sustained

Governance
- equal relations
- flexible structures
- local autonomy

Support
- rewards for collaboration
- sufficient resources
- support services
- resources targeted to needs

Process
- formally agreed-on roles and responsibilities
- time for change to occur
- monitoring process and outcomes

Purpose
- common purpose
- mutually beneficial goals
- collaboration as a group norm

The research question guiding this part of the study was: *Do technology partnerships differ from other kinds of educational partnerships in which features are identified as problematic or successful? If so, why?*

Because neither the preliminary analysis nor the questionnaire was designed to directly address this last research question, this comparative analysis cannot give any definitive answers. However, it does point to promising avenues for further research.

Disagreements About Technology

The general partnership syntheses did not mention disagreements in any of the five categories examined except "purpose," where it was suggested that having a "common purpose" and "mutually beneficial goals" that could be "owned" by everyone was important to minimize disagreements. Technology partnership participants strongly agreed, even to suggesting assigning specific roles to each party in writing before the project began.

However, technology partnership respondents mentioned an array of disagreements, singling out one kind not yet discussed that is unique to these kinds of partnerships. A little more than a fourth of the disagreements mentioned were between other partners and the technology vendor in partnerships that had major hardware and software companies or multimedia production firms as members. Three kinds of problems were mentioned most frequently—slow delivery of promised goods (hardware and software), unavailability of proffered training, and serious contention about the content of materials being collaboratively developed.

Slow Delivery and Insufficient Training

School and university partners often felt the service by the technology partner "after the sale" was not as expected, either because the vendor primarily viewed the partnership as a chance to sell products and services rather than a true collaboration, or because, although well-intentioned, vendors were either too busy to guarantee delivery schedules and training as planned, or too large and bureaucratic to secure the commitment of corporate headquarters. The principal investigator on one grant said, "Over time we got more [goods and training], but I'm not sure we got more than usual people who buy hardware. Corporate headquarters of company 'A' wouldn't commit and company 'B' is always reorganizing, so it was too little, too late on gear and training." In short, the expectations of schools and universities that a partnership with a technology vendor implied a special relationship warranting extra services and attention were often frustrated.

Battles over Collaborative Media Production

Problems over developing materials collaboratively clearly indicates how different organizational cultures can cause conflict. In addition to the contention discussed earlier between a school district and software company jointly developing an educational product, there were two other cases where serious differences arose between the educational partners and the media production staff of the technology partner over the content of educational materials produced. Naturally enough, the educational staffs placed primary emphasis on the teaching and learning objectives of whatever was being produced, and the media producers were primarily interested in its interest level to students. One grant principal investigator said that working with a scriptwriter epitomized this conflict in approach. "It was hard to get him to realize our ideas. We had instructional design goals, he had entertainment goals. It was a knock-down-drag-out to build both into the script. The differences between us were very stark . . . clear differences in conception which were hard to blend."

Two respondents also mentioned "battles" between hardware and software suppliers trying to make their various technologies work together. Project managers sometimes felt caught in between two competing interests, unable to coordinate efforts to go forward. Hardware and software companies usually develop their products in isolation from each other, and seldom work directly with schools when developing educational materials. So these kinds of companies may not share one of the primary values the general syntheses suggest is critical to partnerships—collaboration as an institutional norm. To be successful, such corporations are designed for fierce and highly charged competition that encourages careful guarding of institutional resources and talents and quick claims to proprietary rights. Their organizations and employees may consequently be ill-prepared for collaboration with outsiders. As a production company creative manager said, "The principles we live by in schools and corporations are different. Friction results always. I wish it wasn't there, but that's the way it is. . . . Many feel developing a relationship with teachers, principals and kids costs money and time and doesn't give back to the corporation."

This quote also suggests that many of these kinds of corporations have an instrumental approach to their partnerships with schools—they are ultimately involved in order to develop an educational market for their products or services. Many technology partnerships are different, then, from others in which corporate goals are more diffuse, such as training a productive work force, improving economic competitiveness, or encouraging innovation.

Marketplace Relations

There were other indications that many of the technology corporate partners became involved with schools primarily to sell their products or services. In three cases, major hardware vendors withdrew from the partnership altogether when they were not awarded an exclusive contract for school sales. In two others, the managers of a regional telecommunications company and a major mainframe computer vendor flatly stated that their role in the partnership was to donate goods or services, something they were willing to do in the short run in expectation of substantial future sales.

In another case, a prominent multimedia software company jointly developing products with a school district delivered a single prototype but then declined to provide the promised support for its reproduction so it could be used in multiple schools. It also chose not to develop a second prototype at all. Managers had decided the education market was too risky, and turned attention back to entertainment.

Lastly, in at least one other case a major software company installed a showcase lab in a single school, ushered in school district buyers from other parts of the state, then became unavailable to the first school after multiple other sales, greatly embittering the original district superintendent. He had used federal grant money to make technology purchases and expected a continuing relationship. "Software Company A was *not* a partner. They have no investment in it . . . made a profit from it. It was a new venture for them, now it's standard all over the state. They brought in two visitors a week to see what they'd done. But they didn't share cost and responsibility. We put up the money and took the risks. . . . I made them a ton of money all over the South." Participants spoke of incidents of this kind with a great deal of anger.

In contrast, there were also examples of genuine collaboration. In another state, the same software company that had so upset the superintendent donated extra equipment and in-kind services so that two closely related school districts could have comparable labs, even though one had less money. In another district, corporate technicians servicing computer labs carried messages back and forth between project coordinators and teachers as they moved from school to school, building personal relationships and improving communication between participants. In a final case, a major hardware vendor had been part of educational partnerships for close to 10 years, many of which it had initiated; was actively involved in multiple projects at the time of the interview; and had committed a broad array of resources to continuing these connections in the future.

So, although many technology corporations see their involvement in schools primarily in terms of economic opportunity, that motivation does not always preclude working together collaboratively over the long term. Perhaps these instrumental relations are only a stage these relatively new partnerships are passing through on the way to a more symbiotic and subtle understanding of what schools and technology corporations can do for each other. In studying interorganizational alliances, Intrilagator suggests there is a continuum of relations passing from cooperation through coordination to true collaboration, with each step requiring more interdependence (1992, pp. 2-4). To date, technology partnerships are generally at the cooperative, less interdependent end of this continuum, but that could change in the future.

Lack of Sustained Leadership and Continuing Support

Reference to the general partnership syntheses indicates two other factors that are problematic in technology partnerships—sustained leadership and sufficient support. As suggested by the comings and goings of corporate partners described earlier, many of these partnerships fell victim to multiple changes of personnel. Indeed, the interview sample was low on corporate representatives precisely because original partnership members were so hard to track down. This may be because technology industries are volatile by nature, with many changes of personnel. Or it could be because once a sale was made, the original representative moved on to other projects, leaving support people to follow through as needed, with no continuing presence. These practices, which are "standard operating procedures" in the software and hardware industries, do not lend themselves well to collaborative ventures.

Technology partnership representatives also decried the scramble for resources and institutional support that developed as the federal grants came to an end. Though this scramble often occurs in other kinds of partnerships as well, it appears to be more acute in technology partnerships. Unlike many other educational innovations that form the basis of partnerships, educational technology is expensive to obtain and maintain. In these technology projects, either federal monies or corporate donations were used to make the original capital investment in labs, equipment, and software. But partners uniformly assigned the handling of the continuing needs for maintenance, upgrades, staffing, and ongoing training to the school or school district, few of which were equipped to meet these needs. When asked if the partnership would continue after the grant ended, one university-based project director said, "The local school systems are trying to grapple with that now." Another coordinator said, "There will probably be periodic contact but there is no funding for more, no ongoing training or monthly meetings. . . . Our office is involved in too many other projects. We're overextended and need more staff."

In the face of inadequate institutional support, about half the respondents were actively pursuing other grants to continue projects and maintain the partnership. This led to much stress and uncertainty. There is heavy competition for these outside resources and, even if won, the timing on receiving any resulting support can be tricky. For example, two project coordinators asked outright if the interviewer, whom they had known less than an hour on the telephone, could get them a job.

Lack of Theory and Practical Knowledge

Both the partnership syntheses and the technology project participants emphasize the importance of shared goals and specific assignment of roles and responsibilities. This is complicated in technology partnerships, however, by a lack of clear understanding of what technology in schools can reasonably accomplish. When disagreements arise, it is helpful to be able to refer to some outside authority or expertise for direction. In the case of educational partnerships generally, such reference is usually made either to educational research or professional practice. But because widespread school adoption of educational technology is so recent, research provides few definitive guidelines to follow and practice is undeveloped. Moreover, conditions in each place vary widely. As a result, technology partnership participants often invented implementation processes as they went along. As one project director noted, "The whole first year there was quite a bit of anxiety about what technology would do for teachers. How do we use it?" Another stated, "This is an experiment. You have to be flexible and willing to change." Moreover, the principal scientist for a consulting service contracted to evaluate one project pointed out that the little knowledge that had developed about use of technology in schools was itself changing. "There's a shift going on. In the first generation we were using technology to do old goals better. This [project] is part of the shift to a second generation, to do completely new goals."

Without being able to refer to coherent theory or practice, the coordinators and directors most responsible for the daily oversight of projects often relied on what they knew about educational change generally. Although not prompted to mention particular theories, authors, or works, four managers made direct reference to organizational theories, including those of Fullan (e.g., Fullan and Steigelbauer 1991), Senge (1990a, 1990b), Osborne and Gaebler (1992), and Harvey (1988). Others showed their sources of knowledge by using the vocabulary of educational change or technical innovation. For example, two referred to themselves as "change agents," a concept extensively developed by Rogers and others studying the diffusion of innovations (Rogers and Shoemaker 1971).

One interesting outcome of this lack of clear principles is that the people involved in such technology partnerships used their projects to develop both theory and practice. They attempted to develop models and principles based on their experiences, often pointing with pride to papers they had written, conference presentations they had given, and further research grants they had obtained that focused on synthesizing and evaluating their experiences so they could be shared. Several participants stated that the best thing to come out of their partnership was more formal knowledge about the role technology could play in schools.

Training

When asked what they would change about their projects if given the chance, the largest set of technology partnership responses involved improving teacher training, suggesting that training was viewed as critical to the success of many of the projects, but can be hard to do effectively. Suggestions on training varied widely, including "begin with teachers beyond the basic learning level," "ask for one year to train," "use technology 'mentor' teachers for peer training," and "monitor the quality of inservice training."

It is interesting that only one of the general partnership syntheses mentioned teacher training at all (Grobe 1990). Apparently training is not seen as critical to the success of other kinds of educational partnerships. Yet much of the educational change literature suggests that change efforts often founder due to lack of teacher knowledge and support. It is possible that while teacher training is critical to any educational innovation, it is most obviously needed when teachers are faced with a machine they do not know how to operate. People may associate training with "hard" technologies such as machines more than they do with "soft" technologies such as innovative teaching methods. The principal scientist in an outside consulting agency had this provocative comment about this general effect of technology: "Technology precipitates, brings to a head, things that are otherwise covert." In these cases it made more obvious what is probably a need in other partnerships as well—adequate teacher training.

Group Process and Communication

The general partnership syntheses suggested monitoring progress frequently through ongoing evaluation and feedback, and regular contact among representatives and with the field. Technology participants strongly agreed. Moreover, they used their technical expertise and access to facilitate group communication through electronic mail, faxes, teleconferences, and desktop-published newsletters, brochures, and promotional materials. Their use of technology to improve communication ranged from the sophisticated (one partnership hosted a regional satellite conference), to the elemental (another made frequent use of bicycle messengers for daily communication in a huge urban area with gridlocked traffic). Communication is an area where technology partnerships appear to have the advantage over other kinds of educational partnerships, at least for now. However, this advantage did not extend as much to the school member participants, who often lacked the physical equipment or the infrastructure to take advantage of communications technology, such as dedicated outside telephone lines for telecommunications.

In talking about implementing their projects, technology participants referred to another problem not mentioned in the general partnership syntheses. Several directly mentioned an important point that was assumed, though not stated, in most responses—technical stability and reliability. In every project, technology was seen as the means to a particular end, an end that could not be accomplished if the critical technology needed was absent, broken, unreliable, or overly complex. Having dependable equipment is critical to these kinds of projects. In this sense, technology adds a layer of complexity to the already difficult process of managing a collaboration.

Technology respondents also made a group of suggestions about production of educational materials, including "get a production staff with educational experience," "use existing materials rather than try to develop your own," "leave plenty of time for production," "teach the government [DOE] to be flexible in production schedules," and, most interestingly, "be entrepreneurial . . . use the government seed money to form a partnership with a production house to develop educational materials and use the profits from the product to fund district technology needs and projects."

Educational curriculum and materials development is almost always one of the trickiest parts of any educational innovation, requiring knowledge, dedication, time, and resources. The comments about media production suggest, however, that expectations and routines developed for the production of traditional classroom materials based on speech, print, and group interaction may not apply well to the development of computer-based multimedia materials. These are more complex, requiring special technical skills, more time, more money, more institutional flexibility, and a high degree of collaboration among designers, technicians, and users.

Figure 2, page 102, summarizes these differences between technology partnerships and the general partnership syntheses. These differences are presented as largely arising either from the nature of the corporations involved with technology partnerships, or from the nature of the technology itself.

Figure 2. Unique features of technology partnerships.

Nature of the Corporations Involved
- lack of collaborative ethic and experience
- competition vs. cooperation
- entertainment vs. education
- instrumental relations
- schools as markets
- at one end of the cooperation/collaboration continuum
- short-term involvement

Nature of the Technology
- expensive, complex, and new
- insufficient support
- lack of applicable theory and practice
- need for teacher training
- change in materials development processes
- group focus on technical reliability
- facilitative
- improved group communication

SUMMARY

Overall, technology partnership participants share the joys and frustrations cited by members of other kinds of partnerships, and they give similar advice on making collaborations successful. When discussing which features of their partnerships helped them succeed and which proved problematic, their descriptions and classifications largely correspond to those presented by analysts who have tried to synthesize the collaborative process generally.

Both emphasize the need for top-level administrative involvement, the importance of brokering or linking skills in critical project leaders, development of personal qualities that support collaboration, and the need for sustained leadership. Both underscore the crucial nature of shared purpose and development of mutually beneficial goals that lead to clearly defined roles and responsibilities. Each group suggests there must be sufficient personal and institutional rewards for collaboration as well as adequate resources and support for a project, including allowing sufficient time for expected changes to occur. Each suggests careful monitoring of progress and paying attention to group processes and project outcomes, while allowing for local autonomy and flexibility in structure and procedures.

These commonalities suggest that the experience of interorganizational collaboration is similar regardless of the reasons organizations have for working together. This finding supports social theories of interorganizational behavior such as those of Intrilagator (1986).

At the same time, however, technology partnerships differ from other kinds of educational collaborations in some interesting ways. This exploratory study, though not definitive, suggests that these differences are related to the kinds of corporations involved in technology partnerships and the nature of the technology itself.

The inclusion of hardware and software vendors, multimedia production companies, and telecommunication service providers affects the nature of these partnerships because such firms often lack experience with outside collaboration and value competition rather than cooperation. Moreover, they are often involved with schools for immediate instrumental purposes, and their standard operating procedures discourage long-term involvement with outside organizations.

The nature of the technology itself may also affect these partnerships, largely because it is new, complex to use and integrate, and expensive. These characteristics can lead to inconsistent support, lack of firm theoretical and practical guidelines to follow in implementing a project, a pronounced emphasis on teacher training, and a group focus on technical reliability. However, technology also facilitated group processes by making communication between group members more frequent and rich, using a variety of modalities.

In view of the array of problems and challenges addressed, are such partnerships worthwhile? The participants in this study decisively said yes. It is clear that partnerships are a growing phenomenon, part of the ever-increasing overlap between schools and other major community institutions, particularly businesses and universities. People who involve themselves in partnerships generally enjoy their participation, and have high hopes that their collaboration will make education better, thereby profiting society generally.

These high hopes, however, can mean that partners do not anticipate many of the problems that managing a complex project can bring, the conflict that can result when organizations of disparate natures try to work together, and the time and energy it can take to work it all out successfully. In short, partnerships are not only hard work but hard work usually added to the already busy lives of many of the professionals involved. This is all the more true with technology partnerships, which often add a whole level of complexity to already complicated situations.

Yet the needs partnerships rose to fill are not likely to go away soon, and the trend in education, and perhaps society in general, is increasingly toward disparate groups of people finding ways to work together for their mutual benefit. One project coordinator summed it up well, pointing with excitement to her role as a "bridge" between the research, corporate, and education communities, a "link," which, even if temporary, greatly enriched the experience and understanding of everyone involved. This bridging role is still developing, and as such is fraught with peril for those involved, but it also brings the stimulation of challenge and possibility.

REFERENCES

Campbell, R. F., and Mazzoni, T. L. (1976). *State policymaking for the public schools.* Berkeley, CA: McCutcheon.

Chion-Kennedy, L. (1989). America's leaders speak out on business-education partnerships. In *Compact Institute/Business Leadership Forum* (Washington, DC: National Alliance of Business), 41.

Cuban, L. (1986). *Teachers and machines.* New York: Teachers College Press.

Danzberger, J. P. (1990). *Educational partnerships program: Analysis of project characteristics.* Commissioned Report, Office of Educational Research and Improvement (ED, Programs for the Improvement of Practice). Washington, DC: Institute for Educational Leadership. ERIC no. ED 325 534.

Easton, D. (1965). *A framework for political analysis.* Englewood Cliffs, NJ: Prentice-Hall.

Edelstein, F. S. (1989). *A blueprint for business on restructuring education.* A Corporate Action Package, National Alliance of Business, Inc.

Fassin, Y. (1991). Academic ethos versus business ethics. *International Journal of Technology Management 6*(5/6), 533-46.

Fullan, M. G., and Steigelbauer, S. (1991). *The new meaning of educational change.* New York: Teachers College Press.

Grobe, T., and others. (1990, December). *Synthesis of existing knowledge and practice in the field of educational partnerships.* Commissioned Report, Office for Educational Research and Improvement (ED), Educational Partnerships Study Group. Waltham, MA: Brandeis University, Center for Human Resources. ERIC no. ED 325 535.

Harvey, J. (1988). *The Abilene Paradox and other meditations on management.* Lexington, MA: Lexington Books.

Intrilagator, B. (1986, April). *Collaborating with the schools: A strategy for school improvement.* Paper presented at the 67th Annual Conference of the American Educational Research Association, San Francisco, CA.

Intrilagator, B. (1992, April). *Establishing interorganizational structures that facilitate successful school partnerships.* Paper presented at the Annual Meeting of the American Educational Research Association, San Francisco, CA.

Lasswell, H. (1936). *Politics: Who gets what, when, how.* New York: McGraw-Hill.

Lieberman, A., and Miller, L. (1990, June). Restructuring schools: What matters and what works. *Phi Delta Kappan 17*(10), 759-64.

Mann, D. (1987a, October). Business involvement and public school improvement, Part 1. *Phi Delta Kappan 68*(2), 123-28.

Mann, D. (1987b, November). Business involvement and public school improvement: Part 2. *Phi Delta Kappan 68*(3), 229-32.

McBrierty, V. J., and O'Neill, E. P. (1991). Preface. *International Journal of Technology Management 6*(5/6), 433-34.

Osborne, D., and Gaebler, T. (1992). *Reinventing government: How the entrepreneurial spirit is transforming the public sector.* New York: Addison-Wesley.

Pawley, R. (1992). *Multiorganizational collaborations: An illustration of Intrilagator's model for evaluating educational partnerships.* Master's thesis, University of Washington.

Phillips, D. I. (1991). New alliances: For policy and the conduct of research and education. *International Journal of Technology Management 6*(5/6), 478-87.

Rist, M. (1990, April). Angling for influence. *American School Board Journal 177*(4), 20-25.

Rogers, E., and Shoemaker, F. (1971). *Communication of innovations: A cross-cultural approach.* New York: Free Press.

Sarason, S. (1982). *The culture of the school and the problem of change.* Boston, MA: Allyn & Bacon.

Sarason, S. (1991). *The predictable failure of educational reform.* San Francisco: Jossey-Bass.

Senge, P. (1990a). *The fifth discipline.* New York: Doubleday.

Senge, P. (1990b). The leader's new work: Building learning organizations. *Sloan Management Review 32*(1), 7-32.

Sirotnik, K. (1991). Making school-university partnerships work. *Metropolitan Universities* 2(1), 15-24.

APPENDIX A

Partnership Syntheses

Cates, C. (1986, Spring). Interorganizational collaboration and school improvement. *Teacher Education Quarterly 13*(2), 84-101.

Grobe, T. (1990, December). *Synthesis of existing knowledge and practice in the field of educational partnerships.* Commissioned Report, Office for Educational Research and Improvement (ED), Educational Partnerships Study Group. Waltham, MA: Brandeis University, Center for Human Resources. ERIC no. ED 325 535.

Intrilagator, B. (1986, April). *Collaborating with the schools: A strategy for school improvement.* Paper presented at the 67th Annual Conference of the American Educational Research Association, San Francisco, CA.

King, A. (1986, February 28). *Synthesis of information relating to school and business partnerships.* Report prepared for the U.S. Department of Education, Office of Educational Research and Improvement. Washington, DC.

Phillips. D. (1991). New alliances: For policy and the conduct of research and education. *International Journal of Technology Management 6*(5/6), 478-87.

Sirotnik, K. (1991). Making school-university partnerships work. *Metropolitan Universities* 2(1), 15-24.

Networking in 1993

John Clement
Janice Abrahams*

INTRODUCTION

Date:	02 Mar 1993 11:57:40 -0005 (EST)
From:	"Office of the President" @white-house.gov
To:	KIDCAFE@vm1.nodak.edu
Subject:	Message from President Bill Clinton to KIDCAFE - send you all a thank-you note.

I wanted to thank you for paying attention to the work we're doing here in Washington to get our country moving again. I'm very impressed by your concern about our country's deficit—and your decision to try and help do something about it. And a bake sale is certainly the sweetest way I can think of to reduce the deficit.

It's very important that all Americans understand that we have to work together to make this country a better place for all of us. I'm very happy to see that all of you at Stewart Elementary School already understand that. Someday, when you are teachers, and doctors, and police officers - and some of you are here in Washington - you will be better leaders because you learned the value of cooperation and teamwork while you were growing up in Oxford, Ohio.

Keep working hard, keep working together, and keep working on new ideas.

President Bill Clinton

The year 1993 was one of impressive growth and evolution in networking for education. We begin by examining broader trends in national networking.

During 1993, the Internet and its connected networks once again approximately doubled in size, continuing an extraordinary growth trend.[1] President Clinton's White House established

---

* John Clement is a program officer in the Research, Evaluation, and Dissemination Division, Education and Human Resources Directorate, National Science Foundation. Janice Abrahams is a free-lance network architect and Internet explorer. The opinions expressed in this document are those of the authors and do not represent the views of the National Science Foundation or any other organization.

a connection to the Internet, built a mailing list to send out announcements, and set up an address for incoming electronic mail with a volunteer-run response system. Other federal agencies, hitherto relatively inactive on the net, established public presences.

There were significant developments in the area of network tools, most notably in the evolution of Gopher as a distributed information resource. The establishment of Gophers by many groups, and their interconnection, has provided the rich beginnings of an easily accessible, distributed database on the net.

The public policy arena was marked by increasing recognition of a national information infrastructure as an issue for political debate, with extended discussion focused on connectivity policies. A significant document on the shape of the national information infrastructure was produced (Executive Office of the President 1993).

In business, significant mergers and acquisitions marked an ongoing realignment of corporate strategies preparing to capitalize on the delivery of information, interactive communications, and entertainment.

At the local level, community networks continued to evolve as a resource for the evolution of communities of interest, grass-roots work, and politics: Municipal bulletin boards, Free Nets, and the growth of SeniorNet are three examples. Public commercial network access was provided by a host of new and established companies, from America Online and America Tomorrow through Holonet and Delphi. Internet electronic mail access was provided by nearly every service provider, and a number of providers offered access to a range of Internet capabilities at reasonable rates.

Perhaps most telling is that articles on networking and the Internet—and its use in education—appeared almost routinely in the popular and general scientific press. (Selected articles dating from the second half of the year are listed under "References and Additional Reading" at the end of the chapter.)

Against this background we analyze the year's trends in networking for education. The period is one of rapid growth in numbers of users and of continuing, accelerated adoption of networking as a resource for education. Network tools are under development, connectivity and applications testbeds are being established, and new collaborative projects are being carried out on them.

This is still, however, a period of experimentation and trial rather than one of broad-scale adoption. The educational applications being attempted are in most cases only adjuncts to the curriculum.

In postsecondary settings, trends are for gradually increasing use of networking to support education, in contrast with research, where networking is well established and near-essential in many disciplines. An underlying trend that leads to ongoing change is the pervasive invasion of campus networks into the college culture at many universities. We see collaborative courses being taught by faculty, often between campuses; we see professors offering network bulletin boards as course discussion areas, offering tutorial chat lines and e-mail addresses as the equivalent of "office hours"; assignment delivery via networks; and network-based projects and simulations used as course laboratory areas. The frequency of these applications, though increasing, is still small in relation to the total of campus opportunities.

USERS

The most notable trend, perhaps, is the growth in the number of K-12 users. In the fall of 1993, informal surveys yielded estimates of more than 175,000 user accounts.[2] These are numbers that represent a significant, if still small, fraction of the educators in the United States. Estimates published on the net suggested that more than 600,000 students were within reach of network resources at that time. Projections for the future are for continued rapid growth.

In undergraduate education, numbers are much harder to obtain. There is a clear need to understand how faculty and students are connecting on campuses and for what purposes. Because many colleges now require computers for entering students, and many campuses are extensively networked, the stage is set for widespread changes in access to shared distributed resources for education.

Perhaps the most interesting prospect for growth in K-12 education is the expansion in numbers of directly connected schools and even school districts. Table 1 lists connected school districts and better-established state education networks known as of the end of 1993. Although the state networks offer the largest concentration of resources and the greatest prospects for expanded connectivity, they face expansion problems in providing statewide services to entire educational communities. Growth will require distributing connectivity access and management to the district and school levels; those school districts attempting to grapple with connecting all their schools and classrooms are the current pioneering front for such issues as user training and support, network management, costs, and resource planning, access, and development.

TOOLS

The story of the year in tools is, unquestionably, the growth of Gopher. By November 1993, more than 1,000 Gophers worldwide had been declared, with the "Mother of Gophers" at the University of Minnesota. A survey of hosts on the Internet by the Veronica development group in late November 1993 showed nearly 4,900 unique Gopher servers, up from 528 surveyed by the same method in early December 1992 (Foster 1993). Growth appears to be accelerating: There were just under 4,000 servers in late September, so 922 Gopher servers were added in two months. Table 2, page 110, shows some of the main K-12 educational Gophers.

Table 1. Connection points for education. Some functioning state and regional education networks and schools or school districts with declared domain names on the Internet as of November 1993.

State and regional education networks providing individual dial-up access:
CORE, California Online Resource for Education (12,000 accounts)
FIRN, Florida Information Resource Network (10,000+ accounts)
GC-EDUNET, Georgia (6,000 accounts)
LANENET, Lane Educational Service District, Oregon (3,000 accounts)
NYCENET, New York City Education Network
SEND-IT, North Dakota (1,500 accounts)
TechNet, New Mexico (3,000 accounts)
TENET, Texas Education Network (25,000 accounts)
Virginia's PEN, Virginia's Public Education Network (12,000 accounts)
WEDNet, Washington State Educational Network (8,000 accounts)

Some school districts and schools with declared domain names on the Internet:
Alachua County, FL (acsb.edu)
Bloomfield Hills, MI (mhs87.bloomfield.k12.mi.us)
Boulder Valley School District, Boulder, CO (bvsd.k12.co.us)
Bronx HS of Science, Bronx, NY (bxscience.edu)
Brooklyn Technical HS, Brooklyn, NY (brooktech.edu)
Catlin Gable School, Portland, OR (catlin.edu)
Clearlake HS, Houston, TX (clhs.edu)
Cranston HS, Cranston, RI (crhs.edu)
Davis HS, Davis, CA (under ucdavis.edu)
East High School, Salt Lake City, UT (leopard.east-slc.edu)
East Syracuse Minoa HS, East Syracuse, NY (esm.edu)
Furinkan HS, Fuji Television, Japan (fugisankei.co.jp)
George Washington Carver HS, Philadelphia, PA (hses.edu)
Glenview School District, Glenview, IL (glenvw.ncook.k12.il.us)
Harvey L. Lewis Junior HS, San Diego, CA (lewis.edu)
Highland Park HS, Highland Park, NJ (hphs.edu)
Illinois Math and Science Academy, Aurora, IL (imsa.edu)
Lakeside School, Seattle, WA (lakeside.sea.wa.us)
Monte Vista HS, Cupertino, CA (mvhs.edu)
Montgomery Blair HS, Silver Spring, MD (mbhs.edu)
Park West HS, New York, NY (parkwest.edu)
Penfield HS, Penfield, NY (pcs.edu)
Pittsburgh Public Schools, Pittsburgh, PA (ckp.edu)
Princeton Regional Schools, Princeton, NJ (prs.edu)
Ralph Bunche Elementary School, PS 125M, New York, NY (rbs.edu)
StarkNet, The Stark County School District, Canton, OH (sparcc.ohio.gov)
Thomas Jefferson HS for Science and Technology, Alexandria, VA
    (tjhsst.vak12ed.edu)
Washington HS, Milwaukee, WI (whs.edu)
Woodside District, CA (woodside.k12.ca.us)

Table 2. Some notable education Gophers.

Academy One - education resource of National Public Telecomputing Network (NPTN).

Armadillo - the Texas Studies Gopher. Texas environmental, natural and cultural history and information.

AskERIC - Educational Resources Information Center, ERIC Clearinghouse on Information & Technology.

Bloomfield Hills School District Model High School

Boulder Valley School District - Boulder Valley School District received a grant to hook up some schools directly to the Internet. Both students and teachers (as well as some other people) use it.

Common Knowledge: Pittsburgh - This is the Pittsburgh Public Schools Gopher (PPS Gopher).

Consortium for School Networking (CoSN) East High School, Salt Lake City UT

Empire Internet Schoolhouse - NYSERNET

Iron County School District

k12net Gopher

KIDLINK: Global Networking For Youth 10-15

LaneNet: Lane County Educational Service District, OR

Newton Educational BBS

Poudre-R1 K12 School District (Ft. Collins, CO)

Princeton Regional Schools

StarkNet. The Stark County School District, Canton, Ohio, is a consortium of 12 local school districts, a career center, and affiliated city school districts in Stark County, Ohio.

TIESnet Internet Gopher

TogetherNet, Foundation For Global Unity

Education has its own Gopher success story in the evolution of the AskERIC resource. It started with a simple premise—48-hour guaranteed responses to educational questions, via e-mail, phone, or fax. In 1993, AskERIC responded individually to more than 6,000 distinct questions submitted in this manner.

Responding to the rapid evolution of Gopher technology, AskERIC set up a Gopher server housing a complex of issue digests and summaries, archives, and answers to the best questions educators had asked. In 1993, this resource fulfilled an additional 700,000 specific Gopher queries by users.

Although Gopher has its own interesting evolution and is the most visible case, other tools designed to make information on the network easier to locate and use are being developed and tried that have enormous potential. The World-Wide Web (WWW, or simply "the Web")[3] is beginning to be used to establish databases of "lesson units": multimedia documents combining text, graphics, maps, sounds, and video clips, based on distributed resources and seamlessly embedded inside one another. Such capacities could conceivably be used by a community of educators to build a knowledge base of information materials that would redefine entire curriculum areas. By November 1993, the first specialized Web browser for K-12 educators had appeared in the form of Explorer, which was developed by the UNITE group at the University of Kansas and the Great Lakes Collaborative.

WAIS (Wide Area Information Servers), uniquely offering full-text searching capabilities, has shown continued growth in use and in the number of sources; by the end of 1993, more than 280 different public WAIS textbases were accessible over the Internet, including approximately a dozen WAIS sources of special interest to K-12 educators.

Two developments make these tools especially promising for the future: the appearance of multiplatform implementations (for DOS-based, Windows, and Macintosh OS systems as well as the usual Unix and IBM mainframe systems), and the increasing interoperability of the tools. Today, WAISed databases are widely accessible through Gopher; Gopher and WAIS are both accessible by the Web; and so on.

The next generation of resource identifiers will promote easy access to information by using a standard convention to identify and access resources everywhere on the Internet, thus allowing all databases to be accessed by all toolsets. These universal resource locators (URLs) are a sign of emerging maturity of the Internet.

Another tool with promise is Collage, from the NCSA (National Center for Supercomputing Applications), which offers the possibility of interaction across distributed locations involving whiteboard-like "drawing tablets" as well as text editing and document exchanges. We cannot stop without mentioning Cornell's CU-SeeMe, a way of transmitting slow-scan video over the Internet that has been one of the engines of the Global Schoolhouse collaboration. Users who download the client software can observe classrooms at work and can allow others to observe them.

Two other tools of special application to education are the Guide from the California Technology Project and Alice from TERC (Technical Education Research Centers). The Guide, still in beta version and not widely distributed as this article went to press, offered the promise of a uniform graphical user interface to the core set of capabilities by now typical of state education networks: electronic mail, topic-specific conferences and newsgroups, up- and downloading of materials from the user's machine to the host, Gopher and fixed-location telnet (remote login) access to resources on the Internet. Alice represents an early instance of something different: software specifically designed to support network-based collaborations. Its capabilities include spreadsheets, text, and graphics file exchanges, and reporting structures such as maps for summarizing data. Although Alice servers are designed to reside on the Internet, unfortunately the client version distributed as of this writing does not yet allow access to the servers via anything other than direct modem dial-up. As elsewhere in the world of technology, the choices currently made in the design of these two software packages reflect the present state of thinking about user access and project management rather than the limits of technological capabilities.

RESOURCES

The ERIC Clearinghouse on Elementary and Early Childhood Education and the Center for Early Adolescence at the University of North Carolina (Chapel Hill) are pleased to announce a new list—MIDDLE-L.

This list is open to anyone who has an interest in any aspect of middle level education—classroom teachers, school library media specialists, administrators, parents—anyone.

Subscription requests should be sent to listserv@vmd.cso.uiuc.edu.

Leave the subject line blank. The first line of the message should read: subscribe middle-l YourFirstName YourLastName.

Once you've been notified that your subscription has been accepted, please send a brief note to the list to introduce yourself to other subscribers.

The list is brand new, so you may not find a lot going on—yet. But we have a lot to talk about: questions to ask, resources to announce, experiences (good and bad) to share, etc. So let's get started!

Dianne Rothenberg <rothenbe@ux1.cso.uiuc.edu> ERIC Clearinghouse on Elementary and Early Childhood Education

Jim Rosinia <jim_rosinia@unc.edu> Center for Early Adolescence

We've already mentioned AskERIC. As a resource, both the ERIC Digests and other materials are made available over AskERIC. Although the full ERIC bibliographic database is available for search over the Internet in at least two locations, AskERIC offers a much more user-friendly form of access to the knowledge gained from educational research and practice: not only in the form of personal responses to individual queries, but also by making available responses to good questions asked by other users. AskERIC can be viewed as an experiment in user-expert-database interaction that will benefit not only educators, but also users and information experts in many other disciplines and communities.

Other interesting resources are available and are becoming more widely accessible. Discussion groups of all sorts for education are found in mailing lists and newsgroups; some of the more interesting mailing lists are listed in Table 3.

An interesting resource for education is the WAIS archiving of education-related mailing lists. For example, the full index to the kidsphere mailing list is searchable via WAIS, and it is an invaluable resource to ongoing discussions in all aspects of education. We anticipate more archives being made available via WAIS.

Table 3. Some notable education mailing lists.

ALTLEARN—Alternative Approaches to Learning Discussion (listserv@sjuvm. bitnet)

CESNEWS—Coalition for Essential Schools list (listserv@brownvm.bitnet)

CHATBACK—Planning forum for Chatback UK & International education nets for disabled children (listserv@sjuvm.bitnet)

COSNDISC—Consortium for School Networking discussion group (cosndisc@cren.org)

EDPOLYAN—Education Policy Analysis (listserv@asuacad.bitnet)

EDTECH—A forum for the exchange of ideas and information on education technology (listserv@nic.umass.edu)

ICN—A list for guidance counselors (listserv@ctrvax.vanderbilt.edu)

K12ADMIN—A worldwide list for K-12 administrators, principals, superintendents, and others (listserv@suvm.syr.edu)

KIDS—The kids' part of Kidsnet (kids-request@vms.cis.pitt.edu)

KIDSNET—Global network for use by K-12 children and teachers (kidsnet-request@vms.cis.pitt.edu)

LM_NET—School library/media services (listserv@suvm.bitnet)

MIDDLE-L—For those interested specifically in middle schools (listserv@vmd.cso.uiuc.edu)

NEWEDU-L—Exploration of the way we educate, K through post-grad (listserv@uscvm.bitnet)

RPTCRD—Daily Report Card News Service: News on U.S. education projects that address the America 2000 education goals (listserv@gwuvm.bitnet)

TALKBACK—Kids' forum for CHATBACK, disabled children (listserv@sjuvm.bitnet)

VT-HSNET—VT K-12 School Network (listserv@vtvm1.bitnet)

WORLDGATE EDUCATION NEWSFEED—A forum to share K-12 project ideas and to look for co-participants (weas@cap.gwu.edu)

Storage of curriculum and testing materials is becoming widely accessible. Big Sky Telegraph has more than 600 lesson plans. KC ShareNet has nearly as many. Explorer, the new Web client mentioned earlier, has several hundred curriculum units in mathematics and the natural sciences.

Whole courses and programs of study are being offered over dial-in bulletin boards, although only a few are as yet accessible over the Internet.

ISSUES

The principal issue remains that of access. There has continued to be much discussion in policy circles and network mailing lists about costs and who will bear them. Far too many schools lack widespread access to telephone lines, and cable-based connections are still very rare.

Another issue is that of the level of access. Although terminal-based (that is, dial-up) resources can offer some aspects of full connectivity, full Gopher, Web, WAIS, and file transfer resources are not generally available. The full benefits of the client-server philosophy of design will become available only as more connectivity is made available. We anticipate the expansion of SLIP (serial line IP) and PPP (point-to-point) protocols, by which access to full Internet connectivity can be provided through telephone dial-up.

Other issues that affect the larger community will also hinder progress for networking in education. Perhaps the most serious of these, if we set aside the obvious issue of the need for a rational structure of costs and payments for service, is that of having to play an *in loco parentis* role to minors in reference to access to the full range of free speech that the Internet tolerates. Equally serious are issues of assuring intellectual property rights and of providing for security and privacy where needed. Discussion of these issues, all of great interest, goes well beyond the limited scope of this chapter.

Certain features of growth and evolution of networking will raise issues of their own; for instance, in the next years we look for growth in administrative applications and the gradual merger of instructional and administrative networks.

EVALUATION

Although there were two major international conferences on telecommunications in education during 1993 in the United States (ICTE '93 [International Conference on Technology in Education], in Austin, and Tel•Ed '93 [Symposium on Educational Telecommunications] in Dallas—both in Texas), and the major educational conferences (NECC [National Educational Computing Conference], AERA [American Educational Research Association], NSTA [National Science Teachers Association]) had abundant presentations on networking in education, 1993 still offered relatively slim pickings on process and outcome assessments of networking for education.

The most interesting ongoing work with implications for the future is on the development of frameworks for methodology and synthesis, as represented in articles by Collis, Levin, Riel and coworkers, and others (Collis and Levin 1993; Fowler 1993; Levin and Jacobson 1993; Riel and Fenwick 1993). These frameworks generally offer models and call for larger sample sizes and more comprehensive measurement. In a related vein, a survey paper by Harris (1993) proposes a typology of network-based activities based on examples obtained over the network.

Honey and Henriquez (1993) reported on a survey of 550 U.S. educators who are active users of telecommunications. Among the findings: There is little administrative support for telecommunications activities at school and district levels; most educators are self-taught, and little training is available; and combatting isolation, exchanging ideas with other educators, and obtaining information are basic motivating reasons for using networking as a professional development resource.

In postsecondary education, Manrique and Manrique (1993) report on the use of electronic mail and mailing lists to support college and university faculty teaching international studies courses. Feedback obtained from student end-of-course surveys showed that more constant users had a broad spectrum of uses, including student-faculty and student-student communications and information retrieval beyond class needs; many students request to have their accounts extended after the classes are finished. Schaeffer and Olson (1993a) report on preservice education programs in telecommunications at California postsecondary institutions.

Impact analyses on K-12 educators' professional development include assessments of TERC's Global LabNet project (Ruopp 1993; Gal and DiMauro 1993) and assessments of the use of networking to support collaborative projects by student teachers (McMullen 1993). Student outcome evaluation studies included examinations of impacts on elementary school reading and grammar (Erickson 1993) and second-language comprehension and use (Meagher 1993), as well as more general assessments of collaborative and other skills (Riel and Fenwick 1993; Warner 1993).

COMMUNITIES

> Teachers: We are a media specialist and a language arts teacher preparing to deliver a session on the Internet at a Distance Learning Conference at the University of Georgia in November. We would like to hear from users in grades K-12 about how the Internet has benefitted you and your students. We are also interested in testimonials from teachers as to how the Internet has connected you with colleagues. Tell us how you have shared with each other and learned from the experience. Your messages will be called up at the conference and shared with 600 participants, many of whom are superintendents, principals, teachers, and computer coordinators. This conference is being sponsored by the Georgia State Department of Education. We are especially interested in hearing from our GA colleagues.
>
> Sharon Vansickle, Media Specialist, Norcross High School
> <sharon@norcross.gatech.edu>
> Terrie Adkins, Language Arts Teacher, Norcross High School
> <adkins@norcross.gatech.edu>

The evolution of communities[4] is one sign of the maturation of a given form of human interaction. Network-based communication offers a technology through which communities can form independent of geographical location; the Internet as a unifying version of that technology offers the potential for the formation of very large communities.

The evolution of communities on the Internet can be seen most readily for research-oriented groups in postsecondary educational institutions and laboratories. Notable communities that share network-based communications links, tools, and data include various branches of physics, astronomy, specialized groups in biology (such as the community of researchers interested in the nematode *c. elegans*), and oceanography. The proliferation of mailing lists and newsgroups for nearly every discipline in the panoply of current scholarship and research suggests that many more such communities are in formation.

That there is a community of educators on the Internet is, by such a definition, unquestionable: look again at Table 3. But it is also unquestionable that such communities are relatively embryonic and undifferentiated by comparison to communities in research areas.

Some communities within educational networking are relatively isolated. PSI-NET conferencing servers connect a variety of educational groups: the state mathematics and science supervisors, curriculum specialists involved in the mathematics reform movement, a number of National Education Association projects known collectively as the School Renewal Network, and a number of schools and school systems following the reform principles of Ted Sizer. The PSI-NET servers have recently been linked through a mail gateway to the Internet. Until now, however, the same communications tool that linked them to one another has separated them from others who might have joined their efforts.

Widespread formation of communities of interest in education will follow upon the mutual identification and congregation of specialized groups. Although, as we have seen before, the number of users is large enough, users still largely lack means of finding one another and establishing shared agendas.

REFORM

The real target of networking is, as with the rest of educational technology, the continued development of educators and students: as learners, as teachers, as members of society. Networks will become truly integrated into the educational system only as they become a part of the processes of educational change and curriculum reform. In this connection, it is worthwhile to mention the efforts of the Task Force on Education Network Technology of the National Education Goals Panel, which is at the time of this writing preparing a policy paper for submission to the Goals Panel in early 1994. Tentatively titled "Achieving Educational Excellence by Increasing Access to Knowledge: Discussion Document," the draft is designed to articulate rationales, barriers, and planning guidelines for the use of networking in service to the national movement for education reform. The document has the potential, if accepted and widely disseminated in 1994, of being a key to the widespread adoption of networking at all levels of education.

> Does anyone have some suggestions of outstanding schools in computers and technology at the elementary level? Our school computer and technology committee would like to make some onsite visits to such schools. We are attempting to put together a long-range plan at our school and would like to visit some schools with cutting edge technology in the classroom. Thanks, Bill Wallace <ECHO@TRITON.UNM.EDU> Manzano Day School Albuquerque, NM

FUTURES

As mentioned earlier, immediate prospects for continued evolution are positive. The future of networking appears to include many more educators with access, more state networks, more sophisticated levels of Internet use, continued evolution of interfaces with full migration to Windows and Macintosh platforms, and better tools for storing, indexing, locating, and retrieving materials on the Internet.

The parts of the future of educational networking that seem more obscure are the same parts that appear problematic for educational restructuring and the reform of curriculum: the allocation of resources, people, and time to the school period, day, and year. It is not simply a matter of coming up with excellent projects. Network-using projects will make sense on a national scale, regardless of their technological underpinnings, only if projects are fitted clearly into the curriculum, if good performance is convincingly assessed, and if new styles of learning are worked into the mainstream of educational reform.

SUMMARY: THE STATE OF NETWORKING IN EDUCATION

Nineteen ninety-three has been a good year. There was much growth in resources and numbers of participants, and a good deal of attention was paid to significant issues. The technologies evolved strongly, and we are to the point of seeing truly useful technologies usable across the major hardware platforms that will be employed in schools and postsecondary institutions over the next few years.

We are not yet, however, to the point where the technology has reached so many of our educators that its universal adoption is inevitable. Nor have we reached the point where the impacts of networking are unquestioned.

Most fundamentally, we are not yet at the point where we understand how networking will fit into the schools of the future. In part, this is a failure of vision. One hopes that 1994 will see the articulation of a shared vision of the role that networking can play in the schools and colleges of our country.

NOTES

1. The Internet's "backbone" carried 18.7 billion packets in September 1992, and 36.6 billion packets in September 1993. There were 4,976 networks to the Internet in September 1992, and 16,696 in September 1993. There were 1.1 million "hosts" (connected computers) counted on the Internet in October 1992, and 2.1 million in October 1993 (the latest statistics available as of the time of preparation of this article). Source: InterNIC Gopher and statistics available at ftp.//misc.sri.com/pub/zone.

2. The first approximation to this estimate can be garnered from Table 1, where some of the larger state networks are listed along with the number of accounts registered to them in late 1993.

3. An especially elegant use of the Web is the retrieval and browsing tool Mosaic developed at the National Center for Supercomputing Applications, University of Illinois at Urbana-Champaign (NCSA-UIUC).

4. The term is used here in the sense of groups in which members recognize their fellowship with one another on the basis of shared mission, motives, and interests.

REFERENCES AND ADDITIONAL READING

Allman, William F., and others. (1993, December 6). Pioneering the electronic frontier. *U.S. News and World Report,* 57-62.

Burgess, John. (1993, October 5). Pupils log on and go global. *International Herald Tribune,* special report on international education, 9.

Collis, Betty, and Levin, Jim. (1993, November). *Research on telecommunications and learning: An international perspective.* Paper presented at the 2nd International Symposium on Educational Telecommunications (Tel•Ed '93), Dallas, TX.

Corcoran, Elizabeth. (1993, September 20). Why kids love computer nets. *Fortune,* 103-08.

Davies, G., and Samways, B., eds. (1993). *Teleteaching: Proceedings of the IFIP TC3 Third Teleteaching Conference, Trondeim, Norway, August 1993.* Amsterdam; New York: North-Holland.

Erickson, Barbara J. (1993, November). *Quality of fourth-grade students' compositions written after telecommunications treatment.* Paper presented at the 2nd International Symposium on Educational Telecommunications (Tel•Ed '93), Dallas, TX.

Executive Office of the President. (1993, September). *The National Information Infrastructure: Agenda for action.* Washington, DC: Author.

Foster, Steve. (1993, December 1). Personal communication.

Fowler, L. (1993). A theoretical framework for using email in grades 3-12. In *Rethinking the roles of technology in education.* Ed. N. Estes and M. Thomas. Proceedings of the International Conference on Technology in Education, Cambridge, MA, March 1993. Austin: University of Texas at Austin, College of Education.

The future of technology in education. (1993, November 15). *Business Week,* advertising supplement.

Gal, Shahaf. (1993). Teachers and teaching. *Journal of Research in Rural Education 9*(1), 38-43.

Gal, Shahaf, and DiMauro, Vanessa. (1993, November). *Inquiry into science teaching by a network-mediated science teachers community.* Paper presented at the 2nd International Symposium on Educational Telecommunications (Tel•Ed '93), Dallas, TX.

Glaberson, William. (1993, August 16). Creating electronic editions, newspapers try new roles. *New York Times,* D1, D6.

Harris, Judi. (1993, November). *Educational telecomputing project structures for pre-college online activity design.* Paper presented at the 2nd International Symposium on Educational Telecommunications (Tel•Ed '93), Dallas, TX.

Hezel, Richard. (1993). *Educational telecommunications: The state-by-state analysis.* Syracuse, NY: Hezel Associates.

Holden, Constance. (1993, August 20). Computer networks bring "real science" to the schools. *Science 261,* 980-81.

Honey, Margaret, and Henriquez, H. (1993). *Telecommunications and K-12 education: Findings from a national survey.* New York: Bank Street College of Education.

Levin, Jim, and Jacobson, M. J. (1993, May). *Educational electronic networks and hypertext: Constructing personal and shared knowledge spaces.* Paper presented at the annual meeting of the American Educational Research Association, Atlanta, GA.

Manrique, Cecilia G., and Manrique, Gabriel G. (1993, November). *Taking an electronic carpet ride: A whole new world via electronic mail.* Paper presented at the 2nd International Symposium on Educational Telecommunications (Tel•Ed '93), Dallas, TX.

McMullen, David W. (1993, November). *Project TIE: Student teachers and telecomputing.* Paper presented at the 2nd International Symposium on Educational Telecommunications (Tel•Ed '93), Dallas, TX.

Meagher, Mary E. (1993, November). *Multimedia in bilingual cultural exchange programs via computer networks.* Paper presented at the 2nd International Symposium on Educational Telecommunications (Tel•Ed '93), Dallas, TX.

Riel, Margaret, and Fenwick, Joan. (1993, November). *Telecommunications, educational reform and what work requires of schools.* Paper presented at the 2nd International Symposium on Educational Telecommunications (Tel•Ed '93), Dallas, TX.

Ruopp, R., Gal, S., Drayton, B., and Fisher, M., eds. (1993). *LabNet: Toward a community of practice.* Hillsdale, NJ: Lawrence Erlbaum.

Schaeffer, D. M., and Olson, Patrick C. (1993a, November). *Telecommunications in California teacher education programs.* Paper presented at the 2nd International Symposium on Educational Telecommunications (Tel•Ed '93), Dallas, TX.

Schaeffer, D. M., and Olson, Patrick C. (1993b). The Internet: An essential tool. In *Rethinking the roles of technology in education.* Ed. N. Estes and M. Thomas. Proceedings of the International Conference on Technology in Education, Cambridge, MA, March 1993. Austin: University of Texas at Austin, College of Education.

Schwartz, John. (1993, November 28). Caution: Children at play on information highway. *Washington Post,* A1, A26.

Task Force on Education Network Technology, National Education Goals Panel. (1993, July). *Achieving educational excellence by increasing access to knowledge: Discussion document.* Unpublished draft manuscript. Washington, DC: Author.

U.S. Congress, Office of Technology Assessment. (1993, November). *Making government work: Electronic delivery of federal services.* Washington, DC, report draft available via ftp and Gopher.

U.S. Department of Education. (1993, September). *Using technology to support education reform.* Report prepared for the Office of Research, Office of Educational Research and Improvement. Washington, DC: U.S. Government Printing Office.

Van den Brande, L. (1993). R&D on learning telematics in the European Community. *Journal of Computer Assisted Learning 9,* 75-85.

Warner, Virginia R. (1993, November). *DESERTS: Effects upon man/man's effect on deserts.* Paper presented at the 2nd International Symposium on Educational Telecommunications (Tel•Ed '93), Dallas, TX.

The Eisenhower National Clearinghouse
for Mathematics and Science Education
Working Toward Education Goal 4

Len Simutis
*Director, Eisenhower National Clearinghouse
for Mathematics and Science Education*

In the October 12, 1993, issue, *Education Daily* reported on a poll on the National Education Goals that was conducted by Phi Delta Kappa. This poll found that 88 percent of the public sees world leadership in math and science as a high or very high priority for U.S. education. The goals were developed in 1989 at the Education Summit by the President and the nation's governors, and the federal government has since begun several initiatives to achieve them. The *Excellence in Mathematics, Science, and Engineering Education Act of 1990* provides funds for the Eisenhower National Clearinghouse for Mathematics and Science Education (ENC) and for the Eisenhower Regional Consortia. These programs are to work together to help meet Goal 4, "By the Year 2000, U.S. students will be first in the world in science and mathematics achievement."

ENC is part of the Eisenhower National Program for Mathematics and Science Education in the Office of Educational Research and Improvement (OERI), U.S. Department of Education. The five-year contract for ENC was awarded to the Ohio State University in September 1992. After one year, ENC has made major strides toward the creation of a catalog and database to assist K-12 mathematics and science teachers.

ENC'S MISSION

ENC has defined its mission as:

Encouraging the adoption and use of K-12 curriculum materials and programs which support national goals to improve teaching and learning in mathematics and science by providing better access to resources for all who are interested in creating an effective learning environment.

The Clearinghouse will accomplish this by creating and maintaining a comprehensive, multimedia collection of materials and programs which will be distributed in a timely manner through a national system using both traditional formats and advanced computing and telecommunications technologies.

To accomplish this mission, ENC will provide the following products to teachers, students, and other education professionals:

- A catalog of mathematics and science curriculum materials from federal agencies and other sources available online (via Internet and a toll-free number) in 1994 and on CD-ROM in 1995

- A database including the catalog, evaluations of materials included in the catalog, and information about federal programs serving mathematics and science education that will be accessible online in 1994

- An infrastructure through which users can access information from the Eisenhower Clearinghouse and other databases linked through a federated national database system in 1995

- A permanent repository located in Columbus, Ohio, and a mini-repository located at George Washington University in Washington, DC, for practitioners and others to examine the materials collected by the Clearinghouse in 1994

- Twelve demonstration sites located at the Regional Consortia and repositories in 1994

- An online network through which teachers can communicate with the Clearinghouse and other teachers, and through which they can contribute materials and evaluations of materials to the database in 1994

- Publications about Clearinghouse products and services, print mini-catalogs on topics of importance to teachers, and booklets describing math and science education reform efforts in 1994.

MEETING TEACHER NEEDS

The primary component of the ENC program is the catalog. In 1993, ENC initiated a process to get input from teachers on the structure and content of the catalog, as well as ENC's other planned products and services. Several focus groups were held across the nation to give groups of full-time teachers an opportunity to provide ENC with answers to several questions:

- How do teachers describe curriculum materials?

- How would teachers like print mini-catalogs of Clearinghouse materials to be organized, and what should the topics be?

- How should information about training opportunities, workshops, student support, and other federal programs be organized and cataloged?

- What do teachers expect the Clearinghouse to do for them?

Teachers in the focus groups told ENC that:

- The ENC electronic system must be convenient and easy to use, must allow teachers to construct the kinds of searches that meet their needs, and must be available whenever needed.

- There must be a variety of teaching and learning resources in the Clearinghouse catalog that teachers can use to enhance their curricula, including printed material and nonprint materials such as videotapes, software, optical disks, and interactive resources. Data files that support teaching activities should also be part of the ENC catalog.

The ENC catalog will include all of the kinds of resources that teachers identified as important, and it will be easy to access and use. Planning and initiating the process to make this happen have been the focus of much of ENC's first-year effort.

THE ENC DATABASE AND CATALOG SYSTEM

ENC is building its system using the client/server model. *Clients* are software programs that enable users to search, retrieve, and display information. *Servers* are the computers that house and maintain the data or databases that clients connect with. The client software may reside on a teacher's personal computer, but the server can be next door or many thousands of miles away.

This "distributed" model allows users easy access to a multitude of data sources, because a client can be programmed to interact with a variety of servers in different locations. ENC will develop and distribute client software that can run in Macintosh and PC-Windows environments and will also maintain a terminal-based client at the Clearinghouse computer center to support telephone/modem users.

In practical terms, this means that ENC can provide connections to its own catalog as well as to a number of other databases that contain useful information for teachers. These databases may reside on servers located in various places. The searcher will not need to learn different routines or methods for accessing these disparate resources. Teachers will be able to browse many sources of curriculum information from one vantage point.

Users will connect to and search the Clearinghouse system in a variety of ways. Those who have access to a computer with a modem will be able to dial a free 800 number to connect to the Clearinghouse host computer. Others who have access to the Internet may establish a telnet connection via this network. Commercial services such as Prodigy and America Online are creating Internet "gateways" for their subscribers. Some schools and districts have established network connections for teacher and student use. Because data can be transported much more quickly over networks than telephone lines at this point, the Clearinghouse is encouraging all who have access to Internet services to use this method.

At this time, ENC is planning to support access to several other databases that contain information about curriculum materials, as well as some sources that describe programs and professional development opportunities for teachers and students. As Clearinghouse staff become aware of teacher needs and preferences, they will negotiate agreements to expand the menu of offerings.

Other teachers are often the best source of new ideas. The Clearinghouse will tap this resource by providing online discussion forums. Users will also be able to connect to Clearinghouse reference staff via network or telephone if they need personal assistance, or they can connect to other teachers with common interests through a bulletin board. Those who wish to contribute materials to be considered for inclusion in the ENC collection will be able to send them electronically or by mail. Users who want to comment on the usefulness of particular materials will be able to submit those comments over the network.

ENC is committed to building a catalog that offers not only full descriptions of useful curriculum resources, but also, whenever possible, other information needed to guide informed decision making by teachers. The catalog will include links to page images showing the detailed table of contents or portions of chapters from some printed materials, photographic images of manipulative materials, equipment, and other real objects, and clips or sample portions of audiovisual and software materials.

When authors and developers permit, or when items are in the public domain, the Clearinghouse will provide access to full texts of materials in a textbase. Although this database will grow more slowly than the catalog, users will be able to download or print copies of useful materials and transfer files from software archives.

Finally, the Clearinghouse will locate and attach to descriptive catalog records a variety of quality indicators. These may include citations to or excerpts from published reviews of materials, notations of awards received, information from research articles that studied or evaluated specific materials, information provided by developers and others on field testing, and comments received from users of materials. This evaluative information will serve two important purposes: to help teachers in selecting materials, and to help developers of curriculum resources to study and improve upon existing materials.

What if a teacher does not have the necessary equipment and expertise to access the online catalog? Some ENC products will be available in print and some in other formats, such as CD-ROM. Several print mini-catalogs will be produced each year on topics of particular interest. In addition, in 1994 publications about the catalog, ENC products and services, and reform efforts in math and science will be available. Beginning in 1995, the electronic catalog will be reproduced on CD-ROM, and the full text of some exemplary materials will be available on CD-ROM by 1996.

THE ENC COLLECTION

The materials that ENC collects will come from a variety of sources, but the primary source is federal government agencies. ENC is mandated to collect federally produced K-12 math and science curriculum materials and to collect information on federal programs available to K-12 teachers. Aspen Systems, an ENC subcontractor, has worked closely with the Federal Coordinating Committee for Science, Engineering, and Technology (FCCSET) to produce a publication and an electronic database listing federal programs. Other sources of material for the ENC catalog include publishers, professional organizations, nonprofit organizations, state and local government agencies, science and technology museums and other informal educational organizations, teachers, the Eisenhower Regional Consortia, and existing databases, clearinghouses, and networks.

The most important existing collection of mathematics and science education materials, the ERIC Clearinghouse for Science, Mathematics, and Environmental Education (ERIC/CSMEE), is located in the same building with ENC. The ERIC and ENC staff members are developing clearly defined criteria for the two collections. The major difference between them is that ERIC collects primarily print materials, and ENC will collect materials of all types, including print, video, audio, software, images, and kits. The ERIC collection covers a broader range than the ENC materials will cover, including research, articles in periodicals, and curriculum materials for kindergarten through university graduate and adult education programs. ERIC users include policymakers, researchers, and teacher educators, whereas ENC's primary users will be K-12 teachers.

In general, K-12 instructional materials submitted to ERIC will be transferred to ENC. That transfer process will require carrying them across the hall, a great advantage in having the centers located in the same building. The most likely overlap in the collections will be materials that are defined as "of broad interest." Materials in this category might include curriculum frameworks and standards documents that would be of interest to both ERIC and ENC users. There are plans to make the ERIC database accessible through ENC, but some materials may be cataloged in both systems.

REPOSITORIES AND DEMONSTRATION SITES

As ENC collects information, all of it will be stored in the permanent repository in the ENC offices in Columbus, Ohio. The materials in the permanent repository will be available to teachers and other education professionals for their use at the site. In addition to Columbus, a mini-repository will be located at George Washington University in Washington, DC. The mini-repository will house copies of selected materials from the collection.

The permanent repository and the mini-repository will also house 2 of the 12 ENC demonstration sites. The remaining 10 demonstration sites will be located around the nation at sites designated by the Eisenhower Regional Consortia. Each demonstration site will include the hardware and software necessary to access the ENC catalog and databases and be staffed by a person familiar with its operation. The demonstration sites will also have copies of math and science education CD-ROMs and software for people who visit them to test and to learn to use.

COLLABORATION

Not only the ERIC/CSMEE office is located in the same building as ENC, but so is the National Center for Science Teaching and Learning (NCSTL). All three programs are funded by the U.S. Department of Education, and they have a unique opportunity for collaboration and cooperation in mathematics and science education as they draw upon each other's expertise. In addition, the National Science Foundation-funded State Systemic Initiative program for Ohio is located at the Ohio State University.

In addition to working with the programs located at the Ohio State University, ENC is cooperating with the Eisenhower Regional Consortia in several ways. The Consortia are closely associated with the Regional Education Labs and are charged with collecting and disseminating information and materials to improve mathematics and science education. ENC is providing technical support and consulting with Consortia personnel to assure that data-bases that they develop are compatible with the ENC catalog and database.

ENC and the Consortia are cooperating on the choice of a location and the staffing of 10 of the ENC demonstration sites, as described earlier. They have also worked together to conduct regional teacher focus groups to assess teacher reaction to ENC and Consortia programs and plans. A regional version of the ENC publication that lists the federal math and science education programs has been compiled and will be distributed through the Consortia.

As ENC and the Consortia work toward the achievement of National Education Goal 4, they are tapping the many people and resources that exist throughout the nation for assistance and advice. A major component of ENC's program is collaboration and consultation with education practitioners at many levels. ENC has a 30-member National Steering Committee representing all facets of education and diverse geographic and cultural backgrounds. It also has conducted an annual workshop to acquaint representatives of federal and state agencies, other databases and clearinghouses, professional organizations, and others about its plans and progress. Also, three advisory groups have been organized that will assist ENC with publications, CD-ROM production, and standards for submission.

SUPPORT FOR SYSTEMIC REFORM

Although lack of electronic access for some teachers is a problem now, it should diminish as schools become part of the information age. With few K-12 electronic databases available in the past, schools had no reason to put a computer and network access in every classroom. As projects such as ENC grow, schools will have many reasons to better equip classrooms to take advantage of these resources. The interchange that takes place between ENC users may center around materials, but it will eventually create a change in school practices and in how teachers prepare for their work.

As ENC provides an incentive to schools to change by making information and classroom materials more readily available, it supports the school reform movement. Undoubtedly, the most important way is the creation of a comprehensive collection of K-12 mathematics and science education reform materials. The references to these materials and some of the materials themselves will be available to anyone with access to the ENC catalog and database, and will be included in print materials distributed by ENC. The Clearinghouse is collecting in one place the standards documents, the curriculum frameworks, the assessment strategies, and, most importantly, the materials that support these changes. The teacher thus has the opportunity to access all of them in a "one-stop shopping" environment.

An important way in which ENC supports systemic reform is by promoting the use of technology. ENC will produce some print materials, but the thrust of the project is to encourage use of computer technology in the classroom. If the idea behind systemic reform is to create schools that have the capacity to prepare students for living and working in the next century, they must be familiar with and use computers and networks. A further advantage of using computer technology is that it also makes the classroom a more exciting place for both students and teachers. Anything that encourages learning and promotes a better learning environment supports the spirit of systemic reform and moves the United States closer to meeting its national educational goals.

For further information about the Eisenhower National Clearinghouse for Mathematics and Science Education, please contact Dr. Len Simutis, Director, Eisenhower National Clearinghouse, The Ohio State University, 1929 Kenny Road, Columbus, OH 43210-1079. (614) 292-7784; fax (614) 292-2066; Internet lsimutis@enc.org.

The National Center to Improve Practice
Promoting the Use of Technology in Special Education

Judith Zorfass
Arlene Remz
Patricia Corley
National Center to Improve Practice, Education Development Center

INTRODUCTION

The National Center to Improve Practice (NCIP) is a collaborative project between the Education Development Center, Inc. (EDC) and WGBH Educational Foundation (Boston's Public Television Station). NCIP's mission is to promote change within local schools and districts so that practitioners will effectively use technology, media, and materials (TMM) to improve outcomes for students with disabilities. NCIP is funded by the Department of Education, Office of Special Education Programs (OSEP) for five years, from 1992 to1997.

This article has been written for three purposes:

1. to alert school districts, administrators, teachers, and related services practitioners of the existence of NCIP;

2. to inform them about how the center intends to carry out its mission; and

3. to elicit interest in joining NCIP's efforts.

Now in its second year, NCIP's evolving approach is grounded in the belief that change at the local level is facilitated by change agents who are able to provide stakeholders (administrators, practitioners, parents) with the knowledge, resources, and training they need to embrace and implement innovative uses of TMM. NCIP has developed a "Dynamic Approach to Change" to support these district- or school-level change agents. Although the formal title of the change agent may vary from setting to setting (for example, technology specialist, special education administrator, inclusion specialist, master teacher), the change agent is a key individual in a leadership role who seeks and accepts responsibility for bringing about change in the integration of technology for students with disabilities.

NCIP'S DYNAMIC APPROACH TO CHANGE

NCIP's approach is dynamic in the following ways:

*   It integrates varied components that utilize different media—print, video, telecommunications network, videoconferences—capitalizing on the strengths of each, and building on the interrelationship of the complementary components.

*   It provides technical assistance to change agents so that they can effectively address the needs of teachers, administrators, parents, and students.

- It encourages communication and sharing among people with different sources of knowledge and multiple perspectives, creating a community of learners.

- It incorporates an ever-expanding knowledge base. As change agents try out new strategies, their discussion of issues and their action research findings become part of the growing knowledge base.

Integrates Varied Components

Figure 1 presents the main components of the Dynamic Approach to Change. These include

- Practice Packages

- NCIP InfoNet (telecommunications network)

- Videoconferences.

Figure 1. NCIP components of dynamic approach to change.

Practice Packages. The goal of the Practice Packages is to provide teachers, administrators, and parents with accessible print and video materials that offer a vision of the possible. The Practice Packages will be issued three times within an academic year—September, November, and March—and will be organized around curricular themes such as high- and low-technology tools to support process writing. Decisions about the themes will be driven by NCIP's review of compelling findings drawn from research literature and craft knowledge, as well as recommendations from researchers and practitioners involved in NCIPnet discussions. The Practice Packages will include print materials and an accompanying videotape.

The print component will be modular, containing a series of related newsletters featuring fellow practitioners who are successfully using TMM with students with varying disabilities. NCIP will be sure to include a broad range of TMM applications, including effective low-tech materials that may be most readily accessible to practitioners in the classroom. Change agents can judiciously distribute the various newsletters to teachers, administrators, and parents, providing them access to the information that is most relevant to their work or concerns. These brief vignettes will motivate stakeholders to learn more about particular innovations from the companion materials described later. The vignettes will go beyond descriptions of TMM itself, highlighting contextual factors such as information about instructional practices involving TMM, specific strategies or "hot tips" for effective implementation, organizational supports, parent involvement, and student outcomes.

The accompanying video will provide visual images of these vignettes, as well as other related vignettes of effective practice in different contexts. The video will have a host change agent who introduces each vignette, makes explicit what the video is trying to convey, and asks follow-up questions to encourage active reflection. The video will include detailed demonstrations of relevant TMM when appropriate.

A set of guidelines included with the video will provide a table of contents so viewers can find relevant sections, as well as suggestions for how change agents can use the video (for example, in staff development programs or parent meetings). Each Practice Package will include a list of additional print and video resources that can be ordered from NCIP.

NCIP InfoNet. NCIP InfoNet will be an expanded version of NCIPnet, the telecommunications network currently being used by NCIP. NCIP InfoNet will house a variety of supporting resources that change agents can use to help stakeholders implement the practices highlighted in the Practice Packages. As information brokers, change agents will disseminate resources and materials from the network among stakeholders as appropriate and provide structure and guidance, enabling stakeholders to participate in relevant network discussions.

NCIP InfoNet will contain a vast electronic resource library as well as a series of bulletin boards for knowledge sharing through network conversations. Linked to the instructional practices chronicled in the Practice Packages, both components will provide the breadth and depth of information necessary to promote change. The resource library will provide users with a variety of databased tools (for example, brief research syntheses, hardware and software reviews, software demonstrations, related reference materials) that can be appropriated for training and support. The bulletin boards will offer practitioners and administrators an opportunity to converse with their colleagues featured in the newsletters as well as others in the field who are experimenting with a particular innovation. The craft knowledge that grows out of these discussions will be synthesized and become an integral part of the resource library. For example, a number of practitioners might interactively discuss and review a particular software program from various perspectives. All information formats housed in NCIP InfoNet will be easy to access, understand, and use.

Additionally, an NCIP staff person will be available to guide willing change agents in carrying out action research about the change process itself. This support will enable change agents to reflect on their practice in a more rigorous manner. The results of these action research studies will be synthesized and integrated into the dynamic knowledge base in the resource library.

Videoconferences. NCIP will design and produce videoconferences to further involve and support stakeholders in the change process. The videoconferences will present case studies of schools and districts that are implementing changes. These case studies will highlight the challenges and successes encountered, and illustrate ways in which innovations are being implemented to meet the specific needs of students. The conferences will include video roll-ins to illustrate desired practices and their impact on students. Local participation in these conferences will be facilitated by the change agent, who will receive a set of accompanying materials and guidelines from NCIP. These materials will be designed to maximize interactive engagement among the practitioners, administrators, and parents attending the conference.

Although each of these individual components can stand alone, they derive their power from being meaningfully linked to one another. For example, as practitioners become excited about practices that are introduced in the Practice Packages, they can access more information about specific topics in NCIP InfoNet. Going even further, they can communicate with others about this topic on the network. Then, "primed" for a videoconference on the topic, they become active participants who seek solutions to authentic challenges.

Provides Technical Assistance

NCIP's approach builds in technical assistance to local change agents—those with a background in special education and/or technology who take responsibility for motivating and supporting change. Although the formal title of the change agent may vary from setting to setting, their ability to successfully facilitate the change process rests on the breadth and depth of their knowledge, not only about TMM and special education but also about promoting change. NCIP will provide designated change agents with the following.

Guidelines. NCIP will provide change agents with guidelines to accompany the Practice Packages and the videoconferences. These guidelines will include specific strategies for involving various stakeholders in the change process. For example, the Practice Packages might include a set of guidelines on conducting inservice programs for teachers, discussion or study groups for administrators, or parents' nights around the themes highlighted in the Practice Packages. The guidelines that will be sent prior to videoconferences will give change agents the assistance they need to prepare the audience before the broadcast, engage in activities during the conference, and carry out follow-up tasks. Guidelines will be available in both hard-copy and online formats.

Network Support for the Change Process. Change agents can seek guidance and feedback from NCIP staff via NCIP InfoNet as they implement the approach. In this way, willing change agents will be supported in undertaking action research as they reflect on their own methods and strategies for promoting change. NCIP staff will connect practitioners with researchers from the Literacy Forum and other OSEP-funded literacy projects who are doing significant work in areas of interest or concern. Change agents can also seek assistance from other colleagues in the field who share similar issues, via the bulletin boards on the network.

Conference Workshops. NCIP will organize sessions at annual key regional and national conferences (for example, the Council for Exceptional Children [CEC] and its Technology and Media Division [CEC-TAM], the Association for Supervision and Curriculum Development [ASCD], Closing the Gap, and the National Educational Computing Conference [NECC]). The purpose of these special sessions is to bring together change agents who are in the process of implementing NCIP's Dynamic Approach to Change. During the sessions, persons who have been communicating with one another online will have a chance to meet face-to-face. Topics for presentations and discussions will be driven by the issues discussed on NCIP InfoNet. NCIP will provide facilitators to moderate discussion, as well as speakers who have pertinent information to share. In addition, there will be demonstrations of TMM by change agents, invited speakers, and NCIP staff.

Training Institutes. NCIP will conduct training institutes for change agents, introducing them to NCIP's Dynamic Approach to Change. These institutes will provide change agents with the fundamental skills and strategies they need at the outset to implement NCIP's approach in their local settings.

Encourages Communication and Sharing

NCIP's Dynamic Approach to Change builds in numerous opportunities for communication and knowledge sharing among change agents, practitioners, administrators, and parents within their local settings. At the same time, all participants will have the opportunity to build knowledge and solve problems collaboratively through network discussions among colleagues throughout the country.

Another important linkage will be between practitioners and researchers. As members of the Literacy Forum, researchers around the country have become NCIP collaborators. NCIP staff monitoring NCIP InfoNet will serve as matchmakers, putting researchers and practitioners who have shared areas of interest or concern in touch with one another.

Expands Knowledge Base

The major goal of NCIP's Dynamic Approach to Change is to encourage the translation of ideas and knowledge into practice. NCIP will encourage change agents to carry out action research that focuses on the change process. Action research involves identifying a problem area, gathering data, reflecting on the data, making adjustments grounded in evidence rather than hunches, and assessing the results and revising the questions to study. With the support of an experienced action research facilitator, as well as researchers who are part of our Literacy Forum, change agents will be guided and supported in carrying out action research studies. The results of their studies will be fed back into the expanding knowledge base housed in NCIP InfoNet.

Joining NCIP's Efforts

If you are a change agent who plays a key role in causing change in your school or district in the use of technology for students with disabilities, NCIP wants to hear from you. Even during the development phase of our work this year, there are ways you can become an ongoing collaborator. NCIP has established a user-friendly telecommunications network (NCIPnet) that will evolve into NCIP InfoNet in the years to come. Within NCIPnet, there is a forum called "Views from the Field" (Figure 2). This forum invites change agents to share what they are doing, discuss issues surrounding the uses and implementation of TMM with students with disabilities, ask questions, and share their expertise with others.

If you are interested in participating in the Views from the Field forum, please contact NCIP at (617) 969-4529 (voice and TTY). We will send you the software and manual without cost. The dial-in number for the network is an 800 number. This national project will fulfill its potential only by reaching out to and connecting with change agents in the field.

Figure 2. Joining NCIPnet.

WHAT IS NCIPnet?

NCIPnet is the telecommunications network of the National Center to Improve Practice (NCIP). This electronic mail and bulletin board system is designed for information sharing and efficient communication among practitioners, administrators, researchers, and policymakers who are separated by distance. The purpose of NCIPnet is to help this community share information and ideas about the use of technology, media, and materials (TMM) to improve outcomes for students with disabilities.

WHAT IS VIEWS FROM THE FIELD?

Views from the Field is a forum—a discussion area—within NCIPnet. This forum offers an opportunity for change agents (i.e., people who are promoting the effective use of TMM in their schools or districts) to: discuss how TMM is being used in their schools; join in conversations about effective practice; share information about factors that promote or hinder successful implementation of TMM; ask questions and get advice and recommendations from colleagues in the field; and offer their advice and experience to others. This forum will also provide an opportunity to converse with NCIP staff, as well as researchers, policymakers, and other leaders in the field who participate on NCIPnet.

WHO SHOULD PARTICIPATE IN VIEWS FROM THE FIELD?

The primary participants in the Views from the Field forum are change agents—key individuals who seek and accept responsibility for bringing about change in the integration of technology for students with disabilities. The formal title of the change agent may vary from setting to setting—technology specialist, special education administrator, inclusion specialist, master teacher. In many cases, the change agent has no formal position or title, nevertheless, he or she is a key player in promoting change in the school or district.

HOW DO YOU JOIN NCIPnet?

If you are interested in actively contributing to Views from the Field, all you need is a computer and a modem. We will send you the appropriate software, manual, and a letter explaining how to get started. There will be no cost for you to participate in the network using our toll free dial-in number. For more information call Denise Ethier at NCIP, at 800-225-4276 x 2422 or 617-969-4529 (voice and TTY).

Changing Directions in Higher Education Media and Technology Programs
An Interview with Robert M. Diamond

Donald P. Ely
Professor, Instructional Design, Development and Evaluation
Syracuse University

Many centers for instructional development or faculty development were established at colleges and universities in the late 1960s and early 1970s. Their basic mission was to facilitate the improvement of teaching and learning within the institution. Many focused on the applications of media and technology as primary delivery systems.

One of the pioneers in this movement was Dr. Robert M. Diamond. He began instructional improvement programs at the University of Miami and the State University of New York at Fredonia before he was named Vice Chancellor for Instructional Development at Syracuse University in 1971. He has observed and participated in the movement and offers a 25-year perspective of these programs in the interview that follows.

The Center for Instructional Development at Syracuse University was established to support the University faculty in the improvement of academic courses and programs. Since its inception, more than 100 projects have been undertaken with departments from all parts of the campus. Most of these projects involve the redesign and evaluation of new and existing courses and curricula. The Center has expanded its mission to support programs and services such as the orientation program, the teaching assistant program, an advancement placement program, and evaluation of teaching. Recent efforts are concerned with promotion and tenure procedures and evaluation of teaching. Recent efforts are concerned with promotion and tenure procedures and faculty reward systems. However, with these expanded efforts, the Center has never lost its focus on the improvement of teaching and learning.

One of the hallmarks of CID's program is an instructional development model developed and modified by Bob Diamond. He refers to it in the following interview. It is included here as Figure 1.

The Editor sat down with Bob Diamond to discuss the evolution of instructional development programs in higher education in general and the Syracuse Program in particular. An edited version of that interview begins on page 134.

Figure 1. Process for educational program development. Robert M. Diamond, Center for Instructional Development, Syracuse University. From Robert M. Diamond. (1993). *A systematic approach to course and curriculum design.* San Francisco: Jossey-Bass. Copyright © Robert M. Diamond. Reprinted with permission.

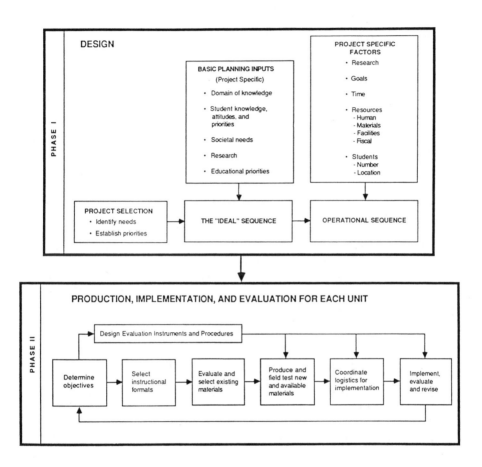

Don: Bob, when did you enter the field?

Bob: It was an evolution rather than directly entering. In the mid-1950s, I was one of the very early television teachers in the public schools and moved from that into heading up one of the closed-circuit operations in a school district on Long Island. At that time I started doing graduate work at New York University with Irene Cypher in the media program there. I had a master's degree in another program at NYU that was completed before I entered.

Don: What was the program called at NYU when you went through it?

Bob: Educational Communications.

Don: And what was the scope of the field at that time?

Bob: The field then was pretty much hardware-oriented; using technology to improve education. That was the focus at NYU and at the national level.

Don: You have spent most of your career in higher education. What have been your major responsibilities in the positions you have held over the years?

Bob: The first position in higher education was in television at San Jose State University where I was an associate professor working part-time for Dick Lewis as television coordinator. I went to San Jose to find ways that we could use television to improve the quality of the academic program there. I think it was a unique opportunity because of the people we were working with at the time: Bob Mager, Jerry Kemp, Jim Brown, and a number of other people who were national leaders in the field. Most important, Dick had a broader vision than the state-of-the-art at that time, focusing on technology as one part of a total system of education. He gave me a unique opportunity to explore and develop. My primary focus was television, but I was able to approach things from a broader perspective and look beyond the technology into the whole content and design of instruction.

Don: From there you went to the University of Miami?

Bob: I was brought into Miami as part of a Ford Grant that was looking at the first two years of the academic program, a newly established university college program. It was there for the first time that I was able to add an integral evaluation component. John Woodard, an expert in evaluation, joined our staff and began to provide the information we would need as we looked at the *design* of courses and programs. During this period, I developed a model which helped show the process, the steps followed, and the questions asked. Part of the model was based on earlier work of Trump that considered large groups, small groups, and independent study.

Don: What was the concept behind your first model?

Bob: Basically it was asking those broader questions. Before you could make certain decisions you needed to ask certain questions. A year or so later, I was informed by some of the folks at Michigan State that what I had developed was an instructional system and that I was an expert in it. Until they had arrived I didn't even know the word "system," but that's basically the evolution. The early model was far more complex than the one we now use.

Don: And was the State University of New York College at Fredonia a natural extension of your Miami effort?

Bob: Yes, because at SUNY-Fredonia I was able to work at all levels of instruction in all disciplines and explore ways to use an entirely new facility. From SUNY-Fredonia, I came to Syracuse.

Don: There seems to be a theme that has gone through each of these positions, and that is: the media and beyond. You looked *beyond* the media; you began to incorporate evaluation when you began to think about the design of courses. Improvement of teaching and learning in higher education is the theme that seems to have run through each of the positions.

Bob: Yes, I really think it's a matter of trying to decide what the best possible course or program would look like as a whole; only when you know where you want to go do you start raising the technology and media questions. I was concerned that we tended to select solutions before we had identified problems and explored alternatives. I think that's the evolution that took place, and as we kept moving, we got more and more into systemic change. I think one of the things that distinguished Syracuse, Fredonia, and Miami from the other universities was the more inclusive model. We didn't start with objectives until we moved back into the whole process and raised some prior questions.

Don: I think there's an increasing interest in improving university teaching as you illustrated in each of your positions. Do you think this effort falls legitimately within the scope of our field?

Bob: I think it's broader than teaching. You can be the best person in the world as a teacher, but if you're not teaching what should be taught, it's a major problem. One of the things that we are finding is that in many programs there are major problems of content and structure. And, quite often, well-taught courses can be not doing what they are expected to do. We find wrong assumptions being made; we find that faculty may have lost touch with what is going on in the outside world, and are making wrong assumptions about the competencies and priorities that students bring to the course. Where I have a problem is when you start talking about "the field." I find that in some ways there are two distinctly different movements evolving from the technology field. Some people within the field focus on technology because that's what they love to do. They're experts in production. Others focus more on process and change.

Don: Is the other the instructional development group?

Bob: Sometimes. You can also call it systems; instructional change, and in some contexts, even faculty development. The problem is that some folks who call themselves instructional developers are in fact product developers. In the broader context, there is a point where media should and must be considered. When I first came to Syracuse, I was accused by some of being anti-television because we weren't using the medium to deliver courses. At that time television just wasn't the appropriate solution; it wasn't cost-effective. We were using it but only where we felt it was the appropriate delivery system. I'm always concerned when you have people in a particular technology selling solutions before they look at problems.

Don: We still have people like that who are trying to promote a medium.

Bob: Well, you've seen it happen. We've killed programmed instruction; we've killed teaching machines; and some of the same problems exist with computers. Unfortunately, so much of what was done was the wrong solution or the right solution done poorly. I think an exciting marriage is now taking place between computers and media. But again, I am very much concerned about the front end. The AECT Division of Instructional Development was at one time beginning to focus on systemic institutional change, but later turned back and became narrower and narrower to the point where its major focus a year ago was on HyperCard. The profession stopped addressing the broader issues of instructional and program improvement.

Don: Maybe this is a cycle that we see repeated in our field. First media, then the broader questions; and later back to media and then the broader questions. What do you think?

Bob: I'm not sure that's the case. It's almost as if we have two different mental sets. The basic question is "What is the field?" There is no question that there is a need for people who have strengths in technology and the design of media. This is particularly true as we began to explore the tremendous potential of multimedia. However, as good as the product of the production group is, their effort will only be successful if a whole series of front-end questions get asked, and that doesn't happen too often; not only questions about the student, the content, and the structure of instructional programs, but questions that address the selection of the delivery system itself. What approach or combination of approaches is cost-effective and efficient? How should technology be used?

Don: Do you think that technology-oriented people need special training to do the things that people on your CID staff do?

Bob: I am not sure if it's specialized training or a different group of people. I find major differences between the people who do evaluation and the people who do instructional development. I find major differences between the media producer and the process person. I look at it in a synergistic way as a combination of outstanding talents. On my staff, I have some people who are extremely good in technology, but they're not going to worry very much about the broad front-end questions or the overall design of a program. We've had the same relationship with professionals in evaluation where we're bringing in support and facilitative individuals with different strengths and perspectives in development and evaluation. The result is far greater than if each worked independently.

Don: So, if you were to look for professionals to work in your Center, where would you look for these people?

Bob: Obviously it depends on the position. You want evaluators who can speak effectively, communicate effectively, and understand the problems of the people they work with. They should write effectively (and a lot of evaluators don't do that particularly well); human skills and a solid base in data collection and interpretation are essential. A certain type of personality is needed for the instructional development personnel. You need a person who has the rare combination of process and interpersonal skills and creativity, while at the same time being well organized. The knowledge and process skills can be taught. A lot of people who have come into the field and called themselves "instructional developers" weren't. They were *product* developers. They had never worked in programs outside of their field, they had never raised the issues and concerns about scope and content and structure of programs. At Syracuse, we literally changed in our hiring procedures. We do an affirmative action search for our interns and then when a position opens, a person can be hired from the intern group without an additional search. Very few institutions are building in the range of experiences an individual needs to do this complex and highly sensitive political work.

Don: Because they've not had on-the-job training?

Bob: Yes, and a broader introduction to being a change agent.

Don: Plus an academic background?

Bob: Yes. This simply was not the case with the people we were interviewing. We were running into all sorts of trouble trying to find people who could do what we needed to have done.

Don: These would be people with just academic backgrounds?

Bob: They tended to come out of an academic department and to have production experience, but few had ever worked in a field other than their own, and never in the role of helping faculty through the design process. And that's what we so desperately needed, people who can fill that support role, that facilitator role.

Don: It seems that you need people who are at home with ideas, who can get along with other people, and yet know the process of instructional development?

Bob: Yes. As I noted earlier, it's an unusual combination because on the one hand, you need someone who is extremely well organized, and, on the other hand, you need somebody who is idealistic, humanistic, and creative. Unfortunately, these characteristics don't often go together.

Don: Right, and not one of those characteristics by itself is sufficient.

Bob: The other thing about the instructional development role, at least as I define it, is that if you're successful, everybody else is going to be successful, and quite often you're not going to be recognized for the significant role you have played. If you have an ego that constantly needs strokes, forget it.

Don: I'd like to talk about your Center. What are the major functions of the Center for Instructional Development?

Bob: It evolved over the years. The interesting thing is that while change has occurred, the instructional development model has stayed consistent. When we first started, our work was primarily at the course level and later some curriculum work. We found from the beginning that if you worked on pieces of courses or smaller units, you didn't have much impact over a period of time. So, with limited dollars, to be cost-effective, we've gone after major change.

Don: Like courses and sequences of courses?

Bob: Yes, whole changes, not piecemeal efforts.

Don: But within that framework, what kind of functions have you performed?

Bob: There are evaluation and needs assessment; the whole front-end analysis; information that you need to know about the student, about the field, what alumni and employers tell us, where the field is going, what exists now, what problems they may be having. The model also forces us to think idealistically: Where do you want to go and what would be the best possible way of getting there, i.e., what would an ideal program be and then how close can we come to the ideal? We use the same process whether it's a curriculum or a course. But then, as we move through the process, there's a point in time where we get into a production mode. We have developed extremely comprehensive student manuals and a wide range of instructional materials, and it's at that point where the media folks start plugging into the system. One sidelight that intrigues me is that we're still doing good old-fashioned programmed instruction because it's a cost-effective way of reaching certain instructional goals.

Don: But you're not committed to any one medium?

Bob: Right. Each medium has, under the correct conditions, a role to play in the instructional process. At CID, we're involved with distance learning; we're developing courses for the use of the armed forces in isolated parts of the world using texts, audiotapes, video, and comprehensive student manuals. We are currently exploring uses of other technology for this program. We've produced video, tape-slide presentations, slides, transparencies, and programmed units. Another facet of our Center has been the broader, facilitative role we have been asked to play on campus. The Center was instrumental in introducing a number of innovative programs, such as Project Advance (a secondary school-university articulation program), a required and comprehensive teaching assistant program which is now a national model, and the University's Academic Support Center. We're playing a key role in a number of campus-wide studies on attrition and program effectiveness. The all-University Compact between students, faculty, and staff was developed here. The Center is also the home of a national project on tenure and promotion and institutional priorities. This project grew out of an on-campus project to focus more faculty energy on the undergraduate experience. A small grant supporting this campus activity has led to a whole series of projects working with colleges, universities, and academic groups throughout the country to facilitate change in the tenure and promotion process.

Don: In some universities they would call this institutional research? Is that what you're doing, in effect?

Bob: Yes, but in a much more applied sense than is common. Our evaluation office is involved in obtaining data for decision makers. Other offices tend to provide the data for state and national reports.

Don: Your evaluation focus is to help make decisions locally?

Bob: Yes. But again, in the Center, we get called on for almost anything under the sun where process skills are required. The staff here is involved in TQM by providing the glue that some of the groups on campus need. We're doing less course development at this time simply because we're being pulled away in other directions.

Don: Can a professor still walk into your Center and say "I'd like to work with you; I am going to be revising a course or a sequence of courses"?

Bob: Sure. In fact, we have recently been meeting with a number of deans to identify course and curriculum initiatives where we can be of help.

Don: Would you say the percentage of that activity has changed over the last dozen years?

Bob: Yes.

Don: Do you want to estimate what it is?

Bob: It's hard because we have that large project with distance education which is all course work and course design, but I think on-campus it may be down 50 percent from what it was five, eight, or ten years ago.

Don: What I am trying to do is to create a catalog of the range of things that you're doing. The basic thesis of this interview is that educational technology (or whatever name you want to use to describe our field) has really come of age in colleges and universities, and we're tending to call it instructional development or . . .

Bob: Don, I'm coming to believe that the word *technology* tends to get in the way because, in effect, in the eye of the beholder, it's a hardware-related role, and I think that in a Center like ours, it would be the wrong word to use. There are tremendous and exciting changes taking place now with opportunities like "multimedia," which opens up new and highly effective instructional options. What people tend to forget, however, is that all the design work must occur before the software gets into the classroom. I find commitments being made to use a sophisticated medium without any understanding of the hard work that must be done long before a lesson is placed on the medium. And I guess the ideal marriage is to make sure you've got the front-end analysis, the objective selection of the appropriate technology, quality production, *and* an effective delivery system. That is something we're struggling with at Syracuse. It's still not as good a marriage between design, media selection, computing, and production as I would like to see.

Don: It seems that at Syracuse and at other universities we are now doing the kinds of things we had hoped to do 25 years ago and more. It seems that we were undervalued for a very long time, but now there's a new recognition of the role we can play in instructional improvement within an institution, and perhaps we have come of age in many postsecondary institutions. Aren't there more centers like CID?

Bob: Yes, but what has happened, interestingly enough, is that they haven't evolved from instructional technology in the media center. I find that for the most part they've evolved from the so-called "faculty development" groups who have moved into the instructional area. As I look around the country, I feel frustrated. Professional faculty in instructional technology, for example, do not understand what is going on with a group like POD (the Professional Organizational Development Network in Higher Education). And this is unfortunate since each area of expertise needs the other. People in faculty development are in the classrooms working with faculty on improvement of instruction, and technology is a part of it. I have recently seen a job opening that, in effect, has such a linkage, but it wasn't in the technology center. But I see centers and professionals that are doing the same thing they were doing 20 to 30 years ago and they're not making the next leap into a broader perspective.

Don: Does that mean that the more traditional programs are only providing support service personnel?

Bob: Yes. When I talk with central administrators and then to directors of instructional support agencies, I get different perspectives. What I hear from central administration is that they're concerned about learning; they're concerned about attrition and retention; they're concerned about job placement of graduates; they're concerned about how to respond to critics who say that we're not paying enough attention to what goes on in our classrooms. They are *not* interested in what most center reports focus on, in the number of items or equipment delivered, or the number of people served. They are after *outcomes*; they are after impact; and I don't think we've done enough work in that area.

Don: What about the marriage with the computer folks? It seems that in many universities there's almost a parallel movement getting the faculty involved in computing. There are computer clusters, computer classrooms, and now there are instructional development efforts that attempt to bring the faculty into that movement. These efforts seem to be parallel, but separate, from what you're doing.

Bob: You're right and it's unfortunate. As I mentioned before, it is something we're trying to work through at Syracuse. Until several weeks ago, the media group's delivery and maintenance reported to my office. They now report to the vice president for computing and I totally support the move. We have retained the production capabilities in CID, but the delivery of the hardware is now combined with all university instructional support services. For example, we were finding that when we looked at the new design of classrooms, the technology was a responsibility of *both* computing and audiovisual media. I don't think you can keep the technologies separate any longer. The question therefore arises, "What *is* the field? Are we into production, into delivery, or are we to play a major role as instructional change agents?" I don't see us preparing the type of professionals education needs if it is to address the problems we face.

Don: I don't see the same kind of instructional development efforts going on with the computing community that I see going on within your organization or others like it, do you?

Bob: No, that's the problem; it's the same problem we've had with every other technology, that is, people selling a solution. Professionals knowledgeable about all technology should be able to help faculty and administrators select and use the best possible combination of resources to address a need.

Don: Media myopia?

Bob: Yes, it's that front end that's missing. It's the issue that we're raising loud and clear here. We've had it in place in all but computing. Only time will tell if our reorganization helps get the proper front-end conversations underway.

Don: Maybe it will happen after computing becomes more commonplace and people feel more comfortable with it. Right now it has the glow, the appeal that television had 20 years ago, and as each medium came along, it became the favored one.

Bob: It's not a new problem. We've managed to do a disservice to media and technology by overselling and poor quality production.

Don: I'd like to close with a final question about the evolution of the field. You and I have now been in the field for more than 25 years; how do you see that it has developed and changed? It's not the same field that we entered, and yet there are elements of it that seem to have been consistent through the years. What do you think about its major changes and emphases over the years? Have they been a natural evolution, opportunistic, or what?

Bob: To be very honest with you, I have not seen the movement in the technology field that I would have liked to see. I feel that it has remained hardware- and production-focused. Early on, when I helped form the Division of Instructional Development [in the Association for Educational Communications and Technology], it was with the hope that we would move in another direction and become instructional change and support agents. The Division started going that way but new leaders brought in a narrower focus as the glamour of technology prevailed. I don't see the concern with the institutional priorities, the concern with what's happening in higher education, and an effort to broaden the scope of our graduates. I think the field has hurt itself by limiting its horizon.

Don: And also concerns for the individual learner?

Bob: Yes, "gutty" questions are not being addressed by the field and I am very concerned that some of the linkages that would have been so natural never happened. It's not as positive a statement as I'd like to make.

Don: But it's not completely lost, because there *are* bright lights, things *have* happened, changes *have* been made. The situation in general has improved, but I don't think you can say that about the entire movement.

Bob: Perhaps. Again, most of the leadership for change has come from outside of this group. It's other professional organizations and their members that are focusing on the broader issues. I don't see the upward professional growth in the technology field. If I look at the centers around the country that are having increasing impact on their campuses, it's a different group of players that are providing leadership. And that concerns me because I think that there are talents in our field that should be used. I believe, in some ways, the field did not shoot high enough. Perhaps I've had a wrong basic assumption about the role the field would play . . . a carryover from working with Dick Lewis. I don't know.

Don: These individuals have been willing to assume a service role?

Bob: Yes, but the service role is not where the needs are. The need is for change; the needs are for change agents; the needs are for people who understand the broadest issues and understand how to deal with them. Many people know what the problems are; the question is how we deal with them.

Don: Thanks, Bob, for your candid comments about the growth, development, and current status of our profession—whatever its name might be.

The Federal Role in
Educational Technology

Malcolm V. Phelps
Chief, Technology and Evaluation Branch
Education Division, National Aeronautics and Space Administration

In 1990, former president George Bush and the nation's governors established six National Education Goals for the year 2000. In response to these National Educational Goals, 16 federal agencies formed what is now known as the Federal Coordinating Council for Science, Engineering, and Technology/Committee on Education and Training (FCCSET/CET). The group's task was to develop an educational strategic plan to ensure U.S. world leadership in science and technology, build a highly trained work force, and increase public understanding of mathematics, science, and technology.

In 1993, FCCSET/CET published the federal strategic plan, *Pathways to Excellence: A Federal Strategy for Science, Mathematics, Engineering, and Technology Education. Pathways to Excellence* delineates a five-year framework and associated milestones that focus federal planning and the resources of the participating agencies toward achieving the requisite or expected level of mathematics, science, and technological competence by all students.

Although FCCSET/CET contains nine interagency working groups to address the President's Goals for the Year 2000, the Educational Technologies Working Group (ETWG) was established to particularly address the President's Goal on technology:

> By the year 2000, with the support of information technologies, all learners and teachers of all ages and at all levels, in all geographic locations and educational settings, will have the required support, knowledge, tools, and infrastructure to have equitable access to scientific information and expertise, technology-based tools, materials for learning and teaching, equipment, innovative curricula, and communities of learners, teachers, and experts.

FCCSET then charged the ETWG to:

> Identify technology-related activities (both Federal and non-Federal) that demonstrate the greatest potential for improving the delivery of science, mathematics, engineering, and technology education; develop resident expertise to understand better the role that technologies can play in their education-related activities; and share information through a standing Educational Technologies Working Group (FCCSET/CET 1993, p. 24).

A DEFINITION OF EDUCATIONAL TECHNOLOGIES

The ETWG defined *educational technology* as the application of computer and communications technologies as an educational resource or tool to facilitate teaching, learning, and research. As part of the planning process, the ETWG identified strategies, priorities, and milestones to increase the use of educational and training technologies in federal educational activities.

Federal activities in mathematics, science, and engineering have resulted in the development of an enormous body of human and material resources, including expertise, information, and scientific instrumentation that could improve the science and mathematics education in our schools. Educational technologies can make these resources available to support teaching, learning, research, and the creation of learning communities of scientists, mathematicians, educators, and students.

More information on how the ETWG defined the applications of educational technology is provided in the ETWG's July 29, 1933, report to FCCSET.

FEDERAL ROLE IN EDUCATIONAL TECHNOLOGY

As noted in *Pathways to Excellence* (1993, p. 24), FCCSET/CET views the federal role in educational technology as supporting:

- Research and development of educational and training technologies

- Infrastructure development for educational technologies

- Implementation of technologies in FCCSET/CET agencies and educational activities.

Research and Development of Educational and Training Technologies

Many promising educational technology products are the result of federal investments in research and development (R&D), but direct federal funding of R&D for educational and training technologies is a tiny fraction of the billions of dollars committed to other major categories of federal R&D. Moreover, according to the Office of Technology Assessment's 1988 report, *Power On! New Tools for Teaching and Learning*, the federal investment in educational technology R&D has fallen since the mid-1980s.

If the federal government is to provide leadership and coordination of technology-based educational programs and materials, staff throughout the FCCSET/CET agencies must be provided with the necessary technology support systems to stay current in the field. These support systems should include:

- State-of-the-art computers for all program officers

- Workstations in appropriate offices

- Connections to electronic facilities (e.g., mail and bulletin boards) and to the Internet for transmission of information and programming

- Networking among and with related agencies

- Exhibit areas where program officers, grantees, proposers, and school officials can have access to direct information about the latest technology

- An ongoing series of workshops and studies to keep abreast of a rapidly changing field.

Infrastructure for Educational Technologies

Education has traditionally not been the impetus for or a primary factor in shaping plans for the development and utilization of technology systems. For example, the U.S. Office of Technology Assessment (1988) indicated that educators have not had a sufficient voice in decision making about the future of the educational telecommunications infrastructure. Yet education's need and demand for access to technology-based resources is clearly accelerating.

To meet the ETWG goal that all learners and teachers have access to the expertise and products of scientific and mathematical inquiry, technology-based tools and materials for learning and teaching, and communities of learners, teachers, and experts, it will be necessary to create, enhance, or extend the nation's technology infrastructure for learning and teaching.

The national technology infrastructure for learning and teaching in science, mathematics, engineering, and technology education encompasses:

- Institutional and organizational arrangements

- Policies and regulatory processes

- Telecommunications networks

- Computers and software

- Technical assistance

- Digital information archives

- Curriculum materials

- Teaching strategies

- The expertise of teachers, educational researchers, mathematicians, scientists, and engineers.

In collaboration with state and local government, private and public educational agencies and institutions, the private sector, and the federal government have opportunities to assist in creating and maintaining a robust national information infrastructure (NII)—one that makes possible more equitable access to the resources needed for modernization of science and mathematics education at all levels. Coordination among agencies and organizations involved in developing and implementing technology-related policies or systems will ensure that such policies and systems will support the needed reforms and innovations in science and mathematics education, and will enable equitable access to such resources on a national basis.

IMPLEMENTATION OF TECHNOLOGIES
IN FCCSET/CET

Activities and Agencies

A major component in meeting the ETWG's principal goal will be the implementation of technologies in FCCSET/CET agencies' educational programs and activities. The FCCSET/CET Elementary and Secondary, Undergraduate, and Graduate Education Working Groups have each established strategic goals for implementing technologies within their respective areas.

The Milestones

The ETWG has established five milestones to measure the progress of the federal agencies in meeting the charge from FCCSET/CET to use educational and training technologies in federal activities. The milestones are as follows:

Milestone 1:   In FY 1993, FCCSET/CET agencies will inventory their educational technology-based activities (e.g., computational mathematics and science tools, learning environments, teaching aids and tutoring systems, and electronic networking and distance learning).

Milestone 2:   Beginning in FY 1994, FCCSET/CET agencies will implement programs that facilitate opportunities for the nation's secondary schools to participate in technology-based research projects involving working relationships with the scientific community.[1]

Milestone 3:   In FY 1994, FCCSET/CET agencies will develop and communicate a vision for establishing the national information infrastructure that supports the needs of the educational community. This vision will reflect input from local, state, and federal agencies and will involve public and private stakeholders.

Milestone 4:   In 1995, FCCSET/CET agencies will sponsor educational technology activities that reflect the national vision and demonstrate significant potential for increasing student performance.

Milestone 5:   Beginning in 1993, the ETWG of the FCCSET/CET Committee will monitor the implementation of Executive Order 12821.[2]

PROGRESS TO MILESTONES

Milestone 1

An inventory of FCCSET/CET agency educational technology-based activities has been completed by staff from 9 of the 16 agencies represented on the ETWG. It identifies programs that support educational technology in mathematics, engineering, and technology education. These agencies are:

- Department of Commerce (DOC)

- Department of Defense (DOD)

- Department of Education

- Department of Energy (DOE)

- Department of Health and Human Services (DHHS)

- Department of Veterans Affairs (VA)

- National Aeronautics and Space Administration (NASA)

- National Science Foundation (NSF)

- U.S. Department of Agriculture (USDA).

Programs that promote the use of technology in the educational process can include the delivery of graduate-level science, mathematics, engineering, and technology courses by means of distance learning technologies; the development of high-quality multimedia science curricula for K-12 schools; and support of the development, production, and dissemination of technology to serve children with disabilities. The federal agencies' inventory is available in the ETWG's July 29, 1993, report to FCCSET/CET.

Milestone 2

In the process of inventorying the activities currently underway, an analysis was conducted of existing projects that contribute to meeting Milestone 2. Several FCCSET/CET agency activities that meet the criteria established by the milestone are now in place. These activities will be accelerated and expanded, and new ones implemented beginning in FY 1994 to meet the Milestone.

The following is a brief summary of current activities being conducted by some federal agencies which address Milestone 2:

- Through the Star Schools Program, the Department of Education supports innovative science applications using a combination of technologies. Funded projects are encouraged to develop activities that permit students at all levels to work collabora-tively with scientists, mathematicians, and other experts via telecommunications. Teacher development activities supported by the Department of Education in FY 1994 will also involve opportunities for high school teachers to enhance their teaching practices by involving experts from the scientific community in technology-based research projects.

- The Education Division of NASA has several programs that contribute to meeting this milestone, including: secondary school educators and students working with scientists on ground-truth studies; the analysis of weather data utilizing satellite receiving systems; the analysis of data from astronomical observatories (such as the Hubble Space Telescope) and Earth-observing satellites.

- At the National Science Foundation, this milestone is addressed primarily through activities conducted by the Division of Teacher Enhancement Programs. Current efforts reach teachers in area schools through institutes and leadership programs run by scientists, members of the scientific community, universities, government agencies, and others. Future efforts will integrate existing NSF networking efforts with the State Systemic Initiatives (SSI).

- The Cooperative Extension Service (CES) is the USDA agency whose mission is to "help people improve their lives through an educational process that uses scientific knowledge focused on issues and needs." This mission is accomplished by the linkage of education and research resources and activities of the USDA, 74 land-grant universities, and 3,150 county administrative units.

Milestone 3

To meet Milestone 3 in FY 1994, the ETWG plans to implement a consensus-building process similar to that being used to develop national standards in science by the National Academy of Sciences (NAS). The NAS approach solicits the participation and input of all federal agencies; local, state, and national resources; and business and industry; and will clarify the roles of public and private stakeholders.

As an important part of this consensus-building process, FCCSET/CET agencies will convene a conference in FY 1994 to develop and communicate a shared national vision for establishing the National Information Infrastructure that supports the needs of the educational community. On August 6, 1993, FCCSET/CET and the Office of Science and Technology Policy (OSTP) hosted a planning meeting where 34 representatives from the federal government, professional education associations, and industry met to begin a discussion on a shared national vision for educational and training technologies. The attendees decided to form a group called the National Coordinating Committee on Technology in Education and Training (NCC-TET) in order to develop a process for achieving a national vision of an NII and what the federal role is in this process. In addition, the NSF has underway four national education network testbeds and a clearinghouse for networking information that will work with major federally supported educational project principal investigators to develop strategies to make use of networking to disseminate their findings, materials, and activities. These efforts, together with two ongoing forums, bring together the directors of the state systemic projects, school district administrators, professional educational society officers, teachers, and others, and will provide avenues by which stakeholders can contribute to the formulation of a national vision and a definition of the federal role in establishing the NII to support the needs of the education community.

Milestone 4

Concomitant with the ETWG's effort to develop a national vision and strategic plan for the implementation of the NII to serve the needs of education, new activities will be planned and implemented that demonstrate the application of computer and information technologies in educational settings to improve student performance, enhance the educational process, and expand the variety of resources available to our schools. Appropriate activities are currently being defined as part of the work of the ETWG.

Milestone 5

The ETWG was assigned the responsibility for monitoring the implementation of Executive Order 12821 by the FCCSET/CET Committee. To date, consultation has occurred between the ETWG and the General Services Administration (GSA) regarding the implementation of the Executive Order. The Coordinating Committee referred to in the Executive Order has now been established and will be responsible for developing implementation policies and procedures.

Individual federal agencies are also developing pilot implementation programs. NASA, for example, is currently finalizing plans for a pilot program at two of its field centers (i.e., federal laboratories)—Lewis Research Center in Cleveland, Ohio, and Johnson Space Center in Houston, Texas.

The USDA continues to have a Memorandum of Understanding (MOU) with the 189 historically black land-grant institutions that enables the transfer of excess federal equipment to those institutions. Also, an MOU was renewed recently with the Hispanic Association of Colleges and Universities (HACU) to enable the Department to transfer excess federal equipment to Hispanic-serving institutions.

PROGRAMMATIC RECOMMENDATIONS

In support of the five milestones, the ETWG has 19 programmatic recommendations concerning the use of educational technology in federal programs during FYs 1995 to 1999. These recommendations are categorized as research and development, implementation, or infrastructure.

Research and Development

Federally sponsored research and development may be the key to laying that foundation and to facilitating the transfer of scientific techniques and technologies to the educational community. Recommendations include:

1. Conduct a thorough study to identify existing and potential federal information resources and the applications of technology relevant to science and mathematics education.

2. Link scientific research with education.

3. Involve practitioners in educational technology research and development activities.

4. Create large-scale testbeds for research on systemic innovations.

5. Develop and disseminate needed software tools.

6. Advance applications and integration of technologies for distance learning.

7. Test innovations that are based on new technologies and new science.

Implementation

FCCSET/CET agencies can make a substantive contribution to assisting schools in the effective implementation of educational technologies into the teaching and learning process. The ETWG makes the following recommendations for activities by FCCSET/CET agencies during FYs 1995-1999:

8. Integrate technological knowledge and skills into increased federal efforts to educate and train leader teachers.

9. Use technology to reach teachers and support teacher exchange of knowledge and expertise.

10. Integrate technological tools, knowledge, and skills into federally supported teacher preparation programs.

11. Build appropriate technology applications into standards and framework development.

12. Integrate technology-based tools, resources, and pedagogical approaches into new instructional materials.

13. Make existing resources more accessible for curriculum development.

14. Develop alternative assessment methods.

Infrastructure

The most effective and efficient means for achieving the goal of equitable access to educational innovations and resources on a national basis may be to create an NII with the following features:

- Innovations and resources, wherever the resources physically reside, are widely accessible through telecommunication networks.

- Networks reflect as coherent a national internetworking infrastructure for education as possible.

- Programs exist that provide teachers and learners with the opportunity to gain the skills, knowledge, tools, and technical assistance necessary to take advantage of networked resources.

- Local places of learning have economically feasible means of accessing networks.

- Teachers are provided with the time and organizational structure that fosters the pursuit of new learning and upgrading of skills.

The most effective and economical NII will be established through the interconnection and expansion of existing local, regional, and national initiatives along with the ongoing incorporation of new, proven technologies. The resulting distributed web of interactive, interconnected networks will enable teachers and students to participate actively in learning, develop local resources to be shared nationally, and acquire and contribute knowledge, experience, and skills.

15. Put federal educational resources in a standard internetwork-accessible form.

16. Establish technical assistance infrastructure and services.

17. Develop networked information services.

18. Review federal-state-local policies and regulations to facilitate instrumentation acquisition.

19. Review technology-related policies and regulatory processes to identify restrictions.

NOTES

1. The original language of Milestone 2 read: "Beginning in FY 1994, CEHR [FCCSET/CET Committee on Education and Human Resources] agencies will *ensure that at least 20% of* the Nation's secondary schools participate in *at least one* technology-based research project involving working relationships with the scientific community." The ETWG felt the level of specificity was arbitrary and limiting, and therefore eliminated reference to a specific percentage target.

2. Milestone 5 was assigned to the ETWG after the publication of *Pathways to Excellence* by FCCSET/CET in response to Executive Order 12821, which establishes federal policy regarding the transfer of education-related federal equipment.

REFERENCES

Federal Coordinating Council for Science, Engineering, and Technology Committee on Education and Human Resources. (1993). *Pathways to excellence: A federal strategy for science, mathematics, engineering, and technology education.* Washington, DC: Author. ERIC no. ED 360 165.

Federal Coordinating Council for Science, Engineering, and Technology Committee on Education and Human Resources, Educational Technologies Working Group. (1993). *July 1993 report to the Subcommittee on Science, Engineering, and Technology Education.* Washington, DC: Author.

United States Congress Office of Technology Assessment. (1988). *Power on! New tools for teaching and learning.* (OTA-SET-379). Washington, DC: U.S. Government Printing Office. ERIC no. ED 295 677.

Alternative Assessment and Technology*

Dorothy Bennett
Jan Hawkins

INTRODUCTION

Considerable attention is now being paid to the reform of testing in this country—going beyond multiple-choice testing that emphasizes facts and small procedures to the development of methods for assessing complex knowledge and performances. This is because goals for education have substantially changed during the last decade, and because changes in assessment are believed to directly influence changes in the classroom. Altering assessment practices is likely to affect curriculum, teaching methods, and students' understanding of the meaning of their work. A newly designed assessment system must accurately measure and *promote* the complex thinking and learning goals that are known to be critical to students' academic success and to their eventual sustained achievement and contribution to their communities.

Two approaches that have shown considerable promise are *performance-based assessment* and *portfolio assessment*. In these approaches, judgments about students' achievement are based on their performances of complex tasks and selections of work over time.

The success of a new approach to assessment carries with it a deep change in how we think about the measurement of cognitive abilities. The view of assessment carried over from the last century is that there are underlying mental traits and that a test is a sample behavior that provides an imperfect measure of the underlying characteristic the test was meant to measure. We are attempting to develop a different paradigm of assessment. The new paradigm *requires* methods like performance assessment or portfolio assessment. Instead of giving a test that consists of a number of varied items believed to constitute a sample of some underlying knowledge or skill, the new approach attempts to record a complex performance that represents a rich array of a student's abilities. Rather than a representative sample, it is meant to be a measure of demonstrated capability.

*This digest was adapted from an article by Dorothy Bennett and Jan Hawkins that appeared in *News from the Center for Children and Technology and the Center for Technology in Education*, Vol. 1, No. 3, March 1992, Bank Street College of Education, 610 West 112th St., New York, NY 10025. As of January 1994, the Center for Technology in Education is affiliated with the Education Development Center, 69 Morton St., New York, NY 10014.

ERIC Digests are in the public domain and may be freely reproduced and disseminated.

This publication was prepared with funding from the Office of Educational Research and Improvement, U.S. Department of Education, under contract no. RR93002009. The opinions expressed in this report do not necessarily reflect the positions or policies of OERI or ED.

A key part of assessment research is developing tasks that will enable students to use and demonstrate a broad range of abilities. Successful tasks will be complex enough to engage students in real thinking and performances, open-ended enough to encourage different approaches, but sufficiently constrained to permit reliable scoring; they will allow for easy collection of records, and they will exemplify authentic work in the disciplines.

THE ROLE OF TECHNOLOGY

How does technology figure in this process of reconfiguring the way students are assessed? Technology has certain unique capabilities that can make crucial contributions to the creation of workable and meaningful forms of alternative assessment. Paper and pencil, video, and computers can give three very different views of what students can do. It's like three different camera angles on the complete picture of a student. You can't reconstruct a total person from just one angle, but with three different views you can triangulate, and discover a much richer portrait of students' abilities.

Well-designed educational technologies can support these new approaches to assessment, and consequently lend themselves to integration into curricula that stress alternative assessment. Computers and video records offer expanded potential for collecting—easily and permanently—different kinds of records of students' work. For example, final products in a variety of media (text, graphics, video, multimedia), students' oral presentations or explanations, interviews that capture students' development and justifications for their work, and in-progress traces of thinking and problem-solving processes can be collected using video and computer technologies. Essential to success is discovering what kind of records is most efficient for scoring yet capture the most important aspects of the different target abilities.

An effort has been underway at the Center for Technology in Education (CTE) to investigate two approaches to assessment based on students' work on complex tasks. They explore the potential that technology holds for facilitating innovative assessment techniques by using videotape and computers. The remainder of this digest describes some of the *performance-based* alternative assessment projects that CTE is working with in collaborative projects with a variety of schools.

PERFORMANCE ASSESSMENT

Performance assessment refers to the process of evaluating a student's skills by asking the student to perform tasks that require those skills. Performances in science might examine the ability to design a device to perform a particular function or to mount an argument supported by experimental evidence. In contrast, answering questions by selecting from among several possible choices, as in multiple-choice tests, is not considered a performance, or at least not a performance that is of primary interest to scientists or science educators.

If you ask scientists what qualities make a good scientist, they might come up with a list like the following: the ability to explain ideas and procedures in written and oral form, to formulate and test hypotheses, to work with colleagues in a productive manner, to ask penetrating questions and make helpful comments when you listen, to choose interesting problems to work on, to design good experiments, and to have a deep understanding of theories and questions in the field. Excellence in other school subjects, such as math, English, and history, requires similar abilities.

The current testing system only taps a small part of what it means to know and carry out work in science or math or English or history, and consequently it drives the system to emphasize a small range of those abilities. In science, the paper-and-pencil testing system has driven education to emphasize just two abilities: recall of facts and concepts, and ability to solve short, well-defined problems. These two abilities do not, in any sense, represent the range of abilities required to be a good scientist. Thus far, CTE has experimented with a number of tasks in the development of technology-based performance assessment records in high school science/mathematics. The tasks and criteria for scoring them are described here.

- **Computer Simulations**. In one science project, CTE has collected data using a computer program called Physics Explorer. Physics Explorer provides students with a simulation environment in which there are a variety of different models, each with a large set of associated variables that can be manipulated. Students conduct experiments to determine how different variables affect each other within a physical system. One task duplicates Galileo's pendulum experiments, where the problem is to figure out what variables affect the period of motion. In a second task, the student must determine what variables affect the friction acting on a body moving through a liquid. Printouts of students' work can be collected and evaluated in terms of the following traits: (1) how systematically they consider each possible independent variable, (2) whether they systematically control other variables while they test a hypothesis, and (3) whether they can formulate quantitative relationships between the independent variables and the dependent variables.

- **Oral Presentations**. This task asks students to present the results of their work on projects to the teacher. These interviews include both a presentation portion, where clarification questions are permitted, and a questioning period, where the students are challenged to defend their beliefs. Students' presentations can be judged in terms of: (1) depth of understanding, (2) clarity, (3) coherence, (4) responsiveness to questions, and (5) monitoring of their listeners' understanding.

- **Paired Explanations**. This task makes it possible to evaluate students' ability to listen as well as to explain ideas. First, one student presents to another student an explanation of a project he or she has completed or a concept (e.g., gravity) he or she has been working on. Then the two students reverse roles. The students use the blackboard or visual aids wherever appropriate. The explainers can be evaluated using the same criteria as for oral presentations. The listeners can be evaluated in terms of: (1) the quality of their questions, (2) their ability to summarize what the explainer has said, (3) their helpfulness in making the ideas clear, and (4) the appropriateness of their interruptions.

- **Progress Interviews**. This is a task in which students are interviewed on videotape about the stages of their project development and asked to reflect upon the different facets of their project work. The task was developed as a means for documenting the degree of progress students make in their understanding of key concepts. Preliminary scoring criteria that have been developed to evaluate these records are: (1) depth of understanding, (2) clarity of explanations, (3) justification of decisions/degree of reflectiveness, (4) use of good examples and explanations, (5) degree of progress made relative to where the student started, and (6) understanding of the bigger picture of the project.

- **Videotaped Demonstrations**. CTE is collecting data on a task that has been developed by a high school teacher in charge of a mechanical engineering program for

11th and 12th graders. Working together on design teams, students design and construct mechanical devices according to a design brief that describes technical specifications. The students must "demonstrate" their work and explain before a panel of judges from the field of engineering how their devices work and why they made certain design decisions. Students are then required to subject the devices to a functional test. For example, one project required students to design a device that can lift and lower "heavy" objects and place them at specified locations. The functional test required students to demonstrate that the devices they constructed could successfully lift and deliver three weights to a specified location in less than four minutes.

The students' performances on this task are evaluated on two levels: the quality of the oral presentation and the quality of the device. The oral presentation can be evaluated in terms of: (1) depth of understanding of the principles and mechanisms, and (2) clarity and completeness of the presentation. The device can be evaluated in terms of: (1) the economy of design (the degree to which there is an economical use of materials), (2) craftsmanship (degree of care in fabrication and assembly of device), (3) aesthetics, (4) creativity (interesting or novel ways of accomplishing the design), and (5) controllability (stability of the device).

These tasks provide interesting windows into students' abilities in the physical sciences. To complete the picture of students' performances, however, this evidence should become part of a larger portfolio of records of their work on a project, such as written descriptions, analyses, and journals.

ADDITIONAL READING

Bruder, Isabelle. (1993, January). Alternative assessment: Putting technology to the test. *Electronic Learning 12*(4), 22-23, 26-28. ERIC no. EJ 457 876.

Clyde, Anne. (1992, January/February). New technology, information access and educational outcomes. *Emergency Librarian 19*(3), 8-14, 16-18. ERIC no. EJ 441 739.

Gray, Bob A. (1991). Using instructional technology with at-risk youth: A primer. *TechTrends 36*(5), 61-63. ERIC no. EJ 441 780.

Magnussun, Kris, and Osborne, John. (1990, April). The rise of competency-based education: A deconstructionist analysis. *Journal of Educational Thought/Revue de la Pensée Educative 24*(1), 5-13. ERIC no. EJ 407 351.

McClure, Robert M., and others. (1992, April). *Alternative forms of student assessment.* Paper presented at the Annual Meeting of the American Educational Research Association, San Francisco, CA, April 20-24, 1992. 46pp. ERIC no. ED 347 209.

Seels, Barbara. (1993, Jan.). *The knowledge base of the evaluation domain.* Paper presented at the Annual Meeting of the Association for Educational Communications and Technology, New Orleans, LA, January 13-17, 1993. 12pp. ERIC no. ED 355 919.

Shavelson, Richard J., and others. (1991). Performance assessment in science. *Applied Measurement in Education 4*(4), 347-62. ERIC no. EJ 446 660.

U.S. Congress. (1992, February). *Testing in American schools: Asking the right questions. Full report.* Washington, DC: Office of Technology Assessment. Rpt. No. OTA-SET-519. ERIC no. ED 340 770. 314pp. (Also available from U.S. Government Printing Office: S/N 052-003-01275-8.)

School-University Partnerships and Educational Technology*

Bernard J. Dodge

According to one recent survey, at least 1,200 partnerships have been established between schools and universities (Wilbur and Lambert 1990). This digest describes current thinking and practice involving the use of educational technology in collaborative activities between schools and universities. It is not intended to be a comprehensive review or synthesis of the literature, but rather a pointer to conceptual overviews and cases. After discussing the features of successful partnerships, this digest will describe four categories of partnerships involving educational technology:

- Staff development about educational technology

- Staff development with distance education technology as a medium

- Research on educational technology

- Development of new educational technologies.

WHAT LEADS TO A SUCCESSFUL PARTNERSHIP?

For a variety of reasons, the relation between universities and schools has been characterized as a "fickle romance" (Wiske 1989). In spite of the differences between schools and universities in reward systems, schedules, roles, and rules, many working partnerships have been created. The most successful projects have been those in which both parties planned and prepared themselves well before starting the partnership, adequate resources were allocated to develop and maintain the activities, and mutual respect between the partners was consciously and systematically nurtured.

*This digest was prepared for the ERIC Clearinghouse on Information Resources by Bernard J. Dodge, Associate Professor, Educational Technology Department, San Diego State University. June 1993.

ERIC Digests are in the public domain and may be freely reproduced and disseminated.

For more information about ERIC or about obtaining ERIC articles and documents, call ACCESS ERIC, 1-800-LET-ERIC.

This publication was prepared with funding from the Office of Educational Research and Improvement, U.S. Department of Education, under contract no. RR93002009. The opinions expressed in this report do not necessarily reflect the positions or policies of OERI or ED.

Among the specific recommendations derived from successful collaborators are these:

- Project goals should be jointly conceived and agreed upon (Knapczyk 1991; Allum 1991).

- Teachers should be actively involved, not just passive recipients (Knapczyk 1991; Allum 1991).

- If teachers are to be involved as equal partners, they must be involved for as much time as the other actors (Wiske 1989).

- Exchanges should be reciprocal; each partner should gain something (Wiske 1989).

- Education should be mutual; each party must develop an appreciation of the other's contribution (Wiske 1989).

- Leadership should rotate among partners as appropriate to their skills (Balajthy 1991).

- Outcomes should be mutually owned (Balajthy 1991).

- The university must be committed to the collaborative ideal and provide financial support if necessary, including stipends or load credit for faculty members (Hillman 1987).

STAFF DEVELOPMENT ABOUT TECHNOLOGY

Many partnerships have been formed with the goal of infusing technology skills into the repertoire of classroom teachers. For example, Balajthy (1991) used a model of consultative consultation in which a team made up of a consultant from the college, a classroom teacher, and several student teachers worked together to create and implement lessons using technology. Byrne, Hittleman, and Marchisotto (1989) designed a voluntary staff development experience in which classroom teachers learned to use telecommunications as a vehicle for student writing. Roseman and Brearton (1989) trained teachers in basic computer use for science education, and then trained a core subset of the original group as trainers and change agents at their own school sites.

STAFF DEVELOPMENT WITH DISTANCE EDUCATION AS A MEDIUM

Collaborative staff development has also been carried out with distance education technology as the medium of delivery, rather than as the content. Pitcher, Rule, and Stowitschek (1986) used two-way audio and video to consult with and train teachers at distant sites on several special education topics. Similarly, Knapczyk (1991) used an audiographic system and fax machines to deliver special education training.

RESEARCH ON EDUCATIONAL TECHNOLOGY

Several partnerships have been established to collaborate on research. These partnerships go beyond the more common arrangement of schools simply granting permission for university researchers to study their classrooms. Instead, an effort is made to jointly establish the goals of the research to the benefit of both sides. The Educational Technology Center at Harvard University has published several thoughtful examinations of the dynamics of this kind of collaboration (Wiske 1989; Lampert 1988). Hillman (1987) describes the problems that occur in implementing research when school sites have not been sufficiently involved in the initial conceptualization of the project.

DEVELOPMENT OF NEW EDUCATIONAL TECHNOLOGIES

The goal of the fourth category of partnership is the development of new educational tools. Typically, school sites provide input into the design process by articulating their needs, testing prototypes, and giving formative feedback. Manatt (1991) describes the creation of a computer-based management system to implement the School Improvement Model. Burger and Stevenson-Burger (1989) built a computerized management tool for schools, while another project (Ritchie and Dodge 1992) developed a tool for student-authored adventure games. The benefit to the school partner in these examples was the possibility of having software customized to its needs. To the university partner, having a field-based source of ideas and evaluation is what made the collaboration work.

An important network of school-university partnerships is the Christopher Columbus Consortium established by Apple Computer in 1989. Each of the more than 40 consortium sites represents a partnership between a university and one or more schools. With Apple serving as the catalyst with an equipment donation, the partnerships each undertook projects intended to improve education at the school site. For descriptions of some of the Christopher Columbus Consortium projects, see Ritchie and Dodge (1992) and Balajthy (1991).

REFERENCES AND ADDITIONAL READING

Allum, K. F. (1991, Fall-Winter). Partners in innovation: School-college collaborations. *EDUCOM Review 26*(3-4), 29-33.

Balajthy, E. (1991, October). *A school-college consultation model for integration of technology and whole language in elementary science instruction. Field study report No. 1991.A.BIAL, Christopher Columbus Consortium Project.* ED 332 155.

Burger, M., and Stevenson-Burger, L. (1989). *Development of a computer-based instructional management system through school-university collaboration.* ED 319 102.

Byrne, M. M., Hittleman, C. G., and Marchisotto, J. (1989). A telecommunications staff development project. *Journal of Staff Development 10*(4), 26-30.

Hillman, S. K., and others. (1987, April). *The collaborative design in advancing the school/college interface.* ED 284 496.

Hord, S. M. (1986, February). A synthesis of research on organizational collaboration. *Educational Leadership 43*(5), 22-26.

Knapczyk, D. (1991). *Improving staff development in rural communities.* ED 345 890.

Lampert, M. (1988). *Teachers' thinking about students' thinking about geometry: The effects of new teaching tools. Technical report 88-1.* Cambridge, MA: Educational Technology Center. ED 294 724.

Manatt, R. P. (1989, Winter). Staff development, teacher evaluation, and a microcomputer. *Journal of Staff Development 10*(1), 48-51.

Pitcher, S., Rule, S., and Stowitschek, J. J. (1986, October). *Inservice training via telecommunications: Almost like being there.* ED 280 639.

Ritchie, D., and Dodge, B. (1992, March). *Integrating technology usage across the curriculum through educational adventure games.* ED 349 955.

Roseman, J. E., and Brearton, M. A. (1989, March). *Computers to enhance science education: An inservice designed to foster classroom implementation.* ED 307 153.

Sirotnik, K. A., and Goodlad, J. I., eds. (1988). *School-university partnerships in action: Concepts, cases, and concerns.* New York: Teachers College Press.

Wilbur, F. P., and Lambert, L. M. (1990). *Linking America's schools and colleges: Guide to partnerships and national directory.* Washington, DC: American Association for Higher Education. ED 340 332.

Wiske, M. S. (1989). *A cultural perspective on school-university collaborative research. Report No. ETC-TP-89-3. Topical paper.* Cambridge, MA: Educational Technology Center. ED 342 051.

Telecommunications and Distance Education*

Alexander Romiszowski

DEVELOPMENTS IN TELECOMMUNICATIONS

Recently a growing number of distance education institutions throughout the world have been utilizing telephone tutorials and audio conferences to supplement print-based interactions (Parker and Olgren 1984; Garrison 1990). A characteristic of this means of distance education by telephone is that communication is *synchronous* in nature. That is, the participants in the discussion or the tutorial are online at the same time, although they may be separated by distance.

Recent developments in telecommunications technologies such as fax machines and electronic mail through computer networks have introduced a new element in the form of rapid *asynchronous* communication. This has the characteristic of the participants being separated in time, even if not necessarily by distance. This form of communication is destined to play an increasingly significant role in future distance educational systems (Mason and Kaye 1989; Kaye 1992; Soby 1992; Cheng, Lehman, and Reynolds 1991).

Another aspect of progress in telecommunications is increasing capacity and greater standardization of electronic communication media. Increasing capacity is a result of the widespread availability of satellites for long-distance communication and the gradual replacement of copper wires by fiber-optic cables of greater capacity. Standardization is being promoted by the gradual implementation of a worldwide Integrated Systems Digital Network (ISDN). The ISDN network will be capable of carrying all types of messages, whether they are in the form of audio, video, text, or computer data, through the same channels in the same digital format. This will enable the messages to be integrated at end user terminals into multimedia presentations (Brewster 1987; Malfitano and Cincotta 1992; Heler, Cooley, and Reitz 1993). This is the impetus for most of the developments in distance education.

*Written by Alexander Romiszowski, Professor, Area of Instructional Design, Development, and Evaluation, School of Education, Syracuse University, Syracuse, New York. June 1993.

ERIC Digests are in the public domain and may be freely reproduced and disseminated.

This publication was prepared with funding from the Office of Educational Research and Improvement, U.S. Department of Education, under contract no. RR93002009. The opinions expressed in this report do not necessarily reflect the positions or policies of OERI or ED.

DEVELOPMENTS IN DISTANCE EDUCATION

The print-based model of correspondence education supported by distance instruction through written messages has survived the test of time and continues to be utilized intensively. However, as distance education has become more institutionalized, other media have been applied. A second generation of distance education through the 1960s and 1970s was characterized by heavy reliance on open broadcast by either radio or television, supported by correspondence instruction and print materials.

The third generation of distance education has been characterized by teleconferencing systems. These began with audio conferencing but progressed to more sophisticated audio-graphic conferencing systems that supported the telephone audio conference with visual and text material (Barker and Goodwin 1992). Another parallel development has been video conferencing. Until recently this was a somewhat expensive alternative to the audio confer-ence, but due to developments in digital computer-based desktop video, it is now becoming economically accessible to an ever-larger section of the educational community (Parker and Olgren 1984; Tremblay 1992).

We are now entering a fourth phase of development of distance education based on the integrated use of new developments in telecommunications and computing and characterized by the integrated use of remote study materials supported by computer-based multimedia teleconferencing (Steinberg 1992). Integrated multimedia computer technology will provide the platform that will most resemble real-time, interactive instruction.

THE TECHNOLOGIES

The various technologies available for telecommunications-based distance education can be schematized as in Figure 1. In the synchronous communication mode, we are witnessing a development from predominantly audio communication by telephone, or ampli-fied telephone in the case of audio conferences, to multimedia interactive real-time commu-nication, either between individuals or groups. The result is that virtually all of the activities that can be undertaken in a conventional classroom situation can also be undertaken over distance, in a form of "virtual reality" (Hiltz 1990).

Figure 1.

	SYNCHRONOUS COMMUNICATION	ASYNCHRONOUS COMMUNICATION
ONE ON ONE	Telephone ↓ (Videophone) ↓ Multimedia Workstation	Facsimile ↓ E-Mail ↓ (Voicemail) ↓ Multimedia Workstation
GROUP LEARNING	Audioconference ↓ Audiographic System ↓ Videoconference ↓ Virtual Classroom	Computer-Conference ↓ Computer-Supported Collaborative Work (CSCW) Environments ↓ Multimedia Network

In the asynchronous communication mode, the predominant medium of the past (print) is being supplemented by voice-messaging facilities and other graphic communication potential so that once more we are working toward an integrated multimedia environment for educational communication. According to Hiltz and Turoff (1978), Vallee (1982), Kearsley (1985), Grief (1988), and Wilkinson and Sherman (1991), we are rapidly becoming a networked society that will adapt to utilizing telecommunications-based communication as easily as face-to-face communication is utilized in society today.

COSTS

The telecommunications option for education is often perceived as being expensive compared to either face-to-face education or the more conventional distance education methods based on print and correspondence by mail. However, this is not a completely accurate perception. Cost calculations that include the communication costs as well as the costs of tutor time in generating feedback messages to students show that telecommunications-based instruction can be more cost-efficient than print-based instruction (Romiszowski and Iskandar 1992). The experience of AT&T in utilizing audiographic teleconferencing has demonstrated cost reductions of more than 50 percent in the real costs of training if these are calculated to include the cost of transport and accommodations of participants from remote sites (Chute 1988). Furthermore, the costs of telecommunication are falling, whereas the costs of educational space, staffing, and transport are rising, so that over time the economical equation will favor the increased use of telecommunications-based education. One should also remember that over the long view it will not be necessary for educational systems to invest in the basic infrastructure for telecommunications, as this is a requirement for society and business in general (Zuboff 1988; Johansen 1988).

POTENTIAL BENEFITS

Given the technological scenario for the future that has just been painted, it is fair to ask whether such future systems are capable of delivering an appropriate level of quality of education. Research on distance education by and large has shown that, when appropriately planned, distance education can be as effective as conventional classroom-based education. Although there are some exceptions in terms of certain types of content or certain groups of students, the move toward integrated multimedia networking may be expected to extend the range of effective distance education applications (Collis 1991; Steinberg 1992; Kaye 1992).

One potential benefit of such integrated networks in distance education is that they may be user-driven. Groups of students may form naturally because of common interests at a given point in time, largely independent of decisions made by any single educational institution. A program of study might be composed of modules of materials pulled in from various institutions as required by the particular individual or group. Potentially, such a development offers the promise of overcoming a major weakness of conventional educational provision, namely, the long reaction time required by institutions to adapt curricula and content to the changing needs of society. To extend the currently popular hypertext/hypermedia jargon, we might look forward to the hyper-school or hyper-university, a network of the world's educational institutions that may be browsed at will by a student interested in planning and following through an individual program of study.

REFERENCES

Barker, B., and Goodwin, R. (1992, April). Audiographics: Linking remote classrooms. *Computing Teacher 19*(7), 11-15.

Brewster, R. L. (1987). *Telecommunications technology.* Chichester, UK: Ellis Horwood.

Cheng, H., Lehman, J., and Reynolds, A. (1991, November). What do we know about asynchronous group computer-based distance learning? *Educational Technology 31*(11), 16-19.

Chute, A. G. (1988). Learning from teletraining. *American Journal of Distance Education 3*, 55-63.

Collis, B. A. (1991). Telecommunications-based training in Europe: A state-of-the-art report. *American Journal of Distance Education 5*(2), 31-40.

Garrison, D. R. (1990). An analysis and evaluation of audio teleconferencing to facilitate education at a distance. *American Journal of Distance Education 4*(3), 13-24.

Grief, I., ed. (1988). *Computer supported cooperative work: A book of readings.* San Mateo, CA: Morgan Kaufmann.

Heler, J., Cooley, V., and Reitz, R. (1993, May). America School 2000 Project: Westfield's technology initiative. *T.H.E. Journal 20*(10), 83-86.

Hiltz, S. R. (1990). Collaborative teaching in a virtual classroom. In *Proceedings of the Third Symposium on Computer-Mediated Communication* (Guelph, Ontario: University of Guelph), 37-55.

Hiltz, S. R., and Turoff, M. (1978). *The network nation: Human communication via computer.* Reading, MA: Addison-Wesley.

Johansen, R. (1988). *Groupware: Computer support for business teams.* New York, NY: Free Press.

Kaye, A. (1992). Learning together apart. In *Collaborative learning through computer conferencing*, ed. A. Kaye (Berlin Heidelberg, Germany: Springer-Verlag), 1-24.

Kearsley, G. (1985). *Training for tomorrow: Distributed learning through computer and communications technology.* Reading, MA: Addison-Wesley.

Malfitano, R., and Cincotta, P. (1992, May). Network for a school of the future. *T.H.E. Journal 20*(10), 70-74.

Mason, R., and Kaye, A., eds. (1989). *Mindweave: Communication, computers and distance education.* London, UK: Pergamon Press.

Parker, L. A., and Olgren, C. A., eds. (1984). *The teleconferencing resource book: A guide to applications and planning.* Amsterdam, Netherlands: Elsevier Science Publishers B.V.

Romiszowski, A. J., and Iskandar, H. (1992, November). *Use of voice-mail tutoring in distance education.* Paper presented at the ICDE World Conference in Distance Education, Bangkok, Thailand.

Soby, M. (1992). Waiting for Electropolis. In *Collaborative learning through computer conferencing*, ed. A. Kaye (Berlin Heidelberg, Germany: Springer-Verlag), 39-50.

Steinberg, E. R. (1992, Spring). The potential of computer-based telecommunications for instruction. *Journal of Computer-Based Instruction 19*(2), 42-46.

Tremblay, W. (1992). Telecourse utilization in American research universities: Institutional context and instructional innovation. *Journal of Instructional Media 19*(3), 191-207.

Vallee, J. (1982). *The network revolution: Confessions of a computer scientist.* Berkeley, CA: And/Or Press.

Wilkinson, T. W., and Sherman, T. M. (1991, November). Telecommunications-based distance education: Who's doing what? *Educational Technology 31*(11), 54-59.

Zuboff, S. (1988). *In the age of the smart machine: The future of work and power.* New York, NY: Basic Books.

Television Violence and Behavior
A Research Summary*

Marilyn E. Smith

INTRODUCTION

The National Association for the Education of Young Children (NAEYC) position statement on media violence and children (1990) reports that violence in the media has increased since 1980 and continues to increase, particularly since the Federal Communication Commission's decision to deregulate children's commercial television in 1982. The NAEYC statement cites the following examples:

- Air time for war cartoons increased from 1.5 hours per week in 1982 to 43 hours per week in 1986.

- In 1980, children's programs featured 18.6 violent acts per hour and now have about 26.4 violent acts each hour.

According to an American Psychological Association task force report on television and American society (Huston et al. 1992), by the time the average child (i.e., one who watches two to four hours of television daily) leaves elementary school, he or she will have witnessed at least 8,000 murders and more than 100,000 other assorted acts of violence on television. Indicating growing concern regarding the issue of television violence, recent commentaries in the *Washington Post* (Harwood 1993; Will 1993; "Televiolence" 1993) highlight:

- a paper by Centerwall (1993) that examines several studies and argues that television violence increases violent and aggressive tendencies in young people and contributes to the growth of violent crime in the United States

- a *Times Mirror* poll, reported in March 1993, that found that the majority of Americans feel that "entertainment television is too violent . . . that this is harmful to society . . . that we as a society have become desensitized to violence."

This digest describes the overall pattern of the results of research on television violence and behavior. Several variables in the relationship between television violence and aggression related to characteristics of the viewers and to the portrayal of violence are identified. Finally, concerns regarding the effects of television violence are summarized.

---

*This digest was prepared by Marilyn E. Smith, Database Coordinator for the ERIC Clearinghouse on Information & Technology, Syracuse University. December 1993.

This publication was prepared with funding from the Office of Educational Research and Improvement, U.S. Department of Education, under contract no. RR93002009. The opinions expressed in this report do not necessarily reflect the positions or policies of OERI or ED.

RESEARCH FINDINGS

The overall pattern of research findings indicates a positive association between television violence and aggressive behavior. A *Washington Post* article (Oldenburg 1992) states that "the preponderance of evidence from more than 3,000 research studies over two decades shows that the violence portrayed on television influences the attitudes and behavior of children who watch it."

Signorielli (1991) finds that:

> Most of the scientific evidence . . . reveals a relationship between television and aggressive behavior. While few would say that there is absolute proof that watching television caused aggressive behavior, the overall cumulative weight of all the studies gives credence to the position that they are related. Essentially, television violence is one of the things that may lead to aggressive, antisocial, or criminal behavior; it does, however, usually work in conjunction with other factors. As aptly put by Dorr and Kovaric (1980), television violence may influence "some of the people some of the time" (pp. 94-95).

CHARACTERISTICS OF VIEWERS

The following characteristics of viewers, summarized by Clapp (1988), have been shown to affect the influence of television violence on behavior.

- **Age.** "A relationship between television violence and aggression has been observed in children as young as 3 (Singer and Singer 1981). Longitudinal data suggest that the relationship is much more consistent and substantial for children in middle childhood than at earlier ages (Eron and Huesmann 1986). Aggression in early adulthood is also related to the amount of violence watched in middle childhood, although it is not related to the amount watched in early adulthood (Eron, Huesmann, Lefkowitz, and Walder 1972). It has been proposed that there is a sensitive period between ages 8 and 12 during which children are particularly susceptible to the influence of television violence (Eron and Huesmann 1986)" (Clapp 1988, pp. 64-65).

- **Amount of television watched.** "Aggressive behavior is related to the total amount of television watched, not only to the amount of violent television watched. Aggressive behavior can be stimulated also by frenetic, hectic programming that creates a high level of arousal in children (Eron and Huesmann 1986; Wright and Huston 1983)" (Clapp 1988, p. 65).

- **Identification with television personalities.** "Especially for boys, identification with a character substantially increases the likelihood that the character's aggressive behavior will be modeled (Huesmann and Eron 1986; Huesmann, Lagerspetz, and Eron 1984)" (Clapp 1988, p. 65).

- **Belief that television violence is realistic.** "Significant relationships have been found between children's belief that television violence is realistic, their aggressive behavior, and the amount of violence that they watch (Huesmann 1986; Huesmann and Eron 1986)" (Clapp 1988, p. 65).

- **Intellectual achievement**. "Children of lower intellectual achievement generally (1) watch more television, (2) watch more violent television, (3) believe violent television reflects real life, and (4) behave more aggressively (Huesmann 1986)" (Clapp 1988, p. 65).

Comstock and Paik (1987, 1991) also identify the following factors that may increase the likelihood of television influence:

- Viewers who are in a state of anger or provocation before seeing a violent portrayal.

- Viewers who are in a state of frustration after viewing a violent portrayal, whether from an extraneous source or as a consequence of viewing the portrayal.

PORTRAYAL OF VIOLENCE

The following are factors related to how the violence is portrayed, which may heighten the likelihood of television influence. Research on these factors is summarized by Comstock and Paik (1987, 1991):

- Reward or lack of punishment for the portrayed perpetrator of violence

- Portrayal of the violence as justified

- Cues in the portrayal of violence that resemble those likely to be encountered in real life. For example, a victim in the portrayal with the same name or characteristics as someone toward whom the viewer holds animosity

- Portrayal of the perpetrator of violence as similar to the viewer

- Violence portrayed so that its consequences do not stir distaste or arouse inhibitions

- Violence portrayed as real events rather than events concocted for a fictional film

- Portrayed violence that is not the subject of critical or disparaging commentary

- Portrayals of violent acts that please the viewer

- Portrayals in which violence is not interrupted by violence in a light or humorous vein

- Portrayed abuse that includes physical violence and aggression instead of or in addition to verbal abuse

- Portrayals, violent or otherwise, that leave the viewer in a state of unresolved excitement.

Comstock and Paik (1991) argue that "these contingencies represent four dimensions: (a) efficacy (reward or lack of punishment); (b) normativeness (justified, consequenceless, intentionally hurtful, physical violence); (c) pertinence (commonality of cues, similarity to the viewer, absence of humorous violence); and (d) susceptibility (pleasure, anger, frustration, absence of criticism)" (pp. 255-56).

CONCERNS

Three major areas of concern regarding the effects of television violence are identified and discussed by the National Association for the Education of Young Children (1990):

- Children may become less sensitive to the pain and suffering of others.

- They may be more likely to behave in aggressive or harmful ways toward others.

- They may become more fearful of the world around them.

Of these, Signorielli (1991) considers the third scenario to be the most insidious:

> Research . . . has revealed that violence on television plays an important role in communicating the social order and in leading to perceptions of the world as a mean and dangerous place. Symbolic victimization on television and real world fear among women and minorities, even if contrary to the facts, are highly related (Morgan 1983). Analysis also reveals that in most subgroups those who watch more television tend to express a heightened sense of living in a mean world of danger and mistrust as well as alienation and gloom (p. 96).

Another concern addressed by the National Association for the Education of Young Children (1990) is the negative effect on children's play of viewing violent television: "In short, children who are frequent viewers of media violence learn that aggression is a successful and acceptable way to achieve goals and solve problems; they are less likely to benefit from creative, imaginative play as the natural means to express feelings, overcome anger, and gain self-control" (p. 19).

REFERENCES

Centerwall, B. S. (1993). Television and violent crime. *Public Interest 111*, 56-77.

Clapp, G. (1988). *Child study research: Current perspectives and applications.* Lexington, MA: Lexington.

Comstock, G., and Paik, H. (1987). *Television and children: A review of recent research.* Syracuse, NY: ERIC Clearinghouse on Information Resources. ED 292 466.

Comstock, G., and Paik, H. (1991). *Television and the American child.* San Diego, CA: Academic.

Dorr, A., and Kovaric, P. (1980). Some of the people some of the time—But which people? In *Children and the faces of television: Teaching, violence, selling.* Ed. E. L. Palmer and A. Dorr (New York: Academic), 183-99.

Eron, L. D., and Huesmann, L. R. (1986). The role of television in the development of prosocial and antisocial behavior. In *The development of antisocial and prosocial behavior: Research, theories, and issues.* Ed. D. Oweus, J. Block, and M. Radke-Yarrow (New York: Academic).

Eron, L. D., Huesmann, L. R., Lefkowitz, M. M., and Walder, L. D. (1972). Does television violence cause aggression? *American Psychologist 27*, 253-63.

Harwood, R. (1993, April 17). Is TV to blame for violence? *Washington Post,* A23.

Huesmann, L. R. (1986). Psychological processes promoting the relation between exposure to media violence and aggressive behavior by the viewer. *Journal of Social Issues 42,* 125-39. EJ 355 099.

Huesmann, L. R., and Eron, L. D. (1986). *Television and the aggressive child: A cross-national comparison.* Hillsdale, NJ: Lawrence Erlbaum.

Huesmann, L. R., Lagerspetz, K., and Eron, L. D. (1984). Intervening variables in the TV violence-aggression relation: Evidence from two countries. *Developmental Psychology 20*(5), 746-77. EJ 308 850.

Huston, A. C., Donnerstein, E., Fairchild, H., Fashbach, N. D., Katz, P. A., Murray, J. P., Rubinstein, E. A., Wilcox, B. L., and Zuckerman, D. (1992). *Big world, small screen: The role of television in American society.* Lincoln, NE: University of Nebraska.

Morgan, M. (1983). Symbolic victimization and real-world fear. *Human Communication Research 9*(2), 146-57. EJ 272 383.

National Association for the Education of Young Children. (1990). NAEYC position statement on media violence in children's lives. *Young Children 45*(5), 18-21. EJ 415 397.

Oldenburg, D. (1992, April 7). Primal screen-kids: TV violence and real-life behavior. *Washington Post,* E5.

Signorielli, N. (1991). *A sourcebook on children and television.* New York: Greenwood.

Singer, J. L., and Singer, D. G. (1981). *Television, imagination and aggression: A study of preschoolers.* Hillsdale, NJ: Lawrence Erlbaum.

Televiolence. (1993, April 17). *Washington Post,* A22.

Will, G. F. (1993, April 8). Yes, blame TV. *Washington Post,* A21.

Wright, J. C., and Huston, A. C. (1983). A matter of form: Potentials of television for young viewers. *American Psychologist 38,* 835-43. EJ 283 455.

Part Four
Leadership Profiles

Introduction

There are special reasons to feature the people and programs of Indiana University's program in Information Systems Technology. The curriculum development effort reported in the section on *The Profession* is a current development in the ongoing saga of that pioneer program. It is worthy of note at this time. The people who have made that program internationally known and respected are not always visible and this seemed like the time to honor them. One purpose of this section is to put the spotlight on individuals who have made significant contributions to the field of educational media and technology. This year the names of two retired Indiana University professors emerged as individuals to be honored. As in the past, these special tributes were written by colleagues of the individuals we have designated as leaders. We have learned much from Carolyn Guss and Mendel Sherman—and from the people they taught. Leadership casts a long shadow and we often find ourselves within it.

Carolyn Guss

Beverly Teach*
*Director, Media Resources, Instructional Support Services,
Indiana University, Bloomington, Indiana*

William J. Cuttill*
*Facilities Coordinator, Office of Integrated Technologies,
Indiana University-Purdue University, Indianapolis, Indiana*

Carolyn Guss was born June 11, 1910, in Indianapolis, the oldest of three children of Mary K. and Edward M. Guss. Carolyn has called "Hi-Lo Acres" home for more than 50 years—100 acres of picturesque, natural beauty in the "hills and 'hollers' " of Brown County, Indiana, about 10 miles east of Bloomington. She shared this country home with longtime friend Harriett Kersey until Harriett's death in 1972 and then with her sister Joan until Joan's death in 1992.

Miss Guss received her B.A. degree in English Literature and Drama from Butler University in 1929 and, at age 19, immediately began her teaching career in the public schools of Indiana. She taught Latin and English, served as school librarian, and supervised the audiovisual program for six years at Kingman High School and for seven years at Amo High School. Although she had planned to teach only a few years before continuing her formal education, more than a decade elapsed before the devoted and popular teacher could tear away from her students and enroll for a master's program at Indiana University.

The field of instructional technology was in its infancy in 1942 when Carolyn Guss enrolled in the only course in audiovisual education at Indiana University. L. C. Larson, the

---

*Beverly Teach is Director of Media Resources, Instructional Support Services, Indiana University-Bloomington. William J. Cuttill is Facilities Coordinator, Office of Integrated Technologies, Indiana University-Purdue University Indianapolis. They have each known Carolyn Guss for more than two decades—Bill since 1967 and Beverly since 1970—when they began their careers in the Selection Department under Carolyn's tutelage. Over these many years, she has been mentor, colleague, and friend.

instructor in that audiovisual course, himself newly arrived and visionary, took only a few months to recognize the potential contributions that his outstanding pupil could make to the developing audiovisual program. Carolyn Guss joined the staff of the Audio-Visual Center at Indiana University in 1942 as Assistant in Administration. She completed her master's degree in Secondary Education that same year, and her doctorate in Education in 1952. She was promoted to full professor in 1961. When she retired in 1975 after 33 years of dedicated leadership and scholarship, Dr. Carolyn Guss, Professor of Education and Associate in Selection, had made a significant contribution to the development of a curriculum and a program that was international in scope and influence.

A pioneer in the field of film evaluation, she became an international authority on the evaluation, selection, and cataloging of educational media. Her dissertation, entitled *A Study of Film Evaluation and Selection Practices in Twelve Universities and Colleges with Recommendations for Improvement*, served as a benchmark for evaluation practices in the area of media selection and as the stimulus and model for numerous scholars in the field. Over the years, she refined the recommendations of this study through teaching, writing numerous articles on evaluation and selection, and conducting workshops. She has consulted with universities, colleges, and community colleges on setting up or improving systems for the bibliographic control of information regarding educational media.

When Carolyn Guss started at IU, there was a small collection of films and lantern slides. With characteristic enthusiasm, she proceeded to develop the young film library collection, carefully evaluating, selecting, and cataloging films for various grade levels and subject matter fields. A classification scheme was developed; a permanent file of film credits, transcribed exactly as they appeared on each film, was created; an evaluation procedure that included the active involvement of subject, utilization, and production specialists was refined. Cataloging standards were such that the IU film catalog was often referred to as "the bible" when accurate bibliographic information was needed. Under Guss's direction, the film library has been recognized nationally and internationally as one of the most comprehensive and useful collections of educational films in the world.

Her areas of instruction expanded correspondingly to encompass evaluation, selection, curricular integration, classification, cataloging, and annotation of educational media. More than 3,000 students have selected her classes as essential components of their programs—to work with her was to work with a recognized authority whose evaluations of media were regular features of leading publications in the educational media field, including *Educational Screen and AV Guide, The Instructor*, and *Teachers Guides to Television*. Dr. Guss has served on approximately 200 advanced degree committees. A few of those receiving degrees under her guidance include Richard W. Gilkey, Jerrold E. Kemp, William G. Oglesby, Edward Minor, William C. Prigge, Irving S. Spigle, and Betty Stoops.

Dr. Guss frequently served as a consultant and lecturer for educational media institutes and workshops throughout the nation. In 1960, she and Margaret Rufsvold co-chaired a feasibility study for the U.S. Office of Education on national bibliographic control of information about newer media. As a result of this study, a national work conference was convened, bringing together national authorities from diverse disciplines. This conference resulted in the Educational Media Council's resolution to establish, for the first time, a national directory of newer educational media. Although the resulting *Educational Media Index* did not survive as a product, the principles embodied in the Guss/Rufsvold conference survived as a founding base for bibliographic control. In 1970, Dr. Guss chaired a conference on *Evaluation in Instructional Systems Technology* that brought together such noted speakers with diverse professional backgrounds and philosophies as Michael Scriven, University of California/Berkeley; Robert Stake, University of Illinois; P. Kenneth Komoski, Educational

Products Information Exchange; Edward Palmer, Children's Television Workshop; and Egon Guba, Indiana University.

Publishers and producers have sought Guss's guidance in media cataloging processes. She has served as consultant to McGraw-Hill, United World, Coronet, and Encyclopaedia Britannica Educational Corporation on media catalogs and the cataloging process in an attempt to create better bibliographic control and retrieval capabilities. By insisting on the need for feedback to producers and emphasizing the partnership producers and consumers must achieve, she has been instrumental in facilitating growth in the quality of instructional films. With Margaret Rufsvold, she co-authored *Guides to Educational Media*, which was published by the American Library Association through four editions.

Carolyn Guss has served the field of education internationally as well as locally and nationally. She has been president of the Indiana Association for Educational Communications and Technology (IAECT) and a member of the Board of Directors of the national AECT, and she chaired the initial Committee on Film Evaluation of AECT. She was the official delegate in 1968 to the international conference on *The Application of Electronic Methods of Cataloging Films and Television Materials* held in Paris, France. She served as director of a four-year Indiana University/Agency for International Development film evaluation project for the purpose of recommending to USAID films that would be appropriate for use in developing countries to assist in education, health, family, and industrial matters. Through this project, scores of international students received instruction and practical experience in media evaluation and utilization, and the films selected reached literally tens of thousands of citizens in developing countries. She served as president, vice president, and secretary of the board of directors of the Educational Film Library Association (EFLA). She was a member of the editorial board for *AV Instruction* (now *Educational Technology Research and Development*), film jury chairperson for the Council on International Nontheatrical Events and the American Film Festival, and served on the advisory board for the Educational Products Information Exchange (EPIE).

Miss Guss's accomplishments have not gone unnoticed. She has memberships in three educational honorary societies: Phi Kappa Phi, Pi Lambda Theta, and Delta Kappa Gamma. Her service to Delta Kappa Gamma, an international honorary society, includes acting as president of the state organization, northeast regional director, international vice president, and international president. She served with such distinction that an annual international scholarship award for advanced graduate study in education was permanently established in her honor. Carolyn also organized and served as first chairperson of the board of directors of the Delta Kappa Gamma Educational Foundation. In recognition of her untiring devotion to the field, her unerring good judgment, and her dedication to serving, she was presented with the Society's annual international achievement award in 1963. In 1965, the Indiana Association for Educational Communications and Technology bestowed on her the Indiana Award for Outstanding Contributions to the Field of Audio-Visual Education; in 1972, the Educational Film Library Association gave her its national award for distinguished leadership; in 1977, the Association for Educational Communications and Technology presented her with the Distinguished Service Award "for the personal example she has set and for her long advocacy of high standards in the evaluation of instructional materials"; in 1982, the Consortium of College and University Media Centers (formerly the Consortium of University Film Centers) awarded her its Silver Reel Award for leadership in developing standards for the selection of audiovisual materials; and in 1992, the American Film and Video Association (formerly the Educational Film Library Association) honored her with its Gold Ribbon Award for distinguished service to the association. The Council on International Nontheatrical Events named her to honorary life membership on its board in recognition of her dedication in improving world understanding through motion pictures. She has been cited in *Who's Who of American Women*, *Who's Who in American Education*, and *The World of Who's Who of Women*. In 1986, the Governor of Indiana named her a Sagamore of the Wabash, the highest personal honor that can be given to recognize those who have rendered distinguished service.

A faculty tribute to Dr. Guss presented upon the occasion of her retirement in 1975 reflects the special qualities that endear her to everyone who knows her:

> Throughout her impressive career, Carolyn has maintained those qualities credited to a truly remarkable individual. Success and honor have come her way, and she has accepted them with humility and grace. She has always regarded human relationships with students and colleagues as her primary responsibility. The students who have been fortunate enough to come under her influence will always be grateful for the professional contribution she has made to their careers, but they will remember her for her human qualities and for the ready help and advice they could always depend on.

Mendel Sherman

Dennis Pett
Professor Emeritus, Indiana University
Bloomington, Indiana

Mendel Sherman has been active as a respected leader in the Audio-Visual/Instructional Technology field for more than 35 years. Starting as a teacher in the elementary schools of Hamilton County, Ohio, he served in public education, the military, and at the university level.

Mendel was born in Newport, Kentucky, and attended elementary and secondary schools in Ohio's Hamilton County schools. He attended the University of Cincinnati where, in 1933, he received an A.B. degree in chemistry and zoology. While a student, he met and married Martha Steincamp. Martha received an undergraduate degree from the Applied Arts College of the University of Cincinnati and a degree in art education. She continued her education in graduate design courses. Martha's interests in the arts were, and continue to be, eclectic, including crafts, music, modern dance, and landscape gardening. Mendel continued his studies in education, receiving an M.Ed. in 1940 from the University of Cincinnati. His master's thesis was titled *An Audio-Visual Program for the Cincinnati Public Schools*.

From 1938 to 1943, Mendel was associated with the Cincinnati schools as an elementary school teacher, assistant principal, and AV coordinator. In the latter role, he prepared the first consolidated audiovisual handbook for all 16mm films, filmstrips, and recordings in the extensive inventory of the Cincinnati Public Schools' AV Library.

Mendel entered military service in 1943 and, after basic training in the Medical Replacement Training Corps, Camp Barkley, Texas, he was transferred to the camp film library. His duties were numerous, including meeting with various instructors on the efficient use of training films and preparing a catalog with descriptions of available materials. Later he attended the Signal Corps Officer Candidate School, and, from November 1944 to February 1945, he was trained as a photographic officer and motion picture cameraman at the Signal Corps Photographic School in Astoria, New York. Mendel was sent to the European theater of operations during the Battle of the Bulge as a replacement photographic officer, but ended up in Paris as officer-in-charge of the Central Film and Equipment Exchange. The next year,

1946, he was promoted to head of the Training Film Operations Branch of the Army Pictorial Division in the European theater of operations. In that role Mendel received a citation for the Army Commendation Ribbon for "outstanding service and meritorious achievement as a training film officer." The same year, he went on a special mission to Denmark for which he received a citation for his service to the Danish military program.

In 1947, Mendel returned to Cincinnati as city-wide AV supervisor responsible for selection, procurement, and distribution of materials and equipment and assistance to teachers and supervisors in the utilization of a broad range of AV materials. He remained in that role until 1955. In addition to handling routine aspects of the position, he organized and conducted numerous workshops and presentations for professional and civic groups throughout the area.

He also produced a film titled *What Makes Plants Grow*, which showed the activities of children and their teacher as they integrated audiovisual materials into a second-grade science unit. This film was widely used in workshops by the science specialist of the U.S. Office of Education. In 1951, Mendel organized a series of telecasts titled *Inside Our Schools*, which were produced in cooperation with *Life* magazine and a local television station. Each morning for one week, crews and their cameras moved from schoolroom to schoolroom to acquaint the viewing public with the teaching and learning that went on in various classrooms. In addition to working with curriculum area supervisors and school administrators to organize the telecasts, Mendel also had the responsibility for breaking in with commentary to interpret scenes as needed. This was an innovative series for those early days of television. In 1954, television was formally added to Mendel's list of responsibilities and, in the next year, he coordinated and produced numerous television programs for the Cincinnati public schools.

In 1955, Mendel completed a Doctorate in Education at the University of Southern California. Building on the interest in television developed in Cincinnati, his dissertation focused on the feasibility of using television to evaluate motion pictures. The *Sherman Film Evaluation Form* he developed for his dissertation was adopted by the periodical *Teaching Tools* and by a number of film evaluation committees. Later in 1955, Mendel moved to Indiana, where he took a joint appointment at Indiana University with the Audio-Visual Center and the School of Education's Division of Educational Media. The division was renamed the Division of Instructional Systems Technology (DIST) in 1969. In his role as an administrator, Mendel was in charge of the Audio-Visual Center's film library from 1955 to 1958, and from 1972 to 1975 was director of the DIST. In his teaching role, he taught several graduate courses, including "Utilization of Audio-Visual Materials" and an experimental course dealing with the design and production of videotaped self-instructional sequences. Closely allied to his teaching were the development and coordination of the department's extensive curriculum and his counseling of graduate students. During the period Mendel directed DIST, I had the privilege of sharing an office area with him. It was a lesson in human relations and a joy to observe his patience and his ability to develop rapport with students from all parts of the globe.

The depth and breadth of Mendel's knowledge and his understanding of the role of media in the broad field of formal and nonformal education are exemplified by the variety of special projects in which he was involved during his tenure at IU:

- He coordinated and/or produced about 30 Saturday morning television programs in cooperation with the Department of Radio and Television.

- For many years, he served as a faculty member of the National Audio Visual Association's annual summer institutes.

- He organized and participated in the annual week-long summer AV conferences from 1956 to 1958 and from 1960 to 1970.

- He organized and participated in the Regional Audio-Visual Leadership Conferences held in the larger school systems of Indiana. These conferences focused on the roles that AV could play in instruction and on the effective utilization of AV materials when integrated in an instructional unit.

- He represented Indiana University in the Midwest Program for Airborne Television Instruction (MPATI). Starting in May 1961, a DC6AB flew in an irregular figure-eight pattern over Montpelier, Indiana, while its two UHF transmitters sent taped lessons in a variety of subjects to elementary and secondary schools throughout a 200-mile radius. The purpose of the project was to bring resources not otherwise readily available to the classroom and to raise the quality of instruction. Mendel provided leadership for this project, which was a forerunner of satellite technology.

- He served as a consultant to the Thailand Ministry of Education, Chulalongkorn University, and The School of Education, with which an IU team was working. In this role he held conferences for Thai media specialists and 222 of the nation's top education officers. Mendel produced a motion picture, *Education Under a Thatched Roof*, which documented a unit approach and the integration of AV materials into Thai elementary education. He also produced several short sequences for Thai television that showed some of the newest practices in health and education.

- He co-directed an National Defense Education Act fellowship grant to develop and conduct a special program for instructional technology specialists who would serve developing institutes of higher learning. The two-year program resulted in completion of specialist or doctorate degrees, depending on the entry level of the participants.

One of Mendel's outstanding attributes was his commitment to service in the AV/IST field. While he was associated with the Cincinnati schools, he was elected president of the Ohio Audio-Visual Director's Association and president of the Cincinnati Film Council. During his years at IU, Mendel was active in associations at the state and national levels. For his service to the state, he was the first recipient of the prestigious Edgar Dale award. As an active member of the Department of Audiovisual Instruction (of the National Education Association), later the Association for Educational Communications and Technology, he served in many roles:

- He joined DAVI in 1947, served on the executive committee beginning in 1958, and was president from 1964 to 1965.

- He chaired the Commission on Professional Standards and Ethics in 1962.

- He co-conducted the first DAVI Field Service Survey in 1954, a week-long effort carried out in Des Moines, Iowa. Most of the changes recommended as a result of the survey were carried out, as reported later in *Educational Screen*.

- He was a consultant and/or speaker at innumerable state and regional conferences and conventions.

- He presented a paper in 1958 on *The Role of Film in Educational Television* at a national conference on educational television called by the U.S. Office of Education. He shared the speakers' platform with Marshall McLuhan, Edgar Dale, and others.

- He participated in five Lake Okoboji Leadership Conferences between 1957 and 1962.

- He served on the American Association of School Librarians/AECT Joint Committee on standards and was co-chairperson of the implementation committee.

- He worked with Gene Faris formulating quantitative standards for audiovisual personnel, equipment, and materials. These standards were adopted by DAVI in October 1965.

After his retirement from Indiana University, Mendel continued his service to education, the field of instructional technology, and his community. In 1987, he received a patent on a device to enable novice tennis players to develop an effective stroke and produced a videotape to demonstrate the device. In 1991, he wrote a booklet, *Videographing the Pictorial Sequence*, for the AECT President's Library. A recent AECT publications catalog notes that it is a best seller. In 1992, Mendel organized a group of residents of Clemson Downs, a retirement community in which he and Martha live, to assist local schools. One project undertaken provides weekly help to the elementary school's homework program for individual students needing assistance. As a part of this program, Mendel conducted training for four sixth-graders on the use of a camcorder. They have completed some remarkable video footage for a tape depicting the cooperation between their elementary school and the retirement community. The retiree group received the Palmetto Pride Award, which is given annually to South Carolina's outstanding volunteer.

Mendel Sherman has made substantial contributions to education by his work in several arenas. This has been accomplished in an easy, unhurried manner by a dependable man of great warmth and kindness who provides a model for those associated with him.

Part Five
The Year in Review

Introduction

There are many professional associations in the field of educational media and technology. The seven that are included in this edition are considered to be the major organizations in North America. Their inclusion is based on longevity, number of members, professional journals published, and visibility. Additional professional associations are listed in part 6, Organizations and Associations in North America.

People in a field organize themselves to improve communications among a group of people with common interests and objectives. They advance the profession by establishing performance standards and usually a code of ethics. All of the associations featured in this part have received recognition for their contributions to the advancement of educational media and technology. In some cases, the scope of interest of one organization overlaps that of another. Some professionals realize that their interests are not contained only within one association, and, therefore, join others that also are compatible with their interests, values, and goals.

The editors plan to continue this section in the *Yearbook* as an important component of an annual status report to the profession.

ADCIS
Association for the Development of Computer-Based Instructional Systems

ADCIS is an international association with a worldwide membership of professionals who are actively involved in the development and use of computer-based instructional technologies. Members work in a wide variety of settings, including business and industry; elementary and secondary schools; junior colleges, colleges, and universities; and vocational and specialized schools; as well as the military and the government.

ADCIS brings together people of many different perspectives and careers, who share the common goal of excellence in instruction through the effective use of computer technology. Their interests range from the most basic concepts of computer literacy to the most advanced concepts in interactive video and artificial intelligence. Information shared is based on the highest-quality research available.

The Association provides an international forum for:

- Intellectual leadership in the field;

- Professional growth opportunities; and

- Integration of theory and practice.

THE ADCIS MISSION AND MEMBERSHIP

The mission of ADCIS is to promote human learning and performance through the use of computer-based technologies. All ADCIS members receive a free subscription to the *Journal of Computer-Based Instruction (JCBI)*, a quarterly periodical that is highly respected as one of the most scholarly publications in the field of computer-based instruction.

ADCIS members also receive reduced registration fees to the annual ADCIS International Conference. This conference attracts more than 750 conferees from around the world. During the five-day meeting, more than 300 presentations are made in the 11 interest areas covered by the Special Interest Groups (SIGs). These presentations are selected from juried papers and bound in a 400-plus-page *Proceedings*, which is received by all conferees. The 37th International Conference will be held February 8-12, 1995, in Anaheim, California, in conjunction with the Annual Conference of the Association for Educational Communications and Technology and InCITE Exposition.

The ADCIS membership divides itself into 11 Special Interest Groups (SIGs). Members receive one free membership in a SIG of their choice; additional SIGs may be joined for $5 each. The 11 SIGs are:

- SIGCBT   Computer-Based Training

- ETSIG   Emerging Technology

- HESIG   Health Education

- HOMEC   Home Economics
- HYPERSIG   Hypermedia
- MISIG   Management Issues
- PUG   Plato User's Group
- SIGAC   Academic Computing
- SIGIVA   Interactive Video/Audio
- SIGTAR   Theory and Research
- SIGTELE   Telecommunications

NEWSLETTERS

ADCIS members receive the *ADCIS News*, an association newsletter that keeps members up-to-date on important developments in the field of computer-based technologies. Each SIG also publishes a newsletter for its members.

NETWORKING

Contacts with professionals who have similar interests or who are working on similar projects or problems are coordinated through the ADCIS headquarters office and through the SIG structure. Members stay in touch with each other through electronic mail.

CURRENT OFFICERS

Cynthia Leshin, President; Rod Sims, Vice President; Tim Spannaus, Immediate Past President; Ed Schwartz, Immediate Past Vice President; Lori Gillespie, Financial Vice President; Steve Harmon, Program Chair; and Carol Norris, Managing Director.

ACCESSING ADCIS SERVICES

Individuals interested in joining ADCIS, subscribing to the *Journal of Computer-Based Instruction*, or receiving registration information for the International Conference should contact ADCIS International Headquarters, 1601 West Fifth Avenue, Suite 111, Columbus, OH 43212. (614) 487-1528. Fax (614) 487-1528. Carol Norris, contact person.

AECT
Association for Educational Communications and Technology

Established in 1923, the Association for Educational Communications and Technology is an international professional association dedicated to the improvement of instruction through the utilization of media and technology. The mission of the association is to provide leadership in educational communications and technology by linking professionals holding a common interest in the use of education technology and its application to the learning process. In the past few years, convention topics have focused on hypermedia, teleconferencing, and converging technologies, and AECT cosponsored the teleconference, "Teaching and Technology: A Critical Link," which addressed issues on the restructuring of public schools and the role of technology. AECT also honors outstanding individuals or groups making significant contributions to the field of educational communications and technology or to the association. (See the separate listing for full information on these awards.)

MEMBERSHIP

AECT members include instructional technologists; media or library specialists; university professors and researchers; industrial/business training specialists; religious educators; government media personnel; school, school district, and state department of education media program administrators and specialists; educational/training media producers; and numerous others whose professional work requires improvement of media and technology in education and training. AECT members also work in the armed forces, in public libraries, in museums, and in other information agencies of many different kinds, including those related to the emerging fields of computer technology.

MEMBERSHIP SERVICES

AECT serves as a central clearinghouse and communications center for its members. The association maintains TechCentral, a national electronic mail network and bulletin board service. Through its various committees and task forces, it compiles data and prepares recommendations to form the basis of guidelines, standards, research, and information summaries on numerous topics and problems of interest to the membership. AECT professional staff members report on government activities of concern to the membership and provide current data on laws and pending legislation relating to the educational media/technology field. AECT also maintains the ECT Foundation, through which it offers a limited number of financial grants to further the association's work. Archives are maintained at the University of Maryland.

CONFERENCES

The 1994 Annual Conference was held February 16-20 in Nashville, Tennessee, and was accompanied by the first International Computing and Instructional Technology Exposition (InCITE). The 1995 Conference will be held February 9-12 in Anaheim, California, together with InCITE.

PUBLICATIONS

AECT maintains an active publication program which includes *TechTrends for Leaders in Education and Training* (6/yr., free with membership); *Educational Technology Research & Development* (4/yr.); various division publications; and a number of books and videotapes, including the following recent titles: *Adoptable Copyright Policy: Copyright Policy and Manuals Designed for Adoption by Schools, Colleges and Universities* (1992); *A Copyright Primer, 2nd Ed.* (1994); *Library Copyright Guide* (1992); *Appraising Audiovisual Media: A Guide for Attorneys, Trust Officers, Insurance Professionals, and Archivists in Appraising Films, Video, Photographs, Recordings, and Other Audiovisual Assets* (1993); *Compressed Video: Operations and Applications* (1993); *The 1992-93 Educational Software Preview Guide* (1992); *Educational Technology: A Review of the Research* (1992); *Evaluating Computer Integration in the Elementary School: A Step by Step Guide* (1990); *Focus on Reform: State Initiatives in Educational Technology* (1992); *Graduate Curricula in Educational Communications and Technology: A Descriptive Directory* (4th ed., 1992); *Videographing the Pictorial Sequence: AECT Presidents' Library Vol. II* (1991); *Teaching and Learning through Technology, the Star Schools Videotape* (one VHS tape, 1989); *TQM for Media Managers* (1994); *Instructional Technology: The Definition and Domains of the Field* (1994).

AFFILIATED ORGANIZATIONS

Because of similarity of interests, a number of organizations have chosen to affiliate with AECT. These include the Association for MultiImage (AMI); Association for Special Education Technology (ASET); Community College Association for Instruction and Technology (CCAIT); Consortium of University Film Centers (CUFC); Federal Educational Technology Association (FETA); Health Science Communications Association (HeSCA); International Association for Learning Laboratories (IALL); International Visual Literacy Association (IVLA); Minorities in Media (MIMS); National Association of Regional Media Centers (NARMC); National Instructional Television Fixed Service Association (NIA/ITFS); New England Educational Media Association; Northwest College and University Council for the Management of Educational Technology; Southeastern Regional Media Leadership Council (SRMLC); and State University of New York Educational Communications Center.

Two additional organizations are also related to the Association for Educational Communications and Technology: the AECT Archives and the AECT ECT Foundation.

AECT DIVISIONS

AECT has nine divisions: Division of Educational Media Management (DEMM); Division of Interactive Systems and Computers (DISC); Division of Instructional Development (DID); Division of School Media Specialists (DSMS); Division of Telecommunications (DOT); Industrial Training and Education Division (ITED); International Division (INTL); Media Design and Production Division (MDPD); and Research and Theory Division (RTD).

CURRENT OFFICERS/MEMBERS OF THE AECT BOARD OF DIRECTORS

Stanley D. Zenor, Executive Director; Kent Gustafson, President; Lynn Milet, President-Elect; Addie Kinsinger, Past President; David Graf, Secretary-Treasurer; and Ron Payne, Jim Stonge, Roberts Braden, Joaquin Holloway, Dave Tiedemann, and Mary Adrion, Board Members.

Further information is available from AECT, 1025 Vermont Avenue NW, Suite 820, Washington, DC 20005. (202) 347-7834. Fax (202) 347-7839.

AMTEC
Association for Media and Technology
in Education in Canada
L'Association des Media et de la Technologie
en Education au Canada

PURPOSE

Canada's national association for educational media and technology professionals, AMTEC is a forum concerned with the impact of media and technology on teaching, learning, and society. As an organization, AMTEC provides national leadership through annual conferences, publications, workshops, media festival awards, ongoing reaction to media and technology issues at the international, national, provincial, and local levels, and linkages with other organizations with similar interests.

MEMBERSHIP

AMTEC's membership is geographically dispersed and professionally diversified. Membership stretches from St. John's, Newfoundland, to Victoria, British Columbia, and from Inuvik, Northwest Territories, to Niagara Falls, Ontario. Members include teachers, consultants, broadcasters, media managers, photographers, librarians/information specialists, educational technology specialists, instructional designers/trainers, technology specialists, artists, and producers/distributors. They represent all sectors of the educational media and technology fields: elementary and secondary schools, colleges, institutes of technology, universities, provincial governments, school boards, military services, health services libraries, and private corporations.

ACTIVITIES

Workshops. AMTEC offers workshops in cooperation with other agencies and associations based on AMTEC members' needs, in addition to the in-depth workshops at the AMTEC annual conference.

Annual Conference. The AMTEC annual conference provides opportunities to meet delegates from across the nation and to attend sessions on the latest issues and developments in such areas as copyright law, instructional design, distance education, library standards, media production, broadcasting and educational technology, media utilization, and visual literacy. AMTEC 94 was held June 12-15, 1994, in Lethbridge, Alberta, and AMTEC 95 is scheduled to be held in May 1995, in Guelph, Ontario.

Awards. AMTEC annually recognizes outstanding individual achievement and leadership in the field through the EMPDAC (Educational Media Producers and Distributors Association of Canada) Achievement Award, the AMTEC Leadership Award, and the Telesat Educational Telecommunications Award. In addition, AMTEC acts as the correspondent for the Commonwealth Relations Trust Bursary for educational broadcasters. This annual bursary provides a three-month study tour of educational broadcasting in the United Kingdom.

Annual Media Festival. AMTEC conducts a national showcase for educational media and technology productions. Awards are presented annually at the AMTEC conference in recognition of outstanding achievement in areas such as television, radio, film, slide, and computer software.

Reaction to Issues. AMTEC provides opportunities for members to contribute to educational media and technology issues and their solutions. The association frequently communicates with other associations and levels of government to resolve issues of concern to the membership.

Publications. Publications include:

- *The Canadian Journal of Educational Communications (CJEC)*, a quarterly covering the latest in research, application, and periodical literature. It also publishes reviews on significant books and films and critiques on computer programs.

- *Media News*, a quarterly newletter that covers the news in the field, including helpful tips, future conferences, comments on current projects, and information about AMTEC members and the AMTEC Board.

- *Membership Directory*, which expands the professional network of members.

In addition, occasional publications are produced to assist members in keeping abreast in the field. These include directories, guidelines, and monographs. AMTEC also operates a mailserv on the Internet.

CURRENT OFFICERS

The AMTEC Board of Directors includes the association's President, Ross Mutton; Past President, Barbara Martin; President-Elect, Al LeBlanc; Secretary/Treasurer, Lillian Carefoot; and three Directors, Bob Christie, Danielle Fortosky, and Dan Malone.

Additional information may be obtained from AMTEC, 3-1750 The Queensway, Suite 1318, Etobicoke, Ontario, Canada M9C 5H5.

ISTE
International Society for Technology in Education

PURPOSE

The International Society for Technology in Education is a nonprofit professional society of educators. Its goals include the improvement of education through the appropriate use of computer-related technology and the fostering of active partnerships between businesses and educators involved in this field. The majority of ISTE's efforts are aimed at precollege education and teacher preparation.

MEMBERSHIP

ISTE members are teachers, administrators, computer coordinators, curriculum coordinators, teacher educators, information resource managers, and educational technological specialists. Approximately 85 percent of the 10,000-person membership is in the United States, 10 percent is in Canada, and the remainder is scattered throughout nearly 100 other countries.

ACTIVITIES

ISTE works to achieve its mission through its publication program, which includes 12 periodicals as well as a wide range of books and courseware, cosponsorship or sponsorship of a variety of conferences and workshops, and its extensive network of regional affiliates, a Private Sector Council, a distance education program, and membership in NCATE (National Council for the Accreditation of Teacher Education).

PUBLICATIONS

Periodical publications include membership periodicals: *The Computing Teacher* (8/yr.); the *Educational Information Resource Manager (IRM) Quarterly*; the *Journal of Research on Computing in Education* (quarterly); and *ISTE Update: People, Events, and News in Education Technology* (newsletter, 8/yr.). Quarterly periodicals for special-interest groups include: *Logo Exchange*, for the SIG Logo; the *Journal of Computing in Teacher Education*, for the Teacher Educators SIG; *HyperNEXUS*, for the Hyper/Multi-Media SIG; the *Journal of Computer Science Education*, for the Computer Science SIG; *T.I.E. News*, for the Telecommunications SIG; and *SIGTC Connections*, for the Technology Coordinator SIG. Other periodicals include the *Microsoft Works in Education*, a quarterly for users of Microsoft Works; and *CAELL Journal* (Computer Assisted English Language Learning Journal), quarterly for teachers of English, foreign languages, and adult literacy.

ISTE also publishes a variety of books and courseware.

CONFERENCES

ISTE is the administrative house for the National Educational Computing Conference (NECC), which was held June 13-15, 1994, in Boston, Massachusetts; NECC '95 will be held in Baltimore in June 1995. ISTE will also be running the third International Symposium on Telecommunications in Education on November 10-13, 1994, in Albuquerque, New Mexico.

CURRENT OFFICERS

The current ISTE Board includes Lajeane Thomas, President; Peggy Kelly, President-Elect; Sally Sloan, Past President; Dennis Bybee, Associate Executive Officer; David Moursund, Executive Officer; Connie Stout; David Brittain; Don Knezek; Kim Allen; Francisco Carocheo; Sheila Cory; Terrie Gray; Terry Killion; Gail Morse; and Gwen Solomon.

For further information, contact Maia Howes, ISTE Executive Secretary, at 1787 Agate Street, Eugene, OR 97403-1923. (503) 346-2414. Fax (503) 346-5890.

IVLA
International Visual Literacy Association

PURPOSE

IVLA, Inc., a nonprofit international association, was established in 1968 to provide a multidisciplinary forum for the exploration, presentation, and discussion of all aspects of visual communication and their applications through visual images, visual literacy, and literacies in general. The association serves as the organizational bond for professionals from many diverse disciplines who are creating and sustaining the study of the nature of visual experiences and literacies and their cognitive and affective bases, and who are developing new means for the evaluation of learning through visual methods. It also encourages the funding of creative visual literacy projects, programs, and research, and promotes and evaluates projects intended to increase the use of visuals in education and communications.

MEMBERSHIP

IVLA members represent a diverse group of disciplines, including fine and graphic artists, photographers, researchers, scientists, filmmakers, television producers, graphic and computer-graphic designers, phototherapists, business communication professionals, school administrators, classroom teachers, visual studies theorists and practitioners, educational technologists, photojournalists, print and electronic journalists, and visual anthropologists.

MEMBER SERVICES

Members of IVLA benefit from opportunities to interact with other professionals whose ideas may be challenging or reinforcing. Such opportunities are provided by the annual conference, information exchanges, research programs, workshops, seminars, presentation opportunities as an affiliate of the Association for Educational Communications and Technology (AECT), and access to the Visual Literacy Collection located in the Center for Visual Literacy at Arizona State University.

PUBLICATIONS

IVLA publishes two periodicals: the *Journal of Visual Literacy* (2 per year) and the *Review*, a visual literacy newsletter. It also publishes an annual book of selected conference readings.

CONFERENCES

The 1994 conference will be held in Tempe, Arizona, October 12-16. The theme will be "Timeless Images: Past, Present, and Future." The 1995 conference is scheduled to be held in Chicago in October 1995.

CURRENT OFFICERS

Ron Sutton, President; Landra Rezabek, President-Elect; Nikos Metallinos, Immediate Past President; Richard Couch, Robert Griffin, and Rune Pettersson, Vice Presidents; Alice D. Walker, Executive Treasurer; and Robert C. Branch, Recording Secretary.

Further information may be obtained from Alice D. Walker, Treasurer, Virginia Tech, Educational Technologies-LRC, Old Security Building, Blacksburg, VA 24061-0232. (703) 231-8992.

NSPI
National Society for Performance and Instruction

NSPI is an international association dedicated to increasing productivity in the workplace through the application of performance and instructional technologies. Founded in 1962, the society promotes the improvement of human performance among governmental, legislative, business, corporate, and educational leaders, and through the national media.

MEMBERSHIP

The 5,500 members of NSPI are located throughout the United States, Canada, and 33 other countries. Members include performance technologists, training directors, human resource managers, instructional technologists, change agents, human factors practitioners, and organizational development consultants. They work in a variety of settings, including business, industry, universities, governmental agencies, health services, banks, and the armed forces.

SERVICES TO NSPI MEMBERS

NSPI offers its members opportunities to grow professionally and personally, to meet and know leaders in the field and learn about new things before they are published for the world at large, to make themselves known in the field, and to pick up new ideas on how to deal with their own political and technical challenges on the job. Membership benefits include subscriptions to *Performance & Instruction* and *News & Notes*; the *Annual Membership Directory*; participation in the annual conference and exposition; access to a variety of resources and individuals to help improve professional skills and marketability; a variety of insurance programs at group rates; leadership opportunities through participation in special projects, 12 major committees, and task forces, or serving as national or chapter officers; an executive referral service; and discounts on publications, advertising, conference registration and recordings, and other society services.

ACTIVITIES

The NSPI Endowment sponsors the Young Academic Program, an awards program for recent recipients of a doctoral degree currently working in academic positions. Designed to promote excellence in the field, the award is given for research on topics related to performance and instructional technology, including literature reviews and/or meta-analyses with implications for performance-enhancing interventions. The recipient of the award of $500 is required to prepare and make a presentation at the annual conference and submit a potentially publishable manuscript.

CONFERENCES

Annual Conference and Expo: San Francisco, California, April 4-8, 1994; Atlanta, Georgia, March 27-31, 1995; Dallas, Texas, April 15-19, 1996; Anaheim, California, April 14-18, 1997; and Chicago, Illinois, March 23-28, 1998.

PUBLICATIONS

NSPI publications include *Performance & Instruction Journal* (10/yr.); *Performance Improvement Quarterly*; *News & Notes* (10/yr.); and the *Annual Membership Directory*.

CURRENT OFFICERS

William Coscarelli, President; Carol Valen, President-Elect; Mark Greene, Vice President—Chapter Development; Noel Villacorta, Vice President—Conferences; Darryl Sink, Vice President—Finance; C. J. Wallington, Vice President—Publications; Clay Carr, Vice President—Research and Development.

Further information is available from NSPI, 1300 L Street NW, Suite 1250, Washington, DC 20005. (202) 408-7969. Fax (202) 408-7972.

SALT
Society for Applied Learning Technology

PURPOSE

The Society for Applied Learning Technology (SALT) is a nonprofit professional membership organization that was founded in 1972. Membership in the society is oriented to professionals whose work requires knowledge and communication in the field of instructional technology. The society provides members a means to enhance their knowledge and job performance by participation in society-sponsored meetings, through subscriptions to society-sponsored publications, by association with other professionals at conferences sponsored by the society, and through membership in special-interest groups and special society-sponsored initiatives and projects.

The society sponsors conferences that are educational in nature and cover a wide range of application areas, such as interactive videodisc in education and training, development of interactive instructional materials, CD-ROM applications in education and training, interactive instruction delivery, and learning technology in the health care sciences. These conferences provide attendees with an opportunity to become familiar with the latest technical information on application possibilities, on technologies, and on methodologies for implementation. In addition, they provide an opportunity for interaction with other professional and managerial individuals in the field.

The society also offers members discounts on society-sponsored journals, conference registration fees, and publications.

PUBLICATIONS

- *Journal of Interactive Instruction Development.* This established quarterly journal meets the needs of instructional systems developers and designers by providing important perspectives on emerging technologies and design technologies.

- *Journal of Medical Education Technologies.* Now in its third year of publication, this exciting journal helps keep readers abreast of developments utilizing technology-based learning systems to train health care professionals and educate students involved in the various health care disciplines.

- *Journal of Educational Technology Systems.* This quarterly publication deals with systems in which technology and education interface, and is designed to inform educators who are interested in making optimum use of technology.

- *Journal of Instruction/Delivery Systems.* Published quarterly, this journal covers interactive multimedia applications. It is devoted to enhancing productivity through appropriate applications of technology in education, training, and job performance.

CONFERENCES

Conferences in 1994 were held February 23-25 in Orlando, Florida, and August 24-26 in Washington, D.C. Conferences for 1995 will be held February 22-24 in Orlando, Florida, and August 23-25 in Washington, DC.

CURRENT OFFICERS

Dr. Nathaniel Macon, Chairman; Raymond G. Fox, President; Dr. Stanley Winkler, Vice President; and Dr. Carl R. Vest, Secretary/Treasurer.

Further information is available from the Society for Applied Learning Technology, 50 Culpeper Street, Warrenton, VA 22186. (703) 347-0055. Fax (703) 349-3169.

Part Six
Organizations and Associations in North America

Introduction

This part of *EMTY 1994* includes annotated entries for several hundred associations and organizations headquartered in North America whose interests are in some manner significant to the fields of instructional technology/educational media, library and information science, communication, computer technology, training/management in business/industry, publishing, and others. They are organized into two general geographic areas: the United States and Canada. The section on the United States includes a classified list with headings designed to be useful in finding subject leads to the alphabetical list. Readers who know only the acronym for an association or organization of interest may refer to the index to obtain its full name.

It was not deemed necessary to include a classified list for Canada because the overall number of organizations listed is considerably smaller than for the United States.

All organizations listed in part 6 were sent a copy of the entry describing the organization that appeared in *EMTY 1993*. Respondents were invited to update and edit these entries, with the proviso that, if no response was received, the entry would be omitted from *EMTY 1994*. However, information on organizations from which a response was received for the 1993 edition are included in this list with an asterisk to indicate that the information is a year old. Organizations for which no response has been received since before 1993 have been omitted. Any organization that has had a name change since the 1993 edition is listed under the new name; a note referring the user to the new name appears under the former name. If information was received that an organization had ceased operations, a note to this effect appears under the organization name in the alphabetical listing.

The reader is reminded that changes in communications and media are frequent and extensive and that the information in this directory is as accurate as possible at the time of publication.

United States

CLASSIFIED LIST

Adult, Continuing, Distance Education
Audio (Records, Audiocassettes and
    Tapes, Telephone, Radio); Listening
Audiovisual (General)
Censorship
Children-, Youth-Related Organizations
Communication
Community Resources
Computers, Computer Software, Computer
    Hardware
Copyright
Databases; Networks
Education (General)
Education (Higher)
Equipment (Manufacturing, Maintenance,
    Testing, Operating)
ERIC-Related
Films—Educational/Instructional/
    Documentary
Films—Theatrical (Film Study, Criticism,
    Production)
Films—Training
Futures
Games, Toys, Drama, Play, Simulation,
    Puppetry

Graphics
Health-Related Organizations
Information Science
Instructional Technology/Design/
    Development
International Education
Libraries—Academic, Research
Libraries—Public
Libraries—Special
Libraries and Media Centers—General,
    School
Microforms; Micrographics
Museums; Archives
Photography
Print—Books
Production (Media)
Publishing
Religious Education
Research
Selection, Collections, Processing (Materials)
Special Education
Training
Video (Cassette, Broadcast, Cable, Satellite,
    Videodisc, Videotex)

Adult, Continuing, Distance Education
(ALA) Reference and Adult Services Division (RASD)
(ALA Round Table) Continuing Library Education Network and Exchange (CLENE)
Association for Continuing Higher Education (ACHE)
Association for Educational Communications and Technology (AECT)
ERIC Clearinghouse on Adult, Career, and Vocational Education (CE)
National University Continuing Education Association (NUCEA)
Network for Continuing Medical Education (NCME)
Superintendent of Documents

Audio (Records, Audiocassettes and Tapes, Telephone, Radio); Listening
American Women in Radio and Television (AWRT)
Clearinghouse on Development Communication
Corporation for Public Broadcasting (CPB)
Federal Communications Commission (FCC)
National Association of Broadcasters (NAB)
Oral History Association
Recording for the Blind
Recording Industry Association of America, Inc. (RIAA)

Audiovisual (General)
Association for Educational Communications and Technology (AECT)
(AECT) Division of Educational Media Management (DEMM)
(AECT) Division of School Media Specialists (DSMS)
Association of AudioVisual Technicians (AAVT)
HOPE Reports
National Audiovisual Center

Censorship
Freedom of Information Center (FOI)

Children-, Youth-Related Organizations
(ALA) Association for Library Service to Children (ALSC)

(ALA) Young Adult Library Services Association (YALSA)
Association for Childhood Education International (ACEI)
Children's Television International, Inc.
Close Up Foundation
Council for Exceptional Children (CEC)
(CEC) Technology and Media Division (TAM)
ERIC Clearinghouse on Elementary and Early Childhood Education (PS)
ERIC Clearinghouse on Disabilities and Gifted Education (EC)
National Association for the Education of Young Children (NAEYC)
National PTA

Communication
Clearinghouse on Development Communication
ERIC Clearinghouse on Information & Technology (IR)
ERIC Clearinghouse on Languages and Linguistics (FL)
ERIC Clearinghouse on Reading, English, and Communication (CS)
Freedom of Information Center (FOI)
International Association of Business Communicators (IABC)
International Communication Association
National Council of the Churches of Christ—Communication Unit
Speech Communication Association (SCA)

Community Resources
Teachers and Writers Collaborative (T&W)

Computers, Computer Software, Computer Hardware
(AECT) Division of Interactive Systems and Computers (DISC)
Association for the Development of Computer-Based Instructional Systems (ADCIS)
Computer-Based Education Research Laboratory (CERL): PLATO and NovaNet
International Society for Technology in Education (ISTE) (formerly International Council for Computers in Education)

MECC (Minnesota Educational Computing Corporation)
OCLC (Online Computer Library Center)
Society for Computer Simulation (SCS)
SOFTSWAP
SpecialNet

Copyright
Copyright Clearance Center (CCC)
International Copyright Information Center (INCINC)

Databases; Networks
ERIC (Educational Resources Information Center) (See separate entries for the various clearinghouses.)
ERIC Document Reproduction Service (EDRS)
ERIC Processing and Reference Facility
SpecialNet

Education (General)
American Association of School Administrators (AASA)
American Montessori Society (AMS)
American Society of Educators (ASE)
Association for Childhood Education International (ACEI)
(AECT) Minorities in Media (MIM)
Association for Experiential Education (AEE)
Association of Teacher Educators (ATE)
Center for Instructional Research and Curriculum Evaluation
Council for Basic Education
Education Development Center, Inc.
ERIC Clearinghouse on Counseling and Student Services (CG)
ERIC Clearinghouse on Educational Management (EA)
ERIC Clearinghouse on Elementary and Early Childhood Education (PS)
ERIC Clearinghouse on Disabilities and Gifted Education (EC)
ERIC Clearinghouse on Rural Education and Small Schools (RC)
ERIC Clearinghouse for Science, Mathematics, and Environmental Education (SE)

ERIC Clearinghouse for Social Studies/Social Science Education (ERIC/ChESS)
ERIC Clearinghouse on Teaching and Teacher Education (SP)
ERIC Clearinghouse on Urban Education (UD)
National Association of Secondary School Principals (NASSP)
National Association of State Boards of Education (NASBE)
National Association of State Educational Media Professionals (NASTEMP)
National Association of State Textbook Administrators (NASTA)
National Center for Appropriate Technology (NCAT)
National Clearinghouse for Bilingual Education
National Council for Accreditation of Teacher Education (NCATE)
National Endowment for the Humanities (NEH)
National Science Foundation (NSF)
National Science Teachers Association (NSTA)

Education (Higher)
American Association of Community Colleges (AACC)
American Association of State Colleges and Universities
Association for Continuing Higher Education (ACHE)
Association of Teacher Educators (ATE)
(AECT) Community College Association for Instruction and Technology (CCAIT)
(AECT) Northwest College and University Council for the Management of Educational Technology
Association for Library and Information Science Education (ALISE)
Consortium of College and University Media Centers
ERIC Clearinghouse for Community Colleges (JC)
ERIC Clearinghouse on Higher Education (HE)
University Film and Video Association (UFVA)

Equipment (Manufacturing, Maintenance, Testing, Operating)

(ALA) Library and Information Technology Association (LITA)

American National Standards Institute (ANSI)

Association of AudioVisual Technicians (AAVT)

EPIE Institute

ERIC Clearinghouse on Assessment and Evaluation (TM)

ITA (formerly International Tape/Disc Association [ITA])

National School Supply and Equipment Association (NSSEA)

Society of Cable Television Engineers (SCTE)

Society of Motion Picture and Television Engineers (SMPTE)

ERIC-Related

ACCESS ERIC

Adjunct ERIC Clearinghouse on Chapter 1 (Compensatory Education) (ADJ/Chapter 1)

Adjunct ERIC Clearinghouse on Clinical Schools (ADJ/CL)

Adjunct ERIC Clearinghouse on Consumer Education (ADJ/CN)

Adjunct ERIC Clearinghouse for ESL Literacy Education (ADJ/LE)

Adjunct ERIC Clearinghouse for United States-Japan Studies (ADJ/JS)

ERIC (Educational Resources Information Center)

ERIC Clearinghouse on Adult, Career, and Vocational Education (CE)

ERIC Clearinghouse on Assessment and Evaluation (TM)

ERIC Clearinghouse for Community Colleges (JC)

ERIC Clearinghouse on Counseling and Student Services (CG)

ERIC Clearinghouse on Educational Management (EA)

ERIC Clearinghouse on Elementary and Early Childhood Education (PS)

ERIC Clearinghouse on Disabilities and Gifted Education (EC)

ERIC Clearinghouse on Higher Education (HE)

ERIC Clearinghouse on Information & Technology (IR)

ERIC Clearinghouse on Languages and Linguistics (FL)

ERIC Clearinghouse on Reading, English, and Communication Skills (CS)

ERIC Clearinghouse on Rural Education and Small Schools (RC)

ERIC Clearinghouse for Science, Mathematics, and Environmental Education (SE)

ERIC Clearinghouse for Social Studies/Social Science Education (SO)

ERIC Clearinghouse on Teaching and Teacher Education (SP)

ERIC Clearinghouse on Urban Education (UD)

ERIC Document Reproduction Service (EDRS)

ERIC Processing and Reference Facility

Films—Educational/Instructional/Documentary

Anthropology Film Center (AFC)

Association of Independent Video and Filmmakers/Foundation for Independent Video and Film (AIVF/FIVF)

Children's Television International, Inc.

CINE Information

Council on International Non-theatrical Events

Film Advisory Board (FAB)

Film Arts Foundation (FAF)

Film/Video Arts, Inc.

National Aeronautics and Space Administration (NASA)

National Alliance for Media Arts and Culture (NAMAC)

National Audiovisual Center (NAC)

National Film Board of Canada (NFBC)

National Information Center for Educational Media (NICEM)

Pacific Film Archive (PFA)

PCR: Films and Video in the Behavioral Sciences

University Film and Video Association

Films—Theatrical (Film Study, Criticism, Production)
Academy of Motion Picture Arts and Sciences (AMPAS)
American Society of Cinematographers
Film Advisory Board (FAB)
Film Arts Foundation (FAF)
Hollywood Film Archive
National Film Information Service (offered by AMPAS)
The New York Festivals (formerly International Film and TV Festival of New York)

Films—Training
American Film and Video Association (AFVA)
(AECT) Industrial Training and Education Division (ITED)
Association of Independent Video and Film-makers/Foundation for Independent Video and Film (AIVF/FIVF)
Council on International Non-theatrical Events
Great Plains National ITV Library (GPN)
National Audiovisual Center (NAC)
National Film Board of Canada (NFBC)
Training Media Association

Futures
Institute for the Future (IFTF)
Office of Technology Assessment (OTA)
World Future Society (WFS)

Games, Toys, Drama, Play, Simulation, Puppetry
North American Simulation and Gaming Association (NASAGA)
Puppeteers of America
Society for Computer Simulation (SCS)

Graphics
International Graphic Arts Education Association (IGAEA)

Health-Related Organizations
American Foundation for the Blind (AFB)
Health Science Communications Association (HeSCA)

Lister Hill National Center for Biomedical Communications of the National Library of Medicine
Medical Library Association (MLA)
National Association for Visually Handicapped (NAVH)
National Library of Medicine
Network for Continuing Medical Education (NCME)

Information Science
International Information Management Congress (IMC)

Instructional Technology/Design/Development
Agency for Instructional Technology (AIT)
Association for Educational Communications and Technology (AECT)
(AECT) Community College Association for Instruction and Technology (CCAIT)
(AECT) Division of Educational Media Management (DEMM)
(AECT) Division of Instructional Development (DID)
Association for the Development of Computer-Based Instructional Systems (ADCIS)
National Society for Performance and Instruction (NSPI)
Office of Technology Assessment (OTA)
Professors of Instructional Design and Technology (PIDT)
Society for Applied Learning Technology (SALT)

International Education
(AECT) International Division (INTL)
(AECT) International Visual Literacy Association, Inc. (IVLA)
East-West Center
Institute of Culture and Communication (East-West Center)
United Nations Department of Public Information, Dissemination Division

Libraries—Academic, Research
American Library Association (ALA)
(ALA) Association of College and Research Libraries (ACRL)

ERIC Clearinghouse on Information & Technology (IR)

Libraries—Public
American Library Association (ALA)
(ALA) Association for Library Service to Children (ALSC)
(ALA) Audiovisual Committee (of the Public Library Association)
(ALA) Library Administration and Management Association (LAMA)
(ALA) Library and Information Technology Association (LITA)
(ALA) Public Library Association (PLA)
(ALA) Reference and Adult Services Division (RASD)
(ALA) Technology in Public Libraries Committee (of the Public Libraries Association)
(ALA) Young Adult Library Services Association (YALSA)
ERIC Clearinghouse on Information & Technology (IR)

Libraries—Special
American Library Association (ALA)
(ALA) Association for Library Service to Children (ALSC)
(ALA) Association of Specialized and Cooperative Library Agencies (ASCLA)
ERIC Clearinghouse on Information & Technology (IR)
Medical Library Association (MLA)
Special Libraries Association (SLA)
Theater Library Association

Libraries and Media Centers—General, School
American Library Association (ALA)
(ALA) American Association of School Librarians (AASL)
(ALA) American Library Trustee Association (ALTA)
(ALA) Association for Library Collections and Technical Services (ALCTS)
(ALA) Association for Library Service to Children (ALSC)

(ALA Round Table) Continuing Library Education Network and Exchange (CLENE)
Association for Educational Communications and Technology (AECT)
(AECT) Division of School Media Specialists (DSMS)
(AECT) National Association of Regional Media Centers (NARMC)
Catholic Library Association (CLA)
Consortium of College and University Media Centers
Council of National Library and Information Associations
ERIC Clearinghouse on Information & Technology (IR)
International Association of School Librarianship (IASL)
Library of Congress
National Alliance for Media Arts and Culture (NAMAC)
National Commission on Libraries and Information Science (NCLIS)
National Council of Teachers of English (NCTE), Commission on Media
On-Line Audiovisual Catalogers (OLAC)

Microforms; Micrographics
See ERIC-related entries.

Museums; Archives
(AECT) Archives
American Federation of Arts (AFA)
Association of Systematics Collections
Computer Museum
George Eastman House (formerly International Museum of Photography at George Eastman House)
Hollywood Film Archive
Museum Computer Network, Inc. (MCN)
Museum of Holography
Museum of Modern Art
National Gallery of Art (NGA)
National Public Broadcasting Archives (NPBA)
Pacific Film Archive (PFA)
Smithsonian Institution

Photography
George Eastman House (formerly International Museum of Photography at George Eastman House)
International Center of Photography (ICP)
Museum of Holography
National Press Photographers Association, Inc. (NPPA)
Photographic Society of America (PSA)
Society for Imaging Science and Technology (IS&T)
Society for Photographic Education (SPE)
Society of Photo Technologists (SPT)

Print—Books
American Library Association (ALA)
Association for Educational Communications and Technology (AECT)
Smithsonian Institution
United Nations Department of Public Information

Production (Media)
American Society of Cinematographers (ASC)
Association for Educational Communications and Technology (AECT)
(AECT) Media Design and Production Division (MDPD)
Association of Independent Video and Filmmakers/Foundation for Independent Video and Film (AIVF/FIVF)
Film Arts Foundation (FAF)

Publishing
Association of American Publishers (AAP)
Government Printing Office (US GPO)
Magazine Publishers of America (MPA)
National Association of State Textbook Administrators (NASTA)
Superintendent of Documents

Religious Education
Catholic Library Association (CLA)
National Religious Broadcasters (NRB)

Research
American Educational Research Association (AERA)

Appalachia Educational Laboratory, Inc. (AEL)
(AECT) ECT Foundation
(AECT) Research and Theory Division (RTD)
Center for Advanced Visual Studies (CAVS)
Center for Technology in Education (CTE)
Center for Instructional Research and Curriculum Evaluation
Clearinghouse on Development Communication
Computer-Based Education Research Laboratory (CERL)
Council for Educational Development and Research (CEDaR)
Education Development Center, Inc.
ERIC Clearinghouses. See ERIC-related entries.
Far West Laboratory for Educational Research and Development (FWL)
HOPE Reports
Institute for Development of Educational Activities, Inc. (IDEA)
Institute for Research on Teaching
Mid-continent Regional Educational Laboratory (McREL)
National Center for Improving Science Education
National Center for Research in Mathematical Sciences Education
National Center for Science Teaching and Learning
National Technical Information Service (NTIS)
National Technology Center (NTC)
The NETWORK
North Central Regional Educational Laboratory (NCREL)
Northwest Regional Educational Laboratory (NWREL)
Office of Technology Assessment (OTA)
Pacific Regional Educational Laboratory (PREL)
Regional Laboratory for Educational Improvement of the Northeast and Islands
Research for Better Schools, Inc.
SouthEastern Regional Vision for Education (SERVE)
Southwest Educational Development Laboratory (SEDL)

Selection, Collections, Processing (Materials)

National Information Center for Educational
Media (NICEM)

Special Education

American Foundation for the Blind (AFB)

(CEC) Council for Exceptional Children,
Technology and Media Division
(TAM)

Council for Exceptional Children (CEC)

ERIC Clearinghouse on Disabilities and
Gifted Education (EC)

National Association for Visually Handicapped (NAVH)

National Technology Center (NTC)

Training

American Management Association (AMA)

American Society for Training and Development (ASTD)

Association for Educational Communications and Technology (AECT)

(AECT) Federal Educational Technology
Association (FETA)

(AECT) Industrial Training and Education
Division (ITED)

ERIC Clearinghouse on Adult, Career, and
Vocational Education (CE)

National Society for Performance and
Instruction (NSPI)

Training Media Association

**Video (Cassette, Broadcast, Cable, Satellite,
Videodisc, Videotex)**

Agency for Instructional Technology (AIT)

American Women in Radio and Television
(AWRT)

Association for Educational Communications and Technology (AECT)

(AECT) Division of Telecommunications
(DOT)

(AECT) National ITFS Association
(NIA/ITFS)

Association of Independent Video and Film-
makers/Foundation for Independent
Video and Film (AIVF/FIVF)

Central Educational Network (CEN)

Children's Television International, Inc.

Close Up Foundation

Community College Satellite Network

Corporation for Public Broadcasting (CPB)

Federal Communications Commission (FCC)

Great Plains National ITV Library (GPN)

International Telecommunications Satellite
Organization (INTELSAT)

International Teleconferencing Association
(ITCA)

International Television Association (ITVA)

ITA (formerly International Tape/Disc
Association [ITA])

National Aeronautics and Space Administration (NASA)

National Association of Broadcasters
(NAB)

National Cable Television Institute (NCTI)

National Federation of Community Broadcasters (NFCB)

National Telemedia Council, Inc. (NTC)

PBS Adult Learning Service (ALS)

PBS ENCORE

PBS VIDEO

Public Broadcasting Service (PBS)

Society of Cable Television Engineers
(SCTE)

Society of Motion Picture and Television
Engineers (SMPTE)

University Film and Video Association
(UFVA)

ALPHABETICAL LIST

Academy of Motion Picture Arts and Sciences (AMPAS). 8949 Wilshire Blvd., Beverly Hills, CA 90211. (310) 247-3000. Fax (310) 859-9351. Bruce Davis, Exec. Dir. An honorary organization composed of outstanding individuals in all phases of motion pictures. Seeks to advance the arts and sciences of motion picture technology and artistry. Presents annual film awards; offers artist-in-residence programs; operates reference library and National Film Information Service. *Membership*: 5,300. *Publications: Annual Index to Motion Picture Credits*; *Academy Players Directory*.

Agency for Instructional Technology (AIT). Box A, Bloomington, IN 47402-0120. (812) 339-2203. Fax (812) 333-4218. Michael F. Sullivan, Exec. Dir., Mardell Raney, Editor-in-Chief. AIT is a nonprofit U.S.-Canadian organization established in 1962 to strengthen education through technology. The Agency provides leadership and service through the development, acquisition, and distribution of technology-based instructional materials. AIT pioneered the consortium process to develop instructional series that meet learners' needs. It has cooperatively produced more than 32 series since 1970. Today, major funding comes from state and provincial departments of education, federal and private institutions, corporate sponsors, and other partners. *Publications: TECHNOS: Quarterly for Education and Technology* is the journal of the Agency for Instructional Technology. It is a forum for the discussion of ideas about the use of technology in education, with a focus on reform. A think piece for decision makers, *TECHNOS Quarterly* focuses on the policy and pedagogical implications of the electronic revolution. ISSN 1060-5649. $20/yr. (four issues). AIT also publishes two product catalogs, one for audiovisual and one for broadcast customers. Materials include video programming, interactive videodiscs, computer software, and supporting print. Its series are broadcast on six continents, reaching nearly 34 million students in North American classrooms each year. Catalogs are available free on request.

American Association of Community Colleges (AACC). One Dupont Cir. NW, Suite 410, Washington, DC 20036. (202) 728-0200. Fax (202) 833-2467. David Pierce, Pres. AACC serves the nation's 1,211 community, technical, and junior colleges through advocacy, professional development, publications, and national networking. The annual convention draws more than 4,000 mid- and top-level administrators of two-year colleges. Staff and presidents offer expertise in all areas of education. Sixteen councils and six commissions address all areas of education. AACC also operates the Community College Satellite Network, providing programming and assistance to colleges. *Membership:* 1,110 institutional, 16 international, 3 foundation, 65 corporate, 75 individual, and 80 educational associate members. *Dues:* Vary for each category. *Meetings:* Annual Convention, April 6-9, 1994, Washington, DC, "Leadership for a Changing World." *Publications: Community College Journal* (bi-mo.); *Community College Times* (bi-weekly newspaper); *College Times*; Community College Press (books and monographs).

(AACC) Community College Satellite Network (CCSN). One Dupont Cir. NW, Suite 410, Washington, DC 20036. (202) 728-0200. Fax (202) 833-2467. Monica W. Pilkey, Dir. An affiliate of AACC, CCSN provides leadership and facilitates distance education, teleconferencing, and satellite training to the nation's community colleges. CCSN offers discounted teleconferences, free program resources, amd general informational assistance in telecommunications. It also coordinates community college satellite downlinks nationally for teleconference users and producers. CCSN meets with its members at various industry trade shows and is very active in the AACC annual convention held each spring. *Membership:* 170 educational institutions. *Dues:* Vary by enrollment numbers. *Publications: Schedule of Programming*, 2/yr., contains listings of live and taped teleconferences for training and staff development; several other publications (free catalog available).

*American Association of School Administrators (AASA). 1801 N. Moore St., Arlington, VA 22209. (703) 528-0700. Fax (703) 528-2146. Richard D. Miller, Exec. Dir. Represents professional administrators and managers in education in the United States and overseas; provides an extensive program of professional development through the National Academy for School Executives (NASE). Also produces publications and audiovisual programs to increase knowledge and skills of administrators. *Membership:* 18,500. *Dues:* $209. *Publications: The School Administrator*; *Leadership News*; numerous books and video programs.

American Association of State Colleges and Universities (AASCU). One Dupont Cir. NW, Suite 700, Washington, DC 20036-1192. (202) 293-7070. Fax (202) 296-5819. James B. Appleberry, Pres. Membership is open to any regionally accredited institution of higher education, and those in the process of securing accreditation, that offers programs leading to the degree of bachelor, master, or doctor, and that are wholly or partially state-supported and state-controlled. Organized and operated exclusively for educational, scientific, and literary purposes, its particular purposes are to improve higher education within its member institutions through cooperative planning, studies, and research on common educational problems and the development of a more unified program of action among its members; and to provide other needed and worthwhile educational services to the colleges and universities it may represent. *Membership:* 375 institutions (university), 28 system, and 7 associate members. *Dues:* Based on current student enrollment at institution. *Publications: MEMO: To the President*; *The Center Associate*; *Office of Federal Program Reports*; *Office of Federal Program Deadlines*. (Catalogs of books and other publications available upon request.)

American Educational Research Association (AERA). 1230 17th St. NW, Washington, DC 20036. (202) 223-9485. Fax (202) 775-1824. William J. Russell, Exec. Dir. AERA is an international professional organization with the primary goal of advancing educational research and its practical application. Its members include educators; administrators; directors of research, testing, or evaluation in federal, state, and local agencies; counselors; evaluators; graduate students; and behavioral scientists. The broad range of disciplines represented includes education, psychology. statistics, sociology, history, economics, philosophy, anthropology, and political science. *Membership:* 20,000. *Dues:* Vary by category—voting, active, student, and international affiliate. *Meetings:* 1994 Annual Convention, April 4-8, New Orleans, LA; 1995 Convention, April 17-21, San Francisco, CA. *Publications: Educational Researcher*; *American Educational Research Journal*; *Journal of Educational Statistics*; *Educational Evaluation and Policy Analysis*; *Review of Research in Education*; *Review of Educational Research*.

*The American Federation of Arts (AFA). Headquarters, 41 E. 65th St., New York, NY 10021. (212) 988-7700. Fax (212) 861-2487. Serena Rattazzi, Dir. National nonprofit museum program and service that organizes and circulates exhibitions of fine arts and media arts to museums, university art galleries, and art centers throughout the United States and abroad. Also provides specialized services to member museums, including reduced-rate programs of fine art insurance, air and surface transport of art, and professional management training. *Institutional Membership:* 520. *Dues:* $220 to $500, institutions; $100 (Friend) to $1,000 (Sustaining) individuals. *Publications:* Newsletter: *ART*, 3/yr.; *MEMO TO MEMBERS* (for institutional members only) (6/yr.). AFA exhibitions are accompanied by illustrated catalogs and/or illustrated brochures. AFA media arts exhibits are also accompanied by program notes.

*American Film and Video Association (AFVA). 8050 N. Milwaukee Ave., P.O. Box 48659, Niles, IL 60714. (708) 698-6440. Fax (708) 823-1561. Kathryn Osen, Acting Exec. Dir.; Larry Skaja, Managing Dir. Formerly the Educational Film Library Association, the AFVA promotes and encourages the use, production, and distribution of quality nontheatrical film, video, and new technology in libraries, schools, and other institutions. *Membership:* 1,200. *Dues:* $55 individual, $210 institution, $315 corporation. *Publications: SightLines* (journal, 6/yr.); *AFVA Bulletin* (newsletter, 6/yr.); *AFVA Evaluations* (annual).

American Foundation for the Blind (AFB). 15 West 16th St., New York, NY 10011. (212) 620-2000; (800) AFB-LINE. Carl R. Augusto, Pres. and Exec. Dir.; Liz Greco, Dir. of Communications. AFB is a leading national resource for people who are blind or visually impaired, the organizations that serve them, and the general public. A nonprofit organization founded in 1921 and recognized as Helen Keller's cause in the United States, AFB has as its mission to enable persons who are blind or visually impaired to achieve equality of access and opportunity that will ensure freedom of choice in their lives. AFB is headquartered in New York City with regional centers in Chicago, Dallas, San Francisco, and Washington, DC. *Meeting:* The Josephine L. Taylor Leadership Institute, March 1994, Washington, DC, "The Future of Uniquely Designed Services (Education, Rehabilitation, etc.) for People Who Are Blind or Visually Impaired." *Publications: AFBnews*; *Journal of Visual Impairment & Blindness*.

American Library Association (ALA). 50 E. Huron St., Chicago, IL 60611. (312) 944-6780. Fax (312) 440-9374. Peggy Sullivan, Exec. Dir. The ALA is the oldest and largest national library association. Its 55,000 members represent all types of libraries—state, public, school, and academic, as well as special libraries serving persons in government, commerce, the armed services, hospitals, prisons, and other institutions. Chief advocate of achievement and maintenance of high-quality library information services through protection of the right to read, educating librarians, improving services, and making information widely accessible. *Membership:* 55,000. *Dues:* Basic dues $38 first year, $75 renewing members. *Meetings:* 1994: Midwinter Meeting, February 5-10, Los Angeles; Annual Conference, June 23-30, 1994, Miami. Theme for both meetings, "Customer Service, the Heart of the Library." 1995: Midwinter Meeting, January 20-26, Cincinnati; Annual Conference, June 22-29, Chicago. *Publications: American Libraries*; *Booklist*; *Choice*; *Book Links*.

(ALA) American Association of School Librarians (AASL). 50 E. Huron St., Chicago, IL 60611. (312) 280-4386. Fax (312) 664-7459. Ann Carlson Weeks, Exec. Dir. Interested in the general improvement and extension of school library media services for children and youth. Activities and projects of the association are divided among 55 committees and 3 sections. *Membership:* 7,690. *Dues:* Membership in ALA (1st yr., $38; 2d yr., $49; 3d and subsequent yrs., $75) plus $35; retired memberships and student membership rates available. *Meetings:* National Conference, November 9-13, 1994, Indianapolis, "Shape the Vision." *Publications: School Library Media Quarterly* (journal, q.); *Presidential Hotline* (newsletter, 2/yr.).

(ALA) American Library Trustee Association (ALTA). 50 E. Huron St., Chicago, IL 60611. (312) 280-2160. Fax (312) 280-3257. Susan Roman, Exec. Dir. Interested in the development of effective library service for people in all types of communities and libraries. Members, as policymakers, are concerned with organizational patterns of service, the development of competent personnel, the provision of adequate financing, the passage of suitable legislation and the encouragement of citizen support for libraries. *Membership:* 1,710. *Dues:* $40 plus membership in ALA. *Publications: ALTA Newsletter*; professional monographs and pamphlets.

*(ALA) Association for Library Collections and Technical Services (ALCTS). 50 E. Huron St., Chicago, IL 60611. (312) 944-6780. Karen Muller, Exec. Dir; Liz Bishoff, Pres., July 1992-June 1993. Dedicated to acquisition, identification, cataloging, classification, and preservation of library materials, the development and coordination of the country's library resources, and aspects of selection and evaluation involved in acquiring and developing library materials and resources. Sections include Acquisition of Library Materials, Cataloging and Classification, Collection Management and Development, Preservation of Library Materials, Reproduction of Library Materials, and Serials. *Membership:* 5,946. *Dues:* $35 plus membership in ALA. *Publications: Library Resources & Technical Services* (q.); *ALCTS Newsletter* (6/yr.).

*(ALA) Association for Library Service to Children (ALSC). 50 E. Huron St., Chicago, IL 60611. (312) 280-2163. Fax (312) 280-3257. Susan Roman, Exec. Dir. Interested in the improvement and extension of library services for children in all types of libraries, evaluation and selection of book and nonbook library materials, and improvement of techniques of library services for children from preschool through the eighth grade or junior high school age. Annual conference and midwinter meeting with the ALA. Committee membership open to ALSC members. *Membership:* 3,600. *Dues:* $35 plus membership in ALA. *Publications: Journal of Youth Services in Libraries*; *ALSC Newsletter.*

(ALA) Association of College and Research Libraries (ACRL). 50 E. Huron St., Chicago, IL 60611-2795. (312) 280-3248. Fax (312) 280-2520. Althea H. Jenkins, Exec. Dir. Represents librarians and promotes libraries of postsecondary, research, and specialized institutions. Has available library standards for colleges, universities, and two-year institutions. Publishes statistics on academic libraries. Committees include Academic Status, Audiovisual, Professional Education, Legislation, Publications, and Standards and Accreditation. Free list of materials available. *Membership:* 11,000. *Dues:* $35 (in addition to ALA membership). *Meetings:* 1995 National Conference, March 24-April 1, Pittsburgh, "Continuity and Transformation: The Promise of Confluence." *Publications: College & Research Libraries*; *College & Research Libraries News*; *Rare Books and Manuscripts Librarianship*; 11 section newsletters; *Choice.*

*(ALA) Association of Specialized and Cooperative Library Agencies (ASCLA). 50 E. Huron St., Chicago, IL 60611. (800) 545-2433, ext. 4399. Fax (312) 280-3257. Andrew Hansen, Exec. Dir. Represents state library agencies, multitype library cooperatives, and libraries serving special clienteles to promote the development of coordinated library services with equal access to information and material for all persons. The activities and programs of the association are carried out by 21 committees, 3 sections, and various discussion groups. Write for free checklist of materials. *Membership:* 1,300. *Dues:* (in addition to ALA membership) $30 for personal members, $50 for organizations, $500 for state library agencies. *Publication: Interface.*

*(ALA) Library Administration and Management Association (LAMA). 50 E. Huron St., Chicago, IL 60611. (312) 280-5038. Karen Muller, Exec. Dir.; James G. Neal, Pres., July 1992-June 1993. Provides an organizational framework for encouraging the study of administrative theory, for improving the practice of administration in libraries, and for identifying and fostering administrative skills. Toward these ends, the association is responsible for all elements of general administration that are common to more than one type of library. These may include: Buildings and Equipment Section (BES); Fundraising & Financial Development Section (FRFDS); Library Organization & Management Section (LOMS); Personnel Administration Section (PAS); Public Relation Section (PRS); Systems & Services Section (SASS); Statistic Section (SS). *Membership:* 5,097. *Dues:* $35 (in addition to ALA membership). *Publication: Library Administration & Management* (q.).

(ALA) Library and Information Technology Association (LITA). 50 E. Huron St., Chicago, IL 60611. (312) 280-4270; (voice) (800) 545-2433, ext. 4270. Fax (312) 280-3257. Linda J. Knutson, Exec. Dir. Concerned with library automation, the information sciences, and the design, development, and implementation of automated systems in those fields, including systems development, electronic data processing, mechanized information retrieval, operations research, standards development, telecommunications, video communications, networks and collaborative efforts, management techniques, information technology, optical technology, artificial intelligence and expert systems, and other related aspects of audiovisual activities and hardware applications. *Membership:* 5,800. *Dues:* $35 plus membership in ALA, $15 for library school students, $25 first year, new members. *Publications: Information Technology and Libraries; LITA Newsletter.*

(ALA) Public Library Association (PLA). 50 E. Huron St., Chicago, IL 60611. (312) 280-5PLA. Fax (312) 280-5029. E-mail U22540@UICVM.UIC.EDU. George M. Needham, Exec. Dir.; Pat Woodrum, Pres., 1993-94; Judith Drescher, Pres., 1994-95. Concerned with the development, effectiveness, and financial support of public libraries. Speaks for the profession and seeks to enrich the professional competence and opportunities of public libraries. Sections include Adult Lifelong Learning, Community Information, Metropolitan Libraries, Public Library Systems, Small and Medium-sized Libraries, Public Policy for Public Libraries, and Marketing of Public Library Services. *Membership:* 7,173. *Dues:* $50, open to all ALA members. *Meetings:* National Conference, March 22-26, 1994, Atlanta, GA, "New Ideas: A PLA Tradition." *Publication: Public Libraries* (bi-mo.).

> **(ALA) Audiovisual Committee (of the Public Library Association)**. 50 E. Huron St., Chicago, IL 60611. (312) 280-5752. Dorothy M. Liegl, Chair. Promotes use of audiovisual materials in public libraries.

> **(ALA) Technology in Public Libraries Committee (of the Public Library Association)**. 50 E. Huron St., Chicago, IL 60611. (312) 280-5752. Susan B. Harrison, Chair. Collects and disseminates information on technology applications in public libraries.

*(ALA) Reference and Adult Services Division (RASD). 50 E. Huron St., Chicago, IL 60611. (312) 280-5752; (800) 545-2433, ext. 4398. Fax (312) 280-3257. Andrew M. Hansen, Exec. Dir. Responsible for stimulating and supporting in every type of library the delivery of reference information services to all groups and of general library services and materials to adults. *Membership:* 5,500. *Dues:* $35 plus membership in ALA. *Publications: RQ* (q.); *RASD Update*; others.

(ALA) Young Adult Library Services Association (YALSA) (formerly Young Adult Services Division). 50 E. Huron St., Chicago, IL 60611. (312) 280-4390. Fax (312) 664-7459. Linda Waddle, Deputy Exec. Dir.; Judy Druse, Pres. Seeks to advocate, promote, and strengthen service to young adults as part of the continuum of total library services, and assumes responsibility within the ALA to evaluate and select books and nonbook media, and to interpret and make recommendations regarding their use with young adults. Committees include Best Books for Young Adults, Recommended Books for the Reluctant Young Adult Reader, Media Selection and Usage, Publishers' Liaison, and Selected Films for Young Adults. *Membership:* 2,223. *Dues:* $35 (in addition to ALA membership), $15 for students. *Publications: Journal of Youth Services in Libraries* (q.).

*(ALA Round Table) Continuing Library Education Network and Exchange (CLENE). 50 E. Huron St., Chicago, IL 60611. (312) 280-4278. Laura Kimberly, Pres. Seeks to provide access to quality continuing education opportunities for librarians and information scientists and to create an awareness of the need for such education in helping individuals in the field to respond to societal and technological changes. *Membership:* 350. *Dues:* Open to all ALA members; individual members $15, $50 for organizations. *Publications: CLENExchange* (q.), available to nonmembers by subscription at $20/yr. U.S. zip, $25 non-U.S. zip.

American Management Association (AMA). 135 W. 50th St., New York, NY 10020-1201. (212) 586-8100. Fax (212) 903-8168. David Fagiano, Pres. and CEO. Founded in 1923, the AMA provides educational forums worldwide where members and their colleagues learn superior, practical business skills and explore best practices of world-class organizations through interaction with each other and expert faculty practitioners. Its publishing program provides tools individuals use to extend learning beyond the classroom in a process of life-long professional growth and development through education. The AMA operates eight management centers and offices in the United States and, through AMA/International, in Brussels, Belgium, and Tokyo, Japan; it also has affiliated centers in Toronto, Canada, and Mexico City, Mexico. AMA offers conferences, seminars, and membership briefings where there is an interchange of information, ideas, and experiences in a wide variety of management topics. AMA publishes approximately 60 books per year, as well as numerous surveys and management briefings. *Publications* (periodicals): *Management Review* (membership); *Compensation & Benefits Review*; *CompFlash*; *Organizational Dynamics*; *HR Focus*; *The President*; *Small Business Reports*; *Supervisory Management*; *Supervisory Sense*; and *Trainer's Workshop.* Other services offered by AMA include AMA Video; Extension Institute (self-study programs in both print and audio formats); Operation Enterprise (young adult program); AMA On-Site (seminars delivered at site of the company's choice); AMA by Satellite (videoconferences); the Information Resources Center (for AMA members only); a management information and library service; and five AMA bookstores. It also cooperates with management associations around the world through correspondent association agreements.

American Montessori Society (AMS). 150 5th Ave., New York, NY 10011. (212) 924-3209. Fax (212) 727-2254. Michael N. Eanes, Natl. Dir. Dedicated to promoting better education for all children through teaching strategies consistent with the Montessori system. Membership is composed of schools in the private and public sectors employing this method, as well as individuals. It serves as a resource center and clearinghouse for information and data on

Montessori, affiliates teacher training programs in different parts of the country, and conducts a consultation service and accreditation program for school members. Sponsors three regional and one national educational conference per year and four professional development symposia under the auspices of the AMS Teachers' Section. *Dues:* Teachers, schoolheads, $37/yr.; parents, $29/yr.; institutions, from $235/yr. and up. *Meetings* (selected): 34th Annual Conference, April 22-24, 1994, Dearborn, MI; 8th Annual Teacher's Section Touring Symposium for Teachers and Parents, April 30-May 1, 1994, Minneapolis, MN; Summer Regional Symposium, August 19-21, 1994, Breckenridge, CO. *Publications: AMS Montessori LIFE* (q.); *Schoolheads* (newsletter); *Montessori in Contemporary American Culture*; *Authentic American Montessori School*; *The Montessori School Management Guide*; occasional papers.

American National Standards Institute (ANSI). 11 W. 42d St., New York, NY 10036. (212) 642-4900. Fax (212) 398-0023. Sergio Mazza, Pres.; Anthony R. O'Neill, Chairman of the Board. ANSI is the coordinator of the U.S. voluntary standards system, approves American National Standards, and represents the United States in the International Organization for Standardization (ISO) and the International Electrotechnical Commission (IEC). The Institute does not write standards or codes, but coordinates those developed through an open consensus process by the approximately 1,300 national and international companies, 30 government agencies, 20 institutional members, and 250 professional, technical, trade, labor, and consumer organizations that compose its membership. *Meetings:* 1994 Annual Public Conference, March 3-4, Washington, DC, "Accessing Global Markets through Standardization." *Publications: Catalog of Standards* (annual) lists more than 8,000 standards for all topic areas; *ANSI Reporter* (mo.), newsletter of the national and international standards community; *Standards Action* (bi-weekly), listing of status of revisions on standards in the United States, international community, Europe, and other foreign national bodies.

*American Society for Training and Development (ASTD). 1640 King St., Box 1443, Alexandria, VA 22313. (703) 683-8100. Fax (703) 683-8103. Curtis E. Plott, Exec. V.P. Leading professional organization for individuals engaged in employee training and education in business, industry, government, and related fields. Members include managers, program developers, instructors, consultants, counselors, suppliers, and academics. The purpose of its extensive professional publishing program is to build an essential body of knowledge for advancing the competence of training and development practitioners in the field. Many special-interest subgroups relating to industries or job functions are included in the organization. *Membership:* 55,000 national plus chapter. *Dues:* $150/yr. individual (group discounts available). *Publications: Training and Development Magazine; Info-Line; ASTD Video Directories; Competency Analysis for Trainers: A Personal Planning Guide; ASTD Directory of Academic Programs in T&D/HRD; Evaluating Training Programs; Training and Development Handbook; National Report; Technical & Skills Training Magazine.* Newsletters: *Focus* (chapter newsletter); *Management Development Report; The Business of Training; Technical Trainer/Skills Trainer.* ASTD also has recognized professional areas, networks, and industry groups, most of which produce newsletters.

American Society of Cinematographers (ASC). 1782 N. Orange Dr., Hollywood, CA 90028. (213) 969-4333. Fax (213) 876-4973. Fax (213) 882-6391. Victor J. Kemper, Pres. ASC is an educational, cultural, and professional organization. Membership is by invitation to those who are actively engaged as directors of photography and have demonstrated outstanding ability. *Membership:* 271, including active, active retired, associates, and honorary members. *Meeting:* Annual ASC Awards, February 27, 1994, Beverly Hills, CA. *Publications: American Cinematographer Video Manual; American Cinematographer Film*

Manual (7th ed.); *Anton Wilson's Cinema Workshop* (4th ed.); *The Cinema of Adventure, Romance, & Terror*; *The Light on Her Face*; and *American Cinematographers Magazine*.

American Society of Educators (ASE). 1429 Walnut St., Philadelphia, PA 19102. (215) 563-3501. Fax (215) 563-1588. Diane Falten, Mng. Ed. A multifaceted professional organization that serves the nation's teachers by providing information and evaluation of media resources and technologies for effective classroom use. *Membership:* 41,000. *Dues:* $29/yr., $47/yr. foreign. *Publications: Media and Methods; School Executive.*

American Women in Radio and Television (AWRT). 1650 Tyson Blvd., Suite 200, McLean, VA 22102-3915. (703) 506-3290. Fax (703) 506-3266. Ellen Teplitz, Mgr. of Association Services. Terri Dickerson-Jones, Exec. Dir. Organization of professionals in the electronic media, including owners, managers, administrators, and those in creative positions in broadcasting, satellite, cable, advertising, and public relations. The objectives are to work worldwide to improve the quality of radio and television; to promote the entry, development, and advancement of women in the electronic media and allied fields; to serve as a medium of communication and idea exchange; and to become involved in community concerns. Organized in 1951. Student memberships available. *Membership:* 40 chapters. *Dues:* $125/yr. *Publications: News and Views; Resource Directory; Careers in the Electronic Media; Sexual Harassment* (pamphlet).

Anthropology Film Center (AFC). Box 493-87504, 1626 Canyon Rd., Santa Fe, NM 87501. (505) 983-4127. Carroll Williams, Dir. Offers the Documentary Film Program, a 30-week full-time course in 16mm film production and theory and summer workshops. Also provides consultation, research, 16mm film equipment sales and rental, facilities rental, occasional seminars and workshops, and a specialized library. *Publications: An Ixil Calendrical Divination* (16mm color film); *First Impressions of Ixil Culture* (16mm color film).

Appalachia Educational Laboratory, Inc. (AEL). 1031 Quarrier St., P.O. Box 1348, Charleston, WV 25325. (304) 347-0400. (800) 624-9120 (outside WV). (800) 344-6646 (in WV). Terry L. Eidell, Exec. Dir. One of 10 Office of Educational Research and Improvement (OERI) regional educational laboratories designed to help educators and policymakers solve educational problems in their schools. Using the best available information and the experience and expertise of professionals, AEL seeks to identify solutions to education problems, tries new approaches, furnishes research results, and provides training to teachers and administrators. AEL serves Kentucky, Tennessee, Virginia, and West Virginia.

Association for Childhood Education International (ACEI). 11501 Georgia Ave., No. 315, Wheaton, MD 20902. (301) 942-2443. Fax (301) 942-3012. Lucy Prete Martin, Ed. and Dir. of Publications. Concerned with children from infancy through early adolescence. ACEI publications reflect careful research, broad-based views, and consideration of a wide range of issues affecting children. Many are media-related in nature. The journal (*Childhood Education*) is essential for teachers, teachers-in-training, teacher educators, day care workers, administrators, and parents. Articles focus on child development and emphasize practical application. Regular departments include book reviews (child and adult); reviews of films, pamphlets, and software; research; and classroom idea-sparkers. Articles address timely concerns. Five issues are published yearly, including a theme issue devoted to critical concerns. *Membership:* 14,000. *Dues:* $45/yr. *Publications: Childhood Education* (official journal) with *ACEI Exchange* (insert newsletter); *Journal of Research in Childhood Education*; professional division newsletters (*Focus on Infancy, Focus on Early Childhood*, and *Focus on Later Childhood/Early Adolescence*); *Developmental Continuity Across Preschool* *and Primary Grades: Implications for Teachers*; *Developmentally Appropriate Middle Level Schools*; *Common Bonds: Antibias Teaching in a Diverse Society*; *Childhood 1892-1992*; *Infants and Toddlers with Special Needs and Their Families* (position paper); and pamphlets.

Association for Continuing Higher Education (ACHE). Continuing Education, Trident Technical College, P.O. Box 118067, CE-P, Charleston, SC 29423-8067. (803) 722-5546. Fax (803) 722-5520. Wayne Whelan, contact person. The Association for Continuing Higher Education is an institution-based organization of colleges, universities, and individuals dedicated to the promotion of lifelong learning and excellence in continuing higher education. ACHE encourages professional networks, research, and exchange of information for its members and advocates continuing higher education as a means of enhancing and improving society. *Membership:* 1,622 individuals in 674 institutions. *Dues:* $50/yr. professionals, $225/yr. institutional. *Publications: Journal of Continuing Higher Education* (3/yr.); *5 Minutes* (newsletter, 10/yr.); *Proceedings* (annual).

Association for Educational Communications and Technology (AECT). 1025 Vermont Ave. NW, Suite 820, Washington, DC 20005. (202) 347-7834. Fax (202) 347-7839. Stanley Zenor, Exec. Dir; Kent Gustafson, Pres. AECT is an international professional association concerned with the improvement of learning and instruction through media and technology. It serves as a central clearinghouse and communications center for its members, who include instructional technologists; media or library specialists; religious educators; government media personnel; school, school district, and state department of education media program administrators and specialists; and educational/training media producers. AECT members also work in the armed forces, in public libraries, in museums, and in other information agencies of many different kinds, including those related to the emerging fields of computer technology. The AECT National Convention and InCITE Exposition was held February 16-20, 1994, in Nashville, Tennessee, at the Opryland Hotel. The 1995 convention will be held in Anaheim, California, February 8-12. *Membership:* 4,500, plus 9,000 additional subscribers, 9 divisions, 15 national affiliates, 46 state and territorial affiliates, and more than 30 national committees and task forces. *Dues:* $65/yr. regular, $26/yr. student and retired. *Meetings:* 1994 Annual Convention and InCITE Exposition, February 16-20, 1994, Nashville, TN; 1995 Convention and Exposition, February 8-12, Anaheim, CA. *Publications: TechTrends* (6/yr., free with membership; $36/yr. nonmembers); *Report to Members* (6/yr., newsletter); *Educational Technology Research and Development* (q., $30/yr. member; $20/yr. student and retired; $45/yr. nonmembers); various division publications; several books; videotapes.

Because of similarity of interests, the following organizations have chosen to affiliate with the Association for Educational Communications and Technology. (As many as possible have been polled for inclusion in *EMTY*.)

- Community College Association for Instruction and Technology (CCAIT)

- Consortium of College and University Media Centers (CCUMC)

- Federal Educational Technology Association (FETA)

- Health Sciences Communications Association (HeSCA)

- International Association for Learning Laboratories (IALL)

- International Visual Literacy Association, Inc. (IVLA)

- Minorities in Media (MIM)

- National Association of Regional Media Centers (NARMC)

- National Instructional Television Fixed Service Association (NIA/ITFS)

- New England Educational Media Association (NEEMA)

- Northwest College and University Council for the Management of Educational Technology (NW/MET)

- Southeastern Regional Media Leadership Council (SRMLC)

Two additional organizations are also related to the Association for Educational Communications and Technology:

- AECT Archives

- AECT ECT Foundation

Association for Educational Communications and Technology (AECT) Divisions:

*(AECT) Division of Educational Media Management (DEMM). 1025 Vermont Ave. NW, Suite 820, Washington, DC 20005. (202) 347-7834. Ron Payne, Pres. Seeks to develop an information exchange network and to share information about common problems, solutions, and program descriptions of educational media management. Develops programs that increase the effectiveness of media managers; initiates and implements a public relations program to educate the public and administrative bodies as to the use, value, and need for educational media management; and fosters programs that will help carry out media management responsibilities effectively. *Membership:* 780. *Dues:* One division membership included in the basic AECT membership; additional division memberships $10/yr. *Publication: Media Management Journal.*

*(AECT) Division of Instructional Development (DID). 1025 Vermont Ave. NW, Suite 820, Washington, DC 20005. (202) 347-7834. Ann Shore, Pres. DID is composed of individuals from business, government, and academic settings concerned with the systematic design of instruction and the development of solutions to performance problems. Members' interests include the study, evaluation, and refinement of design processes; the creation of new models of instructional development; the invention and improvement of techniques for managing the development of instruction; the development and application of professional ID competencies; the promotion of academic programs for preparation of ID professionals; and the dissemination of research and development work in ID. *Membership:* 726. *Dues:* One division membership included in the basic AECT membership; additional division memberships $10/yr. *Publications: DID Newsletter*; occasional papers.

(AECT) Division of Interactive Systems and Computers (DISC). 1025 Vermont Ave. NW, Suite 820, Washington, DC 20005. (202) 347-7834. Sharon Smaldino, Pres. Concerned with the generation, access, organization, storage, and delivery of all forms of information used in the processes of education and training. DISC promotes the networking of its members to facilitate sharing of expertise and interests. *Membership:* 883. *Dues:* One division membership included in the basic AECT membership; additional division memberships $10/yr. *Publication:* Newsletter.

*(AECT) Division of School Media Specialists (DSMS). 1025 Vermont Ave. NW, Suite 820, Washington, DC 20005. (202) 347-7834. Mary Mock Miller, Pres. DSMS promotes communication among school media personnel who share a common concern in the development, implementation, and evaluation of school media programs; and strives to increase learning and improve instruction in the school setting through the utilization of educational media and technology. *Membership:* 902. *Dues:* One division membership included in the basic AECT membership; additional division memberships $10/yr. *Publication:* Newsletter.

(AECT) Division of Telecommunications (DOT). 1025 Vermont Ave. NW, Suite 820, Washington, DC 20005. (202) 347-7834. Mark Rainey, Pres. Seeks to improve education through use of television and radio, video and audio recordings, and autotutorial devices and media. Aims to improve the design, production, evaluation, and use of telecommunications materials and equipment; to upgrade competencies of personnel engaged in the field; to investigate and report promising innovative practices and technological developments; to promote studies, experiments, and demonstrations; and to support research in telecommunications. Future plans call for working to establish a national entity representing instructional television. *Membership:* 607. *Dues:* One division membership included in the basic AECT membership; additional division memberships $10/yr. *Publication:* Newsletter.

*(AECT) Industrial Training and Education Division (ITED). 1025 Vermont Ave. NW, Suite 820, Washington, DC 20005. (202) 347-7834. Joanne Willard, Pres. Seeks to promote the sensitive and sensible use of media and techniques to improve the quality of education and training; to provide a professional program that demonstrates the state of the art of educational technology as a part of the AECT convention; to improve communications to ensure the maximum use of educational techniques and media that can give demonstrable, objective evidence of effectiveness. *Membership:* 273. *Dues:* One division membership included in the basic AECT membership; additional division memberships $10/yr. *Publication:* Newsletter.

(AECT) International Division (INTL). 1025 Vermont Ave. NW, Suite 820, Washington, DC 20005. (202) 347-7834. Boscoe W. Lee, Pres. Seeks to improve international communications concerning existing methods of design; to pretest, use, produce, evaluate, and establish an approach through which these methods may be improved and adapted for maximum use and effectiveness; to develop a roster of qualified international leaders with experience and competence in the varied geographic and technical areas; and to encourage research in the application of communication processes to support present and future international social and economic development. *Membership:* 295. *Dues:* One division membership included in the basic AECT membership; additional division memberships $10/yr. *Publication:* Newsletter.

*(AECT) Media Design and Production Division (MDPD). 1025 Vermont Ave. NW, Suite 820, Washington, DC 20005. (202) 347-7834. Donna Zingelman, Pres. Seeks to provide formal, organized procedures for promoting and facilitating interaction between commercial and noncommercial, nontheatrical filmmakers, and to provide a communications link for filmmakers with persons of similar interests. Also seeks to provide a connecting link between creative and technical professionals of the audiovisual industry. Advances the informational film producer's profession by providing scholarships and apprenticeships to experimenters and students and by providing a forum for discussion of local, national, and universal issues. Recognizes and presents awards for outstanding films produced and for contributions to the state of the art. *Membership:* 318. *Dues:* One division membership included in the basic AECT membership; additional division memberships $10/yr. *Publication:* Newsletter.

(AECT) Research and Theory Division (RTD). 1025 Vermont Ave. NW, Suite 820, Washington, DC 20005. (202) 3477834. James D. Klein, Pres. Seeks to improve the design, execution, utilization, and evaluation of educational technology research; to improve the qualifications and effectiveness of personnel engaged in educational technology research; to advise the educational practitioner as to use of the research results; to improve research design, techniques, evaluation, and dissemination; to promote both applied and theoretical research on the systematic use of educational technology in the improvement of instruction; and to encourage the use of multiple research paradigms in examining issues related to technology in education. *Membership:* 452. *Dues:* One division membership included in the basic AECT membership; additional division memberships $10/yr. *Publication:* Newsletter.

Association for Educational Communications and Technology (AECT) Affiliate Organizations:

(AECT) Community College Association for Instruction and Technology (CCAIT). New Mexico Military Institute, 101 W. College Blvd., Roswell, NM 88201. (505) 624-8381. Bruce McLaren, Pres. A national association of community and junior college educators interested in the discovery and dissemination of information about problems and processes of teaching, media, and technology in community and junior colleges. Facilitates member exchange of data, reports, proceedings, personnel, and other resources; sponsors AECT convention sessions and social activities. *Membership:* 200. *Dues:* $10. *Publications:* Regular newsletter; irregular topical papers.

(AECT) Federal Educational Technology Association (FETA). c/o Applied Science Associates, Inc., 8201 Corporate Dr., Suite 900, Landover, MD 20785. (703) 506-5664. Stuart Weinstein, Pres. FETA is dedicated to the improvement of education and training through research, communication, and practice. It encourages and welcomes members from all government agencies, federal, state, and local; from business and industry; and from all educational institutions and organizations. FETA encourages interaction among members to improve the quality of education and training in any arena, but with specific emphasis on government-related applications. *Meetings:* Meets in conjunction with AECT InCITE and concurrently with SALT's Washington meeting in August. *Publication:* Newsletter (occasional).

(AECT) Health Sciences Communications Association (HeSCA). See separate listing.

(AECT) International Visual Literacy Association, Inc. (IVLA). Concordia University, 7141 Sherbrook St. West, Montreal, Quebec H4B 1R6, Canada. Nikos Metallinos, Pres. Provides a multidisciplinary forum for the exploration of modes of visual communication and their application through the concept of visual literacy; promotes development of visual literacy and serves as a bond between the diverse organizations and groups working in that field. *Dues:* $40 regular; $20 student. *Meeting:* Tempe, AZ, October 1994. *Publications: Journal of Visual Literacy; Readings from Annual Conferences.*

[handwritten: Correct address is on p 189]

(AECT) Minorities in Media (MIM). Center for Instructional Media and Technology, Virginia State University, Box 5002-N, Petersburg, VA 23803. Dr. Vykuntapathi Thota, Pres. Seeks to encourage the effective use of educational media in the teaching/learning process; provide leadership opportunities in advancing the use of technology as an integral part of the learning process; provide a vehicle through which minorities might influence the use of media in institutions; develop an information exchange network to share information common to minorities in media; study, evaluate, and refine the educational technology process as it relates to the education of minorities; and encourage and improve the production of materials for the education of minorities. *Membership:* 100. *Dues:* $10. *Publication:* Annual newsletter.

*(AECT) National Association of Regional Media Centers (NARMC). Special Projects Center, 1150 Education Ave., Punta Gorda, FL 33950. Janet Williams, Pres. Seeks to foster the exchange of ideas and information among educational communications specialists responsible for the administration of regional media centers, through workshops, seminars, and national meetings. Studies the feasibility of developing joint programs that could increase the effectiveness and efficiency of regional media services. Disseminates information on successful practices and research studies conducted by regional media centers. *Membership:* 268 regional centers, 70 corporations. *Dues:* $45. *Publications: etin* (q. newsletter); *Annual Report.*

(AECT) National ITFS Association (NIA). 3421 M St. NW, Suite 1130, Washington, DC 20007; Educational Communications, University of Wisconsin-Milwaukee, P.O. Box 413, Milwaukee, WI 53201. (414) 229-5470. Fax (414) 229-4777. Theodore Steinke, Chair, Bd. of Dirs. Established in 1978, NIA/ITFS is a nonprofit, professional organization of Instructional Television Fixed Service (ITFS) licensees, applicants, and others interested in ITFS broadcasting. The goals of the association are to gather and exchange information about ITFS, to gather data on utilization of ITFS, and to act as a conduit for those seeking ITFS information or assistance. The NIA represents ITFS interests to the FCC, technical consultants, and equipment manufacturers. The association provides its members with a quarterly newsletter and an FCC regulation update as well as information on excess capacity leasing and license and application data. *Meeting:* Meets with AECT and InCITE, February 17, 1994, Nashville, TN. *Publications: National ITFS Association Newsletter* (q.); FCC regulation update.

*(AECT) Northwest College and University Council for the Management of Educational Technology. University of Lethbridge, 4401 University Dr., Lethbridge, AB T1K 3M4, Canada. George Berg, Pres. The first regional group representing institutions of higher education in Alberta, Alaska, British Columbia, Idaho, Montana, Oregon, and Washington to receive affiliate status in AECT. Membership is restricted to media managers with campus-wide responsibilities for educational technical services in the membership region. Corresponding membership is available to those who work outside the membership region. An annual conference and business meeting are held the last weekend of October each year, rotating throughout the region. Current issues under consideration include managing emerging telecommunication technologies, copyright, accreditation, and certification. Organizational goals include identifying the unique status problems of media managers in higher education and improving the quality of the major publication. *Membership:* approx. 85. *Dues:* $35. *Publication: NW/MET Bulletin.*

Other AECT-Related Organizations:

(AECT) Archives. University of Maryland at College Park, Hornbake Library, College Park, MD 20742. Thomas Connors, Archivist, National Public Broadcasting Archives. (301) 405-9988. Fax (301) 314-9419. A collection of media, manuscripts, and related materials representing important developments in visual and audiovisual education and in instructional/educational technology. The collection is housed as part of the National Public Broadcasting Archives. Maintained by the University of Maryland at College Park in cooperation with AECT. Open to researchers and scholars.

(AECT) ECT Foundation. 1025 Vermont Ave. NW, Suite 820, Washington, DC 20005. Hans-Erik Wennberg, Pres. The ECT Foundation is a nonprofit organization whose purposes are charitable and educational in nature. Its operation is based on the conviction that improvement of instruction can be accomplished, in part, by the continued investigation and application of new systems for learning and by periodic assessment of current techniques for the communication of information. In addition to awarding scholarships, internships, and fellowships, the foundation develops and conducts leadership training programs for emerging professional leaders.

Association for Experiential Education (AEE). 2885 Aurora Ave., #28, Boulder, CO 80303-2252. (303) 440-8844. (303) 440-9581. Barbara A. Baker, Exec. Dir. AEE believes that the learner and the teacher should use the most powerful and effective means to interact with each other and their environments, and to deal with the tasks at hand. Experience-based education emphasizes direct experience to increase the quality of learning. AEE helps to advance, expand, conceptualize, and formalize the experiential learning process. *Membership:* 1,900. *Dues:* $50-$75 individuals, $175 organizations. *Meeting:* 22nd International Conference, November 3-6, 1994, Austin, TX, "Experiential Education for the 21st Century: A Critical Resource." *Publications: Jobs Clearinghouse; The Journal of Experiential Education;* books and directories.

Association for Library and Information Science Education (ALISE). Penney DePas, CAE, Exec. Dir. 4101 Lake Boone Tr., Suite 201, Raleigh, NC 27607-4916. Seeks to advance education for library and information science and produces annual *Library and Information Science Education Statistical Report.* Open to professional schools offering graduate programs in library and information science; personal memberships open to educators employed in such institutions; other memberships available to interested individuals. *Membership:* 650 individuals, 85 institutions. *Dues:* institutional, $250 full; $150 associate; $75 international; personal, $40 full-time; $20 part-time, student, retired. *Publications: Journal of Education for Library and Information Science;* directory; *Library and Information Science Education Statistical Report.*

Association for the Development of Computer-Based Instructional Systems (ADCIS). International Headquarters, 1601 W. Fifth Ave., Suite 111, Columbus, OH 43212. (614) 487-1528. Fax (614) 488-8354. Carol Norris, contact person. Cynthia Leshin, Pres. International association with a worldwide membership of professionals who are actively involved in the development and use of computer-based instructional technologies. Members work in business and industry; elementary and secondary schools; junior colleges, colleges, and universities; vocational and specialized schools; and the military and the government. An annual international conference, membership in special-interest groups, and networking for members provide an international forum for intellectual leadership in the field, professional growth opportunities, and the integration of theory and practice. *Membership:* 1,650. *Dues:*

individuals, $60; students, $25. *Meetings:* 1994 Annual Conference, February 16-20, Nashville, TN; 1995 Conference, February 8-12, Anaheim, CA (in conjunction with AECT and InCITE). *Publications: ADCIS News* (members only); *The Journal of Computer-Based Instruction (JCBI)* (q.); *The Conference Proceedings* (annual).

*Association of American Publishers (AAP). 220 E. 23d St., New York, NY 10010. (212) 689-8920. Ambassador Nicholas A. Veliotes, Pres. A group of approximately 220 companies whose members produce the majority of printed materials sold to U.S. schools, colleges, libraries, and bookstores, as well as to homes. Range of member interests is reflected in textbooks; religious, scientific, and media books; instructional systems; software; audio- and videotapes; records; cassettes; slides; transparencies; and tests. Provides its members with information concerning trade conditions, markets, copyrights, manufacturing processes, taxes, duties, postage, freight, censorship movements, government programs, and other matters of importance. *Membership:* 220 companies. *Dues:* Vary. *Publication: AAP Monthly Report.*

*Association of Audio-Visual Technicians (AAVT). P.O. Box 101264, Denver, CO 80250-1264. (303) 698-1820. Fax (303) 777-3261. Elsa C. Kaiser, Exec. Dir. Proposes to increase communication and to assist audiovisual services and production technicians in their work; holds seminars in conjunction with most of the major audiovisual shows. Also has a lending library of old service manuals for rent by AAVT members. *Membership:* 1,200. *Dues:* $35 individuals, $65 institutions. *Publication: Fast Foreword.*

Association of Independent Video and Filmmakers/Foundation for Independent Video and Film (AIVF/FIVF). 625 Broadway, 9th Floor, New York, NY 10012. (212) 473-3400. Fax (212) 677-8732. Ruby Lerner, Exec. Dir. The national trade association for independent video and filmmakers, representing their needs and goals to industry, government, and the public. Programs include domestic and foreign festival liaison for independents, screenings and seminars, insurance for members and groups, and information and referral services. Recent activities include monitoring status of independent work on public television, advocacy for cable access, and lobbying for modifications in copyright law. *Dues:* $45 individuals, $75 libraries, $100 nonprofit organizations, $150 business/industry, $25 students. *Publications: The Independent Film and Video Monthly; The AIVF Guide to International Film and Video Festivals; The AIVF Guide to Film and Video Distributors; The Next Step: Distributing Independent Films and Videos; Alternative Visions: Distributing Independent Media in a Home Video World; Directory of Film and Video Production Resources in Latin America and the Caribbean.*

*Association of Systematics Collections (ASC). 730 11th St. NW, 2d Floor, Washington, DC 20001. (202) 347-2850. Fax (202) 347-0072. K. Elaine Hoagland, Exec. Dir. Fosters the care, management, and improvement of biological collections and promotes their utilization. Institutional members include private, free-standing museums, botanical gardens, zoos, college and university museums, and public institutions, including state biological surveys, agricultural research centers, the Smithsonian Institution, and the U.S. Fish and Wildlife Service. The ASC also represents affiliate societies, keeps members informed about funding and legislative issues, and provides technical consulting for such subjects as collection permits, care of collections, and taxonomic expertise. *Membership:* 76 institutions, 22 societies, 1,200 newsletter subscribers. *Dues:* Depend on the size of collections. *Publication: ASC Newsletter* (for members and nonmember subscribers, bi-mo.).

*Association of Teacher Educators (ATE). Suite ATE, 1900 Association Dr., Reston, VA 22091. (703) 620-3110. Fax (703) 620-9530. Gloria Chernay, Exec. Dir. The ATE serves as a national voice for issues related to preservice, graduate, and inservice teacher education. It also provides opportunities for professional growth and development through its publications and national conferences, workshops, and academies on current issues in teacher education. *Membership:* 3,500 individuals, 500 libraries. *Dues:* $65 regular members, $45 libraries, $20 students and retired. *Publications: Action in Teacher Education* (quarterly); *ATE Newsletter* (bi-mo.); *Education and the Family* (Allyn and Bacon 1992); *Restructuring the Education of Teachers into the 21st Century* (ATE 1991); *The Handbook of Research on Teacher Education* (Macmillan 1990).

*Catholic Library Association (CLA). 461 W. Lancaster Ave., Haverford, PA 19041. (215) 649-5250. Anthony Prete, Exec. Dir.; Maria Ferrante, contact person. Provides educational programs, services, and publications for Catholic libraries and librarians. *Membership:* 1,500. *Dues:* $45 individuals. *Publications: Catholic Library World* (q.); *Catholic Periodical and Literature Index* (q. with annual cumulations).

*Center for Advanced Visual Studies/MIT (CAVS). 40 Massachusetts Ave., Cambridge, MA 02139. (617) 253-4415. Fax (617) 253-1660. Otto Piene, Dir. Founded in 1968 by Gyorgy Kepes, CAVS offers a unique situation in which artists explore and realize artwork in collaboration with scientists and engineers. Has done significant work on lasers, holography, video, kinetics, environmental art, and sky art.

*Center for Instructional Research and Curriculum Evaluation. 1310 S. 6th St., Champaign, IL 61820. (217) 333-3770. Robert E. Stake, Dir. A unit within the College of Education, University of Illinois, the center is primarily active in conducting curriculum research in the United States, but has been of considerable interest to program evaluation specialists in foreign countries.

Center for Technology in Education (CTE). Bank Street College of Education, 610 West 112th St., New York, NY 10025. (212) 222-6700. Dr. Jan Hawkins, Dir. One of 25 university-based national education and development centers supported by the Office of Educational Research and Improvement (OERI) in the U.S. Office of Education to help strengthen student learning in the United States. These centers conduct research on topics that will help policy makers, practitioners, and parents meet the national education goals by the year 2000. In addition to addressing specific topics, most of these centers focus on children at risk. Many are also cooperating with other universities, and many work with elementary and secondary schools. All have been directed by OERI to make sure the information they produce reaches parents, teachers, and others who can use it to make meaningful changes in America's schools.

Central Educational Network (CEN). 1400 E. Touhy, Suite 260, Des Plaines, IL 60018-3305. (708) 390-8700. Fax (708) 390-9435. James A. Fellows, Pres. Provides general audience and instructional television programming and ITV services. *Membership:* PTV stations and educational agencies.

Children's Television International (CTI)/GLAD Productions, Inc. 8000 Forbes Pl., Suite 201, Springfield, VA 22151. (800) 284-4523. Ray Gladfelter, Pres.; Susan Johnson, Dir. of Customer Services. An educational organization that develops, produces, and distributes a wide variety of color television programming and television-related materials as a resource to aid children's social, cultural, and intellectual development. Program areas cover language arts, science, social studies, and art for home, school, and college viewing. *Publications:* Teacher's guides that accompany instructional television series and catalogues.

*CINE Information. 215 W. 90th St., New York, NY 10024. (212) 877-3999. Barbara Margolis, Exec. Dir. CINE Information is a nonprofit educational organization established to develop sound methods and tools for the more effective use of film by community groups and educational programmers. It produces and distributes materials about film and videotape use and produces films on topics of social and cultural importance. Newest releases include an Academy Award nominee for Best Documentary feature in *Adam Clayton Powell*, which was also broadcast on PBS's *The American Experience* series, and American Film Festival winner, *Are We Winning, Mommy? America and the Cold War. Mommy* was also featured at the Berlin, Toronto, Chicago, and Park City, Utah, Film Festivals. *Publication: In Focus: A Guide to Using Films*, by Linda Blackaby, Dan Georgakas, and Barbara Margolis, a complete step-by-step handbook for film and videotape users, with detailed discussions of how to use film and tape in educational, cultural, and fundraising activities.

Clearinghouse on Development Communication. 1815 N. Fort Myer Dr., 6th Floor, Arlington, VA 22209. (703) 527-5546. Fax (703) 527-4661. Valerie Lamont, Acting Dir. A center for materials and information on applications of communication technology to development problems. Operated by the Institute for International Research and funded by the Bureau for Research and Development of the U.S. Agency for International Development. Visitors and written requests for information are welcome, and an electronic bulletin board, CDCNET, is available to individuals with computer communications software and modems. *Dues:* Subscription, $10. *Publications: Development Communication Report* (q.); other special reports, information packages, project profiles, books, bulletins, and videotapes.

Close Up Foundation. 44 Canal Center Plaza, Alexandria, VA 22314. (703) 706-3300; (800) 765-3131. Fax (703) 706-0002. Stephen A. Janger, Pres. A nonprofit, nonpartisan civic education organization promoting informed citizen participation in public policy and community service. Programs reach more than a million participants a year. *Publications: Current Issues*; *The Bill of Rights: A User's Guide*; *Perspectives*; *International Relations*; *The American Economy*; documentary videotapes on domestic and foreign policy issues. Close Up brings 24,000 secondary and middle school students and teachers and older Americans each year to Washington for week-long government studies programs, produces television programs on the C-SPAN cable network for secondary school and home audiences, and conducts the Citizen Bee for high school students.

Computer-Based Education Research Laboratory (CERL). CERL, as a research laboratory dedicated to research on and the development of systems for the delivery of cost-effective, interactive, computer-based education (CBE), will be phased out as a department of the University of Illinois during 1994. The NovaNET system and courseware, which use a custom-designed, low-cost mainframe and satellite communications for continent-wide availability of CBE, will continue to be maintained by and accessible through University Communications, 359 Engineering Research Laboratory, 103 S. Mathews Ave., Urbana, IL 61801. (217) 244-4298. Fax (217) 244-4667.

*The Computer Museum. 300 Congress St., Boston, MA 02210. (617) 426-2800. Fax (617) 426-2943. Dr. Oliver Strimpel, Exec. Dir. The world's only computer museum occupies 55,000 square feet in a renovated historic building on Boston's waterfront. Dedicated to inspiring people of all ages and backgrounds about computers, the museum illustrates the evolution, use, and impact of computers from the mammoth machines of the past to state-of-the-art technology via 125 interactive exhibits, including a giant Walk-Through Computer™, displays, films, and animation; re-creations of vintage computer installations; and the most extensive collection of computers and robots in the world. The museum now exports its most dynamic interactive exhibits to museums and science centers around the globe. *Membership:* 1,400. *Dues:* $35 individuals, $50 family. *Publications: The Computer Museum Annual* (annual journal); *The Computer Museum News* (q. newsletter); Education Group Tour Planner, Educational Activities Kit (in English and Spanish).

Consortium of College and University Media Centers. 121 Pearson Hall-MRC, Iowa State University, Ames, IA 50011. (515) 294-1811. Fax (515) 294-8089. Don Rieck, Exec. Dir. A professional group of higher education media personnel whose purpose is to improve education and training through the effective use of educational media. Assists educational and training users in making films, video, and educational media more accessible. Fosters cooperative planning among university media centers. Gathers and disseminates information on improved procedures and new developments in instructional technology and media center management. *Membership:* 325. *Dues:* $140/yr. constituents; $40 active; $140 sustaining (commercial); $20 students; $100 associates. *Publications: Leader* (newsletter to members); *University and College Media Review* (journal).

Copyright Clearance Center, Inc. (CCC). 222 Rosewood Dr., Danvers, MA 01923. (508) 750-8400. Fax (508) 750-4744. Joseph S. Alen, Pres. and CEO. An organization through which corporations, academic and research libraries, information brokers, government agencies, copyshops, bookstores, and other users of copyrighted information may obtain authorizations and pay royalties for photocopying these materials in excess of exemptions contained in the U.S. Copyright Act of 1976. In addition to offering a Transactional Reporting Service (TRS), CCC also offers the Annual Authorization Service (AAS), an annual-license program serving photocopy permission needs of large U.S. corporations, and the Academic Permissions Service (APS), which provides photocopy authorizations in academic settings, specifically for authorizing anthologies and coursepacks. *Membership:* over 2,000 users, over 8,500 foreign and domestic publishers, 1.5 million publications. *Dues:* Vary. *Publications: COPI: Catalog of Publisher Information* (2/yr., $42 issue, $84/yr.); *CopyFacts: The Guide to Rights Holders, Titles, and Fees for the APS* (2/yr., $40 issue, $80/yr.).

Corporation for Public Broadcasting (CPB). 901 E St. NW, Washington, DC 20004. (202) 879-9800. Richard W. Carlson, Pres. and CEO. A private, nonprofit corporation authorized by the Public Broadcasting Act of 1967 to develop noncommercial television and radio services for the American people, while insulating public broadcasting from political pressure or influence. CPB supports station operations and funds radio and television programs for national distribution. CPB sets national policy that will most effectively make noncommercial radio and television and other telecommunications services available to all citizens. *Publications: CPB Report* (bi-weekly, 3 yrs. for $25); *Annual Report*; *CPB Public Broadcasting Directory* ($15).

Council for Basic Education. 1319 F St. NW, Suite 900, Washington, DC 20004-1152. (202) 347-4171. Fax (202) 347-5047. A. Graham Down, Pres. A vocal force advocating a broadly defined curriculum in the liberal arts for all students in elementary and secondary schools. *Membership:* 4,000. *Dues:* $40 members; $25/yr. subscribers. *Publications: Basic Education*; *Perspective* (q., 2 yrs. for $75 members or $45 subscribers); various reports and books.

Council for Educational Development and Research (CEDaR). 2000 L St. NW, Suite 601, Washington, DC 20036. (202) 223-1593. Dena G. Stoner, Exec. Dir. Members are educational research and development institutions. Aims to advance the level of programmatic, institutionally based educational research and development and to demonstrate the importance of research and development in improving education. Provides a forum for professional personnel in member institutions. Coordinates national dissemination program. Other activities include research, development, evaluation, dissemination, and technical assistance on educational issues. *Membership:* 15. *Publication: R&D Preview.*

*Council for Exceptional Children (CEC). 1920 Association Dr., Reston, VA 22091. (703) 620-3660. Fax (703) 264-9494. Jeptha Greer, Exec. Dir. A membership organization providing information to teachers, administrators, and others concerned with the education of handicapped and gifted children. Maintains a library and database on literature on special education; prepares books, monographs, digests, films, filmstrips, cassettes, and journals; sponsors annual convention and conferences on special education; provides on-site and regional training on various topics and at varying levels; provides information and assistance to lawmakers on education of the handicapped and gifted; coordinates a political action network on the rights of exceptional persons. *Membership:* 55,000. *Dues:* Professionals, $60-80, depending on state of residence; students, $26-26.50, depending on state of residence. *Publications: Exceptional Children; Teaching Exceptional Children; Exceptional Child Educational Resources;* numerous other professional publications dealing with the education of handicapped and gifted children.

(CEC) Technology and Media Division (TAM). Council for Exceptional Children, 1920 Association Dr., Reston, VA 22091. (703) 620-3660. The Technology and Media Division (TAM) of the Council for Exceptional Children (CEC) encourages the development of new applications, technologies, and media for use as daily living tools by special populations. This information is disseminated through professional meetings, training programs, and publications. TAM members receive four issues annually of the *Journal of Special Education Technology* containing articles on specific technology programs and applications, and five issues of the TAM newsletter, providing news of current research, developments, products, conferences, and special programs information. *Membership:* 1,500. *Dues:* $10 in addition to CEC membership.

Council of National Library and Information Associations. 1700 18th St. NW, Suite B-1, Washington, DC 20009. (718) 990-6735. Fax (718) 380-0353. Marie F. Melton, R.S.M., Secy/Treas. The council is a forum for discussion of many issues of concern to library and information associations. *Membership:* 21 associations. *Dues:* Inquire. *Meetings:* Councils meet in May and December in New York City.

Council on International Non-theatrical Events. 1001 Connecticut Ave. NW, Suite 638, Washington, DC 20036. (202) 785-1136. Fax (202) 785-4114. Richard Calkins, Exec. Dir. Coordinates the selection and placement of U.S. documentary, television, short subject, and didactic films in more than 200 overseas film festivals annually. A Golden Eagle Certificate is awarded to each professional film considered most suitable to represent the United States in international competition. A CINE Eagle Certificate is awarded to winning adult amateur-, youth-, and university student-made films. Prizes and certificates won at overseas festivals are presented by embassy representatives at an annual awards luncheon. Deadlines for receipt of entry forms are 1 February and 1 August. *Meeting:* 36th Annual CINE Showcase and Awards, March 3-4, 1994, Washington, DC. *Publications: CINE Annual Yearbook of Film and Video Awards; Worldwide Directory of Film and Video Festivals and Events* (annual); *CINE News* (q.).

East-West Center. 1777 East-West Rd., Honolulu, HI 96848. (808) 944-7666. Fax (808) 944-7333. E-mail culture@ewc. Geoffrey M. White, Dir. The U.S. Congress established the East-West Center in 1960 to foster mutual understanding and cooperation among the governments and peoples of the Asia-Pacific region, including the United States. Principal funding for the center comes from the U.S. government, with additional support provided by private agencies, individuals, and corporations, and more than 20 Asian and Pacific governments. The Program for Cultural Studies pursues research on areas of public policy interest such as education, media, family, religion, the arts, and human rights in which cultural values, identities, and histories become matters of voiced concern. Program research focuses particularly on ways in which culture enters the public sphere and impacts on national integration and international relations, taking into account the increasingly powerful role of film, video, and other mass media in shaping perceptions of culture, gender, and nationality. *Publication: East-West Film Journal.*

Education Development Center, Inc. 55 Chapel St., Newton, MA 02160. (617) 969-7100. Fax (617) 244-3436. Janet Whitla, Pres. Seeks to improve education at all levels, in the United States and abroad, through curriculum development, institutional development, and services to the school and the community. Produces filmstrips and videocassettes, primarily in connection with curriculum development and teacher training. *Publications: Annual Report*; *EDC News* (newsletter, 2/yr.).

Educational Film Library Association. See listing for American Film and Video Association (AFVA).

EPIE Institute (Educational Products Information Exchange). 103 W. Montauk Highway, Hampton Bays, NY 11946. (516) 728-9100. Fax (516) 728-9228. P. Kenneth Komoski, Exec. Dir. Involved primarily in assessing educational materials and providing product descriptions/citations of virtually all educational software. All of EPIE's services, including its Curriculum Alignment Services for Educators, are available to schools and state agencies as well as individuals. *Publications: The Educational Software Selector (T.E.S.S.)* (annual); *The Educational Software Selector Database: TESS*, available to members of the States Consortium for Improving Software Selection; EPIE's newsletter, *EPIEgram* (9/yr.), is published by Sterling Harbor Press, Box 28, Greenport, NY 11944.

ERIC (Educational Resources Information Center). U.S. Department of Education/OERI, 555 New Jersey Ave. NW, Washington, DC 20208-5720. (202) 219-2289. Fax (202) 219-1817. Internet eric@inet.ed.gov. Robert Stonehill, Dir. ERIC is a nationwide information network that provides access to the English-language education literature. The ERIC system consists of 16 Clearinghouses, 5 Adjunct Clearinghouses, and system support components that include the ERIC Processing and Reference Facility, ACCESS ERIC, and the ERIC Document Reproduction Service (EDRS). ERIC actively solicits papers, conference proceedings, literature reviews, and curriculum materials from researchers, practitioners, educational associations and institutions, and federal, state, and local agencies. These materials, along with articles from nearly 800 different journals, are indexed and abstracted for entry into the ERIC database. The ERIC database—the largest education database in the world—now contains almost 800,000 records of documents and journal articles. Users can access the ERIC database online, on CD-ROM, or through print and microfiche indexes. ERIC microfiche collections, which contain the full text of most ERIC documents, are available for public use at nearly 900 locations worldwide. Reprints of ERIC documents, on microfiche or in paper copy, can also be ordered from EDRS. A list of the ERIC Clearinghouses, together with full addresses, telephone numbers, and brief scope notes describing the areas they cover, follows here. *Dues: None. Publications: Resources in Education; Current Index to Journals in Education.*

ERIC Clearinghouse on Adult, Career, and Vocational Education (CE). Ohio State University, Center on Education and Training for Employment, 1900 Kenny Rd., Columbus, OH 43210-1090. (614) 292-4353; (800) 848-4815. Fax (614) 292-1260. Internet ericacve@magnus.acs.ohio-state.edu. Susan Imel, Dir. All levels of adult and continuing education from basic literacy training through professional skill upgrading. The focus is upon factors contributing to the purposeful learning of adults in a variety of situations usually related to adult roles (e.g., occupation, family, leisure time, citizenship, organizational relationships, retirement, and so forth). Includes input from Adjunct ERIC Clearinghouse on Consumer Education.

ERIC Clearinghouse on Assessment and Evaluation (TM) (formerly Tests, Measurement and Evaluation). Catholic University of America, 210 O'Boyle Hall, Washington, DC 20064-4035. (202) 319-5120. Fax (202) 319-6692. Internet eric_ae@cua.edu. Lawrence M. Rudner, Dir. All aspects of tests and other measurement devices. The design and methodology of research, measurement, and evaluation. The evaluation of programs and projects. The application of tests, measurement, and evaluation devices/instrumentation in education projects and programs.

ERIC Clearinghouse for Community Colleges (JC) (formerly Junior Colleges). University of California at Los Angeles (UCLA), Math-Sciences Bldg., Rm. 8118, 405 Hilgard Ave., Los Angeles, CA 90024-1564. (310) 825-3931. Fax (310) 206-8095. Internet eeh3usc@mvs.oac.ucla.edu. Arthur M. Cohen, Dir. Development, administration, and evaluation of two-year public and private community and junior colleges, technical institutes, and two-year branch university campuses. Two-year college students, faculty, staff, curricula, programs, support services, libraries, and community services. Linkages between two-year colleges and business/industrial/community organizations. Articulation of two-year colleges with secondary and four-year postsecondary institutions.

ERIC Clearinghouse on Counseling and Student Services (CG) (formerly Counseling and Personnel Services). University of North Carolina at Greensboro, School of Education, Greensboro, NC 27412-5001. (919) 334-4114; (800) 414-9769. Fax (919) 334-4116. Internet bleuerj@iris.uncg.edu. Garry R. Walz, Dir. Preparation, practice, and supervision of counselors at all educational levels and in all settings. Theoretical development of counseling and guidance, including the nature of relevant human characteristics. Use and results of personnel practices and procedures. Group process (counseling, therapy, dynamics) and case work.

ERIC Clearinghouse on Disabilities and Gifted Education (EC) (formerly Handicapped and Gifted Children). Council for Exceptional Children, 1920 Association Dr., Reston, VA 22091-1589. (703) 264-9474. Fax (703) 264-9494. Internet kmclane-@inet.ed.gov. Bruce Ramirez, Acting Dir. All aspects of the education and development of persons (of all ages) who have disabilities or who are gifted, including the delivery of all types of education-related services to these groups. Includes prevention, identification and assessment, intervention, and enrichment for these groups in both regular and special education settings.

ERIC Clearinghouse on Educational Management (EA). University of Oregon, 1787 Agate St., Eugene, OR 97403-5207. (503) 346-5043; (800) 438-8841. Fax (503) 346-2334. Internet ppiele@oregon.uoregon.edu. Philip K. Piele, Dir. All aspects of the governance, leadership, administration, and structure of public and private educational organizations at the elementary and secondary levels, including the provision of physical facilities for their operation.

ERIC Clearinghouse on Elementary and Early Childhood Education (PS). University of Illinois, College of Education, 805 W. Pennsylvania Ave., Urbana, IL 61801-4897. (217) 333-1386. Fax (217) 333-3767. Internet ericeece@ux1.cso.uiuc.edu. Lilian G. Katz, Dir. All aspects of the physical, cognitive, social, educational, and cultural development of children, from birth through early adolescence. Among the topics covered are: prenatal and infant development and care; parent education; home and school relationships; learning theory research and practice related to children's development; preparation of early childhood teachers and caregivers; and educational programs and community services for children.

ERIC Clearinghouse on Higher Education (HE). George Washington University, One Dupont Cir. NW, Suite 630, Washington, DC 20036-1183. (202) 296-2597. Fax (202) 296-8379. Internet eriche@inet.ed.gov. Jonathan D. Fife, Dir. All aspects of the conditions, programs, and problems at colleges and universities providing higher education (i.e., four-year degrees and beyond). This includes: governance and management; planning; finance; inter-institutional arrangements; business or industry programs leading to a degree; institutional research at the college/university level; federal programs; legal issues and legislation; professional education (e.g., medicine, law, etc.) and professional continuing education.

ERIC Clearinghouse on Information & Technology (IR) (formerly Information Resources). Syracuse University, 4-194 Center for Science and Technology, Syracuse, NY 13244-4100. (315) 443-3640; (800) 464-9107. Fax (315) 443-5448. Internet eric@ericir.syr.edu. AskERIC (question-answering service via Internet) ask-eric@ericir.syr.edu. Michael B. Eisenberg, Dir. Educational technology and library and information science at all academic levels and with all populations, including the preparation of professionals. The media and devices of educational communication as they pertain to teaching and learning (in both conventional and distance education settings). The operation and management of libraries and information services. All aspects of information management and information technology related to education.

ERIC Clearinghouse on Languages and Linguistics (FL). Center for Applied Linguistics, 1118 22d St. NW, Washington, DC 20037-0037. (202) 429-9292. Fax (202) 659-5641. Internet cal@guvax.georgetown.edu. Charles Stansfield, Dir. Languages and language sciences. All aspects of second language instruction and learning in all commonly and uncommonly taught languages, including English as a second language. Bilingualism and bilingual education. Cultural education in the context of second language learning, including intercultural communication, study abroad, and international educational exchange. All areas of linguistics, including theoretical and applied linguistics, sociolinguistics, and psycholinguistics. Includes input from Adjunct ERIC Clearinghouse on Literacy Education for Limited-English-Proficient Adults.

ERIC Clearinghouse on Reading, English, and Communication (CS) (formerly Reading and Communication Skills). Indiana University, Smith Research Center, Suite 150, 2805 E. 10th St., Bloomington, IN 47408-2698. (812) 855-5847; (800) 759-4723. Fax (812) 855-4220. Internet ericcs@ucs.indiana.edu. Carl B. Smith, Dir. Reading and writing, English (as a first language), and communications skills (verbal and nonverbal), kindergarten through college. Includes family or intergenerational literacy. Research and instructional development in reading, writing, speaking, and listening. Identification, diagnosis, and remediation of reading problems. Speech communication (including forensics), mass communication (including journalism), interpersonal and small group interaction, oral interpretation, rhetorical and communication theory, and theater/drama. Preparation of instructional staff and related personnel in all the above areas.

ERIC Clearinghouse on Rural Education and Small Schools (RC). Appalachia Educational Laboratory, 1031 Quarrier St., P.O. Box 1348, Charleston, WV 25325-1348. (304) 347-0465; (800) 624-9120. Fax (304) 347-0487. Internet u56d9@wvnvm.wvnet.edu. Craig Howley, Dir. Curriculum and instructional programs and research/evaluation efforts that address the education of students in rural schools or districts, small schools wherever located, and schools of districts wherever located that serve American Indian and Alaskan natives, Mexican Americans, and migrants, or that have programs related to outdoor education. Includes the cultural, ethnic, linguistic, economic, and social conditions that affect these educational institutions and groups. Preparation programs, including related services, that train education professionals to work in such contexts.

ERIC Clearinghouse on Science, Mathematics, and Environmental Education (SE). Ohio State University, 1929 Kenny Road, Columbus, OH 43210-1080. (614) 292-6717. Fax (614) 292-0263. Internet ericse@osu.edu. David L. Haury, Dir. Science, mathematics, engineering/technology, and environmental education at all levels. The following topics when focused on any of the above broad scope areas: applications of learning theory; curriculum and instructional materials; teachers and teacher education; educational programs and projects; research and evaluative studies; applications of educational technology and media.

ERIC Clearinghouse for Social Studies/Social Science Education (SO). Indiana University, Social Studies Development Center, 2805 E. Tenth St., Suite 120, Bloomington, IN 47408-2698. (812) 855-3838. Fax (812) 855-0455. Internet ericso@ucs. indiana.edu. John Patrick, Dir. All aspects of social studies and social science education, including values education (and the social aspects of environmental education and sex education), international education, comparative education, and cross-cultural studies in all subject areas (K-12). Ethnic heritage, gender equity, aging, and social bias/discrimination topics. Also covered are music, art, and architecture as related to the fine arts. Includes input from the Adjunct ERIC Clearinghouse for U.S.-Japan Studies.

ERIC Clearinghouse on Teaching and Teacher Education (SP) (formerly Teacher Education). American Association of Colleges for Teacher Education, One Dupont Cir. NW, Suite 610, Washington, DC 20036-1186. (202) 293-2450. Fax (202) 457-8095. Internet jbeck@inet.ed.gov. Mary E. Dilworth, Dir. School personnel at all levels. Teacher recruitment, selection, licensing, certification, training, preservice and inservice preparation, evaluation, retention, and retirement. The theory, philosophy, and practice of teaching. Organization, administration, finance, and legal issues relating to teacher education programs and institutions. All aspects of health, physical, recreation, and dance education.

ERIC Clearinghouse on Urban Education (UD). Teachers College, Columbia University, Institute for Urban and Minority Education, Main Hall, Rm. 303, Box 40, 525 W. 120th St., New York, NY 10027-9998. (212) 678-3433; (800) 601-4868. Fax (212) 678-4048. Internet ef29@columbia.edu. Erwin Flaxman, Dir. The educational characteristics and experiences of the diverse racial, ethnic, social class, and linguistic populations in urban (and suburban) schools. Curriculum and instruction of students from these populations and the organization of their schools. The relationship of urban schools to their communities. The social and economic conditions that affect the education of urban populations, with particular attention to factors that place urban students at risk educationally, and ways that public and private sector policies can improve these conditions.

ACCESS ERIC. Aspen Systems Corp., 1600 Research Blvd., Rockville, MD 20850-3172; 1-800-LET-ERIC [538-3742]. Fax (301) 251-5767. Internet acceric@inet.ed.gov. Beverly Swanson, ERIC Project Dir. Toll-free service provides access to the information and services available through the ERIC system. Staff will answer questions as well as refer callers to education sources. ACCESS ERIC also produces several publications and reference and referral databases that provide information about both the ERIC system and current education-related issues and research. *Publications: A Pocket Guide to ERIC; All About ERIC; The ERIC Review;* the Conclusion Brochure series; *Catalog of ERIC Clearinghouse Publications; ERIC Calendar of Education-Related Conferences; ERIC User's Interchange; Directory of ERIC Information Service Centers. Databases:* ERIC Digests Online (EDO); Education-Related Information Centers; ERIC Information Service Providers; ERIC Calendar of Education-Related Conferences. (The databases are available through GTE Education Services on a subscription basis.)

Adjunct ERIC Clearinghouse for ESL Literacy Education (ADJ/LE). Center for Applied Linguistics, 1118 22d St. NW, Washington, DC 20037-0037. (202) 429-9292, Ext. 200. Fax (202) 659-5641. Internet cal@guvax.georgetown.edu. Marilyn Gillespie, Dir.

Adjunct ERIC Clearinghouse for United States-Japan Studies (ADJ/JS). Indiana University, Social Studies Development Center, 2805 E. 10th St., Suite 120, Bloomington, IN 47408-2373. (812) 855-3838. Fax (812) 855-0455. C. Frederick Risingerr, Dir.

Adjunct ERIC Clearinghouse on Chapter 1 (Compensatory Education) (ADJ/Chapter 1). Chapter 1 Technical Assistance Center, PRC Inc., 2601 Fortune Cir. E., One Park Fletcher Bldg., Suite 300-A, Indianapolis, IN 46241-2237. (317) 244-8160; (800) 456-2380. Fax (317) 244-7386. Sheila M. Short, Coord.

Adjunct ERIC Clearinghouse on Clinical Schools (ADJ/CL). American Association of Colleges for Teacher Education, One Dupont Cir. NW, Suite 610, Washington, DC 20036-1186. (202) 293-2450. Fax (202) 457-8095. Internet iabdalha@inet.ed.gov. Ismat Abdal-Haqq, contact person.

Adjunct ERIC Clearinghouse on Consumer Education (ADJ/CN). National Institute for Consumer Education, 207 Rackham Bldg., West Cir. Dr., Eastern Michigan University, Ypsilanti, MI 48197-2237. (313) 487-2292; (800) 336-6423. Fax (313) 487-7153. Internet cse_bonner@emunix.emich.edu. Rosella Bannister, Dir.

ERIC Document Reproduction Service (EDRS). 7420 Fullerton Rd., Suite 110, Springfield, VA 22153-2852. (703) 440-1400; (800) 443-ERIC [3742]. Fax (703) 440-1408. Internet edrs@gwuvm.gwu.edu. Peter M. Dagutis, Dir. Operates the document delivery arm of the ERIC system. Furnishes microfiche and/or paper copies of most ERIC documents. Address purchase orders to the preceding address. Fax order and delivery service available.

ERIC Processing and Reference Facility. 1301 Piccard Dr., Suite 300, Rockville, MD 20850-4305. (301) 258-5500; (800) 799-ERIC (3742). Fax (301) 948-3695. Internet ericfac@inet.ed.gov. Ted Brandhorst, Dir. A centralized information processing facility serving all components of the ERIC network, under policy direction of Central ERIC. Services provided include acquisitions, editing, receiving and dispatch, document control and analysis, lexicography, computer processing, file maintenance, and database management. Receives and edits abstracts from 16 ERIC Clearinghouses for publication in *Resources in Education (RIE)*; updates and maintains the *Thesaurus of ERIC Descriptors*. Publications: *Resources in Education*; *Source Directory*; *Report Number Index*; *Clearinghouse Number/ED Number Cross Reference Listing*; *Title Index*; *ERIC Processing Manual*; numerous other listings and indexes.

Far West Laboratory for Educational Research and Development (FWL). 730 Harrison St., San Francisco, CA 94107-1242. (415) 565-3000. Fax (415) 565-3012. Dr. Dean Nafziger, Exec. Dir. Far West Laboratory for Educational Research and Development serves the four-state region of Arizona, California, Nevada, and Utah, working with educators at all levels to plan and carry out school improvements. The mission of FWL is to challenge and enable educational organizations and their communities to create and sustain improved learning and development opportunities for their children, youth, and adults. To accomplish its mission, FWL directs resources toward: advancing knowledge; developing products and programs for teachers and learners; providing assistance to educational agencies; communicating with outside audiences to remain informed and to inform others about the results of research, development, and exemplary practice; and creating an environment in which diverse educational and societal issues can be addressed and resolved. Far West Laboratory maintains a reference library.

Federal Communications Commission (FCC). 1919 M St. NW, Washington, DC 20554. Patti Grace Smith, Deputy Dir. of Policy/Public Information and Reference Services. The FCC is a federal government agency regulating interstate and international communications by radio, television, wire, satellite, and cable in the United States and its territories and possessions. It allocates frequencies and channels for different types of communication activities, issues amateur and commercial radio operators' licenses, and regulates rates of many types of interstate communication services. Public Service Division: Consumer Assistance Branch (202) 632-7000. Fax (202) 632-0274. TT (202) 632-6999. Public Policy Planning Branch (202) 632-0244. Martha Contee, Chief, Public Service Div. (PSD). *Publications:* Fact Sheets, Information Bulletins, and Public Notices pertaining to FCC-regulated services.

Film Advisory Board (FAB). 1727-1/2 Sycamore, Hollywood, CA 90028. (213) 874-3644. Fax (213) 969-0635. Elayne Blythe, Pres. Previews and evaluates films and film-type presentations in all formats, makes recommendations for improved family entertainment fare, and presents awards of excellence to outstanding motion pictures, television programs, videos, and audiotapes, and for innovations in these industries. Technical awards are also presented, as are awards for outstanding contributions to the entertainment industry and for the most promising newcomers. Awards of excellence are presented for videocassettes; the FAB Award Winner Seal is featured worldwide on many of the family and child videocassettes for Prism, RCA Columbia, Rhino, Turner, Fox, and others. Supplies film list to many national organizations encouraging them to support FAB award-winning products. *Membership:* 450. *Dues:* $40/yr. *Publication: Film Advisory Board Newsletter*, monthly film list distributed to studios, libraries, churches, public relations firms, youth groups, PTAs, clubs, and colleges. Now rating home videos with Film Advisory Board (FAB) Rating System, the only official rating system other than the MPAA. *FAB Rating Categories:* C=Children (ages 10 and under); F=Family (all ages); *PD=Parental Discretion; **PD-M=Parental Discretion-Mature (ages 13 and over). Categories replaced as of March 1, 1993: *M=Mature and **VM=Very Mature. FAB's system was the first to use content descriptions with its rating categories.

Film Arts Foundation (FAF). 346 9th St., 2d Floor, San Francisco, CA 94103. (415) 552-8760. Gail Silva, Dir. Service organization designed to support and promote independent film and video production. Services include low-cost 16mm and Super-8 editing facility, festivals file, resource library, group legal plan, association health options, seminars, workshops, annual film and video festival, grants program, monthly publication, work-in-progress screenings, proposal and distribution consultation, nonprofit sponsorship of selected film and video projects, and advocacy for independent film and video. *Membership:* 2,500 plus. *Dues:* $35. *Publication: Release Print.*

Film/Video Arts, Inc. 817 Broadway, New York, NY 10003. (212) 673-9361. Fax (212) 475-3467. Karen Helmerson, Deputy Dir. Film/Video Arts is a nonprofit media arts center dedicated to the advancement of emerging and established media artists of diverse backgrounds. F/VA provides support services that include low-cost production equipment and facilities, education and training, exhibition, and grant and employment opportunities. F/VA offers scholarship assistance to women, African-Americans, Latinos, Asians, and Native Americans. *Dues:* $40/individuals, $60/nonprofit organizations (Oct. 1-Sept. 30).

Freedom of Information Center (FOI). 20 Walter William Hall, University of Missouri, Columbia, MO 65211. (314) 882-4856. Kathleen Edwards, Center Mgr. Collects and indexes material on actions by government, media, and society affecting the flow of information at international, national, state, and local levels. The center answers questions on the federal FOI Act, censorship issues, access to government at all levels, privacy, ethics, bar-press guidelines, and First Amendment issues. *Publications:* Back issues of FOI publications available for purchase.

George Eastman House (formerly International Museum of Photography at George Eastman House). 900 East Ave., Rochester, NY 14607. (716) 271-3361. Fax (716) 271-3970. James L. Enyeart, Dir. World-renowned museum of photography and cinematography established to preserve, collect, and exhibit photographic art and technology, film materials, and related literature. Services include archives, traveling exhibitions, research library center for the conservation of photographic materials, and photographic print service. Educational programs, films, symposia, and internship stipends offered. *Dues:* $40 libraries; $50 families;

$40 individuals; $25 students or senior citizens; $75 Contributors; $125 Sustainers; $250 Patrons; $500 Benefactors; $1,000 George Eastman Society. *Publications: IMAGE; Microfiche Index to Collections; Newsletter; Annual Report: The George Eastman House and Gardens; Masterpieces of Photography from the George Eastman House Collections;* and exhibition catalogues.

*Government Printing Office (US GPO). North Capitol and H Sts. NW, Washington, DC 20401. (202) 512-2395. Fax (202) 512-2250 for publications and order information. The GPO provides printing and binding services to Congress and the agencies of the federal government, and distributes and sells government publications through its Superintendent of Documents sales and depository library programs.

Great Plains National ITV Library (GPN). PO Box 80669, Lincoln, NE 68501-0669. (402) 472-2007; (800) 228-4630. Fax (402) 472-1785. Lee Rockwell, Dir. Acquires, produces, promotes, and distributes educational video series and singles. Offers more than 200 videotape (videocassette) courses and related teacher utilization materials. Available for purchase or, in some instances, lease. Also distributes instructional videodiscs and CD-ROMs. *Publications: GPN Educational Video Catalog* (annual); *GPNewsletter* (q.); periodic brochures.

Health Sciences Communications Association (HeSCA). 6728 Old McLean Village Dr., McLean, VA 22101. (703) 556-9324. Fax (703) 556-8729. Cheryl Kilday, Assoc. Dir. HeSCA is an international nonprofit organization dedicated to the promotion and sharing of ideas, skills, resources, and techniques to enhance communication and education in the health sciences. HeSCA is actively supported by leading medical and veterinary schools, hospitals, medical associations, and businesses. *Membership:* 350. *Dues:* $90 individual; $135 institutional ($90 additional institutional dues); $55 retirees; $70 students; $1,000 sustaining; all include subscription to the journal and newsletter). *Meeting:* World Congress on Biomedical Communications, June 18-23, 1994, Orlando, FL. *Publications: Journal of Biocommunications; Feedback* (newsletter); *Patient Education Sourcebook Vol. II; 1993 Media Festivals and LRC Catalogue.*

Hollywood Film Archive. 8344 Melrose Ave., Hollywood, CA 90069. (213) 933-3345. D. Richard Baer, Dir. Archival organization for information about feature films produced worldwide, from the early silents to the present. Offers comprehensive movie reference works for sale, including *Variety Film Reviews* (1907-1990) and the *American Film Institute Catalogs* (1911-20, 1921-30, 1931-40, 1961-70), as well as the *Film Superlist* series, which provides information both on copyrights and on motion pictures in the public domain, and *Harrison's Reports and Film Reviews* (1919-1962). *Publications:* Reference books.

*HOPE Reports. 58 Carverdale Dr., Rochester, NY 14618-4004. (716) 442-1310. Fax (716) 442-1725. Thomas W. Hope, Pres. and Chair. Provides reports for the presentation audiovisual/video communication field, covering statistical and financial status, sales, salaries, trends, and predictions. Also provides calendar scheduling service of national/international events. Makes private surveys and has consulting service. *Publications: Contract Production for the '90s; Video Post-Production; Media Market Trends V; Educational Media Trends through the 1990's; LCD Panels and Projectors; Overhead Projection System; Presentation Slides and Computer Graphics; Educational Media Trends; Producer & Video Post Wages & Salaries; Noncommercial AV Wages & Salaries, II; Corporate Media Salaries, V.*

Institute for Development of Educational Activities, Inc. (IDEA). 259 Regency Ridge, Dayton, OH 45459. (513) 434-6969. Fax (513) 434-5203. Action-oriented research and development organization, originating from the Charles F. Kettering Foundation, established to assist the educational community in bridging the gap that separates research and innovation from actual practice in the schools. Goal is to design and test new responses to improve education and to create arrangements that support local application. Main activities include: developing new and improved processes, systems, and materials; training local facilitators to use the change processes; providing information and services about improved methods and materials. Sponsors an annual fellowship program for administrators and conducts seminars for school administrators and teachers.

Institute for Research on Teaching. College of Education, MSU, East Lansing, MI 48824. (517) 355-1737. E-mail penny@msu.bitnet. Penelope Peterson and Jere Brophy, Co-Dirs. Funded primarily by the U.S. Department of Education and Michigan State University; conducts research on the continuing problems of practice encountered by teaching professionals, the teaching of subject matter disciplines in elementary schools (through the Center for the Learning and Teaching of Elementary Subjects), and publishes numerous materials detailing this research. *Publications:* Research series; occasional papers; annual catalog.

Institute for the Future (IFTF). 2744 Sand Hill Rd., Menlo Park, CA 94025-7020. (415) 854-6322. Fax (415) 854-7850. J. Ian Morrison, Pres. Works with organizations to plan their long-term futures. Helps them to evaluate the external environment and take advantage of the opportunities offered by new technologies. Founded in 1968, IFTF has emerged as a leader in action-oriented research for business, industry, and governments, having worked with more than 300 organizations. Typical projects include environmental scanning, strategic planning assistance, policy analyses, and market outlooks and evaluations for new products and next-generation technologies. The success of the organization is based on several unique strengths, including a pragmatic futures orientation, studies of emerging technologies, networking of ideas and people, and use of scenarios to identify and analyze issues and options. *Publications:* List available from IFTF free of charge.

Institute of Culture and Communication. East-West Center, 1777 East-West Rd., Honolulu, HI 96848. (808) 944-7666. Geoffrey M. White, Dir. A program of the East-West Center, which was established by the U.S. Congress "to promote better relations and understanding among the nations of Asia, the Pacific and the United States through cooperative study, training and research." The Institute is organized around four programs: Multiculturalism; Core Values; Cultural Change; and Culture and Development.

International Association of Business Communicators (IABC). One Hallidie Plaza, Suite 600, San Francisco, CA 94102. (415) 433-3400. Fax (415) 362-8762. Norman G. Leaper, Pres. IABC is the worldwide association for the communication and public relations profession. It is founded on the principle that the better an organization communicates with all its audiences, the more successful and effective it will be in meeting its objectives. IABC is dedicated to fostering communication excellence, contributing more effectively to organizations' goals worldwide, and being a model of communication effectiveness. *Membership:* 11,000 plus. *Dues:* $180 in addition to local and regional dues. *Meetings:* 1994, June 12-15, Boston, MA; 1995, June 11-14, Toronto, ON. *Publication: Communication World.*

*International Association of School Librarianship (IASL). Box 1486, Kalamazoo, MI 49005. (616) 343-5728. Jean E. Lowrie, Exec. Secy. Seeks to encourage development of school libraries and library programs throughout the world, to promote professional preparation of school librarians and continuing education programs, to achieve collaboration among school libraries of the world, and to facilitate loans and exchanges in the field. *Membership:* 900 plus. *Dues:* $20 personal and institution for North America, Europe, Japan, and Australia; $15 for all other countries; based on membership for associations. *Publications: IASL Newsletter* (q.); *Annual Proceedings*; *Persons to Contact*; *Indicators of Quality for School Library Media Programs*; *Books and Borrowers*; occasional papers.

International Center of Photography (ICP). 1130 Fifth Ave., New York, NY 10128. (212) 860-1777. Fax (212) 360-6490. ICP Midtown, 1133 Avenue of the Americas, New York, NY 10036. (212) 768-4680. Fax (212) 768-4688. Cornell Capa, Dir.; Phyllis Levine, Dir. of Public Information. A comprehensive photographic institution whose exhibitions, publications, collections, and educational programs embrace all aspects of photography from aesthetics to technique; from the 18th century to the present; from master photographers to newly emerging talents; from photojournalism to the avant garde. Changing exhibitions, lectures, seminars, workshops, museum shops, and screening rooms make ICP a complete photographic resource. *Membership:* 7,000. *Dues:* $50 individual membership, $60 double membership, $125 Supporting Patron, $250 Photography Circle, $500 Silver Card Patron, $1,000 Gold Card Patron; corporate memberships available. *Publications: Library of Photography*; *Encyclopedia of Photography—Master Photographs from PFA Collection*; *Man Ray in Fashion*; *Quarterly Program Guide*; *Quarterly Exhibit Schedule.*

*International Communication Association. Box 9589, Austin, TX 78766. (512) 454-8299. Fax (512) 454-4221. Robert L. Cox, Exec. Dir. Established to study human communication and to seek better understanding of the process of communication. Engages in systematic studies of communication theories, processes, and skills, and disseminates information. *Membership:* 2,400. *Dues:* $40-$l,450. *Publications: Human Communication Research* (q.); *The Guide to Publishing in Scholarly Communication*; *Communication Theory* (q.); *Journal of Communication* (q.); *Communication Yearbook.*

International Copyright Information Center (INCINC). c/o Association of American Publishers, 1718 Connecticut Ave. NW, 7th Floor, Washington, DC 20009-1148. (202) 232-3335. Fax (202) 745-0694. MCI mail aapdc. Carol A. Risher, Dir. Assists developing nations in their efforts to translate and/or reprint copyrighted works published in the United States.

International Council for Computers in Education (ICCE). See listing for International Society for Technology in Education (ISTE).

International Film and TV Festival of New York. See listing for The New York Festivals.

International Graphic Arts Education Association (IGAEA). 4615 Forbes Ave., Pittsburgh, PA 15213-3796. (412) 621-6941. Lenore D. Collins, Pres. (401) 456-8703. Fax (401) 456-8379. An organization of professionals in graphic arts education and industry, dedicated to promoting effective methodology in teaching, relevant educational research and efficient dissemination of information concerning graphic arts, graphic communications, and related fields. To achieve these goals, the IGAEA sponsors conferences, publications, and industry liaison programs. The association has recently revised its mission and now includes and invites not only graphic arts educators but teachers of graphic design, technology education, journalism, photography, and any other field relating to visual/graphic communications and imaging technology. *Membership:* approx. 700. *Dues:* $20 regular; $12 associate (retired); $5 student; $10 library; $50-$200 sustaining members based on number of employees. *Meetings:* 1994, July 31-August 5, Menonomie, WI; 1995, August 6-11, Warrensburg, MO. *Publications: Visual Communications Journal; Research and Resource Reports.*

*International Information Management Congress (IMC). 1650 38th St., #205W, Boulder, CO 80301. (303) 440-7085. Fax (303) 440-7234. Jack Lacy, Exec. Dir.; Janice Marean, Dir. of Administrative Services. An international trade association for the document imaging industry, the IMC supports education in the information management field through the exchange of information, technical journals and monographs, and conferences and exhibits in different parts of the world. *Membership:* 30 associations, 70 sustaining company members. *Dues:* $120 affiliates; $200 associations; varies for sustaining members. *Publication: IMC Journal* (bi-mo.).

International Museum of Photography at George Eastman House. See listing for George Eastman House.

International Society for Technology in Education (ISTE) (formerly International Council for Computers in Education [ICCE]). 1787 Agate St., Eugene, OR 97403-1923. (503) 346-4414. Fax (503) 346-5890. E-mail iste@oregon.uoregon.edu. David Moursund, CEO; Maia S. Howes, Exec. Secy. The largest nonprofit professional organization dedicated to the improvement of all levels of education through the use of computer-based technology. Technology-using educators from all over the world rely on ISTE for information, inspiration, ideas, and updates on the latest electronic information systems available to the educational community. ISTE is a prominent information center and source of leadership to communicate and collaborate with educational professionals, policymakers, and other organizations worldwide. *Membership:* 12,000 individual members, 75 organizational affiliates, 25 Private Sector Council members. *Dues:* $46 individuals, $215 all-inclusive memberships (U.S.); $1,500 to $5,000, Private Sector Council members. *Meeting:* NECC '94, June 13-15, Boston, MA. *Publications: The Computing Teacher* (8/yr.); *The Update Newsletter* (7/yr.); *The Journal of Research on Computing in Education* (q.); *The Information Resource Manager (IRM) Quarterly*; guides to instructional uses of computers at the precollege level and in teacher training, about 80 books, and a range of independent study courses that carry graduate-level credit.

International Tape/Disc Association. See listing for ITA.

International Telecommunications Satellite Organization (INTELSAT). 3400 International Dr. NW, Washington, DC 20008. (202) 944-7500. Fax (202) 944-7890. Irving Goldstein, Dir. Gen. and CEO; Tony A. Trujillo, Mgr., Public and External Relations. Dedicated to the design, development, construction, establishment, operation, and maintenance of the global telecommunications satellite system that currently provides most of the world's international overseas telecommunications links and virtually all live international television services. *Membership:* 128 countries. *Publications: INTELSAT News* (q.); *INTELSAT Annual Report.*

International Teleconferencing Association (ITCA). 1150 Connecticut Ave. NW, Suite 1050, Washington, DC 20036. (202) 833-2549. Fax (202) 833-1308. Debra A. Schartz, Managing Dir.; Debora A. Schwartz, Mgr., Assoc. Services. Seeks to provide a clearinghouse for the exchange of information amoung users, researchers, and providers in the field of teleconferencing. *Membership:* 1,400. *Dues:* $500 organizational; $100 individual; $250 small business; $1,000 sustaining; $2,000 Gold sustaining; $30 student. *Meeting:* ITCA '94, June 19-22, Dallas, TX. *Publications: ITCA Connections Newsletter* (mo.); *Videoconferencing Room Directory; Member Directory.*

ITA (formerly International Tape/Disc Association [ITA]). 505 Eighth Ave., New York, NY 10018. (212) 643-0620. Fax (212) 643-0624. Henry Brief, Exec. V.P.; Charles Van Horn, Exec. Dir. An international association providing a forum for the exchange of management-oriented information on global trends and innovations that impact the magnetic and optical media and related industries. Members include magnetic and optical media manufacturers, rights holders to video programs, recording and playback equipment manufacturers, and audio and video duplicators. For more than 20 years, ITA has provided vital information and educational services throughout the magnetic and optical media industries. By promoting a greater awareness of marketing, merchandising, and technical developments, the association serves all areas of the audio, video, and data industries. *Membership:* 450 corporations. *Dues:* Corporate membership dues. *Meetings:* 24th Annual Seminar, March 9-13, 1994, Tucson, AZ; REPLItech International, April 12-14, 1994, Munich, Germany; REPLItech International, June 14-16, 1994, Santa Clara, CA. (REPLItech is a seminar and trade show aimed at duplicators and replicators of magnetic and optical media.) *Publications: ITA Membership Newsletter; Seminar Proceedings; 1993 International Source Directory.*

ITVA (International Television Association). 6311 N. O'Connor Rd., Suite 230, LB51, Irving, TX 75039. (214) 869-1112. Fax (214) 869-2980. Fred M. Wehrli, Exec. Dir. Founded in 1968, ITVA's mission is to advance the video profession, to serve the needs and interests of its members, and to promote the growth and quality of video and related media. Association members are video professionals working in or serving the corporate, governmental, institutional, or educational markets. ITVA provides professional development opportunities through local, regional, and national workshops, video festivals, and publications. The networking opportunities available to members are another principal benefit. ITVA welcomes anyone who is interested in professional video and is seeking to widen his/her horizons either through career development or networking. *Membership:* 9,000, 77 commercial member companies. *Dues:* $125 individuals; $350 organizational; $40 students; $1,500 commercial sustaining; $625 commercial associate. *Meeting:* June 7-11, 1994, Anaheim, CA (in conjunction with INFOCOMM International), "Unlocking the Human Potential." *Publications: ITN (International Television News)* (6/yr.); *Membership Directory* (annual); *Handbook of Treatments; It's a Business First . . . and a Creative Outlet Second.*

Library of Congress. James Madison Bldg., 101 Independence Ave. SE, Washington, DC 20540. (202) 707-5000. Fax (202) 707-1389. Contact the National Reference Service, (202) 707-5522. The Library of Congress is the major source of research and information for the Congress. In its role as the national library, it catalogs and classifies library materials in some 470 languages, distributes the data in both printed and electronic form, and makes its vast collections available through interlibrary loan and on-site to anyone over high school age. It contains the world's largest television and film archive, acquiring materials through gift, purchase, and copyright deposit. The collections of the Motion Picture, Broadcasting, and Recorded Sound Division include 150,000 motion picture titles; 80,000 television broadcasts; 500,000 radio transcriptions; and 2,600,000 other sound recordings. Bibliographic data in the computerized Library of Congress Information System is now available for online searching over the Internet. The Internet address for telnet (connecting) to LOCIS is locis.loc.gov. The numeric address is 140.147.254.3. In 1992, the library had 900 readers and visitors and performed 1,385,053 direct reference services. *Publications:* Listed in *Library of Congress Publications in Print* (free from Office Systems Services).

Lister Hill National Center for Biomedical Communications. National Library of Medicine, 8600 Rockville Pike, Bethesda, MD 20894. (301) 496-4441. Fax (301) 402-0118. Daniel R. Masys, M.D., Dir. The center conducts research and development programs in three major

234 \ Organizations and Associations in North America

categories: Computer and Information Science; Biomedical Image and Communications Engineering; and Educational Technology Development. Major efforts of the center include its involvement with the Unified Medical Language System (UMLS) project; research and development in the use of expert systems to embody the factual and procedural knowledge of human experts; research in the use of electronic technologies to distribute biomedical information not represented in text and in the storage and transmission of x-ray images over the Internet; and the development and demonstration of new educational technologies, including the use of microcomputer technology with videodisc-based images, for training health care professionals. A Learning Center for Interactive Technology serves as a focus for displaying new and effective applications of educational technologies to faculties and staff of health sciences educational institutions and other visitors, and health professions educators are assisted in the use of such technologies through training, demonstrations, and consultations.

Magazine Publishers of America (MPA). 919 Third Ave., 22nd Floor, New York, NY 10022. (212) 872-3700. Fax (212) 888-4217. Donald D. Kummerfeld, Pres. MPA is the trade association of the consumer magazine industry. MPA promotes the greater and more effective use of magazine advertising, with ad campaigns in the trade press and in MPA member magazines, presentations to advertisers and their ad agencies, and magazine days in cities around the United States. MPA runs educational seminars, conducts surveys of its members on a variety of topics, represents the magazine industry in Washington, D.C., maintains an extensive library on magazine publishing, and carries on other activities. *Membership:* 230 publishers representing more than 1,200 magazines. *Meetings:* American Magazine Conference: 1994, October 23-25, Laguna Niguel, CA; 1995, November 5-9, Boca Raton, FL. *Publications: Newsletter of Consumer Marketing; Newsletter of Research; Newsletter of International Publishing; Magazine; Washington Newsletter.*

MECC (Minnesota Educational Computing Corporation). 6160 Summit Dr. N., Minneapolis, MN 55430-4003. (612) 569-1500; (800) 685-MECC. Fax (612) 569-1551. Dale LaFrenz, Pres.; Dean Kephart, Dir., Marketing Communications. MECC is the leading producer of K-12 educational software in the United States and an emerging player in the rapidly growing home market. For the past 20 years, MECC has provided children and young adults with high-quality educational software that helps them develop a lifelong love of learning. More than 80 million MECC products have been sold to homes and schools since MECC was established in 1973. MECC creates learning opportunities that are fun and provides teachers and parents with products that use technology to enhance learning. MECC products take a child-centered approach, celebrating the uniqueness of individual children and cultivating their talents. MECC software helps children to combine learning with imagination. In addition to software products, MECC offers emerging technology products and an annual international conference. MECC currently offers 150 MAC/DOS/Apple titles to schools for instructional use. The 24 MAC and 20 DOS titles included in the offering lead the industry in quantity and quality. In the home market, MECC offers 10 fun-loving titles on both the DOS and MAC platforms. The company takes great pride in its flagship product, *The Oregon Trail,* which is found in the hands of more kids than any other education product produced. Now *Amazon Trail, DynoPark Tycoon, My Own Stories,* and *Odell Down Under* are carrying on the tradition of excellence.

Medical Library Association (MLA). 6 N. Michigan Ave., Suite 300, Chicago, IL 60602. (312) 419-9094. Fax (312) 419-8950. June H. Fulton, Pres.; Carla J. Funk, Exec. Dir. MLA is a professional organization of 5,000 individuals and institutions in the health sciences information field, dedicated to fostering medical and allied scientific libraries, promoting professional excellence and leadership of its members, and exchanging medical literature among its members. *Membership:* 3,743 individuals, 1,281 institutions. *Dues:* $65-$110 individuals, $25 students; $175-$410 institutional dues depend on number of periodical subscriptions. *Meeting:* May 13-19, 1994, San Antonio, TX, "Enduring Values, Emerging Roles." *Publications: MLA News* (newsletter, 10/yr.); *Bulletin of the Medical Library Association* (q.); monographs.

Mid-continent Regional Educational Laboratory (McREL). Denver Office: 2550 S. Parker Rd., Suite 500, Aurora, CO 80014. (303) 337-0990. Kansas City Office: 4709 Belleview Ave., Kansas City, MO 64112. (816) 756-2401. C. L. Hutchins, Exec. Dir. One of 10 Office of Educational Research and Improvement (OERI) regional educational laboratories designed to help educators and policymakers solve educational problems in their schools. Using the best available information and the experience and expertise of professionals, McREL seeks to identify solutions to education problems, tries new approaches, furnishes research results, and provides training to teachers and administrators. McREL serves Colorado, Kansas, Nebraska, Missouri, Wyoming, North Dakota, and South Dakota.

Museum Computer Network (MCN). 8720 Georgia Ave., Suite 501, Silver Spring, MD 20910. (301) 585-4413. Fax (301) 495-0810. Michele Devine, Admin. Diane Zorich, Pres. As a not-for-profit professional association, membership in MCN means access to professionals committed to using computer technology to achieve the cultural aims of museums. Members include novices and experts, museum professionals, and vendors and consultants, working in application areas from collections management to administrative computing. Activities include an annual conference, educational workshops, advisory services, special projects, and publication of a quarterly newsletter. *Membership dues:* Sponsor $250; vendor $150; institution $100; individual $50. *Meeting:* Annual Conference, August 28-September 3, 1994, Washington, DC. *Publications: Spectra* (newsletter); *CMI.* Subscription to *Spectra* is available to libraries only for $60 plus $10 surcharge for delivery.

Museum of Holography. 11 Mercer St., New York, NY 10013. (212) 925-0581. Fax (212) 334-8039. Martha Tomko, Dir. Housed in a landmark cast-iron building, the museum boasts the world's largest collection of holograms (three-dimensional images). Through its extensive exhibition and education programs, the museum shows the work of artists working in the medium and explains how holograms are made, how they work, and how they have become useful tools in art, science, and technology. The museum also maintains a library, a collection of slides and photographs, and an artist-in-residence program. *Publication: Holosphere.*

Museum of Modern Art, Circulating Film and Video Library. 11 W. 53d St., New York, NY 10019. (212) 708-9530. Fax (212) 708-9531. William Sloan, Libr. Sponsors film study programs and provides film rentals and sales. *Publication: Circulating Film and Video Catalog Vols. 1 and 2.*

National Aeronautics and Space Administration (NASA). NASA Headquarters, Code FET, Washington, DC 20546. (202) 358-1540. Fax (202) 358-3048. E-mail mphelps@nasamail.nasa.gov. Dr. Malcolm V. Phelps, Chief, Technology and Evaluation Branch. Frank C. Owens, Dir., Education Division. From elementary through postgraduate school, NASA's educational programs are designed to capture students' interests in science, mathematics, and technology at an early age; to channel more students into science, engineering, and technology career paths; and to enhance the knowledge, skills, and experiences of teachers and university faculty. NASA's educational programs include NASA Spacelink (an electronic information system); videoconferences (90-minute interactive staff development videoconferences to be delivered to schools via satellite); NASA Select (informational and educational television programming); and ISY (International Space Year) Videoconferences (two live, interactive videoconferences that provide an opportunity for secondary school students to interact with space scientists and engineers). Additional information is available from the Education Division at NASA Headquarters and counterpart offices at the nine NASA field centers. Over 180,000 educators make copies of Teacher Resource Center Network materials each year, and thousands of teachers participate in interactive video teleconferencing, use Spacelink, and watch NASA Select. Current publications are available through Publications, (202) 453-8424.

National Alliance for Media Arts and Culture (NAMAC). 655 13th St., Suite 201, Oakland, CA 94612. (510) 451-2717. Fax (510) 451-2715. Julian Low, Dir. A nonprofit organization dedicated to increasing public understanding of and support for the field of media arts in the United States. Members include media centers, cable access centers, universities, and media artists, as well as other individuals and organizations providing services for production, education, exhibition, distribution, and preservation of video, film, audio, and intermedia. NAMAC's information services are available to the general public, arts and nonarts organizations, businesses, corporations, foundations, government agencies, schools, and universities. *Membership:* 200 organizations, 150 individuals. *Dues:* Institutional ranges from $50 to $250/yr. depending on annual budget; $30/yr. individual. *Publications: Media Arts Information Network*; *NAMAC Directory* (published biennially, available for $25 to nonmembers).

National Association for the Education of Young Children (NAEYC). 1509 16th St. NW, Washington, DC 20036-1426. (202) 232-8777; (800) 424-2460. Fax (202) 328-1846. Marilyn M. Smith, Exec. Dir.; Pat Spahr, contact person. Dedicated to improving the quality core and education provided to young children (birth-8 years). *Membership:* Nearly 90,000. *Dues:* $25. *Meeting:* 1994 Annual Conference, November 30-December 3, Atlanta, GA. *Publications: Young Children* (journal); more than 60 books, posters, videos, and brochures.

*National Association for Visually Handicapped (NAVH). 22 W. 21st St., 6th Floor, New York, NY 10010. (212) 889-3141. Lorraine H. Marchi, Founder/Exec. Dir.; Eva Cohan, Asst. to Exec. Dir. (or) 3201 Balboa St., San Francisco, CA 94121. (415) 221-3201. Serves the partially sighted (not totally blind). Offers informational literature for the layperson and the professional, most in large print. Newsletters for adults—*Seeing Clearly*—and for children—*In Focus*—are published at irregular intervals and distributed free throughout the English-speaking world. Maintains a loan library (free) of large-print books. Provides counseling and guidance for the visually impaired and their families and the professionals and paraprofessionals who work with them. *Membership:* 12,000. *Dues:* Basic membership $35 for individuals. *Publications: Visual Aids and Informational Material Catalog*; *Large Print Loan Library*; two newsletters; informational pamphlets on topics ranging from *Diseases of the Macula* to knitting and crochet instructions.

*National Association of Broadcasters (NAB). 1771 N St. NW, Washington, DC 20036-2891. (202) 429-5300. Fax (202) 429-5343. Edward O. Fritts, Pres. and CEO. A trade association that represents commercial broadcasters. Encourages development of broadcasting arts and seeks to strengthen and maintain the industry so that it may best serve the public. *Membership:* 7,500 radio and television stations, and associate members. *Dues:* Based on station revenue for radio and on market size for television. *Publications: TV Today*; *RadioWeek*.

National Association of Secondary School Principals (NASSP). 1904 Association Dr., Reston, VA 22091. (703) 860-0200. Fax (703) 476-5432. Robert Mahaffey, Dir., Publications and Marketing. Provides a national voice for secondary education, supports promising and successful educational practices, conducts research, examines issues, and represents secondary education at the federal level. *Membership:* 40,000. *Publications: NASSP Bulletin; NASSP NewsLeader; Curriculum Report; Legal Memorandum; Schools in the Middle; TIPS for Principals; AP Special; Practitioner and Leadership Magazine.*

National Association of State Boards of Education (NASBE). 1012 Cameron St., Alexandria, VA 22314. (703) 684-4000. Fax (703) 836-2313. Brenda Lilienthal Welburn, Exec. Dir.; Andrew Stamp, contact person. Studies problems and improves communication among members, exchanges information, provides educational programs and activities, and serves as a liaison with other educators' groups. *Membership:* 650. *Publications: The State Board Connection* (member newsletter, 4/yr.); *Issues in Brief* (4/yr.); guides for policymakers and practitioners; task force reports.

*National Association of State Textbook Administrators (NASTA). Division of Textbook Administration, Texas Education Agency, 1701 N. Congress Ave., Austin, TX 78701-1494. (512) 463-9601. Fax (512) 475-3612. Dr. Ira Nell Turman, Pres. NASTA's purposes are (1) to foster a spirit of mutual helpfulness in adoption, purchase, and distribution of textbooks; (2) to arrange for study and review of textbook specifications; (3) to authorize special surveys, tests, and studies; and (4) to initiate action leading to better-quality textbooks. NASTA is not affiliated with any parent organization and has no permanent address. It works with the Association of American Publishers and the Book Manufacturers Institute. Services provided include a working knowledge of text construction, monitoring lowest prices, sharing adoption information, identifying trouble spots, and discussions in the industry. *Membership:* The textbook administrator from each of the states that adopts textbooks at the state level. *Dues:* $25 individual. *Publication:* Newsletter for members (2/yr.).

National Audiovisual Center (NAC). National Archives and Records Administration, 8700 Edgeworth Dr., Capitol Heights, MD 20743. (301) 763-1896; (800) 788-6282. Fax (301) 763-6025. George Ziener, Dir. Central information and distribution source for more than 8,000 audiovisual programs produced by or for the U.S. government. Materials are made available for sale or rent on a self-sustaining basis, at the lowest price possible. *Publications: Media Resource Catalog* (1991), listing 600 of the latest and most popular programs, is available free. Also available free are specific subject listings such as science, history, medicine, and safety and health. There is a free quarterly update that lists significant additions to the collection. A computer bulletin board has been available for information searches and production orders since late 1993.

National Cable Television Institute (NCTI). 801 West Mineral Ave., Littleton, CO 80120-4501. (303) 797-9393. Fax (303) 797-9394. Byron K. Leech, Pres.; Don Oden, Dir. of Admissions. The largest independent provider of cable television training in the world. The Institute "partners" with cable television companies to provide a fully managed training program. Offers a five-level career path that leads employees through self-study in all technical areas of the cable television system. NCTI also offers training in new and specialized technologies for the broadband telecommunications professional. An NCTI Certificate of Graduation is recognized throughout the cable television industry as a symbol of technical achievement and competence. Call, fax, or write for a *free* Training Kit.

*National Center for Appropriate Technology (NCAT). P.O. Box 3838, Butte, MT 59702. (406) 494-4572. Fax (406) 494-2905. George Turman, Pres. A nonprofit corporation with a mission to advance the research, development, and widespread adoption of appropriate technologies in the major program areas of energy conservation, sustainable agriculture, affordable housing, environmental protection, and sustainable economic development. NCAT operates national technical assistance services and distributes several how-to and educational publications. *Publications: Connections: A Curriculum in AT for the Fifth and Sixth Grades; Energy Education Guidebook; Photovoltaics in the Pacific Islands;* others. Free publications catalog is available from NCAT Publications, P.O. Box 4000, Dept. EMTY, Butte, MT 59702.

The National Center for Improving Science Education. 2000 L St. NW, Suite 603, Washington, DC 20036. (202) 467-0652. Fax (202) 467-0659. BITNET sentar@-gwuvm.gwu.edu. Senta A. Raizen, Dir./300 Brickstone Square, Suite 900, Andover, MA 01810. (508) 470-1080. (508) 475-9220. Internet janeta@neirl.org. Janet Anglis, Dir. of Communications. A division of The NETWORK, Inc. (a nonprofit organization dedicated to educational reform) that works to promote changes in state and local policies and practices in science curriculum, teaching, and assessment through research and development, evaluation, technical assistance, and dissemination. *Publications: Science and Technology Education for the Elementary Years: Frameworks for Curriculum and Instruction; Developing and Supporting Teachers for Elementary School Science Education; Assessment in Elementary School Science Education; Getting Started in Science: A Blueprint Elementary School Science Education; Building Scientific Literacy: Blueprint for the Middle Years; Science and Technology Education for the Middle Years: Frameworks for Curriculum and Instruction; Assessment in Science Education: The Middle Years; Developing and Supporting Teachers for Science Education in the Middle Years; Elementary School Science for the 90s; The High Stakes of High School Science; Future of Science in Elementary Schools: Educating Prospective Teachers.* Publications catalog is available from The NETWORK on request.

National Center for Research in Mathematical Sciences Education. University of Wisconsin at Madison, Wisconsin for Education Research, 1025 West Johnson St., Madison, WI 53706. (608) 263-4285. Dr. Thomas Romberg, Dir. One of 25 university-based national education and development centers supported by the Office of Educational Research and Improvement (OERI) in the U.S. Office of Education to help strengthen student learning in the United States. These centers conduct research on topics that will help policy makers, practitioners, and parents meet the national education goals by the year 2000. In addition to addressing specific topics, most of these centers focus on children at risk. Many are also cooperating with other universities, and many work with elementary and secondary schools. All have been directed by OERI to make sure the information they produce reaches parents, teachers, and others who can use it to make meaningful changes in America's schools.

National Center for Science Teaching and Learning. Ohio State University, Room 104, Research Center, 1314 Kinnear Rd., Columbus, OH 43212. (614) 292-3339. Dr. Arthur L. White, Dir. One of 25 university-based national education and development centers supported by the Office of Educational Research and Improvement (OERI) in the U.S. Office of Education to help strengthen student learning in the United States. These centers conduct research on topics that will help policy makers, practitioners, and parents meet the national education goals by the year 2000. In addition to addressing specific topics, most of these centers focus on children at risk. Many are also cooperating with other universities, and many work with elementary and secondary schools. All have been directed by OERI to make sure the information they produce reaches parents, teachers, and others who can use it to make meaningful changes in America's schools.

National Clearinghouse for Bilingual Education (NCBE). The George Washington University, 1118 22d St. NW, Washington, DC 20037. (202) 467-0867; (800) 321-NCBE. Joel Gomez, Dir. NCBE is funded by the U.S. Department of Education, Office of Bilingual Education and Minority Languages Affairs, to provide information on the education of limited-English-proficient students to practitioners, administrators, researchers, policy-makers, and parents. NCBE collects and disseminates information on print resources, software and courseware, video resources, and organizations. Provides computerized access to bulletin board, bibliographic database, and resources databases. *Publications: FORUM* (bi-mo. newsletter); *Focus* (occasional papers); program information guides.

National Commission on Libraries and Information Science (NCLIS). 1110 Vermont Ave. NW, Suite 820, Washington, DC 20005-3522. (202) 606-9200. Fax (202) 606-9203. Peter R. Young, Exec. Dir. A permanent independent agency of the U.S. government charged with advising the executive and legislative branches on national library and information policies and plans. The commission reports directly to the White House and the Congress on the implementation of national policy; conducts studies, surveys, and analyses of the nation's library and information needs; appraises the inadequacies and deficiencies of current resources and services; promotes research and development activities; conducts hearings and issues publications as appropriate; and develops overall plans for meeting national library and information needs and for the coordination of activities at the federal, state, and local levels. *Membership:* 15 commissioners, 14 appointed by the president and confirmed by the Senate; ex-officio, the Librarian of Congress. *Publication: Annual Report.*

National Council for Accreditation of Teacher Education (NCATE). 2010 Massachusetts Ave. NW, Suite 200, Washington, DC 20036. (202) 466-7496. Fax (202) 296-6620. Arthur E. Wise, Pres. A consortium of professional organizations that establishes standards of quality and accredits professional education units in schools, colleges, and departments of education. Interested in the self-regulation and improvement of standards in the field of teacher education. *Membership:* 500 colleges and universities, 26 educational organizations. *Publications: Standards, Procedures and Policies for the Accreditation of Professional Education Units; Teacher Education: A Guide to NCATE-Accredited Colleges and Universities; Quality Teaching* (newsletter, 3/yr.).

National Council of Teachers of English (NCTE), Commission on Media. 1111 W. Kenyon Rd., Urbana, IL 61801-1096. (217) 328-0977. Fax (217) 328-9645. Miles Myers, Exec. Dir.; Carole Cox, Commission Dir. An advisory body that identifies key issues in teaching of media. Reviews current projects and recommends new directions and personnel to undertake them, monitors NCTE publications on media, and suggests program ideas for the annual convention. *Membership:* 68,000 individual, 125,000 subscribers. *Dues:* $40 individual, $50 institutions. *Publications: English Journal* (8/yr.); *College English* (8/yr.); *Language Arts* (8/yr.); *English Education* (q.); *Research in the Teaching of English* (q.); *Teaching English in the Two-Year College* (q.); *College Composition and Communication* (q.); *English Leadership Quarterly* (q.); *Quarterly Review of Doublespeak* (q).

National Council of the Churches of Christ in the U.S.A. Communication Dept., 475 Riverside Dr., New York, NY 10115. (212) 870-2574. Fax (212) 870-2030. Rev. Dr. J. Martin Bailey, Dir. Ecumenical arena for cooperative work of Protestant and Orthodox denominations and agencies in broadcasting, film, cable, and print media. Offers advocacy to government and industry structures on media services. Services provided include liaison to network television and radio programming; film sales and rentals; distribution of information about syndicated religious programming; syndication of some programming; cable television and emerging technologies information services; news and information regarding work of the National Council of Churches, related denominations, and agencies. Works closely with other faith groups in Interfaith Broadcasting Commission. Online communication via Ecunet/NCCLink. *Membership:* 32 denominations. *Publication: EcuLink.*

National Endowment for the Humanities (NEH). 1100 Pennsylvania Ave. NW, Rm. 420, Washington, DC 20506. (202) 608-8278. James Dougherty, Asst. Dir., Media Program. Independent federal grant-making agency that supports research and educational programs grounded in the disciplines of the humanities. The Media Program supports film and radio programs in the humanities for public audiences, including children and adults. *Publication: Humanities Projects in Media* (guidelines).

National Federation of Community Broadcasters (NFCB). 666 11th St. NW, Suite 805, Washington, DC 20001. (202) 393-2355. Lynn Chadwick, Pres. NFCB represents its members in public policy development at the national level and provides a wide range of practical services. *Membership:* 90 stations, 100 (assoc.) stations and production groups. *Dues:* Based on income, from $75 to $500 for associates; $400 to $2,500 for participants. *Publications: Legal Handbook; Audio Craft* (1989 edition); *Community Radio News; NFCB's Guide to Political Broadcasting for Public Radio Stations; NFCB's Guide to Volunteer Management.*

National Film Board of Canada (NFBC). 1251 Avenue of the Americas, 6th Floor, New York, NY 10020. (212) 596-1770. Fax (212) 595-1779. John Sirabella, U.S. Marketing Mgr./Nontheatrical Rep. Established in 1939, the NFBC's main objective is to produce and distribute high-quality audiovisual materials for educational, cultural, and social purposes.

National Film Information Service (offered by the Academy of Motion Picture Arts and Sciences). 8949 Wilshire Blvd., Beverly Hills, CA 90211-1972. (310) 247-3000. The purpose of this organization is to provide an information service on film. The service is fee-based and all inquiries must be accompanied by a self-addressed stamped envelope.

National Gallery of Art (NGA). Department of Education Resources: Art Information and Extension Programs, Washington, DC 20565. (202) 842-6273. Ruth R. Perlin, Head. This department of NGA is responsible for the production and distribution of educational audiovisual programs, including interactive technologies. Materials available (all loaned free to schools, community organizations, and individuals) range from films, videocassettes, and color slide programs to videodiscs. A free catalog of programs is available upon request. Two videodiscs on the gallery's collection are available for long-term loan. *Publication: Extension Programs Catalogue.*

National Information Center for Educational Media (NICEM). P.O. Box 40130, Albuquerque, NM 87196. (505) 265-3591; (800) 468-3453. E-mail tnaccessi@technet.nm.org. Marjorie M. K. Hlava, Pres., Access Innovations, Inc.; Patrick Sauer, Mng. Dir., NICEM. In conjunction with the Library of Congress, NICEM is a centralized facility that collects, catalogs, and disseminates information about nonbook materials of many different kinds. Its mission is to build and expand the database to provide current and archival information about nonbook educational materials; to apply modern techniques of information dissemination that meet user needs; and to provide a comprehensive, centralized nonbook database used for catalogs, indexes, multimedia publications, special search services, machine-readable tapes, and online access. NICEM services include NICEMEZ (user-defined searches of the database, fee set at editorial time rate, one-day turnaround) and AVxpress ("Document" delivery of any media title [in print] found in NICEM or in any other listing of media material, in cooperation with Dynamic Information in Burlingame, CA). The NICEM masterfile is also available on DIALOG File 46, and on CD-ROM (AVOnline via SilverPlatter); (NICEM AVmarc via BiblioFile); and will soon be available in MARC version on CD-ROM from CASPR, Inc., for cataloging from the Macintosh platform. A 45,000 unit subset of NICEM titles is carried on the Human Resource Information Network, via National Standards Association. *Clients,*

Users: School districts, media resource centers, corporate and educational research professionals, media consultants. *Publications:* Indexes to audiovisual educational materials.

*National Library of Medicine. 8600 Rockville Pike, Bethesda, MD 20894. (301) 496-6095. Donald A. B. Lindberg, M.D., Dir.; Robert Mehnert, Public Information Officer. Collects, organizes, and distributes literature on biomedicine; seeks to apply modern technology to the flow of biomedical information to health professionals; and supports development of improved medical library resources for the country. Responsible for MEDLINE, SDILINE, CATLINE, SERLINE, CANCERLIT, AVLINE, and TOXLINE. Maintains a collection of 20,000 health science audiovisual materials; supervises the Lister Hill Center for Biomedical Communications and the National Center for Biotechnology Information. Maintains eight regional medical libraries. *Publication: National Library of Medicine News* (newsletter, 6/yr.).

National Press Photographers Association, Inc. (NPPA). 3200 Croasdaile Dr., Suite 306, Durham, NC 27705. (919) 383-7246. Fax (919) 383-7261. Charles Cooper, Exec. Dir. An organization of professional news photographers who participate in and promote photojournalism in publications and through television and film. Sponsors workshops and contests; maintains a tape library and collections of slides in the field. *Membership:* 11,000. *Dues:* $55 professional, $30 student. *Publications: News Photographer*; membership directory; *Best of Photojournalism Books.*

*National PTA. 700 N. Rush St., Chicago, IL 60611. (312) 787-0977. Fax (312) 787-8342. Pat Henry, Pres.; Tari Marshall, Dir. of Communications. Advocates for the education, health, safety, and well-being of children and teens. Provides parenting education and leadership training to PTA volunteers. *Membership:* 6.8 million. *Dues:* Varies by local unit. *Sample Publications: PTA Today* (magazine); *What's Happening in Washington* (legislative newsletters); numerous brochures for parents, such as *Help Your Child Get the Most Out of Homework* and *How to Talk to Your Children and Teens about AIDS.* Catalog available.

National Public Broadcasting Archives (NPBA). Hornbake Library, University of Maryland at College Park, College Park, MD 20742. (301) 405-9255. Thomas Connors, Archivist. NPBA brings together the archival record of the major entities of noncommercial broadcasting in the United States. NPBA's collections include the archives of the Corporation for Public Broadcasting (CPB), the Public Broadcasting Service (PBS), and National Public Radio (NPR). Other organizations represented include the Midwest Program for Airborne Television Instruction (MPATI), the Public Service Satellite Consortium (PSSC), America's Public Television Stations (APTS), and the Joint Council for Educational Telecommunications (JCET). NPBA also makes available the personal papers of many individuals who have made significant contributions to public broadcasting, and its reference library contains basic studies of the broadcasting industry, rare pamphlets, and journals on relevant topics, plus up-to-date clippings from the PBS press clipping service. NPBA also collects and maintains a selected audio and video program record of public broadcasting's national production and support centers and of local stations. Oral history tapes and transcripts from the NPR Oral History Project are also available at the archives. The archives are open to the public from 9 am to 5 pm, Monday through Friday. Research in NPBA collections should be arranged by prior appointment. For further information, call (301) 405-9988.

National Religious Broadcasters (NRB). 7839 Ashton Ave., Manassas, VA 22110. (703) 330-7000. Fax (703) 330-7100. E. Brandt Gustavson, Pres. NRB essentially has two goals: (1) to ensure that religious broadcasters have access to the radio and television airwaves, and

(2) to encourage broadcasters to observe a high standard of excellence in their programming and station management for the clear presentation of the gospel. Holds national and regional conventions. *Membership:* 800 organizational stations, program producers, agencies, and individuals. *Dues:* Based on income. *Meetings:* 1994, 51st Annual Convention, January 29-February 1, Washington, DC; 1995, 52nd Annual Convention, February 11-14, Nashville, TN. *Publications: Religious Broadcasting Magazine* (mo.); *Annual Directory of Religious Media*; *Religious Broadcasting Resources Library Brochure*; *Religious Broadcasting Cassette Catalog*.

National School Supply and Equipment Association (NSSEA). 8300 Colesville Rd., Suite 250, Silver Spring, MD 20910. (301) 495-0240. Fax (301) 495-3330. Tim Holt, Exec. V.P. A service organization of 1,200 manufacturers, distributors, retailers, and independent manufacturers' representatives of school supplies, equipment, and instructional materials. Seeks to maintain open communications between manufacturers and dealers in the school market, to find solutions to problems affecting schools, and to encourage the development of new ideas and products for educational progress. *Meetings:* 1994: Ed Expo '94, April 14-17, Santa Clara, CA; 78th NSSGA Annual Fall Show (members only), November 17-20; 1995: Ed Expo '95, March 16-19, Dallas, TX. *Publications: Tidings*; *Annual Membership Directory*.

National Science Foundation (NSF). 4201 Wilson Blvd., Arlington, VA 22230. (703) 306-1234. Michael Fluharty, Chief, Media Relations and Public Affairs. Primary purposes of this agency of the federal government are to increase the nation's base of scientific knowledge; encourage research in areas that can lead to improvements in economic growth, productivity, and environmental quality; promote international cooperation through science; and develop and help implement science education programs to aid the nation in meeting the challenges of contemporary life. Grants go chiefly to universities and research organizations. Applicants should refer to the *NSF Guide to Programs*. Scientific material and media reviews are available to help the public learn about NSF-supported programs. Information is also electronically disseminated through STIS at no cost but the users' long-distance phone charges. For start-up assistance contact via e-mail: stis-request@NSF.gov (Internet) or stis-req@NSF (BITNET), or phone: (703) 306-0214 (voice mail).

National Science Teachers Association (NSTA). 1840 Wilson Blvd., Arlington, VA 22201. (703) 243-7100. Fax (703) 243-7177. Bill Aldridge, Exec. Dir. A national nonprofit association of science teachers ranging from kindergarten through university level. NSTA conducts one national and three regional conventions and provides numerous programs and services, including awards and scholarships, inservice teacher workshops, professional certification, a major curriculum reform effort, and more. It has position statements on many issues, such as teacher preparation, laboratory science, and the use of animals in the classroom. It is involved in cooperative working relationships in a variety of projects with educational organizations, government agencies, and private industries. *Membership:* 50,000. *Dues:* $52/yr. individual or institutional (includes one journal and other benefits). *Meetings:* National: 1994, March 30-April 2, Anaheim, CA; 1995, March 23-26, Philadelphia, PA. Area: 1994, October 13-15, Portland, OR; November 3-5, Minneapolis, MN; December 15-17, Las Vegas, NV. *Publications: Science and Children* (8/yr., journal for elementary teachers); *Science Scope* (8/yr., journal for middle-level teachers); *The Science Teacher* (9/yr., for high school teachers); *Journal of College Science Teaching* (6/yr., journal for college teachers); *NSTA Reports!* (6/yr., newspaper for K-college teachers, free to all NSTA members); *Quantum* (magazine for physics and math high school students); books (free catalog available).

*National Society for Performance and Instruction (NSPI). 1300 L St. NW, Suite 1250, Washington, DC 20005. (202) 408-7969. Fax (202) 408-7972. Paul Tremper, Exec. Dir. NSPI is an international association dedicated to increasing productivity in the workplace through the application of performance and instructional technologies. Founded in 1962, its members are located throughout the United States, Canada, and 30 other countries. The society offers an awards program recognizing excellence in the field. The Annual Conference and Expo are held in the spring. *Membership:* 5,000. *Dues:* $125, active members; $40, students and retirees. *Publications: Performance & Instruction Journal* (10/yr.); *Performance Improvement Quarterly*; *News & Notes* (newsletter, 10/yr.); *Annual Membership Directory.*

*National Technical Information Service (NTIS). Public Affairs Office, Springfield, VA 22161. (703) 487-4650. Fax (703) 321-8547. NTIS is a self-supporting agency of the U.S. Department of Commerce that actively collects, organizes, and distributes technical information generated by United States and foreign governments in all areas of science and technology. There are 2 million titles in the NTIS permanent archives, some of which date as far back as 1945, with approximately 63,000 new titles added annually. Reprints from the entire collection are available at any time, whether a report dates from 20 years ago or last month. In addition, NTIS provides government-generated computer software and computerized data files, on both tape and diskette, through its Federal Computer Products Center. To keep pace with technology transfer activities, the NTIS Center for the Utilization of Federal Technology licenses federal inventions and makes them available to private industry. In the area of foreign technology, NTIS has recently increased its holdings—up to a third of the reports entering the collection are now from foreign sources. Access to the collection is through a printed catalog, *The Government Reports Announcements & Index*, online, or via CD-ROM of the NTIS Bibliographic Database. Most main commercial online services and optical disk publishers offer access to the NTIS Bibliographic Database. To request a free catalog describing NTIS products and services, contact the NTIS Order Desk at the preceding address and ask for PR827/NCB. *Publication: NTIS Alerts* (covers new research in 167 subject categories and custom combinations; 2/mo. on annual subscription basis).

National Technology Center. American Foundation for the Blind, 15 W. 16th St., New York, NY 10011. (212) 620-2080. Evaluations Laboratory: (212) 620-2051. Fax (212) 620-2137. Elliot M. Schreier, Dir. The center has three components: National Technology Information System, Evaluations Laboratory, and Research and Development Laboratory. Provides a resource for blind and visually impaired persons and professionals in education, rehabilitation, and employment; their families; and rehabilitation professionals, educators, researchers, manufacturers, and employers. The NTC also develops products to enhance education, employment, mobility, and independent living opportunities for blind and visually impaired people worldwide.

National Telemedia Council Inc. (NTC). 120 E. Wilson St., Madison, WI 53703. (608) 257-7712. Fax (608) 257-7714. Dr. Marti Tomas, Pres.; Marieli Rowe, Exec. Dir. The NTC is a national not-for-profit organization dedicated to promoting media literacy, or critical television viewing skills, for children and youth. This is done primarily through work with teachers, parents, and caregivers. NTC activities include the development of the Media Literacy Clearinghouse and Center; the Teacher Idea Exchange (T.I.E.); national conferences and regional and local workshops; Sponsor Recognition Awards for companies and corporate entities for their support of programs deemed to be outstanding; the Jessie McCanse Award for individual contribution to media literacy. *Dues:* $30 basic membership; $50 contributing; $100 patron. *Publications: Telemedium* (newsletter, q.); *Telemedium UPDATE.*

*National University Continuing Education Association (NUCEA). One Dupont Cir. NW, Suite 615, Washington, DC 20036. (202) 659-3130. Fax (202) 785-0374. Robert Comfort, Pres.; Kay J. Kohl, Exec. Dir.; Ruth Futrovsky, Dir. of Pubs.; J. Noah Brown, Dir. of Govt. Relations & Public Affairs. An association of public and private institutions concerned with making continuing education available to all population segments and to promoting excellence in the continuing higher education community. NUCEA has an annual national conference and several professional development seminars throughout the year, and many institutional members offer university and college film rental library services. *Membership:* 400 institutions; 2,000 professionals. *Dues:* Vary according to membership category. *Publications:* Monthly newsletter; quarterly occasional papers; scholarly journal; *Independent Study Catalog*; *Guide to Certificate Programs at American Colleges and Universities*; *Conferences and Facilities Directory*; NUCEA-ACE/Macmillan Continuing Higher Education book series; *Lifelong Learning Trends* (a statistical factbook on continuing higher education); *Directory of Black Professionals in Continuing Education*; membership directory; other publications relevant to the field.

The NETWORK, Inc. 300 Brickstone Square, Suite 900, Andover, MA 01810. (508) 470-1080. Fax (508) 475-9220. Internet janeta@neirl.org. Janet Angelis, Dir. of Communications. A research and service organization providing training, research and evaluation, technical assistance, and materials to schools, educational organizations, and private sector firms with educational interests. *Publications: Portrait of Our Mothers: Using Oral History in the Classroom*; *Juggling Lessons: A Curriculum for Women Who Go to School, Work, and Care for Their Families*; *An Action Guide for School Improvement*; *Making Change for School Improvement: A Simulation Game*; *Report on National Dissemination Efforts: Volumes I-X*; *The Effective Writing Teacher*; *Cumulative Writing Folder*; *Developing Writing and Thinking Skills Across the Curriculum: A Practical Program for Schools*; *Five Types of Writing Assignments*. Publications catalog is available upon request.

Network for Continuing Medical Education (NCME). One Harmon Plaza, 7th Floor, Secaucus, NJ 07094. (201) 867-3550. Fax (201) 867-2491. Jim Disque, Exec. Dir. Produces and distributes videocassettes to hospitals for physicians' continuing education. Programs are developed for physicians in the practice of General Medicine, Anesthesiology, Emergency Medicine, Gastroenterology, and Surgery. Physicians who view all the programs can earn up to 25 hours of Category 1 (AMA) credit and up to 20 hours of Prescribed (AAFP) credit each year. *Membership:* More than 1,100 hospitals provide NCME programs to their physicians. *Dues:* Subscription fees: VHS-$1,820/yr. Sixty-minute videocassettes are distributed to hospital subscribers twice per month, except during the summer, when one per month is distributed.

The New York Festivals (formerly the International Film and TV Festival of New York). Admin. offices: 780 King St., Chappaqua, NY 10514. (914) 238-4481. Bilha Goldberg, Vice Pres. An annual competitive festival for industrial and educational film and video productions, filmstrips and slide programs, multi-image business theater and interactive multimedia presentations, and television programs. Entry fees begin at $100. First entry deadline is August 1.

*North American Simulation and Gaming Association (NASAGA). P.O. Box 20590, Indianapolis, IN 46220. (317) 782-1553. John del Regato, Exec. Sec. Provides a forum for the exchange of ideas, information, and resources among persons interested in simulation and games. Assists members in designing, testing, using, and evaluating simulations and/or games and in using these as research tools. Sponsors various conferences. *Membership:* 600. *Dues:* $50 regular, $10 student. *Publication: Simulation and Games* (q.).

North Central Regional Educational Laboratory (NCREL). 1900 Spring Rd., Suite 300, Oak Brook, IL 60521. (708) 571-4700. Jeri Nowakowski, Exec. Dir. One of 10 Office of Educational Research and Improvement (OERI) regional educational laboratories designed to help educators and policymakers solve educational problems in their schools. Using the best available information and the experience and expertise of professionals, NCREL seeks to identify solutions to education problems, tries new approaches, furnishes research results, and provides training to teachers and administrators. NCREL serves Minnesota, Wisconsin, Iowa, Illinois, Michigan, Indiana, and Ohio.

Northwest Regional Educational Laboratory (NWREL). 101 SW Main St., Suite 500, Portland, OR 97204. (503) 275-9500. Fax (503) 275-9489. Robert R. Rath, Exec. Dir. One of 10 Office of Educational Research and Improvement (OERI) regional educational laboratories, NWREL assists education, government, community agencies, and business and labor in bringing about improvement in educational programs and processes by developing and disseminating effective educational products and procedures, including applications of technology. Provides technical assistance and training in educational problem solving. Evaluates effectiveness of educational programs and processes. NWREL serves Alaska, Idaho, Oregon, Montana, and Washington. *Membership:* 817. *Dues:* None. *Publication: Northwest Report* (newsletter).

OCLC Online Computer Library Center, Inc. 6565 Frantz Rd., Dublin, OH 43017-3395. (614) 764-6000. Fax (614) 764-6096. Internet nha_dean@oclc,org. K. Wayne Smith, Pres. and CEO. Nita Dean, Mgr., Public Relations. A nonprofit membership organization that engages in computer library service and research and makes available computer-based processes, products, and services for libraries, other educational organizations, and library users. From its facility in Dublin, Ohio, OCLC operates an international computer network that libraries use to catalog books, order custom-printed catalog cards and machine-readable records for local catalogs, arrange interlibrary loans, and maintain location information on library materials. OCLC also provides online and offline reference products and services for the electronic delivery of information. More than 17,000 libraries contribute to and/or use information in the OCLC Online Union Catalog. *Publications: OCLC Newsletter* (6/yr.); *OCLC Reference News* (6/yr.); *Annual Report*; *Annual Review of Research.*

Office of Technology Assessment (OTA). U.S. Congress, Washington, DC 20510-8025. (202) 228-6938. Fax (202) 228-6098. E-mail kfulton@ota.gov. Kathleen Fulton, Proj. Dir. (contact for education). Established by Congress to study, report on, and assess the significance and probable impact of new technological developments on U.S. society and to advise Congress on public policy implications and options. Recent assessments focusing on technology and education issues include *Elementary and Secondary Education for Science and Engineering, A Technical Memorandum* (1989); *Higher Education for Science and Engineering, A Background Paper* (1989); *Linking for Learning: A New Course for Education* (1989); *Critical Connections: Communication for the Future* (1990); *Computer Software and Intellectual Property, A Background Paper* (1990). In addition, the assessment, *Power On! New Tools for Teaching & Learning* (1988), includes an interim staff paper on "Trends and Status of Computers in Schools: Use in Chapter 1 Programs and Use with Limited English Proficient Students" (March 1987). Two assessments are currently in progress: Vocational Education Assessment Instruments (Spring 1994) and Teachers and Technology (January 1995). *Publications:* For a list, contact the publishing office at (202) 224-8996.

On-line Audiovisual Catalogers (OLAC). c/o Columbia University Health Sciences Library, 701 West 168th St., New York, NY 10032. (212) 305-1406. Fax (212) 234-0595. Johanne LaGrange, Treas. Formed as an outgrowth of the ALA conference, OLAC seeks to permit members to exchange ideas, computer files, and information and to interact with other agencies that influence audiovisual cataloging practices. *Membership: 725. Dues:* Available for single or multiple years, ranges from $10 to $27 individual, $16 to $45 institutional. *Publication: OLAC Newsletter.*

*Oral History Association. 1093 Broxton Ave, No. 720, Los Angeles, CA 90024. (310) 825-0597. Fax (310) 206-1864. Richard Candida Smith, Exec. Sec. Seeks to develop the use of oral history as primary source material and to disseminate oral history materials among scholars. *Membership:* 1,400. *Dues:* $50 individual, $25 student, $75 contributing, $500 life; $75 institution, $120 sponsoring institution; $50 library (nonvoting). *Publications: Oral History Association Newsletter* (q.); *Oral History Review*; *Oral History Evaluation Guidelines*; *Annual Report and Membership Directory*; *Oral History and the Law*; *Oral History in the Secondary School Classroom*; *Using Oral History in Community History Projects*; *Oral History Evaluation Guidelines.*

Pacific Film Archive (PFA). University Art Museum, 2625 Durant Ave., Berkeley, CA 94720. (510) 642-1437 (library); (510) 642-1412 (general). Fax (510) 642-4889. Edith Kramer, Dir. and Curator of Film; Nancy Goldman, Head, PFA Library and Film Study Center. Sponsors the exhibition, study, and preservation of classic, international, documentary, animated, and avant-garde films. Provides on-site research screenings of films in its collection of over 6,000 titles. Provides access to its collections of books, periodicals, stills, and posters (all materials are noncirculating). Offers UAM members reference and research services to locate film and video distributors, credits, stock footage, etc. Library hours are 1pm-5pm weekdays. *Membership:* Through parent organization, the University Art Museum. *Dues:* $35 individual and nonprofit departments of institutions. *Publication: UAM/PFA Calendar* (6/yr.).

Pacific Regional Educational Laboratory (PREL). 1164 Bishop St., Suite 1409, Honolulu, HI 96813. (808) 532-1900. John W. Kofel, Exec. Dir. One of 10 Office of Educational Research and Improvement (OERI) regional educational laboratories designed to help educators and policymakers solve educational problems in their schools. Using the best available information and the experience and expertise of professionals, PREL seeks to identify solutions to education problems, tries new approaches, furnishes research results, and provides training to teachers and administrators. PREL serves American Samoa, Commonwealth of the Northern Mariana Islands, Federated States of Micronesia, Guam, Hawaii, Republic of the Marshall Islands, and Republic of Palau.

PCR: Films and Video in the Behavioral Sciences. Special Services Bldg., Pennsylvania State University, University Park, PA 16802. (814) 863-3102; purchasing info, (800) 826-0132. Fax (814) 863-2574. Thomas McKenna, Mng. Ed. Collects and makes available to professionals 16mm films and video in the behavioral sciences judged to be useful for university teaching and research. A free catalog of the films in PCR is available. The PCR catalog now contains some 1,400 films in the behavioral sciences (psychology, psychiatry, anthropology, animal behavior, sociology, teaching and learning, and folklife). Some 7,000 professionals now use PCR services. Films and tapes are available on loan for a rental charge. Many films may also be purchased. Films may be submitted for international distribution. Contact the managing editor through PCR.

Photographic Society of America (PSA). 3000 United Founders Blvd., Suite 103, Oklahoma City, OK 73102. (405) 843-1437. Terry S. Stull, Operations Mgr. A nonprofit organization for the development of the arts and sciences of photography and for the furtherance of public appreciation of photographic skills. Its members, largely amateurs, consist of individuals, camera clubs, and other photographic organizations. Divisions include color slide, motion picture, nature, photojournalism, travel, pictorial print, stereo, and techniques. Sponsors national, regional, and local meetings, clinics, and contests. Request dues information from preceding address. *Meetings:* 1994, International Conference, Colorado Springs, CO; 1995, International Conference, Williamsburg, VA. *Publication: PSA Journal.*

*Professors of Instructional Design and Technology (PIDT). Center for Media and Teaching Resources, Indiana University, Bloomington, IN 47405-5901. (812) 855-2854. Fax (812) 855-8404. Dr. Thomas M. Schwen, contact person. An organization designed to encourage and facilitate the exchange of information among members of the instructional design and technology academic and corporate communities. Also serves to promote excellence in academic programs in instructional design and technology and to encourage research and inquiry that will benefit the field while providing leadership in the public and private sectors in its application and practice. Membership consists of faculty employed in higher education institutions whose primary responsibilities are teaching and research in this area; their corporate counterparts; and other persons interested in the goals and activities of the PIDT. *Membership:* 300. *Dues:* None.

Public Broadcasting Service (PBS). 1320 Braddock Pl., Alexandria, VA 22314-1698. (703) 739-5000. National distributor of national public television programming, obtaining all programs from member stations or independent producers. PBS also offers educational services for teachers, students, and parents including: PTV; The Ready to Learn Service; MATHLINE; PBS Online; and Learning Link. Owned and operated by the licensees through annual membership fees. Funding for technical distribution facilities in part by the Corporation for Public Broadcasting. PBS services include national promotion, program acquisition and scheduling, legal services, development and fundraising support, engineering and technical studies, and research. Of special interest are: K-12 Learning Services, providing learning resources for elementary and secondary school teachers and students; the Adult Learning Service, which offers telecourses through college/public television station partnerships; and PBS VIDEO, which offers PBS programs for rent or sale to educational institutions. PBS is governed by a board of directors elected by licensees for three-year terms. *Membership:* 175 licensees; 346 stations.

> **PBS Adult Learning Service (ALS).** 1320 Braddock Pl., Alexandria, VA 22314-1698. (800) 257-2578. Fax (703) 739-8495. Will Philipp, Dir. Contact ALS Customer Service. The mission of ALS is to help colleges, universities, and public television stations increase learning opportunities for distance learners; enrich classroom instruction; update faculty; train administrators, management, and staff; and provide other educational services for local communities. A pioneer in the widespread use of video and print packages incorporated into curricula and offered for credit by local colleges, ALS began broadcasting telecourses in 1981. Since that time, over 2 million students have earned college credit through telecourses offered in partnership with more than two-thirds of the nation's colleges and universities. In 1988, ALS established the Adult Learning Satellite Service (ALSS) to provide colleges, universities, businesses, hospitals, and other organizations with a broad range of educational programming via direct satellite. *Membership:* 500-plus colleges, universities, hospitals, government agencies, and Fortune 500 businesses are now ALSS Associates. Organizations that are not

Associates can still acquire ALS programming, but at higher fees. *Dues:* $1,500/yr.; multisite and consortia rates are available. *Publications: ALSS Programming Line-Up* (catalog of available programming, 3/yr.); *The Agenda* (news magazine about issues of interest to distance learning and adult learning administrators); and *Changing the Face of Higher Education* (an overview of ALS services).

PBS ENCORE. 1320 Braddock Pl., Alexandria, VA 22314. (703) 739-5225. Bonnie Green, Prog. Assoc. Distributes PBS programs with extant broadcast rights to public television stations. *Publication: PBS Encore A to Z Listing.*

PBS VIDEO. 1320 Braddock Pl., Alexandria, VA 22314. (703) 739-6602; (800) 344-3337. Fax (703) 739-5269. Jon Cecil, Dir., PBS VIDEO Marketing. Markets and distributes PBS television programs for sale on videocassette or videodisc to colleges, public libraries, schools, governments, and other organizations and institutions. *Publications: PBS VIDEO Catalog*; *PBS VIDEO Check It Out*; *PBS Video News*; and *PBS VIDEO Visions.*

Puppeteers of America. 5 Cricklewood Path, Pasadena, CA 91107. (818) 797-5748. Gayle Schulter, Membership Officer. Founded in 1937 to promote and develop the art of puppetry. It has a large collection of films and videotapes for rent in its audiovisual library and offers books, plays, and related items from the Puppetry Store. Puppeteers is a national resource center that offers workshops, exhibits, a puppetry exchange, and regional festivals. *Membership:* 2,200. *Dues:* Various classes of membership, which range from $15 to $50. *Meetings:* 1994 National Festival, July 13-17, St. Paul, MN; 1995 National Festival, July 23-29, Bryn Mawr, PA. *Publications:* Annual directory; bi-monthly newsletter; quarterly journals.

Recording for the Blind (RFB). 20 Roszel Rd., Princeton, NJ 08540. (609) 452-0606. Fax (609) 987-8116. Ritchie L. Geisel, Pres. and CEO; Laurie Facciarosso, Public Inf. Officer. RFB is a national, nonprofit organization, providing recorded textbooks, library services, and other educational resources to people who cannot read standard print because of a visual, physical, or perceptual disability. It is supported by volunteers and contributions from individuals, corporations, and foundations. RFB services include a lending library with master tapes of 80,000 titles for students from grade 5 through graduate school; recordings of educational books not available in other accessible formats (about 3,000 are recorded each year by volunteers); bibliographic and subject reference services with lists of search results available in large print, braille, or recorded formats; books on computer diskettes for purchase (more than 400 titles are available); and a fee-based service that produces printed materials in accessible formats for commercial interests, government agencies, and nonprofit organizations seeking to comply with the Americans with Disabilities Act. *Dues:* RFB consumers pay a one-time registration fee of $37.50 which entitles them to a lifetime of borrowing privileges. *Publications: RFB Issues* (for service providers); *RFB Impact* (for donors); *RFB News Cassette* (for consumers).

Recording Industry Association of America, Inc. (RIAA). 1020 19th St. NW, Suite 200, Washington, DC 20036. (202) 775-0101. Fax (202) 775-7253. Jason S. Berman, Pres.; Tim Sites, Vice Pres. Communications (contact person). Compiles and disseminates U.S. industry shipment statistics by units and wholesale/retail dollar equivalents; establishes industry technical standards; conducts audits for certification of gold and platinum records and video awards; acts as the public information arm on behalf of the U.S. recording industry; provides antipiracy intelligence to law enforcement agencies; presents an RIAA cultural award for contributions to cultural activities in the United States; and acts as a resource center for recording industry research projects. *Membership:* 200 sound recording manufacturers. *Publications: RIAA Annual Report*; *Inside RIAA* (newsletter); press releases.

The Regional Laboratory for Educational Improvement of the Northeast and Islands. 300 Brickstone Square, Suite 900, Andover, MA 01810. (508) 470-0098. Fax (508) 475-9220. Internet janeta@neirl.org. Janet Angelis, Dir. of Communications. One of 10 regional educational laboratories funded in part by the U.S. Department of Education's Office of Educational Research and Improvement (OERI). The laboratory works to achieve educational improvement by linking schools and classrooms in the Northeast and Islands region (New England, New York, Puerto Rico, and the Virgin Islands) with R&D-based knowledge and confirmed practical experience, complementing and multiplying the activities and accomplishments of existing organizations. *Membership:* Open to individuals, schools, or other organizations committed to improving education. *Meetings:* The Designing Learner Centered Schools Annual Conference, November 1994; Multiage Conference, March 1994; Regional Alliance for Mathematics and Science Education Reform Annual Conference, March 1994. *Publications: Kindle the Spark: An Action Guide Committed to the Success of Every Child*; *Continuing to Learn: A Guidebook for Teacher Development*; *Education by Charter: Restructuring School Districts*; *Building Bridges of Learning and Understanding: A Collection of Classroom Activities on Puerto Rican Culture*; *Managing Change in Rural Schools: An Action Guide*; *Mentoring: A Resource and Training Guide for Educators*; *Work in Progress: Restructuring Ten Maine Schools*; *CaMaPe: An Organizational and Educational Systems Approach to Secondary School Development*; *Building Systems for Professional Growth: An Action Guide*; *The Copernican Plan: Restructuring the American High School*; *The DeWitt Wallace-Reader's Digest Fund Study Conference: Developing a Framework for the Continual Professional Development of Administrators in the Northeast.* Publications catalog is available upon request.

Research for Better Schools, Inc. (RBS). 444 North Third St., Philadelphia, PA 19123-4107. John E. Hopkins, Exec. Dir. One of 10 Office of Educational Research and Improvement (OERI) regional educational laboratories designed to help educators and policymakers solve educational problems in their schools. Using the best available information and the experience and expertise of professionals, RBS seeks to identify solutions to education problems, tries new approaches, furnishes research results, and provides training to teachers and administrators. RBS serves Delaware, Maryland, New Jersey, Pennsylvania, and the District of Columbia.

Smithsonian Institution. 1000 Jefferson Drive SW, Washington, DC 20560. (202) 357-2700. Fax (202) 786-2515. Robert McCormick Adams, Secy. An independent trust instrumentality of the United States that conducts scientific, cultural, and scholarly research; administers the national collections; and performs other educational public service functions, all supported by Congress, trusts, gifts, and grants. Includes 16 museums, including the National Museum of Natural History, the National Museum of American History, the National Air and Space Museum, and the National Zoological Park. Museums are free and open daily except December 25. The Smithsonian Institution Traveling Exhibition Service (SITES) organizes exhibitions on art, history, and science and circulates them across the country and abroad. *Membership:* Smithsonian Associates (Resident and National Air and Space). *Dues:* Vary. *Publications: Smithsonian*; *Air & Space/Smithsonian*; *The Torch* (staff newsletter, mo.); *Research Reports* (semitechnical, q.); *Smithsonian Runner* (for and about American Indians and Smithsonian-related activities, 6/yr.); Smithsonian Institution Press Publications, 470 L'Enfant Plaza, Suite 7100, Washington, DC 20560.

Society for Applied Learning Technology (SALT). 50 Culpeper St., Warrenton, VA 22186. (703) 347-0055. Raymond G. Fox, Pres. The society is a nonprofit, professional membership organization that was founded in 1972. Membership in the society is oriented to professionals whose work requires knowledge and communication in the field of instructional technology. The society provides members a means to enhance their knowledge and job performance by participation in society-sponsored meetings, through subscription to society-sponsored publications, by association with other professionals at conferences sponsored by the society, and through membership in special interest groups and special society-sponsored initiatives/projects. In addition, the society offers members discounts on society-sponsored journals, conferences, and publications. *Membership:* 900. *Dues:* $45. *Publications: Journal of Educational Technology Systems*; *Journal of Interactive Instructional Development*; *Journal of Medical Education Technologies*. Send for list of books.

Society for Computer Simulation (SCS). P.O. Box 17900, San Diego, CA 92177-7900. (619) 277-3888. Fax (619) 277-3930. Bill Gallagher, Exec. Dir. Founded in 1952, SCS is a professional-level technical society devoted to the art and science of modeling and simulation. Its purpose is to advance the understanding, appreciation, and use of all types of computer models for studying the behavior of actual or hypothesized systems of all kinds. Sponsors standards and local, regional, and national technical meetings and conferences, such as Eastern & Western Simulation Multiconferences, Summer Computer Simulation Conference, Winter Simulation Conference, International Simulation Technology Conference (SIMTEC), National Educational Computing Conference (NECC), and others. *Membership:* 1,900. *Dues:* $60. *Publications: Simulation* (mo.); Simulation series (q.); *Transactions of SCS* (q.). Additional office in Ghent, Belgium.

*Society for Imaging Science and Technology (IS&T) (formerly Society of Photographic Engineering). 7003 Kilworth Ln., Springfield, VA 22151. (703) 642-9090. Fax (703) 642-9094. Calva Lotridge, Exec. Dir. Seeks to advance the science and engineering of imaging materials and equipment and to develop means for applying and using imaging techniques in all branches of engineering and science. *Membership:* 3,000; 17 chapters. *Publication: Journal of Imaging Science and Technology*.

Society for Photographic Education (SPE). P.O. Box 222116, Dallas, TX 75222-2116. (817) 273-2845. Fax (817) 273-2846. M. L. Hutchins, Exec. Dir. An association of college and university teachers of photography, museum photographic curators, writers, and publishers. Promotes higher standards of photographic education. *Membership:* 1,700. *Dues:* $55. *Meetings:* March 1994, Chicago; March 1995, Atlanta. *Publications: Exposure*; newsletter.

Society of Cable Television Engineers (SCTE). 669 Exton Commons, Exton, PA 19341. (215) 363-6888. Fax (215) 363-5898. William W. Riker, Pres. SCTE is dedicated to the technical training and further education of members. A nonprofit membership organization for persons engaged in engineering, construction, installation, technical direction, management, or administration of cable television and broadband communication technologies. Also eligible for membership are students in communications, educators, government and regulatory agency employees, and affiliated trade associations. *Membership:* 11,000. *Dues:* $40/yr. *Publication: The Interval*.

*Society of Motion Picture and Television Engineers (SMPTE). 595 W. Hartsdale Ave., White Plains, NY 10607-1824. (914) 761-1100. Fax (914) 761-3115. Lynette Robinson, Exec. Dir. Fosters the advancement of engineering and technical aspects of motion pictures, television, and allied arts and sciences; disseminates scientific information in these areas; and sponsors lectures, exhibitions, classes, and conferences. Open to those with clearly defined interest in the field. *Membership:* 9,500. *Dues:* $65. *Publications:* Booklets and reports related to nonbook media, such as *SMPTE Journal*; *Special Effects in Motion Pictures*; test films.

Society of Photo Technologists (SPT). 6535 S. Dayton, Suite 2000, Englewood, CO 80111. (303) 799-1632. Karen A. Hone, contact person. An organization of photographic equipment repair technicians, which improves and maintains communications between manufacturers and independent repair technicians. *Membership:* 1,000. *Dues:* $60-$250. *Publications: SPT Journal*; *SPT Parts and Services Directory*; *SPT Newsletter*; *SPT Manuals—Training and Manufacturer's Tours*.

Society of Photographic Engineering. See listing for Society for Imaging Science and Technology (IS&T).

SOFTSWAP. 1210 Marina Village Pkwy #100, Alameda, CA 94501. (510) 814-6630. Fax (510) 814-0195. Gloria Gibson, contact person. Part of CUE, Inc., a nonprofit organization that promotes the use of technology in the classroom, SOFTSWAP is an inexpensive yet high-quality library of many teacher-developed and commercial educational programs for use in Apple, IBM, and MAC computers. These copyrighted programs are organized onto disks that are sold for a nominal charge, with permission to copy. *Membership:* Approx. 7,000 (CUE, Inc.). *Dues:* $25/yr. *Meetings:* 1994, May 5-7, Palm Springs, CA, "Technology of Education: Mosaic of the Future"; October 27-29, Santa Clara, CA. *Publication: CUE Newsletter*, 6/yr.

SouthEastern Regional Vision for Education (SERVE). University of North Carolina at Greensboro, P.O. Box 5367, Greensboro, NC 27435-3277. (919) 334-3211; (800) 755-3277. Roy H. Forbes, Exec. Dir. One of 10 Office of Educational Research and Improvement (OERI) regional educational laboratories designed to help educators and policymakers solve educational problems in their schools. Using the best available information and the experience and expertise of professionals, SERVE seeks to identify solutions to education problems, tries new approaches, furnishes research results, and provides training to teachers and administrators. SERVE serves Alabama, Florida, Georgia, Mississippi, North Carolina, and South Carolina.

Southwest Educational Development Laboratory (SEDL). 211 East Seventh St., Austin, TX 78701. (512) 476-6861. Preston C. Kronkosky, Exec. Dir. (512) 476-6861. One of 10 Office of Educational Research and Improvement (OERI) regional educational laboratories designed to help educators and policymakers solve educational problems in their schools. Using the best available information and the experience and expertise of professionals, SEDL seeks to identify solutions to education problems, tries new approaches, furnishes research results, and provides training to teachers and administrators. SEDL serves Arkansas, Louisiana, New Mexico, Oklahoma, and Texas.

Special Libraries Association (SLA). 1700 18th St. NW, Washington, DC 20009-2508. (202) 234-4700. Fax (202) 265-9317. David R. Bender, Exec. Dir. SLA is an international professional organization of more than 14,000 librarians, information managers, and brokers serving business, research, government, universities, media, museums, and institutions that use or produce specialized information. Founded in 1909, the goal of the association is to advance the leadership role of special librarians in the information society. SLA encourages its members to increase their professional competencies and performance by offering continuing education courses, workshops, and middle management and executive management courses. *Membership:* 14,000 plus. *Dues:* $75 individual. *Meeting:* 1994 Annual Conference, June 11-16, Atlanta, GA. *Publications: SpeciaList* (mo. newsletter); *Special Libraries* (q.); bibliographic aids in library and information services.

SpecialNet. Part of GTE Educational Network Services. 1090 Vermont Ave. NW, Suite 800, Washington, DC 20005. (202) 408-7021; (800) 659-3000. Fax (202) 628-8216. Mike McLean, contact person. A computerized, fee-charging information database emphasizing special education resources.

Speech Communication Association (SCA). 5105 Backlick Rd., Bldg. E, Annandale, VA 22003. (703) 750-0533. James L. Gaudino, Exec. Dir. A voluntary society organized to promote study, criticism, research, teaching, and application of principles of communication, particularly of speech communication. *Membership:* 7,000. *Dues:* $75. *Publications: Spectra Newsletter* (mo.); *Quarterly Journal of Speech; Communication Monographs; Communication Education; Critical Studies in Mass Communication; Journal of Applied Communication Research; Text and Performance Quarterly; Speech Communication Teacher; Index to Journals in Communication Studies through 1990; Speech Communication Directory of SCA and the Regional Speech Communication Organizations* (CSSA, ECA, SSCA, WSCA). For additional publications, request brochure.

*Superintendent of Documents. U.S. Government Printing Office, Washington, DC 20402. (202) 783-3238. Fax (202) 512-2250. Functions as the principal sales agency for U.S. government publications. Has over 20,000 titles in its active sales inventory. For information on the scope of its publications, write for the free Subject Bibliography index listing of over 240 subject bibliographies on specific topics. Of particular interest are SB 258, *Grants and Awards;* SB 114, *Directories and Lists of Persons and Organizations;* SB 73, *Motion Pictures, Films and Audiovisual Information;* SB 207, *Small Business;* SB 85, *Financial Aid for Students.*

Teachers and Writers Collaborative (T&W). 5 Union Square W., New York, NY 10003. (212) 691-6590. Nancy Larson Shapiro, Dir. Sends writers and other artists into New York public schools to work with teachers and students on writing and art projects. Hosts seminars, workshops, and lectures. Publishes a magazine and books on teaching writing, featuring creative work from across the United States and beyond. *Dues:* $35/yr. basic membership. *Publications: Teachers & Writers* (magazine, 5/yr.); *The Story in History; The T&W Handbook of Poetic Forms; The T&W Guide to Walt Whitman; Personal Fiction Writing; Blazing Pencils; Like It Was: A Complete Guide to Writing Oral History; Origins; Moving Windows: Evaluating the Poetry Children Write; Poetic Forms: 10 Audio Programs.* Request free publications catalog for list of titles.

*Telecommunications Research and Action Center (TRAC). Box 12038, Washington, DC 20005. (202) 462-2520. Samuel Simon, counsel. Seeks to educate telecommunications consumers, to improve broadcasting, and to support local and national media reform groups and movements. *Dues:* $25/yr. *Publications: After Divestiture: What the AT&T Settlement Means for Business and Residential Telephone Service; Citizens' Media Directory; A Citizens' Primer on the Fairness Doctrine; Phonewriting: A Consumer's Guide to the New World of Electronic Information Services.*

Theater Library Association (TLA). 111 Amsterdam Ave., Rm. 513, New York, NY 10023. (212) 870-1670. Richard M. Buck, Secy./Treas. Seeks to further the interests of collecting, preserving, and using theater, cinema, and performing arts materials in libraries, museums, and private collections. *Membership:* 500. *Dues:* $20 individual, $25 institutional. *Publications: Broadside* (q.); *Performing Arts Resources* (membership annual).

Training Media Association. 198 Thomas Johnson Dr., Suite 206, Frederick, MD 21702. (301) 662-4268. Robert A. Gehrke, Exec. Dir. An organization dedicated to the protection of film and videotape copyright and copyright education. *Membership:* 75. *Dues:* Based on number of employees. *Publication: The Monthly.*

*United Nations Department of Public Information, Dissemination Division. United Nations, Rm. S-1037 A, New York, NY 10017. (212) 963-6835. Fax (212) 963-6914. Chief, *Information Dissemination Service*, Rm. S-0260. (212) 963-6824. Fax (212) 963-4642. *Film, Video and Radio Distribution*, Rm. S-0805. (212) 963-6982. Fax (212) 963-6869. *Print and Electronic Materials Distribution*, Rm. S-0260. (212) 963-1258. Fax (212) 963-4642. Vadim Perfiliev, Dir. The Department of Public Information produces and distributes films, radio, video, still pictures, charts, posters, and various publications on the United Nations and its activities. Distribution is worldwide and is done in part through a network of United Nations information centers, as well as via distributors and direct from U.N. Headquarters in New York. Information products are provided in a number of different languages, mainly in the six official U.N. languages: Arabic, Chinese, English, French, Russian, and Spanish.

*University Film and Video Association (UFVA). c/o Loyola Marymount University, Communication Arts Department, Los Angeles, CA 90045. (310) 338-3033. Fax (310) 338-3030. Donald J. Zirpola, Pres. Members are persons involved in the arts and sciences of film and video. Promotes film and video production in educational institutions, fosters study of world cinema and video in scholarly resource centers, and serves as central source of information on film/video instruction, festivals, grants, jobs, production, and research. *Membership:* Approx. 800. *Dues:* Individuals $35; students $15; institutions $75; commercial firms $150. *Publications: Journal of Film and Video; UFVA Digest;* membership directory.

World Future Society (WFS). 4916 St. Elmo Ave., Bethesda, MD 20814-6089. (301) 656-8274. Edward Cornish, Pres. Organization of individuals interested in the study of future trends and possibilities. *Membership:* 30,000. *Dues:* For information, please write to preceding address. *Meetings:* 1994 Annual Meeting, July 25-26, Cambridge, MA, "Toward the New Millennium: Living, Learning, and Working"; 1995 Annual Meeting, July 19-20, Atlanta, GA. *Publications: The Futurist: A Journal of Forecasts, Trends and Ideas About the Future; Futures Research Quarterly; Future Survey.* The society's bookstore offers audio- and videotapes, books, and other items.

Canada

This section on Canada includes information on 10 Canadian organizations whose principal interests lie in the general fields of education, educational media, instructional technology, and library and information science. Organizations listed in the 1993 *EMTY* were contacted for updated information and changes have been made accordingly.

ACCESS NETWORK. 3720 76 Ave., Edmonton, AB T6B 2N9, Canada. (403) 440-7777. Fax (403) 440-8899. Don Thomas, Pres. and CEO; Jean Campbell, Gen. Mgr., Educational Services and Enterprises; Malcolm Knox, Gen. Mgr., Television; Jackie Rollans, Gen. Mgr., CKUA AM.FM. ACCESS NETWORK is the registered trade name of the Alberta Educational Communications Corporation, which was established in 1973 to consolidate a variety of educational media services developing at that time in the province. ACCESS NETWORK acquires, develops, produces, and distributes curriculum-related video and audio programs and print support to Alberta schools. Intended primarily for use in Alberta classrooms, ACCESS NETWORK productions are now available for national and international distribution. In 1985, the corporation launched a province-wide educational television service, which is available by cable, satellite, and off-air transmitters to 85 percent of Alberta's population. CKUA AM.FM broadcasts music, cultural, and educational programming through a province-wide transmitter network.

Association for Media and Technology in Education in Canada (AMTEC). 3-1750 The Queensway, Suite 1818, Etobicoke, ON M9C 5H5, Canada. Ross Mutton, Pres. Promotes applications of educational technology in improving education and the public welfare. Fosters cooperation and interaction; seeks to improve professional qualifications of media practitioners; organizes and conducts media and technology meetings, seminars, and annual conferences; stimulates and publishes research in media and techhology. *Membership:* 550. *Dues:* $80.25 individual, $32.10 student and retiree. *Meeting:* 1994 Annual Conference, AMTEC '94, June 12-15, Lethbridge, AB, "Winds of Change." *Publications: Canadian Journal of Educational Communication* (q.); *Media News* (q.); *Membership Directory* (with membership).

Canadian Book Publishers' Council (CBPC). 250 Merton St., Suite 203, Toronto, ON M4S 1B1 Canada. (416) 322-7011. Fax (416) 322-6999. Jacqueline Hushion, Exec. Dir. CBPC members publish and distribute an extensive list of Canadian and imported learning materials in a complete range of formats from traditional textbook and ancillary materials to CDs and interactive video. The primary markets for CBPS members are schools, universities and colleges, bookstores, and libraries. CBPC also provides exhibits throughout the year and works through a number of subcommittees and groups within the organization to promote effective book publishing. *Membership:* 48 companies, educational institutions, or government agencies that publish books as an important facet of their work.

Canadian Broadcasting Corporation (CBC)/Société Radio-Canada (SRC). 1500 Bronson Ave., Box 8478, Ottawa, ON K1G 3J5, Canada. (613) 724-1200; (613) 738-6779. Fax (613) 738-6742. Gerard Veilleux, Pres. and CEO; Charlotte O'Dea, Senior Dir. of Corporate Communications. The CBC is a publicly owned corporation established in 1936 by an Act of the Canadian Parliament to provide a national broadcasting service in Canada in the two official languages. CBC services include English and French television networks; English and French AM Mono and FM Stereo radio networks virtually free of commercial advertising; CBC North, which serves Canada's North by providing radio and television programs in English, French, and seven native languages; Newsworld, a 24-hour national satellite to cable English-language news and information service funded entirely by cable subscription and commercial advertising revenues; and Radio Canada International, a shortwave radio service that broadcasts in seven languages and is managed by CBC and financed by External Affairs. The CBC is financed mainly by public funds voted annually by Parliament.

Canadian Education Association/Association canadienne d'éducation (CEA). 252 Bloor St. W., Suite 8-200, Toronto, ON M5S 1V5, Canada. (416) 924-7721. Fax (416) 924-3188. Robert E. Blair, Exec. Dir.; Suzanne Tanguay, Communications Officer. The Canadian equivalent of the U.S. National Education Association. *Membership:* 400 individual, 44 associate, 116 school board. *Dues:* $90 individual, $365 associate, 9.9 cents per pupil for school board. *Publications: CEA Handbook; Education Canada* (q.); *CEA Newsletter* (9/yr.); *Violence in the Schools; Criteria for Admission to Faculties of Education in Canada: What You Need to Know; First Nations and Schools: Triumphs and Struggles; The Canadian Education Association: The First 100 Years 1891-1991; The Multi-Grade Classroom: Myth and Reality; French Immersion Today; Heritage Language Programs in Canadian School Boards.*

Canadian Film Institute (CFI). 2 Daly, Ottawa, ON K1N 6E2, Canada. (613) 232-6727. Fax (613) 232-6315. Serge Losique, Exec. Dir.; Brian Wilson, Dir., Non-Theatrical Services. Established in 1935, the Institute promotes the study of film and television as cultural and educational forces in Canada. It distributes over 6,000 films and videos on the sciences and the visual and performing arts through the Canadian Film Institute Film Library. *Publications: Canadian Film* (series of monographs); *Northern Lights* (programmer's guide to the Festival of Festivals Retrospective); *Switching on to the Environment* (critical guide).

Canadian Library Association. 200 Elgin St., Suite 602, Ottawa, ON K2P IL5, Canada. (613) 232-9625. Fax (613) 563-9895. Françoise Hebert, Pres.; Patricia Cavill, Pres.-Elect (officers change July 1994); Karen Adams, Exec. Dir. *Membership:* 3,200 individual, 850 organization. *Dues:* Range from $50 to $1,600. *Publication: Feliciter* (member newsletter, 10/yr.)

Canadian Museums Association/Association des musées canadiens (CMA/AMC). 280 Metcalfe St., Suite 400, Ottawa, ON K2P 1R7, Canada. (613) 567-0099. Fax (613) 233-5438. John G. McAvity, Exec. Dir. Seeks to advance public museum service in Canada. *Membership:* 2,000. *Publications: Museogramme* (semimo. newsletter); *Muse* (q. journal); *Directory of Canadian Museums* (listing all museums in Canada plus information on government departments, agencies, and provincial and regional museum associations).

National Film Board of Canada (NFBC). 1251 Avenue of the Americas, 16th Floor, New York, NY 10020. (212) 596-1770. Fax (212) 595-1779. John Sirabella, U.S. Marketing Mgr./Nontheatrical Rep. Established in 1939, the NFBC's main objective is to produce and distribute high-quality audiovisual materials for educational, cultural, and social purposes.

Ontario Film Association, Inc. (also known as the Association for the Advancement of Visual Media/l'association pour l'avancement des médias visuels). 3-1750 The Queensway, Suite 1341, Etobicoke, ON M9C 5H5, Canada. (416) 761-6056. Margaret Nix., Exec. Dir. A nonprofit organization whose primary objective is to promote the sharing of ideas and information about film and video through seminars, workshops, screenings, and publications. Sponsors the annual Grierson Documentary Seminar on film and video, and the Annual Showcase of film and video, a marketplace for buyers. *Membership:* 193. *Dues:* $65 personal, $110 institutional/commercial, $199 extended institutional. *Publication: Visual Media/Médias Visuels* (5/yr.).

Part Seven
Graduate Programs

Doctoral Programs in Instructional Technology

This directory presents information on 51 doctoral (Ph.D. and Ed.D.) programs in instructional technology, educational communications/technology, media services, and closely allied programs in 28 states. Notification of the closing of one program is also included. Information in this section for 40 of the programs was obtained from, and updated by, the institutional deans, chairs, or their representatives, in response to an inquiry questionnaire mailed to them during the fall of 1993. Updated information was requested with the proviso that, if no reply was received, information provided for the 1993 edition would be used; programs for which no information has been received since 1992 or before would be dropped. Eleven programs for which the information was updated for the 1993 edition but no response was forthcoming for this edition are indicated by an asterisk (*).

Entries provide as much of the following information as was provided by respondents: (1) name and address of the institution; (2) chairperson or other individual in charge of the doctoral program; (3) types of degrees offered and specializations, including information on positions for which candidates are prepared; (4) special features of the degree program; (5) admission requirements, including minimal grade point average; (6) number of full-time and part-time faculty; (7) number of full-time and part-time students; (8) types of financial assistance available; and (9) the number of doctoral degrees awarded in 1993.

Directors of advanced professional programs for instructional technology/media specialists should find this information useful as a means of comparing their own offerings and requirements with those of institutions offering comparable programs. This listing should also assist individuals seeking a school at which to pursue advanced graduate studies in locating institutions that best suit their interests and requirements.

Additional information on the programs listed, including instructions on applying for admission, may be obtained by contacting individual program coordinators. General or graduate catalogs usually are furnished for a minimal charge; specific program information normally is sent at no charge.

In endeavoring to provide complete listings, we are greatly indebted to those individuals who responded to our requests for information. Although considerable effort has been expended to ensure completeness of the listings, there may be institutions within the United States or its territories that now have programs or that have been omitted. Readers are encouraged to furnish new information to the publisher who, in turn, will follow up for the next edition of *EMTY*.

Institutions in this section are listed alphabetically by state.

ALABAMA

Alabama State University. Library Education Media, School of Education, P.O. Box 271, Montgomery, AL 36195. (205) 293-4107. Fax (205) 241-7192. Katie R. Bell, Ph.D. Coord., Library Education Media, School of Education. *Specializations:* M.Ed., AA Certification, and Ed.S., preparation for K-12 school media programs. *Degree Requirements:* 36 semester hours; thesis required for Ed.S.; 300-clock-hour practicum (100 each in elementary, high school, and other library settings). *Faculty:* 2 part-time. *Students:* 1 full-time; 21 part-time. *Financial Assistance:* Assistantships available for full-time students. *Doctoral Degrees Awarded 1 July 1992-30 June 1993:* 2.

University of Alabama. School of Library and Information Studies, The University of Alabama, Box 87052, Tuscaloosa, AL 35487-0252. (205) 348-1523. Fax (205) 348-3746. J. Gordon Coleman, Jr., Asst. Dean and Assoc. Prof., Doctoral Program, School of Library and Information Studies. *Specializations:* Ph.D. in Librarianship with specializations in library management, information studies, youth services, library media studies, historical studies. *Features:* Program is designed to fit the needs of the student using the resources of the entire university. Students may prepare for careers in teaching and research in colleges and universities or for innovative practice in the profession. *Admission Requirements:* Master's in library science, instructional technology, or equivalent; Miller Analogies score of 55 or GRE score of 1,650; 3.5 graduate GPA. *Faculty:* 10 full-time; 1 part-time. *Students:* 4 full-time; 12 part-time. *Financial Assistance:* Fellowships, assistantships, scholarships. *Doctorates Awarded 1992-93:* 3 (program began 1988; intentionally small).

CALIFORNIA

United States International University. School of Education, 10455 Pomerado Rd., San Diego, CA 92131. (619) 693-4595. Fax (619) 693-8562. E-mail marfern@eis.calstate.edu. Dr. Maria Teresa Fernàndez, contact person. *Specializations:* Computer Education. The Ed.D. program prepares individuals to serve in a variety of positions: school district coordinators for instructional computing, specialists in designing learning strategies and training programs, university directors of learning resources, and change agents in industry and the military having teaching or training as a primary concern. *Features:* Program involves required courses in leadership, cognitive theory, global education, research and statistics; and specialization courses, including problem solving, authoring languages and applications, issues in computer education, curriculum theory and design, and instructional systems development. *Admission Requirements:* Admission to graduate program recommended by committee of faculty to the Chair of the Education Department, evaluation of GRE or Miller Analogies Test score(s), candidate's vita, three letters of recommendation, statement of purpose for study, and final committee interview. *Minimum Degree Requirements:* 95 units, 19 courses. *Faculty:* 14 full-time; 5 part-time. *Students:* 25. *Financial Assistance:* A limited number of graduate assistantships offered in conjunction with research and development work undertaken at the university. *Doctorates Awarded 1992-93:* 10.

University of California at Los Angeles. Graduate School of Education, Los Angeles, CA 90024-1521. (310) 825-8326; (310) 825-1838. Fax (310) 206-6293. Aimee Dorr, Prof. of Education, Learning and Instruction Specialization, Div. of Educational Psychology, graduate School of Education. *Specializations:* Offers Ph.D. and Ed.D. programs. Ph.D. program prepares graduates for research, teaching educational technology, and consultancies in the development of instructional materials. Ed.D. program prepares graduates for leadership roles in the development of instructional materials and educational technologies. *Features:* The program addresses the design and utilization principles and processes underlying all effective applications of instructional technologies and their products. Television, microcomputer-based, and multimedia systems are encouraged. *Admission Requirements:* Superior academic record, combined GRE score of 1,000 or better. For the Ed.D. program, two or more years of relevant field experience is desirable. *Faculty:* 4 full-time; 2 part-time. *Students:* 10-15 in M.A., Ph.D., and Ed.D. programs. *Financial Assistance:* Fellowships, loans, and resident advisors. *Doctorates Awarded 1993:* Data not reported.

University of Southern California. School of Education, Los Angeles, CA 90089-0031. (213) 740-3476. Fax (213) 746-8142. Edward J. Kazlauskas, Prof., Prog. Chair, Instructional Technology. *Specializations:* M.A., Ph.D., Ed.D. to prepare individuals to teach instructional technology; manage educational media/training programs in business or industry, research and development organizations, and higher educational institutions; perform research in instructional technology and media; and deal with computer-driven technology. Satellite Ed.D. program in Silicon Valley in northern California. *Features:* Special emphasis upon instructional design, systems analysis, and computer-based training. *Admission Requirements:* A bachelor's degree and satisfactory performance (combined score of 1,000) on the GRE aptitude test. *Faculty:* 5 full-time; 1 part-time. *Students:* 5 full-time; 41 part-time. *Financial Assistance:* Part-time work available (instructional technology-related) in the Los Angeles area and on the university campus.

COLORADO

University of Colorado at Denver. School of Education, Campus Box 106, P.O. Box 173364, Denver, CO 80217-3364. (303) 556-4881. Fax (303) 556-4822. R. Scott Grabinger, Chair of Instructional Technology Program, School of Education. *Specializations:* Ph.D. in instructional technology, in instructional development, and/or instructional computing for use in business/industry and higher education. *Features:* Courses in management and consulting, emphasizing instructional development, interactive video technologies, evaluation, and internship opportunities in a variety of agencies. *Admission Requirements:* Satisfactory GPA, GRE, writing/publication background, letters of recommendation, transcripts, and application form. *Faculty:* 4-1/2 full-time; 4 part-time. *Students:* 16 part-time; 2 full-time. *Financial Assistance:* Corporate internships are available. *Doctorates Awarded 1992-93:* 2.

University of Northern Colorado. College of Education, Greeley, CO 80639. (303) 351-2687. Fax (303) 351-2312. Edward P. Caffarella, Prof., Chair, Educational Technology, College of Education. *Specializations:* Ph.D. in Educational Technology with emphasis areas in instructional development/design, interactive technology, and technology integration. *Features:* Graduates are prepared for careers as instructional technologists, course designers, trainers, instructional developers, media specialists, and human resource managers. *Admission Requirements:* GPA of 3.2, three letters of recommendation, congruency between applicant's statement of career goals and program goals, GRE combined test score of 1,650, and interview with faculty. *Faculty:* 6 full-time; 2 part-time. *Students:* 39 doctoral, 69 M.A., 23 graduate certification. *Financial Assistance:* A limited number of Colorado Fellowships are available for full-time incoming students; graduate and teaching assistantships are available for full-time students. *Doctorates Awarded 1992-93:* 1.

CONNECTICUT

University of Connecticut. U-64, Storrs, CT 06269-2064. (203) 486-0181. Fax 486-0210. E-mail sbrown@UConnvm.UConn.edu, or myoung@UConnvm.UConn.edu. Scott W. Brown, Chair; Michael Young, contact person. *Specializations:* The emphasis in Educational Technology is a specialization within the Program of Cognition and Instruction, in the Department of Educational Psychology. *Features:* The emphasis in Educational Technology is a unique program at UConn. It is co-sponsored by the Department of Educational Psychology in the School of Education and the Psychology Department in the College of Liberal Arts and Sciences. The emphasis in Educational Technology within the Cognition and Instruction Program seeks to provide students with knowledge of theory and applications regarding the use of advanced technology to enhance learning and thinking. The Ed. Tech. emphasis provides suggested courses, and opportunities for internships and independent study experiences that are directed toward an understanding of both the effects of technology on cognition and instruction, and the enhancement of thinking and learning with technology. Facilities include the UCEML computer lab featuring Mac and IBM networks and a multimedia development center. The School of Education also features a multimedia classroom/auditorium renovated in 1993 for Mac and IBM computer displays and peripherals, including videodisc, CD-ROM, interactive videotape, and fiber connections to our broadcast studio. Faculty research interests include interactive videodisc for anchored instruction and situated learning, telecommunications for cognitive apprenticeship, technology-mediated interactivity for generative learning, and in cooperation with the National Research Center for Gifted and Talented (a collaboration with Yale and the U. of Georgia, housed at UConn), research on the use of technology to enhance cooperative learning and the development of gifted performance in all students. *Admission Requirements:* Admission to the graduate school at UConn, GRE test completion or other evidence of success at the graduate level. Previous experience in a related area of technology, education, or training is a plus. *Faculty:* The program in Cognition and Instruction has 5 full-time faculty; 2 full-time faculty administer the emphasis in Educational Technology. *Students:* Data not reported. *Financial Assistance:* Graduate assistantships, research fellowships, teaching assistantships, and federal and minority scholarships are available competitively. *Doctorates Awarded 1992-93:* 2.

FLORIDA

Florida State University. Instructional Systems Program, Department of Educational Research, College of Education, 305 Stone Bldg., Tallahassee, FL 32306. (904) 644-8785. Fax (904) 644-8776. Walter Dick, Prof. and Program Leader. *Specializations:* Ph.D. degree in instructional systems with specializations for persons planning to work in academia, business, industry, government, or military. *Features:* Core courses include systems and materials development, analysis of media, project management, psychological foundations, current trends in instructional design, and research and statistics. Internships are also required. *Admission Requirements:* Total score of 1,000 on the verbal and quantitative sections of the GRE, or a GPA of 3.0 for the last two years of undergraduate study; international students, TOEFL score of 550. *Faculty:* 6 full-time; 4 part-time. *Students:* 44. *Financial Assistance:* Some graduate research assistantships on faculty grants and contracts; university fellowships. *Doctorates Awarded 1992-93:* 15.

Nova Southeastern University. Fischler Center for the Advancement of Education, 3301 College Ave., Fort Lauderdale, FL 33314. (800) 986-3223. Fax (305) 476-4764. Johanne Peck, M.S. and Ed.S. Programs for Teachers. *Specializations:* M.S. and Ed.S. in Educational

Media. *Minimum Degree Requirements:* M.S., 36 semester hours, including a practicum experience; Ed.S. data not reported. *Faculty:* 2 full-time. *Students:* 56. *Financial Assistance:* NDSL; Federal Stafford Loan, Unsubsidized Federal Stafford Loan, SLS. *Doctorates Awarded 1993:* Data not reported.

University of Florida. College of Education, Gainesville, FL 32611. (904) 392-0705, ext. 600; (904) 392-0705. Fax (904) 392-9193. Lee Mullally, Assoc. Prof., Chair, Educational Media and Instructional Design Program, College of Education. *Specializations:* Ph.D. and Ed.D. programs that stress theory, research, training, teaching, evaluation, and instructional development. *Admission Requirements:* A composite score of at least 1,000 on the GRE, an undergraduate GPA of 3.0 minimum and a graduate GPA of 3.5 minimum, and three letters of recommendation. *Faculty:* 2 full-time. *Students:* 15 full- and part-time. *Financial Assistance:* A few scholarships through the Graduate School. *Doctorates Awarded 1992-93:* 2.

GEORGIA

*Georgia State University. College of Education, Atlanta, GA 30303-3083. (404) 651-2510. Fax (404) 651-2546. Francis D. Atkinson, Coord., Instructional Technology Programs, Dept. of Curriculum and Instruction. *Specializations:* Ph.D. in Instructional Technology. *Admission Requirements:* Three letters of recommendation, handwritten and autobiographical sketch, admission tests, and acceptance by department. *Faculty:* 2 full-time; 6 part-time. *Students:* 3 full-time; 12 part-time. *Financial Assistance:* Assistantships, paid internships, student loans and grants. *Doctorates Awarded 1991-92:* 0.

University of Georgia. College of Education, 607 Aderhold Hall, Athens, GA 30602-7144. (706) 542-3810. Fax (706) 542-4032. James R. Okey, Chair, Dept. of Instructional Technology. *Specializations:* M.Ed, Ed.S., Ed.D, and Ph.D. for leadership positions as specialists in instructional design and development. The program offers advanced study for individuals with previous preparation in instructional media and technology, as well as a preparation for personnel in other professional fields requiring a specialty in instructional systems/instructional technology. Representative career fields for graduates include designing/developing/evaluating new courses, tutorial programs, and instructional materials in a number of different settings; military/industrial training; medical/dental/nursing professional schools; allied health agencies; teacher education/staff development centers; state/local school systems; higher education/teaching/research; and publishers/producers of instructional products (textbooks, workbooks, films, etc.). *Features:* Minor areas of study available in a variety of other departments. Personalized programs are planned around a common core of courses; practica, internships, and/or clinical experiences. Research activities include special assignments, applied projects, and task forces, as well as thesis and dissertation studies. *Admission Requirements:* Application to graduate school, satisfactory GRE score, other criteria as outlined in Graduate School Bulletin. *Faculty:* 11 full-time. *Students:* 40 full-time. *Financial Assistance:* Graduate assistantships available. *Doctorates Awarded 1992-93:* 5.

ILLINOIS

Northern Illinois University. College of Education, DeKalb, IL 60115. (815) 753-0464. Fax (815) 753-9371. Dr. Gary L. McConeghy, Chair, Instructional Technology, College of Education—LEPS. *Specializations:* Ed.D. in Instructional Technology, emphasizing instructional design and development, computer education, media administration, production, and preparation for careers in business, industry, and higher education. *Features:* Considerable flexibility in course selection, including advanced seminars, internships, individual study, and research. Program is highly individualized. A total of 60 courses offered by several departments, including Library Science, Radio/Television/Film, Art, Journalism, Educational Psychology, and Research and Evaluation. *Admission Requirements:* 2.75 undergraduate GPA, 3.5 M.S. GPA; combined score of 1,000 on GRE; a writing sample; and three references. *Faculty:* 5 full-time; 5 part-time. *Students:* 78 part-time. *Financial Assistance:* Assistantships available at times in various departments. *Doctorates Awarded 1992-93:* 5.

*Southern Illinois University. School of Education, Box 1049, Edwardsville, IL 62026. (618) 692-2328. Fax (618) 692-3359. William P. Ahlbrand, Assoc. Dean and Ed.D. Program Dir. *Specializations:* Ed.D. (all-school degree) in instructional processes emphasizing theory and research, teaching, evaluation, and instructional systems design and development. Doctoral graduates are employed in public school systems and universities, generally in the Midwest. *Admission Requirements:* GRE verbal and quantitative composite of 1020, master's GPA of B+; usually admit only 10 students per year. *Faculty:* 8 full-time. *Students:* 4 full- and part-time. *Financial Assistance:* Doctoral assistantships and Graduate School fellowships. *Doctorates Awarded 1991-92:* 6.

Southern Illinois University at Carbondale. College of Education, Carbondale, IL 62901-4610. (618) 536-2441. Fax (618) 453-4244. Billy G. Dixon, Prof., Chair, Dept. of Curriculum and Instruction, College of Education. *Specializations:* Ph.D. in education including specialization in instructional technology. *Features:* All specializations are oriented to multiple education settings. *Admission Requirements:* 3.25 GPA or better; Miller Analogies Test or GRE score; letters of recommendation; and a writing sample. *Faculty:* 5 full-time; 5 part-time. *Students:* 25. *Financial Assistance:* Six graduate scholarships available, as well as a university fellowship program. *Doctorates Awarded 1992-93:* 2.

University of Illinois at Urbana-Champaign. College of Education, Champaign, IL 61820. (217) 244-3391. Fax (217) 244-4572. Graduate Programs Office, Dept. of Curriculum and Instruction, College of Education. *Specializations:* Ph.D., Ed.D. programs (including advanced certificate program) with emphasis in the following areas: preparation of university research faculty, materials/training designers, computer resources managers, and continuing professional teacher training. *Features:* Programs designed to accommodate individuals with diverse background preparations. *Admission Requirements:* Master's degree, 4.0 out of 5.0 GPA, GRE at least 50th percentile in two of Verbal, Quantitative, and Analytic; a sample of scholarly writing in English; TOEFL scores, including scores on Test of Written English and Test of Spoken English for non-English-speaking students. *Faculty:* 8 full- and part-time. *Students:* 20 full- and part-time. *Financial Assistance:* Fellowships for very highly academically talented; assistantships for 20-25 percent; some tuition fee waivers. *Doctorates Awarded 1992-93:* 5.

University of Illinois at Urbana-Champaign. Department of Educational Psychology, 210 Education Bldg., 1310 S. 6th St., Champaign, IL 61820. (217) 333-2245. Fax (217) 244-7620. E-mail cwest@uiuc.edu. Charles K. West, Prof., Div. of Learning and Instruction, Dept. of Educational Psychology. *Specializations:* Ph.D. in educational psychology with emphasis in instructional psychology, instructional design, and educational computing. *Features:* Individually tailored program. Strongly research-oriented with emphasis on applications of cognitive science to instruction. *Admission Requirements:* Excellent academic record, high GRE scores, and strong letters of recommendation. *Faculty:* 17. *Students:* 35. *Financial*

Assistance: Scholarships, research assistantships, and teaching assistantships available. *Doctorates Awarded 1992-93:* 7.

INDIANA

Indiana University. School of Education, Bloomington, IN 47405. (812) 855-1791. Fax (812) 855-3044. Charles Reigeluth, Prof., Chair, Dept. of Instructional Systems Technology, School of Education. *Specializations:* Offers Ph.D. and Ed.D. degrees. For details on this program, see the article, "Preparing Instructional Technologists for the 21st Century," by James Pershing, in this volume.

Purdue University. School of Education, W. Lafayette, IN 47907-1442. (317) 494-5673. Fax (317) 496-1622. James D. Russell, Prof. of Educational Computing and Instructional Development, Dept. of Curriculum and Instruction. *Specializations:* Ph.D. programs in instructional research and development or educational computing. *Admission Requirements:* GPA of 3.0 or better, three recommendations, scores totaling 1,000 or more on the GRE, statement of personal goals. *Faculty:* 6 full-time. *Students:* 10 full-time; 30 part-time. *Financial Assistance:* Assistantships and fellowships. *Doctorates Awarded 1992-93:* 8.

IOWA

Iowa State University. College of Education, Ames, IA 50011. (515) 294-6840. Fax (515) 294-9284. E-mail mrs@iastate.edu. Michael Simonson, Prof., Curriculum and Instruction Dept., College of Education. *Specializations:* Ph.D. in education with emphasis in instructional computing, instructional design, and technology research. *Features:* Practicum experiences related to professional objectives, supervised study and research projects tied to long-term studies within the program, development and implementation of new techniques, teaching strategies, and operational procedures in instructional resources centers and computer labs. Participates in the Iowa Distance Education Alliance, Iowa's Star Schools Project. *Admission Requirements:* Top half of undergraduate class, autobiography, three letters of recommendation, GRE general test scores. *Faculty:* 3 full-time; 3 part-time. *Students:* 21 full-time; 20 part-time. *Financial Assistance:* 10 assistantships. *Doctorates Awarded 1992-93:* 6.

University of Iowa. College of Education, Iowa City, IA 52242. (319) 335-5577. Fax (319) 335-5386. Lowell Schoer, Prof., Psychological and Quantitative Foundations, College of Education. *Specializations:* Ed.D. and M.A. with specializations in Classroom Instruction, Computer Applications, Instructional Development, Media Production, and Training and Human Resource Development. *Features:* Flexibility in planning to fit individual needs, backgrounds, and career goals. The program is interdisciplinary, involving courses within divisions of the College of Education, as well as in the schools of Business, Library Science, Radio and Television, Linguistics, and Psychology. *Admission Requirements:* A composite score of at least 1,000 on GRE (verbal and quantitative) and a 3.2 GPA on all previous graduate work for regular admission. (Conditional admission may be granted.) Teaching or relevant experience may be helpful. *Minimum Degree Requirements:* 60 semester hours of approved coursework—16 in core, 18 in specialization, 6 outside College of Education, 6 in a project, the rest in electives. *Faculty:* 4 full-time; 3 part-time. *Students:* 90 full- and part-time. *Financial Assistance:* Special assistantships (in the College of Education) for which students in any College of Education program may compete. Application deadlines for the special assistantships is 1 February. *Doctorates Awarded 1992-93:* Data not reported.

KANSAS

Kansas State University. College of Education, Manhattan, KS 66506-5301. (913) 532-5904. Fax (913) 532-7304. John Parmley, Chair, Secondary Education. *Specializations:* Ph.D. and Ed.D. programs in Instructional Design, other specializations in development. *Faculty:* 3. *Students:* 15. *Financial Assistance:* Data not available. *Doctorates Awarded 1992-93:* 6.

MARYLAND

The Johns Hopkins University. Center for Technology in Education, Division of Education, Baltimore, MD 21218. (410) 646-3000. Fax (410) 646-2310. Sarah McPherson, Coord., M.S. Technology for Educators, Ed.D. Technology for Special Education, Div. of Education. *Specialization:* M.S. in Technology for Educators, Ed.D. in Technology for Special Education.

University of Maryland. College of Library and Information Services, College Park, MD 20742-4345. (301) 405-2038. Fax (301) 314-9145. Diane Barlow, Dir., Student Services, College of Library and Information Services. *Specializations:* Ph.D. in Library Science and Educational Technology/Instructional Communication. *Features:* Program is broadly conceived and interdisciplinary in nature, using the resources of the entire campus. The student and the advisor design a program of study and research to fit the student's background, interests, and professional objectives. Students prepare for careers in teaching and research in information science and librarianship and elect concentrations including educational technology/instructional communication. *Admission Requirements:* Baccalaureate degree (the majority enter with master's degrees in library science, educational technology, or other relevant disciplines), GRE general tests, three letters of recommendation, and a statement of purpose. Interviews required when feasible. *Faculty:* 15 full-time; 16 part-time. *Students:* 20 full-time. *Financial Assistance:* Some fellowships starting at $8,800, with remission of tuition; some assistantships also available. *Doctorates Awarded 1991-92:* 0.

MASSACHUSETTS

Boston University. School of Education, 605 Commonwealth Ave., Boston, MA 02215. (617) 353-3519. Fax (617) 353-3924. Gaylen B. Kelley, Prof., Chair, Program in Educational Media and Technology, School of Education; David Whittier, Dir., Instructional Materials Center. *Specializations:* Ed.D. specializing in instructional design/development for developing and teaching academic programs in instructional technology in community colleges and universities; or specialization in such application areas as business and industrial training, biomedical communication, or international development projects. Program specializations in instructional development, media production and design, and instructional facilities design for media and technology. Students participate in mandatory research sequence and may elect courses in other university schools and colleges. *Features:* Doctoral students have a great deal of flexibility in program planning and are encouraged to plan programs that build on prior education and experience that lead to specific career goals; there is strong faculty participation in this process. *Admission Requirements:* Three letters of recommendation,

Miller Analogies Test or GRE test score(s), undergraduate and graduate transcripts, completed application form with statement of goals. Minimum GPA is 2.7 with Miller Analogies Test score of 50. *Degree Requirements:* 60 credit hours, comprehensive exam., dissertation. *Faculty:* 1 full-time; 11 part-time. *Students:* 46. *Financial Assistance:* Some assistantships and fellowships. *Doctorates Awarded 1992-93:* 5.

MICHIGAN

University of Michigan. Educational Studies, Ann Arbor, MI 48109-1259. (313) 763-0612. Fax (313) 763-1229. Patricia Baggett, Assoc. Prof., Dept. of Educational Studies. *Specializations:* Ph.D. sequences in Educational Technology and Science Education, Educational Technology and Mathematics Education, and Educational Technology and Literacy. *Minimum Degree Requirements:* 60 credit hours beyond B.A. (trimester). *Faculty:* 1 full-time, 7 part-time. *Students:* Data not reported. *Doctoral Degrees Awarded 1992-93:* 0 (new program). See also listing in Educational Computing Programs.

Wayne State University. College of Education, Detroit, MI 48202. (313) 577-1728. Fax (313) 577-3606. Rita C. Richey, Prof., Program Coord., Instructional Technology Programs, Div. of Administrative and Organizational Studies, College of Education. *Specializations:* Ed.D. and Ph.D. programs to prepare individuals for leadership in business, industry, health care, and the K-12 school setting as instructional development specialists; media or learning resources managers or consultants; specialists in instructional video; and computer-assisted instruction specialists. *Features:* Guided experiences in instructional design and development activities in business and industry are available. *Admission Requirements:* Master's, GPA of 3.5, GRE, and Miller Analogies Test, strong professional recommendations, and an interview. *Faculty:* 5 full-time; 5 part-time. *Students:* 135 full- and part-time. *Financial Assistance:* Contract industrial internships, university scholarships. *Doctorates Awarded 1992-93:* 7.

MINNESOTA

*University of Minnesota. College of Education, Minneapolis, MN 55455. (612) 624-2034. Fax (612) 626-7496. Gregory C. Sales, Assoc. Prof., Curriculum and Instructional Systems, College of Education. *Specializations:* Ph.D. in Education is offered through the graduate school. Areas of study include instructional design and technology, computer-based instruction, and instruction research. *Features:* Internships and special field experiences. *Admission Requirements:* 3.0 GPA, Miller Analogies Test 60 or higher, GRE (required as of 9/93). *Faculty:* 2.5 full-time; 1 part-time. *Students:* 115 full- and part-time. *Financial Assistance:* Determined on an individual basis. *Doctorates Awarded 1991-92:* 4.

MISSOURI

University of Missouri-Columbia. College of Education, 212 Townsend Hall, Columbia, MO 65211. (314) 882-3832. Fax (314) 884-5455. E-mail wedmanjf@missou1.missouri.edu. John F. Wedman, Assoc. Prof., Educational Technology Program, Curriculum and Instruction Dept., College of Education. *Specializations:* Ph.D. in Instructional Theory and Practice. The program emphasizes learning and instructional design, electronic performance support systems (including multimedia development), and change processes. *Features:* Program includes a major in Instructional Theory and Practice with two support areas (i.e., Educational

Psychology and Computer Science), research tools, and R&D apprenticeship experiences. The program is rapidly expanding, providing the cornerstone for improving mathematics, science, and technical education. These areas have been identified for enhancement and supported with an annual R&D budget of over $150,000. *Admission Requirements:* Graduate GPA above 3.2 and a combined score of 1,500 or better on the GRE; letters of recommendation; and a statement of purpose. *Faculty:* 3 full-time, 4 part-time, plus selected faculty in related fields. *Students:* 16. *Financial Assistance:* Graduate assistantships with tuition waivers; numerous academic scholarships ranging from $200 to $10,000. *Doctorates Awarded 1993:* 3.

NEBRASKA

*University of Nebraska. Teachers College, Lincoln, NE 68588-0515. (402) 472-2018. Fax (402) 472-8317. E-mail: dbrooks@unlinfo.unl.edu. David Brooks, Prof., Coord., Teachers College. *Specializations and Features:* Ph.D. and Ed.D. programs are in administration, curriculum, and instruction with an emphasis in instructional technology (IT). Students in these programs demonstrate competencies for professions in instructional design, research in IT, and training by developing appropriate portfolios. Within the context of a balanced graduate experience in IT, extensive experiences in the use of CD-ROM technologies are possible. *Admission Requirements:* Admission standards are set by the graduate college. *Faculty:* 3 full-time faculty teach in the IT program; 5 are involved in CD-ROM design and production. *Financial Assistance:* Scholarship and externally based funding support available. *Doctorates Awarded 1991-92:* 1.

NEW JERSEY

Rutgers-The State University of New Jersey. The Graduate School, New Brunswick, NJ 08903. (908) 932-7447. Fax (908) 932-6916. Lea P. Stewart, Prof., Dir., Ph.D. Program in Communication, Information and Library Studies, The Graduate School. *Specializations:* Ph.D. programs in communication; information and communication in management and organizational processes; information systems, structures, and users; information and communication policy and technology; and library and information services. *Features:* Program provides doctoral-level coursework for students seeking theoretical and research skills for scholarly and professional leadership in the information and communication fields. *Admission Requirements:* Typically, students should have completed a master's degree in information studies, communication, library science, or related field. The undergraduate GPA should be 3.0 or better. The GRE is required; TOEFL is also required for foreign applicants whose native language is not English. *Faculty:* 42 full- and part-time. *Students:* 93 full- and part-time. *Financial Assistance:* Assistantships and Title II-B fellowships. *Doctorates Awarded 1992-93:* 7.

NEW YORK

New York University. School of Education, New York, NY 10003. (212) 998-5177. Fax (212) 995-4041. Francine Shuchat Shaw, Assoc. Prof., Dir., Educational Communication and Technology Program; Donald T. Payne, Assoc. Prof., Doctoral Advisor, Educational Communication and Technology Program, 239 Greene St., Suite 300, School of Education. *Specializations:* Ph.D., Ed.D. in education for the preparation of individuals to perform as instructional media designers, developers, and producers in education, business and industry, health and medicine, community services, government, and other fields; to coordinate media communications programs in educational television centers, museums, schools, corporations, health and medicine, and community organizations; to serve as directors and supervisors in audiovisual programs in all settings listed; and to teach in educational communications and instructional technology programs in higher education. *Features:* Emphasizes theoretical foundations, in particular a cognitive perspective of learning and instruction and their implications for designing media-based learning environments; participation in special research and production projects in multi-image, television, microcomputers, and computer-based interactive multimedia systems. *Admission Requirements:* Combined score of 1,000 minimum on GRE, responses to essay questions and interview related to academic and/or professional preparation and career goals. *Faculty:* 2 full-time; 10 part-time. *Students:* 15 full-time; 35 part-time. *Financial Assistance:* Several graduate and research assistantships and some financial aid and work-study programs. *Doctorates Awarded 1992-93:* 2.

*State University of New York at Buffalo. Graduate School of Education, Buffalo, NY 14214. (716) 636-3164. Fax (716) 645-2481. Taher A. Razik, Prof. of Education, Dept. of Educational Organization, Administration and Policy, 480 Baldy Hall. *Specializations:* Ph.D., Ed.D., and Ed.M. in instructional design systems and management. Emphasis is on the systems approach, communication, and computer-assisted instruction and model building, with a specific focus on the efficient implementation of media in instruction. *Features:* The program is geared to instructional development, systems analysis, systems design and management in educational and noneducational organizations; research is oriented to the analysis of communication and information theory. Laboratories are available to facilitate student and faculty research projects in educational and/or training settings. Specifically, the knowledges and skills are categorized as follows: planning and designing; delivery systems and managing; and evaluating. *Admission Requirements:* Satisfactory scores on the Miller Analogies Test and/or GRE, minimum 3.0 GPA, sample of student writing, and personal interview. *Faculty:* 3 full-time; 3 part-time. *Students:* 25 full- and part-time. *Financial Assistance:* Some graduate assistantships and various fellowships (apply by March 10). *Doctorates Awarded 1991-92:* 3.

Syracuse University. School of Education, Syracuse, NY 13244-2340. (315) 443-3703. Fax (315) 443-5732. Philip L. Doughty, Prof., Chair, Instructional Design, Development, and Evaluation Program, School of Education. *Specializations:* Ph.D. and Ed.D. degree programs for instructional design of programs and materials, educational evaluation, human issues in instructional development, media production (including computers and videodisc), and educational research and theory (learning theory, application of theory, and educational and media research). Graduates are prepared to serve as curriculum developers, instructional developers, program and product evaluators, researchers, resource center administrators, communications coordinators, trainers in human resource development, and higher education instructors. *Features:* Field work and internships, special topics and special issues seminar, student- and faculty-initiated minicourses, seminars and guest lecturers, faculty-student formulation of department policies, and multiple international perspectives. *Admission Requirements:* A master's degree from an accredited institution and GRE (V, Q & A) scores. *Faculty:* 5 full-time; 4 part-time. *Students:* 43 full-time; 36 part-time. *Financial Assistance:* Some fellowships, scholarships, and graduate assistantships entailing either research or administrative duties in instructional technology. *Doctorates Awarded 1992-93:* 8.

OHIO

The Ohio State University. College of Education, Columbus, OH 43210. (614) 292-4872. Fax (614) 292-7900. Robert Lawson, Dept. of Educational Policy and Leadership, College of Education. *Specializations:* Ph.D. in Instructional and Interactive Technologies, within the program area of Instructional Design and Technology, for the preparation of individuals to perform research and to teach in higher education, administer comprehensive media services, or engage in research, production, and development of leadership functions in higher education and related educational agencies. *Features:* Interdisciplinary work in other departments (journalism, communications, radio and television, computer and information science); individual design of doctoral programs according to candidate's background, experience, and goals; and internships provided on campus in business and industry and in schools; integrated school media laboratory, microcomputer, and videodisc laboratories. *Admission Requirements:* Admission to graduate school and specific program area in the College of Education, GRE general test (Ph.D. only), minimum 2.7 GPA, and satisfactory academic and professional recommendations. *Faculty:* 5 full-time; 1 part-time. *Students:* 11 full-time, 3 part-time. *Financial Assistance:* Some assistantships. *Doctorates Awarded 1992-93:* 6.

*The Ohio State University. College of the Arts, Department of Art Education, 340 Hopkins Hall, 128 North Oval Mall, Columbus, OH 43210. (614) 292-0259. Fax (614) 292-4401. E-mail scott+@osu.edu. Dr. Tony Scott, Prog. Coord., Program in Electronic Media in Art Education. *Specializations:* Ph.D. and M.A. in Art Education with specializations in the teaching and learning of computer graphics and computer-mediated art; multimedia production and its curricular implications; electronic networking in the arts; multicultural aspects of computing; hypermedia applications for teaching and art education research; and the application of computing to arts administration, galleries, and museums. *Features:* Students with previous experience in computing in the arts or art education will be eligible for consideration for membership in The Advanced Computing Center for the Arts and Design (ACCAD), an interdisciplinary research center within the College of the Arts. The program will also be closely linked with The Wexner Center for the Arts on the Ohio State campus. Students may study the application of computing to art education in concert with one of the other specialties offered by the Department of Art Education: studies in the teaching of art criticism, art history and aesthetics; multicultural and cross-cultural approaches to art education; classroom-based research in art education; the professional development of art teachers, and arts administration. *Faculty:* 3 full-time in specialty; 19 in department. *Students:* 15 full-time. *Financial Assistance:* Graduate teaching associate positions that carry tuition and fee waivers and pay a monthly stipend; various fellowship programs for applicants with high' GRE scores. *Doctorates Awarded 1991-92:* 0 (new program).

University of Toledo. College of Education and Allied Professions, Toledo, OH 43606-3390. (419) 537-3846. Fax (419) 537-3853. Amos C. Patterson, Prof., Dir. of Academic Programs, College of Education and Allied Professions. *Specializations:* Ph.D. and Ed.D. *Features:* Research and theory in the areas of instructional design, development, evaluation, computers, video, and training and human resources development. Emphasis is in the empirical study of systematic processes in instructional technology. Residency requirement of one year or three full-time summer quarters, depending on Ph.D. or Ed.D. option. Option of one or two minor areas of study to be included in total program hours. *Admission Requirements:* GRE score of 1,000, combined totals, Miller Analogies Test at or above 50th percentile, three letters of recommendation, official transcripts of undergraduate and graduate work, and autobiographical details. *Faculty:* 7 full-time, 2 part-time. *Students:* 10 full-time; 16 part-time. *Financial*

Assistance: Graduate assistantships for research and teaching, Board of Trustee scholarships and grants (tuition only). *Doctorates Awarded 1992-93:* 2.

OKLAHOMA

University of Oklahoma. Department of Educational Psychology, 820 Van Vleet Oval, Norman, OK 73019-0260. (405) 325-5974. Fax (405) 325-3242. Raymond B. Miller, Prog. Area Coord., Dept. of Educational Psychology. *Specializations:* Ph.D. in instructional psychology and technology. *Features:* The program is built around a core of learning and cognition, instructional design, and research methods. Students' programs are tailored to their professional goals within the areas of emphasis within instructional psychology and technology, e.g., instructional design, computer applications, management of technology programs. *Admission Requirements:* A minimum of 3.25 GPA in all graduate work or 3.0 in the last 60 hours of undergraduate work, GRE scores, three letters of recommendation. *Faculty:* 10 full-time; 2 part-time. *Financial Assistance:* Assistantships, out-of-state fee waivers, graduate scholarships (both general and targeted minorities). *Doctorates Awarded 1992-93:* 1.

PENNSYLVANIA

*Pennsylvania State University. 270 Chambers Bldg., University Park, PA 16802. (814) 865-0473. Fax (814) 865-3315. D. W. Johnson, Prof. in Charge. *Specializations:* Ph.D. and Ed.D. in instructional systems design, development, management, evaluation, and research in instructional endeavors within business, industrial, medical, health, religious, higher education, and public school settings. Present research emphases are on instructional development, dissemination, implementation, and management; interactive video; computer-based education; and visual learning. *Features:* A common thread throughout all programs is that candidates have basic competencies in the understanding of human learning; curriculum; instructional design, development, and evaluation; and research procedures. Practical experience is available in mediated independent learning, research, instructional development, computer-based education, and dissemination projects. *Admission Requirements:* GRE or Miller Analogies Test, TOEFL, transcript, two letters of recommendation. *Faculty:* 6 full-time; 2 affiliates; 2 part-time. *Students:* Approx. 260 full- and part-time. *Financial Assistance:* Some assistantships, graduate fellowships, student aid loans. *Doctorates Awarded 1991-92:* 10.

University of Pittsburgh. School of Education, Pittsburgh, PA 15260. (412) 612-7254. Fax (412) 648-5911. Barbara Seels, Assoc. Prof., Prog. Coord., Program in Instructional Design and Technology, Dept. of Instruction and Learning, School of Education. *Specializations:* Ed.D. and M.Ed. programs for the preparation of instructional technologists with skills in designing, developing, using, evaluating, and managing processes and resources for learning. Certification option for instructional technologists available. *Features:* Program prepares people for positions in which they can effect educational change through instructional technology. Program includes three competency areas: instructional design, technological delivery systems, and communications research. *Admissions Requirements:* Submission of written statement of applicant's professional goals, three letters of recommendation, demonstration of English proficiency, satisfactory GPA, sample of professional writing, GRE, and personal interviews. *Faculty:* 3 full-time. *Students:* 44. *Financial Assistance:* Tuition scholarships and assistantships may be available. *Doctorates Awarded 1992-93:* 9.

TENNESSEE

University of Tennessee. College of Education, Department of Curriculum and Instruction, Knoxville, TN 37996-3400. (615) 974-6800. Dr. Al Grant, Coord., Instructional Media and Technology Program. *Specializations:* M.S. in Ed. and Ed.S. in the Department of Curriculum and Instruction, concentration in Instructional Media and Technology; Ph.D., College of Education, concentration in Instructional Media and Technology, Ed.D. in Curriculum and Instruction, concentration in Instructional Media and Technology. *Features:* Coursework in media management, advanced software production, utilization, research, theory, psychology, instructional computing, television, and instructional development. Coursework will also meet the requirements for state certification as Instructional Materials Supervisor in the public schools of Tennessee. *Admission Requirements:* Send for the Graduate Catalog, The University of Tennessee. *Media Faculty:* 1 full-time, with additional assistance from Curriculum and Instruction and university faculty. *Doctorates Awarded 1992-93:* 1.

TEXAS

East Texas State University (Commerce, TX) no longer has a doctoral program in instructional technology.

*Texas A&M University. College of Education, College Station, TX 77843. (409) 845-7276. Fax (409) 845-9663. Ronald D. Zellner, Assoc. Prof., Coord., Educational Technology Program, College of Education. *Specializations:* Ph.D. and Ed.D. programs to prepare individuals to teach college and university courses in educational technology, manage learning resource centers, and apply educational technology skills and knowledge in various settings related to communication and instructional processes in higher education, public education, business and industry, and public and private agencies. *Features:* The doctoral programs are flexible and interdisciplinary; degrees are established and granted in conjunction with the Department of Curriculum and Instruction and other departments in the College of Education; specialization areas include computer applications (CAI, CMI, interactive video), media, and video production; program provides laboratories, equipment, and a PBS television station. *Admission Requirements:* GPA 3.0, GRE 800. *Faculty:* 4 full-time; 1 part-time. *Students:* 4 full-time; 1 part-time. *Financial Assistance:* Several teaching assistantships. *Doctorates Awarded 1991-92:* 1.

The University of Texas. College of Education, Austin, TX 78712. (512) 471-5211. Fax (512) 471-4607. DeLayne Hudspeth, Assoc. Prof., Area Coord., Instructional Technology, Dept. of Curriculum and Instruction, College of Education. *Specializations:* Ph.D. program emphasizes research, design, and development of instructional systems and communications technology. *Features:* The program is interdisciplinary in nature, although certain competencies are required of all students. Programs of study and dissertation research are based on individual needs and career goals. Learning resources include a model LRC, computer labs and classrooms, a color television studio, interactive multimedia lab, and access to a photo and graphics lab. *Admission Requirements:* Minimum 3.0 GPA and a score of at least 1,100 on the GRE. *Faculty:* 4 full-time; 2 part-time. Many courses are offered cooperatively by other departments, including Radio-TV Film, Computer Science, and Educational Psychology. *Students:* 31. *Financial Assistance:* Assistantships may be available to develop instructional materials, teach undergraduate computer literacy, and assist with research projects. There are also some paid internships. *Doctorates Awarded 1992-93:* 9.

UTAH

Brigham Young University. Department of Instructional Science, 201 MCKB, BYU, Provo, UT 84602. (801) 378-7072. Fax (801) 378-4017. E-mail paul_merrill@byu.edu. Paul F. Merrill, Prof., Chair. *Specializations:* M.S. and Ph.D. degrees are offered in instructional science and technology. In the Ph.D. program, students may specialize in instructional design, research and evaluation, instructional psychology, literacy education, or second language acquisition. *Features:* Course offerings include principles of learning, instructional design, assessing learning outcomes, evaluation in education, empirical inquiry in education, project and instructional resource management, quantitative reasoning, microcomputer materials production, naturalistic inquiry, and more. Students are required to participate in internships and projects related to development, evaluation, measurement, and research. *Admission Requirements:* General university requirements plus GRE entrance examination. Applications will not be considered without GRE scores. *Faculty:* 10 full-time. *Students:* 59. *Financial Assistance:* Internships and tuition waivers. *Doctorates Awarded 1992-93:* 1. Students agree to live by the BYU Honor Code.

*Utah State University. College of Education, Logan, UT 84322-2830. (801) 750-2694. Fax (801) 750-2693. Don C. Smellie, Prof., Chair, Dept. of Instructional Technology, College of Education. *Specializations:* Ph.D. in Educational Technology. Offered for individuals seeking to become professionally involved in instructional development in corporate education, public schools, community colleges, and universities. Teaching and research in higher education is another career avenue for graduates of the program. *Features:* The doctoral program is built on a strong master's and specialist's program in instructional technology. All doctoral students complete a core with the remainder of the course selection individualized, based upon career goals. *Admission Requirements:* 3.0 GPA, successful teaching experience or its equivalent, a combined verbal and quantitative score of 1,100 on the GRE, written recommendations, and a personal interview. *Faculty:* 9 full-time; 7 part-time. *Students:* 120 M.S./M.Ed. candidates; 5 Ed.S. candidates; 24 Ph.D. candidates. *Financial Assistance:* Approximately 18 to 26 assistantships (apply by June 1). *Doctorates Awarded 1991-92:* 3.

VIRGINIA

University of Virginia. Curry School of Education, Ruffner Hall, Charlottesville, VA 22903. (804) 924-7471. Fax (804) 924-7987. John B. Bunch, Assoc. Prof., Coord. Instructional Technology Program, Dept. of Educational Studies. *Specializations:* Ed.D. or Ph.D. degrees offered with focal areas in media production, interactive multimedia, and K-12 educational technologies. For specific degree requirements, write to the address above or refer to the UVA *Graduate Record. Faculty:* 3 full-time. *Doctorates Awarded 1992-93:* 3.

*Virginia Polytechnic Institute and State University. College of Education, Blacksburg, VA 24061-0313. (703) 231-5598. Fax (703) 231-3717. Thomas M. Sherman, Prog. Area Leader, Instructional Systems Development, Curriculum and Instruction. *Specializations:* Ed.D. and Ph.D. in Instructional Technology. Preparation for education, business, and industry. *Features:* Areas of emphasis are instructional design, educational computing, evaluation, and media management. Facilities include 70 computer lab microcomputers (IBM, Macintosh), interactive video, speech synthesis, and telecommunications. *Admission Requirements:* 3.3 GPA for master's degree, interview, three letters of recommendation, transcripts of previous academic work. *Faculty:* 8 full-time; 5 part-time. *Students:* 10 full-time; 8 part-time. *Financial*

Assistance: 10 assistantships, tuition scholarships, and contracts with other agencies. *Doctorates Awarded 1991-92:* 1.

WASHINGTON

University of Washington. College of Education, Seattle, WA 98195. (206) 543-1877. Fax (206) 543-8439. E-mail billwinn@u.washington.edu. William D. Winn, Prof. of Education, College of Education. *Specializations:* Ph.D. and Ed.D. for individuals in business, industry, higher education, public schools, and organizations concerned with education or communication (broadly defined). *Features:* Emphasis on instructional design as a process of making decisions about the shape of instruction; additional focus on research and development in such areas as message design (especially graphics and diagrams); electronic information systems; interactive instruction via videodisc, videotex, and computers. *Admission Requirements:* GRE scores, letters of reference, transcripts, personal statement, master's degree or equivalent in field appropriate to the specialization, 3.5 GPA in master's program, two years of successful professional experience and/or experience related to program goals. *Faculty:* 2 full-time; 3 part-time. *Students:* 12 full-time; 32 part-time. *Financial Assistance:* Assistantships awarded competitively and on basis of program needs; other assistantships available depending on grant activity in any given year. *Doctorates Awarded 1992-93:* 2.

WEST VIRGINIA

*West Virginia University. College of Human Resources and Education, Morgantown, WV 26506. (304) 293-3803. Fax (304) 293-7300. David McCrory Prof., Chair; George Maughan, Coord., Technology Education, Communication and Information Systems Sequence of Study. *Specializations:* M.A. and Ed.D. degree programs in history of technical development, research, college teaching, instructional systems design, instructional development, and communication and information systems. *Admission Requirements:* GRE and Miller Analogies Test, minimum GPA 3.0. *Faculty:* 4 full-time; 2 part-time. *Students:* 10 full-time; 6 part-time. *Financial Assistance:* Two teaching assistantships, three research assistantships. *Doctorates Awarded 1991-92:* 3.

WISCONSIN

University of Wisconsin-Madison. School of Education, Madison, WI 53706. (608) 263-4670. Michael Streibel, Prof., Dept. of Curriculum and Instruction, School of Education. *Specializations:* Ph.D. programs to prepare college and university faculty. *Features:* The program is coordinated with media operations of the university. Traditional instructional technology courses are processed through a social, cultural, and historical frame of reference. Current curriculum emphasizes communication, perception, and cognitive theories, critical cultural studies, and theories of textual analysis and instructional development. Strength in small-format video production and computers. *Admission Requirements:* Previous experience in instructional technology preferred, previous teaching experience, minimum 3.0 GPA on last 60 undergraduate credits, acceptable scores on GRE for Ph.D., and a minimum 3.0 GPA on all graduate work. (Note: Exceptions may be made on some of these requirements if all others are acceptable.) *Faculty:* 3 full-time; 1 part-time. *Students:* 23. *Financial Assistance:* A few stipends of approximately $1,000 a month for 20 hours of work per week; other media jobs are also available.

Master's Degree and Six-Year Programs
in Instructional Technology

During the fall semester of 1993, an inquiry-questionnaire was sent to the program chairs or their representatives for the 192 programs listed in the 1993 yearbook. Responses were received from 122 of the programs, three of which notified us that the programs had been discontinued. Information that was updated in 1993 is also included in this edition for 28 additional programs, which are indicated by an asterisk (*) before the name of the institution. Forty-two programs for which no information has been received since 1992 or before have been dropped from this listing.

Each entry in the directory contains as much of the following information as is available: (1) name and mailing address of the institution; (2) name, academic rank, and title of program head or the name of a contact person; (3) name of the administrative unit offering the program; (4) minimum degree requirements; (5) number of full-time and part-time faculty; and (6) number of students who graduated with master's degrees from the program in 1993 or during the one-year period between 1 July 1992 and 30 June 1993. The availability of six-year specialist/certificate programs in instructional technology and related media is indicated where appropriate following the description of the master's program.

Several institutions appear in both this list and the list of graduate programs in educational computing, either because their computer technology programs are offered separately from the educational/instructional technology programs, or because they are separate components of the overall educational technology program.

To ensure completeness of this directory, considerable effort has been expended. However, readers who know of either new programs or omissions are encouraged to provide information to the publisher who, in turn, will follow up on them for the next edition of *EMTY*. Information on any programs that have been discontinued would also be most welcome.

Individuals who are interested in any of these graduate programs are encouraged to make direct contact with the head of the program to obtain the most recent information available.

Institutions in this section are arranged alphabetically by state.

ALABAMA

Alabama State University. Library Education Media, School of Education, P.O. Box 271, Montgomery, AL 36195. (205) 293-4107. Fax (205) 241-7192. Katie R. Bell, Ph.D. Coord., Library Education Media, School of Education. *Specializations:* M.Ed., AA Certification, and Ed.S., preparation for K-12 school media programs. *Degree Requirements:* 36 semester hours; thesis required for Ed.S.; 300-clock-hour practicum (100 each in elementary, high school, and other library settings); research project required for M.Ed. and AA Certification. *Faculty:* 2 part-time. *Students:* 1 full-time; 21 part-time. *Financial Assistance:* Assistantships available for full-time students. *Master's Degrees Awarded 1 July 1992-30 June 1993:* 5. An advanced certificate program is available (see Specializations).

Auburn University. Educational Foundations, Leadership, and Technology, 2084 Haley Center, Auburn, AL 36849. (205) 844-4291. Fax (205) 844-5785. Susan H. Bannon, Coord., Educational Media. *Specializations:* School Library Media Specialist Certification, Instructional Design Specialist. The Instructional Design program has a concentration in computers and interactive technologies. *Degree Requirements:* School Library Media: 48 quarter hours minimum with 32 qtr. hrs. in educational media required; 8 qtr. hrs. in educational media prerequisites. Instructional Design: 48 qtr. hrs. minimum. *Faculty:* 20 full-time; 14 part-time. *Students:* 5 full-time; 28 part-time. *Financial Assistance:* Graduate assistantships. *Master's degrees awarded 1 July 1992-30 June 1993:* 10. The school also offers a sixth-year program only for school library media specialist.

Jacksonville State University. Instructional Media Division, Jacksonville, AL 36265. (205) 782-5011. Martha Merrill, Coord., Dept. of Educational Resources, Instructional Media Div. *Specializations:* M.S. in Education with emphasis on instructional media. *Minimum Degree Requirements:* 33 semester hours including 24 in library media; thesis optional. *Faculty:* 2 full- and part-time. *Students:* 30 full- and part-time. *Master's Degrees Awarded 1 July 1992-30 June 1993:* Data not reported.

University of Alabama. School of Library and Information Studies, Tuscaloosa, AL 35487-0252. (205) 348-4610. Fax (205) 348-3746. Philip M. Turner, Prof., Dean. *Specializations:* M.L.S., Ed.S., M.F.A., Ph.D. *Minimum Degree Requirements:* M.L.S., 36 semester hours, no thesis; Ed.S., 30 semester hours, no thesis; M.F.A., 48 semester hours, creative project; Ph.D., 48 semester hours, dissertation. *Faculty:* 11 full-time; 3 part-time. *Students:* 120 full-time; 100 part-time. *Financial Assistance:* 21 graduate assistantships. *Master's Degrees Awarded 1 July 1992-30 June 1993:* 64. The school also offers a six-year specialist degree program in instructional technology.

University of South Alabama. College of Education, 307 University Blvd., Mobile, AL 36688. (205) 460-6201. Fax (205) 460-7830. Richard L. Daughenbaugh, Prof., Dept. of Behavioral Studies and Educational Technology, College of Education. *Specializations:* M.Ed. program in Educational Media for state school library media certification; M.S. program in Instructional Design for employment in business, industry, the military, etc.; the Ed.S. in Educational Media leads to higher certification in library media. *Minimum Degree Requirements:* 58 quarter hours including 42 in media; thesis optional. *Faculty:* 3 full- and part-time. *Students:* 51 full- and part-time. *Financial Assistance:* Assistantships. *Master's Degrees Awarded 1 July 1992-30 June 1993:* Data not reported. The school also offers a six-year specialist degree program in Instructional Technology for the improvement of teaching.

ARIZONA

Arizona State University. Educational Media and Computers, Education, FMC Payne 146, Tempe, AZ 85287-0111. (602) 965-7192. Fax (602) 965-8887. Gary G. Bitter, Coord., Educational Media and Computers. *Specialization:* Master's degree. *Minimum Degree Requirements:* 33 semester hours, including 21 hours educational media and computers, 9 hours education, 3 hours outside program, 3-hour practicum/internship required, comprehensive exam required. *Faculty:* 7 full-time. *Students:* 104 full-time; 42 part-time. *Financial Assistance:* Assistantships. *Master's Degrees Awarded 1 July 1992-30 June 1993:* 24.

Arizona State University. Learning and Instructional Technology, FPE-0611, ASU, Tempe, AZ 85287-0611. (602) 965-3384. Fax (602) 965-0300. Nancy Archer, Admissions Secy., contact person. *Specializations:* M.A. in Learning, M.Ed. in Instructional Technology. *Minimum Degree Requirements:* 30 semester hours; comprehensive exam required; M.A. requires thesis. *Faculty:* 5. *Students:* 40. *Financial Assistance:* Graduate assistantships available for qualified applicants. *Master's Degrees Awarded 1 July 1992-30 June 1993:* 15.

University of Arizona. School of Library Science. 1515 E. First St., Tucson, AZ 85719. (602) 621-3565. Fax (602) 621-3279. C. D. Hurt, Prof. and Dir., School of Library Science. *Specialization:* Master's degree. *Minimum Degree Requirements:* 36 graduate semester hours including 12 hours of core courses and a computer proficiency requirement; comprehensive required; thesis optional. *Faculty:* 7. *Master's Degrees Awarded 1992 Calendar Year:* 74.

ARKANSAS

Arkansas Tech University. School of Education, Russellville, AR 72801. (501) 968-0434. Fax (501) 964-0811. Connie Zimmer, Asst. Prof., Coord., Master of Instructional Technology. *Specializations:* M.Ed. in Instructional Technology, six-year program. *Features:* Program includes Library Media Education, Training Program, Media Production, Computer Education, and Technology Coordinator. *Minimum Degree Requirements:* 36 credit hours for M.Ed., thesis optional, practicum available. *Faculty:* 1 full-time, 3 part-time. *Students:* 2 full-time, 50 part-time. *Financial Assistance:* Graduate assistantships available. *Master's Degrees Awarded 1 July 1992-30 June 1993:* 10. ATU is located off I-40 between Little Rock and Fort Smith, AR, in what is known as the Arkansas River Valley.

University of Central Arkansas. Educational Media/Library Science Department, Campus Box 4918, Conway, AR 72035. (501) 450-5463. Fax (501) 450-5468. Selvin W. Royal, Prof., Chair, Applied Academic Technologies. *Specializations:* M.S. Educational Media/Library Science: Track 1—School Library Media, Track 2—Public Information Agencies, Track 3—Media Information Studies. *Minimum Degree Requirements:* 36 semester hours, optional thesis, practicum (for Track 1), professional research paper. *Faculty:* 5 full-time; 3 part-time. Students: 8 full-time; 25 part-time. *Financial Assistance:* 3 to 4 graduate assistantships each year. *Master's Degrees Awarded 1 July 1992-30 June 1993:* Data not reported. Advanced certificate program is available for Track 1 to a Master's School Library Media Specialist.

CALIFORNIA

*California State University-Chico. College of Communication and Education, Chico, CA 95929-0504. (916) 898-5367. Fax (916) 898-4345. John Ittelson, Prof., Advisor, Instructional Technology Prog. *Specializations:* M.A. in Information and Communication Studies, Instructional Technology. *Minimum Degree Requirements:* 30 semester hours; thesis or project required. *Faculty:* 3 full-time. *Students:* 10 full-time. *Master's Degrees Awarded 1 July 1991-30 June 1992:* 5.

*California State University-Dominguez Hills. School of Education, Carson, CA 90747. (310) 516-3524. Fax (310) 516-3518. Peter Desberg, Prof., Coord., Computer-Based Education Program. *Specializations:* M.A., Certificate in Computer-Based Education. *Minimum Degree Requirements:* 30 semester hours including a master's project; 15 hours for the certificate. *Faculty:* 4 full-time. *Students:* 90 full-time and part-time. *Master's Degrees Awarded 1 July 1991-30 June 1992:* 15. An advanced certificate program is available.

California State University-Los Angeles. School of Education, Los Angeles, CA 90032-8143. (213) 343-4346; (213) 343-4330. Fax (213) 343-4318. James H. Wiebe, Prof., Div. of Educational Foundations, School of Education. *Specialization:* M.A. *Minimum Degree Requirements:* 45 quarter hours including 33 in media, including 2 options in the M.A. degree program: (1) computer education, and (2) instructional media and design. *Admission Requirements:* B.A. or B.S., 2.75 GPA, GRE not required. *Faculty:* 6 full-time. *Students:* 30. *Financial Assistance*: Contact Student Financial Services Office at (213) 343-3240 for information. *Master's Degrees Awarded 1993:* 20.

*California State University-Northridge. Department of Radio-TV-Film, 18111 Nordhoff St., Northridge, CA 91330. Lili Berks, Grad. Coord., LSUN, Dept. of Radio-Television-Film. *Specializations:* M.A. with emphasis in Screenwriting or Film/TV Theory and Criticism; M.A. in Corporate Educational Media; M.A. in Media Management. *Minimum Degree Requirements:* 30 semester hours, thesis/project for screenwriting, comprehensive exam or thesis option for theory/criticism. *Faculty:* 12 full- and part-time. *Students:* 30 full- and part-time. *Master's Degrees Awarded 1 July 1991-30 June 1992:* 4.

California State University-San Bernardino. 5500 University Parkway, San Bernardino, CA 92407. (909) 880-5677. (909) 880-7011. E-mail rsantiag@wiley.csusb.edu or rsantiag@mcvax.csusb.edu. Dr. Rowena Santiago, Prog. Coord. *Specializations:* M.A. The program has two emphases: video production and computer application. These emphases allow students to choose courses related to the design and creation of video products or courses involving lab and network operation of advanced microcomputer applications. *Minimum Degree Requirements:* 48 units including a master's project (33 units completed in residence); GPA of 3.0 (B), grades of "C" (2) or better in all courses. *Faculty:* 4 full-time. *Students:* 48 part-time, 31 of which have been classified. *Master's Degrees Awarded September 1992-June 1993:* 3. Advanced certificate programs in Computer Technology and in Educational Technology are available.

San Diego State University. Educational Technology, San Diego, CA 92182-0311. (619) 594-6718. E-mail harrison@vesvax.snsu.edu. Patrick Harrison, Prof., Chair, Dept. of Educational Technology. *Specialization:* Master's degree in Educational Technology with specializations in Computers in Education, Workforce Education and Lifelong Learning. *Minimum*

Degree Requirements: 36 semester hours including 6 prerequisite hours, GRE combined total 950 Verbal and Quantitative scores. *Faculty:* 6 full-time. *Students:* 110. *Financial Assistance:* Graduate Assistantships. *Master's Degrees Awarded 1993:* 40. The Educational Technology Department participates in a College of Education joint doctoral program with The Claremont Graduate School.

San Francisco State University. School of Education, Department of Instructional Technologies, 1600 Holloway Ave., San Francisco, CA 94132. (415) 338-1509. Fax (415) 338-7019. Eugene Michaels, Chair & Prof. *Specializations:* Master's degree with emphasis on Training and Designing Development, Instructional Computing, and Instructional and Interactive Video. *Minimum Degree Requirements:* 30 semester hours, field study thesis or project required. *Faculty:* 3 full-time; 4-7 part-time. *Students:* 160. *Master's Degrees Awarded 1 July 1992-30 June 1993:* Data not reported. The school also offers an 18-unit Graduate Certificate in Training Systems Development, which can be incorporated into the master's program.

*San Jose State University. Instructional Technology Program, School of Education, San Jose, CA 95192-0076. (408) 924-3620. Fax (408) 924-3713. Robert Stephens, Assoc. Prof., Chair, Instructional Technology Program, Educational Leadership and Development Div. *Minimum Degree Requirements:* 30 semester hours including 24 in instructional technology, 6 elective from outside program; competency exams in word processing, database management, and spreadsheets. *Faculty:* 7 full-time; 5 part-time. *Students:* 10 full-time; 300 part-time. *Master's Degrees Awarded 1 July 1991-30 June 1992:* 32. A cooperative doctorate (Ed.D.) with the University of California was scheduled to begin in January 1993.

United States International University. School of Education, 10455 Pomerado Rd., San Diego, CA 92131. (619) 693-8562. E-mail mfernand@sanac.usiu.edu. Dr. Maria Teresa Fernandez, Assoc. Prof., School of Education; Dr. Bill Hampton, contact person. *Specialization:* M.A. in Computer Education. *Features:* Tailored to meet computer literacy, problem solving, software applications, curriculum development, and integrating microcomputers into instructional needs of classroom teachers, curriculum coordinators, and district-level specialists from the United States and a number of international countries. *Minimum Degree Requirements:* 45 units, 9 courses. *Faculty:* 10. *Students:* 400. *Financial Aid:* Internships, minority scholarships, government loans. *Master's Degrees Awarded 1993:* 45. Dr. Richard Pfeiffer from Northwestern University will join the faculty in the spring of 1994. His field is developing expert systems. Dr. Hampton's field is Hypermedia and Learning.

University of California-Los Angeles. Graduate School of Education, Los Angeles, CA 90024-1521. (310) 825-8326; (310) 825-1838. Fax (310) 206-6293. Aimee Dorr, Prof., Learning and Instruction Specialization, Div. of Educational Psychology, Graduate School of Education. *Specialization:* M.A. only. *Minimum Degree Requirements:* 36 quarter units, pass written comprehensive exam or complete research thesis. *Faculty:* 4 full-time; 2 part-time. *Students:* 10-15 in M.A., Ph.D., and Ed.D. programs. *Financial Assistance:* Fellowships, loans, resident advisors. *Master's Degrees Awarded 1993:* 3.

University of Southern California. Instructional Technology, Division of Curriculum and Instruction, Los Angeles, CA 90007-0031. (213) 740-3476. Fax (213) 746-8142. Ed Kazlauskas, Prof., Chair, Dept. of Curriculum and Teaching, School of Education. *Specialization:* Master's degree. *Minimum Degree Requirements:* 31 semester hours, thesis optional. *Faculty:* 5 full-time; 1 part-time. *Students:* 1 full-time; 9 part-time. *Master's Degrees Awarded 1 July 1992-30 June 1993:* 3.

COLORADO

*University of Colorado-Denver. Instructional Technology Program, School of Education, Denver, CO 80217-3364. (303) 556-4881. Fax (303) 556-4822. David H. Jonassen, Prof. and Chair, Instructional Technology Program, School of Education. *Specialization:* Master's degree. *Minimum Degree Requirements:* For several tracks, including instructional computing, corporate training and development, library/media and instructional technology, 36 semester hours including comprehensive; project or internship required. *Faculty:* 9 full-time; 1 part-time. *Master's Degrees Awarded:* 38.

University of Northern Colorado. College of Education, Greeley, CO 80639. (303) 351-2687. Fax (303) 351-2312. Edward F. Caffarella, Prof., College of Education. *Specializations:* M.A. in Educational Technology; M.A. in Educational Media. *Minimum Degree Requirements:* 36 semester hours; comprehensive exam. *Faculty:* 5 full-time; 2 part-time. *Students:* 6 full-time; 86 part-time. *Financial Assistance:* Graduate assistantships and loans. *Master's Degrees Awarded 1 July 1992-30 June 1993:* 25. Ph.D. program is also offered.

CONNECTICUT

Fairfield University. Graduate School of Education and Allied Professions, Fairfield, CT 06430. (203) 254-4000, ext. 2697. Fax (203) 254-4087. Dr. Ibrahim M. Hefzallah, Prof., Co-Dir. of Media/Educational Technology Program; Dr. John Schurdak, Assoc. Prof., Co-Dir., Computers in Education/Educational Technology Program. *Specializations:* M.A. in Media/Educational Technology (includes instructional development, television production, or a customized course of study); Computers in Education. *Minimum Degree Requirements:* 33 semester hours and comprehensive exam; C.A.S., 30 credits beyond the M.A. and research project at the end. *Faculty:* 2 full-time; 9 part-time. *Students:* 60 part-time. *Financial Assistance:* Work study, graduate assistantships. *Master's Degrees Awarded 1 July 1992-30 June 1993:* 10. A Certificate of Advanced Studies in Media/Educational Technology is available, which includes instructional development, television production, and media management; customized course of study also available.

Southern Connecticut State University. School of Library Science and Instructional Technology, 501 Crescent St., New Haven, CT 06515. (203) 397-4530. Fax (203) 397-4677. Nancy Disbrow, Chair, School of Library Science and Instructional Technology. *Specializations:* M.S. in Instructional Technology; Sixth-Year Professional Diploma Library-Information Studies (student may select area of specialization in instructional technology). *Minimum Degree Requirements:* For instructional technology only, 30 semester hours including 21 in media with comprehensive examination; 36 hours without examination. For sixth year: 30 credit hours with 6 credit hours of core requirements, 9-15 credit hours in specialization. *Faculty:* 1 full-time. *Students:* 37 full- and part-time in M.S./IT program. *Financial Assistance:* Graduate assistantship: salary $1,800 per semester; assistants pay tuition and a general university fee sufficient to defray cost of student accident insurance. *Master's Degrees Awarded 1 July 1992-30 June 1993:* 1. The school also offers a Professional Diploma in Library Information Studies; students may select instructional technology as area of specialization.

DISTRICT OF COLUMBIA

Gallaudet University. School of Education, 800 Florida Ave. NE, Washington, DC 20002-3625. (202) 651-5535 (voice or TDD). Fax (202) 651-5710. E-mail renomeland@gallua.bitnet. Ronald E. Nomeland, Prof., Chair, Dept. of Educational Technology. *Specializations:* M.S. in Special Education/Deafness with specialization in Educational Computing, Instructional Design, and Media Product Development. *Features:* Combines educational technology skills with study in special education and deafness to prepare graduates for positions in programs serving deaf and other disabled learners as well as in regular education programs, or in government and industry. *Minimum Degree Requirements:* 36 semester hours, including 26 in educational media and a comprehensive exam; optional practicum. *Faculty:* 3 full-time; 1 part-time. *Students:* 15. *Financial Assistance:* Partial tuition waiver; graduate assistantships. *Master's Degrees Awarded 1 July 1992-30 June 1993:* 6.

FLORIDA

*Barry University. School of Education, 11300 Northeast Second Ave., Miami Shores, FL 33161. (305) 899-3608. Fax (305) 899-3630. Sister Evelyn Piche, Dean, School of Education; Joel S. Levine, Prof. and Dir. of Computer Education Programs. *Specializations:* Master's degree and Education Specialist degree in Computer Science Education and Computer Applications in Education. *Minimum Degree Requirements:* Master's degree—36 semester credit hours including directed research; Education Specialist degree—36 semester hours including directed research and seminar on Computer-Based Technology in Education. *Faculty:* 4 full-time; 6 part-time. *Students:* 5 full-time; 5 part-time. *Financial Assistance:* Assistantships, discounts to educators. *Master's Degrees Awarded 1 July 1991-30 June 1992:* 30.

Florida State University. Department of Educational Research, College of Education, Stone Bldg., Tallahassee, FL 32306. (904) 644-8785. Fax (904) 644-8776. Dr. Walter Dick, Prof. and Prog. Leader, Instructional Systems Prog. *Specialization:* M.S. in Instructional Systems. *Minimum Degree Requirements:* 36 semester hours; 2-4-hour internship required; written comprehensive exam. *Faculty:* 6 full-time; 4 part-time. *Students:* 50, most of them full-time. *Financial Assistance:* Some graduate research assistantships on faculty grants and contracts; university fellowships for high GRE students. *Master's Degrees Awarded 1 July 1992-30 June 1993:* 22. A specialist degree program is now being offered for students with or without the M.S. in Instructional Systems.

Nova Southeastern University. Fischler Center for the Advancement of Education, 3301 College Ave., Fort Lauderdale, FL 33314. (800) 986-3223. Fax (305) 476-4764. Johanne Peck, M.S. and Ed.D. Programs for Teachers. *Specializations:* M.S. and Ed.S. in Educational Media. Master's degree program based on modules. *Minimum Degree Requirements:* 36 semester hours, including a practicum experience. *Faculty:* 2 full-time. *Students:* 56. *Financial Aid:* NDSL; Federal Stafford Loan, Unsubsidized Federal Stafford Loan, SLS. *Master's Degrees Awarded 1982-93:* 19.

*University of Central Florida. College of Education, Orlando, FL 32816. (407) 275-2153. Fax (407) 823-5135. Richard Cornell, Instructional Systems; Donna Baumbach, Educational Media, Dept. of Educational Services, Educational Media/Instructional Technology Programs, College of Education. *Specializations:* M.A. in Instructional Systems; M.Ed. in Educational Media. *Minimum Degree Requirements:* 36-45 semester hours; practicum required in both programs; thesis, project, or additional coursework required. *Students:* 10 full-time; 108 part-time. *Faculty:* 32 full-time; 5 part-time. *Financial Assistance:* Graduate assistantships in department and college. *Master's Degrees Awarded 1 July 1991-30 June 1992:* 30. A doctorate in C&I with an emphasis in Instructional Technology is also offered.

University of Florida. Educational Media and Instructional Design, Gainesville, FL 32611. (904) 392-0705. Fax (904) 392-9193. Lee J. Mullally, Assoc. Prof. and Prog. Leader, Educational Media and Instructional Design. *Specialization:* Master's degree. *Minimum Degree Requirements:* 36 semester hours including 24 in educational media and instructional design; thesis optional. *Faculty:* 2 full-time. *Students:* 20 full- and part-time. *Master's Degrees Awarded 1 July 1992-30 June 1993:* 6. The Education Specialist Program is an advanced degree program and has the same requirements for admission as the Ph.D. and Ed.D. programs.

University of Miami. School of Education and Allied Professions, Coral Gables, FL 33124. The educational technology program has been discontinued.

University of South Florida. School of Library and Information Science, Tampa, FL 33620. (813) 974-3520. Fax (813) 974-6840. Kathleen de la Peña McCook, Prof., Dir., School of Library and Information Science. *Specialization:* Master's degree. *Minimum Degree Requirements:* 36 semester hours, thesis optional. *Faculty:* 7 full-time; 5 part-time. *Master's Degrees Awarded 1991-92:* 106.

GEORGIA

Georgia Southern University. College of Education, Statesboro, GA 30460. (912) 681-5307. Fax (912) 681-5093. Jack A. Bennett, Prof., Dept. of Educational Leadership, Technology, and Research. *Specialization:* M.Ed. *Minimum Degree Requirements:* 60 quarter credit hours, including a varying number of hours of media for individual students. *Financial Assistance:* See graduate catalog for general financial aid information. *Faculty:* 3 full-time. *Master's Degrees Awarded 1992-93:* Data not reported. The school also offers a six-year specialist degree program.

*Georgia State University. College of Education, Atlanta, GA 30303-3083. (404) 651-2510. Fax (404) 651-2546. Francis T. Atkinson, Coord., Instructional Technology Programs, Dept. of Curriculum and Instruction, School of Education. *Specialization:* M.S. in Instructional Technology. *Minimum Degree Requirements:* 60 quarter hours; comprehensive exam; internship required. *Faculty:* 2 full-time; 6 part-time. *Students:* 10 full-time; 65 part-time. *Financial Assistance:* Assistantships, paid internships, student loans and grants. *Master's Degrees Awarded 1 July 1991-30 June 1992:* 6. An advanced certificate program in Library/Media is available.

University of Georgia. College of Education, 607 Aderhold Hall, Athens, GA 30602. (706) 542-3810. Fax (706) 542-4032. Jame R. Okey, Prof., Chair, Dept. of Instructional Technology, College of Education. *Specializations:* Master's degree in Instructional Technology; master's degree in Computer-Based Education. *Minimum Degree Requirements:* 60 or more quarter hours in each master's degree; both have an oral examination and/or portfolio presentation. *Faculty:* 11 full-time. *Students:* 20 full-time; 120 part-time. *Financial Assistance:* Limited assistance. *Master's Degrees Awarded 1993:* 5 Computer-Based Education; 19 Instructional

Technology. The school also offers a 45-hour, six-year specialist degree program in instructional technology and a doctoral program.

Valdosta State University. School of Education, 1500 N. Patterson St., Valdosta, GA 31698. (912) 333-5927. Fax (912) 333-7167. E-mail cprice@grits.valdosta.peachnet.edu. Catherine B. Price, Assoc. Prof., Dept. of Instructional Technology. *Specializations:* Master's degree with two tracks: Library/Media or Technology Applications. The program has a strong emphasis on technology. *Minimum Degree Requirements:* 65 quarter credits. *Faculty:* 4 full-time; 2 part-time. *Students:* 112. *Financial Assistance:* Variety, including graduate assistantships. *Master's Degrees Awarded 1993:* 13. A six-year program is pending approval.

West Georgia College. Department of Media Education, Education Center, Carrollton, GA 30118. (404) 836-6558. Fax (404) 836-6729. Price Michael, Prof., Chair, Media Education Dept. *Specializations:* M.Ed. with specialization in Media and add-on certification for students with master's degrees in other disciplines. *Minimum Degree Requirements:* 60 quarter hours minimum, including practicum. Additional hours may be required for state certification. *Faculty:* 3 full-time. *Students:* 3 full-time; 126 part-time. *Financial Assistance:* One graduate assistantship for the department. *Master's Degrees Awarded 1 July 1992-30 June 1993:* 15. The school also offers a six-year specialist degree program.

HAWAII

University of Hawaii-Manoa. Educational Technology Department, 1776 University Ave., Honolulu, HI 96822. (808) 956-7671. Fax (808) 956-3905. Geoffrey Z. Kucera, Prof., Chair, Educational Technology Dept. *Specializations:* M.Ed. in Educational Technology with specialization in Instructional Development and in Computer Technology. *Minimum Degree Requirements:* 39 semester hours (27 in educational technology, 3 in practicum, 3 in internship, 6 in electives), thesis and non-thesis available. *Faculty:* 4 full-time; 3 part-time. *Students:* 4 full-time; 12 part-time. *Financial Assistance:* Consideration given to meritorious second-year students for tuition waivers and scholarship applications. *Master's Degrees Awarded 1 July 1992-30 June 1993:* 6.

IDAHO

Boise State University. Instructional & Performance Technology, 1910 University Drive, Boise, ID 83725. (208) 385-1312. Fax (208) 385-4081. E-mail aiteisle@idbsu.idbsu.edu. Dr. Mark E. Eisley, Dir., Instructional/Performance Technology *Specialization:* M.S. in Instructional & Performance Technology available in a traditional campus setting or via computer-mediated conferencing to students located anywhere on the North American continent. The program has been fully accredited by the Northwest Association of Schools and Colleges and is the recipient of an NUCEA award for Outstanding Credit Program offered by distance education methods. *Minimum Degree Requirements:* 33 semester hours in instructional and performance technology and related coursework; project/thesis required or non-thesis option available (included in 33 credit hours). *Faculty:* 2 full-time; 5 part-time. *Students:* Approx. 125. *Financial Assistance:* DANTES provides funding to some military personnel, and low-interest student loans are available to those who are eligible. *Master's Degrees Awarded 1993:* 33.

ILLINOIS

Chicago State University. Department of Library Science and Communications Media, Chicago, IL 60628. (312) 995-2278. Janice Bolt, Prof., Chair, Dept. of Library Science and Communications Media. *Specialization:* Master's degree. Program has been approved by NCATE: AECT/AASL through accreditation of University College of Education; State of Illinois Entitlement Program. *Minimum Degree Requirements:* 36 semester hours; thesis optional. *Faculty:* 4 full-time. *Master's Degrees Awarded 1992-93:* 45.

Governors State University. College of Arts and Sciences, University Park, IL 60466. (708) 534-5000, ext. 2432. Fax (708) 534-7895. Michael Stelnicki, Prof., Instructional and Training Technology, College of Arts and Sciences. *Specializations:* M.A. in Communication with I and IT major. *Features:* Emphasizes three professional areas—Instructional Design, Performance Analysis, and Design Logistics. *Minimum Degree Requirements:* 36 credit hours (trimester), all in instructional and performance technology; internship/advanced field project required. Metropolitan Chicago area based. *Faculty:* 2 full-time. *Students:* 45 part-time. *Master's Degrees Awarded 1992-93:* 10.

*Northeastern Illinois University. 5500 N. St. Louis, Chicago, IL 60625. (312) 794-2958. Fax (312) 794-6243. Christine C. Swarm, Prof., Coord. of Instructional Media Program. *Specializations:* Master's degrees with Educational Computer area of concentration or School Media Center online courses. *Faculty:* 2 full-time; 1.5 part-time. *Students:* 42 part-time. *Master's Degrees Awarded 1 July 1991-30 June 1992:* 22.

Northern Illinois University. Instructional Technology Faculty, LEPS Department, DeKalb, IL 60115. (815) 753-0464. Fax (815) 753-9371. Dr. Gary L. McConeghy, Chair, Instructional Technology. *Specializations:* M.S.Ed. in Instructional Technology with specializations in Instructional Design, Microcomputers, or Media Administration. *Minimum Degree Requirements:* 39 semester hours, practicum and internship highly recommended. *Faculty:* 5 full-time; 5 part-time. *Students:* 106 part-time. *Financial Assistance:* Assistantships available at times in various departments. *Master's Degrees Awarded 1 July 1992-30 June 1993:* 24.

Rosary College. Graduate School of Library and Information Science, River Forest, IL 60305. (708) 524-6850. Fax (708) 524-6657. Michael E. D. Koenig, Dean. *Specialization:* Master of Library and Information Science. *Minimum Degree Requirements:* 36 semester hours. A particularly relevant area of concentration is the School Library Media Program which, upon completion of the degree and with required education courses, meets the requirements for an Illinois Media Specialist (K-12) Certificate. *Faculty:* 11 full-time; 16 part-time. *Students:* 420 (204 FTE). *Financial Assistance:* Yes. *Master's Degrees Awarded 1 July 1992-30 June 1993:* 170. The school also offers post-master's certificate programs in Law Librarianship, Library Administration, and Technical Services, and several joint-degree programs.

*Southern Illinois University at Carbondale. College of Education, Carbondale, IL 62901-4610. (618) 536-2441. Fax (618) 453-1646. Billy G. Dixon, Chair, Dept. of Curriculum and Instruction. *Specializations:* M.S. in Education; specializations in Instructional Development and Computer-Based Instruction. *Features:* The ID program emphasizes nonschool (primarily corporate) learning environments. *Minimum Degree Requirements:* 32 semester hours plus thesis or 36 credit hours without thesis. *Faculty:* 6 full-time; 4 part-time. *Students:* 30 full-time; 45 part-time. *Financial Assistance:* Some graduate assistantships and scholarships available to qualified students. *Master's Degrees Awarded 1 July 1991-30 June 1992:* 11.

Southern Illinois University at Edwardsville. Instructional Technology Program, School of Education, Edwardsville, IL 62026-1125. (618) 692-3277. Charles Nelson, Coord., Dept. of Educational Leadership Program. *Specialization:* Master's degree with concentrations in Library/Media Specialist or Instructional Systems Design Specialist. *Minimum Degree Requirements:* 36 semester hours; thesis optional. *Faculty:* 6 part-time. *Master's Degrees Awarded 1992-93:* 18.

University of Illinois at Urbana-Champaign. College of Education, Champaign, IL 61820. (217) 244-3391. Fax (217) 244-4572. Graduate Programs Office, Dept. of Curriculum and Instruction, College of Education. *Specialization:* Master's degree. *Minimum Degree Requirements:* 32 semester hours with emphasis on Theory and Design of Interactive Instructional Systems, Educational Psychology, and Educational Policy Studies. *Faculty:* 15. *Students:* 20. *Financial Assistance:* Fellowships for very highly academically talented; assistantships for about 10-15 percent; some tuition waivers. *Master's Degrees Awarded 1 July 1992-30 June 1993:* 15. The school also offers a six-year specialist degree program in Instructional Technology.

University of Illinois at Urbana-Champaign. Department of Educational Psychology, 210 Education Bldg., 1310 S. Sixth St., Champaign, IL 61820. (217) 333-2245. Fax (217) 244-7620. E-mail cwest@uiuc.edu. Charles K. West, Prof., Div. of Learning and Instruction, Dept. of Educational Psychology. *Specializations:* M.A., M.S., and Ed.M. with emphasis in instructional psychology, instructional design, and educational computing. *Minimum Degree Requirements:* 8 units for Ed.M., 6 units and thesis for M.A. or M.S. *Faculty:* 17. *Students:* 11. *Financial Assistance:* Scholarships, research assistantships, and teaching assistantships available. *Master's Degrees Awarded 1993:* 0.

Western Illinois University. Media and Educational Technology, 37 Horrabin Hall, Macomb, IL 61455. (309) 298-1952. Fax (309) 298-2222. E-mail bo_barker@bgu.edu. Bruce O. Barker, Chair, Dept. of Media and Educational Technology. *Specialization:* Master's degree in Instructional Technology & Telecommunication. New program is now offered with emphasis in distance education, telecommunications, and instructional technology. *Minimum Degree Requirements:* 32 semester hours, thesis or practicum. *Faculty:* 6. *Students:* 12. *Financial Assistance:* Graduate and research assistantships, internships, residence hall assistants, veterans' benefits, and loans and part-time employment. *Master's Degrees Awarded in 1993:* New program.

INDIANA

Indiana State University. Media Technology, Terre Haute, IN 47809. (812) 237-2937. Fax (812) 237-4348. Dr. James E. Thompson, Prog. Coord., Dept. of Educational Foundations and Media Technology. *Specializations:* Master's degree; six-year Specialist Degree program in Instructional Technology. *Minimum Degree Requirements:* 32 semester hours, including 18 in media; thesis optional. *Faculty:* 5 full-time. *Students:* 15 full-time; 10 part-time. *Financial Assistance:* Assistantships, fellowships. *Master's Degrees Awarded 1 July 1993:* Data not reported. A six-year program is available.

Indiana University. School of Education, Bloomington, IN 47405. (812) 855-1791. Fax (812) 855-3044. Charles Reigeluth, Chair and Prof., Dept. of Instructional Systems Technology. For information on this program, see the article in this volume, "Preparing Instructional Technologists for the 21st Century," by James A. Pershing.

Purdue University. School of Education, W. Lafayette, IN 47907-1442. (317) 494-5673. Fax (317) 496-1622. James Russell, Prof., Educational Computing and Instructional Development, Dept. of Curriculum and Instruction. *Specializations:* Master's degree, Educational Specialist, and Ph.D. in Educational Computing and Instructional Development. Master's program started in 1982 and specialist and doctoral in 1985. *Admission Requirements:* GPA of 3.0 or better; 3 letters of recommendation; statement of personal goals; total score of 1,000 or more on GRE for Ph.D. admission. *Minimum Degree Requirements:* Master's—36 semester hours (15 in computer or instructional development, 9 in education, 12 unspecified); thesis optional. Specialist—60-65 semester hours (15-18 in computer or instructional development, 30-35 in education; thesis, internship, and practicum required). *Faculty:* 6 full-time. *Students:* 8 full-time; 10 part-time. *Financial Assistance:* Assistantships and fellowships. *Master's Degrees Awarded 1 July 1992-30 June 1993:* 8.

IOWA

Iowa State University. College of Education, Ames, IA 50011. (515) 294-6840. Fax (515) 294-9284. Michael Simonson and Roger Volker, Profs. and Coords., Curriculum and Instructional Technology (including media and computers). *Specialization:* M.S. in Curriculum and Instructional Technology. *Minimum Degree Requirements:* 30 semester hours; thesis required. *Faculty:* 3 full-time; 3 part-time. *Students:* 20 full-time; 20 part-time. *Financial Assistance:* 10 assistantships available. *Master's Degrees Awarded 1 July 1992-30 June 1993:* 10.

University of Iowa. College of Education, Iowa City, IA 52242. Lowell Schoer, Prof., Chair, Psychological and Quantitative Foundations. *Specialization:* Master's degree with concentrations in Classroom Instruction, Computer Applications, Instructional Development, Media Production, and Training and Human Resource Development. *Minimum Degree Requirements:* 35 semester hours of approved coursework (16 in core, 12 in specialization, 7 in electives). *Faculty:* 7. *Students:* 100 plus. *Financial Assistance:* Teaching, research, and production assistantships. *Master's Degrees Awarded 1993:* 15. A six-year program is available.

KANSAS

Emporia State University. School of Library and Information Management, Emporia, KS 66801. (316) 341-5203. Fax (316) 341-5997. E-mail mlhale@twsuvm. Martha L. Hale, Dean, School of Library and Information Management. *Specialization:* Master's of Library Science (ALA accredited program). *Features:* The program is also available in Colorado and other out-of-state sites. Video courses are being developed. *Minimum Degree Requirements:* 42 semester hours, comprehensive examination. *Faculty:* 12 full-time; 30 part-time. *Students:* Approx. 60 full-time; approx. 500 part-time in all sites. *Master's Degrees Awarded 1 July 1992-30 June 1993:* 98. The school also offers a School Library Certification program, which includes 27 hours of the MLS program.

Kansas State University. College of Education, Manhattan, KS 66506. (913) 532-5525. Fax (913) 532-7304. John Parmley, Chair, Secondary Education. *Specialization:* Master's degree in Instructional Design or Instructional Development. *Minimum Degree Requirements:* 30 semester hours, including 21 in media; thesis optional. *Faculty:* 3. *Students:* 25. *Financial Assistance:* Assistantships. *Master's Degrees Awarded 1993:* Data not reported.

KENTUCKY

University of Louisville. School of Education, Louisville, KY 40292. (502) 588-0609. Fax (502) 852-4563. E-mail crrude@ulkyvm.louisville.edu. Carolyn Rude-Parkins, contact person, Occupational Education. *Specialization:* M.Ed., Occupational Education Training and Development with Instructional Technology track. The program focuses on training and development for a business/industry audience; technology courses are appropriate for business or school audiences. *Minimum Degree Requirements:* 30 semester hours; thesis optional. *Faculty:* 5. *Students:* Data not reported. *Financial Assistance:* Graduate assistantships in the school. *Master's Degrees Awarded 1993:* 17 in training with 3 in technology track.

LOUISIANA

Louisiana State University. School of Library and Information Science, Baton Rouge, LA 70803. (504) 388-3158. Fax (504) 388-1465. Bert R. Boyce, Dean, Prof., School of Library and Information Science. *Specializations:* M.L.I.S., C.L.I.S. (post-master's certificate), Louisiana School Library Certification. *Minimum Degree Requirements:* M.L.I.S., 37 hours; comprehensive examination; one semester full-time residence; completion of degree program in five years. *Faculty:* 10 full-time. *Students:* 84 full-time; 83 part-time. *Financial Assistance:* A large number of graduate assistantships are available to qualified students. *Master's Degrees Awarded 1 July 1992-30 June 1993:* Data not reported. An advanced certificate program is available.

McNeese State University. Burton College of Education, Dept. of Administration, Supervision, and Educational Technology, P.O. Box 91815, Lake Charles, LA 70609-1815. (318) 475-5421. Fax (318) 475-5467. Dr. Virgie M. Dronet. *Specialization:* M.Ed. in Educational Technology with concentrations in educational technology, computer education, and instructional technology. *Minimum Degree Requirements:* 30 semester hours for educational technology or instructional technology, 36 hours for computer education. *Faculty:* 2 full-time; 5 part-time. *Students:* 24. *Financial Assistance:* 4 graduate assistantships per year (teaching and lab). *Master's Degrees Awarded 1 July 1992-30 June 1993:* 12. Advanced certificate programs are offered in Computer Literacy and Computer Education.

MARYLAND

The Johns Hopkins University. Center for Technology in Education, Division of Education, Baltimore, MD 21218. (410) 646-3000. Fax (410) 646-2310. Sarah McPherson, Coord., M.S. Technology for Educators, Ed.D. Technology for Special Education, Div. of Education. *Specialization:* Master's degree. *Minimum Degree Requirements:* 36 semester hours, 8 required courses in computer-related technology and media, with remaining courses being electives in other education areas. *Faculty:* 2 full-time; 8 part-time. *Master's Degrees Awarded 1993:* 12.

Towson State University. College of Education, Baltimore, MD 21204. (410) 830-2576. Gary W. Rosecrans, Assoc. Prof., Instructional Technology Prog., General Education Dept. *Specializations:* Master's degrees with concentrations available in Instructional Design and Development and School Library Media. *Minimum Degree Requirements:* 36 graduate semester hours without thesis; 33 graduate semester credits with thesis. *Faculty:* 5 full-time,

2 adjunct. *Financial Assistance:* Graduate assistantships, work-study, scholarships. *Master's Degrees Awarded 1993:* 12.

University of Maryland. College of Library and Information Services, 4105 Hornbake Library Bldg., South Wing, College Park, MD 20742-4345. (301) 405-2033. Fax (301) 314-9145. Ann E. Prentice, Dean and Prof. *Specialization:* Master's of Library Science, including specialization in school library media; Doctorate in Library and Information Services. *Minimum Degree Requirements:* 36 semester hours for MLS; thesis option. *Faculty:* 15 full-time; 9 part-time. *Students:* 251 MLS, 12 Ph.D. *Master's Degrees Awarded 1993:* 101 MLS, 3 Ph.D.

University of Maryland, Baltimore County (UMBC). Department of Education, 5401 Wilkens Ave., Baltimore, MD 21228. (410) 455-2310. Fax (410) 455-3986. Dr. Diane M. Lee, Coord. Grad. Progs. in Education. *Specializations:* Master's degrees in School Instructional Systems, Post-Baccalaureated Teacher Certification, English as a Second Language, Training in Business and Industry. *Minimum Degree Requirements:* 36 semester hours, including 18 in systems development for each program; an internship is required. *Faculty:* 13 full-time; 10 part-time. *Students:* 239 full-time; 289 part-time. *Master's Degrees Awarded 1993:* 61.

Western Maryland College. Department of Education, Main St., Westminster, MD 21157. (410) 857-2507. Fax (410) 857-2515. Mary H. Hackman, Acting Coord., Media/Library Science Program, Dept. of Education. *Specializations:* M.S. in Media/Library Science; Educational Media Generalist, Level II. *Minimum Degree Requirements:* 34 credit hours, including 19 in media and 6 in education; comprehensive examination. *Faculty:* 1 full-time; 7 part-time. *Students:* 120 full- and part-time. *Master's Degrees Awarded 1993:* 20.

MASSACHUSETTS

Boston University. School of Education, 605 Commonwealth Ave., Boston, MA 02215. (617) 353-3519. Fax (617) 353-3924. Gaylen B. Kelley, Prof., Prog. Dir. of Educational Media and Technology, Div. of Instructional Development; David Whittier, Dir., Instructional Materials Center. *Specialization:* Master's degree. *Minimum Degree Requirements:* 32 semester hours; thesis optional. *Faculty:* 1 full-time; 11 part-time. *Students:* 20. *Master's Degrees Awarded 1993:* 15. The school also offers a six-year specialist degree program Certificate of Advanced Graduate Specialization (C.A.G.S.) in Instructional Technology and a corporate training program. For general graduate admissions information, call the Graduate Admissions Office at (617) 353-4237.

Bridgewater State College. Library Media Program, Room L211, Maxwell Library Bldg., Bridgewater, MA 02325. (508) 697-1370. Fax (508) 697-1729. Richard Neubauer, Prof., Coord., Library Media Program. *Specialization:* M.Ed. in Library Media Studies, State Certification as a Library Media Specialist N-12. *Minimum Degree Requirements:* 36 semester hours; thesis and practicums required. *Faculty:* 2 full-time, 6 part-time. *Students:* 58 in degree program, 30 non-degree. *Financial Assistance:* Graduate assistantships, graduate internships. *Master's Degrees Awarded 1993:* 11. The school also offers a Certificate of Advanced Graduate Study in Educational Leadership. This is a fully integrated program of library science, technology, and teacher education that focuses on "cutting edge" technology.

*Harvard University. Graduate School of Education, Appian Way, Cambridge, MA 02138. (617) 495-9373. Fax (617) 495-9268. Gerry Lesser, Prof., Chair; Yesha Sivan, Coord., Technology in Education. *Specialization:* M.Ed. in Technology in Education. *Features:* The TIE program is a concentration within the Human Development and Psychology Department. Students focus on the interaction between technology (computers, television, etc.) and education (at any level). The program is designed to provide both a sound theoretical foundation and practical experience in areas related to effective use of educational technologies, with emphasis on educational design and research issues rather than technical production skills. *Minimum Degree Requirements:* Students must complete 8 courses per year: 1 core course, 3 technology-related courses, 2 human development courses, 2 electives. *Faculty:* 1 full-time; 7 part-time. *Students:* Approx. 30. *Financial Assistance:* Within the school's policy. *Master's Degrees Awarded 1 July 1991-30 June 1992:* 30. An advanced certificate program is available.

Simmons College. Graduate School of Library and Information Science, 300 The Fenway, Boston, MA 02115-5898. (617) 521-2801. Fax (617) 521-3192. Robert D. Stueart, Dean; Dr. James C. Baughman, Dir., Unified Media Specialist Prog. *Specializations:* M.S., specialist preparation for Unified Media Specialist Joint Degree (for Teacher Certification) with Education Department. *Features:* The program prepares individuals for a variety of careers—technology/media emphasis being only one. There are special programs for Unified Media Specialist and Archives Management with strengths in information science/systems, media management, etc. *Minimum Degree Requirements:* 36 semester hours; practicum/internship required for UMS; research projects, independent studies possible. *Faculty:* 13.5 full-time; 12 part-time. *Students:* 66 full-time; 374 part-time. *Financial Assistance:* Grants and scholarships are available. *Master's Degrees Awarded 1993:* Data not reported. A Doctor of Arts in Administration is also offered.

University of Massachusetts-Boston. Graduate College of Education, 100 Morrissey Blvd., Boston, MA 02125. (617) 287-7622 or 287-5980. Fax (617) 265-7173. Canice H. McGarry, Instructional Design Prog. *Specialization:* M.Ed. in Instructional Design; Graduate Certificate in Educational Technology (fall 1994). *Minimum Degree Requirements:* 36 semester hours; thesis or project required. *Faculty:* 1 full-time; 9 part-time. *Students:* 85 part-time. *Financial Assistance:* Graduate assistantships providing tuition plus stipend. *Master's Degrees Awarded 1993:* 26.

MICHIGAN

University of Michigan. Educational Studies, Ann Arbor, MI 48109. (313) 763-0612. Fax (313) 763-1229. Patricia Baggett, Assoc. Prof., Dept. of Educational Studies. *Specialization:* Master's degree, Computers in Education. *Minimum Degree Requirements:* 30 credit hours (trimester). *Faculty:* 1 full-time; 7 part-time. *Master's Degrees Awarded 1993:* 4.

Wayne State University. College of Education, Detroit, MI 48202. (313) 577-1728. Fax (313) 577-3606. Instructional Technology Prog., Div. of Administrative and Organizational Studies. Rita Richey, Prof. and Prog. Coord. *Specialization:* Master's degrees in Business and Human Services Training, K-12 Educational Technology. *Minimum Degree Requirements:* 36 semester hours, including required project; internship recommended. *Faculty:* 3 full-time; 5 part-time. *Master's Degrees Awarded 1993:* 47. The school also offers a six-year specialist degree program in Instructional Technology.

MINNESOTA

Mankato State University. Library Media Education, Mankato, MN 56002. (507) 389-5210. Fax (507) 389-5751. Frank Birmingham, Prof., Chair, Library Media Education. *Specialization:* Master's degree. *Minimum Degree Requirements:* 51 quarter hours, including 27 in media. *Faculty:* 4 full-time. *Master's Degrees Awarded 1993:* 20. The school also offers a six-year specialist degree program in Library Media Education.

St. Cloud State University. College of Education, St. Cloud, MN 56301-4498. (612) 255-2022. Fax (612) 255-4778. John G. Berling, Prof., Dir., Center for Information Media. *Specializations:* Master's degrees in Information Technologies, Educational Media, and Human Resources Development/Training. *Minimum Degree Requirements:* 51 quarter hours with thesis; 54 quarter hours, Plan B; 57 quarter hours, portfolio; 200-hour practicum is required for media generalist licensure—coursework applies to Educational Media master's program. *Faculty:* 30 full- and part-time. *Students:* 167 full- and part-time. *Master's Degrees Awarded 1993:* 24. The school also offers a 45-quarter-credit, six-year specialist degree.

*University of Minnesota. Curriculum and Instructional Systems, 130 Peik Hall, 159 Pillsbury Dr. SE, Minneapolis, MN 55455. (612) 624-2034. Fax (612) 626-7496. Gregory C. Sales, Prof., Chair, Curriculum and Instructional Systems. *Specializations:* M.A., M.Ed. *Minimum Degree Requirements:* 44 quarter hours, including 22 in Instructional Systems. A thesis is required for the M.A., a practicum for the M.Ed. *Faculty:* 4, 4 associates. *Master's Degrees Awarded 1 July 1991-30 June 1992:* 2 M.A., 10 M.Ed.

MISSISSIPPI

Jackson State University. Dept. of Educational Foundations and Leadership, P.O. Box 17175, Jackson, MS 39217-0175. This program has been discontinued.

University of Southern Mississippi. School of Library and Information Science, Box 5146, Hattiesburg, MS 39406-5146. (601) 266-4228. Fax (601) 266-5723. Joy M. Greiner, Assoc. Prof., Dir., School of Library and Information Science. *Specialization:* Master's degree; dual master's in Library Science and History. *Minimum Degree Requirements:* 38 semester hours, comprehensive required. *Faculty:* 6. *Students:* Data not reported. *Master's Degrees Awarded 1993:* 44.

MISSOURI

*Central Missouri State University. Department of Special Services and Instructional Technology, Warrensburg, MO 64093. (816) 543-8636. Fax (816) 543-4167. Kenneth Brookens, Prof., Instructional Technology. *Specialization:* Certification only; master's degree currently offered only in associated programs. *Minimum Degree Requirements:* 32 semester hours in master's degree programs in Administration and Supervision, Library Science, or Curriculum and Instruction; certification, 18 hours. *Faculty:* 2 full-time. *Financial Assistance:* Graduate assistantship. *Master's Degrees Awarded 1 July 1991-30 June 1992:* 0. The school also offers a certification program in learning resources through the Library Science program.

University of Missouri-Columbia. College of Education, 212 Townsend Hall, Columbia, MO 65211. (314) 882-3828. Fax (314) 884-5455. E-mail wedmanjf@mizzou1.missouri.edu. John F. Wedman, Assoc. Prof., Coord., Educational Technology Prog., Curriculum and Instruction Dept., College of Education. *Specialization:* Master's degree emphasizing instructional design, development, and evaluation. The program is rapidly moving into the areas of performance support systems and multimedia design, production, and application. *Minimum Degree Requirements:* 32 semester hours including 16 hours of upper-level graduate work. *Faculty:* 3 full-time, 4 part-time. *Students:* 15. *Financial Assistance:* Graduate assistantships with tuition waivers; numerous academic scholarships. *Master's Degrees Awarded 1993:* 8. An Education Specialist degree program is also available.

*University of Missouri-St. Louis. School of Education, St. Louis, MO 63121. (314) 553-5944. Donald R. Greer, Assoc. Prof., Coord. of Educational Technology, Dept. of Educational Studies, School of Education. *Specialization:* Master's degree. *Minimum Degree Requirements:* 32 semester hours, including 18 in media. *Faculty:* 1 full-time; 1 part-time. *Master's Degrees Awarded 1989-90:* 5.

Webster University. Instructional Technology, St. Louis, MO 63119. Fax (314) 968-7118. Paul Steinmann, Assoc. Dean and Dir., Graduate Studies and Instructional Technology. *Specialization:* Master's degree. *Minimum Degree Requirements:* 33 semester hours, including 24 in media; internship required. State Certification in Media Technology is a program option; six-year program not available. *Faculty:* 4. *Students:* 8 full-time; 22 part-time. *Financial Assistance:* Government loans and limited state aid. *Master's Degrees Awarded 1993:* 12.

MONTANA

*University of Montana. School of Education, Missoula, MT 59812. (406) 243-2563. Fax (406) 243-4908. Geneva T. Van Horne, Prof. of Library/Media, School of Education. *Specializations:* Master's degree; K-12 School Library Media specialization. *Minimum Degree Requirements:* 36 semester credit hours, 28 in media; thesis optional. *Faculty:* 3.5 full-time. *Students:* 17 (School Library Media Certification). *Financial Assistance:* Contact the University of Montana Financial Aid Office. *Master's Degrees Awarded 1 July 1991-30 June 1992:* 5. The school has a School Library Media Certification endorsement program in addition to the master's program.

NEBRASKA

University of Nebraska at Kearney. Kearney, NE 68849. (308) 234-8513. Fax (308) 234-8157. E-mail fredrickson@platte.unk.edu. Dr. Scott Fredrickson, Dir. of Instructional Technology. *Specializations:* M.S. in Instructional Technology, M.S. in Educational Media/Specialist in Educational Media. *Minimum Degree Requirements:* Information not reported. *Faculty:* 4 full-time; 6 part-time. *Students:* 45. *Master's Degrees Awarded 1993:* Approx. 17.

*University of Nebraska-Lincoln. Instructional Technology, Teachers College, Lincoln, NE 68588. (402) 472-2018. Fax (402) 472-8317. David W. Brooks, Prof., Coord., Instructional Technology, Teachers College. *Specialization:* Master's degree. *Minimum Degree Requirements:* 36 semester hours, including 24 in media; thesis optional. *Faculty:* 4 full-time.

Master's Degrees Awarded 1 July 1991-30 June 1992: 3. The school also offers an advanced certificate program.

University of Nebraska-Omaha. Department of Teacher Education, College of Education, Kayser Hall 208D, Omaha, NE 68182. (402) 554-2211. Fax (402) 554-3491. Verne Haselwood, Prof., Educational Media Prog. in Teacher Education. *Specializations:* M.S. in Education, M.A. in Education, both with Educational Media concentration. *Minimum Degree Requirements:* 36 semester hours, including 24 in media; practicum required; thesis optional. *Faculty:* 2 full-time; 3 part-time. *Students:* 12 full-time; 55 part-time. *Financial Assistance:* Contact Financial Aid Office. *Master's Degrees Awarded 1993:* 12. The school also offers an advanced certificate program in Educational Administration and Supervision.

NEW JERSEY

Glassboro State College. See listing for Rowan College of New Jersey.

Montclair State College. Department of Reading and Educational Media, Upper Montclair, NJ 07043. Robert R. Ruezinsky, Dir. of Media and Technology. *Specializations:* No degree program exists. Two certification programs, A.M.S. and E.M.S, exist on the graduate level. *Minimum Degree Requirements:* 18-21 semester hours of media and technology are required for the A.M.S. program and 30-33 hours for the E.M.S. program. *Faculty:* Includes 5 administrators and 1 adjunct, teaching on an overload basis. *Students:* Data not reported. *Master's Degrees Awarded 1993:* Data not reported.

Rowan College of New Jersey. School and Public Librarianship, Glassboro, NJ 08028. (609) 863-5324. Regina Pauly, Graduate Advisor and Prog. Coord. for School and Public Librarianship. *Specialization:* Master's degree. *Minimum Degree Requirements:* 39 semester hours, including required thesis project. *Faculty:* 1 full-time; 3 part-time. *Master's Degrees Awarded 1993:* 11. A six-year program is available.

Rutgers-The State University of New Jersey. School of Communication, Information and Library Studies, New Brunswick, NJ 08903. (908) 932-8824. Fax (908) 932-6916. Dr. Betty J. Turock, Chair, Dept. of Library and Information Studies. *Specializations:* M.L.S. degree with specializations in Information Retrieval, Technical and Automated Services, Reference, School Media Services, Youth Services, Management and Policy Issues, Generalist Studies. A new course on Multimedia Structure, Organization, Access, and Production is being offered. *Minimum Degree Requirements:* 36 semester hours, in which the hours for media vary for individual students; practicum of 100 hours. *Faculty:* 18 full-time; 6 adjuncts. *Students:* 140 full-time; 210 part-time. *Financial Assistance:* Scholarships, fellowships, and graduate assistantships available. *Master's Degrees Awarded 1993:* Data not reported. The school also offers a six-year specialist certificate program.

William Paterson College. School of Education, 300 Pompton Rd., Wayne, NJ 07470. (201) 595-2140. Fax (201) 595-2585. Dr. Amy G. Job, Librarian, Assoc. Prof., Coord., Prog. in Library/Media, Curriculum and Instruction Dept. *Specializations:* M.Ed. for Educational Media Specialist, Associate Media Specialist. *Minimum Degree Requirements:* 33 semester hours, including research projects and practicum. *Faculty:* 6 full-time; 2 part-time. *Students:* 30 part-time. *Financial Assistance:* Limited. *Master's Degrees Awarded 1993:* 4.

NEW YORK

Fordham University. Communications Department, Bronx, NY 10458. Edward A. Wachtel, Assoc. Prof. and Chair; James A. Capo, Assoc. Prof., Dir. of Graduate Studies, Communications Dept. *Specialization:* Master's degree. *Minimum Degree Requirements:* 30 semester hours; internship or thesis required. *Faculty:* 9. *Students:* 31. *Financial Assistance:* Scholarships and assistantships. *Master's Degrees Awarded 1993:* 8.

Ithaca College. School of Communications, Ithaca, NY 14850. (607) 274-3242. Fax (607) 274-1664. E-mail herndon@ithaca.edu. Sandra L. Herndon, Prof., Chair, Graduate Corporate Communications; Roy H. Park, School of Communications. *Specialization:* M.S. in Corporate Communications. *Minimum Degree Requirements:* 36 semester hours; required seminar. *Faculty:* 8 full-time. *Students:* Approx. 25 full-time, 15 part-time. *Financial Assistance:* Full- and part-time research/lab assistantships. *Master's Degrees Awarded 1993:* 25.

*New School for Social Research. Media Studies Program, 2 W. 13th St., New York, NY 10011. (212) 229-8903. Fax (212) 645-0661. Mark Schulman, Chair, Communication Dept. *Specialization:* M.A. in Media Studies. *Minimum Degree Requirements:* 36 semester hours and thesis; 39 credit hours for non-thesis option. *Faculty:* 2 full-time; 30 part-time. *Students:* 40 full-time; 135 part-time. *Financial Assistance:* Assistantships, work-study, federal and state loans. *Master's Degrees Awarded 1 July 1991-30 June 1992:* 75.

New York Institute of Technology. School of Education-Instructional Technology, Old Westbury, NY 11568. (Also in NYC.) (516) 686-7777. Fax (516) 626-7602. Helen Greene, Dean, School of Education. *Specializations:* Master's degree in Instructional Technology with specializations for teachers and for trainers; Computers in Education Certificate. *Minimum Degree Requirements:* 12 credits core; 18 credits specialization; and 6 credits of electives. *Faculty:* 5 full-time; 4 part-time. *Financial Assistance:* Graduate assistantships, institutional and alumni scholarships, Stafford loans. *Master's Degrees Awarded 1993:* 41.

New York University. School of Education, 239 Greene St., Suite 300, New York, NY 10003. (212) 998-5187. Fax (212) 995-4041. Francine Shuchat Shaw, Assoc. Prof. and Dir., Prog. in Educational Communication and Technology. *Specialization:* M.A. in Education with program emphasis on design and production, application and evaluation of materials and environments for all instructional technologies. *Minimum Degree Requirements:* 36 semester hours including final master's project. *Faculty:* 2 full-time; 10 part-time. *Students:* 25 full-time, 35 part-time. *Financial Assistance:* Graduate and research assistantships and some financial aid and work-study programs from the University and the School of Education. *Master's Degrees Awarded 1 July 1992-30 June 1993:* 15. The school also offers a post-M.A. 30-point Certificate of Advanced Study in Education.

New York University-Tisch School of the Arts. Interactive Telecommunications Program, 721 Broadway, New York, NY 10003. (212) 998-1880. Fax (212) 998-1898. Red Burns, Prof., Chair, The Interactive Telecommunications Program/Institute of Film and Television. *Specialization:* Master's degree. *Minimum Degree Requirements:* 60 semester hours (15 courses at 4 credit hours each; program is 2 years for full-time students), including 5-6 required courses and thesis. *Faculty:* 3 full-time, 32 adjunct. *Students:* 150. *Financial Assistance:* Graduate assistantships. *Master's Degrees Awarded 1993:* Data not reported.

St. John's University. Division of Library and Information Science, 8000 Utopia Parkway, Jamaica, NY 11439. (718) 990-6200. Fax (718) 380-0353. James Benson, Dir., Div. of Library and Information Science. *Specializations:* M.L.S. with specializations in School Media,

Public, Academic, Law, Health/Medicine, Business, Archives. Double degree programs: Pharmacy and M.L.S., Government and Politics and M.L.S. *Minimum Degree Requirements:* 36 semester hours; comprehensive; practicum (school media required). *Faculty:* 7 full-time; 14 adjunct. *Students:* 170. *Financial Assistance:* Assistantships and fellowships (1 for school media in 1993). *Master's Degrees Awarded in 1993:* 62. The school also offers a 24-credit Advanced Certificate program.

State University College of Arts and Science. School of Professional Studies, 204 Satterlee Hall, Potsdam, NY 13676. (315) 267-2527. (315) 267-2771. E-mail lichtnc@snypotvx.bitnet. Norman Licht, Coord., Instructional Technology and Media Management; Dr. Charles Mlynarczyk, Chair, Education Department. *Specializations:* Master of Science in Education with concentration in Instructional Technology and Media Management. *Minimum Degree Requirements:* 33 semester hours. *Faculty:* 7. *Master's Degrees Awarded 1993:* 26.

State University of New York at Albany. School of Education, 1400 Washington Ave., Albany, NY 12222. (518) 442-5032. Fax (518) 442-5032. Karen Swan (ED114A), contact person, Instructional Design and Technology Prog. *Specialization:* Master's degree with concentrations in Curriculum Theory, Instructional Design, Program Evaluation, Language in Education, and Teaching and Learning of Academic Disciplines. *Minimum Degree Requirements:* 30 semester hours at the graduate level, including at least 3 credits (1 course) each in curriculum development, instruction, technology, and research; at least 6 credits in the foundations of education; and 12 credits in the student's chosen area of specialization as developed with his/her advisor. *Faculty:* 3. *Students:* 128. *Financial Assistance:* Loans, TAP (depending on eligibility). *Master's Degrees Awarded 1993:* 24.

*State University of New York at Buffalo. Graduate School of Education, 480 Baldy Hall, Amherst, NY 14260. (716) 645-3164. Fax (716) 645-4281. Taher A. Razik, Prof., Instructional Design and Management, Dept. of Educational Organization, Administration, and Policy. *Specialization:* M.Ed. in Instructional Design and Management. *Minimum Degree Requirements:* 32 semester hours, including 21 hours in Instructional Design and Management; thesis or project required. *Faculty:* 3. *Students:* 12. *Financial Assistance:* Some graduate assistantships are available. *Master's Degrees Awarded 1 July 1991-30 June 1992:* 3.

State University of New York at Buffalo. School of Information and Library Studies, Buffalo, NY 14260. (716) 645-2411. Fax (716) 645-3775. E-mail wakefld@aixl.ucok.edu. George S. Bobinski, Dean. *Specialization:* Master's degree. *Minimum Degree Requirements:* 36 semester hours, including 15 in media; thesis optional. *Faculty:* 9 full-time; 6 part-time. *Students:* 3 full-time; 36 part-time. *Financial Assistance:* 12-18 assistantships available, plus fellowships and scholarships. *Master's Degrees Awarded 1993:* 21.

Syracuse University. School of Education, Syracuse, NY 13244-2340. (315) 443-3703. Fax (315) 443-5732. Philip Doughty, Prof., Chair, Instructional Design, Development and Evaluation Prog. *Specializations:* M.S. degree programs for Instructional Design of programs and materials, Educational Evaluation, human issues in Instructional Development, Media Production (including computers and videodisc), and Educational Research and Theory (learning theory, application of theory, and educational and media research). Graduates are prepared to serve as curriculum developers, instructional developers, program and product evaluators, researchers, resource center administrators, communications coordinators, trainers in human resource development, and higher education instructors. *Features:* Field work and internships, special topics and special issues seminar, student- and faculty-initiated minicourses, seminars and guest lecturers, faculty-student formulation of department policies, and multiple international perspectives. *Minimum Degree Requirements:* 30 semester hours; comprehensive and intensive examinations required. *Faculty:* 5 full-time; 4 part-time. *Students:* 31 full-time; 57 part-time. *Financial Assistance:* Some fellowships, scholarships, and graduate assistantships entailing either research or administrative duties in instructional technology. *Master's Degrees Awarded 1 July 1991-30 June 1992:* 23. The school also offers an advanced certificate program.

*Teachers College, Columbia University. Box 221, 525 W. 120th St., New York, NY 10027. (212) 678-3834. Fax (212) 678-4048. Robert P. Taylor, Chair, Dept. of Communication, Computing and Technology in Education. *Specializations:* M.A. in Computing in Education; M.A. or M.Ed. in Instructional Technology and Media; M.A., M.Ed. in Communication. *Minimum Degree Requirements:* M.A., 32 semester hours; graduate project. *Faculty:* 5. *Students:* 200. *Financial Assistance:* Direct scholarship, some assistantships, some work on grant projects. *Master's Degrees Awarded 1 July 1991-30 June 1992:* Approx. 50.

NORTH CAROLINA

Appalachian State University. Department of Library Science and Educational Foundations, Boone, NC 28608. John H. Tashner, Prof., Coord., Dept. of Library Science and Educational Foundations, College of Education. *Specialization:* Master's degree. *Minimum Degree Requirements:* 36 semester hours, including 15 in Computer Education; thesis optional. *Faculty:* 2. *Students:* 10. *Financial Assistance:* 4 graduate assistantships. *Master's Degrees Awarded 1993:* 2.

East Carolina University. Department of Library Studies and Educational Technology, Greenville, NC 27858-4353. (919) 757-6621. Fax (919) 757-4368. Lawrence Auld, Assoc. Prof., Chair. *Specializations*: M.L.S.; areas of specialization include School Media, Community College Librarianship, and Public Librarianship. M.L.S. graduates are eligible for North Carolina School Media Coordinator certification and North Carolina Public Library certification. *Minimum Degree Requirements:* Minimum of 38 semester hours in Library Science and Media. *Faculty:* 8 full-time. *Students:* 6 full-time; 45 part-time. *Financial Assistance:* A limited number of assistantships are available. *Master's Degrees Awarded 1 July 1992-30 June 1993:* 21. A 14-hour post-master's program for School Media Supervisor certification is also offered.

North Carolina Central University. School of Education, 238 Farrison-Newton Communications Bldg., Durham, NC 27707. (919) 560-6218. Dr. Marvin E. Duncan, Prof., Dir., Graduate Prog. in Educational Technology. *Specialization:* M.A. with special emphasis on Instructional Development/Design. *Minimum Degree Requirements:* 33 semester hours, including 21 in Educational Technology; thesis or project required unless student has already written a thesis or project for another master's program. *Features:* The master's program in educational technology is designed to prepare graduates to serve as information and communication technologists in a variety of professional ventures, among which are institutions of higher education (college resource centers); business; industry; and professional schools, such as medicine, law, dentistry, and nursing. The program is also designed to develop in students the theory, practical tools, and techniques necessary to analyze, design, and manage an instructional resources center. Many of our students teach in two- and four-year colleges. *Faculty:* 3 full-time; 1 part-time. *Students:* 25 full-time; 40 part-time. *Financial Assistance:* Assistantships and grants available. *Master's Degrees Awarded 1993:* Data not reported.

University of North Carolina. School of Education, Chapel Hill, NC 27514. (919) 962-3791. Fax (919) 962-1533. Ralph E. Wileman, Prof., Chair, Educational Media and Instructional Design, School of Education. *Specialization:* M.Ed. in Educational Media and Instructional Design. *Minimum Degree Requirements:* 36 semester hours, including a 3-hour practicum; comprehensive examination. *Faculty:* 2 full-time. *Students:* 17 full-time. *Financial Assistance:* Assistantships in many schools throughout the university. *Master's Degrees Awarded 1993:* 7.

OHIO

Miami University. School of Education and Allied Professions, Oxford, OH 45056. (513) 529-3736. Joe Waggener, Assoc. Prof. Degree programs in Instructional Technology have been discontinued.

***The Ohio State University**. College of Education, 29 W. Woodruff Ave., 122 Ramseyer Hall, Columbus, OH 43221. (614) 292-4872. Fax (614) 292-7900. Marjorie Cambre, Assoc. Prof., prog. contact person, Instructional Design and Technology. *Specializations:* M.A. in Instructional Design and Technology with specialties in Educational Computing, Interactive Technologies, and Video; Library Media Certification. *Minimum Degree Requirements:* M.A. degree—50 quarter hours, including an individualized number of hours in media; thesis optional. *Faculty:* 6 full-time; 1 part-time. *Students:* 86 M.A. students—20 full-time; 66 part-time. *Financial Assistance:* Some assistantships available. *Master's Degrees Awarded 1 July 1991-30 June 1992:* Approx. 20.

The Ohio State University. College of the Arts, Department of Art Education, 340 Hopkins Hall, 128 North Oval Mall, Columbus, OH 43210. (614) 292-0259. Fax (614) 292-4401. E-mail scott+@osu.edu. Dr. Tony Scott, Prog. Coord., Prog. in Electronic Media in Art Education. *Specializations:* Ph.D. and M.A. in Art Education with specializations in the teaching and learning of computer graphics and computer-mediated art; multimedia production and its curricular implications; electronic networking in the arts; multicultural aspects of computing; hypermedia applications for teaching and art education research; and the application of computing to arts administration, galleries, and museums. *Faculty:* 3 full-time in specialty; 19 in department. *Students:* 15 full-time in specialty. *Financial Assistance:* Graduate teaching associate positions that carry tuition and fee waivers and pay a monthly stipend; various fellowship programs for applicants with high GRE scores. *Master's Degrees Awarded 1993:* 3 directly related to program.

***Ohio University**. College of Education, McCracken Hall, Athens, OH 45701-2979. (614) 593-4457. Fax (614) 593-0177. Dr. John W. McCutcheon, Asst. Prof., Coord., Educational Media Program. *Specialization:* M.Ed. in Educational Media Management. *Minimum Degree Requirements:* 52 quarter hours, including 26 in Educational Media. *Faculty:* 3 full-time; 2 part-time. *Students:* 24 full-time; 5 part-time. *Master's Degrees Awarded 1 July 1991-30 June 1992:* 3.

University of Cincinnati. College of Education, 608 Teachers College Bldg., Cincinnati, OH 45221-0002. (513) 556-3577. Randall Nichols, Dept. of Curriculum and Instruction. *Specialization:* M.A. in Curriculum and Instruction with an emphasis in Instructional Systems Technology. *Minimum Degree Requirements:* 54 quarter hours; written examination; thesis or research project. *Faculty:* 2. *Students:* 15. *Financial Assistance:* Scholarships and assistantships available. *Master's Degrees Awarded 1993:* Approx. 5.

*University of Toledo. College of Education and Allied Professions, Toledo, OH 43606-3390. (419) 537-3846. Fax (419) 537-3853. Amos C. Patterson, Prof., Dir. of Academic Programs. *Specialization:* M.Ed. in Educational Media. *Minimum Degree Requirements:* 48 quarter hours, including 36 in media; master's project. *Faculty:* 7 full-time; 2 part-time. *Students:* 13 full-time; 14 part-time (in graduate program). For more details, see the listing for Doctoral Programs. The school also offers a six-year specialist degree program in educational technology.

Wright State University. College of Education and Human Services, 244 Millett Hall, Dayton, OH 45435. (513) 873-2509 or (513) 873-2182. Fax (513) 873-3301. Dr. Bonnie K. Mathies, Chair, Dept. of Educational Technology, Vocational Education and Allied Programs. *Specializations:* M.Ed. in Educational Media or Computer Education, or for Media Supervisor or Computer Coordinator; M.A. in Educational Media or Computer Education. *Minimum Degree Requirements:* M.Ed. requires a comprehensive examination that, for this department, is the completion of a portfolio and videotaped presentation to the faculty; the M.A. incorporates a 9-hour thesis; students are eligible for Supervisor's Certificate after completion of C&S; Computer Coordinator or C&S; Media Supervision programs. *Faculty:* 2 full-time; 13 part-time, adjuncts, and other university full-time faculty and staff. *Students:* 61 part-time (not including Computer Education students). *Financial Assistance:* Graduate assistantships available, including three positions in the College's Educational Resource Center; limited number of small graduate scholarships. *Master's Degrees Awarded 1 July 1992-30 June 1993:* 8.

OKLAHOMA

Central State University. See University of Central Oklahoma (name changed July 1991).

Southwestern Oklahoma State University. School of Education, Weatherford, OK 73096. (405) 772-6611. Fax (405) 772-5447. Lessley Price, Asst. Prof., Coord. of Library/Media Prog., School of Education. *Specialization:* M.Ed. in Library/Media Education. *Minimum Degree Requirements:* 32 semester hours, including 24 in library/media. *Faculty:* 1 full-time, 2 part-time. *Master's Degrees Awarded 1993:* 8.

*University of Central Oklahoma. 100 N. University Dr., Edmond, OK 73034. (405) 341-2980, ext. 5886. Fax (405) 341-4964. Dr. Judith E. Wakefield, Assoc. Prof. *Specializations:* M.Ed. in Instructional Media; Library Media Specialist Certification. *Minimum Degree Requirements:* 32 graduate hours in Educational Research, Educational Media, Curriculum and Instruction, and electives. *Faculty:* 3 full-time; 1 part-time. *Students:* 4 full-time; 51 part-time. *Financial Assistance:* Yes. *Master's Degrees Awarded 1 July 1991-30 June 1992:* 12. The school also offers an advanced certificate program.

University of Oklahoma. Department of Educational Psychology, 820 Van Vleet Oval, Norman, OK 73019-0260. (405) 325-5974. Fax (405) 325-3242. Raymond B. Miller, Educational Technology Prog. Area Coord. *Specializations:* M.Ed. in Educational Technology as a Generalist or with emphasis on Computer Applications or Instructional Design; dual degree in Library Science and Educational Technology. *Minimum Degree Requirements:* 32 semester hours for the Generalist and Computer Applications options; 39 hours for the Instructional Design program; 60 hours for the dual degree; comprehensive examination required for all programs. *Faculty:* 10 full-time; 2 part-time. *Students:* 43 full- and part-time. *Financial*

Assistance: Assistantships; out-of-state fee waivers; general and targeted minorities graduate scholarships. *Master's Degrees Awarded 1 July 1992-30 June 1993:* 6.

OREGON

Portland State University. School of Education, P.O. Box 751, Portland, OR 97207. (503) 725-4678. Fax (503) 725-4882. E-mail joyce@loki.cc.pdx.edu. Joyce Petrie, Prof., Coord., Educational Media, School of Education. *Specialization:* Master's degree in Educational Media. *Minimum Degree Requirements:* 45 quarter hours, including 42 in media; thesis optional. *Faculty:* 3 full-time; 4 part-time. *Master's Degrees Awarded 1993:* 35.

Western Oregon State College. Department of Secondary Education, Monmouth, OR 97361. Richard C. Forcier, Prof., Dir., Div. of Information Technology, Dept. of Secondary Education. *Specialization:* Master's degree in Information Technology. *Features:* Offers advanced courses in Library Management, Media Production, Instructional Systems, Instructional Development, and Computer Technology. Some specialization in distance delivery of instruction and computer-interactive video instruction. *Minimum Degree Requirements:* 45 quarter hours, including 36 in media; thesis optional. *Faculty:* 3 full-time; 4 part-time. *Students:* 3 full-time; 210 part-time. *Master's Degrees Awarded 1 July 1992-30 June 1993:* 12.

PENNSYLVANIA

Drexel University. College of Information Studies, Philadelphia, PA 19104. (215) 895-2474. Fax (215) 895-2494. Richard H. Lytle, Prof. and Dean, College of Information Studies. *Specialization:* M.S. and M.S.I.S. degrees. *Minimum Degree Requirements:* 48 quarter hours taken primarily from six functional groupings: Technology of Information Systems; Principles of Information Systems; Information Organizations; Collection Management; Information Resources and Services; and Research. *Faculty:* 18. *Students:* 331. *Master's Degrees Awarded 1993:* 87 M.S. and 3 M.S.I.S.

Lehigh University. Lehigh University College of Education, Bethlehem, PA 18015. (215) 758-3231. Fax (215) 758-6223. Leroy J. Tuscher, Prof., Coord., Educational Technology Program. *Specialization:* Master's degree with emphasis in Interactive Digital Multimedia for Teaching and Learning. *Minimum Degree Requirements:* 30 semester hours, including 9 in media; thesis optional. *Faculty:* 3 full-time; 2 part-time. *Financial Assistance:* University graduate and research assistantships, graduate student support as participants in R&D projects. *Master's Degrees Awarded 1992-93:* 15.

*Pennsylvania State University. Division of Adult Education and Instructional Systems, 27D Chambers Bldg., University Park, PA 16802. (814) 865-0473. Fax (814) 865-3315. D. W. Johnson, Prof. in Charge, Instructional Systems Prog. *Specializations:* M. Ed., M.S. in Instructional Systems. *Minimum Degree Requirements:* 30 semester hours, including either a thesis or project paper. *Faculty:* 6 full-time; 2 affiliate; 2 part-time. *Students:* Approx. 260. *Financial Assistance:* Some assistantships, graduate fellowships, student aid loans. *Master's Degrees Awarded 1 July 1991-30 June 1992:* 23.

Rosemont College. Rosemont College Graduate Studies, 1400 Montgomery Ave., Rosemont, PA 19010-1699. (610) 526-2982; (800) 531-9431 outside 610 area code. Fax (610) 525-2930. E-mail rosemont@villum.bitnet. Dr. Robert J. Siegfried, Dir. *Specializations:* M.Ed. in

Technology in Education, Certificate in Advanced Graduate Study in Technology in Education for those who already hold a master's degree. *Minimum Degree Requirements:* Completion of 12 units (36 credits) and comprehensive exam. *Students:* Approx. 110. *Financial Assistance:* Graduate assistantships, internships, Stafford student loans, and Supplemental Loans to Students. *Master's Degrees Awarded 1993:* 19.

Shippensburg University. Dept. of Communications and Journalism, 1871 Old Main Drive, Shippensburg, PA 17257. (717) 532-1521. Dr. C. Lynne Nash, Dept. Chair. *Specialization:* Master's degree with emphasis on mass communications. *Minimum Degree Requirements:* 30 semester hours in media/communications studies; thesis optional. *Faculty:* 8. *Students:* 35. *Financial Assistance:* Graduate assistantships, federal aid. *Master's Degrees Awarded 1993:* 5.

University of Pittsburgh. Instructional Design and Technology, School of Education, Pittsburgh, PA 15260. (412) 612-7254. Fax (412) 648-5911. Barbara Seels, Assoc. Prof., Coord., Program in Instructional Design and Technology, Dept. of Instruction and Learning. *Specialization:* Ed.D. and M.Ed. programs for the preparation of instructional technologists with skills in designing, developing, using, evaluating, and managing processes and resources for learning. Certificate option for instructional technologists available. *Features:* Program prepares people for positions in which they can effect educational change through instructional technology. Program includes three competency areas: instructional design, technological delivery systems, and communications research. *Minimum Degree Requirements:* 36 trimester hours, including 18 in instructional technology, 9 in core courses, and 9 in electives; comprehensive examination. *Faculty:* 3 full-time. *Students:* 66—22 master's, 44 doctoral. *Master's Degrees Awarded 1993:* Data not reported. The school also offers a 45-credit specialist certification program.

RHODE ISLAND

*Rhode Island College. 600 Mt. Pleasant Ave., Providence, RI 02908. (410) 456-8170. James E. Davis, Assoc. Prof., Chair, Dept. of Administration, Curriculum, and Instructional Technology. *Specialization:* M.S. in Instructional Technology. *Minimum Degree Requirements:* 30 semester hours, including 18 hours minimum in Instructional Technology, 6 hours in related disciplines, 3-6 hours in Humanistic and Behavioral Sciences; written comprehensive examination required. *Faculty:* 2 full-time; 3 part-time. *Students:* 4 full-time; 34 part-time. *Financial Assistance:* Contact college for options and details on available aid. *Master's Degrees Awarded 1 July 1991-30 June 1992:* 5. An individualized program at the sixth-year level is also offered.

The University of Rhode Island. Graduate School of Library and Information Studies, Rodman Hall, Kingston, RI 02881-0815. (401) 792-2947. Fax (401) 792-4395. Elizabeth Futas, Prof. and Dir. *Specializations:* M.L.I.S. degree. Offers accredited master's degree with specialities in Archives, Law, Health Sciences, and Rare Books Librarianship. *Minimum Degree Requirements:* 42 semester-credit program offered in Rhode Island and regionally in Boston and Amherst, MA, and Durham, NH. *Faculty:* 8 full-time; 20 adjunct. *Students:* 250-plus. *Financial Assistance:* 6 half-time graduate assistantships, some scholarship aid. *Master's Degrees Awarded 1993:* 60.

SOUTH CAROLINA

University of South Carolina. Educational Psychology Department, Columbia, SC 29208. (803) 777-6609. Dr. Margaret Gredler, Prof., Chair, Educational Psychology Dept. *Specialization:* Master's degree. *Minimum Degree Requirements:* 33 semester hours, including 3 each in administration, curriculum, and research, 9 in production, and 3 in instructional theory; no thesis required. *Faculty:* 3. *Students:* 5. *Master's Degrees Awarded 1993:* 1.

Winthrop University. Division of Leadership, Counseling and Media, Rock Hill, SC 29733. (803) 323-2151. George H. Robinson, Coord., Educational Media Prog., School of Education. *Specialization:* M.Ed. in Educational Media. *Features:* Students completing this program qualify for certification as a school library media specialist in South Carolina and most other states. *Minimum Degree Requirements:* 36-45 semester hours, including 15-33 in media, depending on media courses a student has had prior to this program; no thesis. *Faculty:* 2 full-time; 5 part-time. *Students:* 4 full-time; 34 part-time. *Financial Assistance:* Graduate assistantships of $1,500 per semester plus tuition. *Master's Degrees Awarded 1 July 1992-30 June 1993:* 11.

TENNESSEE

East Tennessee State University. College of Education, Box 70684, Johnson City, TN 37614-0684. (615) 929-5848. Fax (615) 929-4235. Dr. Rudy Miller, Prof., Dir. Media Services, Dept. of Curriculum and Instruction. *Specializations:* M.Ed. in Instructional Media (Library), M.Ed. in Instructional Technology. *Minimum Degree Requirements:* 39 semester hours, including 18 hours in instructional technology. *Faculty:* 2 full-time. *Students:* 36. *Master's Degrees Awarded 1993:* 6. A six-year program is under development.

Middle Tennessee State University. Department of Educational Leadership, Murfreesboro, TN 37132. (615) 898-2855. Ralph L. White, Prof. and Chair, Dept. of Educational Leadership. *Specialization:* Master's degree. *Minimum Degree Requirements:* 33 semester hours, including 15 in media; no thesis required. *Faculty:* 2 full-time. *Master's Degrees Awarded 1993:* Data not reported.

University of Tennessee-Knoxville. College of Education, Knoxville, TN 37996-3400. (615) 974-6800. Dr. Alfred D. Grant, Coord., Graduate Media Prog., Dept. of Curriculum and Instruction. *Specialization:* M.S. in Education, concentration in Instructional Media and Technology. *Minimum Degree Requirements:* 33 semester hours, thesis optional. *Faculty:* 1. *Master's Degrees Awarded 1993:* 3. The Department of Curriculum and Instruction also offers a six-year specialist degree program in Curriculum and Instruction with a concentration in Instructional Media and Technology.

TEXAS

East Texas State University. Department of Secondary and Higher Education, East Texas Station, Commerce, TX 75429-3011. (903) 886-5607. Fax (903) 886-5603. Dr. Robert S. Munday, Prof., Head, Dept. of Secondary and Higher Education. *Specialization:* Master's degree in Learning Technology and Information Systems with emphasis on Educational Micro Computing, Educational Media and Technology, and Library and Information Science. *Minimum Degree Requirements:* 30 semester hours with thesis, 36 without thesis. M.Ed.

(Educational Computing), 30 hours in ed. tech.; M.S. (Educational Media and Technology), 21 hours in ed. tech.; M.S. (Library and Information Science), 15 hours in library/information science, 12 hours in ed. tech. *Faculty:* 3 full-time; 4 part-time. *Students:* 900. *Financial Assistance:* Graduate assistantships in teaching, graduate assistantships in research, scholarships, federal aid program. *Master's Degrees Awarded 1993:* 20. A six-year program is available.

*Prairie View A&M University. Department of School Services, Prairie View, TX 77446-0036. (409) 857-3018. Fax (409) 857-2911. Dr. Marion Henry, Dir., Educational Media and Technology Prog. *Specialization:* Master's degree in Educational Media and Technology. *Minimum Degree Requirements:* 36 semester hours in media; no thesis required. *Faculty:* 3 full-time; 1 part-time. *Students:* 22. *Financial Assistance:* None. *Master's Degrees Awarded 1 July 1991-30 June 1992:* 6.

*Texas A&M University. College of Education, College Station, TX 77843-3256. (409) 845-7276. Fax (409) 845-9663. Ronald D. Zellner, Coord., Educational Technology Prog. *Specialization:* Master's degree, broad base with emphasis in Television or Computer Applications. *Minimum Degree Requirements:* 37 semester hours; no thesis; practicum or internship course. *Faculty:* 4 full-time; 1 part-time. *Students:* 15 full-time; 5 part-time. *Financial Assistance:* General teaching assistantships. *Master's Degrees Awarded 1 July 1991-30 June 1992:* 12.

Texas Tech University. College of Education, Box 41071, Lubbock, TX 79409. (806) 742-2377. Fax (806) 742-2179. E-mail bprice@tenet.edu. Robert Price, Assoc. Prof., Dir., Instructional Technology Prog. *Specializations:* Master's degree with emphasis in Educational Computing or Learning Resources. *Minimum Degree Requirements:* 39 semester hours; no thesis. *Faculty:* 3 full-time; 2 part-time. *Master's Degrees Awarded 1992-93:* 12.

*University of North Texas. College of Education, Box 13857, Denton, TX 76203-3857. (817) 565-3790. Fax (817) 565-2185. Jan Young, Chair, Dept. of Computer Education and Cognitive Systems, College of Education. *Specialization:* Master's degree. *Minimum Degree Requirements:* 36 semester hours, including 27 hours in Instructional Technology and Computer Education; no thesis. *Faculty:* 8. *Master's Degrees Awarded 1992-93:* 35.

University of Texas-Austin. College of Education, Austin, TX 78712. (512) 471-5211. DeLayne Hudspeth, Assoc. Prof., Coord., Area of Instructional Technology, Dept. of Curriculum and Instruction, College of Education. *Specialization:* Master's degree. *Minimum Degree Requirements:* 30-36 semester hours minimum depending on selection of program; 18 in Instructional Technology plus research course; thesis optional. A 6-hour minor is required outside the department. *Faculty:* 4 full-time; 2 part-time. *Master's Degrees Awarded 1993:* 22.

The University of Texas-Southwestern Medical Center at Dallas. 5323 Harry Hines Blvd., MC8881, Dallas, TX 75235-8881. (214) 648-5378. Fax (214) 648-5353. Dr. Mary F. Whiteside, Dir., Media Development Graduate Prog., Biomedical Communications Dept. *Specializations:* M.A. in Biomedical Communications with an emphasis in media development and instructional design. *Minimum Degree Requirements:* 36 semester hours; thesis required. *Faculty:* 4 (in media development). *Students:* Program limited to 6 full-time students each year. *Financial Assistance:* Student assistantships available when budget permits. *Master's Degrees Awarded 1993:* 4.

UTAH

Brigham Young University. Department of Educational Psychology, 201 MCKB, Provo, UT 84602. (801) 378-5097. Fax (801) 378-4017. E-mail paul_merrill@byu.edu. Paul F. Merrill, Prof., Chair. *Specializations:* M.S. and Ph.D. degrees in instructional science and technology. In the M.S. program, students may specialize in instructional design and production, computers in education, or research and evaluation. *Minimum Degree Requirements:* 6 semester hours of prerequisite credit in technical writing and A/V production; 14 hrs. of core credit in instructional design, statistics, assessing learning outcomes, computer applications, and evaluation; 3 credit hrs. of internship; 9 hrs. of specialization; and 6 hrs. of project or thesis. *Admission Requirements:* General university requirements, plus GRE entrance examination. Application will not be considered without GRE scores. *Faculty:* 10 full-time. *Students:* 30 M.S., 59 Ph.D. *Financial Assistance:* Internships and tuition waivers. *Other:* Students agree to live by the BYU Honor Code. *Master's Degrees Awarded 1993:* 5.

*Utah State University. Department of Instructional Technology, Logan, UT 84322-2830. (801) 750-2694. Fax (801) 750-2693. Dr. Don C. Smellie, Prof., Head, Dept. of Instructional Technology. *Specializations:* M.S. and Ed.S. with concentrations in the areas of Instructional Development, Interactive Learning, Educational Technology, and Information Technology/School Library Media Administration. *Features:* Programs in Information Technology/School Library Media Administration and Master Resource Teacher/Educational Technology are also delivered via an electronic distance education system. *Minimum Degree Requirements:* M.S.—60 quarter hours, including 45 in media; thesis or project option. Ed.S.—45 quarter hours if M.S. is in the field, 60 hours if it is not. *Faculty:* 9 full-time; 7 part-time. *Students:* 52 full-time; 68 part-time (in graduate program). *Financial Assistance:* Fellowships and assistantships. *Master's Degrees Awarded 1 July 1991-30 June 1992:* 36.

VIRGINIA

*James Madison University. Department of Secondary Education, Library Science and Educational Leadership, Harrisonburg, VA 22807. (703) 568-6486. Fax (703) 568-6920. Alvin Pettus, Head, Dept. of Secondary Education, Library Science and Educational Leadership. *Specialization:* Master's degree. *Minimum Degree Requirements:* 33 semester hours, including 21 in media; thesis optional. *Faculty:* 3 full-time; 2 part-time. *Master's Degrees Awarded 1 July 1991-30 June 1992:* 1.

Radford University. Educational Studies Department, College of Education, P.O. Box 6959, Radford, VA 24142. (703) 831-5736. Fax (703) 831-6053. Richard A. Buck, Educational Media Dept. *Specialization:* Master's degree in Educational Media. *Minimum Degree Requirements:* 33 semester hours; thesis optional; practicum required. *Faculty:* 3 full-time; 2 part-time. *Students:* 4 full-time; 29 part-time. *Financial Assistance:* Graduate assistantships available. *Master's Degrees Awarded 1 July 1992-30 June 1993:* 7.

University of Virginia. Curry School of Education, Ruffner Hall, Charlottesville, VA 22903. (804) 924-7471. Fax (804) 924-7987. John D. Bunch, Assoc. Prof., Coord., Instructional Technology Prog., Dept. of Educational Studies. *Specializations:* M.Ed., Ed.S. (Educational Specialist), Ph.D. and Ed.D. degrees offered, with focal areas in Media Production, Interactive Multimedia, and K-12 Educational Technologies. *Minimum Degree Requirements:* For specific degree requirements, write to the address above or refer to the UVA *Graduate Record.*

Faculty: 3 full-time. *Degrees Awarded 1 July 1992-30 June 1993:* 4 master's, 2 Ed. Specialist, 3 doctoral.

Virginia Commonwealth University. Division of Teacher Education, Richmond, VA 23284. (804) 367-1324. Fax (804) 367-1323. Dr. Sheary Johnson, Asst. Prof., Core Coord. of Instructional Technology, Dept. of Teacher Education. *Specialization:* Master's Degree in Curriculum and Instruction with a specialization in Library Media. *Minimum Degree Requirements:* 36 semester hours; internship (field experience); externship (project or research study); comprehensive examination. *Faculty:* 2 full-time. *Students:* 40 part-time. *Financial Assistance:* Graduate assistantship in School of Education. *Master's Degrees Awarded 1 July 1992-30 July 1993:* 4.

*Virginia Polytechnic Institute and State University (Virginia Tech). College of Education, Blacksburg, VA 24061-0313. (703) 231-5598. Fax (703) 231-3717. Thomas M. Sherman, Prof., Prog. Area Leader, Instructional Systems Development, Curriculum and Instruction. *Specializations:* M.S. in Instructional Technology, with emphasis on Training and Development, Educational Computing, Evaluation, and Media Management. *Features:* Facilities include 70-computer laboratory (IBM, Macintosh), interactive video, speech synthesis, telecommunications. *Minimum Degree Requirements:* 30 semester hours, including 15 in Instructional Technology; thesis optional. *Faculty:* 8 full-time; 5 part-time. *Students:* 8 full-time; 15 part-time. *Financial Assistance:* Assistantships are sometimes available, as well as opportunities with other agencies. *Master's Degrees Awarded 1 July 1991-30 July 1992:* 3. An advanced certificate program is available.

Virginia State University. School of Education, Petersburg, VA 23803. (804) 524-5934. Vykuntapathi Thota, Prog. Dir., Dept. of Educational Leadership. *Specializations:* M.S., M.Ed. *Minimum Degree Requirements:* 30 semester hours plus thesis for M.S.; 33 semester hours plus project for M.Ed.; comprehensive examination. *Faculty:* 1 full-time.

WASHINGTON

University of Washington. Department of Education, Seattle, WA 98195. (206) 543-1877. Fax (206) 543-8439. E-mail billwinn@u.washington.edu. William D. Winn, Prof., Prog. in Educational Communication and Technology, School of Education. *Specialization:* Master's degree. *Minimum Degree Requirements:* 45 quarter hours, including 24 in media; thesis optional. *Faculty:* 2 full-time. *Master's Degrees Awarded 1993:* 8.

Western Washington University. Woodring College of Education, Bellingham, WA 98225-9087. (206) 676-3381. Tony Jongejan, Assoc. Prof., Instructional Technology Prog., Dept. of Educational Administration and Foundations. *Specializations:* M.Ed. for Curriculum and Instruction, with emphasis in Instructional Technology, elementary and secondary programs; Adult Education; Master's Degree with emphasis on Instructional Design and Multimedia Development for education and industry persons; and Learning Resources (Library Science) for K-12 school librarians only. *Minimum Degree Requirements:* 52 quarter hours (15 hours in instructional technology, 24 hours in education-related courses, 0 hours outside education); thesis required; internship and practicum possible. *Financial Assistance:* Standard financial assistance for graduate students, some special assistance for minority graduate students. *Faculty:* 3.5 full-time; 8 part-time. *Students:* 4 full-time, 20 part-time. *Master's Degrees Awarded 1992-93:* 10.

WISCONSIN

University of Wisconsin-La Crosse. Educational Media Program, Rm. 109, Morris Hall, La Crosse, WI 54601. (608) 785-8000. Fax (608) 785-8909. Russ Phillips, Dir., Educational Media Prog., College of Education. *Specializations:* Master's degree with specializations in Initial Instructional Library Specialist, License 901; Instructional Library Media Specialist, License 902 (39 credits); Instructional Technology Specialist, License 903; or Instructional Library Media Supervisor (contact director). *Minimum Degree Requirements:* 30 semester hours, including 15 in media; no thesis. *Faculty:* 2 full-time; 4 part-time. *Students:* 21. *Financial Assistance:* Guaranteed student loans, graduate assistantships. *Master's Degrees Awarded 1993:* 11.

University of Wisconsin-Madison. School of Education, 225 North Mills St., Madison, WI 53706. (608) 263-4670. Fax (608) 263-9992. Michael Streibel, Prof., Dept. of Curriculum and Instruction. *Specializations:* Ph.D. programs to prepare college and university faculty; master's degree. *Faculty:* 3 full-time; 1 part-time. *Students:* 23 Ph.D., 27 M.S. *Financial Assistance:* A few stipends of approximately $1,000/mo. for 20 hours of work per week; other media jobs are also available. *Master's Degrees Awarded 1993:* Data not reported. For additional information, see listing in Doctoral Programs.

University of Wisconsin-Oshkosh. College of Education and Human Services, 800 Algoma Blvd., Oshkosh, WI 54901-8666. (414) 424-1490. Richard R. Hammes, Prof., Chair, Dept. of Human Services and Professional Leadership. *Specialization:* M.S. in Educational Leadership with special emphasis in Library/Media. *Minimum Degree Requirements:* 36 semester hours; thesis optional. *Faculty:* 7. *Students:* Approx. 30. *Financial Assistance:* Limited graduate assistantships. *Master's Degrees Awarded 1993:* 8.

University of Wisconsin-Stout. Menomonie, WI 54751. (715) 232-1202. Fax (715) 232-1441. E-mail hartzr@uwstout.edu. Dr. Roger L. Hartz, Prog. Dir., Media Technology Prog. *Specializations:* M.S.; specialization in Training and Human Resource Development available; curricular tracks may be developed in Instructional Development, Media Production, Media Management, and School Media. Note: This is an Educational/Instructional Technology program, not a Mass Media, Media Arts, or Broadcast Media program. *Minimum Degree Requirements:* 32 semester hours, including 15 in media; thesis optional. Coursework is drawn from many departments across the university; internship or field study strongly recommended. *Faculty:* 2 full-time; 2 part-time. *Students:* 8 full-time; 6 part-time. *Financial Assistance:* Limited numbers of graduate and teaching assistantships available; on-campus employment available; out-of-state tuition waivers for some international students. *Master's Degrees Awarded 1993:* 10.

Graduate Programs in
Educational Computing

When the directory of graduate programs in educational computing first appeared in the *1986 EMTY*, there were only 50 programs. This year's listing consists of 53 such programs in 25 states, down from the 1993 total of 71 programs in 31 states, the District of Columbia, and the Virgin Islands. The information in this section has been revised and updates the information assembled in *EMTY 1993*. Individuals who are considering graduate study in educational computing should contact the institution of their choice for current information. It should be noted that some programs that appear in this listing also appear in the listings of master's and six-year programs and doctoral programs.

Copies of the entries from the *1993 EMTY* were sent to the programs with a request for updated information and/or corrections, with the proviso that, if no response was received and the information in the 1993 edition was not current, the entry would be dropped. Programs from which a response was received in 1993 but not in 1994 are indicated with an asterisk (*). It should be noted that not all of the information in these descriptions is necessarily correct for the current year.

We would like to express our appreciation to the 36 program administrators who complied with our request for the 1994 edition. Of the remaining programs, 17 had been updated in the 1993 edition; 22 have been dropped for lack of response since 1992 or before. Our special thanks go to those who notified us of the status of programs that have been discontinued.

Data in this section include as much of the following information as was provided to us: the name of the institution and the program, telephone and fax numbers, e-mail addresses, a contact person, the degree(s) offered, admission requirements, minimum requirements for each degree, the number of faculty, the number of students currently enrolled, information on financial assistance, and the number of degrees awarded.

This section is arranged alphabetically by state and name of institution.

ARIZONA

Arizona State University. Educational Media and Computers, FMC Payne 146, Tempe, AZ 85287-0111. Dr. Gary Bitter, Coord., Educational Media and Computers. (602) 965-7192. Fax (602) 965-8887. *Specializations:* M.A. and Ph.D. in Educational Media and Computers. Master's program started in 1971 and doctorate started in 1976. *Minimum Degree Requirements:* Master's—33 semester hours (21 hours in educational media and computers, 9 hours in education, 3 hours outside education); thesis not required; internship, comprehensive exam, and practicum required. Doctorate—93 semester hours (24 hours in educational media and computers, 57 hours in education, 12 hours outside education); thesis, internship, and practicum required. *Admission Requirements:* MAT/TOEFL. *Faculty:* 7 full-time. *Students:* M.A., 104 full-time; 42 part-time. Ph.D., 10 full-time; 7 part-time. *Financial Assistance:* Full-time support research and graduate assistantships are available. *Degrees Awarded 1 July 1992-30 June 1993:* M.A., 24; Ph.D., 1.

CALIFORNIA

*San Diego State University. Department of Educational Technology, San Diego, CA 92182-0311. (619) 594-6718. Dr. Pat Harrison, Chair, Dept. of Educational Technology. *Specializations:* M.A. in Education with specializations in Educational Technology and Educational Computing. *Minimum Degree Requirements:* 36 semester hours (3 hours in education, hours in computers and outside education not specified); practicum required. *Admission Requirements:* GRE, 950 combined score; GPA 2.5 last 60 units of undergraduate work; evidence of writing competence. *Faculty:* 6 full-time. *Students:* 20 full-time; 80 part-time. *Financial Assistance:* Graduate assistantships, fellowships. *Degrees Awarded 1 July 1991-30 June 1992:* M.A., 40; Ph.D., 1.

United States International University. Department of Education, 10455 Pomerado Rd., San Diego, CA, 92131. (619) 693-4721; (619)-693-4595. Fax (619) 693-4771. Dr. Maria T. Fernandez, Prof., Computer Education. *Specializations:* M.A. and Ed.D. in Computer Education. Master's and doctoral programs started in 1983. *Admission Requirements:* Application, $30 fee, all college transcripts; 2 recommendations for M.A; 3 recommendations, GRE/MAT, writing test, and interview for Ed.D. *Minimum Degree Requirements:* Master's—45 quarter credit hours (30 hours in computers, 15 hours in education, 0 hours outside education); practicum required. Doctorate—95 quarter credit hours (60 hours in computers, 35 hours in education, 0 hours outside education); dissertation, internship, and practicum required. *Faculty:* 4 full-time; 4 part-time. *Students:* M.A., 50; Ed.D., 25. *Financial Assistance:* Loans are available. *Degrees Awarded 1993:* Data not reported.

COLORADO

*University of Colorado at Colorado Springs. School of Education, P.O. Box 7150, Colorado Springs, CO, 80933-7150. (719) 593-3266. Fax (719) 593-3554. Dr. Doris M. Carey, Dir., Educational Computing and Technology. *Specializations:* M.A. in Curriculum and Instruction with an emphasis in Educational Computing and Technology with emphasis on Educational Computing in K-College, Computer-Based Training, and Instructional Design. Master's program started in 1983. *Minimum Degree Requirements:* 33 semester hours (27 hours required in educational technology; 6 hours in education; 0 hours outside education); no thesis, internship, or practicum required. *Admission Requirements:* GRE or Miller Analogies Test; transcripts; four letters of recommendation; interview. *Faculty:* 1 full-time; 6 part-time. *Students:* 2 full-time; 51 part-time. *Degrees Awarded 1 July 1991-30 June 1992:* M.A., 14.

CONNECTICUT

Fairfield University. Graduate School of Education and Allied Professions, Fairfield, CT 06430. (203) 254-4000, ext. 2697. Fax (203) 254-4087. Dr. Ibrahim Hefzallah, Prof. of Educational Technology; Dr. John J. Schurdak, Assoc. Prof., Co-Directors, Computers in Education/Educational Technology Program. *Specializations:* M.A. in two tracks: (1) Computers in Education, or (2) Media/Educational Technology (for school media specialists, see listing of Master's Programs). *Minimum Degree Requirements:* 33 semester credits; comprehensive examination. *Admission Requirements:* Bachelor's degree and, for foreign students, TESOL Exam minimum score of 550. *Faculty:* 2 full-time; 9 part-time. *Students:* 60 part-time. *Financial Assistance:* Work study, graduate assistantships. *Degrees Awarded 1 July 1992-30*

June 1993: 10. An advanced certificate program in Media/Educational Technology is also available.

*University of Hartford. Educational Computing and Technology, 200 Bloomfield Ave., West Hartford, CT 06117. (203) 243-4277. Dr. Marilyn Schaffer, Assoc. Prof. of Educational Computing and Technology. *Specialization:* M.Ed. in Educational Computing. Master's program started in 1985. *Minimum Degree Requirements:* 30 semester hours (21 hours in computers, 9 hours in education); no thesis or practicum required; internships available. *Faculty:* 2 full-time; 24 part-time. *Students:* 35.

FLORIDA

Barry University. School of Education, 11300 N.E. Second Ave., Miami Shores, FL 33161. (305) 899-3608. Fax (305) 899-3630. E-mail levine@buvax.barry.edu. Sister Evelyn Piche, Dean, School of Education, and Joel S. Levine, Assoc. Prof. and Dir. of Computer Education Programs. *Specializations:* Master's and Education Specialist degrees in (1) Computer Science Education and (2) Computer Applications in Education. *Minimum Degree Requirements:* Master's degree—36 semester credit hours including Directed Research; Education Specialist degree—36 semester hours including Directed Research and Seminar on Computer-Based Technology in Education. *Faculty:* 5 full-time; 18 part-time. *Students:* 95. *Financial Assistance:* Assistantships, discounts to educators. *Master's Degrees Awarded 1 July 1992-30 June 1993:* 52.

Florida Institute of Technology. Science Education Department, 150 University Blvd., Melbourne, FL 32901-6988. (407) 768-8000, ext. 8126. Fax (407) 768-8000 ext. 7598. E-mail fronk@sci-ed.fit.edu. Dr. Robert Fronk, Dept. Head. *Specialization:* Master's degree options in Computer Education and in Instructional Technology; Ph.D. degree options in Computer Education and in Instructional Technology. *Admission Requirements:* GPA 3.0 for regular admission; 2.75 for provisional admission. *Minimum Degree Requirements:* Master's—48 quarter hours (18 in computer, 18 in education, 12 outside education); no thesis or internship required; practicum required. *Faculty:* 6 full-time. *Students:* 10 full-time; 9 part-time. *Financial Assistance:* Graduate student assistantships (full tuition plus stipend) available. *Degrees Awarded in 1993:* Master's, 5; Ph.D., 3.

Jacksonville University. Department of Education, 2800 University Blvd. N., Jacksonville, FL 32211. (904) 744-3950. Dr. Daryle C. May, Dir., Teacher Education and M.A.T. Prog. *Specialization:* M.A. in Teaching in Computer Education. Master's program started in 1983. *Minimum Degree Requirements:* 36 semester hours (21 hours in computer, 15 hours in education, 0 hours outside education); no thesis, internship, or practicum required; comprehensive exam required. *Faculty:* 5 full-time; 2 part-time. *Students:* 10. *Financial Assistance:* 40 percent scholarship to all local teachers. *Degrees Awarded 1993:* Master's, 10.

GEORGIA

Georgia State University. MSEIT Dept., Atlanta, GA 30303. (404) 651-2510. Fax (404) 651-2546. Dr. Skip Atkinson, Prof. *Specializations:* M.A. and Ph.D. in Instructional Technology. *Minimum Degree Requirements:* Master's—60 quarter hours (25 hours in computers, 35 hours in education); thesis required; no internship or practicum is required. Doctorate—90 quarter hours (35 hours in computers, 40 hours in education, 15 hours outside education);

thesis required; no internship or practicum is required. *Faculty:* 3. *Students:* 50. *Degrees Awarded 1993:* M.A., 12; Ph.D., 5.

University of Georgia. College of Education, Athens, GA 30602-7144. (706) 542-3810. Fax (706) 542-4032. Dr. James R. Okey, Chair, Dept. of Instructional Technology. *Specialization:* M.Ed. in Computer-Based Education. *Minimum Degree Requirements:* 60 quarter credit hours (25 hours in computers, 10 hours in education, 25 hours not specified [55 hours with applied project]); thesis not required; internship and practicum optional. *Faculty:* 11 full-time. *Students:* 16. *Degrees Awarded 1993:* Data not reported.

HAWAII

University of Hawaii-Manoa. Educational Technology Department, 1776 University Ave., Honolulu, HI 96822. (808) 956-7671. Fax (808) 956-3905. Dr. Geoffrey Z. Kucera, Prof. and Chair, Educational Technology Dept. *Specializations:* M.Ed. in Educational Technology. Specialization in Computer Technology has three options: (a) Computer-Based Learning, (b) Courseware Development, and (c) Information Center Management. Program began in 1983. *Admission Requirements:* GPA 3.0, GRE min. 50th percentile standing. *Minimum Degree Requirements:* 39 semester credit hours (27 in computing, 6 in instructional design, 6 electives); thesis available; practicum and internship required. *Faculty:* 4 full-time; 3 part-time. *Students:* 5 full-time. *Degrees Awarded 1993:* M.Ed., 6.

ILLINOIS

Concordia University. 7400 Augusta, River Forest, IL 60305-1499. (708) 209-3023. Fax (708) 209-3176. Dr. Paul T. Kreiss, Assoc. Dean, School of Graduate Studies. *Specialization:* M.A. in Mathematics Education/Computer Science Education. Master's program started in 1987. *Admission Requirements:* GPA 2.85 or above, 2.25 to 2.85 provision status; bachelor's degree from regionally accredited institution; two letters of recommendation; GRE required in cases of inadequate evidence of academic proficiency. *Minimum Degree Requirements:* 48 quarter hours; no thesis, internship, or practicum required. *Faculty:* 3 full-time; 8 part-time. *Students:* 3 full-time; 36 part-time. *Financial Assistance:* A number of graduate assistantships; Stafford Student loans and Supplement Loan for Students. *Degrees Awarded 1993:* M.A., 4.

Governors State University. College of Education, University Park, IL 60466. (708) 534-4380. Fax (708) 534-8451. E-mail j_meyer@acs.gsu.bgu.edu. Dr. John Meyer, University Prof. *Specialization:* M.A. in Education (with Computer Education as specialization). Master's program started in 1986. *Minimum Degree Requirements:* 36-39 semester hours (15 hours in computer, 21-24 hours in education, 0 hours outside education); thesis/project and practicum required; internship not required. *Faculty:* 2 full-time; 7 part-time. *Students:* 46. *Degrees Awarded 1993:* M.A., 11.

*National-Louis University (formerly National College of Education). Department of Computer Education, 2840 Sheridan Rd., Evanston, IL 60201. (708) 475-1100, ext. 2355. Fax (708) 256-1057. Dr. Marianne G. Handler, Chair, Dept. of Computer Education. *Specializations:* M.Ed., M.S., C.A.S. (Certificate of Advanced Studies) in Computer Education, and Ed.D. in Instructional Leadership with minor concentration in computer education. Master's program started in 1983, specialist in 1983, and doctoral in 1984. *Admission Requirements:* GPA 3.0

of 4.0; Miller Analogies Test 3.3. *Minimum Degree Requirements:* Master's—34 semester hours (24 hours in computers, 10 hours in education, and 0 hours outside education); thesis optional; no internship or practicum is required. Specialist, C.A.S.—30 semester hours (26 hours in computers, 4 hours in education, 0 hours outside education); no thesis, internship, or practicum is required. Doctorate—63 semester hours (14 hours in computers, 37 hours in education, 0 hours outside education); thesis and internship required; practicum not required. *Faculty:* 3 full-time. *Students:* M.Ed. and M.S., 52; C.A.S., 13; Ed.D., 4. *Financial Assistance:* Fellowship program based on need. *Degrees Awarded 1 July 1992-30 June 1992:* M.S. and M.Ed., 16; Ph.D., 0.

Northern Illinois University. Instructional Technology Faculty, LEPS Department, DeKalb, IL 60115. (815) 753-0464. Fax (815) 753-9371. Dr. Gary L. McConeghy, Chair, Instructional Technology Faculty. *Specialization:* M.S.Ed. in Instructional Technology with a concentration in Microcomputers in School-Based Settings. Master's program started in 1968. *Admission Requirements:* GPA 2.75; GRE 800 combined scores; two references. *Minimum Degree Requirements:* 39 hours (27 hours in technology, 9 hours in education, 0 hours outside education); no thesis, internship, or practicum is required. *Faculty:* 5 full-time; 5 part-time. *Students:* 106 part-time. *Financial Assistance:* Some assistantships available at various departments on campus. *Degrees Awarded 1993:* M.S.Ed., 20. See also the listing of Master's Programs.

INDIANA

*Purdue University. School of Education, Department of Curriculum and Instruction, West Lafayette, IN 47907-1442. (317) 494-5673. Fax (317) 494-0587. Dr. James Russell, Prof., Educational Computing and Instructional Development. *Specializations:* M.S., Ed.S., and Ph.D. in Educational Computing and Instructional Development. Master's program started in 1982 and specialist and doctoral in 1985. *Admission Requirements:* GPA of 3.0 or better; three letters of recommendation; statement of personal goals; total score of 1,000 or more on GRE for Ph.D. admission. *Minimum Degree Requirements:* Master's—36 semester hours (15 in computer or instructional development, 9 in education, 12 unspecified); thesis optional. Specialist—60-65 semester hours (15-18 in computer or instructional development, 30-35 in education); thesis, internship, and practicum required. Doctorate—90 semester hours (15-18 in computer or instructional development, 42-45 in education); thesis, internship, and practicum required. *Faculty:* 6 full-time. *Students:* 10 full-time; 12 part-time. *Financial Assistance:* Assistantships and fellowships. *Degrees Awarded 1 July 1991-30 June 1992:* Ph.D., 4; master's, 10. See also listing in Master's Programs.

IOWA

*Dubuque Tri-College Department of Education (a consortium of Clarke College, The University of Dubuque, and Loras College). Graduate Studies, 1450 Alta Vista, Dubuque, IA 52001. (319) 588-7842. Fax (319) 588-7964. Judy Decker, Clarke College, (319) 588-6425. *Specializations:* M.A. in Education in Technology (a multimedia perspective for instructional development); M.A. in Education in Media (includes Iowa licensure for media specialists K-6 or 7-12). *Admission Requirements:* Minimum GPA 2.5 on 4.0 scale; GRE (verbal and quantitative) or Miller Analogies Test; application form and $25 application fee; and letters of recommendation. *Minimum Degree Requirements:* 22 semester hours in computer courses, 12 in education, 3 electives. Predominantly summer program. *Faculty:* Technology, 1 full-time;

1 part-time. Media, 3 part-time. *Students:* Technology, 8 part-time. Media, 23 part-time. *Financial Assistance:* Student loans. *Degrees Awarded 1 July 1991-30 June 1992:* 0 (program is new).

Iowa State University. College of Education, Ames, IA 50011. (515) 294-6840. E-mail mrs@iastate.edu. Dr. Michael R. Simonson, Prof. *Specializations:* M.S., M.Ed., and Ph.D. in Curriculum and Instructional Technology with specializations in Instructional Computing, Instructional Design, and Distance Education. Master's and doctoral programs started in 1967. Participates in Clova Distance Education Alliance: Clova Star Schools Project. *Admission Requirements:* M.S. and M.Ed., three letters; top half of undergraduate class; autobiography. Ph.D., the same plus GRE. *Minimum Degree Requirements:* Master's—30 semester hours; thesis required; no internship or practicum is required. Doctorate—78 semester hours, thesis required; no internship or practicum is required. *Faculty:* 3 full-time; 5 part-time. *Students:* 20 full-time; 20 part-time. *Financial Assistance:* 10 assistantships. *Degrees Awarded 1993:* Ph.D., 6; M.S. and M.Ed., 10.

Teikyo Marycrest University. Department of Computer Science and Mathematics, 1607 W. 12th St., Davenport, IA 52804. (319) 326-9252. Fax (319) 326-9250. Mark McGinn, Dept. Head. *Specialization:* M.S. in Computer Science. *Admission Requirements:* Bachelor's degree in Computer Science from an accredited institution, or complete all preparatory courses *and* have a working knowledge of an assembly language, Pascal, and at least one other high-level programming language. *Minimum Degree Requirements:* 27 graduate semester hours plus 6 hours thesis; 36 graduate semester hours non-thesis. *Faculty:* 5 full time. *Students:* Data not available. *Degrees Awarded in 1993:* M.S., 5.

KANSAS

Kansas State University. Computer Education, 363 Bluemont Hall, Manhattan, KS 66506. (913) 532-7686. Fax (913) 532-7304. E-mail dmcgrath@ksuvm.bitnet. Dr. Diane McGrath, contact person. *Specializations:* M.S. in Secondary Education with an emphasis in Computer Education; Ph.D. and Ed.D. in Curriculum & Instruction with an emphasis in Computer Education. Master's program started in 1982; doctoral in 1987. *Admission Requirements:* M.S.—B average in undergraduate work; one programming language; TOEFL score of 590 or above. Ph.D./Ed.D.—B average in undergraduate and graduate work; one programming language, GRE or MAT; three letters of recommendation. *Minimum Degree Requirements:* M.S.—30 semester hours (minimum of 12 in Computer Education); thesis, internship, or practicum not required, but all three are possible. Ph.D.—90 semester hours (minimum of 21 hours in Computer Education or related area approved by committee; 9 hours in doctoral seminars and research; 21 hours for dissertation research); thesis required; internship and practicum not required but available. Ed.D.—94 semester hours (minimum of 18 hours in Computer Education or related area approved by committee; 6 hours in doctoral seminars and research; 10 hours for dissertation research; 12 hours of internship); thesis required. *Faculty:* 3.5 full-time. *Students:* 35 M.S., 35 doctoral. *Financial Assistance:* Some assistantships available. *Degrees Awarded 1993:* Ph.D., 4; M.S., 8.

MARYLAND

The Johns Hopkins University. Center for Technology in Education, Division of Education, Baltimore, MD 21218. (410) 646-3000. Fax (410) 646-2310. Sarah McPherson, Coord., M.S. Technology for Educators, Ed.D. Technology for Special Education, Div. of Education. *Specialization:* Master's degree. *Minimum Degree Requirements:* 36 semester hours, 8 required courses in computer-related technology and media, with remaining courses being electives in other education areas. *Faculty:* 2 full-time; 8 part-time. *Degrees Awarded 1993:* M.S., 12.

MASSACHUSETTS

Fitchburg State College. Division of Graduate and Continuing Education, 160 Pearl St., Fitchburg, MA 01420-2697. (508) 345-2151, ext. 3183. Fax (508) 345-7207. Dr. Sandra Miller-Jacobs, Chair, Special Education. *Specialization:* Educational Technology Certificate program designed to give teachers and administrators the skills to know how and when to use computer technology in their programs; use of the computer both as a teaching tool and as a means to examine curricula and teaching effectiveness are emphasized. This program may be applied to any of the master's degree or CAGS programs in Education. *Admission Requirements:* Bachelor's degree from accredited institution. *Minimum Certificate Requirements:* 15 semester hours of designated credit with a cumulative average of 3.0.

Lesley College. 29 Everett St., Cambridge, MA 02138-2790. (617) 349-8419. Dr. Nancy Roberts, Prof. of Computer Education. *Specializations:* M.A. in Computers in Education; C.A.G.S. in Computers in Education; Ph.D in Education with a Computers in Education major. Master's program started in 1980. Master's degree program is offered off-campus at 22 sites in 10 states; contact Professional Outreach Associates [(800) 843-4808] for information. *Minimum Degree Requirements:* Master's—33 semester hours in computers (number of hours in education and outside education not specified); integrative final project in lieu of thesis; no internship or practicum is required. Specialist—36 semester hours (hours in computers, education, and outside education not specified); thesis, internship, practicum not specified. Ph.D. requirements available on request. *Faculty:* 5 full-time; 90 part-time on the master's and specialist levels. *Students:* 440 on master's level; 5 on specialist level.

University of Massachusetts-Lowell. College of Education, One University Ave., Lowell, MA 01854. (508) 934-4621. Fax (508) 934-3005. E-mail lebaronj@woods.uml.edu. Dr. John LeBaron, Assoc. Prof., College of Education. *Specializations:* M.Ed. in Curriculum and Instruction; C.A.G.S. in Curriculum and Instruction; Ed.D. in Leadership in Schooling. (Note: Technology and Learning Environments is a component of each of the programs.) Master's, specialist, and doctoral programs started in 1984. *Admission Requirements:* M.Ed.— undergraduate degree from accredited college or university with a minimum GPA of 2.75 on a 4.0 scale; Miller Analogies Test or GRE. C.A.G.S. and Ed.D.—master's degree from an accredited college or university with a minimum GPA of 3.00 on a 4.0 scale; Miller Analogies Test or GRE. *Minimum Degree Requirements:* Master's—33 semester hours (hours in computers, education, and outside education not specified); no thesis or internship is required; practicum required. Doctorate—60 semester hours beyond master's plus dissertation (hours in computers, education, and outside education not specified); thesis, residency, and comprehensive examination required. *Faculty:* 20 full-time; 16 part-time. *Students:* (professional education graduate programs) 121 full-time; 362 part-time. *Financial Assistance:* Limited assistantships available. *Degrees Awarded 1993:* Doctoral, 11; master's and CAGS, 138.

MICHIGAN

University of Michigan. Educational Studies, Ann Arbor, MI 48109. (313) 763-0612. Fax (313) 763-1229. Patricia Baggett, Assoc. Prof. *Specialization:* Master's degree in Computers in Education. *Minimum Degree Requirements:* 30 trimester credit hours. *Faculty:* 1 full-time; 7 part-time. *Students:* Data not reported. *Degrees Awarded in 1993:* Master's, 4.

MINNESOTA

*Mankato State University. Educational Technology Program, L.M.E., Mankato, MN 56002. (507) 389-1965. Fax (507) 389-5751. Kenneth C. Pengelly, Prof. and Coord. of Educational Technology M.S. Prog. *Specialization:* M.S. in Educational Technology, K-12 specialization. Master's program started in 1986. *Admission Requirements:* Miller Analogies Test. *Minimum Degree Requirements:* 51 quarter credit hours (6-15 hours in computers, 12-15 hours in education, 12-18 hours [optional] outside education); 60-hour internship required. *Faculty:* 4 full-time; 5 part-time. *Students:* 15-20 part-time. *Degrees Awarded 1 July 1991-30 June 1992:* M.S., 5.

*University of Minnesota. Department of Curriculum and Instructional Systems, 130 Peik Hall, 159 Pillsbury Dr. SE, Minneapolis, MN 55455. (612) 624-2034. Dr. Gregory Sales, Curriculum and Instructional Systems. *Specializations:* M.Ed., M.A., Ph.D. in Instructional Design and Technology. Master's and doctoral programs started in 1972. *Minimum Degree Requirements:* Master's—45 quarter credit hours (18 hours in technology, 45 hours in education, 0 hours outside education); M.A. thesis (4 credits) required; practicum required for M.Ed. Doctorate—136 quarter credit hours; thesis (36 credits) required. *Faculty:* Not specified. *Students:* M.A. and M.Ed., 75; Ph.D., 40. *Financial Assistance:* Not specified. *Degrees Awarded 1 July 1991-30 June 1992:* Not specified.

MISSOURI

Fontbonne College. 6800 Wydown Blvd., St. Louis, MO 63105. (314) 862-3456. Dr. Mary K. Abkemeier, Master of Science in Computer Education. *Specializations:* M.S. in Computer Education. Master's program started in 1986. *Admission Requirements:* B.S. from accredited school; three letters of recommendation; GPA 2.5 or master's degree. *Minimum Degree Requirements:* 33 semester hours. *Faculty:* 3 full-time; 7 part-time. *Students:* 110 part-time. *Financial Assistance:* Title II funding for St. Louis City full-time school teachers. *Degrees Awarded 1993:* M.S., 14.

Northwest Missouri State University. Department of Computer Science, Maryville, MO 64468. (816) 562-1600. Fax (816) 562-1484. E-mail 0100205@northwest.missouri.edu. Phillip J. Heeler, Prof., Dir., School Computer Studies Prog., Dept. of Computer Science. *Specializations:* M.S. in School Computer Studies; M.S.Ed. in Educational Uses of Computers; M.S.Ed. in Using Computers in Specific Disciplines. *Admission Requirements:* GRE General Exam, writing samples. *Minimum Degree Requirements:* 32 semester hours for each of the three master's degree programs. The first includes 26 credit hours of core computer courses; the second includes 14 credit hours of core computer courses and 12 hours of educational courses; and the third requires 7 hours of core computer courses, 12 hours of education courses, and 7 hours in technology-related areas. *Faculty:* 6. *Students:* 10. *Financial Assistance:* Graduate assistant appointments. *Degrees Awarded 1993:* Master's, 10.

NEW YORK

Buffalo State College. 1300 Elmwood Ave., Buffalo, NY 14222-1095. (716) 878-4923. Dr. Thomas G. Kinsey, Coord. of M.S. in Education in Educational Computing. *Specializations:* M.S. in Ed. in Educational Computing. Master's program started in 1988. *Minimum Degree Requirements:* 33 semester hours (18 hours in computers, 12-15 hours in education, 0 hours outside education); thesis or project required; no internship or practicum is required. *Faculty:* 10 part-time. *Students:* 75. *Degrees Awarded 1993:* Master's, 11.

Iona College. 715 North Ave. NW, New Rochelle, NY 10801. (914) 633-2578. Robert Schiaffino, Asst. Prof. and Coord., Educational Computing Prog. *Specializations:* M.S. in Educational Computing. Master's program started in 1982. *Admission Requirements:* GPA 3.0 or better. *Minimum Degree Requirements:* 36 hours—trimester basis ("all hours listed in educational computing"). *Faculty:* 6 full-time; 8 part-time. *Students:* Data not reported. *Financial Assistance:* Federal student loan programs, veterans' benefits, various scholarships, graduate assistantships, work-study programs. *Degrees Awarded 1993:* M.S., 10.

*Long Island University. C. W. Post, Brookville, NY 11548; Brooklyn Campus, Brooklyn, NY 11201; Rockland Campus, Orangeburg, NY 10962. School of Education, Advisor of Educational Technology, (516) 299-2199. *Specialization:* M.S. in Education, concentration in Computers in Education. One of the oldest and most established programs on the East Coast. Master's program started in 1985. *Minimum Degree Requirements:* 36 semester hours for M.S.; technology project required; evening courses. Special programs available, some on weekends. *Faculty:* 5 full-time; 15 part-time. *Students:* Approx. 587 across three campuses. *Financial Assistance:* Assistance is available.

*Pace University. Department of Educational Administration, 1 Martine Ave., White Plains, NY 10606. (914) 422-4198. Fax (914) 422-4311. Dr. Lawrence Roder, Chair. *Specialization:* M.S. in Curriculum and Instruction with a concentration in Computers and Education. Master's program started in 1986. *Admission Requirements:* GPA 3.0; interview; application. *Minimum Degree Requirements:* 33 semester hours (15 hours in computers, 18 hours in educational administration). *Faculty:* 2 full-time; 12 part-time. *Students:* 60. *Financial Assistance:* Assistance is available. *Degrees Awarded 1 July 1991-30 June 1992:* M.S., 20.

State University College of Arts and Science at Potsdam. 204 Satterlee Hall, Potsdam, NY 13676. (315) 267-2527. Fax (315) 267-2771. E-mail lichtnc@snypotvx.bitnet. Dr. Norman Licht, Prof. of Education. *Specializations:* M.S. in Education, Instructional Technology, and Media Management with Educational Computing concentration. Master's program started in 1981. *Minimum Degree Requirements:* 33 semester hours (15 hours in computers, 18 hours in education, 0 hours outside education); thesis not required; internship or practicum required. *Faculty:* 6 full-time; 4 part-time. *Students:* 110. *Degrees Awarded 1993:* Data not reported.

State University of New York at Stony Brook. Department of Technology and Society, College of Engineering and Applied Sciences, Stony Brook, NY 11794. (516) 632-8767. Fax (516) 632-7809. E-mail tliao@sbccmail. Dr. Thomas T. Liao, Prof. and Chair. *Specializations:* M.S. in Technological Systems Management with concentration in Educational Computing. Master's program started in 1979. *Admission Requirements:* B.A. or B.S. in Sciences, Mathematics, or Social Sciences; GRE. *Minimum Degree Requirements:* 30 semester hours (hours in computer, education, and outside education not specified); thesis required; internship or practicum not specified. *Faculty:* 4 full-time; 6 part-time. *Students:* 20. *Financial Assistance:* Teaching or research assistantships. *Degrees Awarded 1993:* M.S., 10.

NORTH CAROLINA

Appalachian State University. Department of Library Science and Educational Foundations, Boone, NC 28608. (704) 262-2243. Dr. John H. Tashner. *Specialization:* M.A. in Educational Media (Instructional Technology-Computers). Master's program started in 1986. *Minimum Degree Requirements:* 36 semester hours; thesis optional; internship required. *Admission Requirements:* Selective. *Faculty:* 2 full-time; 1 part-time.

North Carolina State University. Department of Curriculum and Instruction, P.O. Box 7801, Raleigh, NC 27695-7801. (919) 515-1779. Dr. Ellen Vasu, Assoc. Prof., Dept. of Curriculum and Instruction. *Specializations:* M.Ed. and M.S. in Instructional Technology-Computers (program track within one master's in Curriculum and Instruction). Master's program started in 1986. *Minimum Degree Requirements:* 36 semester hours; thesis optional; practicum required. *Faculty 1990-91:* 3 full-time. *Students:* 18.

Western Carolina University. Cullowhee, NC 28723. (704) 227-7415. Dr. Don Chalker, Head, Dept. of Administration, Curriculum and Instruction. *Specializations:* M.A.Ed. in Supervision, with concentration in Educational Technology-Computers. Master's program started in 1987. *Minimum Degree Requirements:* 41 semester hours (18 hours in computers, 20 hours in education, 3 hours outside education); internship required. *Faculty:* 25-plus full-time. *Students:* 13.

NORTH DAKOTA

Minot State University. 500 University Ave. W., Minot, ND 58707. (701) 857-3817. Fax (701) 839-6933. Dr. James Croonquist, Dean, Graduate School. *Specializations:* M.S. in Audiology, M.S. in Education of the Deaf, M.S. in Elementary Education, M.S. in Learning Disabilities, M.S. in Special Education, M.S. in Speech-Language Pathology, M.A.T. in Mathematics, M.S. in Criminal Justice, M.A.T. in Science, M.M.E. in Music, M.S. in School Psychology. Master's program started in 1964. *Admission Requirements:* Application with $20 fee, three letters of recommendation, 300-word autobiography, transcripts. *Minimum Degree Requirements:* 45 quarter hours (hours in computers, education, and outside education vary according to program). *Faculty:* 84 full-time; 26 part-time. *Students:* 142. *Financial Assistance:* Loans, teaching assistantships, research assistantships, tuition waivers, scholarships. *Degrees Awarded 1993:* Master's, 65.

OHIO

*The Ohio State University. 236 Ramseyer Hall, 29 W. Woodruff Ave., Columbus, OH 43210-1177. (614) 292-4872. Dr. Marjorie A. Cambre, Assoc. Prof., The Ohio State University. *Specializations:* M.A. and Ph.D. in Computers in Education in the Program Area of Instructional Design and Technology. For additional information, see listings for Doctoral and Master's Programs.

Wright State University. College of Education and Human Services, 244 Millett Hall, Dayton, OH 45435. (513) 873-2509 or (513) 873-2182. Fax (513) 873-3301. Dr. Bonnie K. Mathies, Chair, Dept. of Educational Technology, Vocational Education, and Allied Programs. *Specializations:* M.Ed. in Computer Education; M.Ed. for Computer Coordinator; M.A. in Computer Education. Master's programs started in 1985. *Admission Requirements:*

2.7 GPA for regular admission; GRE or Miller Analogies Test. *Minimum Degree Requirements:* 48 quarter hours (hours in computers, education, and outside education not specified); thesis required for M.A. degree only; comprehensive examination in the form of the completion of a portfolio and a videotaped presentation to the faculty for M.Ed.; eligible for Supervisor's Certificate after completion of C&S; Computer Coordinator program. *Faculty:* 2 full-time; 9 part-time adjuncts and other university full-time faculty and staff. *Students:* 2 full-time; 31 part-time. *Financial Assistance:* Graduate assistantships available, including three positions in the College's Educational Resource Center; limited number of small graduate scholarships. *Degrees Awarded 1993:* M.A. and M.Ed., 11.

OKLAHOMA

The University of Oklahoma. Department of Educational Psychology, 820 Van Vleet Oval, Norman, OK 73019. (405) 325-1521. Fax (405) 325-3242. E-mail tragan@aardvark.ucs.uoknor.edu. Dr. Tillman J. Ragan, Prof. *Specialization:* M.Ed. in Educational Technology with Computer Applications emphasis. For additional options in Educational Technology, see the listing for Master's Programs. *Admission Requirements:* 3.0 GPA over last 60 hours of undergraduate work or at least 12 credit hours of graduate work with a 3.0 GPA from an accredited college or university. *Minimum Degree Requirements:* 32 semester hours (12 hours in computers, 21 hours in education [including computers 12]); internship required. *Faculty:* 10 full-time; 2 part-time. *Students:* 5 full-time; 24 part-time. *Financial Assistance:* Assistantships; out-of-state fee waivers; graduate scholarships (both general and targeted minorities). *Degrees Awarded 1 July 1992-30 June 1993:* M.Ed., 7.

TEXAS

*Texas A&M University. Department of Interdisciplinary Education, Educational Technology Program, College Station, TX 77843. (409) 845-7276. Fax (409) 845-9663. Dr. Ronald Zellner, Coord., Educational Technology. *Specializations:* M.Ed. in Educational Technology, emphasis in computer applications. Master's program started in 1984. *Admission Requirements:* GPA, 3.0; GRE 800. *Minimum Degree Requirements:* 37 semester hours (12 hours in computers, 6 hours in education); internship or practicum required. *Faculty:* 4 full-time; 1 part-time. *Students:* Data not available. *Financial Assistance:* Teaching assistantships available. *Degrees Awarded 1 July 1991-30 June 1992:* M.Ed., 12.

Texas Tech University. College of Education, Box 41071, TTU, Lubbock, TX 79409. (806) 742-2362. Fax (806) 742-2179. Dr. Robert Price, Dir., Instructional Technology. *Specializations:* M.Ed. in Instructional Technology (Educational Computing emphasis); Ed.D. in Instructional Technology. Master's program started in 1981; doctoral in 1982. *Admission Requirements:* M.Ed., GRE score of 800+; GPA of 2.7 on last 30 hours of undergraduate program. Ed.D., GRE score of 1050; GPA of 2.7 on last 30 hours. *Minimum Degree Requirements:* Master's—39 hours (24 hours in computing, 15 hours in education or outside education); practicum required. Doctorate—87 hours (45 hours in educational technology, 18 hours in education, 15 hours in resource area or minor); practicum required. *Faculty:* 3 full-time; 3 part-time. *Students:* Approximately 25 FTE. *Financial Assistance:* Teaching and research assistantships available ($7,500/9 months). *Degrees Awarded 1 July 1992-30 June 1993:* Ed.D., 2; M.Ed., 7.

*Texas Wesleyan University. School of Education, 1201 Wesleyan, Fort Worth, TX 76105. (817) 531-4952. Dr. R. J. Wilson, Coord., Information Processing Technology. *Specialization:* M.S.Ed. in Information Processing Technology. Master's program started in 1982. *Admission Requirements:* Undergraduate GPA 2.75 for conditional admission; 3.0 GPA for regular admission. *Minimum Degree Requirements:* 36 semester hours (18 hours directly related to Information Processing Technologies). Additional certification in IPT without a degree is also an option. *Faculty:* 1.5 full-time. *Students:* 18. *Financial Assistance:* Partial tuition waivers available to full-time teachers. *Degrees Awarded 1 July 1991-30 June 1992:* M.S.Ed., 14.

*University of North Texas. Department of Computer Education and Cognitive Systems, Box 5155-UNT, Denton, TX 76203. (817) 565-3790. Fax (817) 565-2185. Dr. Jon Young, Chair. *Specializations:* M.S. in Computer Education and Cognitive Systems; Information Processing Technology Endorsement Levels I and II. Master's program started in 1987. *Admission Requirements:* Minimum GRE scores of 400 on verbal and 400 on quantitative with total score of 900; minimum of 18 undergraduate hours in education, personnel training and management, or the behavioral sciences. *Minimum Degree Requirements:* 36 semester hours (33 in computers, 6 in education); thesis, internship, practicum not specified. *Faculty:* 8 full-time tenure track; 4 non-tenure track lecturers. *Students:* M.S., 85; doctoral minors, 12. *Financial Assistance:* Teaching fellowships in spring and fall semesters; teaching assistantships available as computer laboratory consultants (contact is Dr. Kathlyn Y. Canaday, (817) 565-4436). *Degrees Awarded 1 July 1991-30 June 1992:* M.S., 33; doctoral, 0—program is still pending.

VIRGINIA

George Mason University. Center for Interactive Educational Technology, Mail Stop 4B3, 4400 University Dr., Fairfax, VA 22030-4444. (703) 993-2052. Fax (703) 993-2013. Dr. Charles S. White, Coord. of Instructional Technology Academic Programs. *Specializations:* M.Ed. in Instructional Technology with tracks in Instructional Design and Development, School-Based Technology Coordinator, Instructional Applications of Technology, Computer Science Educator; M.Ed. in Special Education Technology (S.E.T.); Ph.D. with specialization in Instructional Technology or Special Education Technology. Master's program started in 1983 and doctoral in 1984. *Admission Requirements:* Teaching or training experience; introductory programming course or equivalent; introductory course in educational technology or equivalent. *Minimum Degree Requirements:* M.Ed. in Instructional Technology, 36 hours; practicum/internship/project required. M.Ed. in Special Education Technology, 36-42 hours. Ph.D., 56-62 hours beyond master's degree for either specialization. *Faculty:* 5 full-time; 5 part-time. *Students:* M.Ed.-I.T.—6 full-time; 36 part-time. M.Ed.-S.E.T.—10 full-time; 8 part-time. Ph.D.—10 part-time. *Financial Assistance:* Assistantships and tuition waivers available for full-time (9 credits) graduate students. *Degrees Awarded 1 July 1992-30 June 1993:* M.Ed.-I.T., 10; M.Ed.-S.E.T., 7; Ph.D., 3.

*Hampton University. School of Liberal Arts and Education, 301 A Phenix Hall, Hampton, VA 23668. (804) 727-5751. Fax (804) 727-5084. Dr. JoAnn W. Haysbert, Prof. and Coord. of Graduate Programs in Education. *Specialization:* M.A. in Computer Education. Master's program started in 1983. *Admission Requirements:* Completed application; B.A. from accredited college or university; acceptable GRE scores; two letters of recommendation from professional educators; undergraduate record of above-average scholarship. *Minimum Degree Requirements:* 36 semester hours (21 hours in computers, 15 in education, 0 hours outside education); practicum required. *Faculty:* 4 part-time. *Students:* 32 part-time. *Financial Assistance:* Limited number of teaching, research, laboratory, or resident hall assistantships are available to qualified graduate students, as well as fellowships. Also available are guaranteed student loans and college work-study and tuition assistance grant programs. *Degrees Awarded 1 July 1991-30 June 1992:* M.A., 4.

*Virginia Polytechnic Institute and State University. Instructional Systems Development, College of Education, War Memorial Hall, Blacksburg, VA 24061-0313. (703) 231-5598. Fax (703) 231-3717. Thomas M. Sherman, Prof., Prog. Area Leader, Instructional Systems Development, Curriculum and Instruction. *Specializations:* Ed.D. and Ph.D. programs in Instructional Technology. *Features:* Areas of emphasis are Instructional Design, Educational Computing, Evaluation, Media Management, Speech Synthesis, and Telecommunications. *Admission Requirements:* 3.3 GPA for master's degree; three letters of recommendation; transcripts of previous academic work. *Faculty:* 8 full-time; 5 part-time. *Students:* 6 full-time; 6 part-time. *Financial Assistance:* 10 assistantships; tuition scholarships; contracts with other agencies. *Degrees Awarded 1 July 1991-30 June 1992:* Master's, 2; doctoral, 1.

WASHINGTON

Eastern Washington University. Department Computer Science, Cheney, WA 99004-2495. (509) 359-7092. Fax (509) 359-2215. Dr. Donald R. Horner, Prof. of Computer Science. *Specializations:* M.Ed. in Computer Education (elementary); M.Ed. in Computer Education (secondary); M.S. in Computer Education (Interdisciplinary). Master's program started in 1983. *Admission Requirements:* GRE, at least 3.0 GPA for last 90 quarter credits (60 semester credits). *Minimum Degree Requirements:* M.S., 52 quarter hours (30 hours in computers, 0 hours in education, 8 hours outside education—not specifically computer science; the hours do not total to 52 because of freedom to choose where Methods of Research is taken, where 12 credits of supporting courses are taken, and where additional electives are taken); thesis not required (a research project with formal report is required, although it need not be a thesis in format); internship and/or practicum not required. M.S., 52 quarter hours divided between computer science and another science or mathematics; one area is primary and includes a research project; the second area generally requires fewer hours than the primary. M.Ed., 48 quarter hours minimum (24 hours in computer science, 16 hours in education, 8 hours outside education). Most projects involve the use of high-level authoring systems to develop educational products. *Faculty:* 3 full-time. *Students:* About 35. *Financial Assistance:* Some research and teaching fellowships; financial assistance. *Degrees Awarded 1 July 1992-30 June 1993:* M.S. and M.Ed., 5.

Western Washington University. Woodring College of Education, Bellingham, WA 98225. (206) 650-3090. Fax (206) 650-6526. Dr. Tony Jongejan, Assoc. Prof. of Education. *Specializations:* M.Ed. in Instructional Technology with Elementary, Secondary, Administrative, or Adult Education emphasis. *Minimum Degree Requirements:* 52 quarter hours (15 hours in computers, 24 hours in education, 0 hours outside education); thesis required; internship and practicum possible. *Faculty:* 4 full-time; 2 part-time. *Students:* 30. *Financial Assistance:* Work study, graduate assistantships. *Degrees Awarded 1993:* M.Ed., 10.

316 \ Graduate Programs

WISCONSIN

Edgewood College. Department of Education, 855 Woodrow St., Madison, WI 53711. (608) 257-4861, ext. 2293. Fax (608) 257-1455. E-mail schmied@edgewood.edu. Dr. Joseph E. Schmiedicke, Chair, Dept. of Education. *Specializations:* M.A. in Education with emphasis on Computer-Based Education. Master's program started in 1987. *Admission Requirements:* 2.75/4.0 GPA. *Minimum Degree Requirements:* 36 semester hours (18 hours in computers, 30 hours in education, 6 hours outside education). *Faculty:* 2 full-time; 3 part-time. *Students:* 115. *Degrees Awarded 1993:* M.A., 6.

Scholarships, Fellowships, and Awards

In the instructional technology/media-related fields, various scholarships, fellowships, and awards have been established. Many of these are available to those who either are or will be pursuing advanced degrees at the master's, six-year specialist, or doctoral levels.

Because various colleges, universities, professional organizations, and governmental agencies offer scholarships, fellowships, and awards and may wish to have them included in this section, it would be greatly appreciated if those aware of such financial awards would contact either the editors or the publisher for inclusion of such entries in the next edition of *EMTY*.

We are greatly indebted to the staff members of the Association for Educational Communications and Technology (AECT) for assisting with this section.

Information is furnished in the following sequence:

- Overview of AECT and ECT Foundation Awards

- AECT Awards

- ECT Foundation Awards

AECT AND ECT FOUNDATION AWARDS

The Association for Educational Communications and Technology recognizes and rewards the outstanding achievement of its members and associates through a program that provides for three major annual awards—Achievement, Special Service, and Distinguished Service—and through the ECT Foundation, which provides awards in the areas of leadership, scholarship, and research.

AECT encourages members and associates to apply for these awards, and to disseminate information about the awards to professional colleagues. Specific information about each award is available from the AECT national office. The annual deadline for submitting most award applications is October 15.

All ECT Foundation and AECT awards are presented during the AECT National Convention and InCITE Exposition.

For additional information on all awards, please contact:

AECT Awards Program
1025 Vermont Ave. NW
Suite 820
Washington, DC 20005
(202) 347-7834

AECT Awards

The Association for Educational Communications and Technology (AECT) provides for three annual awards:

Special Service Award: Granted to a person who has shown notable service to AECT as a whole or to one of its programs or divisions (nominee must have been a member of AECT for at least 10 years and must not be currently an AECT officer, board member, or member of the Awards Committee).

Distinguished Service Award: Granted to a person who has shown outstanding leadership in advancing the theory and/or practice of educational communications and technology over a substantial period of time (nominee need not be an AECT member but must not have received this award previously).

Annual Achievement Award: Honors the individual who during the past year has made the most significant contribution to the advancement of educational communications and technology (nominee need not be a member of AECT, and the award can be given to the same person more than once).

AECT/SIRS Intellectual Freedom Award (in conjunction with the Social Issues Resources Services Inc.): Recognizes a media specialist at any level who has upheld the principles of intellectual freedom as set forth in AECT's publication "Media, the Learner, and Intellectual Freedom" and provides $1,000 for the individual and $1,000 for the media center of the recipient's choice (recipient must be a personal member of AECT).

ECT Foundation Awards

The ECT Foundation, a nonprofit organization that carries out the purposes of AECT that are charitable and educational in nature, coordinates the following awards:

AECT National Convention Internship Program: Provides complimentary registration and housing at the annual conference plus a cash award for four full-time graduate students (applicants must be a member of AECT and enrolled in a recognized program in educational communications and technology).

Richard B. Lewis Memorial Award: Presented to the outstanding school district media utilization program along with a cash award (awarded to either a public or private school having media utilization programs in place).

AECT Leadership Development Grants: Supports innovative leadership development activities undertaken by affiliates, divisions, or regions with cash grants (special consideration will be given to proposals that demonstrate a commitment to leadership development, that propose programs unique to the applicant's organization, and that include activities of potential benefit to other AECT programs).

AECT Memorial Scholarship Award: Donations given in memory of specific past leaders of the field provide a scholarship fund that gives annual cash grants to AECT members enrolled in educational technology graduate studies (three letters of recommendation are required).

Dean and Sybil McClusky Research Award: Recognizes the year's outstanding doctoral thesis proposal that has been approved by the student's university and offers a cash reward to defray the research expenses (the winner must agree to complete the proposed study).

Robert M. Gagné Instructional Development Research Award: Recognizes the most significant contribution by a graduate student to the body of knowledge on which instructional development is based with a plaque and a cash prize (the research must have been done in the past three years while the candidate was enrolled as a graduate student).

James W. Brown Publication Award: Recognizes the outstanding publication in the field of educational technology in any media format during the past year with a cash award (excluded from consideration are doctoral, master's, or other types of dissertations prepared in fulfillment of degree program requirements).

ETR&D Young Scholar Award: Recognizes a fresh, creative approach to research and theory in educational technology by a young scholar (applicant must be an individual who does not hold a doctorate degree or who has received a doctorate degree within the past three years).

Young Researcher Award: Recognizes an outstanding unpublished report of research of an experimental, descriptive, or historical nature by a researcher who has not yet attained the doctorate or is less than three years beyond the degree (jointly published papers are not accepted).

AECT Special Service Award

Qualifications

- Award is granted to a person who has shown notable service to AECT. This service may be to the organization as a whole, one of its programs, or one of its divisions.

- Nominee currently must be a member of AECT and have at least 10 years of service to AECT.

Disqualifications

- Recipient may not now be serving as an elected officer of AECT nor as a member of the board of directors.

- Nominee must not be currently serving as a member of the AECT Awards Committee.

Nomination

Nominations are judged and selected on the basis of an outstanding contribution to a division, committee, commission, or program of AECT but not to an affiliate organization. Please provide as much information as you can.

- Write in 100 words or less why you think nominee should receive this award. Include a description of nominee's contribution.

- What year did nominee join AECT?

AECT Distinguished Service Award

Qualifications

- Award is granted to a person who has shown outstanding leadership in advancing the theory and/or practice of educational communications and technology over a substantial period of time.

- The nominee need not be a member of AECT.

- Award may be given posthumously.

Disqualifications

- Nominee must not have received this award previously.

- Nominee must not be currently serving as a member of the AECT Awards Committee.

Nomination

Nominations are judged primarily on the distinction or magnitude of the nominee's leadership in advancing the field rather than the association.

Categories

- The following categories suggest areas in which the nominee may have rendered distinguished service to the field. The nominee may not be represented in these areas. Use those that apply or add others.

    •Leadership   •Research/Theory   •Development/Production   •Writing

    •Major Contribution to Education Outside the United States

AECT Annual Achievement Award

Qualifications

- Recipient may be an individual or a group.

- The AAA honors the individual who during the past year has made the most significant contribution to the advancement of educational communications and technology.

- The nominee need not be a member of AECT.

- The contribution being honored should be publicly visible—a specific thing or event.

- It must be timely—taking place within approximately the past year.

- Award can be given to the same person more than once.

Nomination

The nature of this award precludes the use of a single checklist or set of categories for nomination. The nomination and selection are inherently subjective. You are asked simply to present a succinct argument in favor of your nominee. Your statement ought to answer the following questions:

- What is the specific achievement being honored?

- What impact has this achievement had, or is likely to have, on the field?

- How is the nominee connected with the achievement?

ECT Foundation
1995 AECT/SIRS Intellectual Freedom Award

Purpose: To recognize, annually, a media professional at any level who has upheld the principles of intellectual freedom as set forth in *Media, the Learner, and Intellectual Freedom: A Handbook*, published by AECT.

Award: The award shall consist of:

1. a plaque and $1,000 for the winning media professional, to be presented at the AECT National Convention and InCITE Exposition;

2. a plaque plus $1,000 for the media center designated by the recipient;

3. the opportunity for the recipient to present a session on intellectual freedom at the AECT National Convention and InCITE Exposition.

Selection: The following criteria will be used in the selection process:

1. The recipient will be a media specialist at any level.

2. The recipient will be a member of AECT.

3. The recipient shall not have received another intellectual freedom award in the same year if that award was sponsored by SIRS, Inc.

4. The recipient will meet at least one of the following criteria:

   - has developed and implemented an exemplary selection policy/ challenge procedure for educational nonprint material.

   - has developed an innovative information program on intellectual freedom for nonprint media.

   - has upheld intellectual freedom principles in the face of a challenge to educational nonprint media.

   - has been active in the establishment and/or continuation of a coalition relating to intellectual freedom.

   - has been active in the development of a legal base for the continued enjoyment of intellectual freedom.

Selection
Committee: A subcommittee of the AECT Intellectual Freedom Committee is responsible for the selection of the winner.

ECT Foundation
1995 AECT National Convention
Internship Program

Awards: Four students will be chosen as convention interns. The winners will receive complimentary convention registration, complimentary housing, and $200 cash award. The interns will be expected to arrive at the convention on the day before the convention and to stay until the close of the convention. (Applicants are encouraged to request financial support for transportation and on-site expenses from their institutions or state affiliate organizations.)

Program
Activities: Each intern will be expected to participate fully in a coordinated program of activities. These activities include private seminars with selected association and professional leaders in the field, observation of the AECT governance and program committees, and behind-the-scenes views of the convention itself. Each intern will also be responsible for specific convention-related assignments, which will require approximately 15 hours of time during the convention. A former intern, who is now a member of the AECT Leadership Development Committee, will serve as the program coordinator.

Eligibility: To qualify for consideration, an applicant must be a full-time student throughout the current academic year in a recognized graduate program in educational communications and technology, and must be a member of AECT. (Applicant may join AECT when applying for the award.)

Application
Process: To apply for the internship program, qualified graduate students must complete and return an application form and must submit two letters of recommendation.

ECT Foundation
1995 Richard B. Lewis Memorial Award

Award: $750, provided by the Richard B. Lewis Memorial Fund for "Outstanding School District Media Utilization," is awarded to the winner.

Selection
Process: The winner will be selected by a unified committee appointed from the divisions of Educational Media Management (DEMM) and School Media Specialists (DSMS) of the Association for Educational Communications and Technology, and the National Association of Regional Media Centers (NARMC).

Selection
Criteria: • Evidence of strong media utilization as gathered from:

                    1. special utilization studies conducted by or for the school district;

                    2. specific instances of good utilization as described in writing by school district or other personnel.

                 • Evidence of having provided in the school district budget means of implementing good utilization programs in its schools and of the degree to which AECT/ALA media standards are met for services, equipment, and personnel.

                 • Assessment of applicant's statements as to how the $750 (if awarded) would be spent, such as for:

                    1. attending national, regional, or state conferences or workshops related to media utilization;

                    2. selecting media specialist(s) to attend advanced training programs;

                    3. buying software or hardware needed to improve media utilization programs;

                    4. other purposes (indicating especially creative approaches).

                 • Recognition by an AECT state, regional, or national affiliate organization or representative, or from a National Association of Regional Media Centers state or regional representative:

                    1. through prior recognition or awards;

                    2. through a recommendation.

Eligibility: All school districts, public and private, having media utilization programs in place, and conforming to the preceding criteria, are eligible.

Other: The winning district will receive a plaque as part of this award.

ECT Foundation
1995 Leadership Development Grants

Grants: Grants of up to $500 are provided by the ECT Foundation and administered
            by the AECT Leadership Development Committee. The grants are awarded
            to assist AECT affiliates, AECT divisions, and AECT regional organizations
            to undertake leadership development activities that will improve participants'
            skills as leaders in the professional organization or in educational technology.

Selection: Grant awards will be recommended by the Leadership Committee's Subcommittee
            on Leadership Development Grants.

Selection
Criteria: All AECT state affiliates, divisions, and regional organizations are eligible
            for these competitive grants. An application from a previous grant recipient
            will not be considered unless a summary report has been submitted to the
            Leadership Development Committee and the AECT national office. Organi-
            zations that have not received a grant in the past are particularly invited to
            apply. Funds must be intended for some unique aspect or function not
            previously undertaken. Proposals that demonstrate a commitment to leader-
            ship development, that propose programs that are unique to the applicant's
            organization, and that include activities or products of potential benefit
            to other AECT programs will be given special consideration.

Awards: The awards will be presented during the AECT National Convention and
            InCITE Exposition.

ECT Foundation
1995 AECT Memorial Scholarships

Awards: One scholarship of $1,000 and one scholarship of $750 are awarded to graduate students in educational communications/technology to carry out a research project in the field. The scholarships may be used to assist the recipients to further their education in a summer session or academic year of graduate study at any accredited college or university in the United States or Canada. Programs of study may be at the master's or doctoral level.

Eligibility: All recipients must be members of AECT and accepted in or enrolled in a graduate-level degree program as outlined above.

Selection
Criteria: Selections will be based on the following:

1. scholarship;

2. experience related to the field of educational media, communications, or technology, such as employment, field experience, course work, assistantships, publications, etc.;

3. service to the field through AECT activities and membership in other related professional organizations;

4. three letters of recommendation from persons familiar with the candidate's professional qualifications and leadership potential;

5. the candidate's own knowledge of key issues and opportunities facing the educational communications/technology field today, with respect to the candidate's own goals.

ECT Foundation
1995 Dean and Sybil McClusky
Research Award

Award: $1,000 is available to honor two outstanding doctoral research proposals in
                    educational technology, as selected by a jury of researchers from AECT's
                    Research and Theory Division. Each winner will be awarded $500.

Guidelines
for Preparing
and Submitting
Papers: Submitted proposals may follow acceptable formats of individual schools but
                    must include at least:

                    1. The definition of the problem including a statement of significance;

                    2. A review of pertinent literature;

                    3. Research hypothesis to be examined;

                    4. Research design and procedures including statistical techniques.

                    Applicants are encouraged to review pages 157-61 of Stephen Isaac and
                    William B. Michaels, *Handbook in Research and Evaluation*, Robert R.
                    Knapp, San Diego, CA, 1971.

Eligibility: Applicants must be presently enrolled in a doctoral program in educational
                    technology and have obtained committee acceptance of their proposal. The
                    winner will be expected to sign a statement that the proposed doctoral study
                    will be completed in accordance with the sponsoring university's graduate
                    school policies (including any time limitations) or be required to return the
                    funds received.

ECT Foundation
1995 Robert M. Gagné Award for Graduate Student
Research in Instructional Technology

Purpose:	To provide recognition and financial assistance for outstanding research by a graduate student in the field of instructional development.
Description:	The Robert M. Gagné Award Fund is coordinated by the ECT Foundation, a nonprofit organization sponsored and controlled by the Association of Educational Communications and Technology (AECT). The Division of Instructional Development will solicit nominations for the Gagné Award and will select the winner. The ECT Foundation is responsible for the administration of the award fund and will issue the cash award to the recipient.
Award:	Up to $500 is awarded for the most significant contribution to the body of knowledge upon which instructional development is based. The Gagné Award competition is sponsored by the Association for Educational Communications and Technology (AECT) and its Division of Instructional Development. A jury of scholars will select the winning contribution. The award will be presented to the recipient during the AECT National Convention.
Eligibility:	The work must have been completed after December 31, 1991, while the award candidate was enrolled as a graduate student.
Nomination Procedure:	You may nominate any individual (including yourself) for the Gagné Award.

ECT Foundation
1995 James W. Brown Publication Award

Award:	$300 will be given to the author or authors of an outstanding publication in the field of educational technology.
Eligibility:	Nominated items are not restricted to books or print; they may be in any media format (film, video, broadcast program, book, etc.). Any nonperiodic publication in the field of educational technology is eligible if it bears a publication date of 1993 or 1994.
Guidelines for Nominations:	Nominations are solicited from all possible sources: AECT members, media-related publishers and producers, authors themselves, the AECT nonperiodic publications committee, and others.
Criteria:	Nominated publications shall be judged on the basis of:

1. Significance of the item's content for the field of media/instructional technology, as defined in the *Definition of Educational Technology*, published by AECT in 1977, or in any subset of the publication.

2. Professional quality of the item.

3. Potential impact of the item's content on the field of media/instructional technology, as defined in the *Definition of Educational Technology*.

4. Technical quality of the item.

ECT Foundation
1995 ETR&D Young Scholar Award

Award: $500 will be presented to the winner. Additionally, the winning paper will be published in *ETR&D*, the refereed scholarly research journal published by the Association for Educational Communications and Technology (AECT).

For: The best paper discussing a theoretical construct that could guide research in educational technology, considered worthy by a panel of judges.

Eligibility: An individual who does not hold a doctorate degree or who received a doctorate not more than three years ago as of September 1, 1994.

Guidelines
for Preparing
and Submitting
Papers: 1. Papers must deal with research and theory in educational technology and must include:

- A problem area stated within a well-explicated theoretical construct;

- Supporting citations and analyses of related research;

- A concluding discussion centering on what directions future research might take, with specific regard to variables, subjects, settings, etc., and, if appropriate, suggestions concerning other theoretical constructs that should be taken into consideration;

2. The paper should not be a report of a specific study.

3. A fresh, imaginative approach—which may go beyond the data—is encouraged.

4. The paper must be an original unpublished work.

5. The paper should be a maximum of 35 double-spaced typewritten pages.

6. The paper must be submitted in publishable journal format and must conform to the *American Psychological Association Style Manual*, 3d ed.

Selection
of
Winner: The selection of the winning paper will be the responsibility of the editor and editorial board of *ETR&D*. Only the best paper judged worthy of the award will win. (There may not be a recipient of this award every year.)

ECT Foundation
1995 Young Researcher Award

Award: $500 for the best report of an experimental, descriptive, or historical study in educational technology. The Young Researcher award competition is sponsored by the Research and Theory Division of the Association for Educational Communications and Technology (AECT). A jury of scholars will select the best contribution for presentation at the AECT National Convention and InCITE Exposition. The winner will receive the cash award plus a certificate suitable for framing.

Eligibility: Anyone who is not more than three years beyond a doctorate as of December 31, 1994. A doctorate is not required. Jointly published papers are not acceptable.

Guidelines
for Preparing
and Submitting
Papers: Papers must report an original, unpublished research effort of an experimental, descriptive, or historical nature and must include the following:

1. problem area stated within a well-explicated theoretical construct(s);

2. supporting citations and analyses of related research;

3. exemplary reporting of research design or procedures and full description of statistical procedures where applicable;

4. concluding discussion that centers on directions for future research and implications for future directions in the field.

Other: Manuscripts may be a maximum of 35 double-spaced typewritten pages. The manuscript must be submitted in publishable journal format and must conform to the *American Psychological Association Style Manual*, 3d ed. The author's name should be included *only* on the cover sheet. All manuscripts will be coded and reviewed "blind."

Part Eight
Mediagraphy

Print and Nonprint Resources

Nancy R. Preston
Consultant
ERIC Clearinghouse on Information & Technology
Syracuse University
Syracuse, New York

Introduction

CONTENTS

This resource list includes media-related journals, books, ERIC documents, and journal articles of interest to practitioners, researchers, students, and others concerned with educational technology and educational media. The emphasis in this section is on *currency*; the vast majority of books cited here were published in 1993. ERIC documents and journal articles were all *announced* in the ERIC database in 1993, but many of them were issued in the latter half of the previous year and bear a 1992 publication date. Media-related journals include those listed in past issues of *EMTY* and new entries in the field.

SELECTION

Items were selected for the Mediagraphy in several ways. The ERIC (Educational Resources Information Center) Database was the source for ERIC document and journal article citations. Most of these entries are from a subset of the database selected by the directors of the ERIC Clearinghouse on Information Resources as being the year's most important database entries for this field. Media-related journals were either retained on the list or added to the list when they met one or more of the following criteria: were from a reputable publisher; had a broad circulation; were covered by indexing services; were peer reviewed; filled a gap in the literature. Journal data were verified using *Ulrich's International Periodicals Directory 1992-93*. Finally, the complete contents of the Mediagraphy were reviewed by the editors of *EMTY 1994*.

OBTAINING RESOURCES

Media-Related Periodicals and Books. Publisher, price, and ordering/subscription address are listed wherever available.

ERIC Documents. ERIC documents can be read in microfiche at any library holding an ERIC microfiche collection. The identification number beginning with ED (for example, ED 332 677) is used to find the document in the collection. ERIC documents can also be ordered from the ERIC Document Reproduction Service. Prices charged depend upon format chosen (microfiche or paper copy), length of the document, and method of shipping. Online orders, fax orders, and expedited delivery are available.

To find the closest library with an ERIC microfiche collection, contact:

ACCESS ERIC
1600 Research Blvd.
Rockville, MD 20850-3172
1-800-LET-ERIC (538-3742)
Internet: ACCERIC@GWUVM.GWU.EDU

To order ERIC documents, contact:

ERIC Document Reproduction Service (EDRS)
7420 Fullerton Rd., Suite 110
Springfield, VA 22153-2852
voice: 1-800-443-ERIC (443-3742), 1-703-440-1400
fax: 703-440-1408
Internet: EDRS@GWUVM.GWU.EDU

Journal Articles. Journal articles can be obtained in one of the following ways: (1) from a library subscribing to the title; (2) through interlibrary loan; (3) through the purchase of a back issue from the journal publisher; or (4) from an article reprint service. Articles noted as being available from the UMI (University Microfilms International) reprint service can be ordered using their ERIC identification numbers (numbers beginning with EJ, such as EJ 421 772).

University Microfilms International (UMI)
Article Clearinghouse
300 North Zeeb Rd.
Ann Arbor, MI 48106
1-800-521-0600 ext. 2533, 2534 (toll-free in U.S.)
1-800-343-5299 ext. 2533, 2534 (toll-free in Canada)

ARRANGEMENT

Mediagraphy entries are classified according to major subject emphasis under the following headings:

- Artificial Intelligence and Robotics
- CD-ROM
- Computer-Assisted Instruction
- Databases and Online Searching
- Distance Education
- Educational Research
- Educational Technology

- Electronic Publishing
- Information Science and Technology
- Instructional Design and Training
- Libraries and Media Centers
- Media Technologies
- Simulation and Virtual Reality
- Telecommunications and Networking

Mediagraphy

ARTIFICIAL INTELLIGENCE AND ROBOTICS

Media-Related Periodicals

Artificial Intelligence Abstracts. Bowker A & I Publishing, 121 Chanlon Rd., New Providence, NJ 07974. mo.; $495. Primarily for the specialist; includes abstracts of journal articles, reports, research documents, and other sources about artificial intelligence.

Intelligent Tutoring Media. Learned Information, 143 Old Marlton Pike, Medford, NJ 08055. q.; $125. Concerned with the packaging and communication of knowledge using advanced information technologies. Studies the impact of artificial intelligence, hypertext, and interactive video.

International Journal of Robotics Research. MIT Press, 55 Hayward St., Cambridge, MA 02142. bi-mo.; $80 indiv., $176 inst., $50 students and retired. Interdisciplinary approach to the study of robotics for researchers, scientists, and students.

Journal of Artificial Intelligence in Education. Association for Advancement of Computing in Education, Box 2966, Charlottesville, VA 22902. q.; $65 indiv., $88 libraries. International journal publishes articles on how intelligent computer technologies can be used in education to enhance learning and teaching. Reports on research and developments, integration, and applications of artificial intelligence in education.

Knowledge-Based Systems. Butterworth-Heinemann Ltd., Turpin Transactions, Ltd., Distribution Centre, Blackhorse Rd., Letchworth, Herts SG6 1HN, England. q.; £165. Interdisciplinary and applications-oriented journal on fifth-generation computing, expert systems, and knowledge-based methods in system design.

Mind and Machines. Kluwer Academic Publishers, Box 358, Accord Station, Hingham, MA 02018-0358. q.; $157. Discusses issues concerning machines and mentality, artificial intelligence, epistemology, simulation, and modeling.

Books

Lajoie, Susanne P., and Derry, Sharon J., eds. (1993). **Computers as cognitive tools.** Lawrence Erlbaum Associates, 365 Broadway, Hillsdale, NJ 07642. 392pp. $32.50 (paper). Essays representing two opposing camps: one evolving out of the intelligent tutoring movement, which employs artificial intelligence technologies in the service of student modeling and precision diagnosis, and the other emerging from a constructivist/developmental perspective that promotes exploration and social interaction.

Journal Articles

Bossinger, June, and Milheim, William D. (1993, July). The development and application of expert systems: A national survey. **Educational Technology, 33**(7), 7-17. EJ 465 833. (Available UMI.) Covers uses of expert systems, types of computers and software used, and expert systems shells and development costs.

Caro, Denis H. J. (1992, May). Expert support systems in an emergency management environment: An evaluative framework. **Educational and Training Technology International, 29**(2), 132-42. EJ 447 549. (Available UMI.) Presents a decision matrix construct for selection of an ESS for casualty disposition training, and describes four system options of simulation models that deal with emergency management.

Gisolfi, A., and others. (1993, January). Enhancing the learning process with expert systems. **Educational Technology, 33**(1), 25-32. EJ 457 883. (Available UMI.) Highlights an expert system that was developed to enhance the learning process in the field of grammatical constructs. Addressed are representing the natural language, parsing, LOGOOP (Logo in Object Oriented Programming), and user system interface.

CD-ROM

Media-Related Periodicals

CD-ROM Databases. Worldwide Videotex, Box 138, Babson Park, Boston, MA 02157. mo.; $150 U.S., $190 elsewhere. Descriptive listing of all databases being marketed on CD-ROM with vendor and system information.

CD-ROM Librarian. Meckler Publishing Corp., 11 Ferry Lane W., Westport, CT 06880-5808. 11/yr.; $82. Information about optical technologies relevant to libraries and information centers.

CD-ROM Professional. Pemberton Press, Inc., 11 Tannery Lane, Weston, CT 06883. bi-mo.; $86 U.S., $101 Canada and Mexico, $121 foreign airmail. Assists publishers, librarians, and other information professionals in the selection, evaluation, purchase, and operation of CD-ROM systems.

Books

Shelton, James, ed. (1993). **CD-ROM finder** (5th ed.). Learned Information, 143 Old Marlton Pike, Medford, NJ 08055. $69.50. Directory of more than 1,400 CD-ROM titles, including product content, hardware/software requirements, and market data.

Journal Articles

CD R: The next stage in CD ROM evolution. (1993, March). **CD ROM Professional, 6**(2), 79-83. EJ 459 992. (Available UMI.) Provides an overview of CD-ROM and describes features of CD Recordable (CD R) technology, including disc capacity, data transfer rate, mastering, and multiple write session.

James, Jonathan K. (1993, July). CD-ROM in the information marketplace—A comprehensive study from UMI. **CD-ROM Professional, 6**(4), 102, 104-05. EJ 465 736. (Available UMI.) Discusses results of a telephone survey of academic, private, corporate, and secondary school libraries to track the use of CD-ROM in the library industry, monitor market share levels, and identify trends.

Thiel, Thomas J. (1993, March). Costs of CD ROM production—What they are and how to overcome them. **CD ROM Professional, 6**(2), 43-46. EJ 459 987. (Available UMI.) Describes three steps in CD-ROM production: (1) information base creation; (2) data preparation, conversion, and verification; and (3) indexing and premastering.

COMPUTER-ASSISTED INSTRUCTION

Media-Related Periodicals

Apple Library Users Group Newsletter. Apple Computer, 10381 Bandley Dr., Cupertino, CA 95014. 4/yr.; free. For people interested in using Apple and Macintosh computers in libraries and information centers.

BYTE. Box 550, Hightstown, NJ 08520-9886. mo.; $29.95. Current articles on computer hardware, software, and applications, and reviews of computer products.

CALICO Journal. Computer Assisted Language and Instruction Consortium, 014 Language Building, Duke University, Durham, NC 27706. q.; $35 indiv., $65 inst. Provides information on the applications of technology in teaching and learning languages.

Collegiate Microcomputer. Rose-Hulman Institute of Technology, Department of Mathematics, Terre Haute, IN 47803. q.; $34. Features articles about instructional uses of microcomputers in college and university courses.

Compute. Compute Publications, Inc., Box 3244, Harlan, IA 51593-3244. mo.; $19.94. Specifically designed for users of IBM PC, Tandy, and compatible machines at home, at work, and in the school.

Computer Book Review. 735 Ekekela Pl., Honolulu, HI 96817. 6/yr.; $30. Reviews books on computers and computer-related subjects.

Computers and Education. Pergamon Press, 660 White Plains Rd., Tarrytown, NY 10591-5153. 8/yr.; $581. A theoretical refereed journal that emphasizes research project reports.

Computers and People. Berkeley Enterprises, Inc., 815 Washington St., Newtonville, MA 02160. bi-mo.; $24.50. Covers all aspects of information processing systems with articles, reviews, and games.

Computers and the Humanities. Kluwer Academic Publishers, Box 358, Accord Station, Hingham, MA 02018-0358. bi-mo.; $66 indiv., $189.50 inst. Contains scholarly articles on computer applications in the humanities.

Computers in Human Behavior. Pergamon Press, Inc., 660 White Plains Rd., Tarrytown, NY 10591-5153. q.; £180 ($288 U.S.). Addresses the psychological impact of computer use on individuals, groups, and society.

Computers in the Schools. Haworth Press, 10 Alice St., Binghamton, NY 13904. q.; $34 indiv., $75 inst., $115 libraries. Features articles that combine theory and practical applications of small computers in schools for educators and school administrators.

Computing Teacher. International Society for Technology in Education, University of Oregon, 1787 Agate St., Eugene, OR 97403-9905. 8/yr.; $47 nonmembers, $28.80 members, $23 student members. Focuses on teaching about computers, using computers in teaching and teacher education, and the computer's impact on curricula.

Digest of Software Reviews: Education. School & Home Courseware, Inc., 3999 N. Chestnut Diagonal, Suite 333, Fresno, CA 93726-4797. mo.; $147.50. Compiles software reviews from more than 60 journals and magazines that emphasize critical features of the instructional software for grades K-12.

Dr. Dobb's Journal. M & T Publishing, Inc., 411 Boreal Ave., Suite 100, San Mateo, CA 94402-3516. mo.; $29.97. Articles on the latest in operating systems, programming languages, hardware design and architecture, data structures, and telecommunications; in-depth hardware and software reviews.

Education & Computing. Elsevier Science Publishers, 655 Avenue of the Americas, New York, NY 10010. q; $166. For educators, computer scientists, and decision makers in government, education, and industry, with emphasis on the technical developments in information technology.

Education Technology News. Business Publishers, Inc., 951 Pershing Dr., Silver Spring, MD 20910-4464. bi-w.; $267.54. For teachers and those interested in educational uses of computers in the classroom. Feature articles on applications and educational software.

Electronic Learning. P.O. Box 53797, Boulder, CO 80322-3797. 8/yr.; $23.95. Professional magazine for media specialists, teachers, and administrators that stresses nontechnical information about uses of computers, video equipment, and other electronic devices.

Home Office Computing. Scholastic, Inc., Box 53561, Boulder, CO 80321-1346. mo.; $19.97, foreign $27.97. For professionals who use computers and do business at home.

InCider-A Plus. IDG Communications, Box 58618, Boulder, CO 80322-8616. mo.; $27.97. A magazine for Apple computer users. Reviews new developments in software and hardware and provides how-to articles.

InfoWorld. InfoWorld Publishing, 155 Bovet Rd., Suite 800, San Mateo, CA 94402. w.; $110. News and reviews of PC hardware, software, peripherals, and networking.

Journal of Computer Assisted Learning. Journal Subscription Department, Box 87, Blackwell Scientific Publications Ltd., Osney Mead, Oxford OX2 0DT, England. q.; $49.50 indiv., $197 inst. Articles and research on the use of computer-assisted learning.

Journal of Computer-Based Instruction. Association for the Development of Computer Based Instructional Systems, International Headquarters, 1601 West Fifth Ave., Suite 111, Columbus, OH 43212. q.; $36 nonmembers, single copy $10. Contains both scholarly research and descriptions of practical CBI techniques.

Journal of Educational Computing Research. Baywood Publishing Co., 26 Austin Ave., Box 337, Amityville, NY 11701. q.; $75 indiv., $120 inst. Publishes new research in the theory and applications of educational computing in a variety of content areas and with various ages.

Journal of Research on Computing in Education. International Society for Technology in Education, University of Oregon, 1787 Agate St., Eugene, OR 97403-9905. q.; $65 nonmembers. A technical publication emphasizing current computer research and advances as they apply to all levels of education.

MacWorld. MacWorld Communications, Inc., Box 54529, Boulder, CO 80322-4529. mo.; $30. Describes software, tutorials, and applications for users of the Macintosh microcomputer.

Microcomputer Index. Learned Information, Inc., 143 Old Marlton Pike, Medford, NJ 08055-8750. bi-mo.; $159. Abstracts of literature on the use of microcomputers in business, education, and the home.

Microcomputer Industry Update. Industry Market Reports, Inc., Box 681, Los Altos, CA 94022. mo.; $295. Abstracts of product announcements and reviews of interest appearing in weekly trade press.

Nibble. Mindcraft Publishing Corp., Box 256, Lincoln, MA 01773-0002. mo.; $26.95 U.S., $39.95 elsewhere. Type-in programs for Apple II owners, covering utilities, applications, software reviews, and more.

PC Magazine: The Independent Guide to IBM-Standard Personal Computing. Ziff-Davis Publishing Co., Box 54093, Boulder, CO 80322. bi-w.; $29.97. Comparative reviews of computer hardware and general business software programs.

PC Week. Ziff-Davis Publishing Co., 10 Presidents Landing, Medford, MA 02155-5146. w.; $160, free to qualified personnel. Provides current information on and analyses of hardware, software, and peripherals for the IBM PC as well as buyers' guides and news of the industry.

PC World. PC World Communications, Inc., Box 55029, Boulder, CO 80322-5029. mo.; $29.90 U.S., $49.90 Canada and Mexico, $75.90 elsewhere. Contains new reports on hardware, software, and applications of the IBM PC.

School Tech News. Business Publishers, Inc., 951 Pershing Dr., Silver Spring, MD 20910-4464. mo.; $41. Reports on current developments in computer-based instruction that affect teachers directly.

Social Science Computer Review. Duke University Press, 6697 College Station, Durham, NC 27708. q.; indiv. $36, institutions $72. Features include software reviews, new product announcements, and tutorials for beginners.

Software Digest Ratings Report. National Software Testing Laboratories, Plymouth Corporate Center, Box 1000, Plymouth Meeting, PA 19462. 15/yr.; $445. For IBM personal computer users. Each issue reports the ratings for one category of IBM PC software, based on multiple-user tests.

Software Magazine. Sentry Publishing Co., Inc., 1900 W. Park Dr., Westborough, MA 01581. 17/yr.; $60 U.S, $72 Canada, $125 elsewhere (free to qualified personnel). Focuses on selecting and using business software. Gives addresses of vendors and features of new products.

Software Reviews on File. Facts on File, 460 Park Ave. S., New York, NY 10016. mo.; $210. Condensed software reviews from over 150 publications. Features software for all major microcomputer systems and programming languages.

Teaching and Computers. Scholastic, Inc., 730 Broadway, New York, NY 10003-9538. 6/yr.; $23.95. For the elementary school teacher, with articles on applications of computer-assisted instruction and integrating computers into the classroom environment.

Books

Bailey, Gerald D., ed. (1993). **Computer-based integrated learning systems.** Educational Technology Publications, 700 Palisade Ave., Englewood Cliffs, NJ 07632. 184pp. $32.95. Fifteen chapters provide an introduction to integrated learning systems; a model for improving their performance; factors involved in their implementation; staff development; administrators' and teachers' roles; instructional effectiveness of integrated learning systems; their future; and design experiments for integrating technology into learning.

Bruce, Bertram C., and Rubin, Andee. (1993). **Electronic QUILLS: A situated evaluation of using computers for writing in classrooms.** Lawrence Erlbaum Associates, 365 Broadway, Hillsdale, NJ 07642. 232pp. $22.50 (paper). Centers on the words and experiences of teachers and students who have used QUILL, a software package developed by the authors to aid writing instruction.

Katz, Martin R. (1993). **Computer-assisted career decision making.** Lawrence Erlbaum Associates, 365 Broadway, Hillsdale, NJ 07642. 296pp. $29.95 (paper). Discusses career decision making, career guidance, a computerized system of career guidance, and the interplay among them.

Maddux, Cleborne D., Johnson, D. LaMont, and Willis, Jerry W. (1992). **Educational computing: Learning with tomorrow's technologies.** Allyn and Bacon, 160 Gould St., Needham Heights, MA 02194. 340pp. $42. Covers the role of computers in society and in schools; using computers to facilitate teaching in traditional ways or to improve teaching methods; the history of computing and computing equipment; and issues and trends in educational computing.

Mandinach, Ellen B., and Cline, Hugh F. (1993). **Classroom dynamics: Implementing a technology-based learning environment.** Lawrence Erlbaum Associates, 365 Broadway, Hillsdale, NJ 07642. 280pp. $27.50 (paper). Reports on an attempt to introduce change in schools using a computer-based curriculum innovation for teaching higher-order thinking skills to middle and high school students.

Only the best: Annual guide to highest-rated education software. 1994 edition. (1994). Association for Supervision and Curriculum Development, Curriculum/Technology Resource Center, 1250 N. Pitt St., Alexandria, VA 22314-1403. 120pp. $25. (A cumulative edition from 1985-1993 is available as a Microsoft Works 2.0 database for either IBM or Macintosh computers; $99.) Covers 136 highest-rated computer software programs for educators, together with 25 highly promising new products and 83 programs recommended for special education. Information provided for each program includes the producer, subject, grade level, hardware requirements, cost, description, tips for use, and evaluation/conclusions.

Rowe, A. H. Helga. (1993). **Learning with personal computers.** Australian Council for Educational Research, Radford House, Frederick St., Hawthorn, Victoria 3122, Australia. 334pp. Addresses a wide range of practical and theoretical issues for teachers and school administrators who are introducing computers into classrooms.

ERIC Documents

Brown, William L., and Stevens, Betty L. (1992). **Using the microcomputer to equate ratings of student writing samples.** Paper presented at the American Educational Research Association, San Francisco, CA, April 20-24, 1992. 11pp. ED 352 926. Describes a study to determine whether student writing portfolios could be rated reliably by trained judges; study the effects on student ratings of the differential leniency of the judges; and ascertain the effects of writing-prompt difficulty and its interactions with rater leniency.

Doornekamp, B. Gerard. (1992). **The valuation by students of the use of computers in education.** Paper presented at the European Conference on Educational Research, Enschede, The Netherlands, June 22-25, 1992. 17pp. ED 352 929. Describes research of the Technology Enriched Schools Project to examine factors affecting students' valuation of computers.

Jordan, William R., and Follman, Joseph M., eds. (1993). **Using technology to improve teaching and learning. Hot topics: Usable research.** Victoria, BC: British Columbia

Ministry of Attorney-General; Palatka, FL: SouthEastern Regional Vision for Education. 83pp. ED 355 930. (Also available from: NEFEC/SERVE, Route 1, Box 8500, 3841 Reid St., Palatka, FL 32177; $7.) Discusses the need to restructure learning environments to support the active use of technology by teachers, and examines attitudes and roles that evolve among successful technology-using teachers.

Overbaugh, Richard C. (1993). **Critical elements of computer literacy for teachers.** Paper presented at the Annual Meeting of the National Society of Educators and Scholars, Evansville, IN, March 1993. 25pp. ED 355 922. Addresses general domains that comprise computer literacy for educators and suggests a two-stage and a four-stage model leading to teacher competence in hardware, software, applications, and management.

Phillips, Jeanne, and Soule, Helen. (1992). **A comparison of fourth graders' achievement: Classroom computers versus no computers.** Paper presented at the Annual Meeting of the Mid-South Educational Research Association (21st, Knoxville, TN, November 11-13, 1992). 24pp. ED 354 874. Assessed whether classroom-based microcomputer applications can help improve students' performance on standardized tests, and which subject areas such programs are most effective in for fourth graders in two Mississippi schools.

The survey of microcomputers in schools (1992): Report. (1992). Shelton, CT: Market Data Retrieval, Inc. 55pp. ED 352 930 (available in microfiche only). Based on reports from 85 percent of all public, private, and Catholic schools in the United States, offers statistics for rate of microcomputer installation; occurrence of microcomputers in public, private, and Catholic schools; and microintensity (i.e., number of pupils per computer in a school).

Journal Articles

Allen, Alma A., and Mountain, Lee. (1992, November). When inner city black children go online at home. **Computing Teacher, 20**(3), 35-37. EJ 454 691. (Available UMI.) Describes a study that provided inner-city, fourth-grade, African-American students in Texas with hardware to participate in a telecommunications network to determine whether participation would increase their scores on statewide fifth-grade math tests.

Cennamo, Katherine S. (1992-93). Students' perceptions of the ease of learning from computers and interactive video: An exploratory study. **Journal of Educational Technology Systems, 21**(3), 251-63. EJ 462 945. Focuses on a study that investigated preservice teachers' preconceptions of the ease of achieving various learning outcomes (i.e., psychomotor, affective, verbal, and intellectual).

Clariana, Roy B. (1993, Spring). The motivational effect of advisement on attendance and achievement in computer-based instruction. **Journal of Computer-Based Instruction, 20**(2), 47-51. EJ 467 343. (Available UMI.) Describes a study of at-risk high school students that investigated the motivational and instructional effects of advisement in computer-based instruction on learners of varying ability and locus of control orientations.

Gibbons, Andrew S., and others. (1993, May). The future of computer-managed instruction (CMI). **Educational Technology, 33**(5), 7-11. EJ 464 362. (Available UMI.) Examines CMI in terms of the management function, the current tutorial method that focuses on verbal learning, the relationship to performance and practice, conflicting goals in computer-based training, and the psychology of learning.

Handler, Marianne G. (1993, March). Preparing new teachers to use computer technology: Perceptions and suggestions for teacher educators. **Computers and Education, 20**(2), 147-56. EJ 461 638. (Available UMI.) Discussion of preservice teacher education in computer technology focuses on a survey of teachers who had completed their first year of teaching that examined their perceptions of how prepared they were to use computers in the classroom.

Hartley, James. (1993, January). Writing, thinking and computers. **British Journal of Educational Technology, 24**(1), 22-31. EJ 465 798. (Available UMI.) Considers three levels of computer-aided writing: (1) simple word processors, (2) computer-aided writing programs, and (3) higher-level computer-aided processing.

Hooper, Simon. (1992). Cooperative learning and computer based instruction. **Educational Technology Research and Development, 40**(3), 21-38. EJ 462 851. (Available UMI.) Discusses cognitive effects; design of effective software for cooperative groups, including accountability, interdependence, interaction, ability grouping, age, collaborative skills, and group processing; and recommendations for future research.

Jih, Hueyching Janice, and Reeves, Thomas Charles. (1992). Mental models: A research focus for interactive learning systems. **Educational Technology Research and Development, 40**(3), 39-53. EJ 462 852. (Available UMI.) Addresses interactivity; human factors research; human/computer interface issues; individual differences, including learning styles and prior experience; cognitive load; measuring mental models; and future research.

Lazzaro, Joseph J. (1993, June). Computers for the disabled. **Byte, 18**(7), 59, 61-62, 64. EJ 464 342. (Available UMI.) Describes adaptive technology for personal computers that accommodate disabled users and may require special equipment, including hardware, memory, expansion slots, and ports.

McDaniel, Ernest, and others. Computers and school reform. **Educational Technology Research and Development, 41**(1), 73-78. EJ 462 811. (Available UMI.) Discusses ways in which computers can be used to help school reform by shifting the emphasis from information transmission to information processing.

Milheim, William D. (1993). Computer based voice recognition: Characteristics, applications, and guidelines for use. **Performance Improvement Quarterly, 6**(1), 14-25. EJ 457 942. Describes computer-based voice recognition technology, including disadvantages, and identifies vocabulary, training requirements, and ability to understand continuous speech as the basic characteristics of voice recognition systems.

Norton, Priscilla. (1992, August). When technology meets the subject matter disciplines in education. Part three: Incorporating the computer as method. **Educational Technology, 32**(8), 35-44. EJ 450 461. (Available UMI.) Focuses on the potentials of the microcomputer as a classroom instructional method. Covers programming, computer literacy, software applications, and problem-solving applications.

Pelletier, Pierre. (1992). Word processing as a support to the writing process. **International Journal of Instructional Media, 19**(3), 249-57. EJ 457 838. (Available UMI.) Investigates the theoretical basis of the writing process and describes the possibilities of word processing as a tool to support it.

Reeves, Thomas C. (1993, Spring). Pseudoscience in computer-based instruction: The case of learner control research. **Journal of Computer-Based Instruction, 20**(2), 39-46. EJ 467 342. (Available UMI.) Presents a critique of published learner control studies that highlights problems with definitions of learner control, theoretical foundations, treatment duration, outcome measures, sample sizes, and conclusions.

Saiedian, Hossein. (1993). An interactive computer based conferencing system to accommodate students' learning process. **Journal of Educational Technology Systems, 21**(2), 109-23. EJ 457 869. Describes an integrated computer-based conferencing and mail system called ICMS (Integrated Conferencing and Mail System) that was developed to encourage students to participate in class discussions more actively.

Stinson, Joseph. (1993, March-April). Technology outlook on math and science: Conversations with experts. **Media and Methods, 29**(4), 24-27. EJ 461 552. Discusses the use of educational technology for science and math instruction in elementary and secondary schools through conversations with six curriculum specialists and administrators.

Strommen, Erik F., and Frome, Francine S. (1993). Talking back to Big Bird: Preschool users and a simple speech recognition system. **Educational Technology Research and Development, 41**(1), 5-16. EJ 462 806. (Available UMI.) Describes a study that examined the effectiveness of one configuration of automatic speech recognition software and hardware with 36 three-year-olds and a comparison control group of 20 adults.

Valauskas, Edward J. (1993, July). Education online: Interactive K-12 computing. **Online, 17**(4), 89-91. EJ 465 823. (Available UMI.) Suggests imaginary and currently possible uses of computers to keep children's curiosity alive and improve teaching.

Watson, J. Allen, and others. (1992). Logo mastery and spatial problem solving by young children: Effects of Logo language training, route strategy training, and learning styles on immediate learning and transfer. **Journal of Educational Computing Research, 8**(4), 521-40. EJ 458 009. Describes a study that examined preschoolers' abilities to learn problem solving with Logo, learn new strategies to use during problem solving, and transfer computer learning to other settings.

Winn, William, and Bricken, William. (1992, December). Designing virtual worlds for use in mathematics education: The example of experiential algebra. **Educational Technology, 32**(12), 12-19. EJ 456 186. (Available UMI.) Examines learning theory, including knowledge construction; knowledge representation, including the symbol systems of algebra; and spatial algebra.

DATABASES AND ONLINE SEARCHING

Media-Related Periodicals

CompuServe. 5000 Arlington Centre Blvd., Columbus, OH 43220. mo.; $30. Gives current news about computer communication and information retrieval, in-depth articles on issues and techniques, and software and book reviews.

Data Sources. Ziff-Davis Publishing Co., One Park Ave., New York, NY 10016. 2/yr.; $440. A guide to the information processing industry. Covers equipment, software, services, and systems, and includes profiles of 10,000 companies.

Database. Online, Inc., 462 Danbury Rd., Wilton, CT 06897. bi-mo.; $99 U.S. and Canada, $121 Mexico, $134 foreign airmail. Includes articles on new databases and techniques for searching online databases as well as new products information and news updates.

Database Searcher. Meckler Publishing, 11 Ferry Lane W., Westport, CT 06880-5808. mo.; $98. Includes techniques, new products, conferences, and tips and techniques for searching.

Directory of Online Databases. Gale Research Inc., 835 Penobscot Building, Detroit, MI 48226. q.; $190 U.S., $240 elsewhere. Identifies over 4,500 databases that are publicly available to online service users. Includes information on database selection and vendors.

Information Today. Learned Information, Inc., 143 Old Marlton Pike, Medford, NJ 08055. 11/yr.; $39.95. For users and producers of electronic information services. Articles and news about the industry, calendar of events, and product information.

Journal of Database Administration. Idea Group Publishing, 4811 Jonestown Rd., Suite 230, Harrisburg, PA 17109-9159. q.; $60 indiv., $105 inst. Provides state-of-the-art research to those who design, develop, and administer DBMS-based information systems.

Link-Up. Learned Information, Inc., 143 Old Marlton Pike, Medford, NJ 08055. bi-mo.; $25 U.S., $48 elsewhere. For individuals interested in small computer applications; covers hardware, software, communications services, and search methods.

Online. Online, Inc., 462 Danbury Rd., Wilton, CT 06897-2126. 6/yr.; $99 U.S. and Canada, $121 Mexico, $134 foreign airmail. For online information system users. Articles cover a variety of online applications for general and business use.

Online Review. Learned Information, Inc., 143 Old Marlton Pike, Medford, NJ 08055. bi-mo.; $99. An international journal of online information systems featuring articles on using and managing online systems, training and educating online users, developing search aids, and creating and marketing databases.

Resource Sharing and Information Networks. Haworth Press, 10 Alice St., Binghamton, NY 13904. semi-ann.; $28 indiv., $85 inst. A forum for ideas on the basic theoretical and practical problems faced by planners, practitioners, and users of network services.

ERIC Documents

Kriz, Harry M. (1992). **A public-use, full-screen interface for SPIRES databases**. Paper distributed at the SPIRES Fall Workshop, Chapel Hill, NC, October 12-14, 1992. 57pp. ED 352 991. Describes the techniques for implementing a full-screen, custom SPIRES interface for a public-use library database.

Journal Articles

Keays, Thomas. (1993, January). Searching online database services over the Internet. **Online, 17**(1), 29-33. EJ 457 924. (Available UMI.) Describes how to use the Internet to access commercial online database services, such as DIALOG, and discusses the advantages in terms of costs, reference services, and accessibility.

Woolliams, Peter, and Gee, David. (1992, October). Accounting for user diversity in configuring online systems. **Online Review, 16**(5), 303-11. EJ 456 120. (Available UMI.) Discusses cognitive psychology; ethnocentricity; online systems and their organizational setting; models for organization culture; corporate culture; international systems and country-specific cultures; and Trompenaar's model of culture.

DISTANCE EDUCATION

Media-Related Periodicals

American Journal of Distance Education. Pennsylvania State University, School of Education, 403 S. Allen St., Suite 206, University Park, PA 16801-5202. 3/yr.; $30. Focuses on professional trainers, adult educators, college teachers, and others interested in the latest developments in methods and systems for delivering education to adults.

Appropriate Technology. Intermediate Technology Publications, Ltd., 103-105 Southampton Row, London WC1B 4HH, England. q.; $27 indiv., $37 inst. Articles on low-cost, small-scale technology, particularly for developing countries.

Development Communication Report. Clearinghouse on Development Communication, 1815 N. Ft. Myer Dr., Suite 600, Arlington, VA 22209. q.; $10 (free to readers in developing countries). Applications of communications technology to international development problems such as agriculture, health, and nutrition.

Distance Education. University College of Southern Queensland Press, Darling Heights, Toowoomba, Queensland 4350, Australia. semi-ann.; $65 (Australian currency). Papers on the history, politics, and administration of distance education.

International Council for Distance Education Bulletin. Open University, Regional Academic Services, Walton Hall, Milton Keynes MK7 6AA7, England. 3/yr.; $65. Reports on activities and programs of the ICDE.

Journal of Distance Education. Canadian Association for Distance Education, 151 Slater St., Ottawa, Ontario K1P 5N2, Canada. 2/yr.; $40. Aims to promote and encourage scholarly work of empirical and theoretical nature relating to distance education in Canada and throughout the world.

Open Learning. Longman Group UK Ltd., Journals Dept., 4th Ave., Harlow, Essex CM19 5AA, England. 3/yr.; $72, single copy $25. Academic, scholarly publication on any aspects of open and distance learning anywhere in the world. Includes issues for debate and research notes.

Research in Distance Education. Centre for Distance Education, Athabasca University, Box 10,000, Athabasca, Alberta T0G 2R0, Canada. q.; free. A forum for the discussion of issues surrounding the process of conducting research within the field of distance education.

Books

Burge, Elizabeth J., and Roberts, Judith M. (1993). **Classrooms with a difference: A practical guide to the use of conferencing technologies.** 104pp. The Ontario Institute for Studies in Education, 252 Bloor St. West, Toronto, Ontario M5S 1V6, Canada. 102pp. Available from ERIC as ED 364 206. Explores the factors and dynamics needed for learning and teaching in new classrooms that are created by four conferencing technologies: audio, audiographic, computer, and compressed video.

Van den Brande, Lieve. (1993). **Flexible and distance learning.** John Wiley & Sons, Baffins Lane, Chichester, West Sussex PO19 1UD, England. 263pp. $195. Provides a detailed view of the current world situation of real implementations of flexible and distance learning, emphasizing training and retraining initiatives through new technologies and telecommunications.

Willis, Barry. (1993). **Distance education: A practical guide.** Educational Technology Publications, 700 Palisade Ave., Englewood Cliffs, NJ 07632. 152pp. $29.95. Designed for use by faculty and administrators seeking to plan, develop, and implement distance education programs and learning materials. Includes summaries of comparative research; roles and responsibilities of faculty involved in distance education; a step-by-step process model for designing, developing, evaluating, and revising instruction; strategies for the design, creation, implementation, and administration of inservice training programs; and discussion of academic policy issues and organizational challenges.

ERIC Documents

Brunner, Cornelia. (1992). **Gender and distance learning.** New York, NY: Center for Technology in Education. 12pp. ED 352 953. (Also available from Center for Technology in Education, c/o Bank Street College Bookstore, 610 W. 112th St., New York, NY 10025; $3.) Examines distance learning from a gender perspective, including culturally sanctioned differences in technological expectations that have real implications for the future of distance learning.

Jones, Judy I., and others. (1992). **Distance education: A cost analysis.** Des Moines, IA: Iowa State Dept. of Education, FINE (First in the Nation in Education) Foundation; Ames, IA: Research Institute for Studies in Education. 88pp. ED 355 906. Presents a literature review and data derived from a cost analysis that utilized face-to-face, telephone, and written interviews to identify costs required to design, build, and install a distance education system.

Romiszowski, Alexander. (1993). **Telecommunications and distance education. ERIC digest.** Syracuse, NY: ERIC Clearinghouse on Information Resources. ED 358 841. (Also available from ERIC Clearinghouse on Information & Technology, 4-194 Center for Science and Technology, Syracuse University, Syracuse, NY 13244-4100; free.) Defines four generations of distance education and describes the technology, benefits, and instructional design issues characteristic of each.

Journal Articles

Adrianson, Lillemor, and Hjelmquist, Erland. (1993, Summer-Fall). Communication and memory of texts in face to face and computer mediated communication. **Computers in Human Behavior, 9**(2-3), 121-35. EJ 461 520. (Available UMI.) Describes an experiment conducted at the University of Göteborg (Sweden) that investigated social and cognitive differences in communication and recall in face-to-face communication versus computer-mediated communication.

Barnard, John (1992, September). Multimedia and the future of distance learning technology. **Educational Media International, 29**(3), 139-44. EJ 457 850. (Available UMI.) Describes recent innovations in distance learning technology, including the use of video technology; personal computers, including computer conferencing, computer-mediated communication, and workstations; multimedia, including hypermedia; Integrated Services Digital Networks (ISDN); and fiber optics.

Farnes, Nick. (1993, February). Modes of production: Fordism and distance education. **Open Learning, 8**(1), 10-20. EJ 459 934. (Available UMI.) Analyzes the historical development of economic and educational systems and considers the relationship between industrialization and distance education.

Hardy, Virginia. (1992, November). Introducing computer mediated communications into participative management education: The impact on the tutor's role. **Educational and Training Technology International, 29**(4), 325-31. EJ 457 931. (Available UMI.) Contrasts the role of the moderator in CMC with the role of the tutor in learner-controlled, or participative, education.

Moore, Michael G. (1993). Is teaching like flying? A total systems view of distance education. **American Journal of Distance Education, 7**(1), 1-10. EJ 462 879. Describes two ways of organizing distance education: using telecommunications to duplicate traditional classroom teaching; and reorganizing educational resources with a total systems perspective, including sources of knowledge, structures of knowledge, and media of communication.

Pisacreta, Edward A. (1993, April). Distance learning and intellectual property protection. **Educational Technology, 33**(4), 42-44. EJ 462 848. (Available UMI.) Examines laws governing intellectual property that affect distance education. Addresses copyright law, particularly the concept of fair use; traditional applications of copyright law in education, including photocopying and the *Classroom Guidelines*; and distance learning and copyright law, including works transmitted via telecommunications.

Steele, Ray L. (1993, March-April). Distance learning delivery systems: Instructional options. **Media and Methods, 29**(4), 12, 14. EJ 461 549. (Available UMI.) Discusses the availability of satellite and cable programming to provide distance education opportunities in school districts. A sidebar provides a directory of distance learning opportunities, including telecommunications networks, cable programming, and satellite programming.

Tremblay, Wilfred. (1992). Telecourse utilization in American research universities: Institutional context and instructional innovation. **International Journal of Instructional Media, 19**(3), 191-207. EJ 457 832. (Available UMI.) Describes a study that examined the extent and perception of the use of telecourses at U.S. research universities.

EDUCATIONAL RESEARCH

Media-Related Periodicals

American Educational Research Journal. American Educational Research Association, 1230 17th St. NW, Washington, DC 20036. q.; $37 indiv., $46 inst. Reports original research, both empirical and theoretical, and brief synopses of research.

Current Index to Journals in Education (CIJE). Oryx Press, 4041 N. Central at Indian School Rd., Phoenix, AZ 85012-3397. mo.; $235. A guide to articles published in some 780 education and education-related journals. Includes complete bibliographic information, annotations, and indexes. Semiannual cumulations available. Contents are produced by the ERIC (Educational Resources Information Center) system, Office of Educational Research and Improvement, U.S. Department of Education.

Education Index. H. W. Wilson, 950 University Ave., Bronx, NY 10452. mo. (except July and August); variable costs. Author-subject index to educational publications in the English language. Cumulated quarterly and annually.

Educational Research. ITPS Ltd., Cheritan House, Andover, Hants SP10 5BE, England. 3/yr.; $90. Reports on current educational research, evaluation, and applications.

Educational Researcher. American Educational Research Association, 1230 17th St. NW, Washington, DC 20036. 9/yr.; $37 indiv., $46 inst. Contains news and features of general significance in educational research.

Research in Science and Technological Education. Carfax Publishing Co., P.O. Box 25, Abington, Oxfordshire OX14 3VE, England. 2/yr.; $109 indiv., $298 inst. Publication of original research in the science and technological fields. Includes articles on psychological, sociological, economic, and organizational aspects.

Resources in Education (RIE). Superintendent of Documents, U.S. Government Printing Office, Washington, DC 20402. mo.; $94 U.S, $117.50 elsewhere. Announcement of research reports and other documents in education, including abstracts and indexes by subject, author, and institution. Cumulative semiannual indexes available. Contents produced by the ERIC (Educational Resources Information Center) system, Office of Educational Research and Improvement, U.S. Department of Education.

ERIC Documents

U.S. Congress. House of Representatives. (1992). **Hearings on reauthorization of the Office of Educational Research and Improvement (OERI). Hearings before the Subcommittee on Select Education of the Committee on Education and Labor.** (102nd Cong., 2d session.) ED 358 825. (Also available from U.S. Government Printing Office, Superintendent of Documents, Congressional Sales Office, Washington, DC 20402.) Argues that at the core of a world-class system of delivery of educational services, there must be a comprehensive process for continual transmission of the best that knowledge synthesis and new experimentation can offer for utilization procedures and practices. Prepared statements from 12 persons indicate the shape that various interests would like the reauthorizing legislation to take.

Journal Articles

Coleman, J. Gordon, Jr. (1992). All seriousness aside: The laughing learning connection. **International Journal of Instructional Media, 19**(3), 269-76. EJ 457 840. (Available UMI.) Discusses theories of humor; variables associated with humor; health benefits derived from humor; developmental stages and humor; effects of humor in children's educational television; and humor in the college environment.

Klein, James D., and Pridemore, Doris R. (1992). Effects of cooperative learning and need for affiliation on performance, time on task, and satisfaction. **Educational Technology Research and Development, 40**(4), 39-47. EJ 462 861. (Available UMI.) Describes a study that was conducted to investigate the effect of cooperative learning and the need for affiliation on performance, time on task, and satisfaction of undergraduates using an instructional television lesson.

Mory, Edna H. (1992). The use of informational feedback in instruction: Implications for future research. **Educational Technology Research and Development, 40**(3), 5-20. EJ 462 850 (Available UMI.) Discusses feedback as reinforcement; modeling of the feedback cycle; response certitude; feedback elaboration; error analyses; and feedback and higher-level tasks.

Woodrow, Janice E. J. (1992, Winter). The influence of programming training on the computer literacy and attitudes of preservice teachers. **Journal of Research on Computing in Education, 25**(2), 200-19. EJ 459 869. (Available UMI.) Reports on a study measuring the change in computer literacy and attitudes toward computers among 36 preservice teachers enrolled in an introductory computer training course focused on developing programming skills.

EDUCATIONAL TECHNOLOGY

Media-Related Periodicals

British Journal of Educational Technology. Council for Educational Technology, Sir Wm. Lyons Road, University Science Park, Coventry CV4 7EZ, England. 3/yr.; $66.50. Published by the National Council for Educational Technology, this journal includes articles on education and training, especially theory, applications, and development of educational technology and communications.

Canadian Journal of Educational Communication. Association of Media and Technology in Education in Canada, AMTEC-CJEC Subscription, 3-1750 The Queensway, Suite 1318, Etobicoke, Ontario M9C 5H5, Canada. q.; $42.80. Articles, research reports, and literature reviews on all areas of educational communication and technology.

Education and Training Technology International. Kogan Page Ltd., Distribution Centre, Blackhorse Road, Letchworth, Herts SG6 1HN, England. q.; £50 ($95 U.S.). Journal of the Association for Educational and Training Technology, emphasizing developing trends in and the efficient employment of educational technology.

Educational Technology. Educational Technology Publications, Inc., 700 Palisade Ave., Englewood Cliffs, NJ 07632. mo.; $119., $139 foreign, $12 single copy. Covers telecommunications, computer-aided instruction, information retrieval, educational television, and electronic media in the classroom.

Educational Technology Abstracts. Carfax Publishing Co., P.O. Box 25, Abington, Oxfordshire OX14 3UE, England. 6/yr.; $159 indiv., $388 inst. An international publication of abstracts of recently published material in the field of educational and training technology.

Educational Technology Research and Development. Association for Educational Communications and Technology, 1025 Vermont Ave. NW, Suite 820, Washington, DC 20005-3516. q.; $45 U.S., $53 foreign, $12 single copy. Focuses on research and instructional development in the field of educational technology.

Journal of Instructional Delivery Systems. 50 Culpeper St., Warrenton, VA 22186. q.; $60 indiv., $75 inst., add $15 postage for foreign countries. Devoted to the issues and applications of technology to enhance productivity in education, training, and job performance.

Journal of Technology and Teacher Education. Association for the Advancement of Computing in Education (AACE), P.O. Box 2966, Charlottesville, VA 22902. q.; $65 indiv., $78 inst.; nonmembers add $10. Serves as an international forum to report research and applications of technology in preservice, inservice, and graduate teacher education.

Knowledge: Creation, Diffusion, Utilization. Sage Publications, Inc., 2455 Teller Rd., Newbury Park, CA 91320. q.; $48 indiv., $124 inst., $17 single copy. (In California, add 7.25%.) An international, interdisciplinary journal examining the nature of expertise and the translation of knowledge into practice and policy.

TechTrends. Association for Educational Communications and Technology, 1025 Vermont Ave. NW, Suite 820, Washington, DC 20005-3516. 6/yr.; $36 U.S., $40 elsewhere, $4 single copy. Features authoritative, practical articles about technology and its integration into the learning environment.

Technology and Learning. Peter Li Education Group, 330 Progress Rd., Dayton, OH 45449. 8/yr.; $24. Publishes features, reviews, news, and announcements of educational activities and opportunities in programming, software development, and hardware configurations.

TECHNOS. Agency for Instructional Technology, Box A, 1111 W. 17th St., Bloomington, IN 47402-0120. q.; $20. A forum for the discussion of ideas about the use of technology in education, with a focus on reform.

T.H.E. Journal (Technological Horizons in Education). T.H.E., 150 El Camino Real, Suite 112, Tustin, CA 92680-3670. 11/yr.; $29 (free to qualified educators). For educators of all levels. Focuses on a specific topic for each issue as well as technological innovations as they apply to education.

Books

Barron, Ann E., and Orwig, Gary W. (1993). **New technologies for education: A beginner's guide.** Libraries Unlimited, P.O. Box 6633, Englewood, CO 80155-6633. 209pp. $27.50. Reviews the advantages, disadvantages, and educational applications of such technologies as CD-ROM, interactive videodisc, digital audio, scanning, digitized video, and telecommunications (computer conferencing, satellite communication, local area networks, and electronic mail).

Duffy, Thomas M., and Jonassen, David H., eds. (1992). **Constructivism and the technology of instruction: A conversation**. Lawrence Erlbaum Associates, 365 Broadway, Hillsdale, NJ 07642. 232pp. $24.95. Essays exploring the implications of constructivism for instructional design, which serve as a dialog between instructional developers and learning theorists.

Eckel, Karl. (1993). **Instruction language: Foundations of a strict science of instruction.** Educational Technology Publications, 700 Palisade Ave., Englewood Cliffs, NJ 07632. 200pp. $37.95. Covers the Instrugram as a common basis of person-to-person and person-to-machine communication; minimum instruction, including both explicit and didactic representation and the notion and flow logic of minimum instruction; instruction, including the sequence proper hierarchy and the general flow of instruction and Instrugram parts; response judging; instructional types; and tracing back the calculation path.

Ely, Donald P., and Minor, Barbara B., eds. (1993). **Educational Media and Technology Yearbook 1993. Volume 19.** Libraries Unlimited, Inc., P.O. Box 6633, Englewood, CO 80155-6633. 369pp. $60. Provides media and instructional technology professionals with an up-to-date, single-source overview and assessment of the field of educational technology. Covers trends, issues, and current developments, and provides leadership profiles and annotated listings of the organizations, agencies, and colleges and universities that serve the field.

Schwartz, Judah L., Yerushalmy, Michal, and Wilson, Beth, eds. (1993). **The geometric supposer: What is it a case of?** Lawrence Erlbaum Associates, 365 Broadway, Hillsdale, NJ 07642. 254pp. $27.50. A case study of education reform and innovation using technology that examines the issue from the views and experiences of software designers, curriculum writers, teachers and students, and researchers and administrators.

Simonson, Michael, ed. (1993). **Research proceedings: 1993 AECT national convention.** Association for Educational Communications and Technology, 1025 Vermont Ave. NW, Suite 820, Washington, DC 20005-3547. 1,000pp. $40 AECT members; $57.50 nonmembers. The 15th annual collection of research papers from AECT's 1993 convention in New Orleans; topics include the effects of technology on learning, cognitive theory, distance education, interactive video, and more. (Also available as ERIC document no. ED 362 144; individual papers, ED 362 145-215.)

ERIC Documents

Brunner, Cornelia. (1992). **Integrating technology into the curriculum: Teaching the teachers.** New York, NY: Center for Technology in Education. 9pp. ED 350 980. Describes a technology integration curriculum created for teachers and administrators based on collaborative research in public schools and the benefits and disadvantages of a variety of teaching formats for students, administrators, and faculty that have been used to promote the integration of technology into classrooms.

Hawkins, Jan. (1993). **Technology and the organization of schooling.** New York, NY: Center for Technology in Education. 10pp. ED 359 933. Discusses technology as the key to realizing two conditions of good schooling: students can learn well when they are actively engaged with multiple resources and people, and they can learn well in environments where they are personally well known.

Hawkins, Jan. (1992). **Technology-mediated communities for learning: Designs and consequences. Technical report no. 21.** New York, NY: Center for Technology in Education. 14pp. ED 349 965. Considers what new forms and images for school have been created and tried, issues that arise as experiments in distance learning are developed, and the effect of these forms on the quality of learning and the social fabric of schooling.

Homework help and home/school communications systems: Examples from AMERICA 2000. Issue briefs. (1993). Washington, DC: U.S. Department of Education, Office of Policy and Planning. 16pp. ED 354 870. Describes programs that have been developed to improve students' attention to and success with homework assignments, including recorded messages by voice mail, live telephone homework help, live cable television shows with support for callers, and drop-in homework centers.

Learning technologies essential for education change. (1992). Washington, DC: Council of Chief State School Officers. 82pp. ED 349 967. Four papers about the use of technologies in education address learning alternatives created with technology, student outcomes of learning technologies, integration of technology into teaching, and planning for learning technologies.

Journal Articles

Brown, John Seely, and Duguid, Paul. (1993, March). Stolen knowledge. **Educational Technology, 33**(3), 10-15. EJ 461 591. (Available UMI.) Discusses situated learning in the workplace and in the classroom. Topics addressed include operationalization versus legitimization of educational theories; instruction versus learning; explicit versus implicit instruction and knowledge; individual versus social context; systems narrowly construed versus systems broadly construed; and legitimate peripheral participation.

Bruder, Isabelle. (1993, January). Alternative assessment: Putting technology to the test. **Electronic Learning, 12**(4), 22-23, 26-28. EJ 457 876. (Available UMI.) Addresses the use of technology in assessment, performance-based assessment, the use of video, technological equity, writing portfolios, and professional development to change educators' views of assessment.

Campoy, Renee. (1992, August). The role of technology in the school reform movement. **Educational Technology, 32**(8), 17-22. EJ 450 458. (Available UMI.) Considers the role of educational technology in two views of the school reform movement: one that demands more from the existing educational system, and one that calls for restructuring of the existing system.

Cousins, J. Bradley, and Leithwood, Kenneth A. (1993). Enhancing knowledge utilization as a strategy for school improvement. **Knowledge: Creation, Diffusion, Utilization, 14**(3), 305-33. EJ 459 907. Discussion of school improvement focuses on a study of Ontario educators that examined their use of various sources of information, including conferences, workshops, and inservice training, for improvement purposes.

Damarin, Suzanne K. (1993, March). School and situated knowledge: Travel or tourism? **Educational Technology, 33**(3), 27-32. EJ 461 594. (Available UMI.) Discusses educational theories; the situated nature of knowledge; perception of experts; and the role of technology in situated learning, including virtual reality, hypertext, and telecommunications.

Goodspeed, Jon, ed., and others. (1993, February). How to find money for technology. **Electronic Learning, 12**(5), 2-27. EJ 459 939. (Available UMI.) A special insert contains several articles on finding money for educational technology. Covers foundations that provide educational funding; funding sources and recently funded programs; stretching available funds; fund-raising ideas; elements of a grant proposal; school/business partnerships; and grant proposals as a vehicle for change.

Jonassen, David H. (1993, January). The trouble with learning environments. **Educational Technology, 33**(1), 35-37. EJ 457 885. (Available UMI.) Describes learning environments, including cognitive flexibility hypertexts, anchored instruction, and computer-supported intentional learning environments.

Knox Quinn, Carolyn. (1992). International Society for Technology in Education. **School Library Media Annual, 10,** 185-86. EJ 454 780. Provides information about the International Society for Technology in Education (ISTE), an organization dedicated to improving education throughout the world by facilitating communication among instructors, media specialists, computer coordinators, information resource managers (IRMs), and administrative users of technology.

Mitchell, Ruth. (1992, November). Measuring up: Student assessment and systemic change. **Educational Technology, 32**(11), 37-41. EJ 454 713. (Available UMI.) Examines the power of performance assessment to influence learning and to effect change in the educational system.

Moja, Teboho (1992, September). Teacher education from classroom broadcasts for the new South Africa. **Educational Media International, 29**(3), 171-74. EJ 457 856. (Available UMI.) Discussion of the educational problems facing South Africa focuses on the possible uses of educational technology, particularly radio, for teacher education.

Poirot, James L., and Knezek, Gerald A. (1992, November). Experimental designs for determining the effectiveness of technology in education. **Computing Teacher, 20**(3), 8-9. EJ 454 689. (Available UMI.) Focuses on research designs for teachers to determine the impact of technology in the classroom. Covers research and the scientific method, qualitative versus quantitative research, and statistical inference.

Reigeluth, Charles M. (1992, November). The imperative for systemic change. **Educational Technology, 32**(11), 9-13. EJ 454 707. (Available UMI.) Considers paradigm shifts in society and the relationship between society and education, and presents features of an information-age educational system based on changes in the workplace.

Reigeluth, Charles M., and Garfinkle, Robert J. (1992, November). Envisioning a new system of education. **Educational Technology, 32**(11), 17-23. EJ 454 709. (Available UMI.) Presents a new image of education called Learning Sphere 2000, which is emerging from the educational needs of an information society.

Rossett, Allison. (1992, November-December). Performance technology for instructional technologists: Comparisons and possibilities. **Performance and Instruction, 31**(10), 6-10. EJ 457 826. (Available UMI.) Examines similarities between performance technology and instructional technology, including a systems approach, reliance upon analysis, theoretical antecedents, causes of performance problems, and anticipating obstacles to the introduction of innovation.

ELECTRONIC PUBLISHING

Media-Related Periodicals

Desktop Communications. International Desktop Communications, Ltd., 530 Fifth Ave., 4th Floor, New York, NY 10036. bi-mo.; $24. Helps small business, corporate, and individual computer users to design and implement innovative and effective newsletters, reports, presentations, and other business communications.

Electronic Publishing: Origination, Dissemination, and Design. John Wiley & Sons, Ltd., Baffins Lane, Chichester, W. Sussex PO19 1UD, England. q.; $185. Covers structured editors, authoring tools, hypermedia, document bases, electronic documents over networks, and text integration.

Publish! PC World Communications, Inc., Box 51967, Boulder, CO 80322-5415. mo.; $23.95. A how-to magazine for desktop publishing.

Journal Articles

Abbott, Anthony. (1992, May). Electronic publishing and document delivery: A case study of commercial information services on the Internet. **Proceedings of the ASIS Mid Year Meeting (Albuquerque, NM, May 27-30, 1992),** 193-206. EJ 450 422. Discusses the electronic publishing activities of Meckler Publishing on the Internet, including a publications catalog, an electronic journal, and tables of contents databases. Also addresses broader issues of commercial network publishing.

Atkinson, Ross. (1993, May). Networks, hypertext, and academic information services: Some longer-range implications. **College and Research Libraries, 54**(3), 199-215. EJ 464 357. (Available UMI.) Discusses issues relating to scholarly information exchange in the networked environment, focusing on the hypermedia model and nonlinear links within and between texts and the implications for authorial control.

Hawkins, Donald T., and others. (1992). Forces shaping the electronic publishing industry of the 1990s. **Electronic Networking: Research, Applications and Policy, 2**(4), 38-60. EJ 458 018. Discusses seven major forces affecting electronic publishing: technology, economics, demographics, social trends, government policies, applications growth, and industry trends.

Stoller, Michael E. (1992, Spring). Electronic journals in the humanities: A survey and critique. **Library Trends, 40**(4), 647-66. EJ 461 665. (Available UMI.) Discusses the use of electronic journals for scholarly communication within the humanities, describes 12 electronic journals that are currently available, and discusses issues they raise for libraries.

INFORMATION SCIENCE AND TECHNOLOGY

Media-Related Periodicals

Bulletin of the American Society for Information Science. ASIS, 8720 Georgia Ave., Suite 501, Silver Spring, MD 20910-3602. bi-mo.; $60 North America, $70 elsewhere, $10 single copy. News magazine concentrating on issues affecting the information field; management reports; opinion; and news of people and events in ASIS and the information community.

Canadian Journal of Information and Library Science/Revue canadienne des sciences de l'information et de bibliothèconomie. CAIS, University of Toronto Press, Journal Dept., 5201 Dufferin St., Downsview, ON M3H 5T8, Canada. q.; nonmembers $95 Canada, $110 elsewhere. Published by the Canadian Association for Information Science to contribute to the advancement of library and information science in Canada.

Datamation. Reed Publishing, 44 Cook St., Denver, CO 80206. 24/yr.; $69 indiv., $47 libraries. Covers semi-technical news and views on hardware, software, and databases, for data and information processing professionals.

Information Processing and Management. Pergamon Press, Inc., 660 White Plains Rd., Tarrytown, NY 10591-5153. £255 ($509 U.S.). An international journal covering data processing, database building, and retrieval.

Information Retrieval and Library Automation. Lomond Publications, Inc., Box 88, Mt. Airy, MD 21771. mo.; $66 U.S., $79.50 foreign. News, articles, and announcements on new techniques, equipment, and software in information services.

Information Services & Use. Elsevier Science Publishers, Box 10558, Burke, VA 22009-0558. bi-mo.; $188. An international journal for those in the information management field. Includes online and offline systems, library automation, micrographics, videotex, and tele-communications.

The Information Society. Taylor and Francis, 1900 Frost Rd., Suite 101, Bristol, PA 19007. q.; $43. Provides a forum for discussion of the world of information, including transborder data flow, regulatory issues, and the impact of the information industry.

Information Technology and Libraries. American Library Association, Library and Information Technology Association, 50 E. Huron St., Chicago, IL 60611-2795. q.; $45 U.S. nonmembers, $50 Canada and Mexico, $55 elsewhere. Articles on library automation, communication technology, cable systems, computerized information processing, and video technologies.

Journal of Documentation. Aslib, Association for Information Management, Publications Department, Information House, 20-24 Old St., London EC1V 9AP, England. q.; £92 members, £105 nonmembers. Describes how technical, scientific, and other specialized knowledge is recorded, organized, and disseminated.

Journal of the American Society for Information Science. Subscription Department, 605 Third Ave., New York, NY 10158-0012. 10/yr.; $395 U.S. nonmembers, $495 Canada and Mexico, $532.50 elsewhere. Publishes research articles in the area of information science.

Books

Bonzi, Susan, ed. (1993). **Proceedings of the 56th Annual Meeting of the American Society for Information Science, October 24-28, 1993, Columbus, Ohio. Volume 30.** (1993). American Society for Information Science, 701 Westchester Ave., White Plains, NY 10604. $38 ASIS members, $47.50 others. 334pp. The theme of the meeting was Integrating Technologies/Converging Professions. The first of three parts, Contributed Papers, presents 37 papers in 10 categories: Electronic Information Policy, Online Searching, Relevance, Bibliometrics, Scientific Communication, Controlling Vocabularies, Interfaces, Integrated Information Center, Information Use and Users, and Theoretical Issues. The second part contains reports/presentations from sessions of Special Interest Groups, and the third provides a list of the Plenary and special sessions. Author and subject indexes are also provided.

Elias, Arthur W. (1993). **The NFAIS Yearbook of the Information Industry 1993.** Learned Information, 143 Old Marlton Pike, Medford, NJ 08055. 130pp. $50, $40 NFAIS members. Covers government influence; new technologies; publishers, producers, and distributors; databases; research; legal actions; and more.

Williams, Martha E., ed. (1993). **Annual Review of Information and Science Technology, volume 28—1993 (ARIST).** Learned Information, 143 Old Marlton Pike, Medford, NJ 08055-8750. $74 for members of the American Society for Information Science, $92.50 nonmembers. A literary source of ideas, trends, and references that offers a comprehensive view of information science technology. Nine chapters cover planning information systems and services, basic techniques and technologies, applications, and the profession.

Williams, Martha E., ed. (1993). **Proceedings of the 14th National Online Meeting.** Learned Information, 143 Old Marlton Pike, Medford, NJ 08055. 452pp. $55. Sixty-two papers by experts from all facets of the electronic information field.

ERIC Documents

Bollier, David. (1992). **The information evolution: How new information technologies are spurring complex patterns of change. Forum report.** Report of the Conference on the Impact of Information Technology, Aspen, Colorado, August 6-9, 1992. 31pp. ED 358 826. (Also available from The Aspen Institute, Communications and Society Program, 1755 Massachusetts Ave. NW, Suite 501, Washington, DC 20036.) Presents a new paradigm for thinking about the impact of information technology—co-evolving complex adaptive systems. Considers the potential of information technologies to stimulate the development of new organizational models for understanding business.

Clinton, William J., and Gore, Albert, Jr. (1993). **Technology for America's economic growth, a new direction to build economic strength.** Washington, DC: Executive Office of the President. 39pp. ED 355 929. Argues that U.S. technology must move in a new direction to build economic strength and spur economic growth. Recommends expanding the traditional roles of support of basic science and mission-oriented technological research, so that the federal government plays a key role in helping private firms develop and profit from innovations.

Journal Articles

Burke, Colin. (1992, December). The other Memex: The tangled career of Vannevar Bush's information machine, the Rapid Selector. **Journal of the American Society for Information Science, 43**(10), 648-57. EJ 454 696. (Available UMI.) Presents an historical overview of Vannevar Bush's efforts to develop a machine for free-form indexing and computerized information retrieval.

Chen, Ching Chih. (1992). Digital vs. analog video on microcomputers: Implications for information management. **Microcomputers for Information Management, 9**(1), 3-16. EJ 450 358. Covers converting analog video to digital data; digital image compression technology;

digital compression and digital video on Macintosh computers; and potential library and information-related applications.

Craven, Timothy C. (1992, October). Use of a general graph-drawing algorithm in the construction of association maps. In Debora Shaw, ed., **Proceedings of the ASIS Annual Meeting (55th, Pittsburgh, PA, October 26-29, 1992), 29,** 32-40. EJ 454 801. Describes research that investigated a method of automatically generating concept association maps that could be useful to abstractors.

Eisenberg, Michael B., and Small, Ruth V. (1993, March-April). Information based education: An investigation of the nature and role of information attributes in education. **Information Processing and Management, 29**(2), 263-75. EJ 462 841. (Available UMI.) Describes the concept of information-based education, provides a theoretical basis for investigating the role of information in education, and begins developing a classification scheme for documenting and distinguishing among information bases.

Frohmann, Bernd. (1992, December). The power of images: A discourse analysis of the cognitive viewpoint. **Journal of Documentation, 48**(4), 365-86. EJ 457 828. Identifies seven discursive strategies that constitute information as a commodity and persons as surveyable information consumers within a market economy: theoretical imperialism, referentiality and reification, representation and processing, radical individualism, knowledge, expert intervention, and instrumental reason.

Lee, Joon Ho, and others. (1993, June). Information retrieval based on conceptual distance in Is-A Hierarchies. **Journal of Documentation, 49**(2), 188-207. EJ 465 723. Discussion of document ranking methods to calculate the conceptual distance between a Boolean query and a document.

McCallum, Sally. (1993, March). Information technology standards: Implementation, maintenance, and coordination. **Wilson Library Bulletin, 67**(7), 43-45, 117-18. EJ 462 910. (Available UMI.) Discusses issues in the information retrieval standards development process, including interdependency among standards, organizational responsibility, scope, and future needs.

McClure, Charles R., and others. (1992, Winter). Design for an Internet based government wide information locator system. **Electronic Networking: Research, Applications and Policy, 2**(4), 6-37. ED 458 017. Summarizes a study that identified and described federal information inventory/locator systems and resulted in the Federal Locator Database—an electronic database describing 250 federal databases.

McClure, Charles R., and others. (1992, October). Identifying and describing federal information inventory/locator systems: Preliminary findings and key issues. In Debora Shaw, ed., **Proceedings of the ASIS Annual Meeting (55th, Pittsburgh, PA, October 26-29, 1992), 29,** 110-19. EJ 454 812. Discussion of federal information policy focuses on a study that was conducted to identify federal information/locator systems.

Newby, Gregory B. (1992, October). An investigation of the role of navigation for information retrieval. In Debora Shaw, ed., **Proceedings of the ASIS Annual Meeting (55th, Pittsburgh, PA, October 26-29, 1992), 29,** 20-25. EJ 454 799. Presents a theoretical framework for navigation in information retrieval systems and describes a prototype retrieval system that was developed to investigate navigation.

Paisley, William. (1993, May). Knowledge utilization: The role of new communication technologies. **Journal of the American Society for Information Science, 44**(4), 222-34. EJ 462 905. (Available UMI.) Reviews the characteristics of electronic communications technologies and their role in knowledge utilization.

Pezzulo, Judy. (1993, May). The human interface with technology. **Computers in Libraries, 13**(5), 20-23. EJ 464 306. (Available UMI.) Discusses the present status of technology use by students in Pennsylvania public school libraries. Considers the role of library media specialists in developing outcome-based curricula to facilitate use of technology tools.

Stephenson, Geoffrey A. (1992). Open information interchange. **Information Services and Use, 12**(3), 235-46. EJ 459 875. Explores the open information interchange (OII) initiative to promote the use of standards in the exchange of information in electronic form.

Wersig, Gernot. (1993, March-April). Information science: The study of postmodern knowledge usage. **Information Processing and Management, 29**(2), 229-39. EJ 462 837. (Available UMI.) Argues that information science is a postmodern science, driven by the need to solve problems caused by classical sciences and technologies.

INSTRUCTIONAL DESIGN AND TRAINING

Media-Related Periodicals

AVC Presentation Development & Delivery. PTN Publishing Co., 445 Broad Hollow Rd., Suite 21, Melville, NY 11747-4722. mo.; $60, $6 single copy. Industry news and applications for those who manage AV, video, or computer presentations.

Data Training: The Monthly Newspaper for Information Trainers. Weingarten Publications, Inc., 25 First St., Cambridge, MA 02141-1810. bi-mo.; $18 U.S., $30 Canada and Mexico, $45 elsewhere (free to qualified readers). Features training in information processing, office automation, and information maintenance.

Human Computer Interaction. Lawrence Erlbaum Associates, 365 Broadway, Hillsdale, NJ 07642. q.; $39 U.S. and Canada, $64 elsewhere, $145 inst. A journal of theoretical, empirical, and methodological issues of user science and of system design.

Instructional Developments. School of Education, Syracuse University, 364 Huntington Hall, Syracuse, NY 13244-2340. 3/yr.; free. Feature articles, research reviews, innovations, and job aids.

Instructional Science. Kluwer Academic Publishers, 101 Philip Dr., Norwell, MA 02061. bi-mo.; $50 indiv., $217 inst. Aimed to promote a deeper understanding of the nature, theory, and practice of the instructional process and the learning resulting from this process.

Journal of Educational Multimedia and Hypermedia. Association for the Advancement of Computing in Education, Box 2966, Charlottesville, VA 22902. q.; $65 indiv., $78 inst., Canada and Mexico add $10, other countries add $15. A multidisciplinary information source presenting research and applications on multimedia and hypermedia tools that allow the integration of images, sounds, text, and data in learning and teaching.

Journal of Educational Technology Systems. Baywood Publishing Co., 26 Austin Ave., Box 337, Amityville, NY 11701. q.; $107 plus $4.50 postage U.S. and Canada, $9.35 postage elsewhere. In-depth articles on completed and ongoing research in all phases of educational technology and its application and future within the teaching profession.

Journal of Interactive Instruction Development. Communicative Technology Corp., Society for Applied Learning Technology, 50 Culpeper St., Warrenton, VA 22186. q.; $60 members, $75 nonmembers. A showcase of successful programs that will give awareness of innovative, creative, and effective approaches to courseware development for interactive technology.

Journal of Technical Writing and Communication. Baywood Publishing Co., 26 Austin Ave., Box 337, Amityville, NY 11701. q.; $36 indiv., $96 inst. Essays on oral and written communication, for purposes ranging from pure research to needs of business and industry.

Journal of Visual Literacy. International Visual Literacy Association, c/o John C. Belland, 122 Ramseyer Hall, 29 West Woodruff Ave., Ohio State University, Columbus, OH 43210. semi-ann.; $12 indiv., $18 libraries. Interdisciplinary forum on all aspects of visual/verbal languaging.

Performance and Instruction. National Society for Performance and Instruction, 1300 L St. NW, Suite 1250, Washington, DC 20005. 10/yr.; $50. Journal of NSPI, intended to promote the advantage of performance science and technology. Contains articles, research, and case studies relating to improving human performance.

Performance Improvement Quarterly. National Society for Performance and Instruction, 1300 L St. NW, Suite 1250, Washington, DC 20005. q.; $20 nonmembers. Represents the cutting edge in research and theory in performance technology.

Training. Lakewood Publications, Inc., 50 S. Ninth, Minneapolis, MN 55402. mo.; $54. News, how-to features, case studies, and opinions on managing training and human resources development activities.

Books

Dempsey, John V., and Sales, Gregory C. (1993). **Interactive instruction and feedback.** Educational Technology Publications, 700 Palisade Ave., Englewood Cliffs, NJ 07632. 380pp. $39.95. Thirteen chapters cover feedback in programmed instruction; text-based feedback; the role of questions in learning; designing instructional feedback for different learning outcomes; motivating learners through CBI feedback; cooperative learning and feedback in technology-based instruction; adapted and adaptive feedback in technology-based instruction; using feedback to adapt instruction for individuals; simulation and gaming;

feedback and certitude in interactive videodisc programs; feedback and emerging instructional technologies; feedforward; and the role of feedback in program evaluation.

Fleming, Malcolm, and Levie, W. Howard, eds. (1993). **Instructional message design: Principles from the behavioral and cognitive sciences** (2d ed.). Educational Technology Publications, 700 Palisade Ave., Englewood Cliffs, NJ 07632. 352pp. $39.95. Seven chapters by 11 contributors discuss the principles of motivation, perceptions, psychomotor factors, learning, concept-learning, problem-solving, and attitude change.

Jonassen, David H., and Grabowski, Barbara L. (1993). **Handbook of individual differences, learning, and instruction.** Lawrence Erlbaum Associates, 365 Broadway, Hillsdale, NJ 07642. 512pp. $34.50 (paper). Describes most of the major differences that exist among normal learners, and demonstrates how to design various forms of instruction and predict the ease with which learners will acquire different skills.

Kaufman, Rober, Rojas, Alicia M., and Mayer, Hanna. (1993). **Needs assessment: A user's guide.** Educational Technology Publications, 700 Palisade Ave., Englewood Cliffs, NJ 07632. 200pp. $34.95. For use by anyone involved in planning, management, administration, organizational change, assessment, evaluation, and renewal. This handbook explains the different types of needs assessments, when each is most appropriate to use, and how to successfully conduct each type of needs assessment.

Pettersson, Rune. (1993). **Visual information** (2d ed.). Educational Technology Publications, 700 Palisade Ave., Englewood Cliffs, NJ 07632. 400pp. $39.95. Seven chapters address communication, perception, literacy and visual language, classification of visuals, visual content, execution of effective visuals, context in graphic design, and media formats.

Spector, J. Michael, Polson, Martha C., and Muraida, Daniel J., eds. (1993). **Automating instructional design: Concepts and issues.** Educational Technology Publications, 700 Palisade Ave., Englewood Cliffs, NJ 07632. 370pp. $39.95. Eleven chapters by 12 contributors provide an overview of the topic and discuss both approaches to and research and development issues in automating instructional design.

Wileman, Ralph E. (1993). **Visual communicating.** Educational Technology Publications, 700 Palisade Ave., Englewood Cliffs, NJ 07632. 160pp. $34.95. Designed as a text in courses on visual literacy as well as a continuing guide and reference source for practitioners in the field. Five chapters address visualization as a new language and a process, visual stimuli, visual thinking, visual design considerations, and field testing and rendering visuals.

ERIC Documents

Baca, Judy Clark, and others, eds. (1992). **Visual communications: Bridging across cultures. Selected Readings from the Annual Conference of the International Visual Literacy Association** (23rd, Washington, D.C., October 1991). 504pp. ED 352 932. Selected papers presented under five topics: Research and Theory, Curriculum Approaches, Text and Graphic Design, Media and Technology, and The Arts.

Lenze, James S. (1993). **Learner generated versus instructor induced visual imagery.** Paper presented at the Annual Conference of the International Visual Literacy Association, Pittsburgh, PA, September 30-October 4, 1992. ED 363 326. Reviews the concepts of imagery, mathemagenic behaviors, and generative imagery, discusses the learner's use of visual imagery, and examines research findings and issues relevant to instructional design.

Reynolds, Lynne, and Ehrlich, Diane. (1992). **Multimedia in industry and education: A decision model for design.** Paper presented at the European Conference on Educational Research, Enschede, The Netherlands, June 22-25, 1992. 5pp. ED 351 003. Presents a decision-making model that uses a systematic approach to design; has as a driving force the needs and goals of a particular learning situation; is derived from traditional instructional system design models; and addresses the potential impact of multimedia as a delivery system/learning tool.

Journal Articles

Banathy, Bela H. (1993, January). Comprehensive systems design in education: Designing education around the learning experience level. **Educational Technology, 33**(1), 33-35. EJ 457 884. (Available UMI.) Discussion of educational systems design describes four systems levels that can be emphasized: learning experience, instructional, administration, and governance levels.

Brethower, Dale M., and Smalley, Karolyn A. (1992, August). Performance based instruction—Part 5: Evaluating performance based instruction. **Performance and Instruction, 31**(7), 33-40. EJ 451 801 (Available UMI.) Presents a model for evaluating performance-based instruction intended for use by human resource development/performance technology professionals.

Cook, E. K., and Kazlauskas, E. J. (1992-93). The cognitive and behavioral basis of an instructional design: Using CBT to teach technical information and learning strategies. **Journal of Educational Technology Systems, 21**(4), 287-302. EJ 464 384. Describes a project developed to create production guidelines for instructional design of computer-based training (CBT) for industrial purposes.

Davidove, Eric A. (1993, March). Using content experts to help produce training. **Performance and Instruction, 32**(3), 18-23. EJ 462 824. (Available UMI.) Describes six guiding principles to help training developers use content experts more efficiently and effectively to ensure that training materials contain accurate, complete, and relevant information.

Dowding, Tim J. (1993, July). The application of a spiral curriculum model to technical training curricula. **Educational Technology, 33**(7), 18-28. EJ 465 834. (Available UMI.) Discusses the characteristics of a spiral curriculum, contributing factors that may have hindered it from being successfully implemented in public school systems, and examples of how it is successfully used in developing technical training curricula.

Hellebrandt, Josef, and Russell, James D. (1993, July). Confirmative evaluation of instructional materials and learners. **Performance and Instruction, 32**(6), 22-27. EJ 467 327. (Available UMI.) Discusses confirmative evaluation of instructional materials and learners that completes a cycle of evaluative steps in order to maintain performance standards of an instructional system.

Lake-Dell Angelo, Marilyn. (1993, June). The parable of the bridge: A study in performance technology. **Educational Technology, 33**(6), 57-59. EJ 465 795. (Available UMI.) Discusses management and leadership roles, assigning tasks to appropriately skilled workers, teamwork, cooperation, task performance, job descriptions, training needs, management goals, rewards, and quality control.

Macchia, Peter, Jr. (1992, July). Total quality education and instructional systems development. **Educational Technology, 32**(7), 17-21. EJ 448 993. (Available UMI.) Explains Total Quality Management (TQM), a participative management style, and examines its relationship to Instructional Systems Development (ISD) as it is used for curriculum development.

McAlpine, Lynn. (1992, November). Cross cultural instructional design: Using the cultural expert to formatively evaluate process and product. **Educational and Training Technology International, 29**(4), 310-15. EJ 457 930. (Available UMI.) Discussion of instructional design models and the use of experts focuses on cultural experts in cross-cultural educational settings.

McAlpine, Lynn. (1992, November-December). Highlighting formative evaluation: An instructional design model derived from practice. **Performance and Instruction, 31**(10), 16-18. EJ 457 827. (Available UMI.) Presents a model for instructional design based on formative evaluation. Discusses other models, data collection methods, and the evaluator's role.

Milheim, William D. (1992, Winter). Performance support systems: Guidelines for system design and integration. **Canadian Journal of Educational Communication, 21**(3), 243-52. EJ 464 356. Describes the components of electronic performance support systems that are used for the provision of information, decision support, and training for on-the-job employees.

Song, Xueshu. (1992). Computer aided decision making in choosing innovative education programs. **International Journal of Instructional Media, 19**(3), 235-42. EJ 457 836. (Available UMI.) Describes the development of a computer-aided decision-making system to assist educational practitioners in curriculum decision making about innovative program features and implementation requirements.

Wedman, John, and Tessmer, Martin. (1993). Instructional designers' decisions and priorities: A survey of design practice. **Performance Improvement Quarterly, 6**(2), 43-57. EJ 461 571. Describes a survey of 73 training professionals involved in course development that was conducted to determine whether and how they included instructional design activities in their projects.

Yelon, Stephen, and Reznich, Christopher. (1992, July). Visible models of course organization. **Performance and Instruction, 31**(6), 7-11. EJ 448 902. (Available UMI.) Discussion of visible models of training course organization covers uses for course designers, six steps to produce a visible model, and benefits for designers, instructors, and students.

LIBRARIES AND MEDIA CENTERS

Media-Related Periodicals

Book Report. Linworth Publishing, 480 E. Wilson Bridge Rd., Suite L, Worthington, OH 43085-2372. 5/school yr.; $39.99 U.S., $47 Canada, $9 single copy. Journal for junior and senior high school librarians provides articles, tips, and ideas for day-to-day school library management, as well as reviews of audiovisuals and software, all written by school librarians.

Collection Building. Neal-Schuman, 100 Varick St., New York, NY 10013. q.; $58.50. Focuses on all aspects of collection building, ranging from microcomputers to business collections to popular topics and censorship.

College and Research Libraries. Association of College and Research Libraries, 50 E. Huron St., Chicago, IL 60611. bi-mo.; $50 U.S. nonmembers, $55 Canada, $60 elsewhere, $12 single copy. Publishes articles of interest to college and research librarians.

Computers in Libraries. Meckler Publishing, 11 Ferry Lane W., Westport, CT 06880-5808. 10/yr.; $80. Covers practical applications of microcomputers to library situations and recent news items.

Electronic Library. Learned Information, Inc., 143 Old Marlton Pike, Medford, NJ 08055. 6/yr.; $99. For librarians and information center managers interested in microcomputer and library automation. Features industry news and product announcements.

Emergency Librarian. Dyad Services, P.O. Box 46258, Station G, Vancouver, BC V6R 4G6, Canada. bi-mo. (except July-August); $47, $42 prepaid. Articles, review columns, and critical analyses of management and programming issues for children's and young adult librarians.

Government Information Quarterly. JAI Press, 55 Old Post Rd., No. 2, P.O. Box 1678, Greenwich, CT 06835-1678. q.; $55 indiv., $110 inst. International journal of resources, services, policies, and practices.

Government Publications Review. Pergamon Press, Inc., Journals Division, 660 White Plains Rd., Tarrytown, NY 10591-5153. 6/yr.; £180 ($290 U.S.). An international journal covering production, distribution, bibliographic control, accessibility, and use of government information in all formats and at all levels.

Information Services and Use. Elsevier Science Publishers, Box 10558, Burke, VA 20009-0558. 6/yr.; $188. Contains data on international developments in information management and its applications. Articles cover online systems, library automation, word processing, micrographics, videotex, and telecommunications.

Journal of Academic Librarianship. Business Office, P.O. Box 8330, Ann Arbor, MI 48107. bi-mo.; $29 indiv., $52 inst. Results of significant research, issues and problems facing academic libraries, book reviews, and innovations in academic libraries.

Journal of Librarianship and Information Science. Bailey Management Systems, 127 Sandgate Rd., Folkestone, Kent CT20 2BL, England. q.; $115. Deals with all aspects of library and information work in the United Kingdom and reviews literature from international sources.

Journal of Library Administration. Haworth Press, 10 Alice St., Binghamton, NY 13904-1580. q.; $38 indiv., $95 inst. Provides information on all aspects of effective library management, with emphasis on practical applications.

Library and Information Science Abstracts. Bailey Management Systems, 127 Sandgate Rd., Folkestone, Kent CT20 2BL, England. mo.; $585. More than 500 abstracts per issue from more than 500 periodicals, reports, books, and conference proceedings.

Library and Information Science Research. Ablex Publishing Corp., 355 Chestnut St., Norwood, NJ 07648. q.; $45 indiv., $95 inst. Research articles, dissertation reviews, and book reviews on issues concerning information resources management.

Library Computer Systems & Equipment Review. Meckler Publishing, 11 Ferry Lane W., Westport, CT 06880-5808. 2/yr.; $225. Features articles on automated systems for library and applications. Each issue focuses on one topic.

Library Hi Tech. Pierian Press, Box 1808, Ann Arbor, MI 48106. q.; $55. Concentrates on reporting on the selection, installation, maintenance, and integration of systems and hardware.

Library Journal. Box 1977, Marion, OH 43305-1977. 21/yr.; $79. A professional periodical for librarians, with current issues and news, professional reading, lengthy book review section, and classifieds.

Library Quarterly. University of Chicago Press, Box 37005, Chicago, IL 60637. q.; $26 indiv., $40 inst., $20 students. Scholarly articles of interest to librarians.

Library Resources and Technical Services. Association for Library Collections and Technical Services, 50 E. Huron St., Chicago, IL 60611. q.; $45 U.S. nonmembers, $55 Canada, $14 single copy. Scholarly papers on bibliographic access and control, preservation, conservation, and reproduction of library materials.

Library Software Review. Meckler Publishing Corp., 11 Ferry Lane W., Westport, CT 06880. q.; $125 U.S., foreign add $18. Articles on software evaluation, procurement, applications, and installation decisions.

Library Trends. University of Illinois Press, Journals Department, 54 E. Gregory, Champaign, IL 61820. q.; $60, $18.50 single copy. Each issue is concerned with one aspect of library and information science, analyzing current thought and practice, and examining ideas that hold the greatest potential for the field.

Microcomputers for Information Management. Ablex Publishing, 355 Chestnut St., Norwood, NJ 07648. q.; $39.50 indiv., $90 inst. Focuses on new developments with microcomputer technology in libraries and in information science in the United States and abroad.

The Public-Access Computer Systems Review. An electronic journal published on an irregular basis by the University Libraries, University of Houston, and sent free of charge to participants of the Public-Access Computer Systems Forum (PACS-L), a computer conference on BITNET. (To join -L, send an e-mail message to LISTSERV@UHUPVM1 (BITNET) or LISTSERV@UHUPVM1.UH.EDU (Internet) that says SUBSCRIBE PACS-L First Name Last Name.) Annual cumulated volume available in print from Order Department, American Library Association, 50 E. Huron St., Chicago, IL 60611. $20; discount to members of the Library and Information Technology Association. Contains articles about all types of computer systems that libraries make available to their patrons and technologies to implement these systems.

Public Libraries. Public Library Association, American Library Association, 50 E. Huron St., Chicago, IL 60611. q.; $50 U.S. nonmembers, $60 elsewhere, $10 single copy. News and articles of interest to public librarians.

Public Library Quarterly. Haworth Press, 10 Alice St., Binghamton, NY 13904. q.; $36 indiv., $95 inst. Addresses the major administrative challenges and opportunities that face the nation's public libraries.

Reference Librarian. The Haworth Press, 10 Alice St., Binghamton, NY 13904-9981. q.; $38 indiv., $95 inst. Each issue focuses on a topic of current concern, interest, or practical value to reference librarians.

RQ. Reference and Adult Services Division, American Library Association, 50 E. Huron St., Chicago, IL 60611-2795. q.; nonmembers $42 U.S., $52 elsewhere, $12 single copy. Covers all aspects of library service to adults, and reference service and collection development at every level and for all types of libraries.

School Library Journal. Box 1978, Marion, OH 43305-1978. mo.; $67 U.S., $91 Canada, $110 elsewhere. For school and youth service librarians. Contains about 2,500 critical book reviews annually.

School Library Media Activities Monthly. LMS Associates, 17 E. Henrietta St., Baltimore, MD 21230. 10/yr.; $44 U.S., $54 elsewhere. A vehicle for distributing ideas for teaching library media skills and for the development and implementation of library media skills programs.

School Library Media Quarterly. American Association of School Librarians, American Library Association, 50 E. Huron St., Chicago, IL 60611. q.; $40 U.S. nonmembers, $50 elsewhere, $12 single copy. For library media specialists, district supervisors, and others concerned with the selection and purchase of print and nonprint media and with the development of programs and services for preschool through high school libraries.

Special Libraries. Special Library Association, 1700 18th St. NW, Washington, DC 20009-2508. q.; $65 nonmembers, $10 single copy. Discusses administration, organization, and operations. Includes reports on research, technology, and professional standards.

The Unabashed Librarian. Box 2631, New York, NY 10116. q.; $30 U.S., $36 elsewhere. Down-to-earth library items: procedures, forms, programs, cataloging, booklists, software reviews.

Voice of Youth Advocates. Scarecrow Press, 52 Liberty St., Metuchen, NJ 08840. bi-mo.; $32.50 U.S., $37.50 others. Contains articles, bibliographies, and media reviews of materials for or about adolescents.

Wilson Library Bulletin. H. W. Wilson Co., 950 University Ave., Bronx, NY 10452. 10/yr.; $52 U.S., $58 elsewhere. Significant articles on librarianship, news, and reviews of films, books, and professional literature.

Books

Cibbarelli, Pamela, ed. (1993). **Directory of library automation software, systems, and services**. Learned Information, 143 Old Marlton Pike, Medford, NJ 08055-8750. 370pp. $79. Detailed descriptions of and comparative information on about 250 currently available microcomputer, minicomputer, and mainframe software packages for library use.

Corbin, John. (1993). **Corbin's library automation handbook**. Oryx Press, 4041 North Central at Indian School Rd., Phoenix, AZ 85012-3397. 224pp. $37.50. A guide to planning to automate or managing an existing system to obtain the maximum results. Covers system initiation, procurement, evaluation, site preparation, staffing, and costs.

Dickinson, Gail K. (1993). **Selection and evaluation of electronic resources**. Libraries Unlimited, P.O. Box 3988, Englewood, CO 80155. 110pp. $21. Simplifies the selection process and the continuing evaluation of resources such as online databases, CD encyclopedias, and magazine indexes.

Hagloch, Susan B. (1993). **Library building projects: Tips for survival**. Libraries Unlimited, P.O. Box 3988, Englewood, CO 80155. 75pp. $27.50. Step-by-step advice manual covering the library construction process from needs assessment to grand opening.

Latrobe, Kathy Howard, and Laughlin, Mildred Knight, comps. (1992). **Multicultural aspects of library media programs**. Libraries Unlimited, P.O. Box 3988, Englewood, CO 80155. 217pp. $27.50. Essays addressing the history of the multicultural movement; multicultural collection development; curriculum and program planning; and needs of specific cultural groups.

Lazzaro, Joseph R. (1993). **Adaptive technologies for learning and work environments**. American Library Association, 50 East Huron St., Chicago, IL 60611. 252pp. $35. Provides a brief overview of adaptive technology, shows how to analyze a library to make adaptive equipment recommendations, and discusses how to install and integrate the equipment.

Morris, Betty J. (1992). **Administering the school library media center** (3d ed.). R. R. Bowker, P.O. Box 31, New Providence, NJ 07974. 567pp. $41. A complete guide to establishing, managing, and evaluating today's school library media center, with new chapters on the impact of *Information Power*, uses of technology, and assessment of programs and personnel.

ERIC Documents

Auerbach, Jacqueline T. (1993). **Utilization of computer-based technology in high school library media centers. A scholarly study**. (Prepared in partial fulfillment of requirements for the degree of Specialist in Education in Library Media Technology, Georgia State University.) 55pp. ED 357 756. Reports on a descriptive study which determined how computer-based technology was being selected, funded, and utilized in high school library media centers and assessed its impact on library media programs.

Boucher, Julie J., and Lance, Keith Curry. (1992). **The roles of libraries in education**. Denver, CO: Colorado State Dept. of Education, State Library and Adult Education Office. 28pp. ED 354 919. Explains three sets of roles libraries play in education: provide access to education; ensure equity in education; and affect academic achievement for individuals and assist them in lifelong learning.

Brandhorst, Ted. (1993). **The Educational Resources Information Center (ERIC)**. Rockville, MD: ERIC Processing and Reference Facility. 28pp. ED 354 884. (Submitted for publication in Allen Kent, ed. (1993), *Encyclopedia of Library and Information Science*, vol. 51, suppl. 14, pp. 208-25.) Marcel Dekker, Inc., 270 Madison Ave., New York, NY 10016. Describes the historical development of ERIC and major events in the development of the system; strategies that contributed to system evolution; policy emphases identified through a 1986-87 redesign study; and statistics revealing the current status of the system.

Burnheim, Robert. (1992, October). **Information literacy: The keystone of the bridge**. Paper presented at the TAFE National Conference on Student Services, Brisbane, Australia, October 14-16, 1992. 15pp. ED 356 775. Draws on the work of two Australian committees to establish the importance of information literacy skills and describes a research project on library services required to support the delivery of competency-based training curriculum.

Doyle, Christina S. (1992). **Outcome measures for information literacy within the National Education Goals of 1990. Final report to National Forum on Information Literacy. Summary of findings**. 18pp. ED 351 033. Summarizes the findings of a study that was conducted for the National Forum on Information Literacy (NFIL) to create a comprehensive definition of information literacy and to develop outcome measures for the concept.

Lance, Keith Curry, and others. (1990). **The impact of school library media centers on academic achievement**. Denver, CO: Colorado State Dept. of Education, State Library and Adult Education Office. 160pp. ED 353 989. Reports on a study that provides evidence of the positive impact of library media centers (LMCs) on academic achievement in 221 Colorado public schools during the 1988-89 school year.

Lesk, Michael. (1992). **Preservation of new technology. A report of the Technology Assessment Advisory Committee to the Commission on Preservation and Access**. Washington, DC: Commission on Preservation and Access. 22pp. ED 352 973. (Also available from Commission on Preservation and Access, 1400 16th St. NW, Suite 740, Washington, DC 20036-2117; $5 prepaid.) Summarizes the application of digital technology to preservation problems for new kinds of media such as audio and videotape and computer disks.

Schiller, Nancy. (1992). **The emerging virtual research library. SPEC kit 186**. Washington, DC: Association of Research Libraries, Office of Management Services. 199pp. ED 356 772. (Also available from Systems and Procedures Exchange Center, Office of Management Services, 1527 New Hampshire Ave. NW, Washington, DC 20036.) Describes the results of a 1992 survey of Association of Research Libraries member libraries to determine the extent to which they are becoming virtual libraries, i.e., libraries in which computer and telecommunications technologies make access to a wide range of information resources possible.

Todd, Ross J., and others. (1992, July). **The power of information literacy: Unity of education and resources for the 21st century**. Paper presented at the Annual Meeting of the International Association of School Librarianship, Belfast, Northern Ireland, July 19-24, 1992. 22pp. ED 354 916. Defines information literacy and describes an action research project that is attempting to place information literacy at the center of a secondary school curriculum.

Journal Articles

Barron, Daniel D. (1993, June). School library media program research and assessment. **School Library Media Activities Monthly, 9**(19), 48-50. EJ 464 335. Reviews recent resources for assessing school library media programs and discusses the importance of program assessment.

Boardman, Edna, and others. (1993, March-April). Censorship and intellectual freedom in the schools. **Book Report, 11**(5), 14-27, 65. EJ 459 896. (Available UMI.) Seven articles highlight access to appropriate information, library material selection, dealing with complaints, potentially controversial titles and topics, the censorship of fiction, and more.

Dillon, Martin, and others. (1993, Spring). Assessing information on the Internet: Toward providing library services for computer-mediated communication. Results of an OCLC research project. **Internet Research, 3**(1), 54-69. EJ 464 380. Describes the OCLC Internet Resource project, which investigated the nature of electronic textual information available through the Internet and the practical and theoretical problems associated with creating machine-readable cataloging (MARC) records using USMARC format for computer files.

Doll, Carol A. (1992, Summer). School library media centers: The human environment. **School Library Media Quarterly, 20**(4), 225-29. EJ 448 977. (Available UMI.) Review of the literature on aspects of human behavior relevant to library media center design discusses personal space, territoriality, privacy, variety, and color.

Donham van Deusen, Jean. (1993, Spring). The effects of fixed versus flexible scheduling on curriculum involvement and skills integration in elementary school library media programs. **School Library Media Quarterly, 21**(3), 173-82. EJ 464 310. (Available UMI.) Describes a study that attempted to determine the effects of scheduling on the curriculum involvement of library media specialists and on the curricular integration of library skills.

Epler, Doris M. (1993, January). Funding equipment needs in school districts. **Computers in Libraries, 13**(1), 46-48. EJ 459 894. (Available UMI.) Provides guidelines for school librarians and educators seeking funds for information technology from service groups, corporations, and foundations.

Giesecke, Joan. (1993, March). Recognizing multiple decision making models: A guide for managers. **College and Research Libraries, 54**(2), 103-14. EJ 461 514. (Available UMI.) Provides a theoretical overview of decision-making models that are applicable to libraries; presents a framework for comparing models; and discusses strategies for library managers for decision making.

Hafner, Arthur W., and others. (1992). Traditional mediation. **Reference Librarian, 17**(37), 3-64. EJ 456 122. Four articles address traditional mediation in library services, including the librarian as mediator, the reference librarian as information intermediary, recommitment to patrons' information needs, and mediation in reference service to extend patron success.

Hopkins, Dianne McAfee. (1993, January). A conceptual model of factors influencing the outcome of challenges to library materials in secondary school settings. **Library Quarterly, 63**(1), 40-72. EJ 459 882. (Available UMI.) Reports on a national study of variables influencing the retention, restriction, or removal of challenged library materials in secondary schools.

Jurow, Susan, and Barnard, Susan B. (1993). Introduction: TQM fundamentals and overview of contents. **Journal of Library Administration, 18**(1-2), 1-13. EJ 469 099. Discusses total quality management (TQM), its benefits to libraries, and possible barriers to its adoption. An overview of the 13 articles included in this theme issue is provided.

King, Hannah. (1993, June). Walls around the electronic library. **Electronic Library, 11**(3), 165-74. EJ 465 768. (Available UMI.) Questions the wisdom of permitting visions of the electronic library to drive budgets and strategic planning.

Knirk, Frederick G. (1992, Summer). New technology considerations for media facilities: Video technologies and space requirements. **School Library Media Quarterly, 20**(4), 205-10. EJ 448 974. (Available UMI.) Discusses requirements for audiovisual media, including space needs of groups, individuals, and library personnel.

Kreiser, Latane C., and Hortin, John. (1993). The history of the curriculum integrated library media program concept. **International Journal of Instructional Media, 19**(4), 313-19. EJ 460 011. (Available UMI.) Relates the development of the concept of curriculum-integrated library media programs in elementary and secondary education.

Kurzweil, Raymond. (1993, March 15). The virtual library. **Library Journal, 118**(5), 54-55. EJ 461 539. (Available UMI.) Discusses the impact of electronic publishing, information networks, and new ways of accessing information on libraries.

Lehmann, Stephen, and Spohrer, James H. (1993, July). The year's work in collection development, 1992. **Library Resources and Technical Services, 37**(3), 299-313. EJ 467 379. (Available UMI.) Reviews the collection development literature of 1992.

Loertscher, David V. (1993, May). Objective: Achievement. Solution: School libraries. **School Library Journal, 39**(5), 30-33. EJ 464 320. (Available UMI.) Discussion of effective education focuses on two studies: one on the impact of school library media centers on student achievement, and another on the value of voluntary reading.

McClure, Charles R., and others. (1993). The role of public libraries in the use of Internet/NREN information sources. **Library and Information Science Research, 15**(1), 7-34. EJ 461 567. Reports on a study that assessed key issues affecting public library roles in the use of nonbibliographic Internet information services and explored possible future roles for public libraries in the NREN.

McClure, Charles R., and others. (1992, May). The role of public libraries in the use of Internet/NREN information services: Preliminary findings. **Proceedings of the ASIS Mid-Year Meeting. Networks, Telecommunications, and the Networked Information Resource Revolution (Albuquerque, NM, May 27-30, 1992)**, 46-62. EJ 450 407. Identifies key issues, including risks and barriers to network use, access, suggested services, professional association role, and committing resources.

McCook, Kathleen de la Pena. (1992, Winter). Where would we be without them? Libraries and adult education activities: 1966-91. **RQ, 32**(2), 245-53. EJ 457 994. (Available UMI.) Reviews the role of public libraries in adult literacy and lifelong learning in the 25 years since the signing of the Adult Education Act.

Minor, Barbara B. (1992). Research from the ERIC files: July 1990 to June 1991. **School Library Media Annual (SLMA), 10**, 83-99. EJ 454 767. Describes research from the ERIC database on school library media programs. Topics discussed include library and information skills instruction; information seeking; educational equity; use of technology; censorship; school library media collections; use studies; role of the library media specialist; collective bargaining and job/certification requirements; and training for media specialists.

Riddick, John F. (1993, July). An electrifying year: A year's work in serials, 1992. **Library Resources and Technical Services, 37**(3), 335-42. EJ 467 382. (Available UMI.) Selectively reviews the serials literature published in 1992.

Robertson, Michelle M. (1992, Summer). Ergonomic considerations for the human environment: Color treatment, lighting, and furniture selection. **School Library Media Quarterly, 20**(4), 211-15. EJ 448 975. (Available UMI.) Discusses variables such as temperature and humidity, noise, illumination, color, and windows, and describes computer workstation requirements.

Saunders, Laverna M. (1992, November). The virtual library revisited. **Computers in Libraries, 12**(10), 51-54. EJ 456 154. (Available UMI.) Discusses searching remote library catalogs and databases; the availability of information through the Internet and other networks; and the expertise needed by library staff to instruct and assist users.

Smith, Kitty. (1993, June). Toward the new millennium: The human side of library automation (revisited). **Information Technology and Libraries, 12**(2), 209-16. EJ 467 291. (Available UMI.) Reexamines human factors of human-machine systems from an individual and organizational behavior standpoint, particularly as they relate to library automation.

Swan, John, and others. (1992). Mediation and the electronic world. **Reference Librarian, 17**(37), 65-90. EJ 456 129. Three articles discuss the issue of the mediator's role in the library of the electronic age.

Van Orden, Phyllis. (1993, July). A kaleidoscope of challenges: Youth services in the 90's. **School Library Journal, 39**(7), 18-21. EJ 469 096. (Available UMI.) Identifies current challenges to children's library services, including inequitable access to information, integration of information skills in the classroom, rising costs, the state of book collections, and the need for research at state and national levels.

Walling, Linda Lucas. (1992, Summer). Granting each equal access. **School Library Media Quarterly, 20**(4), 216-22. EJ 448 976. (Available UMI.) Summarizes federal legislation regarding equal access for students with disabilities and discusses environmental barriers to accessibility in the library media center.

MEDIA TECHNOLOGIES

Media-Related Periodicals

Broadcasting. Broadcasting Publications, 1705 DeSales St. NW, Washington, DC 20036. wk.; $85 U.S., $125 elsewhere. All-inclusive newsweekly for radio, television, cable, and allied business.

CableVision. Cable Publishing Group, 600 S. Cherry St., Suite 400, Denver, CO 80222. 26/yr.; $55. A newsmagazine for the cable television industry. Covers programming, marketing, advertising, business, and other topics.

Communication Abstracts. Sage Publications, Inc., 2455 Teller Rd., Newbury Park, CA 91320. bi-mo.; $114 indiv., $342 inst. Abstracts communication-related articles, reports, and books. Cumulated annually.

Communication Booknotes. Center for Advanced Study in Telecommunications (CAST), Graduate Telecommunications Program, George Washington University, 2020 K St. NW, Suite 240, Washington, DC 20006. bi-mo.; $45 indiv., $95 inst. Newsletter that reviews books and periodicals about mass media, telecommunications, and information policy.

Communications News. American Society of Association Executives, Communications Section, 1575 Eye St. NW, Washington, DC 20005. mo.; $27 (free to qualified personnel). Up-to-date information from around the world regarding voice, video, and data communications.

Document Image Automation (previously **Optical Information Systems Magazine**). Meckler Publishing, 11 Ferry Lane W., Westport, CT 06880-5808. q.; $59 indiv., $115 inst., add $18 for delivery outside U.S. Features articles on the applications of videodisc, optical disc, and teletext systems; future implications; system and software compatibilities; and cost comparisons. Also tracks videodisc projects and covers world news.

Document Image Automation Update (previously **Optical Information Systems Update**). Meckler Publishing, 11 Ferry Lane W., Westport, CT 06880-5808. 12/yr.; $297. News and facts about technology, software, courseware developments, calendar, conference reports, and job listings.

Educational Media International. Kogan Page, Ltd., Distribution Centre, Blackhorse Road, Letchworth, Herts SG6 1HN, England. q.; £35 ($63 U.S.), plus £8 ($17 U.S.) airmail. The official journal of the International Council for Educational Media.

Federal Communications Commission Reports. Superintendent of Documents, Government Printing Office, Washington, DC 20402. w.; price varies. Decisions, public notices, and other documents pertaining to FCC activities.

Historical Journal of Film, Radio, and Television. Carfax Publishing Co., Box 2025, Dunnellon, FL 34430-2025. 4/yr.; $112 indiv., $298 inst. Articles by international experts in the field, news and notices, and book reviews.

International Journal of Instructional Media. Westwood Press, Inc., 23 East 22nd St., New York, NY 10010. q.; $105 plus $5 postage U.S., $10 postage elsewhere. Articles discuss specific applications and techniques for bringing the advantages of a particular instructional medium to bear on a complete curriculum system or program.

Journal of Broadcasting and Electronic Media. Broadcast Education Association, 1771 N St. NW, Washington, DC 20036. q.; $40 U.S., $50 elsewhere, $25 students. Includes articles, book reviews, research reports, and analyses. Provides a forum for research relating to telecommunications and related fields.

Journal of Educational Television. Carfax Publishing Co., Box 25, Abingdon, Oxfordshire OX14 3VE, England. 3/yr.; $70 indiv., $280 inst. This journal of the Educational Television Association serves as an international forum for discussions and reports on developments in the field of television and related media in teaching, learning, and training.

Journal of Popular Film and Television. Heldref Publications, 1319 Eighteenth St. NW, Washington, DC 20036-1802. q.; $37 indiv., $58 inst. Articles on film and television, book reviews, and theory.

Media International. Reed Publishing Services, 151 Wardour St., London W1V 4BN, England. mo.; $95. Contains features on the world's major media developments and regional news reports from the international media scene.

Multimedia and Videodisc Monitor (previously **Videodisc Monitor**). Future Systems, Inc., Box 26, Falls Church, VA 22040. mo.; $347 indiv., $150 educational inst. Describes current events in the videodisc marketplace and in training and development.

Multimedia Review. Meckler Publishing Corp., 11 Ferry Lane W., Westport, CT 06880. 4/yr.; $97. Dedicated to analysis of trends, paradigms, and strategies affecting the creation and production, design and development, and implementation and use of multimedia programs and configuration.

Telematics and Informatics. Pergamon Press, Inc., Journals Division, 660 White Plains Rd., Tarrytown, NY 10591-5153. q.; £215. Intended for the specialist in telecommunications and information science. Covers the merging of computer and telecommunications technologies worldwide.

Video Systems. Intertec Publishing Corp., 9800 Metcalf, Overland Park, KS 66212-2215. mo.; $45, free to qualified professionals. For video professionals. Contains state-of-the-art audio and video technology reports.

Videography. United Newspapers Publications, Inc., 2 Park Ave., 18th Floor, New York, NY 10016. mo.; $30. For the video professional; covers techniques, applications, equipment, technology, and video art.

Books

Considine, David, and Haley, Gail E. (1992). **Visual messages: Integrating imagery into instruction**. Teacher Ideas Press, Libraries Unlimited, P.O. Box 3988, Englewood, CO 80155. 269pp. $26.50. An examination of the media with ideas, strategies, and activities that can easily be integrated into diverse areas of an existing school curriculum to promote media literacy.

Gayeski, Diane M., ed. (1993). **Multimedia for learning: Development, application, evaluation**. Educational Technology Publications, 700 Palisade Ave., Englewood Cliffs, NJ 07632. 184pp. $32.95. Eleven chapters by 10 contributors cover making sense of multimedia, skills required for effective multimedia development, technology transfer, evaluating multimedia platforms, HyperCard and CD-I, DVI in organizational information retrieval and training, virtual reality in education, preparing multimedia designers, evaluating interactive multimedia, the future of the technology, and getting started.

Hakes, Barbara T., Sachs, Steven G., Box, Cecilia, and Cochenour, John. (1993). **Compressed video: Operations and applications**. Association for Educational Communications and Technology, 1025 Vermont Ave. NW, Suite 820, Washington, DC 20005-3547. 456pp. $29.95 AECT members; $37.95 nonmembers. Synthesizes what groups around the country have learned about live, two-way audio and video uses of interactive compressed video; covers planning and system management; and includes user profiles for existing applications.

Hodges, Matthew E., and Sasnett, Russell M. (1993). **Multimedia computing: Case studies from MIT Project Athena**. Addison-Wesley, 1 Jacob Way, Reading, MA 01867. 288pp. $35.50. A concise introduction to multimedia computing, reviews both the human and technical elements involved in multimedia technology and the major issues that will determine its development.

Lochte, Robert H. (1993). **Interactive television and instruction: A guide to technology, technique, facilities design, and classroom management**. Educational Technology Publications, 700 Palisade Ave., Englewood Cliffs, NJ 07632. 160pp. $29.95. Eight chapters cover what interactive television is and how it works; preparing, teaching, and evaluating an interactive television class; the instructor training workshop; and installing classroom equipment. Appendices include information on using the overhead camera and useful forms and handouts.

Maurer, Hermann, ed. (1993). **Educational multimedia and hypermedia annual, 1993.** Association for the Advancement of Computing in Education, P.O. Box 2966, Charlottesville, VA 22902. 660pp. Proceedings of ED-MEDIA 93—World Conference on Educational Multimedia and Hypermedia, Orlando, Florida, June 23-26, 1993.

McKenzie, Jamieson A. (1993). **Power learning in the classroom.** Corwin Press, 2455 Teller Rd., Newbury Park, CA 91320. 70pp. $15. Presents the array of new instructional technologies that will become the basis for creating a generation of citizens prepared for the Information Age.

Schwier, Richard A., and Misanchuk, Earl R. (1993). **Interactive multimedia instruction.** Educational Technology Publications, 700 Palisade Ave., Englewood Cliffs, NJ 07632. 392pp. $39.95. Presents information on interactive multimedia instruction systems and the components of, designing, and resources for interactive multimedia instruction.

Stevens, Gregory I. (1993). **Videos for understanding diversity: A core selection and evaluation guide.** American Library Association, 50 E. Huron St., Chicago, IL 60611. 217pp. $35. A complete guide to classroom use of videos to promote multicultural inclusiveness, with reviews of 126 videos, advice for classroom discussion, ordering information, and more.

ERIC Documents

Ayersman, David J. (1993). **An overview of the research on learning styles and hypermedia environments.** Paper presented at the Annual Convention of the Eastern Educational Research Association, Clearwater, FL, February 17-23, 1993. 18pp. ED 356 756. Provides a conceptual foundation for the development of hypermedia as an instructional tool for addressing individual learning style differences.

Cates, Ward Mitchell. (1992). **Considerations in evaluating metacognition in interactive hypermedia/multimedia instruction.** Paper presented at the Annual Conference of the American Educational Research Association, San Francisco, CA, April 20-24, 1992. 17pp. ED 349 966. Defines metacognition as the set of skills and strategies one uses in monitoring and modifying how one learns; this paper addresses ways in which interactive hypermedia/ multimedia instructional programs might enhance the metacognitive abilities of the learners who use them.

Couch, John D., and others. (1993). **Interdisciplinary study with computer-based multimedia.** Paper presented at the Annual Conference of the International Visual Literacy Association, Pittsburgh, PA, September 30-October 4, 1992. ED 363 316. Reviews the role of interdisciplinary study with computer-based multimedia in the classroom, discusses multimedia courseware and interactive multimedia for science instruction, and considers the importance of visual literacy.

Fletcher, J. D. (1992). **Cost-effectiveness of interactive courseware.** Alexandria, VA: Institute for Defense Analyses. 41pp. ED 355 914. Reviews what is known about the cost-effectiveness of interactive courseware (ICW) and considers effect sizes for two ICW media: computer-based instruction and interactive videodisc instruction.

Gueulette, David G. (1993). **Preparing teachers for using instructional television in diverse cultural settings**. Paper presented at the Annual Conference of the International Visual Literacy Association, Pittsburgh, PA, September 30-October 4, 1992. ED 363 333. Describes the work of a team of researchers at Northern Illinois University (DeKalb) to compile knowledge about the most critical audience factors and their impact on the design and delivery of instruction for international learners in higher education in the United States.

Gutenko, Gregory. (1993). **Selling color: The development and marketing of the NTSC color television broadcasting technology and the implications for HDTV**. ED 358 827. Reviews the introduction and acceptance of color television and the National Television System Committee (NTSC) color standard for the lessons they hold for the future of high-definition television (HDTV).

Hillyer, Kathryn Oliver. (1993). **Seeing through the glitz: Commercial literacy for students**. Paper presented at the Annual Conference of the International Visual Literacy Association, Pittsburgh, PA, September 30-October 4, 1992. ED 363 291. Explores television advertising aimed at children and discusses its regulation, effects on behavior, and sexual stereotypes.

Liu, Min. (1992). **Hypermedia-assisted instruction and second language learning: A semantic-network-based approach**. Paper presented at the Annual Conference of the Eastern Educational Research Association, Hilton Head, SC, March 1992. 32pp. ED 349 954. A literature review examining a hypermedia learning environment from a semantic network basis and the application of such an environment to second language learning.

Lloyd, R. Scott. (1993). **An introduction to educational holography**. Paper presented at the Annual Conference of the International Visual Literacy Association, Pittsburgh, PA, September 30-October 4, 1992. ED 363 327. Explores holograms as educational tools to explain information visually to everyone.

Pinheiro, Edwin J., and Oblinger, Diana. (1993). **Digital multimedia. An IAT technology primer**. Chapel Hill, NC: University of North Carolina, Institute for Academic Technology.; New York, NY: International Business Machines Corporation. ED 358 855. Explains the technology behind digital multimedia and outlines specific uses and advantages.

Public Broadcasting: Ready to teach. How Public Broadcasting can serve the ready-to-learn needs of America's children. A report to the 103rd Congress and the American people. (1993). Washington, DC: Corporation for Public Broadcasting. 98pp. ED 355 920. Three approaches to delivering a national ready-to-learn television service from public broadcasting are explored, along with a fourth option, as follows: (1) universal access; (2) national cable feed; (3) local hybrid; and (4) existing schedule.

Reed, W. Michael, and Rosenbluth, Gwendolyn S. (1992). **The effect of HyperCard programming on knowledge construction and interrelatedness of humanities-based information**. 9pp. ED 355 908. Reports on a study that centered on students as creators rather than users of programs to determine whether collaboratively creating HyperCard stacks affected the amount of knowledge and the interrelatedness of students' informational units.

Rogers, Dwight L. (1992). **Instructional media technology in secondary education**. 25pp. ED 354 862. Reviews the research literature from the early 1980s to the present pertaining to instructional media utilization practices in secondary classrooms.

Sutton, Ronald E. (1993). **Information literacy meets media literacy and visual literacy**. Paper presented at the Annual Conference of the International Visual Literacy Association, Pittsburgh, PA, September 30-October 4, 1992. ED 363 307. Offers current definitions of three media literacies from a theoretical and practical standpoint and discusses their interrelatedness.

Townsend, Frank C., and Townsend, Catherine M. (1992). **Meeting learning needs through multimedia: A look at the way modern technology can help classroom teachers meet the varied instructional needs of students**. 47pp. ED 352 969. This paper builds a case for the use of multimedia to meet students' varied learning needs instead of relying solely on the traditional lecture/textbook/workbook approach.

Journal Articles

Brown, Kenneth. (1993, April-May). Video production in the classroom: Creating success for students and schools. **TechTrends, 38**(3), 32-35. EJ 462 830. (Available UMI.) Describes benefits of integrating video production into high school curricula.

Cambre, Marjorie A., and others. (1992, Spring). Implementation of generative learning principles in interactive video using repurposed video materials. **Journal of Visual Literacy, 12**(1), 35-56. EJ 461 604. Discusses barriers to videodisc use in education and describes two models that integrate curriculum theory and cognitive learning theory in the creation of social studies and foreign language curriculum packages.

Chen, Ching-Chih. (1993, March). Photo CD and other digital imaging technologies: What's out there and what's it for? **Microcomputers for Information Management, 10**(1), 29-42. EJ 464 317. Describes Kodak's Photo CD technology, color desktop publishing, image processing and preservation, image archival storage, and interactive multimedia development.

Collins, Jude, and others. (1992, December). Who's afraid of the big bad box? Children and TV advertising in four countries. **Educational Media International, 29**(4), 245-60. EJ 460 001. (Available UMI.) Describes a study of nine-year-olds in Ireland, Australia, the United States, and Norway that investigated their attitudes to television advertising and the connection to buying patterns in their families.

Fabris, Marta E. (1993). Using multimedia in the multicultural classroom. **Journal of Educational Technology Systems, 21**(2), 163-71. EJ 457 872. Discusses types of multimedia technology, including hypermedia, voice/sound digitizers, scanners, CD-ROMs, videodiscs, and other video equipment; lesson plans for teachers; ideas for student group projects; and sources for multimedia materials.

Fujihara, Hiroko, and others. (1992). Intelligent search in an educational hypertext environment. **Journal of Educational Multimedia and Hypermedia, 1**(4), 401-15. EJ 459 930. Discussion of hypertext for computer-assisted instruction highlights SINS (Semistructured

Intelligent Navigation System), a hypertext system that addresses and solves navigation problems common to hypertext environments.

Hartigan, John M. (1993, May). Multimedia: The marriage broker for television and computers. **CD-ROM Professional, 6**(3), 69-71. EJ 464 271. (Available UMI.) Gives an overview of the development of multimedia, from the combination of film and computer graphics used during the 1960s to present-day jet aircraft simulators.

Heeren, Elske, and Collis, Betty. (1993). Design considerations for telecommunications-supported cooperative learning environments: Concept mapping as a "telecooperation support tool." **Journal of Educational Multimedia and Hypermedia, 2**(2), 107-27. EJ 467 366. Discusses computer-mediated communication, computer-supported cooperative work, distributed learning environments, and frameworks for supporting telecooperation.

Hofmeister, Alan M., and others. (1992, July). Learner diversity and instructional video: Implications for developers. **Educational Technology, 32**(7), 13-16. EJ 448 992. (Available UMI.) Discussion of growing diversity in learners' language and communication skills and increasing use of video in instruction focuses on the use of captioning in instructional video and the implications for educational and industrial training.

Lee, YungBin B., and Lehman, James D. (1993). Instructional cuing in hypermedia: A study with active and passive learners. **Journal of Educational Multimedia and Hypermedia, 2**(1), 25-37. EJ 461 609. Describes a study of undergraduates that investigated the use of hypermedia programs by learners classified as active, passive, or neutral.

Ley, Kathryn, and Klein, James D. (1993). The effect of interactive video and print role models and learner sex on instructional motivation. **Performance Improvement Quarterly, 6**(2), 58-67. EJ 461 572. Describes a study that examined the effect of two types of instructional media—interactive video and print—and learner gender on attitudes toward instruction.

Nelson, Wayne A., and Palumbo, David B. (1992). Learning, instruction, and hypermedia. **Journal of Educational Multimedia and Hypermedia, 1**(3), 287-99. EJ 448 904. Examines the psychological basis of hypermedia as a medium for learning, surveys the characteristics of current hypermedia systems, and suggests ways to make hypermedia systems more valuable as instructional environments.

Simpson, Henry, and others. (1993). Empirical comparison of alternative instructional TV technologies. **Distance Education, 14**(1), 147-64. EJ 467 340. (Available UMI.) Describes a study conducted by the U.S. Navy that compared training effectiveness and user acceptance of live instruction and six different alternative instructional television (ITV) technologies.

Vepierre, Philippe. (1992, December). The computer serving the video: A new technology for all. **Educational Media International, 29**(4), 241-46. EJ 459 999. (Available UMI.) Examines the use of the microcomputer in video production and considers the types of equipment, the management, and the technological capabilities that need to be available to a small producer.

Welsch, Erwin K. (1992, Spring). Hypertext, hypermedia, and the humanities. **Library Trends, 40**(4), 614-46. EJ 461 664. (Available UMI.) Provides historical background on hypertext and hypermedia; discusses their use in the humanities; gives examples of hypersystem applications in the humanities; and examines libraries' roles in the use of hypersystems in the humanities.

Worringham, Richard E. (1992). The video cassette recorder's potential as a tool for development. **International Journal of Instructional Media, 19**(3), 259-67. EJ 457 839. (Available UMI.) Examines the potential of the videocassette recorder (VCR) as a tool for development in technologically poor countries and assesses possible impacts of the VCR on culture and family life.

SIMULATION AND VIRTUAL REALITY

Media-Related Periodicals

Simulation and Gaming. Sage Publications, Inc., 2455 Teller Rd., Newbury Park, CA 91320. q.; $50 indiv., $157 inst. An international journal of theory, design, and research published by the Association for Business Simulation and Experiential Learning.

Simulation/Games for Learning. Distribution Centre, Blackhorse Rd., Letchworth, Herts SG6 1HN, England. q.; £38. Main publication of the Society for the Advancement of Games and Simulations in Education and Training (SAGSET), which aims to encourage and develop the use of simulation and gaming techniques in applications in education and training.

Virtual Reality Report. Meckler Publishing, 11 Ferry Lane W., Westport, CT 06880-5808. 9/yr.; $227. Covers developments in the field of virtual reality and cyberspace.

ERIC Documents

Bricken, Meredith, and Byrne, Chris M. (1992). **Summer students in virtual reality: A pilot study on educational applications of virtual reality technology**. Seattle, WA: University of Washington, Washington Technology Center, Human Interface Technology Laboratory. 14pp. ED 358 853. Describes a study at a technology-oriented day camp undertaken to evaluate VR in terms of usefulness and appeal to students ages 10-15 and to document the students' behavior and opinions as they used VR to construct and explore their own virtual worlds.

McLellan, Hilary. (1993). **Virtual reality: Visualization in three dimensions**. Paper presented at the Annual Conference of the International Visual Literacy Association, Pittsburgh, PA, September 30-October 4, 1992. 9pp. ED 363 322. Presents a discussion of virtual reality as a newly emerging tool for scientific visualization that makes possible multisensory, three-dimensional modeling of scientific data. Describes research efforts and future professional applications.

Merickel, Mark L. (1992). **A study of the relationship between virtual reality (perceived realism) and the ability of children to create, manipulate and utilize mental images for spatially related problem solving**. Paper presented at the Annual Convention of the National School Boards Association, Orlando, FL, April 25-28, 1992. 9pp. ED 352 942. Reports on a study that measured the effects on cognitive ability of children who worked at either a computer workstation or a virtual reality/cyberspace system.

Yildiz, Rauf, and Atkins, Madeleine J. (1992). **How to evaluate multimedia simulations: Learning from the past**. Paper presented at the European Conference on Educational Research, Enschede, The Netherlands, June 22-25, 1992. 7pp. ED 350 978. Identifies and discusses the main criticisms of media research, discusses the state of current interactive video simulation research, and makes recommendations for future research, particularly in the areas of cognitive and attitudinal effectiveness and the theoretical basis of the design of interactive video simulations.

Zwart, Willem Jaap. (1992). **Instructional transaction theory applied to computer simulations**. 4pp. ED 352 945. Argues that Merrill's instructional transaction theory provides a framework that can decrease learners' problems in using computer simulations by specifying transaction shells rather than frames in designing interactive courseware.

Journal Articles

Lintern, Gavan. (1992, December). Flight simulation for the study of skill transfer. **Simulation Games for Learning, 22**(4), 336-50. EJ 459 937. Discusses the issue of similarity, simulation and the design of training devices, an information theory of transfer, invariants for flight control, and experiments involving the transfer of flight skills.

Munro, Allen, and Towne, Douglas M. (1992). Productivity tools for simulation centered training development. **Educational Technology Research and Development, 40**(4), 65-80. EJ 462 863. (Available UMI.) Discusses model-based simulation for training, explains an object-oriented approach, and describes RAPIDS, an authoring system for the production of interactive graphical models.

Neves, Joao S., and Sanyal, Rajib N. (1992, September). UPSIDE DOWN: A cross cultural experiential exercise. **Simulation & Gaming, 23**(3), 370-75. EJ 451 842. (Available UMI.) Describes a game called UPSIDE DOWN that is designed for use in higher education courses or in corporate training to sensitize participants to cultural issues when interacting with groups with different backgrounds.

Shlechter, Theodore M., and others. (1992, Fall). Computer based simulation systems and role playing: An effective combination for fostering conditional knowledge. **Journal of Computer Based Instruction, 19**(4), 110-14. EJ 457 936. (Available UMI.) Examines the effectiveness of SIMNET (Simulation Networking), a virtual reality training simulation system, combined with a program of role-playing activities for helping Army classes to master the conditional knowledge needed for successful field performance.

TELECOMMUNICATIONS AND NETWORKING

Media-Related Periodicals

Canadian Journal of Educational Communication. Association for Media and Technology in Education in Canada, 3-1750 The Queensway, Suite 1318, Etobicoke, ON M9C 5H5, Canada. q; $42.80 Canada, $50 U.S., $58.85 elsewhere. Concerned with all aspects of educational systems and technology.

Computer Communications. Butterworth-Heinemann, Ltd., Turpin Transactions, Ltd., Distribution Centre, Blackhorse Rd., Letchworth, Herts SG6 1HM, England. 10/yr.; £205 in UK and Europe, £225 elsewhere. Focuses on networking and distributed computing techniques, communications hardware and software, and standardization.

Data Communications. Box 473, Hightstown, NJ 08520. mo.; $95 U.S., $105 Canada. Provides users with news and analysis of changing technology for the networking of computers.

EDUCOM Review. EDUCOM, 1112 16th St. NW, Suite 600, Washington, DC 20036-4823. q.; $60 U.S., $75 elsewhere. Features articles on current issues and applications of computing and communications technology in higher education. Reports of EDUCOM consortium activities.

EMMS (Electronic Mail & Micro Systems). International Resource Development, Inc., Box 1716, New Canaan, CT 06840. semi-mo.; $535 U.S., $595 elsewhere. Covers technology, user, product, and legislative trends in graphic, record, and microcomputer applications.

Internet Research (previously **Electronic Networking: Research, Applications, and Policy**). Meckler Corp., 11 Ferry Lane W., Westport, CT 06880. q.; $95. A cross-disciplinary journal presenting research findings related to electronic networks, analyses of policy issues related to networking, and descriptions of current and potential applications of electronic networking for communication, computation, and provision of information services.

Networking Management. Penn Well Publishing Co., Box 2417, Tulsa, OK 74101-2417. mo.; $42 (free to qualified individuals). Covers issues and applications for planning, support, and management of voice data networks.

Telecommunications. Horizon House Publications, Inc., 685 Canton St., Norwood, MA 02062. mo.; $67 U.S., $120 elsewhere (free to qualified individuals). Feature articles and news for the field of telecommunications.

T.I.E. News (Telecommunications in Education). International Society for Technology in Education, 1787 Agate St., Eugene, OR 97403-1923. q.; free to members of the SIG/Tel special interest group. Contains articles on all aspects of educational telecommunications.

Books

Azarmsa, Reza. (1993). **Telecommunications: A handbook for educators**. Garland Publishing, 717 Fifth Ave., Suite 2500, New York, NY 10022. 318pp. $48. A comprehensive introduction to telecommunications and their applications in teaching and learning.

Duning, Becky S., Van Kekerix, Marvin J., and Zaborowski, Leon M. (1993). **Reaching learners through telecommunications: Management and leadership strategies for higher education**. Jossey-Bass Inc., 350 Sansome St., San Francisco, CA 94104. 305pp. $34.95. Offers practical advice to novice and experienced managers on every phase of administering a telecommunications-based education program.

Estrada, Susan. (1993). **Connecting to the Internet: A buyer's guide**. O'Reilly and Associates, 632 Petaluma Ave., Sebastopol, CA 95472. 170pp. $15.95. Consumer-oriented guide to evaluating the offerings of different service providers and choosing the best solution for a particular need.

Fraase, Michael. (1993). **The Mac Internet tour guide: Cruising the Internet the easy way**. Ventana Press, P.O. Box 2468, Chapel Hill, NC 27515. 290pp. with disk. $27.95. An Internet book/disk package exclusively for Macintosh users, with complete information about the Internet, a guide to networked resources, and software for electronic mail, file transfer, and file decompression.

LaQuey, Tracy, and Ryer, J. C. (1993). **The Internet companion: A beginner's guide to global networking**. Addison-Wesley, Reading, MA. 208pp. $12.95. Covers the origins of the Internet, acceptable use, basics of electronic mail, online resources, security issues, "netiquette," and more.

Lynch, Daniel C., and Rose, Marshall T. (1993). **Internet system handbook**. Addison-Wesley, Reading, MA. 900pp. $59.25. Explains Internet protocols in logical succession. Also addresses the historical evolution of the Internet community, the technologies employed, management of the technology for a cohesive infrastructure, and future trends.

Networks now: The 1993 survey of how states use telecommunication networks in education. (1993). EDUCORP Consultants Corp., 1414 Third St. SW, Roanoke, VA 24016. 200pp. $99. Describes the current status of each state's activities to support, operate, and maintain a statewide telecommunications network serving instructional activities. Includes a full report of every state's response and a review of relevant research.

Ruopp, Richard R., Gal, Shahaf, Brayton, Brian, and Pfister, Meghan, eds. (1993). **LabNet: Toward a community of practice**. Lawrence Erlbaum Associates, 365 Broadway, Hillsdale, NJ 07642. 362pp. $29.95 (paper). Describes a three-year project conducted by the Technical Education Research Centers to provide a telecommunications network for the exchange of ideas among high school teachers in 37 states.

Smoot, Carl-Mitchell, and Quarterman, John S. (1993). **Practical internetworking with TCP/IP and UNIX**. Addison-Wesley, 1 Jacob Way, Reading, MA 01867. 432pp. $43.25. Offers a synergistic and practical approach to understanding TCP/IP, how to set up and manage a TCP/IP network, and how to use the tools available in the UNIX operating system.

Tennant, Roy, Ober, J., and Lipow, A. G. (1993). **Crossing the Internet threshold: An instructional handbook**. Library Solutions Press, 2137 Oregon St., Berkeley, CA. 134pp. $45.

ERIC Documents

Educational telecommunications. Final report of the NEA Special Committee on Telecommunications. (1992). Washington, DC: National Education Association. 49pp. ED 358 834. Reports on the work of the NEA Special Committee on Telecommunications to investigate the impact of telecommunications technology on education and make policy recommendations. Discusses the need for leadership among teachers, the potential of distance education to reduce inequity, the need for telephone service in every classroom, and more.

Honey, Margaret, and Henriquez, Andres. (1992). **Telecommunications and K-12 educators: Findings from a national survey**. New York, NY: Center for Technology in Education. 95pp. ED 359 923. Presents a systematic profile of activities currently being undertaken by K-12 educators in telecommunications technology. Describes characteristics of respondents and implications of findings for improving the educational uses of telecommunications.

Johnston, Valerie L. (1992). **Towards a global classroom: Using computer-mediated communications at UAA**. 75pp. ED 356 759. An introduction to computer-mediated communication (CMC) for university faculty. Covers advantages and disadvantages, design issues, CMC for professional development and research, and more. Describes the experiences of the University of Alaska at Anchorage.

K-12 computer networking. ERIC Review. (1993). Rockville, MD: ACCESS ERIC; Washington, DC: Educational Resources Information Center. 33pp. ED 355 940. Explores computer networking in elementary and secondary schools via two principal articles: "Plugging into the 'Net" (Michael B. Eisenberg and Donald P. Ely); and "Computer Networks for Science Teachers." Includes lists of K-12 computer networking resources.

Newman, Denis, and others. (1992). **Local infrastructures for school networking: Current models and prospects. Technical report no. 22**. New York, NY: Center for Technology in Education. 30pp. ED 349 957. Identifies a paradigm shift that must take place in school networking in order to retool the schools with a local technical infrastructure that gives teachers and students immediate access to communication systems and information resources.

Scott, Donna M., and others. (1993). **Teaching collaborative problem solving using computer-mediated communications**. Paper presented at the Annual Meeting of the Association for Educational Communications and Technology, New Orleans, LA, January 13-17, 1993. 9pp. ED 354 869. Reports on research using a system of microcomputers interconnected with electronic meeting system software as a possible means of overcoming the grading and participation disparity problems associated with group work sessions conducted in face-to-face meetings.

Sivin Kachala, Jay P., and Bialo, Ellen R. (1992). **Using computer-based, telecommunications services to serve educational purposes at home. Final report**. New York, NY: Interactive Educational Systems Design, Inc. 55pp. ED 354 853. Addresses the use of computer-based telecommunications services to meet educational needs at home, focusing on services for students in grade 7 through college, including adult education. Lists service providers, network providers with education services, homework hotlines, and other resources.

Tinker, Robert F., and Kapisovsky, Peggy M., eds. (1992). **Prospects for educational telecomputing: Selected readings**. Cambridge, MA: Technical Education Research Center. 164pp. ED 350 992. (Also available from: Technical Education Research Center, 2067 Massachusetts Ave., Cambridge, MA 02140; $15.) Collection of readings intended to stimulate debate on the role of educational telecomputing in school reform and restructuring, and how efforts from the public and private sectors can coordinate to bring about these changes.

U.S. Congress. House of Representatives. Committee on Energy and Commerce. (1992). **Telecommuting. Hearing on H.R. 5082, a bill to promote the use of telecommuting, before the Subcommittee on Telecommunications and Finance of the Committee on Energy and Commerce**. 102d Cong., 2d session. 99pp. ED 352 950. (Also available from U.S. Government Printing Office, Superintendent of Documents, Congressional Sales Office, Washington DC 20402, S/N 102-149.) Focuses on how the developing telecommunications infrastructure can provide major benefits to the environment, employers, and the daily life of working people. Notes that telecommuting hopes to take advantage of technology such as personal computers, modems, fax machines, fiber optics, videoconferencing, and private and public networks to create remote satellite or tele-work centers away from the traditional workplace.

Journal Articles

Arora, Jagdish, and others. (1992). Computer communication networks and their use for information retrieval and dissemination: Basic tutorial and current scenario of networks in India. **Microcomputers for Information Management, 9**(4), 241-61. EJ 461 556. Offers a tutorial on telecommunications that covers the basic concepts, types, techniques, and protocols of data communications.

Collis, Betty, and others. (1993, January). Preparing for an interconnected future: Policy options for telecommunications in education. **Educational Technology, 33**(1), 17-24. EJ 457 882. (Available UMI.) Examines the concept of interconnectivity in society and in the educational system, and presents four scenarios for telecommunications policy in schools.

Connolly, Frank W., and Schneebeck, Chuck. (1993, May-June). The community of electronic learners. **EDUCOM Review, 28**(3), 36-37. EJ 465 745. (Available UMI.) Discusses the formation of communities of electronic learners through computer networks. Covers the responsibilities of electronic communities as outlined in the Bill of Rights and Responsibilities for Electronic Learners.

Gates, Rick. (1993, February). Internet cruising with the Internet Hunt. **Electronic Library, 11**(1), 19-24. EJ 461 621. (Available UMI.) Describes the Internet Hunt, a game designed to challenge and inform librarians about information sources available on the Internet.

Silva, Marcos, and Cartwright, Glenn F. (1993, Summer). The Internet as a medium for education and educational research. **Education Libraries, 17**(2), 7-12. EJ 469 141. (Available UMI.) Examines the use of the Internet as a resource for teaching and research and as a virtual classroom, the reasons for investing in the United States and Canadian national supernetworks, and the implications of the supernetworks for education and librarianship.

Simmonds, Curtis. (1993, March). Searching Internet archive sites with Archie: Why, what, where, and how. **Online, 17**(2), 50, 52-55. EJ 460 024. (Available UMI.) Describes Archie, an online catalog of electronic holdings of anonymous FTP (File Transfer Protocol) archive sites on the Internet.

Index

This index lists names of associations and organizations, authors, titles, and subjects (indicated by bold entries). In addition, acronyms for all organizations and associations are cross-referenced to the full name. Please note that a classified list of U.S. organizations and associations appears on pages 195-253.

AACC. *See* American Association of Community Colleges
AAP. *See* Association of American Publishers
AASA. *See* American Association of School Administrators
AASCU. *See* American Association of State Colleges and Universities
AASL. *See* American Association of School Librarians
AAVT. *See* Association of Audio-Visual Technicians
Abbott, A., 355
Abrahams, Janice, 106-19
Academy of Motion Picture Arts and Sciences, 203
ACCESS ERIC, 226
ACCESS NETWORK, 254
"Accounting for user diversity in configuring online systems," 345
ACEI. *See* Association for Childhood Education International
ACHE. *See* Association for Continuing Higher Education
ACRL. *See* Association of College and Research Libraries
Adaptive Technologies for Learning and Work Environments, 367
ADCIS. *See* Association for the Development of Computer-Based Instructional Systems
ADJ/Chapter 1. *See* ERIC Adjunct Clearinghouse on Chapter 1
ADJ/CL. *See* ERIC Adjunct Clearinghouse on Clinical Schools
ADJ/CN. *See* ERIC Adjunct Clearinghouse on Consumer Education
ADJ/JS. *See* ERIC Adjunct Clearinghouse for United State-Japan Studies
ADJ/LE. *See* ERIC Adjunct Clearinghouse for ESL Literacy Education
Administering the School Library Media Center, 367
Adrianson, L., 347
Adult Literacy Program, Vanderbilt University, 46
Adventure Maker software, 45
AECT. *See* Association for Educational Communications and Technology

AEE. *See* Association for Experiential Education
AEL. *See* Appalachia Educational Laboratory, Inc.
AERA. *See* American Educational Research Association
AFA. *See* American Federation of Arts
AFB. *See* American Foundation for the Blind
AFC. *See* Anthropology Film Center
AFVA. *See* American Film and Video Association
Agency for Instructional Technology, 203
AIT. *See* Agency for Instructional Technology
AIVF/FIVF. *See* Association of Independent Video and Filmmakers/Foundation for Independent Video and Film
ALA. *See* American Library Association
Alabama
    doctoral programs in instructional technology, 258
    graduate programs in instructional technology, 274
Alabama State University, 258, 274
ALCTS. *See* Association for Library Collections and Technical Services
Alice Network Software, 55, 56, 111
ALISE. *See* Association for Library and Information Science
"All seriousness aside," 349
Allen, Alma A., 341
ALS. *See* PBS Adult Learning Service
ALSC. *See* Association for Library Service to Children
ALTA. *See* American Library Trustee Association
"Alternative assessment," 353
AMA. *See* American Management Association
American Association of Community Colleges, 203-4
American Association of School Administrators, 204
American Association of School Librarians, 205
American Association of State Colleges and Universities, 204
American Educational Research Association, 204
American Educational Research Journal, 348
American Federation of Arts, 204-5
American Film and Video Association, 205

American Foundation for the Blind, 205
American Journal of Distance Education, 345, 347
American Library Association, 172, 205-8
American Library Trustee Association, 205-6
American Management Association, 208
American Montessori Society, 208-9
American National Standards Institute, 209
American Psychological Association, 164
American Research Association, 18
American Society for Training and Development, 29, 209
American Society of Cinematographers, 209-10
American Society of Educators, 210
American Women in Radio and Television, 210
AMPAS. *See* Academy of Motion Picture Arts and Sciences
AMS. *See* American Montessori Society
AMTEC. *See* Association for Media and Technology in Education in Canada
Andersen, Dale G., 34
Annual Review of the Information and Science Technology, 357
ANSI. *See* American National Standards Institute
Anthropology Film Center, 210
Appalachia Educational Laboratory, Inc., 210
Appalachian State University, 312
Apple Computer, 157
Apple Library Users Group Newsletter, 336
"The application of a spiral curriculum model to technical training curricula," 362
Appropriate Technology, 345
Arizona
   graduate programs in educational computing, 303
   graduate programs in instructional technology, 275
Arizona State University, 275, 303
Arkansas graduate programs in instructional technology, 275
Arkansas Tech University, 275
Arora, J., 384
Arthur Andersen, Inc., 31
Artificial Intelligence Abstracts, 334
ASC. *See* American Society of Cinematographers
ASC. *See* Association of Systematics Collections
ASCLA. *See* Association of Specialized and Cooperative Library Agencies
ASE. *See* American Society of Educators
AskERIC, 111, 112
Aspen Systems, 123
"Assessing information on the Internet," 369
Assessment, student, 151-54
   technology in, 152
Association for Childhood Education International, 210-11
Association for Continuing Higher Education, 211

Association for Educational Communications and Technology, 2, 181-83, 211-16
   Annual Achievement Award, 318, 321
   archives of, 216
   awards, 317-18, 320-21
   Board of Directors, 6, 8
   Committee on Definition and Terminology, 4, 6-7
   Distinguished Service Award, 318, 320-21
   Division of Educational Media Management, 212
   Division of Instructional Development, 135, 140, 212
   Division of Interactive Systems and Computers, 212
   Division of School Media Specialists, 213
   Division of Telecommunications, 213
   Industrial Training and Education Division, 213
   International Division, 213
   Leadership Development Grants, 318, 325
   Media Design and Production Division, 213-14
   Memorial Scholarship Award, 319, 326
   National Convention Internship Program, 318, 323
   presidential address, 41-43
   Research and Theory Division, 214
   Richard B. Lewis Memorial Award, 318, 324
   SIRS Intellectual Freedom Award, 318, 322
   Special Service Award, 318, 320
   Summer Leadership Development Conference, 42
Association for Experiential Education, 216
Association for Library and Information Science, 216
Association for Library Collections and Technical Services, 206
Association for Library Service to Children, 206
Association for Media and Technology in Education in Canada, 184-85, 254
Association for the Development of Computer-Based Instructional Systems, 179-80, 216-17
Association of American Publishers, 217
Association of Audio-Visual Technicians, 217
Association of College and Research Libraries, 206
Association of Independent Video and Filmmakers/Foundation for Independent Video and Film, 217
Association of Specialized and Cooperative Library Agencies, 206
Association of Systematics Collections, 217
Association of Teacher Educators, 218
ASTD. *See* American Society for Training and Development
ATE. *See* Association of Teacher Educators
Atkins, M. J., 380
Atkinson, R., 355

Auburn University, 274
Audiovisual education, 27
Auerbach, J. T., 368
Automating Instructional Design, 361
AWRT. *See* American Women in Radio and
    Television
AVC Presentation Development & Delivery, 359
Awards, AECT, 317-18
Ayersman, D. J., 375
Azarmsa, R., 382

Baca, J. C., 361
Bailey, Gerald D., 339
Baker, Linda M., 82-105
Balajthy, E., 156
Banathy, B. H., 362
Barnard, J., 347
Barnard, S. B., 370
Barron, A. E., 351
Barron, D. D., 369
Barry University, 279, 305
Bedrick, David, 29
Bennett, Dorothy, 151
Berry, Lou, 7
Big Sky Telegraph, 113
Boardman, E., 369
Boise State University, 30, 281
Bollier, D., 357
Bonzi, S., 356
Book Report, 364, 369
Bossinger, June, 335
Boston University, 264-65, 286
Boucher, J. J., 368
Bowers, C. A., 68
Box, C., 374
Brandhorst, T., 368
Bransford, John, 44-48
Brearton, M. A., 156
Brethower, D. M., 362
Bricken, M., 379
Bricken, W., 343
Bridgewater State College, 286
Brigham Young University, 271, 300
British Journal of Educational Technology,
    342, 350
Broadcasting, 372
Brown, George, 68
Brown, J. S., 353
Brown, K., 377
Brown, William L., 340
Bruce, Bertram C., 339
Bruder, I., 353
Brunner, C., 346, 352
Buffalo State College, 311
*Bulletin of the American Society for Information
    Science,* 355
Burge, E. J., 346
Burger, M., 157

Burke, C., 357
Burnheim, R., 368
Byrne, C. M., 379
Byrne, M. M., 156
Byte, 336, 342

Cablevision, 372
CALICO Journal, 336
California
    **doctoral programs in instructional technol-
        ogy, 258-59**
    **graduate programs in educational comput-
        ing, 304**
    **graduate programs in instructional technol-
        ogy, 276-77**
California State University-Chico, 276
California State University-Dominguez Hills, 276
California State University-Los Angeles, 276
California State University-Northridge, 276
California State University-San Bernardino, 276
California Technology Project, 111
Cambre, M. A., 377
Cameron, Walter A., 29
CamMotion software, 59
Campoy, R., 353
Canadian Book Publishers' Council, 254
Canadian Broadcasting Corporation/Societe
    Radio-Canada, 255
Canadian Education Association/Association
    canadienne d'education, 255
Canadian Film Institute, 255
*Canadian Journal of Educational Communica-
    tion,* 350, 363, 381
*Canadian Journal of Information and Library
    Science,* 355
Canadian Library Association, 255
Canadian Museums Association/Association des
    musees canadiens, 255
Caro, Denis H. J., 335
Carpenter, D., 34
Cartwright, G. F., 385
Cates, W. M., 375
Catholic Library Association, 218
CAVS. *See* Center for Advanced Visual
    Studes/MIT
CBC. *See* Canadian Broadcasting Corporation
CBPC. *See* Canadian Book Publishers' Council
CCAIT. *See* Community College Association for
    Instruction and Technology
CCSN. *See* Community College Satellite
    Network
CCSSO. *See* Council of Chief State School
    Officers
"CD R: The next stage in CD ROM evolution,"
    336
CD ROM Professional, 336, 378
CD-ROM Databases, 335
CD-ROM Finder, 336

"CD-ROM in the information marketplace," 336
CD-ROM Librarian, 335
CD-ROM Professional, 335
CE. *See* ERIC Clearinghouse on Adult Career, and Vocational Education
CEA. *See* Canadian Education Association/Association canadienne d'education
CEC. *See* Council for Exceptional Children
CEDaR. *See* Council for Educational Development and Research
CEN. *See* Central Educational Network
Cennamo, Katherine S., 341
"Censorship and intellectual freedom in the schools," 369
Center for Advanced Visual Studies/MIT, 218
Center for Excellence in Education, Indiana University, 28
Center for Instructional Research and Curriculum Evaluation, 218
Center for Technology in Education, 151-54, 218
Central Educational Network, 218
Central Missouri State University, 288
CERL. *See* Computer-Based Education Research Laboratory
CFI. *See* Canadian Film Institute
CG. *See* ERIC Clearinghouse on Counseling and Student Services
Chen, C. C., 357, 377
Chicago State University, 282
Children's behavior and television violence, 164-68
Children's Television International/GLAD Productions, Inc., 218-19
Christopher Columbus Consortium, 157
Cibbarelli, P., 367
CIJE. *See Current Index to Journals in Education*
CINE Information, 219
CLA. *See* Catholic Library Association
Clapp, G., 165
Clariana, Roy B., 341
Classroom Dynamics, 340
Classrooms with a Difference, 346
Clearinghouse on Development Communication, 219
Clement, John, 106-19
CLENE. *See* Continuing Library Education Network and Exchange
Clients, 122
Cline, Hugh F., 340
Clinton, W. J., 106, 357
Close Up Foundation, 219
CMA/AMC. *See* Canadian Museums Association/Association des musees canadiens
Cochenour, J., 374
Cognition and Technology Group at Vanderbilt, 44
"The cognitive and behavioral basis of an instructional design," 362
Cognitive instructional theory, 27
Coleman, J. G., Jr., 349

Collaborative skills in educational partnerships, 94
Collage, 111
Collection Building, 364
College and Research Libraries, 355, 364, 370
Collegiate Microcomputer, 336
Collins, J., 377
Collis, B., 114, 378, 384
Colloquia at Indiana University Instructional Systems Technology Department, 35
Colorado
doctoral programs in instructional technology, 259
graduate programs in educational computing, 304
graduate programs in instructional technology, 278
Communication Abstracts, 372
"Communication and memory of texts in face to face and computer mediated communication," 347
Communication Booknotes, 372
Communication News, 372
Community College Association for Instruction and Technology, 214
Community College Satellite Network, 203-4
"The community of electronic learners," 384
A Comparison of Fourth Graders' Achievement, 341
"Comprehensive systems design in education," 362
Compressed Video, 374
CompuServe, 344
Compute, 336
"Computer aided decision making in choosing innovative education programs," 363
Computer and Education, 337
"Computer based simulation systems and role playing," 380
"Computer based voice recognition," 342
Computer Book Review, 337
"Computer communication networks and their use for information retrieval and dissemination," 384
Computer Communications, 381
The Computer Museum, 219-20
"The computer serving the video," 378
Computer simulations, 153
Computer skills, Indiana University Instructional Systems Technology Department, 35
Computer technology in schools
advantages of, 66-72
criticism of, 64-65
Computer-Assisted Career Decision Making, 340
Computer-Based Education Research Laboratory, 219
Computer-Based Integrated Learning Systems, 339
Computers and Education, 342

Computers and People, 337
"Computers and school reform," 342
Computers and the Humanities, 337
Computers as Cognitive Tools, 335
"Computers for the disabled," 342
Computers in Human Behavior, 337, 347
Computers in Libraries, 359, 364, 369, 371
Computers in the Schools, 337
Computing Teacher, 337, 341, 354
Comstock, G., 166
"A conceptual model of factors influencing the
    outcome of challenges to library
    materials...," 370
Concordia University, 306
"Confirmative evaluation of instructional
    materials and learners," 362
**Conflict resolution in educational partner-
    ships, 90**
Connecticut
    **doctoral programs in instructional technol-
        ogy, 260**
    **graduate programs in educational comput-
        ing, 304-5**
    **graduate programs in instructional technol-
        ogy, 278**
Connecting to the Internet, 382
Connolly, F. W., 384
Connors, Connie, 65
Consensus in Educational Partnerships, 90, 91
*Considerations in Evaluating Metacognition in
    Interactive Hypermedia/Multimedia
    Instruction,* 375
Considine, D., 374
Consortium of College and University Media
    Centers, 220
*Constructivism and the Technology of Instruc-
    tion,* 351
Constructivism theory, 27
Continuing Library Education Network and
    Exchange, 208
Cook, E. K., 362
"Cooperative learning and computer based
    instruction," 342
Copyright Clearance Center, Inc., 220
Corbin, J., 367
Corbin's Library Automation Handbook, 367
Corley, Patricia, 126-31
Corporation for Public Broadcasting, 220
Cost-Effectiveness of Interactive Courseware,
    375
"Costs of CD ROM production," 336
Couch, J. D., 375
Council for Basic Education, 220
Council for Educational Development and
    Research, 220-21
Council for Exceptional Children, 221
    Technology and Media Division, 221
Council of Chief State School Officers, 74-81
Council of National Library and Information
    Associations, 221

Council on International Non-theatrical Events,
    221
Cousins, J. B., 353
CPB. *See* Corporation for Public Broadcasting
Craven, T. C., 358
*Critical Elements of Computer Literacy for
    Teachers,* 341
"Cross cultural instructional design," 363
Crossing the Internet Threshold, 383
CS. *See* ERIC Clearinghouse on Reading,
    English and Communication
CTE. *See* Center for Technology in Education
CTGV. *See* Cognition and Technology Group at
    Vanderbilt
CTI. *See* Children's Television International
Cuban, Larry, 83
Current Index to Journals in Education, 18, 348
Curriculum at Indiana University Instructional
    Systems Technology Department, 31,
    35-36
Cuttill, William J., 170-73
Cypher, Irene, 134

D&T. *See* Association for Educational Commu-
    nications and Technology, Committee
    on Definition and Terminology
Damarin, S. K., 353
Data Communications, 381
Data modeling and analysis, TERC, 57-60
Data Sources, 344
Data Training, 359
Database, 344
Database Searcher, 344
Datamation, 356
Davidove, E. A., 362
Dean and Sybil McClusky Research Award,
    319, 327
**Definition of field of instructional technology,
    2-17**
DEMM. *See* Association for Educational Com-
    munications and Technology, Division
    of Educational Media Management
Dempsey, J. V., 360
Department of Education, 84-85
    Office of Special Education Programs, 126
Derry, Sharon J., 335
"Design considerations for telecommunications-
    supported cooperative learning environ-
    ments," 378
**Design domain of instructional technology, 3,
    12-13**
"Design for an Internet based government wide
    information locator system," 358
"Designing virtual worlds for use in mathemat-
    ics education," 343
Desktop Communications, 354
"The development and application of expert sys-
    tems," 335

Development Communication Report, 345

Development domain of instructional technology, 3, 12-13

Diamond, Robert M., 132-41

Dickinson, G. K., 367

DID. *See* Association for Educational Communications and Technology, Division of Instructional Development

Digest of Software Reviews: Education, 337

Digital Multimedia, 376

"Digital vs. analog video on microcomputers," 357

Dill, David D., 34

Dillon, M., 369

Directory of Library Automation Software, Systems and Services, 367

Directory of Online Databases, 344

DISC. *See* Association for Educational Communications and Technology, Division of Interactive Systems and Computers

Discipline versus field in instructional technology definition, 13-14

Distance Education, 345, 346, 347, 378

Distance education and telecommunications, 159-63

"Distance learning and intellectual property protection," 347

"Distance learning delivery systems," 348

District of Columbia, graduate programs in instructional technology, 279

Doctor of Education, 35

Doctor of Philosophy in Education, 35

Doctoral programs in instructional technology, 257-72

Document Image Automation, 372

Document Image Automation Update, 372

DOE. *See* Department of Education

Doll, C. A., 369

Domains of instructional technology definition, 3, 12-13

Donham van Deusen, J., 369

Doornekamp, B. Gerard, 340

DOT. *See* Association for Educational Communications and Technology, Division of Telecommunications

Dowding, T. J., 362

Doyle, C. S., 368

Dr. Dobb's Journal, 337

Drexel University, 296

DSMS. *See* Association for Educational Communications and Technology, Division of School Media Specialists

Dubuque Tri-College Department of Education, 307-8

Duffy, T. M., 351

Duguid, P., 353

Duning, B. S., 382

Dynamic approach to change, NCIP, 126-30

EA. *See* ERIC Clearinghouse on Educational Management

East Tennessee State University, 298

East Texas State University, 298-99

Eastern Washington University, 315

East-West Center, 222

EC. *See* ERIC Clearinghouse on Disabilities and Gifted Education

Eckel, K., 351

Economist, 41

ECT Foundation, 216

awards, 317-19, 322-31

Edgewood College, 316

EDRS. *See* ERIC Document Reproduction Service

Education & Computing, 337

Education Daily, 120

Education Development Center, Inc., 222

Education Index, 348

Education Libraries, 385

"Education online," 343

Education Technology News, 337

Education Under a Thatched Roof, 176

Educational and Training Technology International, 335, 347, 350, 363

Educational Computing, 340

Educational computing graduate programs, 303-16

Educational media and technology, current literature, 18-23

Educational Media and Technology Yearbook 1992, 351

Educational Media Index, 171

Educational Media International, 347, 354, 373, 377, 378

Educational Multimedia and Hypermedia Annual, 375

Educational partnerships, 82-105

characteristics of, 95-102

research on, 83-86

starting, 94-95

success measures in, 86-95

Educational Research, 348

Educational Researcher, 348

Educational Resources Information Center. *See* ERIC

The Educational Resources Information Center, 368

Educational technologies, 4

ETWG definition of, 143

versus instructional technology definition, 14

Educational Technologies Working Group, 142-43

Educational Technology, 335, 341, 342, 343, 347, 350, 353, 354, 362, 363, 378, 384

Educational Technology Abstracts, 350

Educational Technology Research and Development, 342, 343, 349, 350, 380

Educational Telecommunications, 383
EDUCOM Review, 381, 384
EduQuest, 50, 52
*The Effect of HyperCard Programming on
    Knowledge Construction...,* 376
"The effect of interactive video and print role
    models...," 378
"The effectiveness of technology in schools,"
    65
"Effects of cooperative learning and need for
    affiliation on performance...," 349
"The effects of fixed versus flexible scheduling
    on curriculum...," 369
Ehrlich, D., 362
Eisenberg, Michael B., 358
Eisenhower National Clearinghouse for Mathe-
    matics and Science Education,
    120-25
    collaboration, 124-25
    collection of, 123-24
    database and catalog system, 122-23
    mission of, 120-21
    repositories and demonstration sites, 124
    systemic reform, 125
    teacher needs, 121-22
Eisenhower Regional Alliance for Mathematics
    and Science Education Reform, 57
"An electrifying year," 371
"Electronic journals in the humanities," 355
Electronic Learning, 337, 353
Electronic Library, 364, 370, 384
Electronic mail, 107
Electronic Networking, 355, 358
Electronic Publishing, 354
"Electronic publishing and document delivery,"
    355
Electronic QUILLS, 339
Elias, A. W., 357
Elliott, M., 41
Ely, D. P., 18-23, 132-41, 351
Emergency Librarian, 364
The Emerging Virtual Research Library, 369
EMMS (Electronic Mail & Micro Systems), 381
"Empirical comparison of alternative instruc-
    tional TV technologies," 378
Emporia State University, 284
ENC. *See* Eisenhower National Clearinghouse
    for Mathematics and Science Education
"Enhancing knowledge utilization as a strategy
    for school improvement," 353
"Enhancing the learning process with expert sys-
    tems," 335
Environmental Snapshots, 56
"Envisioning a new system of education," 354
EPIE Institute (Educational Products Informa-
    tion Exchange), 222
Epler, D. M., 369
"Ergonomic considerations for the human envi-
    ronment," 371

ERIC (Educational Resources Information
    Center), 112, 123, 222-23
    documents, 332-33
ERIC Adjunct Clearinghouse for ESL Literacy
    Education, 226
ERIC Adjunct Clearinghouse for United State-
    Japan Studies, 226
ERIC Adjunct Clearinghouse on Chapter 1, 226
ERIC Adjunct Clearinghouse on Clinical
    Schools, 226
ERIC Adjunct Clearinghouse on Consumer
    Education, 227
ERIC Clearinghouse for Community Colleges,
    223
ERIC Clearinghouse on Adult Career, and Voca-
    tional Education, 223
ERIC Clearinghouse on Assessment and Evalu-
    ation, 223
ERIC Clearinghouse on Counseling and Student
    Services, 223
ERIC Clearinghouse on Disabilities and Gifted
    Education, 223
ERIC Clearinghouse on Educational Manage-
    ment, 224
ERIC Clearinghouse on Elementary and Early
    Childhood Education, 224
ERIC Clearinghouse on Higher Education,
    224
ERIC Clearinghouse on Information and Tech-
    nology, 18, 224
ERIC Clearinghouse on Languages and Linguis-
    tics, 224
ERIC Clearinghouse on Reading, English and
    Communication, 225
ERIC Clearinghouse on Rural Education and
    Small Schools, 225
ERIC Clearinghouse on Science, Mathematics,
    and Environmental Education, 225
ERIC Clearinghouse on Social Studies/Social
    Science Education, 225
ERIC Clearinghouse on Teaching and Teacher
    Education, 225-26
ERIC Clearinghouse on Urban Education, 226
ERIC Document Reproduction Service, 227
ERIC Processing and Reference Facility, 227
Estrada, S., 382
ETR&D Young Scholar Award, 319, 330
ETWG. *See* Educational Technologies Working
    Group
**Evaluation domain of instructional technol-
    ogy, 3, 12-13**
Evaluation in Instructional Systems Technology,
    171
*Excellence in Mathematics, Science and Engi-
    neering Education Act of 1990,* 120
Exiting in educational partnerships, 92
"Experimental designs for determining the effec-
    tiveness of technology in education,"
    354

"Expert support systems in an emergency management environment," 335
Explorer, 111

FAB. *See* Film Advisory Board
Fabris, M. E., 377
FAF. *See* Film Arts Foundation
Fairfield University, 278, 304-5
Far West Laboratory for Educational Research and Development, 227
Farnes, N., 347
FCC. *See* Federal Communications Commission
FCCSET/CET. *See* Federal Coordinating Council for Science, Engineering, and Technology/Committee on Education and Training
Federal Communications Commission, 227
Federal Communications Commission Reports, 373
Federal Coordinating Council for Science, Engineering, and Technology/Committee on Education and Training, 123, 142-54
  implementation, 145
  infrastructure for, 144
  milestones, 145-48
  recommendations, 148-50
Federal Educational Technology Association, 214
Federal role
  in educational technology, 142-54
  and learning technologies, 77-78, 80-81
FETA. *See* Federal Educational Technology Association
Film Advisory Board, 228
Film Arts Foundation, 228
Film/Video Arts, Inc., 228
Fitchburg State College, 309
FL. *See* ERIC Clearinghouse on Languages and Linguistics
Fleming, M., 361
Fletcher, J. D., 375
Flexible and Distance Learning, 346
"Flight simulation for the study of skill transfer," 380
Florida
  doctoral programs in instructional technology, 260-61
  graduate programs in educational computing, 305
  graduate programs in instructional technology, 279-80
Florida Institute of Technology, 305
Florida State University, 260, 279
FOI. *See* Freedom of Information Center
Follman, Joseph M., 340
Fontbonne College, 310
"Forces shaping the electronic publishing industry of the 1990s," 355

Fordham University, 291
Fraase, M., 382
Free Nets, 107
Freedom of Information Center, 228
Frohmann, B., 358
Frome, F. S., 343
Fujihara, H., 377
Fullan, M. G., 100
"Funding equipment needs in school districts," 369
"The future of computer-managed instruction," 341
FWL. *See* Far West Laboratory for Educational Research and Development

Gaebler, T., 100
Gallaudet University, 279
Garfinkle, R. J., 354
Gates, R., 384
Gayeski, D. M., 374
Gee, D., 345
Gender and Distance Learning, 346
General system theory, 27
The Geometric Supposer, 352
George Eastman House, 228-29
George Mason University, 314
George Washington University, 121, 124
Georgia
  doctoral programs in instructional technology, 261
  graduate programs in educational computing, 305-6
  graduate programs in instructional technology, 280-81
Georgia Southern University, 280
Georgia State University, 261, 280, 305-6
Gibbons, Andrew S., 341
Giesecke, J., 370
Giroux, H. A., 70
Gisolfi, A., 335
Global Laboratory Project, TERC, 49-63, 115
Good, Barbara, 7
Goodspeed, J., 353
Gophers, on Internet, 107, 108, 110-11
Gore, A., Jr., 357
Governance in educational partnerships, 95-96
Government Printing Office, 229
Government Publications Review, 364
Governors State University, 282, 306
GPN. *See* Great Plains National ITV Library
GPO. *See* Government Printing Office
Grabowski, B. L., 361
Graduate programs in educational computing, 303-16
"Granting each equal access," 372
Great Plains National ITV Library, 229
Grief, I., 161

Group process in educational partnerships, 94-95, 101
Gueulette, D. G., 376
Guide, California Technology Project, 111
Guides to Educational Media, 172
Guss, Carolyn, 170-73
Gutenko, G., 376

Hafner, A. W., 370
Hagloch, S. B., 367
Hakes, B. T., 374
Haley, G. E., 374
Hampton University, 314-15
Handbook of Individual Differences, Learning, and Instruction, 361
Handler, M. G., 342
Hands-On Elementary Science project, 60
Hardy, V., 347
Hartigan, J. M., 378
Hartley, J., 342
Harvard University, 287
  Educational Technology Center, 157
Harvey, J., 91, 100
Hawaii
  graduate programs in educational computing, 306
  graduate programs in instructional technology, 281
Hawkins, D. T., 355
Hawkins, J., 151, 352
HE. *See* ERIC Clearinghouse on Higher Education
Health Sciences Communications Association, 229
Hearings on Reauthorization of the Office of Educational Research and Improvement, 349
Heeren, E., 378
Heide, Susan, 7
Hellebrandt, J., 362
Henriquez, A., 383
Henriquez, H., 114
HeSCA. *See* Health Sciences Communications Association
"Highlighting formative evaluation," 363
Hillman, S. K., 157
Hillyer, K. O., 376
Hiltz, S. R., 161
Historical Journal of Film, Radio, and Television, 373
"The history of curriculum integrated library media program concept," 370
Hittleman, C. G., 156
Hjelmquist, E., 347
Hlynka, Denis, 5, 7
Hodges, M. E., 374

HOES. *See* Hands-On Elementary Science project
Hofmeister, A. M., 378
Holloway, Bob, 5
Hollywood Film Archive, 229
Home Office Computing, 338
Homework Help and Home/School Communications Systems, 352
Honey, M., 114, 383
Hooper, Simon, 342
HOPE Reports, 229
Hopkins, D. M., 370
How to Evaluate Multimedia Simulations, 380
"How to find money for technology," 353
The Hub, 57
Human Computer Interaction, 359
"The human interface with technology," 359
"Hypertext, hypermedia, and the humanities," 379

IABC. *See* International Association of Business Communicators
IASL. *See* International Association of School Librarianship
IBM, 52, 53
ICP. *See* International Center of Photography
Idaho, graduate programs in instructional technology, 281
IDEA. *See* Institute for Development of Educational Activities
"Identifying and describing federal information inventory/locator systems," 358
IFTF. *See* Institute for the Future
IGAEA. *See* International Graphic Arts Education Association
Illinois
  doctoral programs in instructional technology, 261-63
  graduate programs in educational computing, 306-7
  graduate programs in instructional technology, 282-83
IMC. *See* International Information Management Congress
The Impact of School Library Media Centers on Academic Achievement, 368
"The imperative for systemic change," 354
Implementation in educational partnerships, 87-88
"Implementation of generative learning principles in interactive video....," 377
InCider-A Plus, 338
INCINC. *See* International Copyright Information Center
InCITE, 42

Indiana
  doctoral programs in instructional technology, 263
  graduate programs in educational computing, 307
  graduate programs in instructional technology, 283-84
Indiana State University, 283
Indiana University, 263, 283
Indiana University Instructional Systems Technology Department, 26-40, 29-31
  analysis and design, 32-34
  changes in field, 27
  changes in School of Education, 28
  core courses of, 33
  curriculum elements, 35-36
  curriculum needs assessment survey, 31
  curriculum revision overview, 28
  development and implementation, 34
  effects on faculty, 37
  new curriculum features, 34-36
  rationale for curriculum change, 26-27
  redefinition of degrees, 34-35
  societal changes, 27-28
  strategic planning and direction, 29
  survey of graduates, 30-31
"The influence of programming training on the computer literacy...," 349
Informal learning environments, TERC, 61-62
"Information based education," 358
The Information Evolution, 357
Information Literacy, 368
Information Literacy Meets Media Literacy and Visual Literacy, 377
Information Processing and Management, 356, 358, 359
Information Retrieval and Library Automation, 356
"Information retrieval based on conceptual distance in Is-A hierarchies," 358
"Information science," 359
Information Services and Use, 356, 359, 364
The Information Society, 356
Information Technology and Libraries, 356, 371
"Information technology standards," 358
Information Today, 344
InfoWorld, 338
Inside Our Schools, 175
Institute for Development of Educational Activities, 230
Institute for Research on Teaching, 230
Institute for the Future, 230
Institute of Culture and Communication, 230
Instruction Language, 351
"Instructional cuing in hypermedia," 378
"Instructional designers' decisions and priorities," 363
Instructional Developments, 359
Instructional Media Technology in Secondary Education, 377

Instructional Message Design, 361
Instructional Science, 359
Instructional Systems Technology Department, Indiana University, 26-40
Instructional technology
  doctoral programs in, 257-72
  domains of, 3
  master's degree programs in, 34-35, 273-302
Instructional Technology: The Definition and Domains of the Field, 2
  review and endorsement of, 8
  writing meetings for, 8
Instructional technology definition
  acceptable definition, 10
  background, 2
  chronology of process, 2-10
  conceptual nature of definition, 11-12
  discipline versus field, 13-14
  domains, 12-13
  terminology and glossary, 13-14
  versus educational technology, 14
Instructional Transaction Theory Applied to Computer Simulations, 380
Integrated Systems Digital Network, 159
Integrating Technology into the Curriculum, 352
Intellectual achievement and television violence, 166
"Intelligent search in an educational hypertext environment," 377
Intelligent Tutoring Media, 334
INTELSAT. *See* International Telecommunications Satellite Organization
"An interactive computer based conferencing system to accommodate students' learning process," 343
Interactive Instruction and Feedback, 360-61
Interactive Multimedia Instruction, 375
Interactive Television and Instruction, 374
Interdisciplinary Study with Computer-Based Multimedia, 375
International Assessment of Educational Progress, 64
International Association of Business Communicators, 230
International Association of School Librarianship, 230-31
International Center of Photography, 231
International Communication Association, 231
International Copyright Information Center, 231
International Council for Distance Education Bulletin, 345
International Graphic Arts Education Association, 231-32
International Information Management Congress, 232
International Journal of Instructional Media, 343, 348, 349, 363, 370, 373, 379
International Journal of Robotics Research, 334

International Society for Technology in Education, 186-87, 232
International Telecommunications Satellite Organization, 232
International Teleconferencing Association, 232
International Television Association, 233
International Visual Literacy Association, 188-89, 214
Internet, 106-19
  communities on, 115-16
  educational connections, 109-10
  Gophers, 106, 110-12
  mailing lists on, 112-13
  reform, 116
"The Internet as a medium for education and educational research," 385
The Internet Companion, 382
"Internet cruising with the Internet Hunt," 384
Internet Research, 369, 381
Internet System Handbook, 382
INTL. *See* Association for Educational Communications and Technology, International Division
Intrilagator, B., 102
"Introducing computer mediated communications into participative management education," 347
"Introduction: TQM fundamentals and overview of contents," 370
An Introduction to Educational Holography, 376
"An Investigation of the Role of Navigation for Information Retrieval," 358
Iona College, 311
Iowa
  doctoral programs in instructional technology, 263-64
  graduate programs in educational computing, 307-8
  graduate programs in instructional technology, 284
Iowa State University, 263, 284, 308
IR. *See* ERIC Clearinghouse on Information and Technology
"Is teaching like flying?," 347
IS&T. *See* Society for Imaging Science and Technology
ISDN. *See* Integrated Systems Digital Network
IST. *See* Indiana University Instructional Systems Technology Department
IST. *See* Instructional Systems Technology Department
ISTE. *See* International Society for Technology in Education
ITA, 233
ITCA. *See* International Teleconferencing Association
ITED. *See* Association for Educational Communications and Technology, Industrial Training and Education Division
Ithaca College, 291

ITVA. *See* International Television Association
IVLA. *See* International Visual Literacy Association

Jacksonville State University, 274
Jacksonville University, 305
James, Jonathan K., 336
James Madison University, 300
James S. McDonnell Foundation, 45
James W. Brown Publication Award, 319, 329
Jasper Woodbury Problem-Solving Series, Vanderbilt University, 45, 47
JC. *See* ERIC Clearinghouse for Community Colleges
Jih, H. J., 342
The Johns Hopkins University, 264, 285, 309
Johnsen, J. B., 69
Johnson, D. LaMont, 340
Johnston, V. L., 383
Jonassen, D. H., 351, 353, 361
Jones, J. I., 347
Jordan, William R., 340
Journal of Academic Librarianship, 364
Journal of Artificial Intelligence in Education, 334
Journal of Broadcasting and Electronic Media, 373
Journal of Computer Assisted Learning, 338
Journal of Computer-Based Instruction, 338, 341, 343, 380
Journal of Database Administration, 344
Journal of Distance Education, 346
Journal of Documentation, 356, 358
Journal of Educational Computing Research, 338, 343
Journal of Educational Multimedia and Hypermedia, 360, 377, 378
Journal of Educational Technology Systems, 341, 343, 360, 362, 377
Journal of Educational Television, 373
Journal of Instructional Delivery Systems, 350
Journal of Interactive Instruction Development, 360
Journal of Librarianship and Information Science, 364
Journal of Library Administration, 365, 370
Journal of Popular Film and Television, 373
Journal of Research on Computing in Education, 338, 349
Journal of Technical Writing and Communication, 360
Journal of Technology and Teacher Education, 350
Journal of the American Society for Information Science, 356, 357, 359
Journal of Visual Literacy, 360, 377
Jurow, S., 370

K-12 Computer Networking, ERIC Review, 383
"A kaleidoscope of challenges," 372
Kansas
  doctoral programs in instructional technology, 264
  graduate programs in educational computing, 308
  graduate programs in instructional technology, 284
Kansas State University, 264, 284, 308
Kapisovsky, P. M., 384
Katz, Martin R., 340
Kaufman, R., 361
Kazlauskas, E. J., 362
KC ShareNet, 113
Kearsley, G., 161
Keays, T., 345
Kennedy, Mary, 29
Kentucky, graduate programs in instructional technology, 285
Kernan, John T., 64
Kids Network, 50
King, H., 370
Kinsinger, Addie, 41-43
Klein, J. D., 349, 378
Knapczyk, D., 156
Knezek, G. A., 354
Knirk, F. G., 370
Knowledge: Creation, Diffusion, Utilization, 350, 353
"Knowledge utilization," 359
Knowledge-Based Systems, 334
Knox Quinn, C., 353
Kogan Page, 18
Krieser, Latane C., 370
Kriz, H. M., 345
Kurzweil, R., 370

LabNet, 382
LabNet: Toward a Community of Practice, 57
LabNet Project, TERC, 56-57
Lajoie, Susanne P., 335
Lake-Dell Angelo, M., 363
LAMA. *See* Library Administration and Management Association
Lance, K. C., 368
LaQuey, T., 382
Latrobe, K. H., 367
Laughlin, M. K., 367
Lawrence Erlbaum Associates, 57
Lazzaro, J., 342, 367
Leadership in educational partnerships, 95-96, 99
"Learner diversity and instructional video," 378
Learner Generated Versus Instructor Induced Visual Imagery, 362
"Learning, instruction, and hypermedia," 378

Learning technologies
  definition of, 75
  and federal plans, 77-78, 80-81
  and implementation recommendations, 76-81
  and student performance, 74-81
Learning Technologies Essential for Education Change, 352
Learning Technology Center, Vanderbilt University, 44-48
Learning with Personal Computers, 340
Lee, J. H., 358
Lee, Y. B., 378
Lehigh University, 296
Lehman, J. D., 378
Lehmann, S., 370
Leithwood, K. A., 353
Lenze, J. S., 362
Lesk, M., 368
Lesley College, 309
Levie, W., 361
Levin, Jim, 114
Lewis, Dick, 134
Ley, K., 378
Library Administration and Management Association, 207
Library and Information Science Abstracts, 365
Library and Information Science Research, 365, 371
Library and Information Technology Association, 207
Library Building Projects, 367
Library Computer Systems & Equipment Review, 365
Library Hi Tech, 365
Library Journal, 365, 370
Library of Congress, 233
Library Quarterly, 365, 370
Library Resources and Technical Services, 365, 370, 371
Library Software Review, 365
Library Trends, 355, 365, 379
Link-Up, 344
Linking for Learning, 80
Lintern, G., 380
Lister Hill National Center for Biomedical Communications, 233-34
LITA. *See* Library and Information Technology Association
Literacy in a Science Context Project, 56
Liu, M., 376
Local Infrastructures for School Networking, 383
Lochte, R. H., 374
Loertscher, D. V., 370
Logistical problems in educational partnerships, 88
"Logo mastery and spatial problem solving by young children," 343
Long Island University, 311

Louisiana, graduate programs in instructional technology, 285
Louisiana State University, 285
LTC. *See* Learning Technology Center; Vanderbilt University Learning Technology Center
Lynch, D. C., 382

The Mac Internet Tour Guide, 382
Macchia, P., Jr., 363
MacWorld, 338
Maddux, Cleborne D., 340
Magazine Publishers of America, 234
Mailing lists on Internet, 112-13
Management domain of instructional technology, 3, 12-13
Manatt, R. P., 157
Mandinach, Ellen B., 340
Mankato State University, 288, 310
Manrique, C. G., 115
Manrique, G. G., 115
Marchisotto, J., 156
Marketplace relations in educational partnerships, 98
Maryland
doctoral programs in instructional technology, 264
graduate programs in educational computing, 309
graduate programs in instructional technology, 285-86
Massachusetts
doctoral programs in instructional technology, 264-65
graduate programs in educational computing, 309
graduate programs in instructional technology, 286-87
Master's degree programs in instructional technology, 34-35, 273-302
Math proficiency of students, 64
Maurer, H., 375
Mayer, H., 361
MBL. *See* Microcomputer-based labs
McAlpine, L., 363
McCallum, S., 358
McClure, C. R., 358, 371
McCook, Kathleen de la Pena, 371
McDaniel, E., 342
McKenzie, J. A., 375
McLagan, Patricia A., 29
McLellan, H., 379
MCN. *See* Museum Computer Network
McNeese State University, 285
McREL. *See* Mid-continent Regional Educational Laboratory

MDPD. *See* Association for Educational Communications and Technology, Media Design and Production Division
"Measuring up," 354
MECC (Minnesota Educational Computing Corporation), 234
Media and Methods, 343, 348
Media International, 373
Media production in educational partnerships, 97-98
Media-oriented clearinghouses, 120-68
Medical Library Association, 234-35
"Meditation and the electronic world," 371
Meeting Learning Needs Through Multimedia, 377
"Mental models," 342
Merickel, M. L., 380
Michigan
doctoral programs in instructional technology, 265
graduate programs in educational computing, 310
graduate programs in instructional technology, 287
Microcomputer Index, 338
Microcomputer Industry Update, 338
Microcomputer-based labs, 52-54
Microcomputers for Information Management, 357, 365, 377, 384
Mid-continent Regional Educational Laboratory, 235
Middle Tennessee State University, 298
MIDDLE-L mailing list, 112
Milheim, W. D., 335, 342, 363
MIM. *See* Minorities in Media
Mind and Machines, 334
Minnesota
doctoral programs in instructional technology, 265
graduate programs in educational computing, 310
graduate programs in instructional technology, 288
Minor, B., 351, 371
Minorities in Media, 215
Minot State University, 312
Misanchuk, E. R., 375
Mississippi, graduate programs in instructional technology, 288
Missouri
doctoral programs in instructional technology, 265-66
graduate programs in educational computing, 310
graduate programs in instructional technology, 288-89
Mitchell, R., 354
MLA. *See* Medical Library Association
"Modes of production," 347
Moja, T., 354

Molenda, Michael, 5
Montana, graduate programs in instructional technology, 289
Montclair State College, 290
Moore, M. G., 347
Morris, B. J., 367
Morrison, James L., 34
Mory, E. H., 349
"The motivational effect of advisement on attendance and achievement...," 341
Mountain, Lee, 341
MPA. *See* Magazine Publishers of America
Multicultural Aspects of Library Media Programs, 367
"Multimedia," 378
"Multimedia and the future of distance learning technology," 347
Multimedia and Videodisc Monitor, 373
Multimedia Computing, 374
Multimedia for Learning, 374
Multimedia in Industry and Education, 362
Multimedia Review, 373
Munro, A., 380
Muraida, D. J., 361
Museum Computer Network, 235
Museum of Holography, 235
Museum of Modern Art, Circulating Film and Video Library, 235
Museums as learning environments, 61

NAB. *See* National Alliance of Business; National Association of Broadcasters
NAC. *See* National Audiovisual Center
NAEYC. *See* National Association for the Education of Young Children
NAMAC. *See* National Alliance for Media Arts and Culture
NARMC. *See* National Association of Regional Media Centers
NASA. *See* National Aeronautics and Space Administration
NASAGA. *See* North American Simulation and Gaming Association
NASBE. *See* National Association of State Boards of Education
NASSP. *See* National Association of Secondary School Principals
NASTA. *See* National Association of State Textbook Administrators
A Nation at Risk, 82
National Aeronautics and Space Administration, 235-36
National Alliance for Media Arts and Culture, 236
National Alliance of Business, 82
National Association for the Education of Young Children, 164, 167, 236

National Association for Visually Handicapped, 236
National Association of Broadcasters, 236
National Association of Regional Media Centers, 215
National Association of Secondary School Principals, 236-37
National Association of State Boards of Education, 237
National Association of State Textbook Administrators, 237
National Audiovisual Center, 237
National Cable Television Institute, 237
National Center for Appropriate Technology, 237-38
National Center for Improving Science Education, 238
National Center for Research in Mathematical Sciences Education, 238
National Center for Science Teaching and Learning, 124, 238
National Center for Supercomputing Applications, 111
National Center to Improve Practice, 126-31
  dynamic approach to change, 126-30
  NCIP InfoNet, 128
  practice packages, 127-28
  technical assistance of, 129
  videoconferences, 128-29
National Clearinghouse for Bilingual Education, 238-39
National Commission on Libraries and Information Science, 239
National Council for Accreditation of Teacher Education, 239
National Council for Educational Technology, 18
National Council of Teachers of English Commission on Media, 239
National Council of the Churches of Christ in the U.S. A., 239
National Education Goals, 116, 120, 124
National Endowment for the Humanities, 240
National Federation of Community Broadcasters, 240
National Film Board of Canada, 240, 255
National Film Information Service, 240
National Gallery of Art, 240
National Geographic Society, 50
National Information Center for Educational Media, 240-41
National ITFS Association, 215
National Library of Medicine, 241
National Press Photographers Association, Inc., 241
National PTA, 241
National Public Broadcasting Archives, 241
National Religious Broadcasters, 241-42
National School Supply and Equipment Association, 242
National Science Foundation, 45, 147, 242

National Science Teachers Association, 242
National Society for Performance and Instruc-
 tion, 6, 30, 190-91, 243
National Technical Information Service, 243
National Technology Center, 243
National Telemedia Council Inc., 243
National University Continuing Education Asso-
 ciation, 244
National-Louis University, 306-7
Nature of Science software, 52, 53
NAVH. *See* National Association for Visually
 Handicapped
NCAT. *See* National Center for Appropriate
 Technology
NCATE. *See* National Council for Accreditation
 of Teacher Education
NCATE Guidelines Task Force, 7
NCBE. *See* National Clearinghouse for Bilingual
 Education
NCIP. *See* National Center to Improve Practice
NCIP InfoNet, 128, 130
NCIPnet, 130-31
NCLIS. *See* National Commission on Libraries
 and Information Science
NCME. *See* Network for Continuing Medical
 Education
NCREL. *See* North Central Regional Educa-
 tional Laboratory
NCSA. *See* National Center for Supercomputing
 Applications
NCSTL. *See* National Center for Science Teach-
 ing and Learning
NCTE. *See* National Council of Teachers of
 English
NCTI. *See* National Cable Television Institute
Nebraska
 **doctoral programs in instructional technol-
 ogy, 266**
 **graduate programs in instructional technol-
 ogy, 289-90**
Needs Assessment, 361
NEH. *See* National Endowment for the
 Humanities
Nelson, W. A., 378
The NETWORK, Inc., 244
Network for Continuing Medical Education,
 244
Networked learning, TERC, 54-57
Networking, 106-19
 and education users, 108-10
 and learning technologies, 79-80
Networking Management, 381
"Networks, hypertext, and academic informa-
 tion services," 355
Networks Now, 382
Neves, J. S., 380
New Directions for Science Playgrounds,
 61

New Jersey
 **doctoral programs in instructional technol-
 ogy, 266**
 **graduate programs in instructional technol-
 ogy, 290**
New School for Social Research, 291
New Technologies for Education, 351
"New technology considerations for media facilities," 370
New York
 **doctoral programs in instructional technol-
 ogy, 266-67**
 **graduate programs in educational comput-
 ing, 311**
 **graduate programs in instructional technol-
 ogy, 291-93**
The New York Festivals, 244
New York Institute of Technology, 291
New York University, 134, 266-67, 291
New York University-Tisch School of the Arts,
 291
Newby, G. B., 358
Newman, D., 383
*The NFAIS Yearbook of the Information Indus-
 try 1993,* 357
NFBC. *See* National Film Board of Canada
NFCB. *See* National Federation of Community
 Broadcasters
NGA. *See* National Gallery of Art
NIA. *See* National ITFS Association
Nibble, 338
NICEM. *See* National Information Center for
 Educational Media
Nichols Publishing, 18
North American Simulation and Gaming Asso-
 ciation, 244-45
North Carolina
 **graduate programs in educational comput-
 ing, 312**
 **graduate programs in instructional technol-
 ogy, 293-94**
North Carolina State University, 312
North Central Regional Educational Laboratory,
 245
**North Dakota, graduate programs in educa-
 tional computing, 312**
Northeastern Illinois University, 282
Northern Illinois University, 261-62, 282, 307
Northwest College and University Council for
 the Management of Educational Tech-
 nology, 215
Northwest Missouri State University, 310
Northwest Regional Educational Laboratory, 245
Norton, P., 342
Nova Southeastern University, 260-61, 279
NPBA. *See* National Public Broadcasting Ar-
 chives
NRB. *See* National Religious Broadcasters
NSF. *See* National Science Foundation

NSPI. *See* National Society for Performance and Instruction
NSSEA. *See* National School Supply and Equipment Association
NSTA. *See* National Science Teachers Association
NTC. *See* National Telemedia Council Inc.
NTIS. *See* National Technical Information Service
NUCEA. *See* National University Continuing Education Association
NWREL. *See* Northwest Regional Educational Laboratory
Nyland, Heidi H., 49-63

"Objective: Achievement. Solution: School libraries," 370
Oblinger, D., 376
OCLC Online Computer Library Center, Inc., 245
OERI. *See* Office of Educational Research and Improvement
Office of Educational Research and Improvement, 120, 144
Office of Technology Assessment, 80, 245
Ohio
    doctoral programs in instructional technology, 268-69
    graduate programs in educational computing, 312-13
    graduate programs in instructional technology, 294-95
The Ohio State University, 120-25, 268, 294, 312
Ohio University, 294
Oklahoma
    doctoral programs in instructional technology, 269
    graduate programs in educational computing, 313
    graduate programs in instructional technology, 295-96
OLAC. *See* On-line Audiovisual Catalogers
Olia, Fatemeh, 7
Olson, Patrick C., 115
Ong, W., 67
Online, 343, 344, 345, 385
On-line Audiovisual Catalogers, 246
Online Review, 344, 345
Only the Best: Annual Guide to Highest-Rated Education Software, 340
Ontario Film Association, Inc., 256
"Open information interchange," 359
Open Learning, 346, 347
Optical Data's "Product of the Year" award, 45
Oral History Association, 246
Oral presentations, 153
Oregon, graduate programs in instructional technology, 296

Orwig, G. W., 351
Oryx Press, 18
Osborne, D., 100
OSEP. *See* Office of Special Education Programs
OTA. *See* Office of Technology Assessment
"The other Memex," 357
Outcome Measures for Information Literacy..., 368
Outcome orientation in instructional technology, 11
Overbaugh, Richard C., 341
An Overview of the Research on Learning Styles and Hypermedia Environments, 375

Pace University, 311
Pacific Film Archive, 246
Pacific Regional Educational Laboratory, 246
Paik, H., 166
Paired explanations (in performance assessment), 153
Paisley, W., 359
Palmer, Teresa M., 30
Palumbo, D. B., 378
"The parable of the bridge," 363
Partnerships, school-university, 155-63
Pathways to Excellence: A Federal Strategy for Science, Mathematics, Engineering, and Technology Education, 142, 143
PBS. *See* Public Broadcasting Service
PBS Adult Learning Service, 247-48
PBS ENCORE, 248
PBS VIDEO, 248
PC Magazine, 338
PC Week, 339
PC World, 339
PCR: Films and Video in the Behavioral Sciences, 246
Pelletier, P., 343
Pennsylvania
    doctoral programs in instructional technology, 269
    graduate programs in instructional technology, 296-97
Pennsylvania State University, 269, 296
Performance and Instruction, 354, 360, 362, 363
"Performance based instruction," 362
Performance Improvement Quarterly, 342, 360, 363, 378
"Performance support systems," 363
"Performance technology for instructional technologists," 354
Performance-based assessment, 151, 152-54
Pershing, James A., 26-40
Personal Science Laboratory hardware, 52, 53
Pett, Dennis, 174-77
Pettersson, R., 361
Pezzulo, J., 359
PFA. *See* Pacific Film Archive

Phelps, Malcolm V., 142-54
Phi Delta Kappa, 120
Phillips, Jeanne, 341
Philosophy in instructional technology, 11
"Photo CD and other digital imaging technolo-
gies," 377
Photographic Society of America, 247
Physics Explorer, 153
PIDT. *See* Professors of Instructional Design
and Technology
Pinheiro, E. J., 376
Pinto, Patrick, 29
Pisacreta, E., 347
Pitcher, S., 156
PLA. *See* Public Library Association
Planning in educational partnerships, 87-88
Playgrounds as learning environments, 61
Poirot, J. L., 354
Polson, M. C., 361
Portfolio assessment, 151
Portland State University, 296
Power Learning in the Classroom, 375
"The power of images," 358
The Power of Information Literacy, 369
*Power On! New Tools for Teaching and Learn-
ing,* 80, 143
*Practical Internetworking with TCP/IP and
UNIX,* 382
Prairie View A&M University, 299
PREL. *See* Pacific Regional Educational
Laboratory
"Preparing for an interconnected future," 384
"Preparing new teachers to use computer tech-
nology," 342
*Preparing Teachers for Using Instructional Tele-
vision in Diverse Cultural Settings,* 376
Preservation of new technology, 368
**Preservice education programs at Vanderbilt
University, 47**
Preston, Nancy R., 332-85
Pridemore, Doris R., 349
*Proceedings of the ASIS Annual Meeting (Pitts-
burgh, PA, Oct. 26-29, 1992),* 358
*Proceedings of the ASIS Mid Year Meeting
(Albuquerque, NM, May 27-30, 1992),*
355, 371
*Proceedings of the 56th Annual Meeting of the
American Society for Information
Science, October 24-28, 1993,* 356
*Proceedings of the 14th National Online Meet-
ing,* 357
Process in educational partnerships, 95-96
"Productivity tools for simulation centered train-
ing development," 380
**Professional development activities and learn-
ing technologies, 78-79**
Professors of Instructional Design and Technol-
ogy, 5-6, 247
Progress interviews, 153

**Project coordinator in educational partner-
ships, 90-91**
Prospects for Educational Telecomputing, 384
PS. *See* ERIC Clearinghouse on Elementary and
Early Childhood Education
PSA. *See* Photographic Society of America
"Pseudoscience in computer-based instruction,"
343
Public Broadcasting, 376
Public Broadcasting Service, 247
Public Libraries, 366
Public Library Association, 207
Public Library Quarterly, 366
The Public-Access Computer Systems Review,
365-66
"A public-use, full-screen interface for SPIRES
databases," 345
Publish!, 355
Puppeteers of America, 248
Purdue University, 263, 284, 307
Purpose of educational partnerships, 95-96

Quarterman, J. S., 382
QuickTime, 46

Radford University, 300
RASD. *See* Reference and Adult Services
Division
RBS. *See* Research for Better Schools, Inc.
RC. *See* ERIC Clearinghouse on Rural Educa-
tion and Small Schools
*Reaching Learners Through Telecommunica-
tions,* 382
"Recognizing multiple decision making
models," 370
Recording for the Blind, 248
Recording Industry Association of America,
Inc., 248-49
Reed, W. M., 376
Reeves, T. C., 342, 343
Reference and Adult Services Division, ALA,
207-8
Reference Librarian, 366, 370, 371
The Regional Laboratory for Educational
Improvement of the Northeast and
Islands, 249
Reigeluth, C. M., 354
Reiser, Robert A., 27
Remz, Arlene, 126-31
Research for Better Schools, Inc., 249
"Research from the ERIC files," 371
Research in Distance Education, 346
*Research in Science and Technological Educa-
tion,* 348
*Research Proceedings: 1993 AECT National
Convention,* 352

Resistance (teacher and student), 71
Resource Sharing and Information Networks,
    344
Resources in Education, 349
Reynolds, L., 362
Reznich, C., 363
RFB. *See* Recording for the Blind
**Rhode Island, graduate programs in instruc-
    tional technology, 297**
Rhode Island College, 297
RIAA. *See* Recording Industry Association of
    America, Inc.
Riddick, J. F., 371
RIE. See Resources in Education
Ritchey, Rita C., 2-17
Robert M. Gagne Instructional Development
    Research Award, 319, 328
Roberts, J. M., 346
Robertson, M. M., 371
Rogers, D. L., 377
Rogers, E., 100
Rojas, A. M., 361
The Role of Film in Educational Television, 176
"The role of public libraries in the use of
    Internet/NREN information sources,"
    371
"The role of technology in the school reform
    movement," 353
The Roles of Libraries in Education, 368
Romiszowski, A., 159-63, 347
Rosary College, 282
Rose, M. T., 382
Roseman, J. E., 156
Rosemont College, 296-97
Rosenbluth, G. S., 376
Rossett, A., 354
Rowan College of New Jersey, 290
Rowe, A. H., 340
RQ, 366, 371
RTD. *See* Association for Educational Communi-
    cations and Technology, Research and
    Theory Division
Rubin, Andee, 339
Rufsvold, Margaret, 172
Rule, S., 156
Ruopp, R. R., 382
Russell, J. D., 362
Rutgers-The State University of New Jersey,
    266, 290
Ryer, J. C., 382

Sachs, S. G., 374
Saiedian, H., 343
Sales, G. C., 360
Salisbury, David F., 27
SALT. *See* Society for Applied Learning
    Technology
San Diego State University, 276-77, 304

San Francisco State University, 277
San Jose State University, 134, 277
Sanyal, R. N., 380
Sasnett, R. M., 374
Saunders, L. M., 371
SCA. *See* Speech Communication Association
Schaeffer, D. M., 115
Schiller, N., 369
Schneebeck, C., 384
Schoenberg, Susan L., 49-63
"School and situated knowledge," 353
School Improvement Model, 157
School Library Journal, 366, 370, 372
School Library Media Activities Monthly, 366,
    369
School Library Media Annual, 353, 371
"School library media centers," 369
"School library media program research and
    assessment," 369
School Library Media Quarterly, 366, 369, 370,
    371, 372
School of Education, Indiana University, 26-40
School Tech News, 339
School-university partnerships, 155-63
    **development of new educational technolo-
        gies, 157**
    **research on educational technologies, 156-
        57**
    staff development, 156
    successful, 155-56
Schrage, Michael, 64-65, 66, 67, 68, 70
Schwartz, J. L., 352
Schwier, R. A., 375
Science Challenges, 61
Science proficiency of students, 64
Scientists in Action, Vanderbilt University, 45
Scott, D. M., 383
SCS. *See* Society for Computer Simulation
SCTE. *See* Society of Cable Television
    Engineers
SE. *See* ERIC Clearinghouse on Science, Mathe-
    matics, and Environmental Education
"Searching Internet archive sites with Archie,"
    385
"Searching online database services over the
    Internet," 345
SEDL. *See* Southwest Educational Development
    Laboratory
Seeing Through the Glitz, 376
Seels, Barbara, 2-17
Selection and Evaluation of Electronic Resources,
    367
Selling Color, 376
SeniorNet, 107
SERVE. *See* SouthEastern Regional Vision for
    Education
Servers (computer), 122
Shelton, James, 336
Sherman, Mendel, 174-77
Sherman, T. M., 161

Sherman Film Evaluation Form, 175
Shippensburg University, 297
Shlechter, T. M., 380
Signorielli, N., 165, 167
Silva, M., 385
Simmonds, C., 385
Simmons College, 287
Simonson, M., 352
Simpson, H., 378
Simulation and Gaming, 379, 380
Simulation/Games for Learning, 379, 380
Simutis, Len, 120
Sivin, K., 384
Six-year programs in instructional technol-
    ogy, 273-302
SLA. *See* Special Libraries Association
SLMA. *See School Library Media Annual*
Small, R. V., 358
Smalley, K. A., 362
SMART. *See* Special Multimedia Arenas for
    Refining Thinking
Smith, K., 371
Smith, Marilyn E., 164-68
Smithsonian Institution, 249
Smog Watch program, 61-62
Smoot, C., 382
SMPTE. *See* Society of Motion Picture and
    Television Engineers
SO. *See* ERIC Clearinghouse on Social
    Studies/Social Science Education
Social Science Computer Review, 339
Society for Applied Learning Technology, 192-
    93, 250
Society for Computer Simulation, 250
Society for Imaging Science and Technology,
    250
Society for Photographic Education, 250
Society of Cable Television Engineers, 250
Society of Motion Picture and Television Engi-
    neers, 250-51
Society of Photo Technologists, 251
SOFTSWAP, 251
Software Digest Ratings Report, 339
Software Magazine, 339
Software Publishers Association, 65
Software Reviews on File, 339
Software tools, TERC Global Laboratory
    Project, 52-62
Song, X., 363
Soule, Helen, 341
South Carolina, graduate programs in
    instructional technology, 298
SouthEastern Regional Vision for Education, 251
Southern Connecticut State University, 278
Southern Illinois University, 262
Southern Illinois University at Carbondale, 262,
    282
Southern Illinois University at Edwardsville, 283
Southwest Educational Development Labora-
    tory, 251

Southwestern Oklahoma State University, 295
SP. *See* ERIC Clearinghouse on Teaching and
    Teacher Education
SPE. *See* Society for Photographic Education
Special Libraries, 366
Special Libraries Association, 251-52
Special Multimedia Arenas for Refining
    Thinking assessment project,
    Vanderbilt University, 47
SpecialNet, 252
Spector, J. M., 361
Speech Communication Association, 252
Spitzer, Dean R., 30
Spohrer, J. H., 370
SPT. *See* Society of Photo Technologists
SRC. *See* Canadian Broadcasting
    Corporation/Societe Radio-Canada
St. Cloud State University, 288
St. John's University, 291-92
Staff development in school-university part-
    nerships, 156
State action and learning technologies, 75-76, 77
State University College of Arts and Science at
    Potsdam, 292, 311
State University of New York at Albany, 292
State University of New York at Buffalo, 267,
    292
State University of New York at Stony Brook,
    311
State University of New York College at
    Fredonia, 134
Steele, R. L., 348
Stephens, Paul, 64
Stephenson, G. A., 359
Stevens, Betty L., 340
Stevens, G. I., 375
Stevenson-Burger, L., 157
Stinson, J., 343
"Stolen knowledge," 353
Stoller, M. E., 355
Stowitschek, J. J., 156
Stress in educational partnerships, 88
Strommen, E. F., 343
Student assessment and learning technolo-
    gies, 80
Student performance and learning technolo-
    gies, 74-81
"Students' perceptions of the ease of learning
    from computers and interactive video,"
    341
A Study of Film Evaluation and Selection Prac-
    tices in Twelve Universities and Col-
    leges..., 171
A Study of the Relationship Between Virtual
    Reality..., 380
Summer Students in Virtual Reality, 379
Superintendent of Documents, 252
Support in educational partnerships, 95-96
The Survey of Microcomputers in Schools, 341
Sutton, R. E., 67, 377

Swan, J., 371
Syracuse University, 267, 292-93
    Center for Instructional Development, 132
*A Systemic Approach to Course and Curriculum
    Design,* 133
**Systems paradigm in instructional technology
    definition, 11**

Tabletop and Tabletop Junior software, 58-59
T&W. *See* Teachers and Writers Collaborative
TAM. *See* Council for Exceptional Children,
    Technology and Media Division
"Talking back to Big Bird," 343
Task Force on Education Network Technology,
    116
Taylor, W. D., 69
Teach, Beverly, 170-73
"Teacher education from classroom broadcasts
    for the new South Africa," 354
**Teacher enhancement and curriculum devel-
    opment, TERC, 60-61**
Teachers and Writers Collaborative, 252
Teachers College, Columbia University, 293
Teaching and Computers, 339
Teaching Collaborative Problem Solving..., 383
Teaching Tools, 175
TechTrends, 6, 7, 351, 377
Technology and Learning, 351
Technology and the Organization of Schooling,
    352
Technology Education Research Centers. *See*
    TERC
*Technology for America's Economic Growth, a
    New Direction to Build Economic
    Strength,* 357
Technology for Science curriculum development
    project, 61
Technology in assessment, student, 152
"Technology outlook on math and science," 343
*Technology-Mediated Communities for Learn-
    ing,* 352
TECHNOS, 351
Teikyo Marycrest University, 308
Telecommunications, 381, 382
**Telecommunications and distance education,
    159-63**
Telecommunications and Distance Education,
    347
Telecommunications and K-12 Educators, 383
Telecommunications Research and Action
    Center, 252
Telecommuting, 384
"Telecourse utilization in American research
    universities," 348
Telematics and Informatics, 373
**Television violence
    and children's behavior, 164-68
    research findings, 165**
    portrayal, 166
    viewer characteristics, 165-66
Tennant, R., 383
**Tennessee
    doctoral programs in instructional technol-
        ogy, 270
    graduate programs in instructional tech-
        nology, 298**
TERC
    data modeling and analysis, 57-60
    Global Laboratory Project, 49-63
    software tools, 52-62
    informal learning environments, 61-62
    teacher enhancement and curriculum
        development, 60-61
**Terminology and glossary in instructional
    technology definition, 13-14**
Tessmer, M., 363
Testing, alternative, 151-54
**Texas
    doctoral programs in instructional technol-
        ogy, 270
    graduate programs in educational comput-
        ing, 313-14
    graduate programs in instructional tech-
        nology, 298-99**
Texas A&M University, 270, 299, 313
Texas Tech University, 299, 313
Texas Wesleyan University, 314
T. H. E. Journal, 351
Theater Library Association, 253
Theory and Resistance in Education, 70
Thiel, Thomas J., 336
Thrift, N., 72
T. I. E. News, 381
Times Mirror, 164
Tinker, R. F., 49-63, 384
Todd, R. J., 369
TLA. *See* Theater Library Association
TM. *See* ERIC Clearinghouse on Assessment
    and Evaluation
"Total quality education and instructional sys-
    tems development," 363
"Toward the new millennium," 371
Towards a Global Classroom, 383
Towne, D. M., 380
Townsend, C. M., 377
Townsend, F. C., 377
Towson State University, 285-86
TRAC. *See* Telecommunications Research and
    Action Center
"Traditional mediation," 370
Training, 360
**Training in educational partnerships,
    97, 100**
Training Media Association, 253
Tremblay, W., 348
Trimby, Madeline J., 29
"The trouble with learning environments," 353
Turoff, M., 161

UD. *See* ERIC Clearinghouse on Urban Education

UFVA. *See* University Film and Video Association

Ulrich's International Periodicals Directory 1992-93, 332

UMBC. *See* University of Maryland, Baltimore County

The Unabashed Librarian, 366

United Nations Department of Public Information, Dissemination Division, 253

United States International University, 258, 277, 304

Universal resource locators, 111

University Film and Video Association, 253

University of Alabama, 258, 274

University of Arizona, 275

University of California at Los Angeles, 258-59, 277

University of Central Arkansas, 275

University of Central Florida, 279-80

University of Central Oklahoma, 295

University of Cincinnati, 294

University of Colorado at Colorado Springs, 304

University of Colorado at Denver, 259, 278

University of Connecticut, 260

University of Florida, 261, 280

University of Georgia, 261, 280-81, 306

University of Hartford, 305

University of Hawaii-Manoa, 281, 306

University of Illinois at Urbana-Champaign, 262, 283

University of Iowa, 263-64, 284

University of Louisville, 285

University of Maryland, 264, 286

University of Maryland, Baltimore County, 286

University of Massachusetts-Boston, 287

University of Massachusetts-Lowell, 309

University of Michigan, 265, 287, 310

University of Minnesota, 265, 288, 310

University of Missouri-Columbia, 265-66, 289

University of Missouri-St. Louis, 289

University of Montana, 289

University of Nebraska, 266

University of Nebraska at Kearney, 289

University of Nebraska-Lincoln, 289-90

University of Nebraska-Omaha, 290

University of North Carolina, 294

University of North Texas, 299, 314

University of Northern Colorado, 259, 278

University of Oklahoma, 269, 295-96, 313

University of Pittsburgh, 269, 297

The University of Rhode Island, 297

University of South Alabama, 274

University of South Carolina, 298

University of South Florida, 280

University of Southern California, 259, 277

University of Southern Mississippi, 288

University of Tennessee, 270

University of Tennessee-Knoxville, 298

The University of Texas, 270

The University of Texas-Austin, 299

The University of Texas-Southwestern Medical Center at Dallas, 299

University of Toledo, 268-69, 295

University of Virginia, 271, 300-301

University of Washington, 272, 301

University of Wisconsin-La Crosse, 302

University of Wisconsin-Madison, 272, 302

University of Wisconsin-Oshkosh, 302

University of Wisconsin-Stout, 302

"UPSIDE DOWN," 380

URLs. *See* Universal resource locators

U.S. Congress, House of Representatives, 349, 384

"Use of a general graph-drawing algorithm in the construction of association maps," 358

"The use of informational feedback in instruction," 349

Using Computer-Based Telecommunications Services to Serve Educational Purposes at Home, 384

"Using content experts to help produce training," 362

"Using multimedia in the multicultural classroom," 377

Using Technology to Improve Teaching and Learning, 340

Using the Microcomputer to Equate Ratings of Student Writing Samples, 340

Utah
  doctoral programs in instructional technology, 271
  graduate programs in instructional technology, 300

Utah State University, 271, 300

Utilization domain of instructional technology, 3, 12-13

Utilization of Computer-Based Technology in High School Library Media Centers, 368

Valauskas, E. J., 343

Valdosta State University, 281

Vallee, J., 161

The Valuation by Students of the Use of Computers in Education, 340

Van den Brande, L., 346

Van Orden, P., 372

Vanderbilt University Learning Technology Center, 44-48

Vepierre, P., 378

Video Case Studies on Scientific Sense-Making, TERC, 60

"The video cassette recorder's potential as a tool for development," 379
Video for Exploring the World project, 59
"Video production in the classroom," 377
Video Systems, 374
Videoconferences, NCIP, 128-29
Videographing the Pictorial Sequence, 177
Videography, 374
Videos for Understanding Diversity, 375
Videotaped demonstrations, 153-54
VIEW. *See* Video for Exploring the World
Viewer characteristics in television violence, 165-66
"Views from the Field," 130, 131
Virginia
 doctoral programs in instructional technology, 271-72
 graduate programs in educational computing, 314-15
 graduate programs in instructional technology, 300-301
Virginia Commonwealth University, 301
Virginia Polytechnic Institute and State University (Virginia Tech), 271-72, 301, 315
Virginia State University, 301
"The virtual library," 370
"The virtual library revisited," 371
Virtual Reality, 379
Virtual Reality Report, 379
"Visible models of course organization," 363
VISION 2000 Task Force, 41
Visual Communicating, 361
Visual Communications, 361
Visual Information, 361
Visual Messages, 374
Voice of Youth Advocates, 367

Wagner, Ellen, 7
WAIS (Wide Area Information Servers), 111
Walker, James, 29
Walling, L. L., 372
"Walls around the electronic library," 370
Washington Post, 164, 165
Washington
 doctoral programs in instructional technology, 272
 graduate programs in educational computing, 315
 graduate programs in instructional technology, 301
Watson, J. A., 343
Wayne State University, 265, 287
Webster University, 289
Wedman, J., 363
Welsch, E. K., 379
Wersig, G., 359

West Georgia College, 281
West Virginia, doctoral programs in instructional technology, 272
West Virginia University, 272
Western Carolina University, 312
Western Illinois University, 283
Western Maryland College, 286
Western Oregon State College, 296
Western Washington University, 301, 315
WFS. *See* World Future Society
WGBH Educational Foundation, 126
What Makes Plants Grow, 175
"When inner city black children go online at home," 341
"When technology meets the subject matter disciplines in education," 342
"Where would we be without them?," 371
"Who's afraid of the big bad box?," 377
Wileman, R. E., 361
Wilkinson, T. W., 161
William Paterson College, 290
Williams, M. E., 357
Willis, B., 346
Willis, Jerry W., 340
Wilson, B., 352
Wilson Library Bulletin, 358, 367
Winn, W., 343
Winner, Langdon, 67-68
Winthrop University, 298
Wisconsin
 doctoral programs in instructional technology, 272
 graduate programs in educational computing, 316
 graduate programs in instructional technology, 302
Woodrow, Janice E. J., 349
Woolliams, P., 345
"Word processing as a support to the writing process," 343
Working Group on Typology and Geography of the Field, 5
World Future Society, 253
World-Wide Web, 111
Worringham, R. E., 379
Wright State University, 295, 312-13
"Writing, thinking and computers," 342
WWW. *See* World-Wide Web

YALSA. *See* Young Adult Library Services Association
Yeaman, Andrew R. J., 70-72
"The year's work in collection development," 370
Yelon, S., 363
Yerushalmy, M., 352

YES. *See* Your Explorer Series
Yildiz, R., 380
Young Adult Library Services Association, 208
Young Researcher Award, 319, 331
Your Explorer Series, Vanderbilt University,
    45-46

Zenor, Stan, 6, 8
Zorfass, Judith, 126-31
Zwart, W. J., 380